Number Theoretic Methods in Statistics: Theory and Applications

Number Theoretic Methods in Statistics: Theory and Applications

Guest Editors

Kai-Tai Fang
Yongdao Zhou

MDPI

Basel • Beijing • Wuhan • Barcelona • Belgrade • Novi Sad • Cluj • Manchester

Guest Editors

Kai-Tai Fang
Guangdong Provincial Key Laboratory of Interdisciplinary Research and Application for Data Science (IRADS)
Beijing Normal-Hong Kong Baptist University
Zhuhai
China

Yongdao Zhou
School of Statistics and Data Science
Nankai University
Tianjin
China

Editorial Office
MDPI AG
Grosspeteranlage 5
4052 Basel, Switzerland

This is a reprint of the Special Issue, published open access by the journal *Entropy* (ISSN 1099-4300), freely accessible at: https://www.mdpi.com/journal/entropy/special_issues/00ZUSBR4MQ.

For citation purposes, cite each article independently as indicated on the article page online and as indicated below:

Lastname, A.A.; Lastname, B.B. Article Title. *Journal Name* **Year**, *Volume Number*, Page Range.

ISBN 978-3-7258-7406-4 (Hbk)
ISBN 978-3-7258-7407-1 (PDF)
https://doi.org/10.3390/books978-3-7258-7407-1

Contents

About the Editors . . . . **vii**

Kai-Tai Fang and Yongdao Zhou
Number-Theoretic Methods in Statistics: Theory and Applications
Reprinted from: *Entropy* **2026**, *28*, 147, https://doi.org/10.3390/e28020147 . . . . **1**

Feng Yang and Zheng Zhou
Maxpro Designs for Experiments with Multiple Types of Branching and Nested Factors
Reprinted from: *Entropy* **2024**, *26*, 856, https://doi.org/10.3390/e26100856 . . . . **6**

Yong-Feng Zhou, Yu-Xuan Lin, Kai-Tai Fang and Hong Yin
The Representative Points of Generalized Alpha Skew-t Distribution and Applications
Reprinted from: *Entropy* **2024**, *26*, 889, https://doi.org/10.3390/e26110889 . . . . **21**

Xinyu Chen, Zhenyu Shi, Yuanqi Xie, Zichen Zhang, Achraf Cohen and Shusen Pu
Advancing Continuous Distribution Generation: An Exponentiated Odds Ratio Generator Approach
Reprinted from: *Entropy* **2024**, *26*, 1006, https://doi.org/10.3390/e26121006 . . . . **45**

Qi-Yi Tang and Yu-Xuan Lin
Maximum Entropy-Minimum Residual Model: An Optimum Solution to Comprehensive Evaluation and Multiple Attribute Decision Making
Reprinted from: *Entropy* **2025**, *27*, 203, https://doi.org/10.3390/e27020203 . . . . **73**

Xinyang Li and Xiaoling Peng
Mean Squared Error Representative Points of Pareto Distributions and Their Estimation
Reprinted from: *Entropy* **2025**, *27*, 249, https://doi.org/10.3390/e27030249 . . . . **93**

Qiuying Chen, Zhiming Li and Zhi Li
An Aliasing Measure of Factor Effects in Three-Level Regular Designs
Reprinted from: *Entropy* **2025**, *27*, 680, https://doi.org/10.3390/e27070680 . . . . **124**

Shengli Zhao and Mengru Qin
Two-Level Regular Designs for Baseline Parameterization
Reprinted from: *Entropy* **2025**, *27*, 706, https://doi.org/10.3390/e27070706 . . . . **143**

Mei Zhang and Feng Yang
Federated Semi-Supervised Learning with Uniform Random and Lattice-Based Client Sampling
Reprinted from: *Entropy* **2025**, *27*, 804, https://doi.org/10.3390/e27080804 . . . . **156**

Kai-Tai Fang, Yu-Xuan Lin and Yu-Hui Deng
A Review: Construction of Statistical Distributions
Reprinted from: *Entropy* **2025**, *27*, 1188, https://doi.org/10.3390/e27121188 . . . . **178**

Weiping Zhou, Miaomiao Meng, Min Li and Xue Yang
Construction of Space-Filling Asymmetrical Marginally Coupled Designs
Reprinted from: *Entropy* **2025**, *27*, 1256, https://doi.org/10.3390/e27121256 . . . . **214**

About the Editors

Kai-Tai Fang

Kai-Tai Fang is a professor at Beijing Normal-Hong Kong Baptist University. His research area includes applications of number-theoretic methods in statistics, data science, multivariate analysis, experimental design, and distribution theory. Professor Fang is a reputable statistician. He was elected as a Life Fellow by the Institute of Mathematical Statistics (IMS) in 1992 and a Life Fellow by the American Statistical Association (ASA) in 2001, as well as elective member of the International Statistical Institute (ISI) in 1985. Professor Fang visited Yale University and Stanford University for two years and was invited as a Guest Professor in the Swiss Federal Institute of Technology, and was also a Visiting Professor in the University of North Carolina at Chapel Hill. He was a Vice Director of the Institute of Applied Mathematics, Academia Sinica, Beijing, from 1984 to 1992. He had been Chair Professor of the Department of Mathematics, Hong Kong Baptist University, from 1993 to January 2006, Director of the Statistics Research and Consultancy Centre from 1992 to 2005, and Head of the department from 2002 to 2005. His research interests are in statistics and mathematics—more specifically, in experimental design, multivariate analysis, and data mining. He is also an accomplished author, having published 24 books (including 6 monographs in English) and over 300 refereed papers. He was the co-inventor of the uniform experimental design, which is used by engineers to expedite product development. He developed new methods for inference in generalized multivariate analysis. Prof. Fang received a number of awards. Recently, he received the 2008 State Natural Science Award at the Second Level with Wang Yuan, the 2012 Guangdong Excellent Teacher award by the Guangdong Government, and the 2012 Zhuhai Advanced Teachers award by the Zhuhai Government. Recently, Professor Fang received the 2014 ICSA Distinguished Achievement Award.

Yongdao Zhou

Yongdao Zhou is a professor of the Department of Statistics at Nankai University. His research agenda focuses on experimental design and big data analysis. He received the PhD degree in statistics from Sichuan University, China, in 2008. After graduation, he joined Sichuan University and became a professor in 2015. In 2017, he joined Nankai University, where he is presently a professor in statistics. For continuous spaces, he has developed the theory of data collection methods such as uniform experimental designs, computer experiments, order of addition experiments, etc. For discrete massive data, he has extended the theory of big data subsampling based on the theory of experimental designs. Moreover, he has proposed many efficient methods for the sampling theory in complex cases, approximate Bayesian computation, and graph zero-shot learning. He published more than 80 papers in high-level journals and top conferences of machine learning and 5 monographs. His research publications have won two Best Paper awards. He is the principal investigator of seven national-level projects and five big data analysis projects. He has won the first prize of the Outstanding Achievement Award for Statistical Science Research from the National Bureau of Statistics and the third prize of the National Statistical Science and Technology Progress Award. He is the president of the Association for Applied Statistics of Tianjin.

entropy

MDPI

Editorial

Number-Theoretic Methods in Statistics: Theory and Applications

Kai-Tai Fang [1,2] and Yongdao Zhou [3,*]

[1] Guangdong Provincial Key Laboratory of Interdisciplinary Research and Application for Data Science (IRADS), Beijing Normal-Hong Kong Baptist University, Zhuhai 519087, China; ktfang@bnbu.edu.cn
[2] The Key Laboratory of Random Complex Structures and Data Analysis, The Chinese Academy of Sciences, Beijing 100045, China
[3] School of Statistics and Data Science, Nankai University, Tianjin 300071, China
* Correspondence: ydzhou@nankai.edu.cn

There are many settings in which the key underlying quantities that affect the outcome are unknown, resulting in the unknown inputs often being modeled using random vector variables or stochastic processes. The essence of the Monte Carlo (MC) method is to estimate the mean, quantiles, and/or probability distribution of the outcome. An enhancement of the traditional MC method, the Quasi-Monte Carlo (QMC) method, is a numerical technique used to approximate integrals, particularly in high-dimensional spaces [1,2]. Instead of using the random points of the MC method, QMC methods employ low-discrepancy sequences (also called quasi-random sequences or sub-random sequences), such as the Halton sequence, the Sobol sequence, or the Faure sequence, to achieve faster convergence. Quasi-Monte Carlo method has a rate of convergence close to $O(1/N)$, whereas the rate for the traditional Monte Carlo method is $O(N^{-0.5})$. QMC methods are also called number-theoretic methods (NTMs), and have played an important role in numerical integration in high dimensions, statistical inference, and experimental design, as well as having applications in engineering, biology, economics, and data science.

NTMs are a class of methods that represent a combination of number theory and numerical analysis [3]. Since the 1980s, statisticians have directed their attention to NTMs and their applications in statistics, with the first application of NTMs being an evaluation of the probabilities and moments of a multivariate distribution. Later, Shaw [4] provided a detailed discussion on applications of NTMs in Bayesian statistics, mainly for the numerical computation of posterior density and moments. Fang [5] was the first to apply NTMs to the design of experiments, and proposed new type of design called uniform design. With the exception of integration, this was the first application of NTMs in statistics. Since then, the theory and applications of uniform design developed quickly in China and in other countries. Several monographs on the topic of uniform design were published, see [6–8]. The content of uniform design has also been included in many encyclopedia or handbooks, such as the *Handbook on Statistics*, the *Handbook of Engineering Statistics*, and the *International Encyclopedia of Statistical Science*. Uniform experimental design can be understood as a space-filling design for computer experiments, a fractional factorial design with model uncertainty, a robust design against model specification, and a supersaturated design, and an experimental design that can be applied to experiments with mixtures.

The essence of NTMs is to find representative points (RPs) of the uniform distribution in the experimental domain, such as the unit cube of R^s, the simplex, or another given region. In other words, the main idea of representative points in NTMs is to scatter the point set uniformly in the experimental domain. Those RPs are also called space-filling designs in the field of experimental design [8,9]. Many criteria, such as the uniformity criteria [10,11], maximin distance criterion [12], and low-dimensional projection uniformity [13], have been proposed to assess the space-filling properties of design points. Recently, NTMs have been extended to generate RPs for many useful multivariate distributions and have been systematically applied in statistics [14]. Therefore, the lively interest in the development of the theory and application of NTMs has prompted us to propose this Special Issue on "Number-Theoretic Methods in Statistics: Theory and Applications", which brings together ten contributions that address the topic of NTMs from different methodological and applicative perspectives. Among them, four contributions cover the space-filling properties of factorial designs, as well as some other factorial design-related criteria; four contributions center on the RPs for different distributions; and two contributions focus on the application of NTMs.

As shown in [15], the uniform criterion has a close relationship with generalized minimum aberration criterion of fractional factorial designs. Therefore, discussions of the criteria of factorial design are useful in terms of their space-filling properties, the paper on the "Construction of Space-Filling Asymmetrical Marginally Coupled Designs" by Zhou et al. (Contribution 1) studies marginally coupled designs (MCDs) for computer experiments with both qualitative and quantitative factors, and proposes four approaches to constructing a series of space-filling asymmetrical MCDs based on space-filling symmetrical MCDs or space-filling Latin hypercube designs (LHDs). The obtained asymmetrical MCDs can inherit the low-dimensional space-filling properties of these symmetrical MCDs or LHDs, and are flexible in terms of their run sizes.

In "Maxpro Designs for Experiments with Multiple Types of Branching and Nested Factors", Yang and Zhou (Contribution 2) considered the space-filling design of experiments with branching factors and nested factors by using the maxpro criterion, which is also a type of space-filling criterion. They proposed this novel space-filling criterion based on the maximum projection criterion to evaluate the performance of designs with branching and nested factors, and provided a framework to construct optimal designs under the proposed criterion. Compared with the existing works, the resulting designs have superior space-filling properties across all possible low-dimensional projections. Moreover, their strategy is flexible regarding run size, number of levels, and type of factors, ultimately improving the space-filling properties of such designs.

The paper on "Two-Level Regular Designs for Baseline Parameterization" by Zhao and Qin (Contribution 3) considers the baseline parameterization model of two-level regular fractional factorial designs. The baseline parameterization model is a linear model based on baseline constraints, and is one of the most used models in the analysis of experimental data. The authors made progress on bridging the K-values and word length pattern, and analytically calculate the quantities for two-level regular designs with a higher resolution, which will result in enhanced space-filling properties.

Moreover, a new three-level aliasing pattern was proposed in the paper "An Aliasing Measure of Factor Effects in Three-Level Regular Designs" by Chen, Li and Li (Contribution 4). The aliasing properties of factor effects are more significant than the component effects in the experimental model. The proposed new aliasing pattern for three-level regular designs can be used to evaluate the degree of aliasing among different factors, as well as choosing optimal three-level regular designs. The proposed criterion has a strong relationship with other commonly used criteria such as general minimum lower-order confounding, entropy, minimum aberration, and clear effects. Moreover, the optimal three-level design for all 27-run and some 81-run and 243-run three-level designs is listed in tables, and can be used for practical applications.

Traditional NTMs consider the point set as the representative points of uniform distribution in experimental domains. Currently, the theory of representative points has been extended to other useful distributions, such as the normal distribution, exponential

https://doi.org/10.3390/e28020147

distribution family, skew-t distribution, and so forth. To search the representative points of a given distribution, several criteria have been proposed. The simplest method is to use the Monte Carlo method, the corresponding RPs are then called MC-RPs. Fang and Wang [6] were the first to explore statistical simulation using NTMs. They constructed approximate distributions to $F(x)$ via QMC-based representative points (QMC-RPs). They also considered the representative points under the mean square error (MSE) criterion, the corresponding RPs are called MSE-RPs or principal points [16]. The properties of MC-RPs, QMC-RPs, and MSE-RPs, and their application in statistical simulation, experimental design, geometric probability problems, and finance, have been studied in [14]. Statistical simulation has become a cornerstone in statistical research and applications, and it has been shown that the converge rate can be improved when replacing MC-RPs with QMC-RPs or MSE-RPs. This Special Issue includes four contributions on RPs.

In the paper "The Representative Points of Generalized Alpha Skew-t Distribution and Applications" by Zhou et al. (Contribution 5), the authors studied the construction methods and properties of different types of RPs of the generalized alpha skew-t distribution, such as MC-RPs, QMC-RPs, and MSE-RPs. These three types of RPs are utilized to estimate moments and densities of special distributions with known and unknown parameters, and the authors were able to show that the MSE-RPs perform best across all case studies.

MSE-RPs were also discussed in the paper "Mean Squared Error Representative Points of Pareto Distributions and Their Estimation" by Li and Peng (Contribution 6). Pareto distributions are widely applied in various fields, such as economics, finance, and environmental studies, and this paper demonstrates the uniqueness and existence of MSE-RPs in Pareto distributions under certain parameter settings, as well as providing a theoretical k-means algorithm for the computation of MSE-RPs for Pareto I and Pareto II distributions. Several construction methods for estimating MSE-RPs in different types of Pareto distributions are provided. The effectiveness of the proposed methods for MSE-RPs is compared through simulations and real data studies.

The study "Advancing Continuous Distribution Generation: An Exponentiated Odds Ratio Generator Approach" by Chen et al. (Contribution 7) presents a new methodology for generating continuous statistical distributions, integrating the exponentiated odds ratio within the framework of survival analysis. The benefit of the new method is illustrated through the mathematical properties and statistical properties of the Type 2 Gumbel Weibull-G family of distributions, such as density functions, moments, hazard rate and quantile functions, Rényi entropy, order statistics, and the concept of stochastic ordering.

In the paper "A Review: Construction of Statistical Distributions", Fang, Lin, and Deng (Contribution 8) focused on the methods used to construct discrete or continuous and univariate or multivariate distributions, covering both traditional and newly developed approaches. They consider the classic distributions such as the normal, exponential, gamma, and beta for univariate data, and the multivariate normal, elliptical, and Dirichlet for multidimensional data, and showed these to be necessary for more flexible modeling tools, as well as their construction methods. The approximation to the continuous distributions by different types of representative points is also discussed.

Two contributions to this Special Issue concern the applications of NTMs. The study "Maximum Entropy-Minimum Residual Model: An Optimum Solution to Comprehensive Evaluation and Multiple Attribute Decision Making" by Tang and Lin (Contribution 9) considers the weighting methods of the factors. The authors propose a new model to generate weights based on the maximum entropy–minimum residual (MEMR) principle, directly estimating the relationship between factor weights and the composite indicator. Compared with other weighting methods, the MEMR model is more robust, consistent, and

https://doi.org/10.3390/e28020147

interpretable, and is therefore suitable for all comprehensive evaluation cases involving quantitative factors.

Furthermore, in the paper "Federated Semi-Supervised Learning with Uniform Random and Lattice-Based Client Sampling", Zhang and Yang (Contribution 10) propose a novel federated averaging semi-supervised learning algorithm, called FedAvg-SSL, by using two sampling approaches that rely on MC-RPs and QMC-RPs. The lattice-based sampling method using QMC-RPs proved to provide more balanced client participation through structured deterministic selection. The rigorous convergence analysis showed that FedAvg-SSL achieves a sublinear convergence rate with linear speedup, which was validated through simulation experiments.

Overall, this Special Issue presents a variety of methodologies and applications of number-theoretic methods in statistics, including the construction methods of space-filling designs, different types of representative points such as QMC-RPs and MSE-RPs, and their applications in modeling techniques and federated semi-supervised learning. The benefits of NTMs were valuated according to different aspects in the collected contributions. Further properties, construction methods, and applications of NTMs are welcome in future editions of this Special Issue.

Acknowledgments: We express our thanks to the authors of the above contributions and to the editorial staff of the journal *Entropy* for their support during this work.

Conflicts of Interest: The authors declare no conflicts of interest.

List of Contributions

1. Zhou, W.; Meng, M.; Li, M.; Yang, X. Construction of Space-Filling Asymmetrical Marginally Coupled Designs. *Entropy* **2025**, *27*, 1256.
2. Yang, F.; Zhou, Z. Maxpro Designs for Experiments with Multiple Types of Branching and Nested Factors. *Entropy* **2024**, *26*, 856.
3. Zhao, S.; Qin, M. Two-Level Regular Designs for Baseline Parameterization. *Entropy* **2025**, *27*, 706.
4. Chen, Q.; Li, Z.; Li, Z. An Aliasing Measure of Factor Effects in Three-Level Regular Designs. *Entropy* **2025**, *27*, 680.
5. Zhou, Y.F.; Lin, Y.X.; Fang, K.T.; Yin, H. The Representative Points of Generalized Alpha Skew-t Distribution and Applications. *Entropy* **2024**, *26*, 889.
6. Li, X.; Peng, X. Mean Squared Error Representative Points of Pareto Distributions and Their Estimation. *Entropy* **2025**, *27*, 249.
7. Chen, X.; Shi, Z.; Xie, Y.; Zhang, Z.; Cohen, A.; Pu, S. Advancing Continuous Distribution Generation: An Exponentiated Odds Ratio Generator Approach. *Entropy* **2024**, *26*, 1006.
8. Fang, K.T.; Lin, Y.X.; Deng, Y.H. A Review: Construction of Statistical Distributions. *Entropy* **2025**, *27*, 1188.
9. Tang, Q.Y.; Lin, Y.X. Maximum Entropy-Minimum Residual Model: An Optimum Solution to Comprehensive Evaluation and Multiple Attribute Decision Making. *Entropy* **2025**, *27*, 203.
10. Zhang, M.; Yang, F. Federated Semi-Supervised Learning with Uniform Random and Lattice-Based Client Sampling. *Entropy* **2025**, *27*, 804.

References

1. Niederreiter, H. Quasi-Monte Carto Methods and Pseudo-Random Numbers. *Bull. Am. Math. Soc.* **1978**, *84*, 957–1041. [CrossRef]
2. Niederreiter, H. *Random Number Generation and Quasi-Monte Carlo Methods*; SIAM CBMS-NSF Regional Conference Series in Applied Mathematics; Society for Industrial and Applied Mathematics: Philadelphia, PA, USA, 1992.
3. Hua, L.K.; Wang, Y. *Applications of Number Theory to Numerical Analysis*; Springer and Science Press: Berlin/Heidelberg, Germany; Beijing, China, 1981.
4. Shaw, J.E.H. A quasi-random approach to integration in Bayesian statistics. *Ann. Statist.* **1988**, *16*, 859–914. [CrossRef]

https://doi.org/10.3390/e28020147

5. Fang, K.T. The uniform design: Application of number-theoretic methods in experimental design. *Acta Math. Appl. Sin.* **1980**, *3*, 363–372.
6. Fang, K.T.; Wang, Y. *Number-Theoretic Methods in Statistics*; Chapman and Hall: London, UK, 1994.
7. Fang, K.T.; Li, R.; Sudjianto, A. *Design and Modeling for Computer Experiments*; Chapman and Hall: New York, NY, USA; CRC: Boca Raton, FL, USA, 2006.
8. Fang, K.T.; Liu, M.Q.; Qin, H.; Zhou, Y. *Theory and Application of Uniform Experimental Designs*; Science Press and Springer: Beijing, China, 2018; Volume 221.
9. Santner, T.; Williams, B.; Notz, W. *The Design and Analysis of Computer Experiments*, 2nd ed.; Springer: New York, NY, USA, 2018.
10. Hickernell, F.J. A Generalized Discrepancy and Quadrature Error Bound. *Math. Comp.* **1998**, *67*, 299–322. [CrossRef]
11. Hickernell, F.J. Lattice Rules: How Well Do They Measure Up? In *Random and Quasi-Random Point Sets*; Hellekalek, P., Larcher, G., Eds.; Springer: Berlin/Heidelberg, Germany, 1998; pp. 106–166.
12. Johnson, M.E.; Moore, L.M.; Ylvisaker, D. Minimax and Maxmin Distance Designs. *J. Statist. Plan. Infer.* **1990**, *26*. 131–148. [CrossRef]
13. Sun, F.; Wang, Y.; Xu, H. Uniform projection designs. *Ann. Statist.* **2019**, *47*, 641–661. [CrossRef]
14. Fang, K.T.; Ye, H.; Zhou, Y. *Representative Points of Statistical Distributions: Applications in Statistical Inference*; Chapman and Hall: New York, NY, USA, 2025.
15. Zhou, Y.; Xu, H. Space-Filling Fractional Factorial Designs. *J. Am. Stat. Assoc.* **2014**, *109*, 1134–1144. [CrossRef]
16. Flury, B.D. Principal points. *Biometrika* **1990**, *77*, 33–41. [CrossRef]

https://doi.org/10.3390/e28020147

entropy

MDPI

Article

Maxpro Designs for Experiments with Multiple Types of Branching and Nested Factors

Feng Yang [1] **and Zheng Zhou** [2,*]

[1] School of Mathematical Sciences, Sichuan Normal University, Chengdu 610066, China; yangfeng@sicnu.edu.cn
[2] School of Mathematics, Statistics and Mechanics, Beijing University of Technology, Beijing 100124, China
* Correspondence: zhengzhou@bjut.edu.cn

Abstract: Contemporary experiments often involve special factors known as branching factors. The levels of such factors determine the presence of some certain factors, referred to as nested factors. The design criteria for investigating the goodness of such designs are rarely developed. Furthermore, the existing criteria for such designs pay less attention to the space-filling property of low-dimensional projections of the design. The efficiencies of designs yielded by such criteria can markedly decrease when only a few factors are significant. To address this issue, this paper proposes a novel space-filling criterion based on the maximum projection criterion to evaluate the performance of the designs with branching and nested factors. A framework to construct optimal designs under the proposed criterion is also provided. Compared with the existing works, the resulting designs have better space-filling properties in all possible low-dimensional projections. Moreover, our strategy imposes no constraints on run size, level, and type of any factor, demonstrating its broad applicability.

Keywords: maximum projection; branching and nested; space-filling; criterion

1. Introduction

With the advancement of technology, the structures of experimental factors have become more and more complex. In many experiments, the presence of some factors is determined by the levels of specific factors, where the former factors are called nested factors and the latter factors are called branching factors. The remaining factors, apart from these two kinds, are referred to as shared factors. Here, we revisit the example in [1] to briefly illustrate these three kinds of factors. An experiment aims to optimize the turning process hardened for bearing steel. The factors of the experiment include cutting edge shape, cutting speed, cutting depth, and so on. Hone and chamfer are two commonly used cutting edge shapes, where chamfer length and chamfer angle can be altered when using a chamfered edge. In this experiment, the cutting edge shape is a branching factor, chamfer length and chamfer angle are two nested factors, and the other factors are shared factors. For more examples, see [2–5].

Space-filling designs are commonly used in situations where the relationship between factors and responses is a black box. The core idea behind such designs is to distribute design points evenly across the design space [6,7]. This facilitates a comprehensive exploration of the design space and guarantees that no area remains under-explored. Quasi-Monte Carlo (QMC) methods, such as the good lattice point method [8] and (t,m,s)-nets [9], are commonly used for constructing space-filling designs because they generate low-discrepancy sequences that ensure good coverage of the experimental domain. Another method for constructing space-filling designs is entropy criterion optimization [10]. By maximizing the entropy criterion [11,12], design points are ensured to spread points out [13–15], thus achieving maximum information gain and reducing uncertainty. Refs. [14,16] pointed out that, under the assumption of extremely weak correlation, maximum entropy designs tend to maximin distance designs [17], which are the most classical space-filling designs. Although space-filling designs, QMC methods, and entropy optimization may seem distinct at first glance, they are fundamentally interconnected through their shared goals of efficient sampling and maximizing the information obtained from a system. Therefore, the study of space-filling designs can be viewed as research on maximizing information gain from the experimental domain with a limited number of points, which falls at the intersection of statistics and information theory. In this paper, we primarily investigate the space-filling design method when branching and nested factors are involved.

The presence of branching and nested factors brings numerous challenges for generating the space-filling designs because different trials of an experiment can involve different factors, which are determined by the levels of branching factors. On the other hand, the nested factors are connected to branching factors, meaning that they are not independent. Moreover, such experiments commonly incorporate multiple types of factors, such as qualitative and quantitative factors. These characteristics make traditional space-filling design criteria unsuitable for evaluating designs with branching and nested factors. Naturally, the corresponding design strategies also become invalid. Recently, some studies have proposed space-filling criteria suitable for such experiments and provided corresponding design methods. Ref. [1] proposed the criterion from the perspectives of maximin distance. Unlike traditional criteria, such a criterion firstly assesses the sub-designs (including the nested and shared factors) under each level of each branching factor separately, secondly evaluates the design for shared factors, and then combines all of them to obtain the criteria for the entire design. Ref. [4] proposed a class of linear models suitable for experiments with branching and nested factors and used the D-optimality criterion to find the optimal designs. Ref. [5] proposed a uniformity criterion for such a design and claimed that compared with the criterion proposed by [1], this criterion allows all factors to be either qualitative or quantitative, and it imposes no restrictions on the number of levels for quantitative factors, making it applicable to a wider range of experiments.

However, the projection properties of these strategies are often ignored. In most experiments, only a small portion of factors involved are significant. Ref. [18] suggests that, if we only focus on the overall space-filling property of the design, it may result in poor projection uniformity in the dimensions of the significant factors, thereby reducing the efficiency of the experiment. Ref. [18] proposed a criterion for constructing maximum projection (Maxpro) designs. Optimal designs under this criterion can ensure space-filling properties in projections onto all subsets of factors. Ref. [19] extended this criterion to experiments involving both qualitative and quantitative factors. However, these criteria are not applicable to experiments with branching and nested factors.

In this paper, for experiments with branching and nested factors, we introduce a novel space-filling criterion by extending the Maxpro criterion in [19]. The paper is organized as follows. In Section 2, we provide some preliminaries relevant to this work. Section 3 reviews existing design criteria for experiments with branching and nested factors, pointing out their limitations. Section 4 introduces the novel criterion. Section 5 provides efficient methods for constructing optimal designs under the proposed criterion. Numerical comparisons are provided in Section 6 to demonstrate the effectiveness of the proposed methods. Section 7 concludes this paper.

2. Preliminaries

For a design $\boldsymbol{D}$ with n runs and m factors, where all factors are quantitative, plentiful criteria are proposed to find a "good" design. Ref. [20] suggested to choose designs with a minimal average of squared correlations between factors, defined as

$$\rho^2(\boldsymbol{D}) = \frac{\sum_{i \neq j} \rho_{ij}^2}{m(m-1)}, \quad (1)$$

where ρ_{ij} is the linear correlation between the ith and jth columns. Ref. [16] proposed a criterion to construct the maximin Latin hypercube designs, given by

$$\phi_\lambda(\boldsymbol{D}) = \left\{\sum_{i\neq j} d(\boldsymbol{x}_i, \boldsymbol{x}_j)^{-\lambda}\right\}^{1/\lambda}, \tag{2}$$

where $d(\boldsymbol{x}_i, \boldsymbol{x}_j) = \left(\sum_{k=1}^{m} |x_{ik} - x_{jk}|^p\right)^{1/p}$ is the distance between the points $\boldsymbol{x}_i$ and $\boldsymbol{x}_j$ of the design $\boldsymbol{D}$. Hereinafter, we set $p = 1$. The design points of the resulting design optimized by (2) try to scatter evenly across the design space. Ref. [18] proposed the following performance measure

$$\psi(\boldsymbol{D}) = \left\{\frac{1}{n(n-1)} \sum_{i\neq j} \frac{1}{\prod_{k=1}^{m}(x_{ik} - x_{jk})^2}\right\}^{1/m}. \tag{3}$$

A Maxpro design minimizes the ψ value in (3), which aims to simultaneously optimize the space-filling properties of the design points across all possible subsets of factors.

On the other hand, some researchers focus on the design with multiple types of factors. Suppose that there are p_1 continuous quantitative factors, p_2 discrete quantitative factors, and p_3 qualitative factors, Ref. [19] proposed a new criterion to accommodate multiple types of factors,

$$\psi(\boldsymbol{D}) = \left\{\frac{1}{n(n-1)} \psi^*(\boldsymbol{D})\right\}^{1/(p_1+p_2+p_3)}, \tag{4}$$

where

$$\psi^*(\boldsymbol{D}) = \sum_{i\neq j} \frac{1}{\prod\limits_{k=1}^{p_1} (x_{ik} - x_{jk})^2 \prod\limits_{k=p_1+1}^{p_1+p_2} \left\{|x_{ik} - x_{jk}| + \frac{1}{q_k}\right\}^2 \prod\limits_{k=p_1+p_2+1}^{p_1+p_2+p_3} \left\{I(x_{ik} \neq x_{jk}) + \frac{1}{q_k}\right\}^2},$$

$I(x_{ik} \neq x_{jk})$ is an indicator function, taking the value 1 if x_{ik} is not equal to x_{jk}, and 0 otherwise. Moreover, q_k is the number of levels in the kth column. Before calculating (4), each quantitative factor should be scaled into [0, 1]. Furthermore, Ref. [21] proposed the qualitative–quantitative discrepancy (QQD) to investigate the uniformity performance of the design with m_1 qualitative and m_2 quantitative factors, given by

$$\mathrm{QQD}^2(\boldsymbol{D}) = -\prod_{k=1}^{m_1}\left(\frac{5q_k+1}{4q_k}\right)\left(\frac{4}{3}\right)^{m_2} + \frac{1}{n^2}\sum_{i,j=1}^{n}\left(\frac{5}{4}\right)^{m_1}\left(\frac{6}{5}\right)^{\delta_{ij}(\boldsymbol{D}_1)} \times \prod_{k=m_1+1}^{m_1+m_2}\left(\frac{3}{2} - |\, x_{ik} - x_{jk} \,| + |\, x_{ik} - x_{jk} \,|^2\right),$$

where $\delta_{ij}(\boldsymbol{D}_1)$ represents the coincidence number between the ith and jth points of the qualitative sub-design $\boldsymbol{D}_1$.

3. Existing Criteria and Limitations

Limited researches have been conducted on the experimental designs with branching and nested factors. There are two primary research directions, namely deterministic constructions [22–24] and the criteria. The existing conditions of the deterministic strategy are quite restrictive, while the criteria-based approach offers greater flexibility and adaptability to a variety of situations.

To the best of our knowledge, only two model-independent criteria have been customized for the designs including branching and nested factors. One is proposed by [1], by extending the maximin criterion (2), given by

$$\Phi_\lambda(\boldsymbol{D}) = \left\{ \sum_{i \neq j} \left(\frac{t}{d_S(\boldsymbol{x}_i, \boldsymbol{x}_j)} \right)^\lambda + \sum_{l=1}^{r} \sum_{z=1}^{q_l} \sum_{i,j \in U_l^z} \left(\frac{t + t_l}{d_N(\boldsymbol{x}_i, \boldsymbol{x}_j) + d_S(\boldsymbol{x}_i, \boldsymbol{x}_j)} \right)^\lambda \right\}^{1/\lambda}, \quad (5)$$

where t and t_l are the number of shared factors and nested factors corresponding to the lth branching factor, and U_l^z gathers the row indices where the lth branching factor at level z; besides that, the subscripts S and N mean the projections of design points onto shared and nested factors, respectively. This is the first systemic measure to evaluate the goodness of a design with branching and nested factors. The design strategy suggested by [1] imposed a constraint on the branching factor, requiring it to be an orthogonal array. It also assumed that the nested and shared factors are quantitative with n distinct levels, making it only suitable for a computer experiment. From Formula (5), it is evident that the resulting design takes no account of the space-filling properties between the branching factor and the other factors; that is, such a criterion only considers the space-filling property among the nested and shared factors. Moreover, as mentioned in [19], the criterion in (2) pursues the space-fillingness in full dimensional space, whereas its projection properties in terms of subspaces for dimensions $2, \cdots, m-1$ are not ensured. The measure in (5) originates from (2); as a consequence, it shares the same shortcomings.

Ref. [5] tried to investigate the physical experiment systems with multiple types of factors, and introduced a criterion for experiments in the presence of nested factors from the perspective of uniformity

$$\Psi(\boldsymbol{D}) = \frac{\mathrm{QQD}(\boldsymbol{D_{BS}})}{2^{r+t}} + \sum_{l=1}^{r} \sum_{z=0}^{q_l-1} \frac{\mathrm{QQD}(\boldsymbol{D}_{\boldsymbol{BNS}}^{l,z})}{2^{r-1+t+t_l}}, \quad (6)$$

where $\boldsymbol{D_{BS}}$ is the sub-design that $\boldsymbol{D}$ projects on branching and shared factors; in addition, $\boldsymbol{D}_{\boldsymbol{BNS}}^{l,z}$ represents the sub-design consisting of all rows (consisting of the other branching, associated nested, and shared factor) within the lth branching factor taking level z. However, through our observation, the discrimination sensitivity of criterion (6) is relatively poor. Two illustrative designs with the same Ψ-value are given in Table 1, and their design points are shown in Figure 1. It is clear that the design points of Figure 1a are more space-filling than those of Figure 1b with respect to each level of the branching factor. However, they are considered to be equivalent under the criterion (6), which is inconsistent with the intuition. This indicates that the criterion in (6) fails to distinguish these two designs. On the other hand, although uniform designs perform well under uniformity criteria, their performance may not be satisfactory in terms of other space-filling properties, referring to Figure 1 of [18]. Consequently, the performance of the uniform designs with branching and nested factors in terms of other space-filling properties is still a concern. From the discussion above, a new criterion is required to deal with the experiments with multiple types of branching and nested factors.

Table 1. Two designs with $\Psi = 0.023$.

Run	D_1			D_2		
	B	N	S	B	N	S
1	0	0	5	0	0	7
2	0	1	1	0	1	4
3	0	2	6	0	2	6
4	0	3	3	0	3	2
5	1	0	4	1	0	5
6	1	1	0	1	1	3
7	1	2	7	1	2	0
8	1	3	2	1	3	1

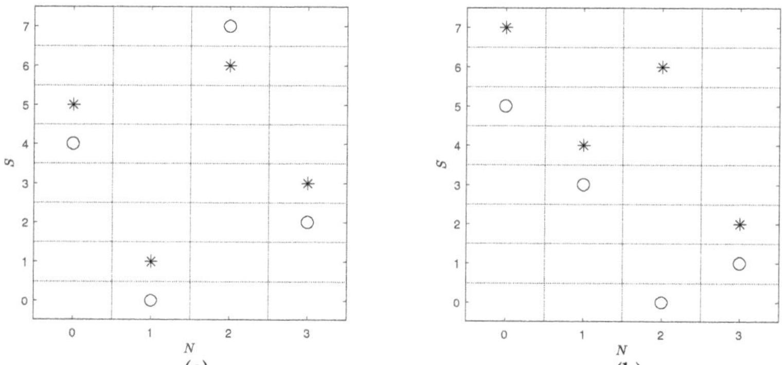

Figure 1. The points for designs in Table 1, where "$*$" corresponds to $B = 0$ and "$\circ$" corresponds $B = 1$. (**a**) D_1; (**b**) D_2.

4. Maxpro Criterion for Experiments with Multiple Types of Branching and Nested Factors

Throughout this paper, for the sake of clarity and without causing confusion, we will often use B, N, and S to represent the branching factor, nested factor, and shared factor, respectively. For simplicity, if there exist m_1 quantitative factors and m_2 qualitative factors, a modified criterion of (4) is given

$$\psi(D) = \left\{ \sum_{i \neq j} \frac{1}{\prod_{k=1}^{m_1} \left\{ |x_{ik} - x_{jk}| + \frac{1}{q_k} \right\}^2 \prod_{k=m_1+1}^{m_1+m_2} \left\{ I(x_{ik} \neq x_{jk}) + \frac{1}{q_k} \right\}^2} \right\}^{1/(m_1+m_2)}. \tag{7}$$

More generally, let there be m factors, each of which can be either qualitative and quantitative. Let $\xi(x_{ik}, x_{jk})$ be a binary function that takes value $\left\{ |x_{ik} - x_{jk}| + \frac{1}{q_k} \right\}^2$ if the kth factor is quantitative and $\left\{ I(x_{ik} \neq x_{jk}) + \frac{1}{q_k} \right\}^2$ otherwise. Then, (7) becomes

$$\psi(D) = \left\{ \sum_{i \neq j} \frac{1}{\prod_{k=1}^{m} \xi(x_{ik}, x_{jk})} \right\}^{1/m}. \tag{8}$$

Now, we develop a new criterion for evaluating the goodness of designs for experiments including multiple types of branching and nested factors, by extending (8). Begin with a simple example where only one branching factor with q_1 levels exists. The Maxpro criterion for such a design can be defined as

$$\Upsilon(\boldsymbol{D}) = \psi(\boldsymbol{D_{BS}}) + \sum_{z=0}^{q_1-1} \psi(\boldsymbol{D}_{\boldsymbol{NS}|b_1=z}),$$

where $\boldsymbol{D}_{\boldsymbol{NS}|b_1=z}$ represents the sub-design of that design $\boldsymbol{D}$ projects onto nested and shared factors where the branching factor is at level z.

More generally, let there be r branching factors, and then the Maxpro criterion should be

$$\Upsilon(\boldsymbol{D}) = \psi(\boldsymbol{D_{BS}}) + \sum_{l=1}^{r} \sum_{z=0}^{q_l-1} \psi(\boldsymbol{D}_{\boldsymbol{B}_{(-l)}\boldsymbol{N}^l\boldsymbol{S}|b_l=z}), \tag{9}$$

where $\boldsymbol{D}_{\boldsymbol{B}_{(-l)}\boldsymbol{N}^l\boldsymbol{S}|b_l=z}$ is the sub-design that consists of all the branching factors (except the lth one), the associated nested factor corresponding to the lth branching factors, and the shared factors, where the lth branching factor takes level z. Essentially, $\boldsymbol{D}_{\boldsymbol{B}_{(-l)}\boldsymbol{N}^l\boldsymbol{S}|b_l=z}, l = 1, \cdots, r, z = 0, \cdots, q_l - 1$ can be regarded as a series of sliced (or small) designs generated according to each level of each branching factor. The first part addresses the overall properties of the branching and shared space, while the second part of (9), related to $\sum_{l=1}^{r} q_l$ small designs involving branching, nested, and shared factors, examines the properties of these small designs at each level of every branching factor. The design with branching and nested factors corresponding to the minimal Υ value is called the optimal Maxpro BNS design, which takes into account the characteristics among the three kinds of factors. This criterion is based on the work of [19]; therefore, it inherits all its advantages and can also handle cases with branching and nested factors. The proposed criterion imposes no restrictions on run size and level, and is suitable for multiple types of factors.

A similar structure of the objective criterion was proposed in [5]. The key difference is that, here, we focus on the Maxpro properties, whereas [5] concentrates on the uniformity. Both criteria are effective for searching optimal designs. However, there is no one-to-one relationship between these two criteria; in other words, the optimal designs under such two criteria can differ. To explain this point, consider all the eight-point designs with one two-level branching factor, one four-level nested factor, and one eight-level shared factor. There are a total of $8! = 40{,}320$ non-isomorphic designs that cannot be obtained from each other through row and level permutations. These designs can be ranked in terms of the uniformity and the Maxpro criterion, (6) and (9), respectively, where under both criteria, the design ranked first is the corresponding best design. There are a total of 1891 combinations of ranking, with 1809 rankings on the Maxpro and 35 rankings on the UD, referring to Figure 2. It indicates the Maxpro criterion offers superior discrimination compared to the UD criterion. To elaborate on this, comparing the two designs colored by red in Figure 2, both of them are ranked 5th in terms of the UD criterion, but their rankings under Maxpro criterion are significantly different, being 7th and 985th, respectively. In fact, they are exactly the two designs in Table 1, where $\boldsymbol{D}_1$ corresponds to the ranking seventh under the Maxpro criterion, and $\boldsymbol{D}_2$ corresponds to another one. Despite both designs having the same UD value, the Maxpro values indicate that the design in Figure 1a is more desirable, which aligns with our intuition. On the other hand, it can be seen that the optimality of one criterion may not lead to the optimality of another. This issue becomes more severe as the number of factors and runs increases. As a result, the proposed criterion is able to distinguish the quality of designs involving branching and nested factors more efficiently.

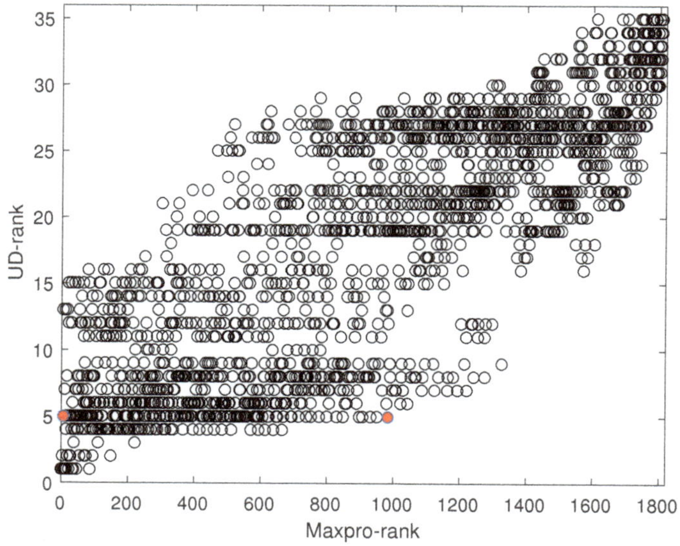

Figure 2. Maxpro rankings versus UD rankings , where the two designs marked by red color share the same UD ranking but different Maxpro rankings.

5. Optimal Design Construction

5.1. Construction Method

Several stochastic algorithms can be utilized to construct the optimal designs, such as the threshold accepting method [7], simulated annealing algorithm [16], and stochastic evolutionary algorithm [25]. A standard procedure is as follows:

1. Start with a beginning design.
2. Develop a neighbor design of the current design by using the coordinate exchange algorithm.
3. Calculate the Y-value for the neighbor design, and then decide whether to replace the current design or not.

Now, we give the method to generate the beginning design with branching and nested factors. Such a design consists of three parts. To spread the design points evenly on each dimension, for the branching and shared parts, U-type designs should be adopted, as well as the nested part corresponding to each level of the branching factors utilizing a smaller U-type design.

Construction 1. *Beginning design:*

1. *Randomly generate an $n \times r$ U-type design $\mathbf{B}$ to accommodate the branching factors.*
2. *For level z of the lth branching factor, randomly generate a smaller $(n/q_l) \times t_l$ U-type design for $l = 1, \cdots, r; z = 0, \cdots, q_l - 1$, say $\mathbf{N}_z^l$, and then integrate them based on the levels of the branching factors to accommodate the nested factor $\mathbf{N}^l$, which corresponds to the lth branching factor.*
3. *Randomly generate an $n \times t$ U-type design $\mathbf{S}$ to arrange the nested factors.*
4. *Let*

$$\mathbf{D} = (\mathbf{B}, \mathbf{N}^1, \cdots, \mathbf{N}^r, \mathbf{S}), \tag{10}$$

which consists of r branching factors, t_l factors nested into the lth branching factors, and t shared factors. Thus, there are $r + \sum_{l=1}^{r} t_l + t$ factors in total.

For the constructed design in (10), assume the level of kth factor is $q_k, k = 1, \cdots, r + \sum_{l=1}^{r} t_l + t$. We give an example to illustrate each step of Construction 1.

Example 1. *Let* $n = 8, r = 1, t_1 = 1, t = 1, q_1 = 2, q_2 = 4, q_3 = 8$, *and then a possible outcome from Steps 1–3 can be*

$$\mathbf{B} = \begin{pmatrix} 0 \\ 1 \\ 0 \\ 0 \\ 1 \\ 1 \\ 0 \\ 1 \end{pmatrix}, \quad \mathbf{N}_0^1 = \begin{pmatrix} 0 \\ 1 \\ 2 \\ 3 \end{pmatrix}, \quad \mathbf{N}_1^1 = \begin{pmatrix} 3 \\ 2 \\ 0 \\ 1 \end{pmatrix}, \quad \mathbf{N}^1 = \begin{pmatrix} \mathbf{0} \\ 3 \\ \mathbf{1} \\ \mathbf{2} \\ 2 \\ 0 \\ \mathbf{3} \\ 1 \end{pmatrix}, \quad \mathbf{S} = \begin{pmatrix} 2 \\ 6 \\ 0 \\ 5 \\ 7 \\ 3 \\ 4 \\ 1 \end{pmatrix},$$

Note that the elements of $\mathbf{N}^1$ *coming from* $\mathbf{N}_0^1$ *are bold, corresponding to the rows where the branching factor is at level* 0. *In Step 4, generate the initial design*

$$\mathbf{D} = (\mathbf{B}, \mathbf{N}^1, \mathbf{S}) = \begin{pmatrix} 0 & \mathbf{0} & 2 \\ 1 & 3 & 6 \\ 0 & \mathbf{1} & 0 \\ 0 & \mathbf{2} & 5 \\ 1 & 2 & 7 \\ 1 & 0 & 3 \\ 0 & \mathbf{3} & 4 \\ 1 & 1 & 1 \end{pmatrix}$$

For simplicity, some sets are introduced to collect the column indices where some sub-designs are located. Let $\delta_B = \{1, \cdots, r\}$, that is, column $i \in \delta_B$ of design $\mathbf{D}$ in (10) is a branching factor. In the same fashion, let $\delta_{N^l} = \{r + 1 + \sum_{p=1}^{l} t_{p-1}, \cdots, r + \sum_{p=1}^{l} t_p\}$ for $l = 1, \cdots, r$, and $\delta_S = \{r + 1 + \sum_{l=1}^{r} t_l, \cdots, r + \sum_{l=1}^{r} t_l + t\}$, corresponding to the column indices where the nested factors are for the lth branching factors and the shared factors, respectively. More generally, let $\delta_{BS} = \delta_B \cup \delta_S$ and $\delta_{B_{(-l)}N^lS} = \delta_B \cup \delta_{N^l} \cup \delta_S \setminus \{l\}$, such as, for $\mathbf{D}$ in Example 1, $\delta_{BS} = \{1, 3\}$ and $\delta_{B_{(-1)}N^1S} = \{2, 3\}$.

To generate a neighbor design that maintains the branching–nested relationship, we provide the following construction by modifying the coordinate exchange algorithm.

Construction 2. *Neighbor design:*

1. *Draw a random column number* u *from* $\{1, \cdots, r + t + \sum_{l=1}^{r} t_l\}$.
2. *If* $u \in \delta_B$, *the selected factor is a branching factor, then exchange two randomly locations* (w_1, w_2) *within the uth column, and also exchange the* w_1 *and* w_2 *rows of the* $\mathbf{N}^u$. *There are* $2 + 2t_u$ *changed elements in total.*
3. *If* $u \in \delta_{N^l}, l = 1, \cdots, r$, *the selected factor is a nested factor nested into the lth branching factor, then exchange two randomly locations* (w_1, w_2) *of the uth column where the associated branching factor has the same level.*
4. *If* $u \in \delta_S$, *the selected factor is a shared factor, then exchange two randomly locations* (w_1, w_2) *of uth column.*

Example 2. *Consider neighbor designs of the current* $\mathbf{D}$ *in Example 1.*

(a) *If* $u = 1$, *turn to Step 2, and suppose* $w_1 = 1, w_2 = 2$; *then, we can obtain* $\mathbf{D}_a$. *Here, if we only swap the first and second elements of the branching factor and ignore the associated nested factor, the branching–nested structure will be disrupted.*

(b) *If* $u = 2$, *go to Step 3. Two selected locations should correspond to the same level of the branching factor (such as level 0), i.e.,* $w_1, w_2 \in \{1, 3, 4, 7\}$. *Let* $w_1 = 1, w_2 = 7$, *and then* *the resulting design is $\boldsymbol{D}_b$. In this situation, if two elements come from different levels of the branching factor, then the branching–nested structure should also be broken.*

(c) *If $u = 3$, proceed to Step 4, and assume $w_1 = 2, w_2 = 3$; then, we have $\boldsymbol{D}_c$.*

$$\boldsymbol{D}_a = \begin{pmatrix} \mathbf{1} & \mathbf{3} & 2 \\ \mathbf{0} & \mathbf{0} & 6 \\ 0 & 1 & 0 \\ 0 & 2 & 5 \\ 1 & 2 & 7 \\ 1 & 0 & 3 \\ 0 & 3 & 4 \\ 1 & 1 & 1 \end{pmatrix}, \ \boldsymbol{D}_b = \begin{pmatrix} 0 & \mathbf{3} & 2 \\ 1 & 3 & 6 \\ 0 & 1 & 0 \\ 0 & 2 & 5 \\ 1 & 2 & 7 \\ 1 & 0 & 3 \\ 0 & \mathbf{0} & 4 \\ 1 & 1 & 1 \end{pmatrix}, \ \boldsymbol{D}_c = \begin{pmatrix} 0 & 0 & 2 \\ 1 & 3 & \mathbf{0} \\ 0 & 1 & \mathbf{6} \\ 0 & 2 & 5 \\ 1 & 2 & 7 \\ 1 & 0 & 3 \\ 0 & 3 & 4 \\ 1 & 1 & 1 \end{pmatrix}.$$

The exchanged elements in $\boldsymbol{D}_a, \boldsymbol{D}_b, \boldsymbol{D}_c$ are in bold.

5.2. Iterative Formulas

From Construction 2, the exchanging strategies depend heavily on the kinds of the selected factor. In each iteration (neighbor design), only a few elements have been changed. Through our observations, the value of (9) relies on $1 + \sum_{l=1}^{r} q_l$ sud-designs, many of which remain unchanged after one iteration. Therefore, the criterion can be efficiently updated without recalculating all parts of (9) at each iteration. The neighbor design of $\boldsymbol{D}$ is denoted by $\boldsymbol{D}^*$. It is feasible to skillfully compute the new $\Upsilon(\boldsymbol{D}^*)$ by leveraging the previous $\psi(\boldsymbol{D}_{\boldsymbol{BS}})$ and $\psi(\boldsymbol{D}_{\boldsymbol{B}_{(-l)}\boldsymbol{N}^l\boldsymbol{S}|b_l=z})$. We have

$$\Upsilon(\boldsymbol{D}^*) = \psi(\boldsymbol{D}^*_{\boldsymbol{BS}}) + \sum_{l=1}^{r}\sum_{z=0}^{q_l-1} \psi(\boldsymbol{D}^*_{\boldsymbol{B}_{(-l)}\boldsymbol{N}^l\boldsymbol{S}|b_l=z}). \tag{11}$$

The computational complexity of (11) consists of two parts. The calculation of the first and second parts will take $O(n^2(r+t))$ and $\sum_{l=1}^{r} O((n^2/q_l)(r-1+t_l+t))$, respectively. In the rest of this section, three possible neighbors from Steps 2, 3, and 4 of Construction 2 are discussed, respectively, and the iterative formulas for them are derived separately.

(a) If $u \in \delta_B$, since the branching factor determines the manner of partitioning, it becomes quite complex, and thus, the iterative formula for the second part of (11) is not considered. The first part of (11) can be updated iteratively. Let $h_{\boldsymbol{BS}}(x_i, x_j) = \prod_{k\in\delta_{BS}} \xi(x_{ik}, x_{jk})$, and x_i and x_j correspond to the ith and jth rows of design $\boldsymbol{D}$. Note that $\boldsymbol{D}^*_{\boldsymbol{BS}}$ is obtained by interchanging the w_1 and w_2 positions of the uth column of $\boldsymbol{D}_{\boldsymbol{BS}}$; then, for $1 \le i \le n$ and $i \ne w_1, w_2$, we have

$$h_{\boldsymbol{BS}}(x_i, x^*_{w_1}) = h_{\boldsymbol{BS}}(x_i, x_{w_1})\frac{\xi(x_{iu}, x_{w_2u})}{\xi(x_{iu}, x_{w_1u})}$$

and

$$h_{\boldsymbol{BS}}(x_i, x^*_{w_2}) = h_{\boldsymbol{BS}}(x_i, x_{w_2})\frac{\xi(x_{iu}, x_{w_1u})}{\xi(x_{iu}, x_{w_2u})},$$

where $x^*_{w_1}$ and $x^*_{w_2}$ are the w_1th and w_2th rows of $\boldsymbol{D}^*_{\boldsymbol{BS}}$. It can be easily derived that

$$\begin{aligned}[\psi(\boldsymbol{D}^*_{\boldsymbol{BS}})]^{r+t} =& [\psi(\boldsymbol{D}_{\boldsymbol{BS}})]^{r+t} + 2\sum_{i(\ne w1,w2)=1}^{n}\left(\frac{1}{h_{\boldsymbol{BS}}(x_i, x^*_{w_1})} - \frac{1}{h_{\boldsymbol{BS}}(x_i, x_{w_1})}\right) \\ &+ 2\sum_{i(\ne w1,w2)=1}^{n}\left(\frac{1}{h_{\boldsymbol{BS}}(x_i, x^*_{w_2})} - \frac{1}{h_{\boldsymbol{BS}}(x_i, x_{w_2})}\right),\end{aligned} \tag{12}$$

for which the computational complexity is $O(n)$.

(b) If $u \in \delta_{N^l}, l = 1, \cdots, r$, assume the selected locations (w_1, w_2) in the uth column correspond to level i_0 of the l_0th branching factor. Clearly, the sub-design for branching and shared factors remains unchanged, and thus, the value for the first part of (11) does not change; that is,

$$[\psi(D^*_{BS})]^{r+t} = [\psi(D_{BS})]^{r+t}.$$

As for the second part of (11), among the $\sum_{l=1}^r q_l$ terms involved, only one of them is subject to change, as follows,

$$\psi(D^*_{B_{(-l)}N^lS|b_l=z})^{r-1+t+t_l} = \begin{cases} \psi(D_{B_{(-l)}N^lS|b_l=z})^{r-1+t+t_l} \\ +2\sum_{i\in I(\neq w1,w2)}\left(\frac{1}{h_{B_{(-l)}N^lS}(x_i,x^*_{w_1})} - \frac{1}{h_{B_{(-l)}N^lS}(x_i,x_{w_1})}\right) \\ +2\sum_{i\in I(\neq w1,w2)}\left(\frac{1}{h_{B_{(-l)}N^lS}(x_i,x^*_{w_2})} - \frac{1}{h_{B_{(-l)}N^lS}(x_i,x_{w_2})}\right), & \text{if } l = l_0 \text{ and } z = z_0, \\ \psi(D_{B_{(-l)}N^lS|b_l=z})^{r-1+t+t_l}, & \text{otherwise,} \end{cases}$$

where I is a set, collecting row indices where the l_0th branching factor takes level z_0. In addition, $h_{B_{(-l)}N^lS}(\cdot,\cdot)$ can be similarly defined as $h_{BS}(\cdot,\cdot)$. The computation will take $O(n/q_{l_0})$, if $l = l_0$ as well as $z = z_0$, and 0 otherwise.

(c) If $u \in \delta_S$, $[\psi(D^*_{BS})]^{r+t}$ can be calculated by (12). In addition, depending on the levels of branching factors at w_1 and w_2 positions, it can be further divided into the following two cases:

(i) The w_1 and w_2 runs of the lth branching factor have the same level, say level c, denoting the corresponding run indices such that the lth branching factor takes level c as I^l_c, then

$$\psi(D^*_{B_{(-l)}N^lS|b_l=z})^{r-1+t+t_l} = \begin{cases} \psi(D_{B_{(-l)}N^lS|b_l=z})^{r-1+t+t_l}, & \text{if } z \neq c, \\ \psi(D_{B_{(-l)}N^lS|b_l=z})^{r-1+t+t_l} \\ +2\sum\limits_{i\in I^l_c(\neq w1,w2)}\left(\frac{1}{h_{B_{(-l)}N^lS}(x_i,x^*_{w_1})} - \frac{1}{h_{B_{(-l)}N^lS}(x_i,x_{w_1})}\right) \\ +2\sum\limits_{i\in I^l_c(\neq w1,w2)}\left(\frac{1}{h_{B_{(-l)}N^lS}(x_i,x^*_{w_2})} - \frac{1}{h_{B_{(-l)}N^lS}(x_i,x_{w_2})}\right), & \text{if } z = c. \end{cases}$$

(ii) The w_1 and w_2 runs of the lth branching factor take two distinct levels, say level c, c', respectively. Similarly, define $I^l_c, I^l_{c'}$, then

$$\psi(D^*_{B_{(-l)}N^lS|b_l=z})^{r-1+t+t_l} = \begin{cases} \psi(D_{B_{(-l)}N^lS|b_l=z})^{r-1+t+t_l}, & \text{if } z \neq c, c', \\ \psi(D_{B_{(-l)}N^lS|b_l=z})^{r-1+t+t_l} \\ +2\sum\limits_{i\in I^l_c(\neq w1,w2)}\left(\frac{1}{h_{B_{(-l)}N^lS}(x_i,x^*_{w_1})} - \frac{1}{h_{B_{(-l)}N^lS}(x_i,x_{w_1})}\right), & \text{if } z = c, \\ \psi(D_{B_{(-l)}N^lS|b_l=z})^{r-1+t+t_l} \\ +2\sum\limits_{i\in I^l_{c'}(\neq w1,w2)}\left(\frac{1}{h_{B_{(-l)}N^lS}(x_i,x^*_{w_2})} - \frac{1}{h_{B_{(-l)}N^lS}(x_i,x_{w_2})}\right), & \text{if } z = c'. \end{cases}$$

In the same fashion, the computational complexity can be given.

Let $k_l = r - 1 + t + t_l$. Overall, the computational complexity of (11) by using the original method is $O(n^2(r+t) + \sum_{l=1}^{r}(n^2/q_l)k_l)$. Theorem 1 summarizes the complexities of the iterative method for three different cases.

Theorem 1. *The computational complexities for* (11) *by using the iterative method are as follows.*

(a) *If a branching factor is selected, the computational complexity is* $O(n + \sum_{l=1}^{r}(n^2/q_l)k_l)$.
(b) *If a nested factor associated with the* l_0*th branching factor is selected, the computational complexity is* $O(n/q_{l_0})$.
(c) *If a shared factor is selected, the computational complexity is* $O(n + \sum_{l=1}^{r}(n/q_l))$.

Assume that each factor has an equal probability of being chosen, then from Step 1 of Construction 2, the probabilities of the three kinds of factors, i.e., branching, nested, and shared factors, being selected in each iteration are $r/(r+t+\sum_{l=1}^{r} t_l)$, $\sum_{l=1}^{r} t_l/(r+t+\sum_{l=1}^{r} t_l)$, and $t/(r+t+\sum_{l=1}^{r} t_l)$, respectively. From Theorem 1, it can be found that the computational complexity has been significantly reduced for each iteration.

6. Numerical Comparisons

In this section, we examine the performances of the low-dimensional projections for the optimal designs with branching and nested factors (for short, BNS designs) under (9), (5), (6), and the random design, (referred to as "Maxpro BNS", "Hung BNS", "UD BNS", and "Random BNS", respectively), across three criteria: (a) the maximin design criterion in (2), (b) the average correlation in (1), and (c) the Maxpro distance criterion in (3), denoted by "Mm", "Ave-corr", and "Maxpro", respectively. For all the criteria, the smaller the better.

Example 3. *Let there be one two-level branching factor, one twenty-level factor nested in the branching factor, and seven forty-level shared factors with forty points. To make a comparison, we have to assume that the branching factor is qualitative, while the rest of the factors are quantitative because Hung's method has such limitations.*

The projected designs of the shared parts onto $2 \leq k \leq 6$ *dimensions, as well as the projected designs of the nested and shared parts onto* $2 \leq k \leq 7$ *dimensions corresponding to each level of the branching factor are investigated, respectively. Only the worst cases are presented, for example, in Figure 3a, there are a total of* $\binom{7}{2} = 21$ *possible two-dimensional projected designs for the shared designs of the Maxpro BNS design, and the "Mm" value for the worst one among them is* 0.1362. *Figure 3 shows that the proposed Maxpro BNS design is the best under "Mm" and "Maxpro", and performs well in terms of "Ave-corr", just behind the Hung BNS design. As expected, the random BNS design is the worst under all the criteria. In addition, after partitioning the nested and shared factors into slices by the levels of the branching factor, from Figures 4–6, it can be easily found that Maxpro BNS behaves substantially better with respect to "Mm", "Ave_corr", and "Maxpro".*

To show that the proposed Maxpro BNS design can achieve better grid stratification than a UD BNS design, another simple example is presented.

Example 4. *Consider a sixteen-run design with one two-level qualitative branching factor, one two-level qualitative factor nested within it, and additionally, two eight-level quantitative and two sixteen-level quantitative shared factors (i.e.,* $r = 1, t_1 = 1, t = 4, q_1 = q_2 = 2, q_3 = q_4 = 8, q_5 = q_6 = 16$*). The optimal designs under Maxpro BNS and UD BNS criterion are listed in Table 2, denoted by* $\mathbf{D}_1$ *and* $\mathbf{D}_2$*, respectively. Scatter points of bivariate projection of* $\mathbf{D}_1$ *and* $\mathbf{D}_2$ *are shown in Figure 7. Note that the two designs are generated by stochastic methods without utilizing any specific structure. Surprisingly, the points of the Maxpro BNS design appear to achieve stratification on grids like the OA-based structure. Focus on Figure 7a, with exactly four points in each of the* 2×2 *grids for any two variables, as well as exactly two red/green points in each of the* 2×2 *grids. However, as depicted in Figure 7b, it is evident that* $\mathbf{D}_2$ *cannot achieve such properties.*

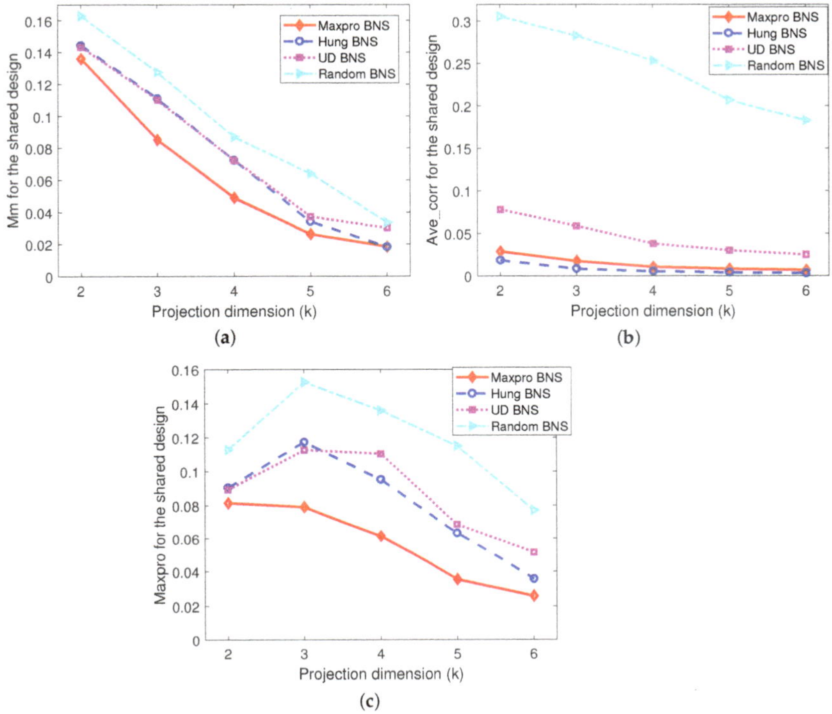

Figure 3. The comparisons of projection designs under "Mm", "Ave_corr", and "Maxpro". (**a**) Mm; (**b**) Ave_corr; (**c**) Maxpro.

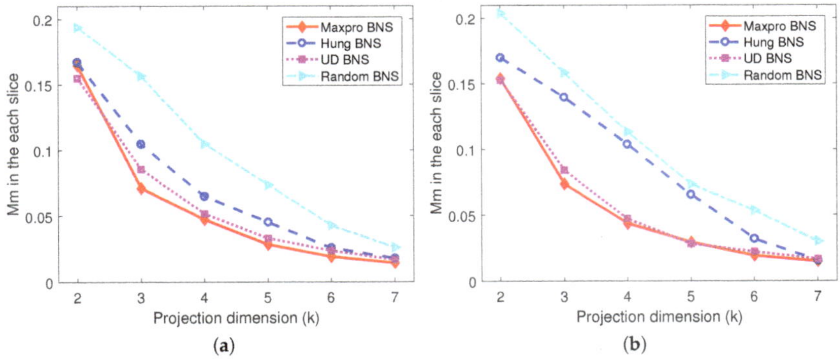

Figure 4. Comparisons of projection designs under "Mm". (**a**) When $B = 0$. (**b**) When $B = 1$.

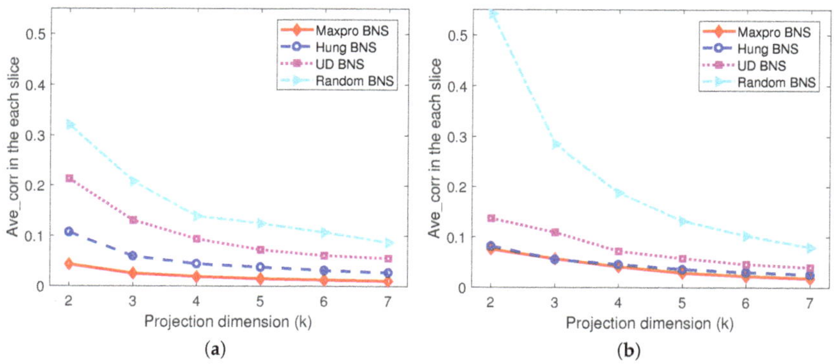

Figure 5. Comparisons of projection designs under "Ave_corr". (**a**) When $B = 0$. (**b**) When $B = 1$.

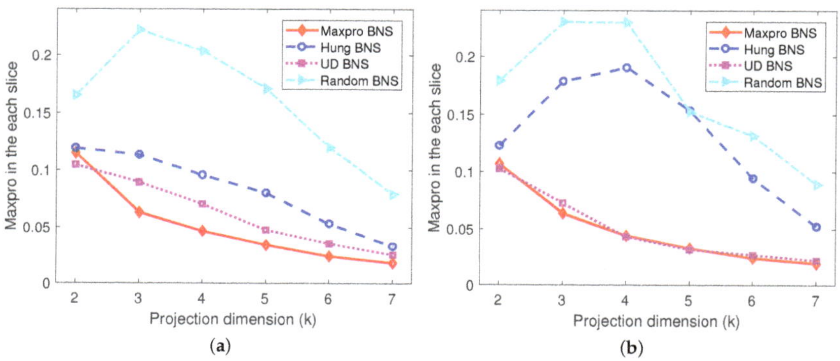

Figure 6. Comparisons of projection designs under "Maxpro". (**a**) When $B = 0$. (**b**) When $B = 1$.

Table 2. The Maxpro BNS design $\boldsymbol{D}_1$ and the UD BNS design $\boldsymbol{D}_2$.

Run	D_1						D_2					
	B	N	S_1	S_2	S_3	S_4	B	N	S_1	S_2	S_3	S_4
1	0	0	3	1	10	12	0	0	4	4	2	8
2	0	0	7	0	3	5	0	0	0	6	6	12
3	0	0	6	6	6	14	0	0	5	2	14	0
4	0	0	1	5	13	6	0	0	2	0	10	4
5	0	1	4	7	8	3	0	1	6	5	8	2
6	0	1	5	3	15	9	0	1	1	3	12	10
7	0	1	2	4	0	11	0	1	3	7	0	14
8	0	1	0	2	5	1	0	1	7	1	4	6
9	1	0	4	5	14	13	1	0	7	4	11	13
10	1	0	3	6	2	2	1	0	5	6	15	5
11	1	0	6	1	11	4	1	0	1	2	3	1
12	1	0	0	7	9	8	1	0	3	0	7	9
13	1	1	1	0	4	10	1	1	0	1	13	7
14	1	1	2	3	12	0	1	1	6	7	5	15
15	1	1	5	2	1	15	1	1	2	5	1	11
16	1	1	7	4	7	7	1	1	4	3	9	3

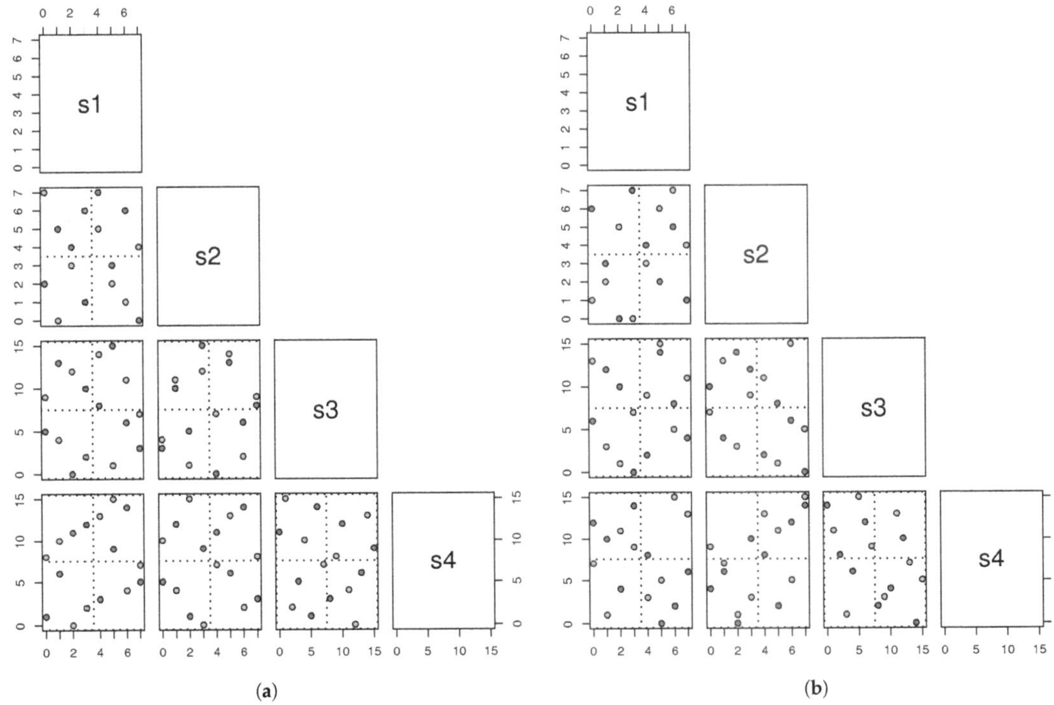

Figure 7. Scatter points of bivariate projections for D_1 and D_2 in Example 4. The red color corresponds to level 0 of the branching factor, while the green color corresponds to level 1 of the branching factor. (**a**) D_1; (**b**) D_2.

7. Discussion

In this paper, we have introduced a novel criterion to quantify the performance of the designs with the branching and nested factors based on the maximum projection principle. We have developed a comprehensive framework for constructing optimal designs under this criterion and demonstrated its advantages through numerical comparisons, particularly in terms of maintaining superior space-filling properties across projections to nearly all subsets of factors. To enhance the efficiency of design optimization, we provide the iterative formulas that significantly reduce the computational complexity involved in the design optimization process.

There are some future research directions from this paper. One significant direction is the theoretical construction of optimal designs under the proposed criterion. There is potential to derive closed-form solutions for optimal designs under certain conditions. Such theoretical results will enhance the efficiency of design construction in practical applications. Another is to verify the performance of Maxpro BNS designs in various modeling contexts. For instance, studying the behavior of Maxpro designs in polynomial regression models or Gaussian process (GP) models. This study could provide valuable insights into their effectiveness in capturing complex relationships in experimental data, which helps to further validate the applicability of the Maxpro BNS designs.

Author Contributions: Conceptualization, F.Y. and Z.Z.; methodology, F.Y. and Z.Z.; writing—original draft preparation, F.Y.; writing—review and editing, F.Y. and Z.Z.; supervision, Z.Z.; funding acquisition, F.Y. All authors have read and agreed to the published version of the manuscript.

Funding: This research was funded by the National Natural Science Foundation of China (No. 12101435), Research Foundation of Sichuan Normal University (No. pt12101435, ky20200919).

Institutional Review Board Statement: Not applicable.

Data Availability Statement: The data presented in this study are available on request from the corresponding author.

Acknowledgments: The authors thank Yongdao Zhou for his help and guidance in preparing this paper.

Conflicts of Interest: The authors declare no conflicts of interest.

References

1. Hung, Y.; Joseph, V.R.; Melkote, S.N. Design and Analysis of Computer Experiments With Branching and Nested Factors. *Technometrics* **2009**, *51*, 354–365. [CrossRef]
2. Decrop, D.; Lammertyn, J.; Goos, P. Optimal experimental design for efficient optical manipulation of magnetic beads seeded in a microwell array. *J. Q. Technol.* **2017**, *49*, 402–417. [CrossRef]
3. Su, H.; Wu, C.J. CME analysis: A new method for unraveling aliased effects in two-level fractional factorial experiments. *J. Q. Technol.* **2017**, *49*, 1–10. [CrossRef]
4. Goos, P.; Jones, B. Optimal Experimental Design in the Presence of Nested Factors. *Technometrics* **2019**, *61*, 533–544. [CrossRef]
5. Yang, F.; Zhou, Z.; Zhou, Y.D. Uniform Designs for Experiments with Branching and Nested Factors. *JMVA* 2024, *under review*.
6. Santner, T.J.; Williams, B.J.; Notz, W.I. *The Design and Analysis of Computer Experiments*; Springer: New York, NY, USA, 2003.
7. Fang, K.T.; Liu, M.Q.; Qin, H.; Zhou, Y.D. *Theory and Application of Uniform Experimental Designs*; Springer: Singapore, 2018.
8. Korobov, N.M. The approximate computation of multiple integrals. *Dokl. Akad. Nauk. SSSR* **1959**, *124*, 1207–1210.
9. Niederreiter, H. *Random Number Generation and Quasi-Monte Carlo Methods*; SIAM: Philadelphia, PA, USA, 1992.
10. Fang, K.T.; Li, R.Z.; Sudjianto, A. *Design and Modeling for Computer Experiments*; Chapman and Hall/CRC: New York, NY, USA, 2006.
11. Shewry, M.C.; Wynn, H.P. Maximum entropy sampling. *J. Appl. Stat.* **1987**, *14*, 165–170. [CrossRef]
12. Mitchell, T.J.; Scott, D.S. A computer program for the design of group testing experiments. *Commun. Stat. Theory Methods* **1987**, *16*, 2943–2955. [CrossRef]
13. Currin, C.; Mitchell, T.; Morris, M.; Ylvisaker, D. Bayesian prediction of deterministic functions, with applications to the design and analysis of computer experiments. *J. Am. Stat. Assoc.* **1991**, *86*, 953–963. [CrossRef]
14. Koehler, J.R.; Owen, A.B. Computer experiments. In *Handbook of Statistics*; Ghosh, S., Rao, C.R., Eds.; Elsevier Science: New York, NY, USA, 1996; Volume 13, pp. 261–308.
15. Lam C.Q. Sequential Adaptive Designs in Computer Experiments for Response Surface Model Fit. Ph.D. Thesis, The Ohio State University, Columbus, OH, USA, 2008.
16. Morris, M.D.; Mitchell, T.J. Exploratory designs for computational experiments. *J. Stat. Plan. Inference* **1995**, *43*, 381–402. [CrossRef]
17. Johnson, M.E.; Moore, L.M.; Ylvisaker, D. Minimax and maximin distance designs. *J. Stat. Plan. Inference* **1990**, *26*, 131–148. [CrossRef]
18. Joseph, V.R.; Gul, E.; Ba, S. Maximum projection designs for computer experiments. *Biometrika* **2015**, *102*, 371–380. [CrossRef]
19. Joseph, V.R.; Gul, E.; Ba, S. Designing Computer Experiments with Multiple Types of Factors: The MaxPro Approach. *J. Q. Technol.* **2020**, *52*, 343–354. [CrossRef]
20. Owen, A. Controlling correlations in Latin hypercube samples. *J. Am. Stat. Assoc.* **1994**, *89*, 1517-1522. [CrossRef]
21. Zhang, M.; Yang, F.; Zhou, Y.D. Uniformity Criterion for Designs with Both Qualitative and Quantitative Factors. *Statistics* **2021**, *55*, 90–109. [CrossRef]
22. Chen, H.; Yang, J.Y.; Lin, D.K.J.; Liu, M.Q. Sliced Latin Hypercube Designs with Both Branching and Nested Factors. *Stat. Probab. Lett.* **2019**, *146*, 124–131. [CrossRef]
23. Chen, H.; Yang, J.Y.; Liu, M.Q. Construction of Improved Branching Latin Hypercube Designs. *Acta Math. Sci.* **2021**, *41*, 1023–1033. [CrossRef]
24. Wei, Q.; Liu, M.Q.; Yang, J.F. Orthogonal Designs with Branching and Nested Factors. *Stat* **2022**, *11*, e447. [CrossRef]
25. Jin, R.; Chen, W.; Sudjianto, A. An Efficient Algorithm for Constructing Optimal Design of Computer Experiments. *J. Stat. Plan. Inference* **2005**, *134*, 268–287. [CrossRef]

entropy

MDPI

Article

The Representative Points of Generalized Alpha Skew-*t* Distribution and Applications

Yong-Feng Zhou [1,†], Yu-Xuan Lin [2,3,†], Kai-Tai Fang [4] and Hong Yin [1,*]

1 School of Mathematics, Renmin University of China, No. 59, Zhongguancun Street, Haidian District, Beijing 100872, China; zyfeng177@ruc.edu.cn
2 Research Center for Frontier Fundamental Studies, Zhejiang Lab, Kechuang Avenue, Zhongtai Sub-District, Yuhang District, Hangzhou 311121, China; yuxuanlin@zhejianglab.com
3 Guangdong Provincial Key Laboratory of Interdisciplinary Research and Application for Data Science, BNU-HKBU United International College, Zhuhai 519087, China
4 Department of Statistics and Data Science, Faculty of Science and Technology, BNU-HKBU United International College, 2000 Jintong Road, Tangjiawan, Zhuhai 519087, China; ktfang@uic.edu.cn
* Correspondence: yinhong@ruc.edu.cn
† These authors contributed equally to this work.

Abstract: Assuming the underlying statistical distribution of data is critical in information theory, as it impacts the accuracy and efficiency of communication and the definition of entropy. The real-world data are widely assumed to follow the normal distribution. To better comprehend the skewness of the data, many models more flexible than the normal distribution have been proposed, such as the generalized alpha skew-*t* (GAST) distribution. This paper studies some properties of the GAST distribution, including the calculation of the moments, and the relationship between the number of peaks and the GAST parameters with some proofs. For complex probability distributions, representative points (RPs) are useful due to the convenience of manipulation, computation and analysis. The relative entropy of two probability distributions could have been a good criterion for the purpose of generating RPs of a specific distribution but is not popularly used due to computational complexity. Hence, this paper only provides three ways to obtain RPs of the GAST distribution, Monte Carlo (MC), quasi-Monte Carlo (QMC), and mean square error (MSE). The three types of RPs are utilized in estimating moments and densities of the GAST distribution with known and unknown parameters. The MSE representative points perform the best among all case studies. For unknown parameter cases, a revised maximum likelihood estimation (MLE) method of parameter estimation is compared with the plain MLE method. It indicates that the revised MLE method is suitable for the GAST distribution having a unimodal or unobvious bimodal pattern. This paper includes two real-data applications in which the GAST model appears adaptable to various types of data.

Keywords: entropy; generalized alpha skew-*t* distribution; kernel density estimation; maximum likelihood estimation; moments; quasi-Monte Carlo; representative points

1. Introduction

Statistical distributions play a crucial role in information theory since they describe the probability characteristics of data or signals, and hence directly affect the accuracy and efficiency of the representation, transmission, compression, and reconstruction of information. Entropy, as the most important measure in the field of information theory, depends on the statistical distribution of the random variable. In many applications of information theory, it requires the assumption of the statistical distribution of the data. Although assumed to follow the normal distribution in most statistical analyses due to mathematical convenience and generality, real-world data frequently exhibit skewness, leading to the demand for more flexible models. The geometric Brownian motion (GBM) as a popular model of stochastic processes assumes that its solutions follow the log-normal distribution. Gupta et al. (2024) [1] indicated that the GBM yields trajectories significantly deviated from the reference distribution when the data do not meet the log-normal assumption. To deal with the limitations in such a scenario, some may consider correcting the model as in [1]. Constructing alternative distributions of the normal distribution has been a common concern.

The skew-normal (SN) distribution is an extension of the normal distribution that allows for skewness, capable of modeling asymmetric data. It was first introduced by Azzalini (1985) [2]. If a random variable Z has a probability density function (pdf) given by

$$\phi(z;s) = 2\phi(z)\Phi(sz), \quad z \in \mathcal{R}, \quad s \in \mathcal{R}, \tag{1}$$

where $\phi(\cdot)$ and $\Phi(\cdot)$ are the pdf and cumulative distribution function (cdf) of the standard normal distribution, then Z follows the SN distribution, denoted as $Z \sim SN(s)$. The parameter s controls the skewness of the distribution. When $s = 0$, the SN distribution reduces to the standard normal distribution. With $s > 0$, the SN distribution is right-skewed, while $s < 0$ implies left skewness.

The skew-t (ST) distribution is an intriguing example among scale mixtures of SN distributions. It was first formulated by Branco and Dey (2001) [3] and later extensively studied by Azzalini and Capitanio (2003) [4]. An ST random variable, $Y \sim ST(s, \nu)$, can be represented as

$$Y = \frac{Z}{\sqrt{V/\nu}}, \tag{2}$$

where $Z \sim SN(s)$ and $V \sim \chi^2_\nu$, i.e., chi-square distribution with ν degrees of freedom, are independent of each other. The moment of Y exists only when the order is less than ν, which is the same condition required as the Student's t-distribution with ν degrees of freedom, denoted by t_ν. The construction method from the SN distribution to the ST distribution is similar to the approach used to derive the Student's t-distribution from the normal distribution. The pdf of the ST distribution is given by

$$f(y;s,\nu) = 2t(y;\nu)T\left(\sqrt{\frac{1+\nu}{y^2+\nu}}sy;\nu+1\right), \quad y \in \mathcal{R}, \quad s \in \mathcal{R}, \tag{3}$$

where $t(\cdot)$ is the pdf of t_ν, and $T(\cdot)$ is the cdf of $t_{\nu+1}$. The parameter ν controls the tail heaviness. As ν approaches infinity, the ST distribution approaches the SN distribution. Lower values of ν result in heavier tails, providing robustness against outliers. Similar to the SN distribution, the parameter s controls the skewness. When $s = 0$, the ST distribution reduces to the Student's t-distribution. Azzalini and Genton (2008) [5] conducted a quite extensive numerical exploration, demonstrating that the ST distribution can adapt well to various empirical problems. They utilized an autoregressive model of order one, $Y(t) = \beta_0 + \beta_1 Y(t-1) + \epsilon(t)$ with $\beta_0 \in \mathcal{R}$ and $|\beta_1| \leq 1$, to fit the 91 monthly interest rates of an Austrian bank. Their results clearly showed that the error components $\epsilon(t)$ have an ST distribution, where the small degrees of freedom parameter signifies heavy tails in the error distribution, allowing the ST model to better manage outliers than the normal distribution. The ST distribution, which combines the characteristics of the Student's t-distribution and the SN distribution, is particularly suitable for the applications in finance that need to model returns with skewness and excess kurtosis, as well as in environmental studies where the focus is on modeling extreme events. Martínez-Flórez et al. (2020) [6] also mentioned other kinds of skew distributions like skew-Student-t distribution, skew-Cauchy distribution, skew-logistic distribution and skew-Laplace distribution. They summarized those distributions as skew-elliptical distributions since those distributions have a unified expression form of the density function as

$$h_Y(y;s) = 2f(y)F(sy), \quad y, s \in \mathrm{R},$$

where $f(\cdot)$ is a symmetric pdf, and $F(\cdot)$ is the corresponding cdf.

Another type of skew distribution is to add a coefficient function with an α argument to the density function. Elal-Olivero (2010) [7] proposed a distribution called alpha-skew-normal (ASN), with a pdf defined as

$$f(x;\alpha) = \frac{(1-\alpha x)^2+1}{2+\alpha^2}\phi(x), \quad x \in \mathcal{R}, \quad \alpha \in \mathcal{R}. \tag{4}$$

If a random variable X has the pdf as (4), we denote it as $X \sim ASN(\alpha)$. This distribution is more flexible than SN and ST distributions since it can be unimodal or multimodal by adjusting the α parameter. When $\alpha = 0$, the ASN distribution reduces to the standard normal distribution, $X \sim N(0,1)$.

Although the ASN distribution is able to model both skew and bimodal data, it has limitations when data have tails thinner or thicker than the normal distribution. In order to fit stock data more accurately, Altun et al. (2018) [8] introduced a new generalized alpha skew-t (GAST) distribution combining the approaches of [4,7]. They combined the GAST distribution with the generalized autoregressive conditional heteroskedasticity (GARCH) model to build a new Value-at-Risk (VaR) prediction model for forecasting daily log returns in three years. They compared the failure rates of the GARCH models under different distribution assumptions including normal, Student's t, ST and GAST. The results showed that the GAST distribution performs the best in the backtesting. The definition of GAST distribution and its properties with proof will be elaborated in the next section.

For an unknown continuous statistical distribution, an empirical distribution of a random sample is a traditional way to approximate the target distribution. However, it often leads to low accuracy, and hence the support points for the discrete approximation, also known as representative points (RPs), are explored in order to preserve the information of the target distribution as much as possible. Representative points have a big potential for applications in statistical simulation and inference, see Fang and Pan (2023) [9] for a comprehensive review. Various kinds of representative points of different statistical distributions have been explored in the literature. Especially for complex distributions, the study on the representative points is necessary. The concept of representative points is to simplify complex probability distributions with discrete points easier to manipulate, facilitating efficient computations and analyses. These points serve as a finite set that approximates the distribution of a random variable that can be either discrete or continuous and either univariate or multivariate. In this paper, we focus on the study of the representative points of the GAST distribution and applications. We first introduce the concepts of three kinds of RPs here, while the specific construction procedures are included in Section 4 with their applications on the estimation of moments and densities.

There are many existing criteria for choosing RPs of a distribution, such as Monte Carlo RPs (MC-RPs), quasi-Monte Carlo RPs (QMC-RPs) and mean square error RPs (MSE-RPs) that will be introduced as follows. In fact, the Kullback–Leibler (KL) divergence or relative entropy of two probability distributions is a good criterion for this purpose. The entropy has been utilized as a measure of the experimental design, for example, Lin et al. (2022) [10]. Due to computational complexity, entropy is not popularly used in generating RPs in applications. Therefore, in this article, we study MC-RPs, QMC-RPs, and MSE-RPs of the Generalized alpha skew-t distribution only.

1.1. Monte Carlo Representative Points

Let X be the population random variable with the cdf $F(x) = P\{X \leq x\}$, $x \in R$. Various Monte Carlo methods provide ways to generate independent identically distributed (i.i.d.) samples $\{x_1, \ldots, x_n\}$ from the population, and $p(x_i) = \frac{1}{n}$, $i = 1, \ldots, n$. The empirical distribution of the random sample is defined as follows:

$$F_n(x) = \frac{1}{n}\sum_{i=1}^{n} I_{\{x_i \leq x\}},$$

where I_A is the indicator function of A. The empirical distribution $F_n(x)$ should be close to $F(x)$ in the sense of consistency. Hence, $F_n(x)$ can be regarded as an approximation of $F(x)$. We denote this empirical distribution of random samples generated by the Monte Carlo method as F_{MC}. Traditional statistical inference is based on the empirical distribution. Efron (1979) [11] proposed a resampling technique, *the bootstrap* method, with which we can take a set of random samples from F_{MC} instead of F. Combined with bootstrap, the MC-RPs have proven to be useful in statistical inference, such as parameter estimation, density estimation and hypothesis testing. However, the MC method has many limitations since the convergence rate of $F_n(x) \to F(x)$ in distribution as $n \to \infty$, given by $O(\frac{1}{\sqrt{n}})$, is too slow. The following two kinds of RPs improve the convergence rate nicely.

1.2. Quasi-Monte Carlo Representative Points

For a high-dimensional integration problem:

$$I(f) = \int_0^1 \cdots \int_0^1 f(y_1, \ldots, y_d) dy_1 \cdots dy_d = \int_{C^d} f(\boldsymbol{y}) d\boldsymbol{y},$$

where f is a continuous function on $C^d = [0,1]^d$. Suppose that $\mathcal{Y} = \{\boldsymbol{y}_1, \ldots, \boldsymbol{y}_n\}$ is a set of n points uniformly scattered in C^d, we can estimate $I(f)$ by

$$\overline{f(\boldsymbol{y})} = \frac{1}{n} \sum_{i=1}^{n} f(\boldsymbol{y}_i), \quad \boldsymbol{y}_i \in \mathcal{Y}.$$

If we generate $\mathcal{Y}$ by the MC method, the convergence rate of $\overline{f(\boldsymbol{y})} \to I(f)$ is $O(1/\sqrt{n})$ as $n \to \infty$. The quasi-Monte Carlo (QMC) method provides many ways for the construction of $\mathcal{Y}$ to increase the convergence rate. Through the QMC method, the convergence rate can reach $O(n^{-1}\log^d n)$ according to Fang et al. (1994) [12]. For further theory studies, readers can refer to Hua and Wang (1981) [13] and Niederreiter (1992) [14]. In the study of [12], the F-discrepancy is used to measure the uniformity of $\mathcal{Y}$ in C^d, which is defined by

$$D(F, F_n) = \sup_{\boldsymbol{x} \in \mathrm{R}^d} |F(\boldsymbol{x}) - F_n(\boldsymbol{x})|, \tag{5}$$

where $F(\boldsymbol{x})$ is the cdf of uniform distribution $U(C^d)$ and $F_n(\boldsymbol{x})$ is the empirical distribution of $\mathcal{Y}$. The $\mathcal{Y}$ that minimizes $D(F, F_n)$ is called QMC-RPs which have equal probability $1/n$.

For the univariate distribution of this paper, the QMC method is designed to sample points that are uniformly distributed on the interval $[0,1]$. If the inverse function of F exists, then the set of n points:

$$\left\{ b_j = F^{-1}\left(\frac{2j-1}{2n}\right), j = 1, \ldots, n \right\}, \tag{6}$$

has been proved to have the minimal F-discrepancy of $1/2n$ from $F(x)$ [12]. Therefore, the set of points $\mathcal{B} = \{b_1, \ldots, b_n\}$ is called the QMC-RPs of $F(x)$. Fang et al. (1994) [12] gave a comprehensive study on QMC methods and their applications in statistical inference, experimental design, geometric probability, and optimization.

1.3. Mean Square Error Representative Points

The concept of MSE-RPs was independently proposed by Cox (1957) [15], Flury (1990) [16] and many others. In the literature, "MSE-RPs" have been called by different names, such as "quantized" and "principal points". Let a random variable $X \sim F(x)$ with finite mean μ and variance σ^2. To provide the best representation of F for a given number

n, we select a set of n representative points having the least mean square error from $F(x)$, and form a discrete distribution $F_{MSE}^{(n)}$. Denote $Y_{MSE}^{(n)} \sim F_{MSE}^{(n)}$ defined as

$$F_{MSE}^{(n)}(y) = \sum_{i=1}^{n} p_i^{(n)} I_{\{b_i^{(n)} \le y\}},$$

with the probability mass function

$$f(y = b_i^{(n)}) = p_i^{(n)}, \quad i = 1, \cdots, n, \tag{7}$$

where $-\infty < b_1^{(n)} < b_2^{(n)} < \cdots < b_n^{(n)} < \infty$ are MSE-RPs of X and $p_1^{(n)}, \cdots, p_n^{(n)}$ are the corresponding probabilities with respect to

$$MSE(Y_{MSE}) = MSE\left(b_1^{(n)}, \cdots, b_n^{(n)}\right) = \int_{-\infty}^{\infty} \min_{i=1,\cdots,n} \left(x - b_i^{(n)}\right)^2 f(x)dx, \tag{8}$$

and

$$\begin{aligned} p_1^{(n)} &= \int_{-\infty}^{(b_1^{(n)}+b_2^{(n)})/2} f(x)dx, \\ p_i^{(n)} &= \int_{(b_{i-1}^{(n)}+b_i^{(n)})/2}^{(b_i^{(n)}+b_{i+1}^{(n)})/2} f(x)dx, \quad i = 2, \ldots, n-1, \\ p_n^{(n)} &= \int_{(b_{n-1}^{(n)}+b_n^{(n)})/2}^{+\infty} f(x)dx. \end{aligned}$$

The MSE-RPs have many useful properties. Graf and Luschgy (2007) [17], and Fei (1991) [18] proved that

$$E\left[Y_{MSE}^{(n)}\right] = E[X], \quad \lim_{n\to\infty} E\left[(X - Y_{MSE}^{(n)})^2\right] = \lim_{n\to\infty}\left[\mathrm{Var}(X) - \mathrm{Var}(Y_{MSE}^{(n)})\right] = 0. \tag{9}$$

Hence, $Y_{MSE}^{(n)}$ converges to X in distribution.

In this paper, Section 2 begins by reviewing the definition and properties of the GAST distribution. To explore the relationship between the classification of the GAST distribution and the three parameters α, s, ν, we apply the uniform design (Wang and Fang 1981 [19]) to arrange the values of parameter combinations, and then depict the corresponding density plots. Section 2 also classifies the GAST distribution according to the number of peaks in the density function with some proofs. The first four order moments and stochastic representation of the GAST distribution are shown in this section. Section 3 mainly introduces a maximum likelihood estimation (MLE) method with a distribution-free quantile estimator: QMC-MLE (Li and Fang 2024 [20]). In this QMC-MLE method, the estimated quantiles of the sample are used to replace the original sample, and then the MLE is performed on the estimated quantiles to obtain the parameter estimates. We explore the parameter estimation effectiveness of QMC-MLE for small samples by simulation in this section. In order to cover both unimodal and bimodal cases, we choose the GAST distribution with different parameter settings as the underlying distributions. In this section, we find that the effectiveness of QMC-MLE in parameter estimation is influenced by the number of peaks of sample. Section 4 calculates the three types of RPs, MC-RPs, QMC-RPs, and MSE-RPs, of the GAST distribution for different sample size n. For MSE-RPs, the calculation process requires a parametric k-means algorithm (Stampfer and Stadlober 2002 [21]). We will compare the estimates of four statistics (mean, variance, skewness and kurtosis) by the three types of RPs of the underlying distributions. Another application of RPs is density estimation. Section 4 combines the kernel density method (Rosenblatt 1956 [22]) and the three types of RPs to estimate the density of the underlying

GAST distributions. Section 5 applies the RPs to real data samples to show the outstanding performance of MSE-RPs under the assumption of a GAST model.

2. Generalized Alpha Skew-*t* Distribution

In this section, we give the definition of the density function of the GAST distribution (Altun et al., 2018 [8]) and list some of its commonly used subdistributions. We set the parameter values by the uniform design method (Wang and Fang 1981 [19]) to fully demonstrate the influence of parameters on the shape of the density function. Section 2.2 discusses how the parameters influence the number of peaks of density under four conditions. Sections 2.3 and 2.4 give the moments and stochastic representation of the GAST distribution, respectively.

2.1. Definition of the GAST Distribution

Definition 1. *(GAST distribution). A random variable X is said to follow the GAST distribution, denoted as $X \sim GAST(\alpha, s, \nu)$, if it has the following pdf*

$$f(x;\alpha,s,\nu) = \frac{(1-\alpha x)^2+1}{c(\alpha,s,\nu)} t(x;\nu) T\left(\sqrt{\frac{1+\nu}{x^2+\nu}} sx; \nu+1\right), \qquad \nu > 2, \quad x \in \mathcal{R}, \tag{10}$$

where

$$c(\alpha,s,\nu) = 1 - \alpha\left[\frac{s}{\sqrt{1+s^2}}\left(\frac{\nu}{\pi}\right)^{1/2}\Gamma\left(\frac{\nu-1}{2}\right)/\Gamma\left(\frac{\nu}{2}\right)\right] + \frac{\alpha^2}{2}\left(\frac{\nu}{\nu-2}\right). \tag{11}$$

Proposition 1. *If a random variable $Y \sim ST(s,\nu)$, the $c(\alpha,s,\nu)$ in (11) can be written as*

$$c(\alpha,s,\nu) = 1 - \alpha E[Y] + \frac{\alpha^2}{2} E\left[Y^2\right]. \tag{12}$$

Proof. We set a random variable $Z \sim SN(\alpha)$. From the Equation (2), the moments of the ST distribution are given by

$$E[Y^m] = \frac{(\nu/2)^{m/2}\Gamma\left(\frac{\nu-m}{2}\right)}{\Gamma\left(\frac{\nu}{2}\right)} E[Z^m]. \tag{13}$$

Henze (1986) [23] has given the general expression of the odd moments of Z, which is

$$E\left[Z^{2k+1}\right] = \sqrt{\frac{2}{\pi}} \frac{\delta}{(1+s^2)^k} \frac{(2k+1)!}{2^k} \sum_{i=0}^{k} \frac{i!(2s)^{2i}}{(2i+1)!(k-i)!}, \quad k = 0, 1, \cdots, n, \tag{14}$$

where $\delta = s/\sqrt{1+s^2}$. The even moments coincide with the standard normal distribution, because $Z^2 \sim \chi_1^2$. Hence, the first two moments of ST distribution are, respectively, given by

$$E[Y] = \frac{\left(\frac{\nu}{\pi}\right)^{1/2}\Gamma\left(\frac{\nu-1}{2}\right)}{\Gamma\left(\frac{\nu}{2}\right)} \delta,$$
$$E\left[Y^2\right] = \frac{\nu}{\nu-2}.$$

Then the Equation (12) is proved. □

The GAST distribution involves several popular useful distributions:

- If $\alpha = 0$, the GAST distribution reduces to the skew-*t* (ST) distribution.
- If $s = 0$, the GAST distribution reduces to the alpha-skew-*t* (AST) distribution.
- If $\alpha = 0$ and $s = 0$, the GAST distribution reduces to the Student's-*t* distribution.
- If $\nu \to \infty$, the GAST distribution reduces to the alpha-skew-normal (ASN) distribution.
- If $\nu \to \infty$, $\alpha = 0$, the GAST distribution reduces to the skew-normal (SN) distribution.

- If $\nu \to \infty$, $\alpha = 0$ and $s = 0$ the GAST distribution reduces to the normal distribution.

In order to depict the GAST densities, especially the characteristics of unimodal or multimodal with different combinations of parameters, the experimental design is used to arrange the parameter values. The uniform design is a number-theoretic method, proposed by Wang and Fang (1981) [19]. As a robust experimental design method, the uniform design has been widely applied in various fields. A uniform design table provides a scientific arrangement of experiments by tabulating the level combinations of factors of interest. Let $U_n(q^s)$ denote a uniform design with n experimental runs and s factors each having q levels. The uniform design table, $U_{16}(16^3)$, adopted in this paper is derived from the website Uniform-Design-Tables (https://fst.uic.edu.cn/isci/research/Uniform_Design_Tables.htm (accessed on 15 September 2024)). In uniform design tables, the levels of factors are labeled by positive integers. For a unit hypercube experimental region $[0,1]^s$, the levels $\{1,2,\ldots,q\}$ usually take values $\{\frac{1}{2q},\frac{3}{2q},\ldots,\frac{2q-1}{2q}\}$. For any hyperrectangle experimental region $[a,b]^s$, a linear transformation $a+(b-a)\frac{i}{2q}$, $i=1,3,\ldots,2q-1$ is applied. Table 1 lists the arrangement of the uniform design table $U_{16}(16^3)$ for the parametric region, $\alpha \times s \times \nu : [-2.6,3.8] \times [-3,3.4] \times [2.5,18.5]$, indicating the 16 kinds of parameter settings.

Figure 1 shows the density plots corresponding to eight parameter settings in Table 1, which are enough to represent the plot of GAST density. As shown in Figure 1, there are four cases in which the pdfs are bimodal and the No. XII and XIV GAST distributions are AST and ST distributions, respectively.

Table 1. The parameter settings according to a uniform design table $U_{16}(16^3)$.

No.	α	s	ν	No.	α	s	ν
I	−2.4	1.6	9	IX	3.2	−2	16
II	−0.8	0.4	3	X	1.2	1.2	15
III	−1.6	−1.6	6	XI	3.6	0.8	11
IV	1.6	−2.4	4	XII	0.4	0	18
V	−1.2	2.4	17	XIII	0.8	−1.2	10
VI	2.4	−0.4	8	XIV	0	3.2	7
VII	−2	−0.8	14	XV	−0.4	−2.8	12
VIII	2.8	2	5	XVI	2	2.8	13

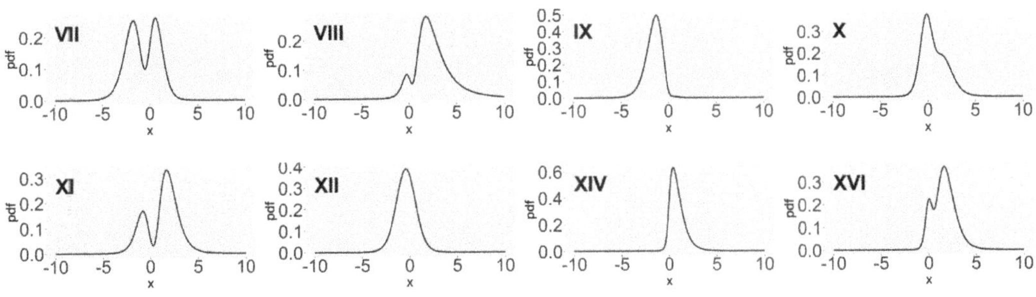

Figure 1. Some plots of GAST densities with parameters in Table 1.

In Section 2.2, we will show how the parameters α, s and ν affect the number of peaks of two special types of the GAST distribution, the AST and ST distributions, leading to the two categories, unimodal and bimodal. The number of peaks in the distribution may affect the parameter estimation. For instance, if the sample size is small and the density function presents a bimodal shape, then the sample is likely to miss the turning points, which will affect the parameter estimation to a certain extent. In addition, the calculation of representative points will also be affected, and the accuracy of derivative density estimation may be reduced.

2.2. Unimodal and Bimodal Properties

Since the density plots of the GAST distribution are varied, we will divide the GAST distribution into two categories: unimodal and bimodal. The number of peaks is determined by the number of zeros of the first derivative of (10). If it has one zero, then the density function is unimodal. If it has three zeros, then the density function is bimodal. To simplify the analysis, we consider the situations under four different parameter combinations of α and s, $(\alpha = 0, s = 0)$, $(\alpha = 0, s \neq 0)$, $(\alpha \neq 0, s = 0)$ and $(\alpha \neq 0, s \neq 0)$. The discussion is as follows:

(1) $\alpha = 0, s = 0$ and $X \sim t(\nu)$

The Student's t-distribution is a well-known unimodal distribution.

(2) $\alpha = 0, s \neq 0$ and $X \sim ST(s, \nu)$

The pdf of $X \sim ST(s, \nu)$, $f(x; s, \nu)$, is given by (3), $\nu > 2$.

Proposition 2. *The skew-t distribution is always unimodal.*

Proof. We derive the first derivative of (3) as follows:

$$f'(x;s,\nu) = 2t'(x;\nu)T\left(sx\sqrt{\frac{\nu+1}{\nu+x^2}};\nu+1\right) + 2t(x;\nu)T'\left(sx\sqrt{\frac{\nu+1}{\nu+x^2}};\nu+1\right), \tag{15}$$

where

$$t(x;\nu) = \frac{\Gamma\left(\frac{\nu+1}{2}\right)}{\sqrt{\pi\nu}\Gamma\left(\frac{\nu}{2}\right)}\left(1+\frac{x^2}{\nu}\right)^{-\frac{\nu+1}{2}} \equiv c\left(1+\frac{x^2}{\nu}\right)^{-\frac{\nu+1}{2}}, \tag{16}$$

$$t'(x;\nu) = -c\left(\frac{2x}{\nu}\right)\left(\frac{\nu+1}{2}\right)\left(1+\frac{x^2}{\nu}\right)^{-\frac{\nu+1}{2}-1} = t(x;\nu)(-x)\left(\frac{\nu+1}{\nu+x^2}\right), \tag{17}$$

$$T'(\cdot) = \left(s\sqrt{\frac{\nu+1}{\nu+x^2}}\right)\left(\frac{\nu}{\nu+x^2}\right)t\left(sx\sqrt{\frac{\nu+1}{\nu+x^2}};\nu+1\right). \tag{18}$$

Substituting (17) and (18) in Equation (15), we obtain that

$$\begin{aligned} f'(x;s,\nu) &= 2(-x)t(x;\nu)\left(\frac{\nu+1}{\nu}\right)\left(\frac{\nu}{\nu+x^2}\right)T(\cdot) \\ &\quad + 2t(x;\nu)\left(s\sqrt{\frac{\nu+1}{\nu+x^2}}\right)\left(\frac{\nu}{\nu+x^2}\right)t\left(sx\sqrt{\frac{\nu+1}{\nu+x^2}};\nu+1\right) \\ &= 2t(x;\nu)\left(\frac{\nu}{\nu+x^2}\right)\left[(-x)\left(\frac{\nu+1}{\nu}\right)T(\cdot) + \left(s\sqrt{\frac{\nu+1}{\nu+x^2}}\right)t\left(sx\sqrt{\frac{\nu+1}{\nu+x^2}};\nu+1\right)\right]. \end{aligned}$$

As $2t(x;\nu)\left(\frac{\nu}{\nu+x^2}\right) > 0$, the solution to $f'(x;s,\nu) = 0$ can be evaluated by solving the next equation:

$$g(x) = (-x)\left(\frac{\nu+1}{\nu}\right)T(\cdot) + \left(s\sqrt{\frac{\nu+1}{\nu+x^2}}\right)t\left(sx\sqrt{\frac{\nu+1}{\nu+x^2}};\nu+1\right) = 0. \tag{19}$$

Since $f(x;s,\nu)$ is symmetric with respect to s:

$$f(x;s,\nu) = f(-x;-s,\nu).$$

The number of peaks is not affected by the sign of s such that we assume $s > 0$. From the expression of (19), we can see that $g(x) > 0$, when $x \in (-\infty, 0]$. When $x \in (0, +\infty)$, we have

$$\left(sx\sqrt{\frac{\nu+1}{\nu+x^2}}\right)' = \left(s\sqrt{\frac{\nu+1}{\nu+x^2}}\right)\left(\frac{\nu}{\nu+x^2}\right) > 0.$$

Hence, $T(\cdot)$ is monotonically increasing, while $t(\cdot)$ is monotonically decreasing. Therefore, we can deduce that $g(x)$ is decreasing when $x \in (0, +\infty)$, i.e., $g(x) \to -\infty$, as $x \to +\infty$. Hence, there is only one solution x_1, s.t. $g(x_1) = 0$. And the ST distribution must be unimodal. □

(3) $\alpha \neq 0, s = 0$ and $X \sim AST(\alpha, \nu)$

The pdf of $X \sim AST(\alpha, \nu)$ is given by

$$f(x;\alpha,\nu) = \frac{(1-\alpha x)^2 + 1}{2c(\alpha,0,\nu)} t(x;\nu) \quad , \nu > 2. \tag{20}$$

Proposition 3. *The pdf of the AST distribution, $f(x;\alpha,\nu)$ as (20), is bimodal if and only if $g(x_1) < 0 < g(x_2)$ and $\alpha \notin \left(-\sqrt{\frac{\nu^2-3}{3\nu^2-3\nu}}, \sqrt{\frac{\nu^2-3}{3\nu^2-3\nu}}\right)$, where*

$$\begin{aligned} g(x) &= (1-\nu)\alpha^2 x^3 + 2\alpha\nu x^2 + (2\alpha^2\nu - 2\nu - 2)x - 2\alpha\nu, \\ x_1, x_2 &= \frac{-4\alpha\nu \mp \sqrt{\Delta}}{2\alpha^2(3-3\nu)}, \ \Delta = 8\alpha^2\left[(3\nu^2 - 3\nu)\alpha^2 + (3-\nu^2)\right]. \end{aligned} \tag{21}$$

Otherwise, it is unimodal. It is worth mentioning that a sufficient condition for $f(x;\alpha,\nu)$ to be unimodal is

$$\alpha \in \left(-\sqrt{\frac{\nu^2-3}{3\nu^2-3\nu}}, \sqrt{\frac{\nu^2-3}{3\nu^2-3\nu}}\right). \tag{22}$$

Proof. Differentiating (20), we obtain

$$f'(x;\alpha,\nu) = \frac{1}{2c(\alpha,0,\nu)}\left[(-2\alpha)(1-\alpha x)t(x;\nu) - \frac{(\nu+1)x}{\nu+x^2} t(x;\nu)\left((1-\alpha x)^2 + 1\right)\right].$$

Since $\frac{1}{2c(\alpha,0,\nu)}$ is a constant, and $t(x;\nu) > 0$, we obtain the equivalent relation expression

$$\begin{aligned} f'(x;\alpha,\nu) = 0 &\iff (-2\alpha)(1-\alpha x)(\nu + x^2) - (\nu+1)x((1-\alpha x)^2 + 1) = 0 \\ &\iff g(x) \equiv (1-\nu)\alpha^2 x^3 + 2\alpha\nu x^2 + (2\alpha^2\nu - 2\nu - 2)x - 2\alpha\nu = 0. \end{aligned} \tag{23}$$

Now our problem is transformed into studying the number of zeros of the function $g(x)$. The first derivative of (23) is

$$g'(x) = (3-3\nu)\alpha^2 x^2 + 4\alpha\nu x + 2\alpha^2\nu - 2\nu - 2 \quad , \quad \nu > 2.$$

This is a quadratic function with a downward opening. The discriminant Δ of $g'(x)$ is as follows:

$$\Delta = 8\alpha^2\left[(3\nu^2 - 3\nu)\alpha^2 + (3-\nu^2)\right].$$

If $\Delta < 0$, namely

$$-\sqrt{\frac{\nu^2-3}{3\nu^2-3\nu}} < \alpha < \sqrt{\frac{\nu^2-3}{3\nu^2-3\nu}},$$

then $g(x)$ is monotonically decreasing. Since $\lim_{x\to-\infty} g(x) = +\infty$, $\lim_{x\to+\infty} g(x) = -\infty$, there must be only one root of $g(x) = 0$, i.e., $f(x;\alpha,v)$ is unimodal. It is worth mentioning that the parameter setting of No.XII in Table 1 fits this condition.

If $\Delta > 0$, then

$$\exists\, x_1 < x_2, \text{ s.t. } g'(x_1) = g'(x_2) = 0, \text{ where } x_1, x_2 = \frac{-4\alpha v \mp \sqrt{\Delta}}{2\alpha^2(3-3v)}.$$

We can obtain that

$$\begin{aligned} g'(x) > 0, &\quad x \in (x_1, x_2), \\ g'(x) < 0, &\quad x \in (-\infty, x_1) \cup (x_2, \infty). \end{aligned}$$

Hence, when $x \in (x_1, x_2)$, $g(x)$ is monotonically increasing. When $x \in (-\infty, x_1) \cup (x_2, \infty)$, $g(x)$ is monotonically decreasing. If $g(x_1) < 0 < g(x_2)$, then $g(x)$ has three zeros, and $f(x;\alpha,v)$ is bimodal. If condition (22) is met, $f(x;\alpha,v)$ is unimodal. To sum up, $f(x;\alpha,v)$ is bimodal if and only if $\Delta > 0$, i.e., condition (22) is not satisfied, and $g(x_1) < 0 < g(x_2)$. Otherwise, it is unimodal. □

(4) $\alpha \neq 0, s \neq 0$ and $X \sim GAST(\alpha,s,v)$

Differentiating the pdf of the GAST distribution as (10), we obtain

$$\begin{aligned} f'(x;\alpha,s,v) = \frac{t(x;v)}{c(\alpha,s,v)} \Bigg\{ &(-2\alpha)(1-\alpha x)T(\cdot) + \left(\frac{-(v+1)x}{v+x^2}\right)\left((1-\alpha x)^2+1\right)T(\cdot) \\ &+ \left((1-\alpha x)^2+1\right)\left(s\sqrt{\frac{v+1}{v+x^2}}\right)\left(\frac{v}{v+x^2}\right)t\left(sx\sqrt{\frac{v+1}{v+x^2}}; v+1\right)\Bigg\}. \end{aligned}$$

Let

$$\begin{aligned} g(x) =& (-2\alpha)(1-\alpha x)T(\cdot) + \left(\frac{-(v+1)x}{v+x^2}\right)\left((1-\alpha x)^2+1\right)T(\cdot) + \\ &\left((1-\alpha x)^2+1\right)\left(s\sqrt{\frac{v+1}{v+x^2}}\right)\left(\frac{v}{v+x^2}\right)t\left(sx\sqrt{\frac{v+1}{v+x^2}}; v+1\right). \end{aligned} \tag{24}$$

Then we have $f'(x;\alpha,s,v) = \frac{t(x;v)}{c(\alpha,s,v)} g(x)$, and we obtain

$$f'(x;\alpha,s,v) = 0 \iff g(x) = 0.$$

Due to the complexity of the $g(x)$, it is difficult to study its zeros. The discussion of such a situation remains to be studied.

2.3. Moments of the GAST Distribution

From the pdf of the GAST distribution in (10), the kth moment of $X \sim GAST(\alpha,s,v)$ is given by

$$E\left[X^k\right] = \frac{E\left[Y^k\right] - \alpha E\left[Y^{k+1}\right] + \frac{\alpha^2}{2} E\left[Y^{k+2}\right]}{c(\alpha,s,v)} \equiv \frac{M_k(\alpha,s,v)}{c(\alpha,s,v)}, \tag{25}$$

where $Y \sim ST(s,v)$. Combined with (13) and (14), we have the first four moments of X in which the $M_k(\alpha,s,v)$ is given as follows

$$
\begin{aligned}
M_1(\alpha,s,\nu) =& \delta\left(\frac{\nu}{\pi}\right)^{1/2}\frac{\Gamma\left(\frac{\nu-1}{2}\right)}{\Gamma\left(\frac{\nu}{2}\right)} - \frac{\alpha\nu}{\nu-2} + \frac{\alpha^2}{2}\left(\frac{\nu}{2}\right)^{3/2}\frac{\Gamma\left(\frac{\nu-3}{2}\right)}{\Gamma\left(\frac{\nu}{2}\right)}\sqrt{\frac{2}{\pi}}\left(\frac{3}{1+s^2}\delta + 2\delta^3\right), \\
M_2(\alpha,s,\nu) =& \frac{\nu}{\nu-2} - \alpha\left(\frac{\nu}{2}\right)^{3/2}\frac{\Gamma\left(\frac{\nu-3}{2}\right)}{\Gamma\left(\frac{\nu}{2}\right)}\sqrt{\frac{2}{\pi}}\left(\frac{3}{1+s^2}\delta + 2\delta^3\right) + \frac{3\alpha^2\nu^2}{2(\nu-2)(\nu-4)}, \\
M_3(\alpha,s,\nu) =& \left(\frac{\nu}{2}\right)^{3/2}\frac{\Gamma\left(\frac{\nu-3}{2}\right)}{\Gamma\left(\frac{\nu}{2}\right)}\sqrt{\frac{2}{\pi}}\left(\frac{3}{1+s^2}\delta + 2\delta^3\right) - \frac{3\alpha\nu^2}{(\nu-2)(\nu-4)} \\
&+ \frac{\alpha^2}{2}\left(\frac{\nu}{2}\right)^{5/2}\frac{\Gamma\left(\frac{\nu-5}{2}\right)}{\Gamma\left(\frac{\nu}{2}\right)}\sqrt{\frac{2}{\pi}}\left(\frac{15}{(1+s^2)^2}\delta + \frac{20}{1+s^2}\delta^3 + 8\delta^5\right), \\
M_4(\alpha,s,\nu) =& \frac{3\nu^2}{(\nu-2)(\nu-4)} - \alpha\left(\frac{\nu}{2}\right)^{5/2}\frac{\Gamma\left(\frac{\nu-5}{2}\right)}{\Gamma\left(\frac{\nu}{2}\right)}\sqrt{\frac{2}{\pi}}\left(\frac{15}{(1+s^2)^2}\delta + \frac{20}{1+s^2}\delta^3 + 8\delta^5\right) \\
&+ \frac{15\alpha^2\nu^3}{2(\nu-2)(\nu-4)(\nu-6)}.
\end{aligned}
$$

2.4. Stochastic Representation the GAST Distribution

Altun (2018) [8] provided a stochastic representation of $X \sim GAST(\alpha,s,\nu)$ as follows.

Theorem 1. *If the random variables $W \sim AST(\alpha,\nu)$ and $Z \sim t(\nu+1)$ are independent, then we have*

$$
W\left|\left\{\sqrt{\frac{1+\nu}{W^2+\nu}}sW > Z\right\}\right. \sim GAST(\alpha,s,\nu) \tag{26}
$$

According to (26) given by [8] , we can generate random samples from the GAST distribution by the following procedure:

Step 1. Generate $W \sim AST(\alpha,\nu)$ and $Z \sim t(\nu+1)$.
Step 2. If $\sqrt{(1+\nu)/(W^2+\nu)}sW > Z$, then keep W. Otherwise, go to Step 1.

3. Parameter Estimation

In parameter estimation, the maximum likelihood estimation has been widely utilized because of its transitivity. Let $\boldsymbol{x} = \{x_1, x_2, \ldots, x_n\}$ be a random sample from the $GAST(x;\alpha,s,\nu)$ distribution. The log-likelihood function is given by

$$
\begin{aligned}
\ell(\alpha,s,\nu \mid \boldsymbol{x}) =& \sum_{i=1}^{n}\log\left[\frac{(1-\alpha x_i)^2+1}{c(\alpha,s,\nu)}\right] + \sum_{i=1}^{n}\log[t(x_i;\nu)] + \\
& \sum_{i=1}^{n}\log\left[T\left(\sqrt{\frac{1+\nu}{x_i^2+\nu}}sx_i;\nu+1\right)\right].
\end{aligned} \tag{27}
$$

By taking the partial derivatives with respect to α, s and ν, we have

$$
\begin{aligned}
\frac{\partial\ell}{\partial\alpha} &= \sum_{i=1}^{n}\frac{(-2x_i)(1-\alpha x_i)c(\alpha,s,\nu) - c_\alpha(\alpha,s,\nu)\left[(1-\alpha x_i)^2+1\right]}{[(1-\alpha x_i)^2+1]c(\alpha,s,\nu)}, \\
\frac{\partial\ell}{\partial s} &= n\frac{-c_s(\alpha,s,\nu)}{c(\alpha,s,\nu)} + \sum_{i=1}^{n}x_i\sqrt{\frac{\nu+1}{x_i^2+\nu}}\omega_i^*, \\
\frac{\partial\ell}{\partial\nu} &= n\frac{-c_\nu(\alpha,s,\nu)}{c(\alpha,s,\nu)} + \sum_{i=1}^{n}\tau_i^* + \sum_{i=1}^{n}\frac{sx_i(x_i^2-1)}{2\sqrt{\frac{\nu+1}{x_i^2+\nu}}(x_i^2+\nu)^2}\omega_i^*,
\end{aligned} \tag{28}
$$

where

$$\omega_i^* = \frac{t\left(\sqrt{\frac{1+\nu}{x_i^2+\nu}} s x_i; \nu+1\right)}{T\left(\sqrt{\frac{1+\nu}{x_i^2+\nu}} s x_i; \nu+1\right)}, \qquad \tau_i^* = \frac{t_\nu(x_i;\nu)}{t(x_i;\nu)}.$$

Remark that $c_\alpha(\alpha,s,\nu)$, $c_s(\alpha,s,\nu)$, $c_\nu(\alpha,s,\nu)$, and $t_\nu(x_i;\nu)$ are the partial derivatives of $c(\alpha,s,\nu)$ and $t(x_i;\nu)$. The solution $(\hat{\alpha},\hat{s},\hat{\nu})$ satisfying $\frac{\partial \ell}{\partial \alpha}=0$, $\frac{\partial \ell}{\partial s}=0$, $\frac{\partial \ell}{\partial \nu}=0$ at the same time is the MLE of (α,s,ν). To solve the system of nonlinear equations in (28), a numerical method is required. In the following subsections, we introduce the algorithm for solving MLE: L-BFGS-B (Byrd et al., 1995 [24]) in Section 3.1. In order to improve estimation accuracy by enhancing sample representativeness, we incorporate a non-parametric quantile estimation method (Harrell and Davis 1982 [25]) introduced in Section 3.2. In Section 3.3, we evaluate the effectiveness of the algorithm and quantile estimation method by simulation. In our study, we use R software version 4.4.1 to conduct simulation.

3.1. L-BFGS-B

L-BFGS-B (Byrd et al., 1995 [24]) is a limited-memory algorithm for solving large nonlinear optimization problems subject to simple bounds on the variables. The essence of the algorithm is a quasi-Newton method. At each iteration, a limited-memory BFGS approximation to the Hessian matrix is updated. This limited-memory matrix is used to define a quadratic model of the objective function, in our study indicating (27). Given a set of samples $\boldsymbol{x}=\{x_i\}_{i=1}^n$, the optimization problem can be formulated as follows:

$$\max_{\alpha,s,\nu} \ell(\alpha,s,\nu \mid \boldsymbol{x}).$$

We summarize the procedures of L-BFGS-B as following Algorithm 1.

Algorithm 1 L-BFGS-B for MLE

- **Input:** Initial guesses for parameters α_0, s_0, ν_0, tolerance ϵ, maximum number of iterations N, bounds $(\alpha_{\min}, s_{\min}, \nu_{\min})$ and $(\alpha_{\max}, s_{\max}, \nu_{\max})$
- **Output:** Estimated parameters $\hat{\alpha}, \hat{s}, \hat{\nu}$
- Initialize $k \leftarrow 0$
- Initialize parameters $\boldsymbol{\theta}^{(0)} \leftarrow (\alpha_0, s_0, \nu_0)$
- **repeat**
  - Compute the gradient $\nabla \ell(\boldsymbol{\theta}^{(k)})$
  - Compute the search direction $\boldsymbol{p}^{(k)}$ using a two-stage approach [24]
  - Project the search direction $\boldsymbol{p}^{(k)}$ to satisfy the bounds
  - Line search: find step size $\lambda^{(k)}$ that maximizes $\ell(\boldsymbol{\theta}^{(k)} + \lambda^{(k)}\boldsymbol{p}^{(k)})$
  - Update parameters: $\boldsymbol{\theta}^{(k+1)} \leftarrow \boldsymbol{\theta}^{(k)} + \lambda^{(k)}\boldsymbol{p}^{(k)}$
  - $k \leftarrow k+1$
- **until** $\|\nabla \ell(\boldsymbol{\theta}^{(k)})\| < \epsilon$ or $k \geq N$
- $(\hat{\alpha}, \hat{s}, \hat{\nu}) \leftarrow \boldsymbol{\theta}^{(k)}$

We chose the L-BFGS-B algorithm because the degree of freedom ν must be greater than 2 for the GAST distribution. If the unconstrained optimization method is used, missing values are likely to appear in the optimization process.

3.2. QMC-MLE

In this subsection, we introduce a method for improving the accuracy of MLE. It is well-known that the accuracy of MLE depends on the sample size to a certain extent. If the sample misses the turning points of the population density, it is less representative, which may lead to lower estimation accuracy. This situation is prone to occur in small sized samples and especially bimodal cases. Fang and Wang (1994) [12] pointed out that the set of equal quantiles $\{p_i = (2i-1)/2n, i = 1,\ldots,n\}$ has the best representativeness in the sense of F-discrepancy. In Section 1, we introduce a QMC method to generate the RPs of a distribution with known parameters. However, for a distribution with unknown parameters, how can we obtain the pth quantile of the distribution F? Harrell and Davis (1982) [25] proposed a distribution-free method: the Harrell–Davis (HD) quantile estimator. We use this estimator to calculate the set of equal quantiles of F, and then substitute these n quantiles into the likelihood function $\ell(\theta \mid x)$ for calculation. Li and Fang (2024) [20] called the MLE method with HD quantile estimator as QMC-MLE, presented below.

Let $\boldsymbol{x} = \{x_1,\ldots,x_n\}$ be a random sample of size n from the GAST distribution. Denote $X_{(i)}$ as the ith largest value in $\boldsymbol{x}$ and $F^{-1}(p)$ as the pth population quantile.

Step 1: Generate a set of points uniformly scattered on $(0,1)$ through

$$p_i = \frac{2i-1}{2n},\ i = 1,\ldots,n.$$

Step 2: Use the Harrell–Davis quantile estimator to process sample:

$$Q(p_i) = \sum_{i=1}^{n} W_{n,i} X_{(i)},$$

where

$$\begin{aligned} W_{n,i} &= \frac{1}{\beta\{(n+1)p_i,(n+1)(1-p_i)\}}\int_{(i-1)/n}^{i/n} y^{(n+1)p_i-1}(1-y)^{(n+1)(1-p_i)-1}\,dy \\ &= I_{i/n}\{p_i(n+1),(1-p_i)(n+1)\} - I_{(i-1)/n}\{p_i(n+1),(1-p_i)(n+1)\}, \end{aligned}$$

and $I_x\{a,b\}$ denotes the incomplete beta function.
Step 3: Let $z_i = Q(p_i)$, for $i = 1,\ldots,n$. Therefore, the $\boldsymbol{x} = (x_1,\ldots,x_n)$ in the log-likelihood function is replaced by $\boldsymbol{z} = (z_1,\ldots,z_n)$ such that the objective function based on the revised sample is

$$\ell(\boldsymbol{\theta}|\boldsymbol{z}) = \sum_{i=1}^{n} \ln(f(z_i;\alpha,s,\nu)). \tag{29}$$

Step 4: Use the L-BFGS-B algorithm to find the MLE of $\boldsymbol{\theta}$ by maximizing (29).

3.3. Simulation

Before the simulation, we introduce four measures of the estimation accuracy: L2.pdf, L2.cdf, absolute bias index (ABI) and Kullback–Leibler (KL) divergence. Denote the true underlying distribution as F in cdf or f in pdf, and the estimated distribution as $\hat{F}$ or $\hat{f}$. The four measures are defined as follows:

- **L2.pdf** between two densities is defined as

$$L_2\left(f,\hat{f}\right) = \left[\int_{-\infty}^{\infty}\left(f(x)-\hat{f}(x)\right)^2 dx\right]^{1/2};$$

- **L2.cdf** between two cdf's is defined as

$$L_2\left(F,\hat{F}\right) = \left[\int_{-\infty}^{\infty}\left(F(x)-\hat{F}(x)\right)^2 dx\right]^{1/2};$$

- **Absolute bias index** (ABI) is used to evaluate the overall estimation bias in parameters in which $\hat{\mu}$ and $\hat{\sigma}$ denote the estimated expectation and standard deviation of the GAST distribution, defined as

$$ABI = \frac{1}{2}\left(\left|\frac{\mu - \hat{\mu}}{\mu}\right| + \left|\frac{\sigma - \hat{\sigma}}{\sigma}\right|\right);$$

- **Kullback–Leibler (KL)** divergence or the so-called relative entropy is used to measure the difference from one probability distribution to another, defined as follows:

$$D_{KL}(F \,||\, \hat{F}) = \int_{-\infty}^{\infty} f(x) \log\left(\frac{f(x)}{\hat{f}(x)}\right) dx.$$

In the simulation, we generate samples by the inverse transformation method and mainly focus on the small sample case. To study both unimodal and bimodal cases, we choose five parameter settings, No.VII, VIII, IX, X and XI, of the GAST distribution from Figure 1 as the underlying distributions, among which the No.VII, VIII, and XI distributions are bimodal. The sample size n is set to be $25, 50, 100$ and 300. After $N = 100$ times of repetition, the average of $(\hat{\alpha}, \hat{s}, \hat{v})$ is set to be the parameters of the estimated GAST distribution. The precision of the estimates is evaluated by L2.pdf, L2.cdf, ABI and KL, summarized in Table 2, in which "plain" indicates the MLE resulting from the original sample $\boldsymbol{x} = (x_1, \ldots, x_n)$, and "qmc" uses the revised sample $\boldsymbol{z} = (z_1, \ldots, z_n)$.

Table 2. The comparisons between the plain MLE and QMC-MLE in four measures ($n = 25, 50, 100, 300$; $N = 100$).

No.	Method	n = 25				n = 50				n = 100				n = 300			
		L2.pdf	**L2.cdf**	**ABI**	**KL**	**L2.pdf**	**L2.cdf**	**ABI**	**KL**	**L2.pdf**	**L2.cdf**	**ABI**	**KL**	**L2.pdf**	**L2.cdf**	**ABI**	**KL**
VII	plain	**0.0326**	0.0469	0.0730	**0.0039**	**0.0133**	**0.0153**	**0.0207**	**0.0012**	**0.0064**	**0.0131**	**0.0260**	**0.0001**	**0.0041**	**0.0056**	0.0098	**0.0001**
VII	qmc	0.0446	**0.0440**	**0.0552**	0.0079	0.0201	0.0218	0.0307	0.0019	0.0163	0.0224	0.0326	0.0008	0.0076	0.0071	**0.0078**	0.0002
VIII	plain	0.0896	0.1161	0.1822	0.0897	0.0575	0.0721	0.1026	0.0256	0.0178	0.0358	0.0809	0.0024	0.0077	0.0186	0.0436	0.0005
VIII	qmc	**0.0670**	**0.0923**	**0.1590**	**0.0830**	**0.0359**	**0.0496**	**0.0749**	**0.0181**	**0.0127**	**0.0286**	**0.0650**	**0.0019**	**0.0058**	**0.0160**	**0.0346**	**0.0004**
IX	plain	**0.0317**	0.0365	0.0321	**0.0073**	0.0185	0.0214	0.0230	0.0034	0.0110	0.0129	0.0172	0.0021	0.0047	0.0049	0.0092	**0.0003**
IX	qmc	0.0302	**0.0363**	**0.0306**	0.0074	**0.0108**	**0.0150**	**0.0160**	**0.0026**	**0.0056**	**0.0082**	**0.0101**	**0.0015**	**0.0029**	**0.0035**	**0.0057**	0.0004
X	plain	**0.0691**	0.0762	0.1443	**0.0097**	0.0453	0.0525	0.0967	0.0056	0.0172	0.0261	0.0525	0.0010	0.0066	0.0125	0.0272	0.0003
X	qmc	0.0570	**0.0663**	**0.1293**	0.0104	**0.0381**	**0.0476**	**0.0886**	**0.0041**	**0.0112**	**0.0207**	**0.0372**	**0.0003**	**0.0058**	**0.0113**	**0.0203**	**0.0002**
XI	plain	0.0689	0.0883	0.1073	**0.0194**	0.0398	0.0487	0.0576	**0.0031**	**0.0134**	**0.0151**	0.0265	**0.0067**	0.0058	**0.0063**	0.0087	**0.0005**
XI	qmc	**0.0563**	**0.0552**	**0.1043**	0.0263	**0.0390**	**0.0342**	**0.0525**	0.0104	0.0279	0.0265	**0.0196**	0.0104	**0.0041**	0.0127	**0.0069**	0.0010

The best performance in the sense of each measure for each pair of distribution type and sample size is highlighted in bold in Table 2. The QMC-MLE method performs better than the plain MLE in most cases, especially for the No.VIII, IX and X distributions. However, for the No.VII and XI distributions, the QMC-MLE has no obvious advantage. The No.IX and X distributions are unimodal, but the No.VIII is bimodal. From the pdf plot of No.VIII distribution, we can see that although it is bimodal, its first peak is not as obvious as the peaks of No.VII and XI distributions. In the pdf plots of No.VII and XI distributions, as x increases, the density function experiences a steep decline after the first peak, while for the No.VIII distribution, the decline lasts only for a short distance before it begins to rise again. Therefore, we have reasons to believe that the QMC-MLE method is more suitable for unimodal functions or bimodal functions of which one peak is not obvious.

In addition, for No.XI GAST distribution, in the sense of KL divergence, the plain MLE is better than the QMC-MLE for all sample sizes. As for the No.XI case under other measures, although the QMC-MLE performs better when $n = 25$ and 50, it becomes less effective for $n = 100$ and 300, which may be caused by the consistency of MLE. According to the discussion above, when we conduct case studies in Section 5, the QMC-MLE will be only used for unimodal samples in parameter estimation, while for bimodal samples, we will use the plain MLE. Nevertheless, this simulation study reveals that the MLE method (both plain and QMC) is appropriate for estimating the GAST parameters due to the small values of four bias measurements.

4. RPs of the GAST Distribution

Recall that in Section 1, we introduced three types of representative points: MC-RPs, QMC-RPs, and MSE-RPs. In this section, we will find these three types of RPs of the GAST distribution for different sample sizes n, and use them to estimate moments and densities in Section 4.1 and Section 4.2, respectively.

4.1. Moment Estimation

For a given n, MC-RPs will be generated by the inverse transformation method. QMC-RPs can be easily obtained by (6) while MSE-RPs are calculated through a parametric k-means algorithm proposed by Stampfer and Stadlober (2002) [21]. We summarize the computation procedure of the k-means algorithm for approximating MSE-RPs of the GAST distribution as follows.

Step 1: For a given pdf $f(x;\alpha,s,\nu)$, the number of RPs: n, and $t=0$, input a set of initial points $b_1^{(t)} < b_2^{(t)} < \cdots < b_n^{(t)}$. Here we take n QMC-RPs as the initial values. Determine a partition of $\mathcal{R}$ as

$$I_i^{(t)} = (a_{i-1}^{(t)}, a_i^{(t)}], \quad i=1,\ldots,n-1, \quad I_n^{(t)} = (a_{n-1}^{(t)}, a_n^{(t)}),$$

where

$$a_0^{(t)} = -\infty, \quad a_i^{(t)} = (b_{i-1}^{(t)} + b_i^{(t)})/2, \quad i=1,\ldots,n-1, \quad a_n^{(t)} = \infty.$$

Step 2: Calculate probabilities

$$p_j^{(t)} = \int_{I_j^{(t)}} f(x;\alpha,s,\nu)dx, \quad j=1,\ldots,n;$$

and the condition means

$$b_j^{(t+1)} = \frac{\int_{I_j^{(t)}} xf(x;\alpha,s,\nu)dx}{\int_{I_j^{(t)}} f(x;\alpha,s,\nu)dx} = \frac{\int_{I_j^{(t)}} xf(x;\alpha,s,\nu)dx}{p_j^{(t)}}.$$

Step 3: If two sets, $\{b_j^{(t)}\}$ and $\{b_j^{(t+1)}\}$ are identical, the process stops and the outputs $\{b_j^{(t)}\}$ as the MSE-RPs of the distribution with probabilities $\{p_j^{(t)}\}$. Otherwise, let $t := t+1$ and go back to **Step 1**.

Let Y be a discrete distribution with probability mass function $P(Y=b_j)=p_j$, $j=1,\ldots,n$, which is an approximate distribution to the GAST distribution. Then, the estimates of mean, variance, skewness and kurtosis can be calculated by

$$\begin{aligned} E[Y] &= \sum_{j=1}^{n} b_j p_j = \mu_Y, & Var[Y] &= \sum_{j=1}^{n} (b_j-\mu_Y)^2 p_j = \sigma_Y^2, \\ Sk[Y] &= \frac{1}{\sigma_Y^3}\sum_{j=1}^{n} (b_j-\mu_b)^3 p_j, & Ku[Y] &= \frac{1}{\sigma_Y^4}\sum_{j=1}^{n} (b_j-\mu_Y)^4 p_j - 3. \end{aligned} \tag{30}$$

We use the No.IX, X and XI as the underlying distributions and consider $n=10,20,30$. It is clear that MC-RPs are random samples of size n. For fair comparisons, we generate N samples of size n and then take the average of the estimated statistics as the results of the MC(N) method. In our study, we choose $N=10,100$. The true parameters and four statistics of the three underlying distribution are listed in Table 3. The bias of the estimated results is summarized in Tables 4–6.

Table 3. True parameters and statistics of the underlying distributions.

No.	α	s	ν	$E(X)$	Var(X)	Sk(X)	Ku(X)
IX	3.2	−2	16	−1.5997	0.7971	−0.7117	1.4857
X	1.2	1.2	15	0.6272	1.7074	0.6258	0.3101
XI	3.6	0.8	11	1.2301	3.0124	−0.2293	0.0633

Table 4. Estimation bias of four statistics for the No.IX distribution $GAST(3.2, -2, 16)$.

Statistics	Category	10	20	30
Mean	MC(10)	−0.1180	−0.1562	−0.0149
	MC(100)	−0.0291	0.0214	0.0132
	QMC	0.0090	0.0031	0.0014
	MSE	**0.0000**	**0.0000**	**0.0000**
Variance	MC(10)	0.1194	0.3288	0.0769
	MC(100)	−0.0024	−0.0212	−0.0044
	QMC	−0.1455	−0.0889	−0.0668
	MSE	**−0.0231**	**−0.0063**	**−0.0029**
Skewness	MC(10)	0.3486	0.1735	0.1472
	MC(100)	0.3667	0.2676	0.2479
	QMC	0.2740	0.1677	0.1227
	MSE	**0.0259**	**0.0045**	**0.0027**
Kurtosis	MC(10)	−2.4314	−1.3967	−0.7850
	MC(100)	−2.3704	−1.6857	−1.3343
	QMC	−2.0406	−1.6037	−1.3769
	MSE	**−0.5136**	**−0.1855**	**−0.0942**

The best performance within each statistic per sample size is highlighted in bold.

Table 5. Estimation bias of four statistics for the No.X distribution $GAST(1.2, 1.2, 15)$.

Statistics	Category	10	20	30
Mean	MC(10)	−0.0472	0.0170	0.1001
	MC(100)	0.0736	0.0219	−0.0217
	QMC	−0.0102	−0.0051	−0.0035
	MSE	**0.0000**	**0.0000**	**0.0000**
Variance	MC(10)	−0.0684	−0.1739	−0.1644
	MC(100)	0.0757	0.1530	0.0124
	QMC	−0.2179	−0.1213	−0.0861
	MSE	**−0.0394**	**−0.0109**	**−0.0051**
Skewness	MC(10)	−0.6435	−0.1809	−0.0803
	MC(100)	−0.2718	−0.1878	−0.1476
	QMC	−0.1634	−0.1104	−0.0873
	MSE	**−0.0106**	**−0.0034**	**−0.0017**
Kurtosis	MC(10)	−1.4404	−0.5846	−0.5425
	MC(100)	−1.3711	−0.8694	−0.6661
	QMC	−1.0604	−0.7846	−0.6516
	MSE	**−0.2881**	**−0.1005**	**−0.0514**

The best performance within each statistic per sample size is highlighted in bold.

The results indicate that the estimates based on MSE-RPs perform the best for all underlying distributions and sample sizes. The performance of MC-RPs is unstable. Sometimes the average estimates of moments based on MC-RPs are more accurate than those based on QMC-RPs, but in general, appear less effective. In addition, we can observe that with the increase in the number n, the overall effect of estimation is better. The estimates of higher-order moments (skewness and kurtosis) are worse than those of lower-order moments (mean and variance).

Table 6. Estimation bias of four statistics for the No.XI distribution $GAST(3.6, 0.8, 11)$.

Statistics	Category	10	20	30
Mean	MC(10)	0.0529	−0.1639	0.0381
	MC(100)	−0.0581	−0.0778	0.0276
	QMC	−0.0189	−0.0082	−0.0032
	MSE	**0.0000**	**0.0000**	**0.0000**
Variance	MC(10)	0.4662	0.1453	−0.3346
	MC(100)	0.2882	−0.0598	−0.0723
	QMC	−0.3569	−0.2171	−0.1635
	MSE	**−0.0705**	**−0.0200**	**−0.0093**
Skewness	MC(10)	−0.2932	−0.1673	−0.0959
	MC(100)	−0.0544	−0.0884	−0.1192
	QMC	−0.1259	−0.0954	−0.0829
	MSE	**−0.0024**	**−0.0051**	**−0.0031**
Kurtosis	MC(10)	−0.9306	−0.7944	−0.6527
	MC(100)	−0.9915	−0.7274	−0.3822
	QMC	−0.9529	−0.7366	−0.6273
	MSE	**−0.3395**	**−0.1294**	**−0.0702**

The best performance within each statistic per sample size is highlighted in bold.

4.2. Kernel Density Estimation

Another application of representative points is density estimation. In the field of signal transmission, the input signal is often converted into discrete data in the transmitter and then reconstructed in the receiver. For a distribution with unknown parameters, how do we use a set of data to construct its overall density function? Here, we introduce a kernel estimation method proposed by Rosenblatt (1956) [22] and Parzen (1962) [26]. Given a fixed number of points $\{x_1, \ldots, x_n\}$ from the original signal, the density estimation of $f(x)$ is given by

$$\hat{f}_h(x) = \frac{1}{n}\sum_{i=1}^{n} k_h(x - x_i) = \frac{1}{nh}\sum_{i=1}^{n} k\left(\frac{x - x_i}{h}\right),$$

where $k(\cdot)$ is the kernel function is the bandwidth and $k_h(y) = \frac{1}{h}k(\frac{y}{h})$. The most popular kernel is the standard normal density function

$$k(x) = \phi(x) = \frac{1}{\sqrt{2\pi}}e^{-\frac{1}{2}x^2}.$$

In our study, we employ the representative points $\{b_1, \ldots, b_n\}$ from the GAST distribution as the samples with their corresponding probabilities $p_i, i = 1, \ldots, n$. The density estimation of $f(x)$ can be extended to

$$\hat{f}_h(x) = \sum_{i=1}^{n} k_h(x - x_i)p_i = \frac{1}{h}\sum_{i=1}^{n} k\left(\frac{x - x_i}{h}\right)p_i.$$

The choice of the bandwidth h is very important. Here, we set a search range $\{0.05, 0.06, \ldots, 1\}$ for h. In the following comparisons, we utilize three types of RPs having sample sizes $n = 10, 20, 30$ for the kernel density estimation of No.IX, X and XI distributions, and evaluate the performances by the minimum L2.pdf between $\hat{f}_h(x; \alpha, s, \nu)$ and $f(x; \alpha, s, \nu)$.

Tables 7–9 show that the kernel density estimation based on MSE-RPs always has the minimum L2.pdf, which decreases as n increases. For the underlying distribution No.IX, we notice that the minimum L2.pdf based on the MSE-RPs with size 10 is only 0.0306, which is even smaller than that based on the QMC-RPs with size 30 (0.0341). Figures 2–4 show the comparing fitting plots of different sets of representative points. It is obvious that the fitting effect increases with n, and the MSE-RPs-based kernel estimation has the best fitting effect, followed by the QMC-RPs-based estimation. It is worth mentioning that for the MC-RPs-based density estimation, due to the randomness of the Monte Carlo method, the density curve fitted out each time differs greatly, and in many cases, it is not sufficient to reconstruct the original density function.

Table 7. The minimum L2.pdf and the corresponding bandwidth h of the kernel density estimation for No.IX distribution.

Method	n	h	min L2.pdf
MC	10	0.50	0.2108
QMC	10	0.30	0.0583
MSE	10	0.24	**0.0306**
MC	20	0.60	0.1300
QMC	20	0.23	0.0418
MSE	20	0.15	**0.0127**
MC	30	0.48	0.1471
QMC	30	0.21	0.0341
MSE	30	0.13	**0.0098**

The best performance within each sample size is highlighted in bold.

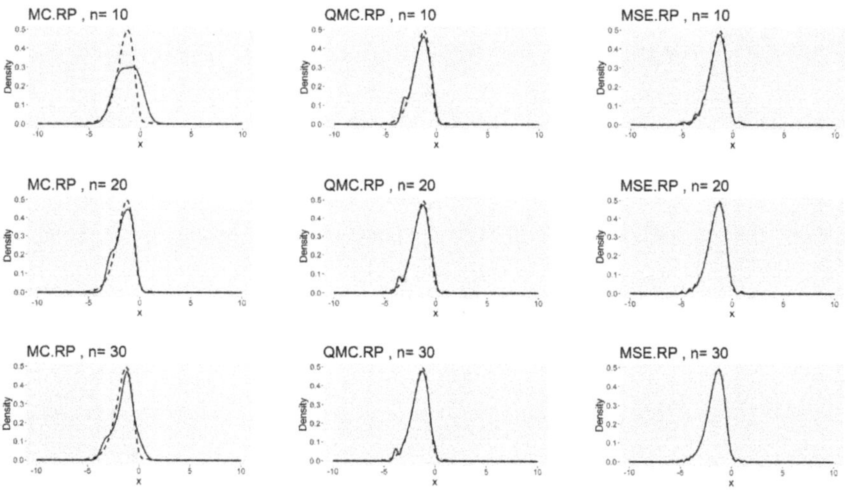

Figure 2. Comparing plots of the fitted densities (in solid lines) by kernel density estimation and the true densities (in dashed lines) for the No.IX distribution.

Table 8. The minimum L2.pdf and the corresponding bandwidth h of the kernel density estimation for No.X distribution.

Method	n	h	min L2.pdf
MC	10	0.90	0.2067
QMC	10	0.36	0.0563
MSE	10	0.29	**0.0305**
MC	20	0.46	0.1504
QMC	20	0.28	0.0379
MSE	20	0.18	**0.0119**
MC	30	0.53	0.1072
QMC	30	0.24	0.0295
MSE	30	0.15	**0.0094**

The best performance within each sample size is highlighted in bold.

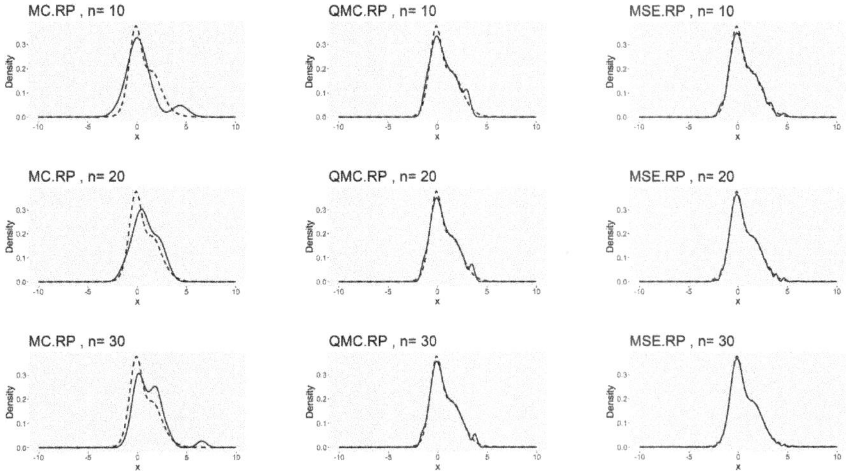

Figure 3. Comparing plots of the fitted densities (in solid lines) by kernel density estimation and the true densities (in dashed lines) for the No.X distribution.

Table 9. The minimum L2.pdf and the corresponding bandwidth h of the kernel density estimation for No.XI distribution

Method	n	h	min L2.pdf
MC	10	0.71	0.1607
QMC	10	0.38	0.0628
MSE	10	0.35	**0.0441**
MC	20	0.57	0.1592
QMC	20	0.29	0.0481
MSE	20	0.22	**0.0212**
MC	30	0.76	0.1392
QMC	30	0.25	0.0382
MSE	30	0.17	**0.0137**

The best performance within each sample size is highlighted in bold.

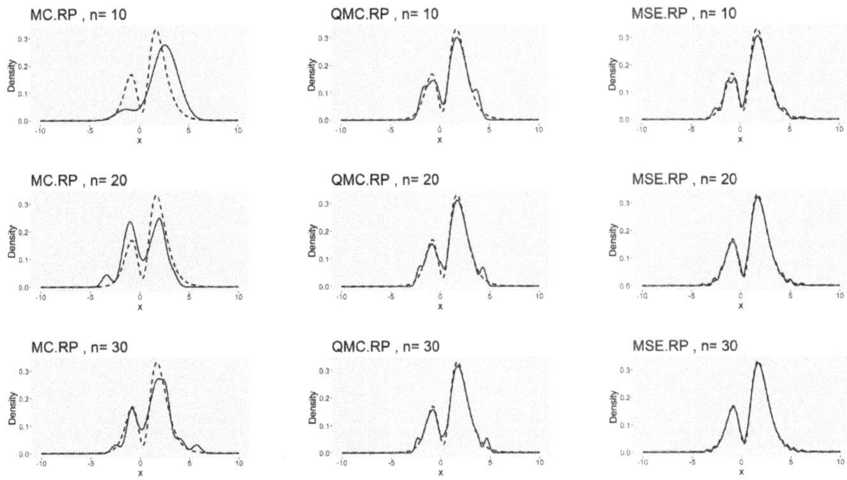

Figure 4. Comparing plots of the fitted densities (in solid lines) by kernel density estimation and the true densities (in dashed lines) for the No.XI distribution.

5. Case Studies

In this section, we will utilize three types of RPs to study real data samples. Before calculating the RPs, we incorporate two additional parameters in the GAST distribution, the location parameter μ and the scale parameter σ, to fit the samples. The pdf is given by

$$f(x;\alpha,s,\nu,\mu,\sigma)=\frac{\left(1-\alpha\left(\frac{x-\mu}{\sigma}\right)\right)^2+1}{\sigma c(\alpha,s,\nu)}t\left(\frac{x-\mu}{\sigma};\nu\right)T\left(\sqrt{\frac{1+\nu}{\left(\frac{x-\mu}{\sigma}\right)^2+\nu}}s\left(\frac{x-\mu}{\sigma}\right);\nu+1\right),$$

where $c(\alpha,s,\nu)$ is the same as that in Formula (11). For the sample data, we choose both unimodal and bimodal types, which are the O_3 data and the Faithful Geyser data.

5.1. O_3 Data

These data are from the website (https://archive.ics.uci.edu/dataset/360/air+quality (accessed on 15 September 2024)), which contains hourly averaged responses from an Air Quality Chemical Multisensor Device in an Italian city. We selected the "PT08.S5(O_3)" (denoted as "O_3" in this article) data as the study object. After setting the interception time from September 1 to November 30 in 2004, and removing the missing values, we derive 90 observations. We summarize the parameter estimation results of $GAST(\alpha,s,\nu,\mu,\sigma)$ obtained by the QMC-MLE in Table 10, providing the estimated GAST model as follows

$$GAST(-0.1518,-0.2030,16.9607,1219.228,385.0162). \tag{31}$$

Table 10. Parameter estimates of the GAST model based on O_3 data.

Parameters	$\hat{\alpha}$	$\hat{s}$	$\hat{\nu}$	$\hat{\mu}$	$\hat{\sigma}$
QMC-MLE	−0.1518	−0.2030	16.9607	1219.228	385.0162

We present the histogram with the fitted density for O_3 data in Figure 5a. After calculating the $\{p_i=(2i-1)/2n, i=1,\ldots,n\}$ quantiles of these data by the HD quantile estimator introduced in Section 3.2, we obtain the associated QQ plot given in Figure 5b. Figure 5 shows the good fitting effect of the GAST model on this unimodal data.

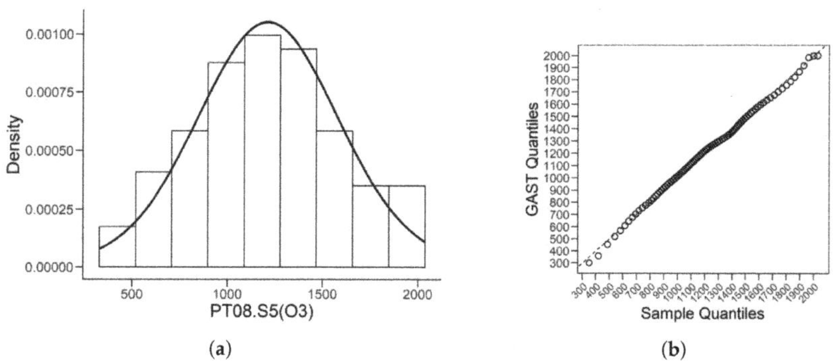

Figure 5. (**a**) is the histogram of O_3 data with fitted GAST density line. (**b**) is the associated QQ plot by HD quantile estimator.

The mean, variance, skewness, kurtosis of the distribution (31) are as follows

$$(1209.544,\ 168359.9,\ 0.0362,\ 0.601).$$

We generate MC-RPs, QMC-RPs and MSE-RPs of size 30, from the GAST model (31) using the methods discussed in Section 4.1. Table 11 summarizes the bias of the estimation of the four statistics based on the MC, QMC, and MSE methods.

Table 11. The estimation bias of the four statistics for the fitted GAST model is based on three types of RPs with size 30.

Method	Mean	Variance	Skewness	Kurtosis
MC	39.6251	−46,385.8384	−0.1111	−1.3819
QMC	−0.1250	−10,554.1427	−0.0121	−0.7845
MSE	0.0048	−579.8522	0.0005	−0.0641

Although the bias of the estimated variance in Table 11 is large in value, it is relatively small compared to the true variance of the model, which is 168,359.9. As shown in Table 11, the MSE-RPs estimate the moments of the model more accurately than the other two types of RPs.

The comparisons of the kernel density estimates based on MC, QMC, and MSE RPs are presented in Figure 6.

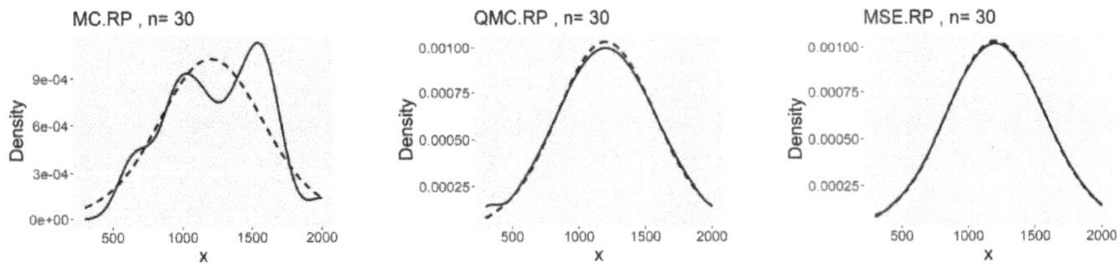

Figure 6. Comparing plots of the fitted densities (in solid lines) by kernel density estimation and the density of the distribution (31).

The corresponding minimum L2.pdf's between the kernel estimates and the density of the model (31) are 0.00237 for MC, 0.00026 for QMC and 0.00025 for MSE. As shown in Figure 6, although the estimated kernel density based on the QMC method is well-fitted, it is not as good as that based on the MSE method at the beginning and at the peak.

5.2. *Faithful Geyser Data*

The Faithful Geyser Data, a commonly used dataset in R software, is a record of the waiting time between eruptions and the duration time of these eruptions for Old Faithful Geyser in Yellow National Park, Wyoming, USA. In this study, we use the waiting-time samples which include 299 observations.

Since these data are bimodal, we use the plain-MLE to estimate parameters. The results are given in the Table 12, providing the GAST model as

$$GAST(-2.4016, -0.2322, 100, 70.6301, 8.7872). \tag{32}$$

Table 12. Parameter estimates of the GAST model based on Faithful Geyser data

Parameters	$\hat{\alpha}$	$\hat{s}$	$\hat{\nu}$	$\hat{\mu}$	$\hat{\sigma}$
Plain-MLE	−2.4016	−0.2322	100	70.6301	8.7872

The histogram with the fitted density for Faithful Geyser data is given in Figure 7a. Denoting $X_{(1)} < \ldots < X_{(n)}$ as the order statistics of this bimodal data, we calculate its quantiles by the traditional estimator:

$$Q_p = (1-g)X_{(j)} + gX_{(j+1)},$$

where $(n+1)p = j + g$ and j is the integral part of $(n+1)p$. The associated QQ plot is given in Figure 7b.

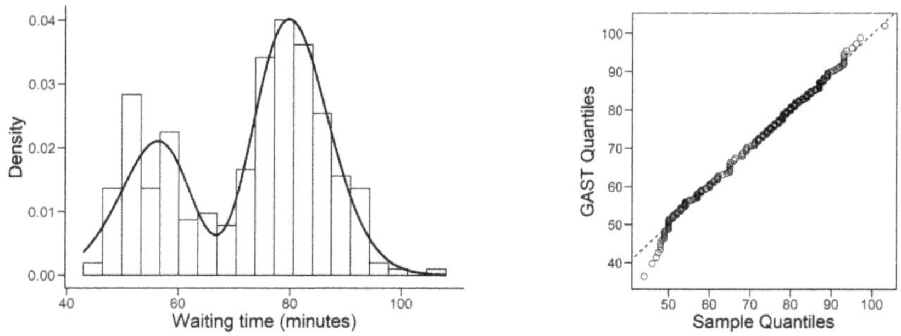

(a) (b)

Figure 7. (**a**) is the histogram of Faithful Geyser data with fitted GAST density line. (**b**) is the associated QQ plot by traditional quantile estimator.

Table 12 shows that the estimated ν is 100, which is the upper bound we set. From this point of view, we can assume that $\nu \to \infty$ in this fitting model. As described in Section 2.1, this model is actually a subdistribution of the GAST: ASN, indicating that the GAST model is flexible since it can adapt to different types of data. From the QQ plot in Figure 7, we notice that when data are less than 50, the scatter point deviates far from the line, which can also be observed from Figure 7a. The fitting curve rises slowly at the beginning, so the sample quantiles will be larger than the GAST quantiles. When the data are greater than 50, where more samples are located, this distribution fits the data well. Hence, the estimated GAST model (32) is still acceptable.

The mean, variance, skewness, and kurtosis of the distribution (32) are

$$(72.3205,\ 192.9088,\ -0.4496,\ -0.8031).$$

We generate MC-RPs, QMC-RPs and MSE-RPs of size 50 from the model (32). The estimation biases of the four statistics are summarized in Table 13.

Table 13. The estimation biases of the four statistics for the fitted GAST model based on three types of RPs with size 50.

Method	Mean	Variance	Skewness	Kurtosis
MC	2.8239	−11.0749	0.02917	0.5070
QMC	0.0010	−2.5761	0.0010	−0.0907
MSE	0.0000	−0.1364	−0.0001	−0.0051

We observe that the MSE-RPs have the same mean as the population expectation, which is described in (9). Compared to MC-RPs and QMC-RPs, the MSE method estimates the moments of the model more accurately. The comparison of the kernel density plots is presented in Figure 8.

The corresponding minimum L2.pdf's between the kernel estimates and the density of the model (32) are 0.0041 for MC, 0.0029 for QMC and 0.0027 for MSE. The MSE-RPs still perform the best.

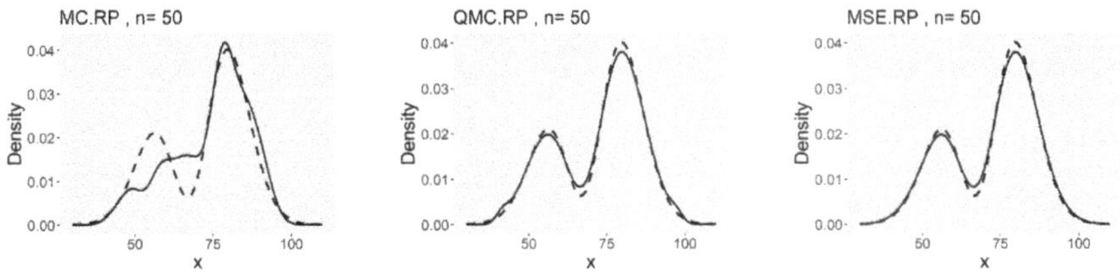

Figure 8. Comparing plots of the fitted densities (in solid lines) by kernel density estimation and the density of the distribution (32).

6. Conclusions

This paper mainly studies different types of representative points of the GAST distribution and the applications of these RPs. The comparative analyses across various sample sizes and both unimodal and bimodal GAST distributions reveal that the RPs obtained by the MSE method consistently outperform the others in the applications of estimating moments and densities. However, the performance on estimating higher-order moments, such as skewness and kurtosis, shows the limitations of RPs on capturing higher-order statistical properties. Therefore, the number of RPs n must adopt a larger value to reduce the bias of higher-order moment estimation. This paper also incorporates QMC-MLE for parameter estimation of the GAST distribution. For unimodal or bimodal data with an unclear peak, the QMC-MLE method improves parameter estimation accuracy. However, in bimodal cases, plain MLE is more effective. Combined with such property, we can model different types of data accordingly.

Author Contributions: Conceptualization, K.-T.F.; Funding acquisition, Y.-X.L.; Methodology, Y.-F.Z. and K.-T.F.; Software, Y.-F.Z.; Writing—original draft, Y.-F.Z.; Writing—review and editing, Y.-X.L., K.-T.F. and H.Y. All authors have read and agreed to the published version of the manuscript.

Funding: This research was funded by China Postdoctoral Science Foundation grant number 2023TQ0326.

Institutional Review Board Statement: Not applicable.

Data Availability Statement: A part of the dataset utilized for case studies in this paper is openly available in UCI Machine Learning Repository at https://archive.ics.uci.edu/dataset/360/air+quality (accessed on 15 September 2024). Another data set for analysis in this paper is obtained from R package *datasets*, named *faithful: Old Faithful Geyser Data*.

Acknowledgments: Our work was supported in part by Research Center for Frontier Fundamental Studies, Zhejiang Lab, and the Guangdong Provincial Key Laboratory of Interdisciplinary Research and Application for Data Science.

Conflicts of Interest: The authors declare no conflicts of interest. The funders had no role in the design of the study; in the collection, analyses, or interpretation of data; in the writing of the manuscript; or in the decision to publish the results.

References

1. Gupta, R.; Drzazga-Szczęśniak, E.; Kais, S.; Szczęśniak, D. The entropy corrected geometric Brownian motion. *arXiv* **2024**, arXiv:2403.06253.
2. Azzalini, A. A class of distributions which includes the normal ones. *Scand. J. Stat.* **1985**, *12*, 171–178.
3. Branco, M.D.; Dey, D.K. A general class of multivariate skew-elliptical distributions. *J. Multivar. Anal.* **2001**, *79*, 99–113. [CrossRef]
4. Azzalini, A.; Capitanio A. Distributions generated by perturbation of symmetry with emphasis on a multivariate skew *t*-distribution. *J. R. Stat. Soc.* **2003**, *65*, 367–389. [CrossRef]
5. Azzalini, A.; Genton, M.G. Robust likelihood methods based on the skew-*t* and related distributions. *Int. Stat. Rev.* **2008**, *76*, 106–129. [CrossRef]
6. Martínez-Flórez, G.; Tovar-Falón, R.; Gómez, H. Bivariate Power-Skew-Elliptical Distribution. *Symmetry* **2020**, *12*, 1327. [CrossRef]
7. Elal-Olivero, D. Alpha-skew-normal distribution. *Proyecciones* **2010**, *29*, 224–240. [CrossRef]

8. Altun, E.; Tatlidil, H.; Ozel, G.; Nadarajah, S. A new generalization of skew-t distribution with volatility models. *J. Stat. Comput. Simul.* **2018**, *88*, 1252–1272. [CrossRef]
9. Fang, K.T.; Pan, J. A Review of Representative Points of Statistical Distributions and Their Applications. *Mathematics* **2023**, *11*, 2930. [CrossRef]
10. Lin, Y.X.; Tang, Y.H.; Zhang, J.H.; Fang, K.T. Detecting non-isomorphic orthogonal design. *J. Stat. Plan. Inference* **2022**, *221*, 299–312. [CrossRef]
11. Efron, B. Bootstrap methods: Another look at the jackknife. *Ann. Stat.* **1979**, *7*, 1–26. [CrossRef]
12. Fang, K.T.; Wang, Y.; Bentler, P.M. Some applications of number-theoretic methods in statistics. *Stat. Sci.* **1994**, *9*, 416–428. [CrossRef]
13. Hua, L.K.; Wang, Y. *Applications of Number Theory to Numerical Analysis*; Springer: Berlin/Heidelberg, Germany; Science Press: Beijing, China, 1981.
14. Niederreiter, H. *Random Number Generation and Quasi-Monte Carlo Methods*; Society Industrial and Applied Mathematics (SIAM): Phiadelphia, PA, USA, 1992.
15. Cox, D.R. Note on grouping. *J. Am. Stat. Assoc.* **1957**, *52*, 543–547. [CrossRef]
16. Flury, B.A. Principal points. *Biometrika* **1990**, *77*, 33–41. [CrossRef]
17. Graf, S.; Luschgy, H. *Foundations of Quantization for Probability Distributions*; Springer: Berlin/Heidelberg, Germany, 2007.
18. Fei, R. Statistical relationship between the representative point and the population. *J. Wuxi Inst. Light Ind.* **1991**, *10*, 78–81.
19. Wang, Y.; Fang, K.T. A note on uniform distribution and experimental design. *Kexue Tongbao* **1981**, *6*, 485–489.
20. Li, Y.N.; Fang, K.T. A new approach to parameter estimation of mixture of two normal distributions. *Commun. Stat.-Simul. Comput.* **2024**, *53*, 1161–1187. [CrossRef]
21. Stampfer, E.; Stadlober, E. Methods for estimating principal points. *Commun. Stat.-Simul. Comput.* **2002**, *31*, 261–277. [CrossRef]
22. Rosenblatt, M. Remarks on some nonparametric estimates of a density function. *Ann. Math. Stat.* **1956**, *27*, 832–837. [CrossRef]
23. Henze, N. A probabilistic representation of the 'skew-normal' distribution. *Scand. J. Stat.* **1986**, *13*, 271–275.
24. Byrd, R.H.; Lu, P.; Zhu, C. A limited memory algorithm for bound constrained optimization. *SIAM J. Sci. Comput.* **1995**, *16*, 1190–1208. [CrossRef]
25. Harrell, F.E.; Davis, C.E. A new distribution-free quantile estimator. *Biometrika* **1982**, *69*, 635–640. [CrossRef]
26. Parzen, E. On estimation of a probability density function and mode. *Ann. Math. Stat.* **1962**, *33*, 1065–1076. [CrossRef]

entropy

MDPI

Article

Advancing Continuous Distribution Generation: An Exponentiated Odds Ratio Generator Approach

Xinyu Chen [1,2,†], Zhenyu Shi [3], Yuanqi Xie [4], Zichen Zhang [5], Achraf Cohen [1] and Shusen Pu [1,*,†]

1 Department of Mathematics and Statistics, University of West Florida, Pensacola, FL 32514, USA; xinyu.chen3@mail.mcgill.ca (X.C.); acohen@uwf.edu (A.C.)
2 Department of Epidemiology, Biostatistics and Occupational Health, McGill University, Montreal, QC H3A 0C7, Canada
3 Department of Communications Engineering, Zhejiang University of Science and Technology, Hangzhou 310018, China; 15906572525@163.com
4 Department of Computer Science, University of West Florida, Pensacola, FL 32514, USA; yxie@uwf.edu
5 Department of Mathematical and Computational Sciences, University of Toronto Mississauga, Mississauga, ON L5L 1C6, Canada; ziichen.zhang@mail.utoronto.ca
* Correspondence: spu@uwf.edu
† These authors contributed equally to this work.

Abstract: This paper presents a new methodology for generating continuous statistical distributions, integrating the exponentiated odds ratio within the framework of survival analysis. This new method enhances the flexibility and adaptability of distribution models to effectively address the complexities inherent in contemporary datasets. The core of this advancement is illustrated by introducing a particular subfamily, the "Type 2 Gumbel Weibull-G family of distributions". We provide a comprehensive analysis of the mathematical properties of these distributions, including statistical properties such as density functions, moments, hazard rate and quantile functions, Rényi entropy, order statistics, and the concept of stochastic ordering. To test the robustness of our new model, we apply five distinct methods for parameter estimation. The practical applicability of the Type 2 Gumbel Weibull-G distributions is further supported through the analysis of three real-world datasets. These real-life applications illustrate the exceptional statistical precision of our distributions compared to existing models, thereby reinforcing their significant value in both theoretical and practical statistical applications.

Keywords: continuous statistical distribution generator; exponentiated odds ratio; survival analysis; methods of estimation; statistical properties

MSC: 62E99; 60E05

1. Introduction

With the ever-increasing complexity and volume of data across various disciplines, developing new statistical distributions has become a paramount area of research. These continuous distributions are essential in modeling, forecasting, and interpreting complex data, facilitating hidden patterns and relationships [1]. Nonetheless, the rapid growth and evolving nature of contemporary data often pose challenges that traditional distributions struggle to cope with, leading to a need for novel statistical distributions [2].

Traditional statistical models often face significant challenges when tasked with generating bathtub-shaped density and hazard rate functions. The concept of the bathtub curve originated in reliability engineering, where it was used to describe the life cycles of mechanical and electronic components. The initial phase of high failure rates, known as infant mortality, is often due to manufacturing defects or initial quality issues. This is followed by a middle phase characterized by a relatively constant failure rate, representing the useful life of the product. The final phase, marked by an increasing failure rate, corresponds to the wear-out period where aging and deterioration dominate [3]. Classical models like the exponential, gamma, and Weibull distributions typically show a monotonic hazard function. This limits their ability to account for the complexities inherent in bathtub-shaped data. The non-monotonic nature of these functions, which involves decreasing hazard rates after an initial peak and increasing rates as the system ages, poses a significant modeling challenge. The inadequacies of these traditional models necessitate the development of more sophisticated statistical techniques to capture the true dynamics of the underlying processes [4].

Over the past several decades, numerous methods for creating new continuous probability distributions have been explored. These include methods such as transformations of random variables, the use of mixed models, and advanced compounding methods [5–8]. Among the recent contributions in this field are the gamma–Topp–Leone–Type II–exponentiated half logistic-G distribution family [9], an enhanced version of the generalized Weibull distribution [10], the innovative modified alpha power Weibull-X distribution set [11], the Topp–Leone type II exponentiated half logistic-G distribution category [12], the modified-half-normal distribution by ref. [13], an inventive extension of the power Lindley distribution [13], the truncated inverse generalized Rayleigh distribution [14], the Ristić–Balakrishnan–Topp–Leone–Gompertz-G family of distributions [15], the odd Gompertz-G distribution family [16], the inverse Burr–generalized distribution series [17], the gamma inverse paralogistic distribution [18], and the shifted generalized truncated Nadarajah–Haghighi distribution by ref. [19].

Traditional distributions such as exponential, Weibull, gamma, and log-logistic have broad applications across various fields. However, they often struggle to model data with complex shapes, such as the bathtub curve. Recent models, such as those described in refs. [9,12,15,19], have successfully generated bathtub shapes, but the complexity of these distributions makes them difficult to comprehend and apply in practical scenarios. Additionally, statistical inference for these models can be challenging. A comprehensive review by Scheidegger et al. [20] highlights a unified perspective on various approaches to modeling such distributions, particularly in water distribution systems. Additionally, Romaniuk and Hryniewicz [21] demonstrated the utility of distributions with linear segments for capturing unique hazard rate functions, such as those encountered in pipeline maintenance cost estimation. Recent developments in reliability modeling, such as the work by Chachra et al. [22], have explored Markovian frameworks within fuzzy settings, providing further flexibility in addressing these challenges. These perspectives underscore the importance of novel methodologies, such as the one proposed in this study, to address the increasing complexity of modern data. The R-transferred exponentiated odds ratio generator introduced in this paper provides a general framework that is both concise and straightforward, as illustrated in Equation (3). This new generator is designed to offer greater flexibility and adaptability, making it well suited for managing the increasing complexity of contemporary datasets.

The foundation of this generator's development lies in survival analysis, drawing inspiration from the extreme values of odds ratio data, as elaborated in Section 3. The generator proposed herein aims to provide a comprehensive framework for the creation of a broad range of distributions, each characterized by unique shapes and properties. This feature allows for more precise modeling and analysis of an extensive variety of data. The adaptability of the proposed generator is illustrated through its application in deriving new families of distributions, demonstrating superior data fitting capabilities compared with traditional methods.

The structure of the remaining sections of this paper is outlined as follows: Section 2 provides a description of the methodology of the new generator. Section 3 presents the new subfamily of distributions generated by the proposed technique and investigates the mathematical properties of the resulting distributions. Four estimation methods are discussed in Section 4 to test the robustness of the model. Section 5 introduces several special cases of the new family of distributions. In Section 6, we evaluate the performance and flexibility of the generator through a set of experiments and comparative analyses. Finally, we conclude the paper and discuss the future directions in Section 7.

2. The New Generator Based on Odds Ratio

Odds ratio quantifies the probability that an individual or component, defined by a specific lifespan following a continuous distribution $H(x, \boldsymbol{\psi})$, will fail or expire at a particular point in time, x [23]. The parameters of the baseline function H are denoted by $\boldsymbol{\psi}$. The odds ratio, expressed as $H(x, \boldsymbol{\psi})/\overline{H}(x, \boldsymbol{\psi})$, has become an important tool for understanding and assessing risk factors, shedding light on the relative probabilities of event outcomes, namely, death or failure [24–26].

This study presents a novel generator developed by integrating the methodologies delineated in [6,27]. This new generator can be efficiently applied to any baseline distribution with a cumulative distribution function (cdf), represented as $R(t)$. It is mathematically defined by the following:

$$F_{\text{RT-EOR-H}}(x;\alpha,\beta) = \int_0^{-\log(1-F_{WG}(x))} r(t)dt \tag{1}$$

$$= R\{-\log(1-F_{WG}(x))\} \tag{2}$$

$$= R\left\{\alpha\left[\frac{H(x,\boldsymbol{\psi})}{\overline{H}(x,\boldsymbol{\psi})}\right]^{\beta}\right\} \tag{3}$$

Here, $r(t)$ and $R(t)$ denote the probability density function (pdf) and cdf of a continuous random variable, respectively. $f_{WG}(x)$, and $F_{WG}(x)$ represent the pdf and cdf of the Weibull-G family of distributions proposed by Bourguignon et al. [6]. $H(x, \boldsymbol{\psi})$ and $\overline{H}(x, \boldsymbol{\psi})$ represent the cdf and the survival function of the baseline distribution, respectively. α and β are positive shape parameters, as defined in [6]. This newly designed generator of continuous distributions is denoted as the R-transferred exponentiated odds ratio generator (RT-EOR-H), denoted as $F_{\text{RT-EOR-H}}(x;\alpha,\beta)$. While $R(t)$ and $H(x, \boldsymbol{\psi})$ are both cdfs, it is advisable to select a simpler format for $H(x, \boldsymbol{\psi})$ in real-life applications.

This new approach provides a comprehensive framework, allowing researchers to delve into the exponentiated odds ratio of any baseline function $H(x, \boldsymbol{\psi})$, embedded within any conceivable distribution $R(t)$. Crucially, this new generator, by permitting the investigation of any baseline function within any distribution R, significantly enhances the flexibility, yielding more accurate, adaptable, and precise predictions. These advancements meet the need for continued evolution in reliability analysis, providing a path for enhanced comprehension of the complexities of survival and risk.

The proposed model in this paper introduces two layers of flexibility, enabling the generation of various families of distributions. As shown in Equation (3), for any given cdf, it can be assigned as either the "outer transformer", $R(t)$, or the "inner driver", $H(x, \boldsymbol{\psi})$. This composite method significantly enhances the flexibility of possible density and hazard rate shapes, especially when using simple cdfs.

Some example subfamilies are presented in Table 1. Additional subfamilies of the proposed model have been discussed in our recent work, including [28,29]. These subfamilies demonstrate the remarkable adaptability of the proposed model and its broad applicability to various complex datasets. When a simple "inner driver" is selected, as in the special case discussed in Section 3, the Type 2 Gumbel Weibull-G family exhibits a straightforward and elegant form. The special cases highlighted in this paper illustrate how this intuitively accessible framework can transform basic distributions, such as uniform and exponential distributions, into highly flexible shapes. Moreover, employing the same distribution for both the inner and outer components introduces intriguing behaviors, which will be addressed in detail in our future work.

Table 1. Families of distributions derived from different $R(t)$.

Distribution	$R(t)$	RT-EOR-H
Uniform	$\frac{t}{\theta}$	$\frac{\alpha}{\theta}\left[\frac{H(x,\boldsymbol{\psi})}{\overline{H}(x,\boldsymbol{\psi})}\right]^{\beta}$
Normal	$\Phi\left(\frac{x-\mu}{\sigma}\right)$	$\Phi\left(\frac{\alpha\left[\frac{H(x,\boldsymbol{\psi})}{\overline{H}(x,\boldsymbol{\psi})}\right]^{\beta}-\mu}{\sigma}\right)$
Gamma	$\frac{1}{\Gamma(k)}\gamma(k,\frac{t}{\theta})$	$\frac{1}{\Gamma(k)}\gamma\left(k,\frac{\alpha}{\theta}\left[\frac{H(x,\boldsymbol{\psi})}{\overline{H}(x,\boldsymbol{\psi})}\right]^{\beta}\right)$
Log-logistic	$\frac{1}{1+(t/c)^{-k}}$	$\frac{1}{1+\left(\frac{\alpha}{c}\left[\frac{H(x,\boldsymbol{\psi})}{\overline{H}(x,\boldsymbol{\psi})}\right]^{\beta}\right)^{-k}}$
Rayleigh	$1-e^{-\frac{t^2}{2\sigma^2}}$	$1-\exp\left\{-\frac{\alpha^2}{2\sigma^2}\left[\frac{H(x,\boldsymbol{\psi})}{\overline{H}(x,\boldsymbol{\psi})}\right]^{2\beta}\right\}$
Weibull	$1-e^{-(t/\lambda)^k}$	$1-\exp\left\{-\left(\frac{\alpha}{\lambda}\left[\frac{H(x,\boldsymbol{\psi})}{\overline{H}(x,\boldsymbol{\psi})}\right]^{\beta}\right)^{k}\right\}$
Type 2 Gumbel	$e^{-\lambda t^{-\delta}}$	$\exp\left\{-\lambda\left(\alpha\left[\frac{H(x,\boldsymbol{\psi})}{\overline{H}(x,\boldsymbol{\psi})}\right]^{\beta}\right)^{-\delta}\right\}$
Lomax	$1-(1+\lambda t)^{-k}$	$1-\left(1+\lambda\alpha\left[\frac{H(x,\boldsymbol{\psi})}{\overline{H}(x,\boldsymbol{\psi})}\right]^{\beta}\right)^{-k}$
Burr XII	$1-(1+t^c)^{-k}$	$1-\left\{1+\left(\alpha\left[\frac{H(x,\boldsymbol{\psi})}{\overline{H}(x,\boldsymbol{\psi})}\right]^{\beta}\right)^{c}\right\}^{-k}$
Pareto	$1-(\frac{\gamma}{t})^k$	$1-\left(\frac{\gamma}{\alpha\left[\frac{H(x,\boldsymbol{\psi})}{\overline{H}(x,\boldsymbol{\psi})}\right]^{\beta}}\right)^{k}$
Lévy	$\mathrm{erfc}\left(\sqrt{\frac{c}{2t}}\right)$	$\mathrm{erfc}\left(\sqrt{\frac{c}{2\alpha\left[\frac{H(x,\boldsymbol{\psi})}{\overline{H}(x,\boldsymbol{\psi})}\right]^{\beta}}}\right)$
Fréchet	$e^{-\lambda t^{\gamma}}$	$\exp\left\{-\lambda\left(\alpha\left[\frac{H(x,\boldsymbol{\psi})}{\overline{H}(x,\boldsymbol{\psi})}\right]^{\beta}\right)^{\gamma}\right\}$
Kumaraswamy	$(1-x^k)^{-\lambda}-1$	$\left\{1-\left(\alpha\left[\frac{H(x,\boldsymbol{\psi})}{\overline{H}(x,\boldsymbol{\psi})}\right]^{\beta}\right)^{k}\right\}^{-\lambda}-1$

3. The Type 2 Gumbel Weibull-G Family of Distributions

To illustrate the applicability of the new generator, we will focus on one of its subfamilies in this paper. Here, we combine the generator with the cdf of Type 2 Gumbel distribution as follows:

$$R(t) = e^{-\lambda t^{-\delta}}, \tag{4}$$

where λ and δ are real numbers and λ is the shape parameter. Then, we obtain the cdf and pdf of a new Type 2 Gumbel Weibull-G (T2GWG) family of distributions as

$$F_{T2GWG}(x) = \exp\left\{-\lambda\alpha^{-\delta}\left[\frac{H(x,\boldsymbol{\psi})}{\overline{H}(x,\boldsymbol{\psi})}\right]^{-\beta\delta}\right\} \tag{5}$$

To avoid over-parameterization, we let $\lambda = 1$, $\delta = 1$, and substitute $\alpha = \alpha^{-1}$; now, the cdf reduces to

$$F_{T2GWG}(x) = \exp\left\{-\alpha\left[\frac{H(x,\boldsymbol{\psi})}{\overline{H}(x,\boldsymbol{\psi})}\right]^{-\beta}\right\} \tag{6}$$

and

$$f_{T2GWG}(x) = \alpha\beta h(x,\boldsymbol{\psi})\frac{H(x,\boldsymbol{\psi})^{-\beta-1}}{\overline{H}(x,\boldsymbol{\psi})^{-\beta+1}}\exp\left\{-\alpha\left[\frac{H(x,\boldsymbol{\psi})}{\overline{H}(x,\boldsymbol{\psi})}\right]^{-\beta}\right\} \tag{7}$$

The T2GWG distribution emerges as a notable variant within the Odd Inverse Weibull-G family [30], distinguished by setting $\lambda = 1$, and serves as an expansion to the Odd Fréchet-G framework [31]. The exploration of this particular distribution's statistical attributes remains relatively uncharted in the existing literature. Because of its straightforwardness and minimal parameter requirements, we delve into the intricacies of the T2GWG distribution as a prime exemplar of the RT-EOR-H generator's potential. This initial exploration sets the stage for a more comprehensive examination of additional models in forthcoming studies.

An interpretation of the T2GWG family of distributions can be given as follows. Let Z be a lifetime random variable with a baseline cdf $H(x, \boldsymbol{\psi})$. The odds ratio that an individual following the lifetime Z will die (failure) at time x is $\dfrac{H(x,\boldsymbol{\psi})}{\overline{H}(x,\boldsymbol{\psi})}$. For a sequence of such independent and identical odds ratios $Z_1, Z_2, \cdots, Z_n$, maximum $M_n = \max(Z_1, Z_2, \cdots, Z_n)$, M_n follows a distribution which converges to the T2GWG distribution as provided in Equation (6) [5,6].

In the subsequent subsections, we delve into the statistical properties of this novel distribution. Our discussion will cover a broad range of topics, including the expansion of the density function, hazard rate and quantile functions, moments, incomplete moments, the generation function, Rényi entropy, order statistics, and stochastic ordering.

3.1. Expansion of the pdf

Consider the following expansion

$$\exp\left\{-\alpha\left[\frac{H(x,\boldsymbol{\psi})}{\overline{H}(x,\boldsymbol{\psi})}\right]^{-\beta}\right\} = \sum_{j=0}^{\infty}\frac{(-1)^j\alpha^j}{j!}\left[\frac{H(x,\boldsymbol{\psi})}{\overline{H}(x,\boldsymbol{\psi})}\right]^{-j\beta}, \tag{8}$$

then the pdf of T2GWG can be expanded as

$$\begin{aligned} f_{\text{T2GWG}}(x) &= \alpha\beta h(x,\boldsymbol{\psi})\frac{H(x,\boldsymbol{\psi})^{-\beta-1}}{\overline{H}(x,\boldsymbol{\psi})^{-\beta+1}}\sum_{j=0}^{\infty}\frac{(-1)^j\alpha^j}{j!}\left[\frac{H(x,\boldsymbol{\psi})}{\overline{H}(x,\boldsymbol{\psi})}\right]^{-j\beta} \\ &= \alpha\beta h(x,\boldsymbol{\psi})\sum_{j=0}^{\infty}\frac{(-1)^j\alpha^j}{j!}\frac{\overline{H}(x,\boldsymbol{\psi})^{\beta+j\beta-1}}{H(x,\boldsymbol{\psi})^{\beta+j\beta+1}} \end{aligned} \tag{9}$$

Moreover, note that

$$\begin{aligned} \overline{H}(x,\boldsymbol{\psi})^{\beta+j\beta-1} &= [1-H(x,\boldsymbol{\psi})]^{\beta+j\beta-1} \\ &= \sum_{k=0}^{\infty}\binom{\beta(j+1)-1}{k}(-1)^k H(x,\boldsymbol{\psi})^k \end{aligned} \tag{10}$$

Then,

$$\begin{aligned} f_{\text{T2GWG}}(x) &= \alpha\beta h(x,\boldsymbol{\psi})\sum_{j=0}^{\infty}\frac{(-1)^j\alpha^j}{j!}\sum_{k=0}^{\infty}\binom{\beta(j+1)-1}{k}\frac{(-1)^k H(x,\boldsymbol{\psi})^k}{H(x,\boldsymbol{\psi})^{\beta+j\beta+1}} \\ &= \alpha\beta h(x,\boldsymbol{\psi})\sum_{j,k=0}^{\infty}\frac{(-1)^{j+k}\alpha^j}{j!}\binom{\beta(j+1)-1}{k}[H(x,\boldsymbol{\psi})]^{k-\beta-j\beta-1} \\ &= \sum_{j,k=0}^{\infty} c_{j,k}\, r_{k-\beta(j+1)-1}(x,\boldsymbol{\psi}) \end{aligned} \tag{11}$$

where

$$c_{j,k} = \frac{\alpha\beta(-1)^{j+k}\alpha^j}{j!(k-\beta(j+1))}\binom{\beta(j+1)-1}{k} \tag{12}$$

and

$$r_{k-\beta-j\beta-1}(x,\boldsymbol{\psi}) = (k-\beta(j+1))h(x,\boldsymbol{\psi})H(x,\boldsymbol{\psi})^{k-\beta(j+1)-1}$$

which is the pdf of the exponentiated generalized (EG) distribution with parameter $\beta^* = k - \beta(j+1)$.

3.2. Hazard Rate and Quantile Functions

Building upon our earlier discussion on the odds ratio and survival analysis, we now delve into the key mathematical structures: the hazard rate function and the quantile function. These are crucial to the deeper understanding and application of survival analysis as they allow the computation of survival probabilities and survival times.

3.2.1. Hazard Rate and Quantile Functions

The hazard rate function (hrf) plays an important role in survival analysis as it defines the instantaneous potential per unit time for the occurrence of an event given survival up to that time. On the other hand, the quantile function is essential in determining the time at which a certain proportion of survival is expected. In the newly proposed family of distributions, these functions take a particularly interesting form as follows.

$$h_{T2GWG}(x) = \frac{\alpha\beta h(x,\boldsymbol{\psi})\frac{H(x,\boldsymbol{\psi})^{-\beta-1}}{\overline{H}(x,\boldsymbol{\psi})^{-\beta+1}}\exp\left\{-\alpha\left[\frac{H(x,\boldsymbol{\psi})}{\overline{H}(x,\boldsymbol{\psi})}\right]^{-\beta}\right\}}{1-\exp\left\{-\alpha\left[\frac{H(x,\boldsymbol{\psi})}{\overline{H}(x,\boldsymbol{\psi})}\right]^{-\beta}\right\}} \tag{13}$$

In addition to the hrf, it is also useful to consider its reciprocal, termed the reverse hazard rate function. This function essentially reflects the hazard function's properties but is viewed from the perspective of the event not occurring.

$$\begin{aligned}\tau_{T2GWG}(x) &= \frac{\alpha\beta h(x,\boldsymbol{\psi})\frac{H(x,\boldsymbol{\psi})^{-\beta-1}}{\overline{H}(x,\boldsymbol{\psi})^{-\beta+1}}\exp\left\{-\alpha\left[\frac{H(x,\boldsymbol{\psi})}{\overline{H}(x,\boldsymbol{\psi})}\right]^{-\beta}\right\}}{\exp\left\{-\alpha\left[\frac{H(x,\boldsymbol{\psi})}{\overline{H}(x,\boldsymbol{\psi})}\right]^{-\beta}\right\}} \\ &= \alpha\beta h(x,\boldsymbol{\psi})\frac{H(x,\boldsymbol{\psi})^{-\beta-1}}{\overline{H}(x,\boldsymbol{\psi})^{-\beta+1}}\end{aligned} \tag{14}$$

3.2.2. Quantile Function

Next, we will focus on the quantile function, which is particularly useful when determining the survival time corresponding to a specific survival probability.

$$F_{T2GWG}(x) = \exp\left\{-\alpha\left[\frac{H(x,\boldsymbol{\psi})}{\overline{H}(x,\boldsymbol{\psi})}\right]^{-\beta}\right\} = p$$

For $0 \le p \le 1$, then, it is sufficient to solve

$$H(x,\boldsymbol{\psi}) = \frac{1}{\left(\frac{\log p}{-\alpha}\right)^{\frac{1}{\beta}}+1} := q \tag{15}$$

Thus, the quantile x_p of the distribution reduces to the quantile x_q of the baseline distribution with cdf $H(x,\boldsymbol{\psi})$ and is given by

$$x_q = H^{-1}(q) \tag{16}$$

3.3. *Moments, Incomplete Moments, and Generating Functions*

3.3.1. Moments

In the field of statistics, moments play a vital role in characterizing the properties of a probability distribution. Moments provide important summary measures of the characteristics of datasets. The first moment about the origin, also known as the mean, measures the location of the distribution. The second central moment is known as the variance, which quantifies the spread or dispersion of the distribution. The third and fourth moments, skewness and kurtosis, respectively, describe the shape of the distribution, capturing aspects of its asymmetry and tailedness. We can present the rth moment of the distributions as

$$E(Y^r) = \sum_{j,k=0}^{\infty} c_{j,k} E(Z_{j,k}^r) \tag{17}$$

where $Z_{j,k}$ is the exponentiated generalized distribution with the parameter $\beta^* = k - \beta(j+1)$ and $c_{j,k}$ is defined by Equation (12).

3.3.2. Incomplete Moments, Conditional Moments, and Moment Generating Function

While moments give us an understanding of the general characteristics of a distribution, they do not always provide sufficient detail about specific intervals or subsets within the data. This is where incomplete moments come into play. Incomplete moments, also known as truncated or restricted moments, are defined similarly to regular moments but are integrated over a subset of the possible range of the variable. They offer a more granular insight into the characteristics of the distribution within specific ranges. This makes them particularly useful when analyzing left- or right-skewed data, or when assessing the impact of outlier observations. The incomplete moment is provided as

$$I_Y(z) = \int_0^z y^s f_{\text{T2GWG}}(y)dy = \sum_{j,k=0}^{\infty} c_{j,k} I_{j,k}(y) \tag{18}$$

where $I_{j,k}(y) = \int_0^z y^s r_{k-\beta(j+1)}(x, \boldsymbol{\psi})$.

The rth conditional moments of the Type 2 Gumbel Weibull-G family of distributions is given by

$$\begin{aligned} E(Y^r|Y \geq a) &= \frac{1}{\overline{F}_{\text{T2GWG}}(a;\alpha,\beta,\boldsymbol{\psi})} \int_t^{\infty} y^r f_{\text{T2GWG}}(y;\alpha,\beta,\boldsymbol{\psi})dy \\ &= \frac{1}{\overline{F}_{\text{T2GWG}}(a;\alpha,\beta,\boldsymbol{\psi})} \sum_{j,k=0}^{\infty} c_{j,k} I_{j,k}(y) \end{aligned} \tag{19}$$

where $I_{j,k}(y)$ is defined above.

The moment generating function is given by

$$M_Y(t) = E(e^{tY}) = \sum_{j,k=0}^{\infty} c_{j,k} E(e^{tZ_{j,k}}) = \sum_{j,k=0}^{\infty} c_{j,k} M_{Z_{j,k}}(t) \tag{20}$$

and the characteristic function is defined as

$$\phi(t) = E(e^{itY}) = \sum_{j,k=0}^{\infty} c_{j,k} E(e^{itZ_{j,k}}) = \sum_{j,k=0}^{\infty} c_{j,k} \phi_{k-\beta(j+1)}(t), \tag{21}$$

where $\phi_{k-\beta(j+1)}(t)$ is the characteristic function of the EG distribution with parameter $\beta^* = k - \beta(j+1)$.

3.4. Rényi Entropy

Rényi entropy is named after the Hungarian mathematician Alfréd Rényi [32]. While Shannon entropy is perhaps the most commonly referenced form of entropy in the field of information theory, characterizing the average uncertainty or unpredictability of a source of information, Rényi entropy provides a more generalized measure. Rényi entropy finds applications in various domains including physics, computer science, statistics, and quantum information theory. For example, in the context of machine learning, it can be used to measure the diversity or complexity of learned models. In statistical physics, it is useful in understanding the thermodynamics of complex systems. The Rényi entropy of this new distribution is

$$\begin{aligned}
I_R(\omega) =& (1-\omega)^{-1}\log\left[\int_{-\infty}^{\infty} f^{\omega}(x)dx\right] \\
=& (1-\omega)^{-1}\{\omega(\log\alpha+\log\beta) \\
&+\log\left[\int_{-\infty}^{\infty} h^{\omega}(x,\boldsymbol{\psi})\frac{H(x,\boldsymbol{\psi})^{\omega(-\beta-1)}}{\overline{H}(x,\boldsymbol{\psi})^{\omega(-\beta+1)}}\exp\left\{-\omega\alpha\left[\frac{H(x,\boldsymbol{\psi})}{\overline{H}(x,\boldsymbol{\psi})}\right]^{-\beta}\right\}\right]\right\}
\end{aligned}$$

where $\omega > 0$ and $\omega \neq 1$. Applying the same expansion technique for the pdf, we obtain

$$\begin{aligned}
I_R(\omega) =& (1-\omega)^{-1}\{\omega(\log\alpha+\log\beta) \\
&+\log\left[\sum_{i=0}^{\infty}\frac{(-1)^i(\omega\alpha)^i}{i!}\int_{-\infty}^{\infty} h^{\omega}(x,\boldsymbol{\psi})\frac{[\overline{H}(x,\boldsymbol{\psi})]^{\omega(\beta-1)+i\beta}}{[H(x,\boldsymbol{\psi})]^{\omega(\beta+1)+i\beta}}dx\right]\right\}
\end{aligned} \tag{22}$$

Consider that

$$\begin{aligned}
\overline{H}(x,\boldsymbol{\psi})^{\omega(\beta-1)+i\beta} &= [1-H(x,\boldsymbol{\psi})]^{\omega(\beta-1)+i\beta} \\
&= \sum_{j=0}^{\infty}\binom{\omega(\beta-1)+i\beta}{j}(-1)^j H(x,\boldsymbol{\psi})^j
\end{aligned} \tag{23}$$

Thus, we can write the Reńyi entropy as

$$\begin{aligned}
I_R(\omega) =& (1-\omega)^{-1}\left\{\omega(\log\alpha+\log\beta)+\log\left[\sum_{i=0}^{\infty}\sum_{j=0}^{\infty}\frac{(-1)^{i+j}(\omega\alpha)^i}{i!}\right.\right. \\
&\times\left.\left.\binom{\omega(\beta-1)+i\beta}{j}\int_{-\infty}^{\infty} h^{\omega}(x,\boldsymbol{\psi})(H(x,\boldsymbol{\psi}))^{j-\omega(\beta+1)-i\beta}dx\right]\right\} \\
=& (1-\omega)^{-1}\left\{\omega(\log\alpha+\log\beta)+\log\left[\sum_{i=0}^{\infty}\sum_{j=0}^{\infty}\frac{(-1)^{i+j}(\omega\alpha)^i}{i!}\right.\right. \\
&\times\binom{\omega(\beta-1)+i\beta}{j}\frac{\omega^{\omega}}{[j-\omega(\beta+1)-i\beta+\omega]^{\omega}} \\
&\times\left.\left.\int_{-\infty}^{\infty}[\frac{j-\omega(\beta+1)-i\beta+\omega}{\omega}h(x,\boldsymbol{\psi})(H(x,\boldsymbol{\psi}))^{\frac{j-\omega(\beta+1)-i\beta}{\omega}}]^{\omega}\right]\right\} \\
=& (1-\omega)^{-1}\left\{\omega(\log\alpha+\log\beta)+\log\left[\sum_{i=0}^{\infty}\sum_{j=0}^{\infty}\frac{(-1)^{i+j}(\omega\alpha)^i}{i!}\right.\right. \\
&\times\binom{\omega(\beta-1)+i\beta}{j}\frac{\omega^{\omega}}{[j-\omega(\beta+1)-i\beta+\omega]^{\omega}}\times e^{(1-\omega)I_{REG}}
\end{aligned} \tag{24}$$

where I_{REG} is the Rényi entropy of the exponentiated generalized distribution with parameter $\beta^* = \dfrac{j-\omega(\beta+1)-i\beta+\omega}{\omega}$.

3.5. Order Statistics

In the field of statistics, order statistics are a fundamental concept that allows for deeper analysis and understanding of sampled data. Specifically, order statistics are the values from a random sample sorted in ascending or descending order. This sorting process provides a powerful perspective on the sample's overall distribution and associated characteristics. Order statistics are used in a variety of applications, including non-parametric statistics (which does not rely on parameters defined in terms of a theoretical or assumed population), reliability engineering, and statistical quality control. They also play a central role in the construction of quantile–quantile plots, which are used to assess whether a dataset follows a particular theoretical distribution.

Let $X_1, X_2, \ldots, X_n$ be independent identically distributed random variables distributed by Equation (7). The pdf of the ith order statistic $f_{i:n}(x)$ is given by

$$\begin{aligned}
f_{i:n}(x) &= \frac{n! f_{T2GWG}(x)}{(i-1)!(n-i)!}[F_{T2GWG}(x)]^{i-1}[1-F_{T2GWG}(x)]^{n-i} \\
&= \frac{n! f_{T2GWG}(x)}{(i-1)!(n-i)!}\sum_{m=0}^{n-i}\binom{n-i}{m}(-1)^m[F_{T2GWG}(x)]^{i-1+m} \\
&= \frac{n! f_{T2GWG}(x)}{(i-1)!(n-i)!}\sum_{m=0}^{n-i}\binom{n-i}{m}(-1)^m \exp\left\{(i-1+m)(-\alpha)\left[\frac{H(x,\boldsymbol{\psi})}{\overline{H}(x,\boldsymbol{\psi})}\right]^{-\beta}\right\} \\
&= \frac{n!}{(i-1)!(n-i)!}\sum_{m=0}^{n-i}\binom{n-i}{m}\frac{(-1)^m}{i+m} f_{T2GWG}(x;(i+m)\alpha,\beta)
\end{aligned} \tag{25}$$

Therefore, we can present $f_{i:n}(x)$ as a linear combination of the T2GWG with parameter (α^*, β), where $\alpha^* = (i+m)\alpha$.

3.6. Stochastic Ordering

Stochastic ordering is a mathematical concept frequently applied in the realm of statistics, probability theory, decision theory, and economics [33]. The most basic form of stochastic ordering is the usual order of real numbers, which extends naturally to random variables: a random variable X is said to be stochastically smaller than another random variable Y if, for every real number x, the probability that X is less than or equal to x is higher than or equal to the probability that Y is less than or equal to x. This gives rise to the concept of one distribution being "stochastically larger" than another, which can be a valuable tool in comparing different probability models or assessing risk. There are several types of stochastic orderings, such as increasing convex order, likelihood ratio order, and hazard rate order, each imposing a different structure on the sets of random variables or distributions. Stochastic ordering is a significant concept because it enables us to make statements about the relative behavior of different random variables or distributions without specifying them precisely. It has been widely used in various fields, such as reliability, insurance, finance, operations research, and queuing theory.

Let $X_1 \sim T2GWG(x;\alpha_1,\beta,\boldsymbol{\psi})$ and $X_2 \sim T2GWG(x;\alpha_2,\beta,\boldsymbol{\psi})$. The likelihood ratio is

$$\begin{aligned}
\frac{f_{X_1}(x)}{f_{X_2}(x)} &= \frac{\alpha_1\beta h(x,\boldsymbol{\psi})\frac{H(x,\boldsymbol{\psi})^{-\beta-1}}{\overline{H}(x,\boldsymbol{\psi})^{-\beta+1}}\exp\left\{-\alpha_1\left[\frac{H(x,\boldsymbol{\psi})}{\overline{H}(x,\boldsymbol{\psi})}\right]^{-\beta}\right\}}{\alpha_2\beta h(x,\boldsymbol{\psi})\frac{H(x,\boldsymbol{\psi})^{-\beta-1}}{\overline{H}(x,\boldsymbol{\psi})^{-\beta+1}}\exp\left\{-\alpha_2\left[\frac{H(x,\boldsymbol{\psi})}{\overline{H}(x,\boldsymbol{\psi})}\right]^{-\beta}\right\}} \\
&= \frac{\alpha_1}{\alpha_2}\exp\left\{(\alpha_2-\alpha_1)\left[\frac{H(x,\boldsymbol{\psi})}{\overline{H}(x,\boldsymbol{\psi})}\right]^{-\beta}\right\}
\end{aligned} \tag{26}$$

Then, we differentiate Equation (26) and obtain

$$\frac{d}{dx}\left(\frac{f_{X_1}(x)}{f_{X_2}(x)}\right) = \frac{\alpha_1}{\alpha_2}\exp\left\{(\alpha_2-\alpha_1)\left[\frac{H(x,\boldsymbol{\psi})}{\overline{H}(x,\boldsymbol{\psi})}\right]^{-\beta}\right\} \times \left[(\alpha_2-\alpha_1)h(x,\boldsymbol{\psi})\frac{H(x,\boldsymbol{\psi})^{-\beta-1}}{\overline{H}(x,\boldsymbol{\psi})^{-\beta+1}}\right] \tag{27}$$

If $\alpha_1 < \alpha_2$, $\frac{d}{dx}\left(\frac{f_{X_1}(x)}{f_{X_2}(x)}\right) < 0$. Thus, it indicates that $X \preceq_{lr} Y$. According to the theorem proposed by ref. [33], both $X \preceq_{hr} Y$ and $X \preceq Y$ hold.

4. Methods of Estimation

4.1. Maximum Likelihood Estimation

We can estimate the unknown parameters of the Type 2 Gumbel Weibull-G family distributions by using the widely used maximum likelihood estimation (MLE). Let $\boldsymbol{\Delta} = (\alpha, \beta, \boldsymbol{\psi})^T$. Then, the log-likelihood for $\boldsymbol{\Delta}$ is defined by

$$\ell(\boldsymbol{\Delta}) = n\log(\alpha) + n\log(\beta) + \sum_{i=1}^{n}\log h(x_i,\boldsymbol{\psi}) - (\beta+1)\sum_{i=1}^{n}\log H(x_i,\boldsymbol{\psi}) + (\beta-1)\sum_{i=1}^{n}\log[1-H(x_i,\boldsymbol{\psi})] - \alpha\sum_{i=1}^{n}\left[\frac{H(x_i,\boldsymbol{\psi})}{1-H(x_i,\boldsymbol{\psi})}\right]^{-\beta} \tag{28}$$

The first derivatives of $\ell(\boldsymbol{\Delta})$ with respect to $\boldsymbol{\Delta}$ are shown as follows:

$$\frac{\partial\ell}{\partial\alpha} = \frac{n}{\alpha} - \sum_{i=1}^{n}\left[\frac{H(x_i,\boldsymbol{\psi})}{1-H(x_i,\boldsymbol{\psi})}\right]^{-\beta} \tag{29}$$

$$\frac{\partial\ell}{\partial\beta} = \frac{n}{\beta} - \sum_{i=1}^{n}\log H(x_i,\boldsymbol{\psi}) + \sum_{i=1}^{n}\log[1-H(x_i,\boldsymbol{\psi})] + \alpha\sum_{i=1}^{n}\left[\frac{H(x_i,\boldsymbol{\psi})}{1-H(x_i,\boldsymbol{\psi})}\right]^{-\beta}\log\left(\frac{H(x_i,\boldsymbol{\psi})}{1-H(x_i,\boldsymbol{\psi})}\right) \tag{30}$$

and

$$\frac{\partial\ell}{\partial\psi_k} = \sum_{i=1}^{n}\frac{1}{h(x_i,\boldsymbol{\psi})}\frac{\partial h(x_i,\boldsymbol{\psi})}{\partial\psi_k} - (\beta+1)\sum_{i=1}^{n}\frac{1}{H(x_i,\boldsymbol{\psi})}\frac{\partial H(x_i,\boldsymbol{\psi})}{\partial\psi_k} - (\beta-1)\sum_{i=1}^{n}\frac{1}{1-H(x_i,\boldsymbol{\psi})}\frac{\partial H(x_i,\boldsymbol{\psi})}{\partial\psi_k} + \alpha\beta\sum_{i=1}^{n}\frac{H(x_i,\boldsymbol{\psi})^{-\beta-1}}{[1-H(x_i,\boldsymbol{\psi})]^{-\beta+1}}\frac{\partial H(x_i,\boldsymbol{\psi})}{\partial\psi_k} \tag{31}$$

where ψ_k is the kth element of the vector $\boldsymbol{\psi}$.

We can maximize the log-likelihood function $\ell(\boldsymbol{\Delta})$ by solving the nonlinear equations $\left(\frac{\partial\ell}{\partial\alpha}, \frac{\partial\ell}{\partial\beta}, \frac{\partial\ell}{\partial\psi_k}\right) = 0$ with numerical methods such as the Newton–Raphson approach.

4.2. Least Square and Weighted Least Square Estimation

The least square (LS) method is a commonly used technique in regression analysis for approximating the solution of overdetermined systems. The method provides the best linear unbiased estimates of the unknown parameters if the errors are homoscedastic and uncorrelated. On the other hand, the weighted least square (WLSE) approach extends the least square technique by incorporating the different variances of the observations.

This method assigns a weight to each data point based on the variance of its error term, placing less emphasis on the observations with higher variances to make the overall model more reliable.

The LSE and WLSE techniques can also provide estimators in the model. The LS estimation is given by

$$\begin{aligned} LS(\boldsymbol{\Delta}) &= \sum_{i=1}^{n}\left(F(x_i,\boldsymbol{\Delta}) - \frac{i}{n+1}\right)^2 \\ &= \sum_{i=1}^{n}\left(\exp\left\{-\alpha\left[\frac{H(x_i,\boldsymbol{\psi})}{\overline{H}(x_i,\boldsymbol{\psi})}\right]^{-\beta}\right\} - \frac{i}{n+1}\right)^2 \end{aligned} \tag{32}$$

By differentiating Equation (32), we have the following:

$$\begin{aligned} \frac{\partial LS}{\partial \alpha} =&2\sum_{i=1}^{n}\left(\exp\left\{-\alpha\left[\frac{H(x_i,\boldsymbol{\psi})}{\overline{H}(x_i,\boldsymbol{\psi})}\right]^{-\beta}\right\} - \frac{i}{n+1}\right) \\ &\times(-1)\left[\frac{H(x_i,\boldsymbol{\psi})}{\overline{H}(x_i,\boldsymbol{\psi})}\right]^{-\beta}\exp\left\{-\alpha\left[\frac{H(x_i,\boldsymbol{\psi})}{\overline{H}(x_i,\boldsymbol{\psi})}\right]^{-\beta}\right\} \end{aligned} \tag{33}$$

$$\begin{aligned} \frac{\partial LS}{\partial \beta} =&2\sum_{i=1}^{n}\left(\exp\left\{-\alpha\left[\frac{H(x_i,\boldsymbol{\psi})}{\overline{H}(x_i,\boldsymbol{\psi})}\right]^{-\beta}\right\} - \frac{i}{n+1}\right) \\ &\times \alpha\log\left(\frac{H(x_i,\boldsymbol{\psi})}{\overline{H}(x_i,\boldsymbol{\psi})}\right)\left[\frac{H(x_i,\boldsymbol{\psi})}{\overline{H}(x_i,\boldsymbol{\psi})}\right]^{-\beta}\exp\left\{-\alpha\left[\frac{H(x_i,\boldsymbol{\psi})}{\overline{H}(x_i,\boldsymbol{\psi})}\right]^{-\beta}\right\} \end{aligned} \tag{34}$$

and

$$\begin{aligned} \frac{\partial LS}{\partial \psi_k} =&2\sum_{i=1}^{n}\left(\exp\left\{-\alpha\left[\frac{H(x_i,\boldsymbol{\psi})}{\overline{H}(x_i,\boldsymbol{\psi})}\right]^{-\beta}\right\} - \frac{i}{n+1}\right) \\ &\times \alpha\beta\frac{\partial H(x_i,\boldsymbol{\psi})}{\partial \psi_k}\frac{H(x_i,\boldsymbol{\psi})^{-\beta-1}}{\overline{H}(x_i,\boldsymbol{\psi})^{-\beta+1}}\exp\left\{-\alpha\left[\frac{H(x_i,\boldsymbol{\psi})}{\overline{H}(x_i,\boldsymbol{\psi})}\right]^{-\beta}\right\} \end{aligned} \tag{35}$$

We can also apply the Newton–Raphson procedure to minimize the least square estimation $LS(\boldsymbol{\Delta})$ by solving the equations $\left(\frac{\partial LS}{\partial \alpha}, \frac{\partial LS}{\partial \beta}, \frac{\partial LS}{\partial \theta_k}\right) = 0$.

Similarly, the WLS estimation can be obtained by minimizing

$$\begin{aligned} WLS(\boldsymbol{\Delta}) &= \sum_{i=1}^{n}\frac{(n+1)^2(n+2)}{i(n-i+1)}\left(F(x_i,\boldsymbol{\Delta}) - \frac{i}{n+1}\right)^2 \\ &= \sum_{i=1}^{n}\frac{(n+1)^2(n+2)}{i(n-i+1)}\left(\exp\left\{-\alpha\left[\frac{H(x_i,\boldsymbol{\psi})}{\overline{H}(x_i,\boldsymbol{\psi})}\right]^{-\beta}\right\} - \frac{i}{n+1}\right)^2 \end{aligned} \tag{36}$$

4.3. Maximum Product Spacing Approach of Estimation

The maximum product spacing (MPS) approach is particularly useful when dealing with unknown or complex distributions [34]. Unlike MLE, the MPS method does not require the explicit formulation of a likelihood function, making it a versatile and robust approach for different types of distributions. The geometric mean of the MPS spacings is given by

$$G(\boldsymbol{\Delta}) = \left\{\prod_{i=1}^{n+1} D_i(x_i,\boldsymbol{\Delta})\right\}^{\frac{1}{n+1}} \tag{37}$$

where

$$D_i = \begin{cases} F(x_1, \boldsymbol{\Delta}), i = 0 \\ F(x_i, \boldsymbol{\Delta}) - F(x_{i-1}, \boldsymbol{\Delta}), i = 2, 3, ..., n \\ 1 - F(x_n, \boldsymbol{\Delta}), i = n+1 \end{cases}$$

Thus, we can maximize

$$\begin{aligned} G(\boldsymbol{\Delta}) = & \left[\exp\left\{ -\alpha \left[\frac{H(x_1, \boldsymbol{\psi})}{\overline{H}(x_1, \boldsymbol{\psi})} \right]^{\beta} \right\} \left(1 - \exp\left\{ -\alpha \left[\frac{H(x_n, \boldsymbol{\psi})}{\overline{H}(x_n, \boldsymbol{\psi})} \right]^{-\beta} \right\} \right) \right. \\ & \left. \times \prod_{i=2}^{n} \left(\exp\left\{ -\alpha \left[\frac{H(x_i, \boldsymbol{\psi})}{\overline{H}(x_i, \boldsymbol{\psi})} \right]^{-\beta} \right\} - \exp\left\{ -\alpha \left[\frac{H(x_{i-1}, \boldsymbol{\psi})}{\overline{H}(x_{i-1}, \boldsymbol{\psi})} \right]^{-\beta} \right\} \right) \right]^{\frac{1}{n+1}} \end{aligned} \quad (38)$$

Equivalently, we can also maximize $W = \log G$

$$\begin{aligned} W(\boldsymbol{\Delta}) = & \frac{1}{n+1} \sum_{i=1}^{n+1} \log D_i(x_i, \boldsymbol{\Delta}) \\ = & \frac{1}{n+1} \left\{ -\alpha \left[\frac{H(x_1, \boldsymbol{\psi})}{\overline{H}(x_1, \boldsymbol{\psi})} \right]^{-\beta} + \log\left(1 - \exp\left\{ -\alpha \left[\frac{H(x_n, \boldsymbol{\psi})}{\overline{H}(x_n, \boldsymbol{\psi})} \right]^{-\beta} \right\} \right) \right. \\ & \left. + \sum_{i=2}^{n} \log\left(\exp\left\{ -\alpha \left[\frac{H(x_i, \boldsymbol{\psi})}{\overline{H}(x_i, \boldsymbol{\psi})} \right]^{-\beta} \right\} - \exp\left\{ -\alpha \left[\frac{H(x_{i-1}, \boldsymbol{\psi})}{\overline{H}(x_{i-1}, \boldsymbol{\psi})} \right]^{-\beta} \right\} \right) \right\} \end{aligned} \quad (39)$$

By solving $\left(\frac{\partial W}{\partial \alpha}, \frac{\partial W}{\partial \beta}, \frac{\partial W}{\partial \psi_k} \right) = 0$, we can obtain the estimators. The partial derivatives are provided in Appendix ??.

4.4. Cramér–Von Mises Approach of Estimation

The Cramér–von Mises method is another approach to estimate the parameters of a distribution [35]. The Cramér–von Mises statistic measures the difference between the empirical distribution function of the data and the cumulative distribution function of the proposed model. This technique has an advantage over methods such as maximum likelihood estimation in that it considers the whole dataset, not just the location and dispersion, resulting in a more comprehensive estimation. We can apply the Cramér–von Mises criterion to obtain the estimators by minimizing the function $S(x; \boldsymbol{\Delta})$ with respect to $\boldsymbol{\Delta}$, where

$$\begin{aligned} S(x; \boldsymbol{\Delta}) = & \frac{1}{12n^2} + \frac{1}{n} \sum_{i=1}^{n} \left(F(x_i; \boldsymbol{\Delta}) - \frac{2i-1}{2n} \right)^2 \\ = & \frac{1}{12n^2} + \frac{1}{n} \sum_{i=1}^{n} \left(\exp\left\{ -\alpha \left[\frac{H(x_i, \boldsymbol{\psi})}{\overline{H}(x_i, \boldsymbol{\psi})} \right]^{-\beta} \right\} - \frac{2i-1}{2n} \right)^2 \end{aligned} \quad (40)$$

Take the first partial derivatives of S, and we can have the following:

$$\begin{aligned} \frac{\partial S}{\partial \alpha} = & \frac{2}{n} \sum_{i=1}^{n} \left(\exp\left\{ -\alpha \left[\frac{H(x_i, \boldsymbol{\psi})}{\overline{H}(x_i, \boldsymbol{\psi})} \right]^{-\beta} \right\} - \frac{2i-1}{2n} \right) \\ & \times (-1) \left[\frac{H(x_i, \boldsymbol{\psi})}{\overline{H}(x_i, \boldsymbol{\psi})} \right]^{-\beta} \exp\left\{ -\alpha \left[\frac{H(x_i, \boldsymbol{\psi})}{\overline{H}(x_i, \boldsymbol{\psi})} \right]^{-\beta} \right\} \end{aligned} \quad (41)$$

$$\frac{\partial S}{\partial \beta} = \frac{2}{n}\sum_{i=1}^{n}\left(\exp\left\{-\alpha\left[\frac{H(x_i,\boldsymbol{\psi})}{\overline{H}(x_i,\boldsymbol{\psi})}\right]^{-\beta}\right\} - \frac{2i-1}{2n}\right) \times \alpha\log\left(\frac{H(x_i,\boldsymbol{\psi})}{\overline{H}(x_i,\boldsymbol{\psi})}\right)\left[\frac{H(x_i,\boldsymbol{\psi})}{\overline{H}(x_i,\boldsymbol{\psi})}\right]^{-\beta}\exp\left\{-\alpha\left[\frac{H(x_i,\boldsymbol{\psi})}{\overline{H}(x_i,\boldsymbol{\psi})}\right]^{-\beta}\right\} \quad (42)$$

$$\frac{\partial S}{\partial \psi_k} = \frac{2}{n}\sum_{i=1}^{n}\left(\exp\left\{-\alpha\left[\frac{H(x_i,\boldsymbol{\psi})}{\overline{H}(x_i,\boldsymbol{\psi})}\right]^{-\beta}\right\} - \frac{2i-1}{2n}\right) \times \alpha\beta\frac{\partial H(x_i,\boldsymbol{\psi})}{\partial \psi_k}\frac{H(x_i,\boldsymbol{\psi})^{-\beta-1}}{\overline{H}(x_i,\boldsymbol{\psi})^{-\beta+1}}\exp\left\{-\alpha\left[\frac{H(x_i,\boldsymbol{\psi})}{\overline{H}(x_i,\boldsymbol{\psi})}\right]^{-\beta}\right\} \quad (43)$$

4.5. Anderson and Darling Approach of Estimation

The Anderson–Darling approach was proposed in ref. [36] to test whether a dataset follows a specific distribution, and can also be used to estimate parameters. This method gives greater weight to the tails of the distribution compared to other methods, like the Kolmogorov–Smirnov test. The Anderson–Darling statistic is minimized to find the parameters of the best-fitting distribution. This estimation method is highly sensitive to deviations in the tails and thus can be more powerful for identifying whether a particular distribution fits the data. The Anderson–Darling estimators can be obtained by minimizing

$$\begin{aligned} AD(\boldsymbol{\Delta}) &= -n - \frac{1}{n}\sum_{i=1}^{n}(2i-1)[\log F(x_i,\boldsymbol{\Delta}) - \log\overline{F}(x_{n+1-i},\boldsymbol{\Delta})] \\ &= -n - \frac{1}{n}\sum_{i=1}^{n}(2i-1)\left[-\alpha\left[\frac{H(x_i,\boldsymbol{\psi})}{\overline{H}(x_i,\boldsymbol{\psi})}\right]^{-\beta} - \log\left(1-\exp\left\{-\alpha\left[\frac{H(x_{n+1-i},\boldsymbol{\psi})}{\overline{H}(x_{n+1-i},\boldsymbol{\psi})}\right]^{-\beta}\right\}\right)\right] \end{aligned} \quad (44)$$

Similarly, we take the first derivatives of $AD(\boldsymbol{\Delta})$ and obtain

$$\frac{\partial AD}{\partial \alpha} = -\frac{1}{n}\sum_{i=1}^{n}(2i-1)\left(-\left[\frac{H(x_i,\boldsymbol{\psi})}{\overline{H}(x_i,\boldsymbol{\psi})}\right]^{-\beta} - \left[\frac{H(x_{n+1-i},\boldsymbol{\psi})}{\overline{H}(x_{n+1-i},\boldsymbol{\psi})}\right]^{-\beta}\frac{\exp\left\{-\alpha\left[\frac{H(x_{n+1-i},\boldsymbol{\psi})}{\overline{H}(x_{n+1-i},\boldsymbol{\psi})}\right]^{-\beta}\right\}}{1-\exp\left\{-\alpha\left[\frac{H(x_{n+1-i},\boldsymbol{\psi})}{\overline{H}(x_{n+1-i},\boldsymbol{\psi})}\right]^{-\beta}\right\}}\right) \quad (45)$$

$$\frac{\partial AD}{\partial \beta} = -\frac{1}{n}\sum_{i=1}^{n}(2i-1)\left[\alpha\log\left(\frac{H(x_i,\boldsymbol{\psi})}{\overline{H}(x_i,\boldsymbol{\psi})}\right)\left[\frac{H(x_i,\boldsymbol{\psi})}{\overline{H}(x_i,\boldsymbol{\psi})}\right]^{-\beta} + \alpha\log\left(\frac{H(x_{n+1-i},\boldsymbol{\psi})}{\overline{H}(x_{n+1-i},\boldsymbol{\psi})}\right)\left[\frac{H(x_{n+1-i},\boldsymbol{\psi})}{\overline{H}(x_{n+1-i},\boldsymbol{\psi})}\right]^{-\beta}\frac{\exp\left\{-\alpha\left[\frac{H(x_{n+1-i},\boldsymbol{\psi})}{\overline{H}(x_{n+1-i},\boldsymbol{\psi})}\right]^{-\beta}\right\}}{1-\exp\left\{-\alpha\left[\frac{H(x_{n+1-i},\boldsymbol{\psi})}{\overline{H}(x_{n+1-i},\boldsymbol{\psi})}\right]^{-\beta}\right\}}\right. \quad (46)$$

$$\frac{\partial AD}{\partial \psi_k} = -\frac{1}{n}\sum_{i=1}^{n}(2i-1)\left[\alpha\beta\frac{H(x_i,\boldsymbol{\psi})^{-\beta-1}}{\overline{H}(x_i,\boldsymbol{\psi})^{-\beta+1}}\frac{\partial H(x_i,\boldsymbol{\psi})}{\partial \psi_k}\right.$$
$$\left. +\alpha\beta\frac{H(x_{n+1-i},\boldsymbol{\psi})^{-\beta-1}}{\overline{H}(x_{n+1-i},\boldsymbol{\psi})^{-\beta+1}}\frac{\partial H(x_{n+1-i},\boldsymbol{\psi})}{\partial \psi_k}\frac{\exp\left\{-\alpha\left[\frac{H(x_{n+1-i},\boldsymbol{\psi})}{\overline{H}(x_{n+1-i},\boldsymbol{\psi})}\right]^{-\beta}\right\}}{1-\exp\left\{-\alpha\left[\frac{H(x_{n+1-i},\boldsymbol{\psi})}{\overline{H}(x_{n+1-i},\boldsymbol{\psi})}\right]^{-\beta}\right\}}\right] \tag{47}$$

4.6. Simulation and Estimation

We combined Monte Carlo simulation with the above estimation techniques to estimate the parameters of distributions. The parameters are set as $\alpha = 2.5, \beta = 0.8$, and $\gamma = 1.3$. The sample sizes $N = 50, 100, 250, 500$, and 1000 were used to generate random samples. For each sample size, the experiment was replicated $N = 1000$ times. Then, the bias and mean squared error (MSE) were calculated for each set of data. Detailed pseudo-code for simulating our proposed model using a Monte Carlo framework is provided in Table 2. Table 3 and Figure 1 show the estimation results. The MSE converges to 0 as N increases, confirming the estimations' stability and reliability in all cases.

Table 2. Pseudo-code for Monte Carlo simulation.

Step	Description
Input	Select a set of true parameters, for example, $\alpha = 2.5$, $\beta = 0.8$, $\gamma = 1.3$. Sample sizes: $N = \{50, 100, 250, 500, 1000\}$. Number of repetitions: $R = 1000$. Initial values for optimization: init_params = $[\alpha_0, \beta_0, \gamma_0]$.
Output	Mean parameter estimates and error metrics for each sample size.
Step 1	Define the model-specific function and transformation rules.
Step 2	Initialize an empty data structure (e.g., table) to store results.
Step 3	For each sample size n in N: 1. Initialize a results container to store parameter estimates and errors. 2. For each replication $r = 1$ to R: • Generate a random sample of size n from the model. • Initialize arrays to store intermediate values (e.g., sample data **X**, estimation errors). • For each data point i in the sample, – Compute y_i using the model with parameters (α, β, γ). – Store y_i in the sample array **X**. – Calculate indices or statistics required for estimation (e.g., MLE, WLS). • Sort **X** in descending order to prepare for estimation. • Apply estimation techniques to compute parameter estimates. • Record the estimation errors in the results container. 3. Compute mean parameter estimates and error metrics (e.g., MSE) for sample size n.
Step 4	Aggregate results for all sample sizes.
Return	Summary of mean parameter estimates and error metrics.

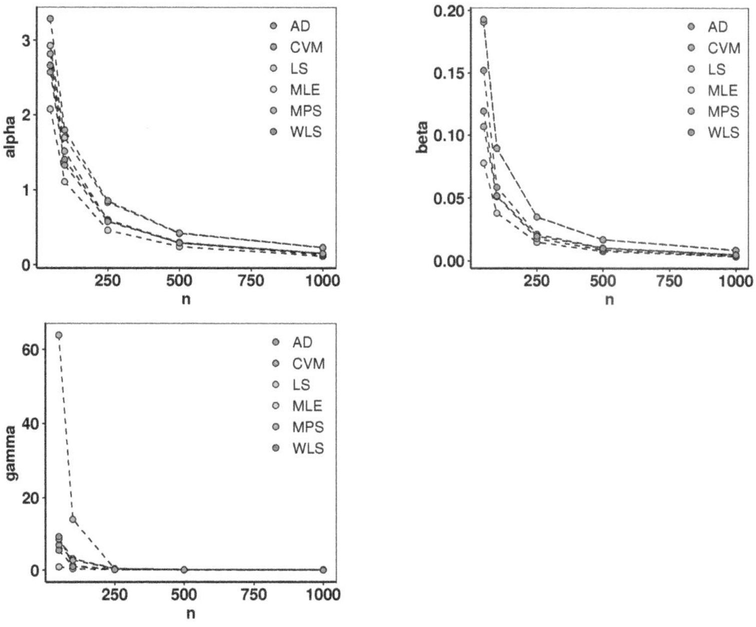

Figure 1. MSE of parameters in Table 3.

Table 3. Different estimations for $\alpha = 2.5, \beta = 0.8, \gamma = 1.3$.

		MLE		LS		WLS		MPS		CVM		AD	
N		Bias	MSE	Bias	MSE	Bias	MSE	Bias	MSE	Bias	MSE	Bias	MSE
50	α	0.0909	2.0761	−0.0418	2.9292	0.0307	2.6645	0.8349	2.8174	0.1095	3.2913	0.1459	2.5743
	β	0.0512	0.0778	0.0107	0.1906	0.0066	0.1520	−0.1492	0.1068	0.0262	0.1929	0.0010	0.1192
	γ	0.1512	0.8690	0.9373	8.7264	0.8477	9.4008	2.4409	63.8413	0.8518	6.9832	0.6359	5.4760
100	α	0.0662	1.1061	0.0595	1.6917	0.0878	1.4001	0.5914	1.5128	0.1357	1.7947	0.1327	1.3275
	β	0.0182	0.0379	−0.0229	0.0897	−0.0158	0.0586	−0.1047	0.0511	−0.0161	0.0895	−0.0163	0.0520
	γ	0.0963	0.3519	0.4901	3.1145	0.2684	1.1972	0.8138	14.1750	0.4755	2.7094	0.2518	0.9787
250	α	0.0203	0.4578	0.0211	0.8317	0.0336	0.5983	0.3204	0.5872	0.0510	0.8502	0.0533	0.5754
	β	0.0097	0.0148	−0.0027	0.0349	−0.0010	0.0211	−0.0544	0.0177	−0.0002	0.0350	−0.0027	0.0197
	γ	0.0265	0.1085	0.1088	0.3554	0.0614	0.1707	0.2180	0.2020	0.1141	0.3529	0.0660	0.1620
500	α	0.0226	0.2394	0.0168	0.4176	0.0220	0.2933	0.2066	0.2890	0.0318	0.4223	0.0321	0.2900
	β	0.0049	0.0075	−0.0015	0.0168	0.0002	0.0102	−0.0335	0.0086	−0.0003	0.0168	−0.0008	0.0100
	γ	0.0189	0.0543	0.0498	0.1280	0.0307	0.0742	0.1269	0.0809	0.0529	0.1282	0.0347	0.0744
1000	α	0.0072	0.1146	0.0071	0.2278	0.0113	0.1497	0.1163	0.1310	0.0146	0.2290	0.0167	0.1504
	β	0.0027	0.0036	−0.0003	0.0086	0.0001	0.0050	−0.0198	0.0039	0.0003	0.0086	−0.0007	0.0050
	γ	0.0079	0.0254	0.0258	0.0673	0.0160	0.0373	0.0691	0.0331	0.0274	0.0673	0.0186	0.0380

5. Special Cases

In this section, we will explore a variety of special cases that emerge from our novel distribution model. By closely examining these unique instances, we aim to illustrate the multifaceted aspects and potential applications of the T2GWG family of distributions.

5.1. Type 2 Gumbel Weibull–Exponential (T2GWE) Distribution

Suppose the baseline distribution $H(x, \boldsymbol{\psi})$ is an exponential distribution with parameter $\gamma > 0$. Then, $h(x;\gamma) = \gamma e^{-\gamma x}$ and $H(x;\gamma) = 1 - e^{-\gamma x}$.

5.1.1. cdf and pdf of the T2GWE Distribution

The cdf of the Type 2 Gumbel Weibull–exponential distribution is presented as

$$F_{T2GWE}(x) = \exp\left\{-\alpha(e^{\gamma x} - 1)^{-\beta}\right\} \tag{48}$$

and the pdf is given by

$$f_{T2GWE}(x) = \beta\alpha(e^{\gamma x} - 1)^{-\beta-1} \exp\left\{\gamma x - \alpha(e^{\gamma x} - 1)^{-\beta}\right\} \tag{49}$$

where $x \geq 0$ and $\alpha, \beta > 0$.

5.1.2. Hazard Rate and Quantile Functions

The hrf is shown as

$$h_{T2GWE} = \frac{\beta\alpha(e^{\gamma x} - 1)^{-\beta-1} \exp\{\gamma x - \alpha(e^{\gamma x} - 1)^{-\beta}\}}{1 - \exp\{-\alpha(e^{\gamma x} - 1)^{-\beta}\}} \tag{50}$$

and the reverse hrf is given by

$$\tau_{T2GWE} = \beta\alpha(e^{\gamma x} - 1)^{-\beta-1} \tag{51}$$

Moreover, the quantile function is obtained as

$$x_p = -\frac{1}{\gamma}\log\left(\left[\frac{\log p}{-\alpha}\right]^{-\frac{1}{\beta}} + 1\right) \tag{52}$$

Figure 2 displays several typical configurations of the pdf and hrf for the T2GWE distribution. The pdf of the T2GWE distribution shows various configurations, including almost symmetric, right-skewed, decreasing, and increasing. Additionally, the hrf of the T2GWE distribution can exhibit a range of shapes, such as decreasing, increasing, and right-skewed.

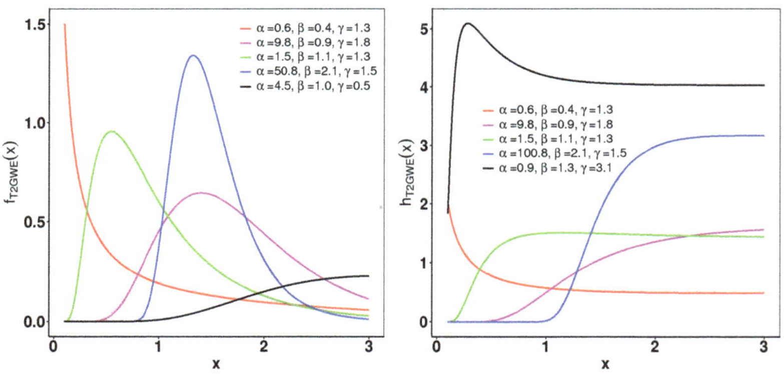

Figure 2. (**left**): The pdf of the T2GWE distribution for different parameters. (**right**): The hrf of the T2GWE for different parameter values.

5.2. *Type 2 Gumbel Weibull–Uniform (T2GWU) Distribution*

Let the baseline distribution $H(x, \boldsymbol{\psi})$ be a uniform distribution with parameter $\gamma > 0$. Then, $h(x, \gamma) = \frac{1}{\gamma}$ and $H(x, \gamma) = \frac{x}{\gamma}$.

5.2.1. cdf and pdf of the T2GWU Distribution

The cdf of the T2GWU distribution is

$$F_{T2GWU} = \exp\left\{-\alpha\left(\frac{x}{\gamma - x}\right)^{-\beta}\right\}, \tag{53}$$

and the corresponding pdf is

$$f_{T2GWU}(x) = \alpha\beta\frac{\gamma x^{-\beta-1}}{(\gamma - x)^{-\beta+1}}\exp\left\{-\alpha\left(\frac{x}{\gamma - x}\right)^{-\beta}\right\}. \tag{54}$$

5.2.2. Hazard Rate and Quantile Functions

The hrf of T2GWU is displayed by

$$h_{T2GWU} = \frac{\alpha\beta\frac{\gamma x^{-\beta-1}}{(\gamma - x)^{-\beta+1}}\exp\left\{-\alpha\left(\frac{x}{\gamma - x}\right)^{-\beta}\right\}}{1 - \exp\left\{-\alpha\left(\frac{x}{\gamma - x}\right)^{-\beta}\right\}}, \tag{55}$$

and the reverse hrf is given by

$$\tau_{T2GWU} = \alpha\beta\frac{\gamma x^{-\beta-1}}{(\gamma - x)^{-\beta+1}}. \tag{56}$$

Moreover, the quantile function can be obtained as

$$x_p = \frac{1}{1 + \left[\frac{\log p}{-\alpha}\right]^{\frac{1}{\beta}}}. \tag{57}$$

Figure 3 shows the plots of the pdf and hrf for the T2GWU distribution with several combinations of parameter values. The pdf plots show different shapes, including right-skewed, decreasing, and increasing. In addition, the hrf plots capture various possibilities such as increasing, decreasing, bathtub, and shallow bathtub.

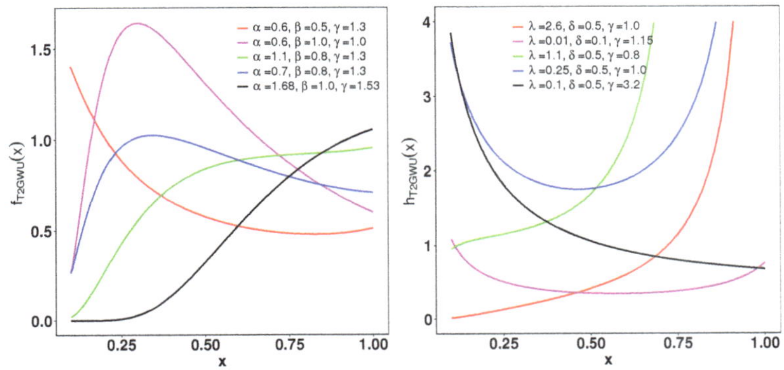

Figure 3. (**left**): Pdf of T2GWU distribution for different values of parameters α, β, and γ. (**right**): Hrf of T2GWU for selected parameters α, β, and γ.

5.3. Type 2 Gumbel Weibull–Pareto (T2GWP) Distribution

If we set $H(x, \boldsymbol{\psi})$ as a Pareto distribution with parameter $\theta, k > 0$, then $h(x, \theta, k) = \frac{k\theta^k}{x^{k+1}}$ and $H(x, \theta, k) = 1 - \left(\frac{\theta}{x}\right)^k$.

5.3.1. cdf and pdf of the T2GWP Distribution

Thus, the cdf of the T2GWP distribution is given by

$$F_{T2GWP} = \exp\left\{-\alpha\left(\left[\frac{x}{\theta}\right]^k - 1\right)^{-\beta}\right\}, \tag{58}$$

with a pdf

$$f_{T2GWP}(x) = \beta\alpha k x^{k-1}\theta^{-k}\left(\left[\frac{x}{\theta}\right]^k - 1\right)^{-\beta-1} \exp\left\{-\alpha\left(\left[\frac{x}{\theta}\right]^k - 1\right)^{-\beta}\right\}. \tag{59}$$

5.3.2. Hazard Rate and Quantile Functions

The hrf of T2GWP is given by

$$h_{T2GWP} = \frac{\beta\alpha k x^{k-1}\theta^{-k}\left(\left[\frac{x}{\theta}\right]^k - 1\right)^{-\beta-1} \exp\left\{-\alpha\left(\left[\frac{x}{\theta}\right]^k - 1\right)^{-\beta}\right\}}{1 - \exp\left\{-\alpha\left(\left[\frac{x}{\theta}\right]^k - 1\right)^{-\beta}\right\}}, \tag{60}$$

and the reverse hrf is

$$\tau_{T2GWP} = \beta\delta\alpha^{-\delta} k x^{k-1}\theta^{-k}\left(\left[\frac{x}{\theta}\right]^k - 1\right)^{-\beta\delta-1}. \tag{61}$$

Moreover, the quantile function is obtained as

$$x_p = \theta\left(\left[\frac{\log p}{-\alpha}\right]^{-\frac{1}{\beta}} + 1\right)^{\frac{1}{k}} \tag{62}$$

Shapes of the pdf and hrf for the T2GWP distribution with selected parameters are shown in Figure 4. The pdfs exhibit a variety of shapes, including right-skewed, decreasing, and increasing. Moreover, hrf plots for the T2GWP distribution display growing, decreasing, and right-skewed forms.

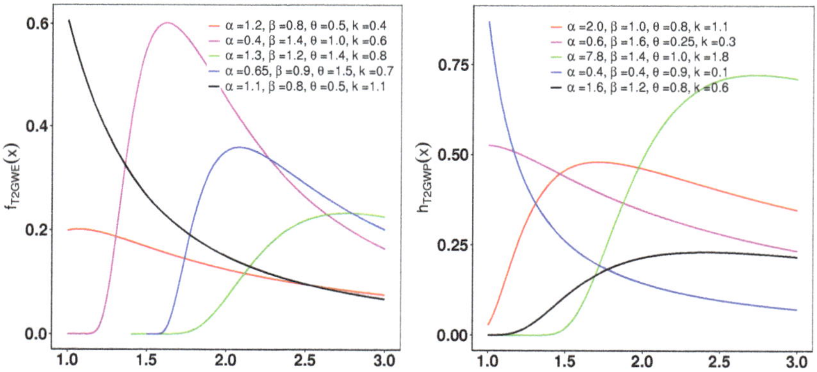

Figure 4. (**left**): The pdf of the T2GWP distribution for selected values of α, β, θ, and k. (**right**): The hrf of the T2GWP for various α, β, θ, and k.

6. Applications

In this section, we will investigate beyond theoretical constructs and delve into the practical implications of our model, demonstrating its applicability using real-world datasets. This will validate the practical utility of our newly devised model and shed light on how it can be effectively employed in handling concrete data-driven scenarios. The objective is to ensure that our theoretical advancements resonate with tangible applications, thereby significantly contributing to both the academic discourse and the operational applications of statistical distributions.

In this section, we present three applications of the Type 2 Gumbel Weibull–uniform and exponential distribution. We compared it with the Exponentiated Gumbel Type 2 (EGT) [37], Weibull Generalized Exponential (WGE) [38], Lomax Gumbel Type 2 (LGT) [39], Type 2 Gumbel (T2G), and gamma distribution (GM) and Weibull distribution (WB). The pdf and cdf of those distributions are provided in Appendix **??**. The goodness-of-fit statistics including the -2log-likelihood statistic, Cramér–von Mises statistic (W^*), Anderson–Darling statistic (A^*), Akaike Information Criterion (AIC), Bayesian Information Criterion (BIC), Consistent Akaike Information Criterion (CAIC), Hannan–Quinn criterion (HQIC), and Kolmogorov–Smirnov test statistic (K-S) and its corresponding p-value are reported.

To evaluate and compare the performance of different models, we can examine their goodness-of-fit statistics. Generally, a model with smaller values in these statistics fits the data better. However, it is important to note that, for the p-values, which are a measure of expectation, a larger value indicates a better fit. To access the data discussed in this section, please refer to the "Declarations" section for guidance.

6.1. Aarset Data

This Aarset dataset recorded the lifetimes of 50 devices [40]. The estimated parameters and the goodness-of-fit statistics are presented in Table 4. Figure 5 presents the plots of the fitted densities alongside the histogram and the expected probability. In Figure 6, the Kaplan–Meier (K–M) survival curve, the theoretical cumulative distribution function and empirical cumulative distribution function (ECDF), and total time on test (TTT) scaled are displayed. The closely matched empirical and theoretical plots suggest that our model is an excellent fit for the given data. Additionally, the TTT scaled plot shows that the model is suitable for a hazard rate structure that is not monotonic.

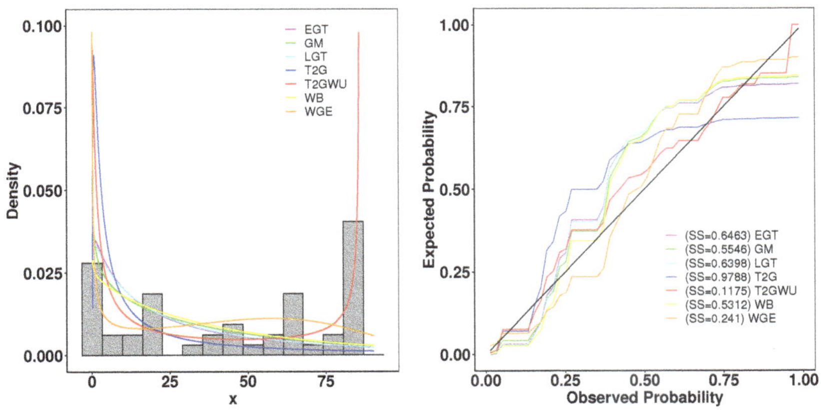

Figure 5. **(left)**: Fitted density superposed on the histogram and observed probability for the Aarset data. **(right)**: Expected probability plots for the Aarset data.

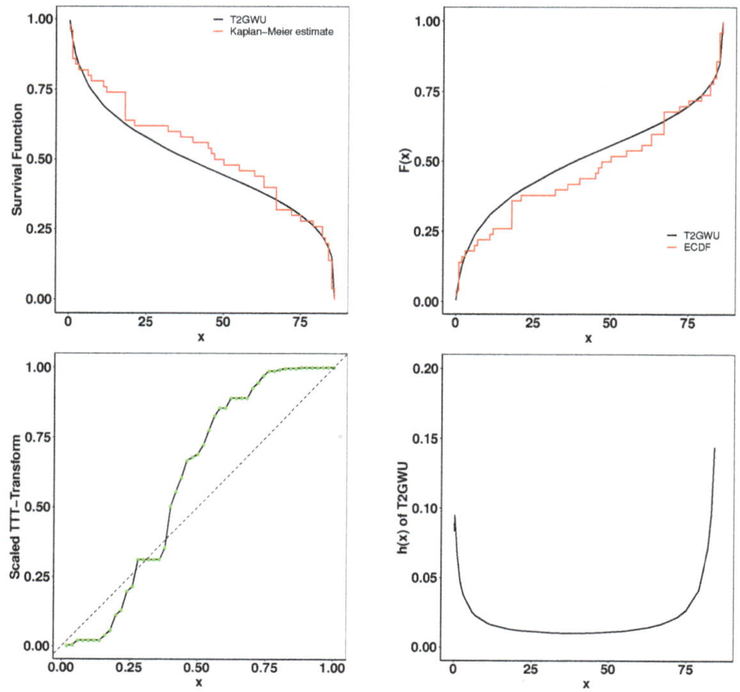

Figure 6. Fitted K-M survival curve, theoretical and empirical cdfs, the TTT statistics, and the hrf for the Aarset data.

Table 4. MLEs and goodness-of-fit statistics for Aarset data.

	Estimates (SE)				Statistics								
Model	α	β	γ		$-2\log L$	AIC	$CAIC$	BIC	$HQIC$	W^*	A^*	**K-S**	**p-Value**
T2GWU	0.6470	0.3112	86.0000	-	361.1643	367.1643	371.0961	372.9003	369.3486	0.3358	2.2924	0.1604	0.1524
EGT	α 1000.1042 (1.0496×10^3)	ϕ 0.1088 (1.7639×10^{-2})	θ 10.3528 (1.1897)	-	492.5518	498.5519	499.0736	504.2880	500.7362	0.6258	3.6601	0.2164	0.0185
WGE	α 0.1742 (0.0620)	θ 0.3851 (0.1028)	γ 0.0778 (0.0257)	-	451.2370	457.2371	457.7588	462.9731	459.4214	0.2120	1.4796	0.1288	0.3778
LGT	α 31.9188 (30.3417)	β 0.0093 (0.0061)	θ 11.6179 (1.2409)	k 0.0959 (0.0154)	491.9342	499.9343	500.8232	507.5824	502.8467	0.6163	3.6145	0.2160	0.0189
T2G	α 2.6477 (0.3898)	ν 0.4633 (0.0444)	-	-	530.0282	534.0281	534.2835	537.8522	535.4844	1.0407	5.5694	0.2855	0.0006
WB	k 0.9488 (0.1195)	λ 44.8440 (6.9313)	-	-	482.0038	486.0037	486.2591	489.8278	487.4600	0.4964	3.0078	0.1933	0.0476
GM	α 0.7995 (0.1376)	β 0.0175 (0.0041)	-	-	480.3804	484.3804	484.6358	488.2045	485.8367	0.4892	2.9700	0.2022	0.0335

6.2. Meeker and Escobar Data

This dataset consists of the running times of 30 devices. From Table 5 and Figure 7, we can compare the Type 2 Gumbel Weibull–uniform distribution with other distributions for various goodness-of-fit methods. As shown in Figure 8, the close resemblance between the fitted empirical and theoretical plots indicates a strong fit of our model to the provided data. Furthermore, the TTT scaled plot provides clear evidence that the model is appropriate for a non-monotonic hazard rate structure.

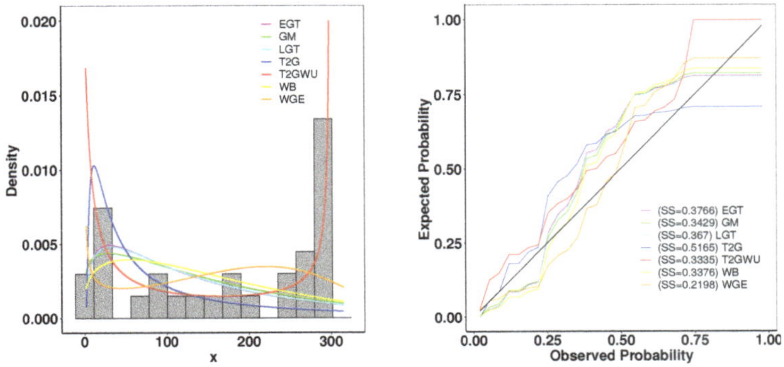

Figure 7. (**left**): Fitted density superposed on the histogram and observed probability for the Aarset data. (**right**): Expected probability plots for the Meeker and Escobar data.

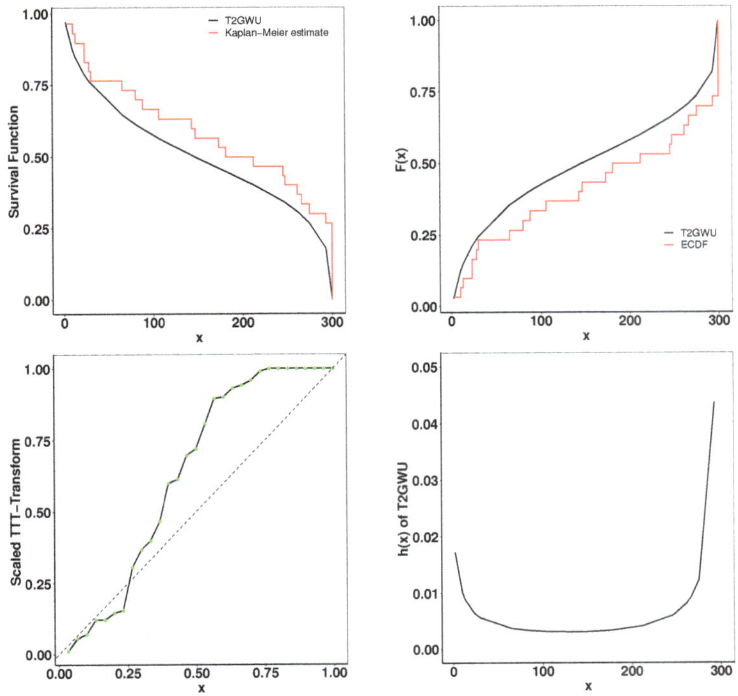

Figure 8. Fitted K-M survival curve, theoretical and empirical cdf, the TTT statistics, and the hrf for the Meeker and Escobar data.

Table 5. MLEs and goodness-of-fit statistics for Meeker and Escobar data.

	Estimates (SE)				Statistics								
Model	α	β	γ		$-2\log L$	AIC	$CAIC$	BIC	$HQIC$	W^*	A^*	K-S	p-Value
T2GWU	0.6825 (8.8328)	0.3305 (0.2076)	300.00 (0.2675)	-	86.4070	92.4070	95.8410	96.6106	93.7518	0.2427	1.6235	0.1894	0.2319
	α	ϕ	θ										
EGT	1000.6472 (1.3869×10^3)	0.1470 (3.1342×10^{-2})	14.7781 (2.0011)	-	374.4318	380.4317	381.3548	384.6353	381.7765	0.3617	2.0879	0.2170	0.1186
	α	θ	γ										
WGE	0.1253 (0.0676)	0.4986 (0.2096)	0.0187 (0.0097)	-	354.3142	360.3143	361.2374	364.5179	361.659	0.1938	1.3025	0.1728	0.3322
	α	β	θ	k									
LGT	20.7564 (19.6057)	0.0065 (0.0040)	15.7890 (1.8170)	0.1303 (0.0240)	374.4282	382.4283	384.0283	388.0331	384.2213	0.3612	2.0865	0.2143	0.1272
	α	ν											
T2G	12.1053 (3.6124)	0.6252 (0.0761)	-	-	396.8938	400.8938	401.3383	403.6962	401.7903	0.5541	3.0254	0.2898	0.0129
	α	β											
WB	1.2626 (0.2042)	186.8126 (27.9960)	-	-	368.6296	372.6296	373.0741	375.4320	373.5261	0.3035	1.8207	0.2221	0.1037
	α	β											
GM	1.1931 (0.2677)	0.0067 (0.0018)	-	-	370.0416	374.0415	374.4860	376.8439	374.938	0.3212	1.9044	0.2172	0.1179

6.3. Chemotherapy Data

This dataset is a subset of data reported by Bekker et al. [41], which represents the survival times (in years) of a group of 45 patients who received chemotherapy treatment alone. The estimates of the parameters and the goodness-of-fit statistics are summarized in Table 6. Figure 9 plots the fitted densities alongside the histogram and the expected probability.

In Figure 10, the K–M survival curve, as well as the theoretical and empirical cdfs, and TTT scaled are displayed.

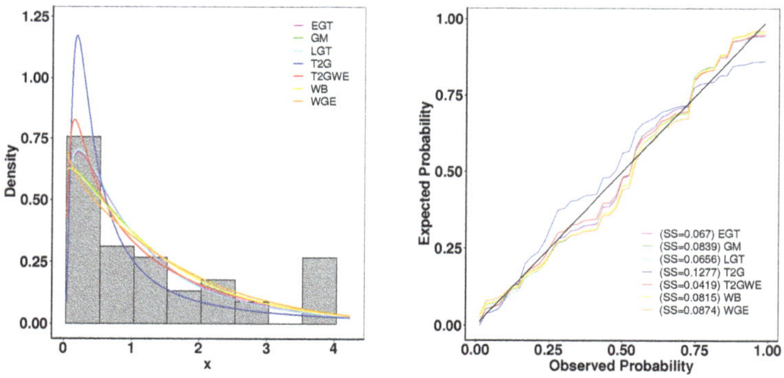

Figure 9. (**left**): Fitted density superposed on the histogram and observed probability for the Chemotherapy data. (**right**): Expected probability plots for the Chemotherapy data.

The above examples evaluate the performance and flexibility of the proposed Type 2 Gumbel Weibull-G family of distributions using three distinct datasets: the Aarset data, Meeker and Escobar data, and Chemotherapy data. The findings are summarized as follows:

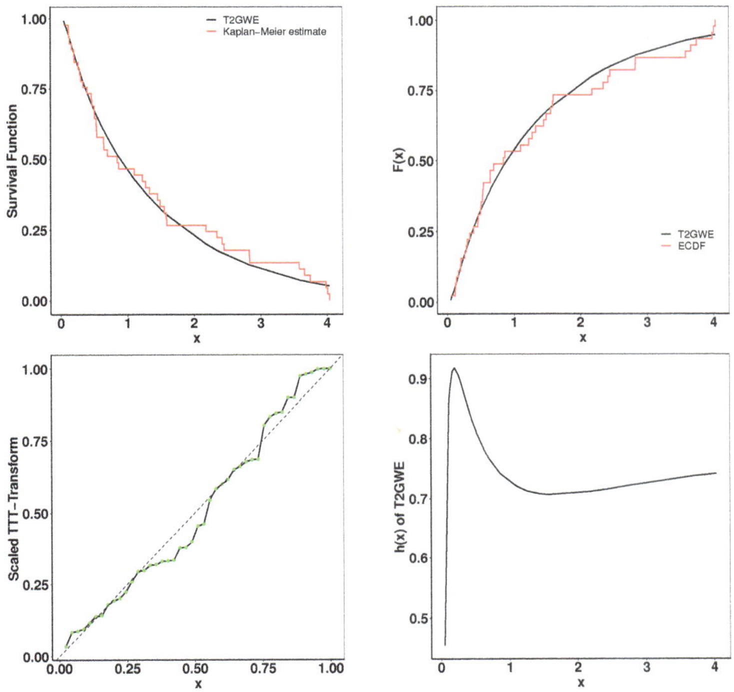

Figure 10. Fitted K-M survival curve, theoretical and empirical cdfs, the TTT statistics, and the hrf for the Chemotherapy data.

Table 6. MLEs and goodness-of-fit statistics for Chemotherapy data.

	Estimates (SE)				Statistics								
Model	α	β	γ		$-2\log L$	AIC	$CAIC$	BIC	$HQIC$	W^*	A^*	K-S	p-Value
T2GWE	1.1328 (0.4388)	0.5416 (0.1170)	1.4015 (0.5530)	-	113.3334	119.3334	119.9188	124.7534	121.3539	0.0415	0.3113	0.0756	0.9421
EGT	α 1000.1282 (3.6913×10^3)	ϕ 0.1452 (7.4598×10^{-2})	θ 7.1554 (3.7373)	-	115.9096	121.9096	122.4949	127.3295	123.9301	0.0608	0.4231	0.0927	0.0926
WGE	α 3.9393 (8.8328)	θ 0.9508 (0.2076)	γ 0.1484 (0.2675)	-	115.9251	121.9251	122.5105	127.3451	123.9457	0.0917	0.6079	0.1120	0.5864
LGT	α 17.9903 (24.8990)	β 0.0196 (0.0298)	θ 7.0332 (1.9777)	k 0.1503 (0.0459)	116.3564	124.3564	125.3564	131.5831	127.0504	0.0610	0.4270	0.0892	0.835
T2G	α 0.4987 (0.0979)	ν 0.8672 (0.0928)	-	-	127.6381	131.6381	131.9238	135.2515	132.9851	0.1430	0.9790	0.1382	0.3253
WB	k 1.0532 (0.1238)	λ 1.3700 (0.2048)	-	-	116.2474	120.2474	120.5331	123.8608	121.5944	0.0813	0.5436	0.1094	0.6146
GM	α 1.1007 (0.2060)	β 0.8205 (0.1928)	-	-	480.3804	120.1815	120.4672	123.7948	121.5285	0.0790	0.5295	0.1106	0.6016

1. **Goodness-of-Fit Analysis:** Across all datasets, the proposed distributions demonstrate superior performance compared to existing models. This is evidenced by their

lower goodness-of-fit statistics, including -2log-likelihood statistic, W^*, A^*, AIC, BIC, CAIC, HQIC, and K-S and its higher p-values. These metrics confirm the robustness of the proposed distributions in capturing complex data patterns.

2. **Empirical and Theoretical Fits:** The fitted densities closely resemble the empirical histograms and expected probability plots, indicating a strong fit. Additionally, survival curves (Kaplan–Meier estimates) and cumulative distribution functions align well with the theoretical models, supporting the applicability of the proposed family to survival analysis.
3. **Hazard Rate Characteristics:** The total time on test (TTT) and hazard rate plots highlight the capability of the proposed distributions to model non-monotonic hazard rate structures, such as bathtub-shaped curves, which are often challenging for traditional distributions.

7. Conclusions

This paper introduces a novel methodology for generating continuous statistical distributions by utilizing the exponentiated odds ratio, which is based on the concepts of survival analysis. The approach described herein constitutes a substantial advancement in the field of statistical modeling, effectively augmenting the flexibility and accuracy of distribution models to effectively address the requirements posed by intricate contemporary data architectures. The major point of this progress lies in the formulation of the "Type 2 Gumbel Weibull-G family of distributions", which has undergone a comprehensive mathematical analysis. The scope of this investigation covered various statistical properties, such as expansions of density functions, moments, hazard rate and quantile functions, Rényi entropy, order statistics, and an examination of stochastic ordering.

In order to assess the robustness and reliability of the new generator, we employed a set of five advanced parameter estimation techniques: maximum likelihood, least square, weighted least square, maximum product spacing, Cramér–von Mises, and Anderson and Darling. The efficacy and utility of the Type 2 Gumbel Weibull-G distributions were further validated through a comprehensive analysis of three datasets obtained from real-world scenarios. These practical implementations demonstrated the superior statistical accuracy of our proposed distributions over existing models, thereby emphasizing their relevance and applicability in both theoretical and practical statistical domains.

As highlighted in our recent work [28,29], the proposed generator shows significant potential for producing a wider variety of density functions, including more bathtub and complex shapes. Our future research endeavors will entail a thorough investigation of several more sub-families within the new generator. This exploration will focus on their distinct properties and potential applications in diverse scenarios, setting them in comparison with other established distribution models. Furthermore, we are now developing an R package (version 4.4.2) with the objective of optimizing the parameter estimate process through the utilization of diverse methodologies. This will result in the improved efficiency of data-fitting procedures, thus increasing the accessibility and practicality of our study for wider applications.

Author Contributions: Conceptualization, S.P. and X.C.; methodology, X.C.; software, X.C. and Z.Z.; validation, X.C., Y.X. and Z.S.; formal analysis, X.C. and Y.X.; investigation, X.C.; resources, X.C.; data curation, X.C. and S.P.; writing—original draft preparation, X.C. and S.P.; writing—review and editing, X.C., Y.X., Z.Z., Z.S. and S.P.; visualization, X.C. and A.C.; supervision, S.P.; project administration, S.P. All authors have read and agreed to the published version of the manuscript.

Funding: This research received no external funding.

Data Availability Statement: All data utilized in this study are openly available on GitHub. The dataset can be accessed through the provided link: https://github.com/shusenpu/Generator_Data, accessed on 15 October 2024. The data can also be accessed using their Digital Object Identifier (DOI): 10.5281/zenodo.10215787. To retrieve the data, visit the following link: https://doi.org/10.5281/zenodo.10215787.

Acknowledgments: The authors wish to thank all members of the CSDA lab at the University of West Florida for their helpful comments on the manuscript.

Conflicts of Interest: The authors declare no conflicts of interest.

Abbreviations

The following abbreviations are used in this manuscript:

T2GWG	The Type 2 Gumbel Weibull-G
cdf	cumulative distribution function
pdf	probability density function
hrf	hazard rate function
Exp-G	exponentiated-G
EGT	Exponentiated Gumbel Type 2
WGE	Weibull Generalized Exponential
LGT	Lomax Gumbel Type 2
T2G	Type 2 Gumbel
EWL	Exponentiated Weibull–logistic distribution
MLE	maximum likelihood estimate
MPS	maximum product spacing estimate
LS	least square estimate
WLS	weighted least square estimate
CVM	Cramér–von Mises estimate
AD	Anderson and Darling estimate
T2GWE	Type 2 Gumbel Weibull–exponential
T2GWU	Type 2 Gumbel Weibull–uniform
T2GWP	Type 2 Gumbel Weibull–Pareto
AIC	Akaike Information Criterion
CAIC	Consistent Akaike Information Criterion
BIC	Bayesian Information Criterion
HQIC	Hannan–Quinn Criterion
W^*	Cramér–von Mises statistic
A^*	Anderson–Darling statistic
K-S	Kolmogorov–Smirnov statistic
ECDF	empirical cumulative distribution function
TTT	total time on test
K-M	Kaplan–Meier

Appendix A. The First Derivatives of H

The first partial derivatives of H in Section 4 with respect to $\alpha, \beta, \delta, \psi_k$ are given by

$$\frac{\partial W}{\partial \alpha} = \frac{1}{n+1}\left\{ -\left[\frac{H(x_1,\boldsymbol{\psi})}{\overline{H}(x_1,\boldsymbol{\psi})}\right]^{-\beta} + \frac{\left[\frac{H(x_n,\boldsymbol{\psi})}{\overline{H}(x_n,\boldsymbol{\psi})}\right]^{-\beta}\exp\left\{-\alpha\left[\frac{H(x_i,\boldsymbol{\psi})}{\overline{H}(x_i,\boldsymbol{\psi})}\right]^{-\beta}\right\}}{1-\exp\left\{-\alpha\left[\frac{H(x_i,\boldsymbol{\psi})}{\overline{H}(x_i,\boldsymbol{\psi})}\right]^{-\beta}\right\}} \right.$$
$$+\sum_{i=2}^{n}\left[\frac{\left[\frac{H(x_i,\boldsymbol{\psi})}{\overline{H}(x_i,\boldsymbol{\psi})}\right]^{-\beta}\exp\left\{-\alpha\left[\frac{H(x_i,\boldsymbol{\psi})}{\overline{H}(x_i,\boldsymbol{\psi})}\right]^{-\beta}\right\}}{\exp\left\{-\alpha\left[\frac{H(x_i,\boldsymbol{\psi})}{\overline{H}(x_i,\boldsymbol{\psi})}\right]^{-\beta}\right\}-\exp\left\{-\alpha\left[\frac{H(x_{i-1},\boldsymbol{\psi})}{\overline{H}(x_{i-1},\boldsymbol{\psi})}\right]^{-\beta}\right\}}\right.$$
$$\left.\left.-\frac{\left[\frac{H(x_{i-1},\boldsymbol{\psi})}{\overline{H}(x_{i-1},\boldsymbol{\psi})}\right]^{-\beta}\exp\left\{-\alpha\left[\frac{H(x_{i-1},\boldsymbol{\psi})}{\overline{H}(x_{i-1},\boldsymbol{\psi})}\right]^{-\beta}\right\}}{\exp\left\{-\alpha\left[\frac{H(x_i,\boldsymbol{\psi})}{\overline{H}(x_i,\boldsymbol{\psi})}\right]^{-\beta}\right\}-\exp\left\{-\alpha\left[\frac{H(x_{i-1},\boldsymbol{\psi})}{\overline{H}(x_{i-1},\boldsymbol{\psi})}\right]^{-\beta}\right\}}\right]\right\} \tag{A1}$$

$$
\begin{aligned}
\frac{\partial W}{\partial \beta} =& \frac{1}{n+1}\Bigg\{\alpha \log\left(\frac{H(x_1,\boldsymbol{\psi})}{\overline{H}(x_1,\boldsymbol{\psi})}\right)\left[\frac{H(x_i,\boldsymbol{\psi})}{\overline{H}(x_i,\boldsymbol{\psi})}\right]^{-\beta} \\
&+\frac{\log\left(\frac{H(x_n,\boldsymbol{\psi})}{\overline{H}(x_n,\boldsymbol{\psi})}\right)\left[\frac{H(x_n,\boldsymbol{\psi})}{\overline{H}(x_n,\boldsymbol{\psi})}\right]^{-\beta}\exp\left\{-\alpha\left[\frac{H(x_i,\boldsymbol{\psi})}{\overline{H}(x_i,\boldsymbol{\psi})}\right]^{-\beta}\right\}}{1-\exp\left\{-\alpha\left[\frac{H(x_i,\boldsymbol{\psi})}{\overline{H}(x_i,\boldsymbol{\psi})}\right]^{-\beta}\right\}} \\
&+\sum_{i=2}^{n}\left[\frac{\log\left(\frac{H(x_i,\boldsymbol{\psi})}{\overline{H}(x_i,\boldsymbol{\psi})}\right)\left[\frac{H(x_i,\boldsymbol{\psi})}{\overline{H}(x_i,\boldsymbol{\psi})}\right]^{-\beta}\exp\left\{-\alpha\left[\frac{H(x_i,\boldsymbol{\psi})}{\overline{H}(x_i,\boldsymbol{\psi})}\right]^{-\beta}\right\}}{\exp\left\{-\alpha\left[\frac{H(x_i,\boldsymbol{\psi})}{\overline{H}(x_i,\boldsymbol{\psi})}\right]^{-\beta}\right\}-\exp\left\{-\alpha\left[\frac{H(x_{i-1},\boldsymbol{\psi})}{\overline{H}(x_{i-1},\boldsymbol{\psi})}\right]^{-\beta}\right\}}\right. \\
&\left.-\frac{\log\left(\frac{H(x_{i-1},\boldsymbol{\psi})}{\overline{H}(x_{i-1},\boldsymbol{\psi})}\right)\left[\frac{H(x_{i-1},\boldsymbol{\psi})}{\overline{H}(x_{i-1},\boldsymbol{\psi})}\right]^{-\beta}\exp\left\{-\alpha\left[\frac{H(x_{i-1},\boldsymbol{\psi})}{\overline{H}(x_{i-1},\boldsymbol{\psi})}\right]^{-\beta}\right\}}{\exp\left\{-\alpha\left[\frac{H(x_i,\boldsymbol{\psi})}{\overline{H}(x_i,\boldsymbol{\psi})}\right]^{-\beta}\right\}-\exp\left\{-\alpha\left[\frac{H(x_{i-1},\boldsymbol{\psi})}{\overline{H}(x_{i-1},\boldsymbol{\psi})}\right]^{-\beta}\right\}}\right]\Bigg)\Bigg\}
\end{aligned}
\tag{A2}
$$

$$
\begin{aligned}
\frac{\partial W}{\partial \psi_k} =& \frac{1}{n+1}\Bigg\{\alpha\beta\frac{H(x_1,\boldsymbol{\psi})^{-\beta-1}}{\overline{H}(x_1,\boldsymbol{\psi})^{-\beta+1}}\frac{\partial H(x_1,\boldsymbol{\psi})}{\partial \psi_k}+\frac{\frac{H(x_n,\boldsymbol{\psi})^{-\beta-1}}{\overline{H}(x_n,\boldsymbol{\psi})^{-\beta+1}}\frac{\partial H(x_n,\boldsymbol{\psi})}{\partial \psi_k}\exp\left\{-\alpha\left[\frac{H(x_n,\boldsymbol{\psi})}{\overline{H}(x_n,\boldsymbol{\psi})}\right]^{-\beta}\right\}}{1-\exp\left\{-\alpha\left[\frac{H(x_n,\boldsymbol{\psi})}{\overline{H}(x_n,\boldsymbol{\psi})}\right]^{-\beta}\right\}} \\
&+\sum_{i=2}^{n}\left[\frac{\frac{H(x_i,\boldsymbol{\psi})^{-\beta-1}}{\overline{H}(x_i,\boldsymbol{\psi})^{-\beta+1}}\frac{\partial H(x_i,\boldsymbol{\psi})}{\partial \psi_k}\exp\left\{-\alpha\left[\frac{H(x_i,\boldsymbol{\psi})}{\overline{H}(x_i,\boldsymbol{\psi})}\right]^{-\beta}\right\}}{\exp\left\{-\alpha\left[\frac{H(x_i,\boldsymbol{\psi})}{\overline{H}(x_i,\boldsymbol{\psi})}\right]^{-\beta}\right\}-\exp\left\{-\alpha\left[\frac{H(x_{i-1},\boldsymbol{\psi})}{\overline{H}(x_{i-1},\boldsymbol{\psi})}\right]^{-\beta}\right\}}\right. \\
&\left.-\frac{\frac{H(x_{i-1},\boldsymbol{\psi})^{-\beta-1}}{\overline{H}(x_{i-1},\boldsymbol{\psi})^{-\beta+1}}\frac{\partial H(x_{i-1},\boldsymbol{\psi})}{\partial \psi_k}\exp\left\{-\alpha\left[\frac{H(x_{i-1},\boldsymbol{\psi})}{\overline{H}(x_{i-1},\boldsymbol{\psi})}\right]^{-\beta}\right\}}{\exp\left\{-\alpha\left[\frac{H(x_i,\boldsymbol{\psi})}{\overline{H}(x_i,\boldsymbol{\psi})}\right]^{-\beta}\right\}-\exp\left\{-\alpha\left[\frac{H(x_{i-1},\boldsymbol{\psi})}{\overline{H}(x_{i-1},\boldsymbol{\psi})}\right]^{-\beta}\right\}}\right]\Bigg)\Bigg\}
\end{aligned}
\tag{A3}
$$

Appendix B. Distributions Used in the Application Section

- Exponentiated Gumbel Type 2 Distribution:

$$F_{EGT}(x) = 1-\left(1-e^{-\theta x^{-\phi}}\right)^{\alpha},$$

$$f_{EGT}(x) = \alpha\phi\theta x^{-\phi-1}e^{-\theta x^{-\phi}}\left(1-e^{-\theta x^{-\phi}}\right)^{\alpha-1},$$

$$\alpha,\phi,\theta > 0$$

- Weibull Generalized Exponential Distribution:

$$F_{WGE}(x) = 1-e^{-a\left[e^{\lambda x}-1\right]^{b}},$$

$$f_{WGE}(x) = ab\lambda e^{\lambda x}\left[e^{\lambda x}-1\right]^{b-1}e^{-a\left[e^{\lambda x}-1\right]^{b}},$$

$$a,b,\lambda > 0$$

- Lomax Gumbel Type 2 Distribution:

$$F_{LGT}(x) = 1-\beta^{\alpha}\left(\beta-\log\left[1-e^{-\theta x^{-k}}\right]\right)^{-\alpha}$$

$$f_{LGT}(x) = \frac{\alpha\beta^{\alpha}\theta k x^{-k-1} e^{-\theta x^{-k}}}{\left[1 - e^{-\theta x^{-k}}\right]} \left[\beta - \log\left[1 - e^{-\theta x^{-k}}\right]\right]^{-(\alpha+1)}$$

$$\alpha, \beta, \theta, k > 0$$

- Type 2 Gumbel Distribution:

$$F_{T2G}(x) = e^{-\theta x^{-\phi}}$$

$$f_{T2G}(x) = \phi\theta x^{-\phi-1} e^{-\theta x^{-\phi}}$$

$$\phi, \theta > 0$$

- Exponentiated Weibull–Logistic Distribution:

$$F_{EWL}(x) = \left(1 - e^{-\alpha e^{\lambda\beta x}}\right)^{\theta}$$

$$f_{EWL}(x) = \theta\left(1 - e^{-\alpha e^{\lambda\beta x}}\right)^{\theta-1}\left(\lambda\alpha\beta e^{\lambda\beta x - \alpha e^{\lambda\beta x}}\right),$$

$$\lambda, \alpha, \beta, \theta > 0.$$

References

1. Rodríguez González, C.A.; Rodríguez-Pérez, A.M.; López, R.; Hernández-Torres, J.A.; Caparrós-Mancera, J.J. Sensitivity Analysis in Mean Annual Sediment Yield Modeling with Respect to Rainfall Probability Distribution Functions. *Land* **2023**, *12*, 35. [CrossRef]
2. Jiang, S.H.; Liu, X.; Wang, Z.Z.; Li, D.Q.; Huang, J. Efficient sampling of the irregular probability distributions of geotechnical parameters for reliability analysis. *Struct. Saf.* **2023**, *101*, 102309. [CrossRef]
3. Klein, J.P.; Moeschberger, M.L. *Survival Analysis: Techniques for Censored and Truncated Data*; Springer Science & Business Media: New York, NY, USA, 2006.
4. Bain, L.J.; Engelhardt, M. Reliability Test Plans for One-Shot Devices Based on Repeated Samples. *J. Qual. Technol.* **1991**, *23*, 304–311. [CrossRef]
5. Cooray, K. Generalization of the Weibull distribution: The odd Weibull family. *Stat. Model.* **2006**, *6*, 265–277. [CrossRef]
6. Bourguignon, M.; Silva, R.B.; Cordeiro, G.M. The Weibull-G family of probability distributions. *J. Data Sci.* **2014**, *12*, 53–68. [CrossRef]
7. Pu, S.; Oluyede, B.O.; Qiu, Y.; Linder, D. A Generalized Class of Exponentiated Modified Weibull Distribution with Applications. *J. Data Sci.* **2016**, *14*, 585–613. [CrossRef]
8. Oluyede, B.; Pu, S.; Makubate, B.; Qiu, Y. The gamma-Weibull-G Family of distributions with applications. *Austrian J. Stat.* **2018**, *47*, 45–76. [CrossRef]
9. Oluyede, B.; Moakofi, T. The Gamma-Topp-Leone-Type II-Exponentiated Half Logistic-G Family of Distributions with Applications. *Stats* **2023**, *6*, 706–733. [CrossRef]
10. Shama, M.S.; Alharthi, A.S.; Almulhim, F.A.; Gemeay, A.M.; Meraou, M.A.; Mustafa, M.S.; Hussam, E.; Aljohani, H.M. Modified generalized Weibull distribution: theory and applications. *Sci. Rep.* **2023**, *13*, 12828. [CrossRef]
11. Emam, W.; Tashkandy, Y. Modeling the Amount of Carbon Dioxide Emissions Application: New Modified Alpha Power Weibull-X Family of Distributions. *Symmetry* **2023**, *15*, 366. [CrossRef]
12. Gabanakgosi, M.; Oluyede, B. The Topp-Leone type II exponentiated half logistic-G family of distributions with applications. *Int. J. Math. Oper. Res.* **2023**, *25*, 85–117. [CrossRef]
13. Sun, J.; Kong, M.; Pal, S. The Modified-Half-Normal distribution: Properties and an efficient sampling scheme. *Commun. -Stat.-Theory Methods* **2023**, *52*, 1591–1613. [CrossRef]
14. Guptha, R.C.S.; Maruthan, S.K. A New Generalization of Power Lindley Distribution and Its Applications. *Thail. Stat.* **2023**, *21*, 196–208.
15. Pu, S.; Moakofi, T.; Oluyede, B. The Ristić–Balakrishnan–Topp–Leone–Gompertz-G Family of Distributions with Applications. *J. Stat. Theory Appl.* **2023**, *22*, 116–150. [CrossRef]
16. Kajuru, J.; Dikko, H.; Mohammed, A.; Fulatan, A. odd Gompertz-G Family of Distribution, its Properties and Applications. *Fudma J. Sci.* **2023**, *7*, 351–358. [CrossRef]
17. Osagie, S.A.; Uyi, S.; Osemwenkhae, J.E. The Inverse Burr-Generalized Family of Distributions: Theory and Applications. *Earthline J. Math. Sci.* **2023**, *13*, 313–351. [CrossRef]
18. Marasigan, A.E. A New Extension of the Inverse Paralogistic Distribution using Gamma Generator with Application. *Mindanao J. Sci. Technol.* **2023**, *21*, 59–80. [CrossRef]

19. Azimi, R.; Esmailian, M. A new generalization of Nadarajah-Haghighi distribution with application to cancer and COVID-19 deaths data. *Math. Slovaca* **2023**, *73*, 221–244.
20. Scheidegger, A.; Leitao, J.P.; Scholten, L. Statistical failure models for water distribution pipes–A review from a unified perspective. *Water Res.* **2015**, *83*, 237–247. [CrossRef]
21. Romaniuk, M.; Hryniewicz, O. Estimation of maintenance costs of a pipeline for a U-shaped hazard rate function in the imprecise setting. *Eksploat. Niezawodn.* **2020**, *22*, 352–362. [CrossRef]
22. Chachra, A.; Kumar, A.; Ram, M. A Markovian approach to reliability estimation of series-parallel system with Fermatean fuzzy sets. *Comput. Ind. Eng.* **2024**, *190*, 110081. [CrossRef]
23. Kleinbaum, D.G.; Klein, M. *Survival Analysis a Self-Learning Text*; Springer: New York, NY, USA, 1996.
24. Tsiatis, A.A.; Davidian, M.; Holloway, S.T. Estimation of the odds ratio in a proportional odds model with censored time-lagged outcome in a randomized clinical trial. *Biometrics* **2023**, *79*, 975–987. [CrossRef] [PubMed]
25. VanderWeele, T.J. Optimal approximate conversions of odds ratios and hazard ratios to risk ratios. *Biometrics* **2020**, *76*, 746–752. [CrossRef] [PubMed]
26. Penner, C.G.; Gerardy, B.; Ryan, R.; Williams, M. The Odds Ratio Product (An Objective Sleep Depth Measure): Normal Values, Repeatability, and Change With CPAP in Patients With OSA: The Odds Ratio Product. *J. Clin. Sleep Med.* **2019**, *15*, 1155–1163. [CrossRef]
27. Alzaatreh, A.; Carl, L.; Felix, F. A new method for generating families of continuous distributions. *Metron* **2013**, *71*, 63–79. [CrossRef]
28. Yang, H.; Huang, M.; Chen, X.; He, Z.; Pu, S. Enhanced Real-Life Data Modeling with the Modified Burr III Odds Ratio–G Distribution. *Axioms* **2024**, *13*, 401. [CrossRef]
29. Roy, S.S.; Knehr, H.; McGurk, D.; Chen, X.; Cohen, A.; Pu, S. The Lomax-Exponentiated Odds Ratio–G Distribution and Its Applications. *Mathematics* **2024**, *12*, 1578. [CrossRef]
30. Al-Moisheer, A.; Elbatal, I.; Almutiry, W.; Elgarhy, M. Odd inverse power generalized Weibull generated family of distributions: Properties and applications. *Math. Probl. Eng.* **2021**, *2021*, 5082192. [CrossRef]
31. ul Haq, M.A.; Elgarhy, M. The Odd Frèchet-G family of probability distributions. *J. Stat. Appl. Probab.* **2018**, *7*, 189–203. [CrossRef]
32. Rényi, A. On measures of entropy and information. In Proceedings of the 4th Berkeley Symposium on Mathematical Statistics and Probability, Berkeley, CA, USA, 20 June–30 July 1961; Volume 1, pp. 547–561.
33. Szekli, R. *Stochastic Ordering and Dependence in Applied Probability*; Springer Science & Business Media: New York, NY, USA, 2012; Volume 97.
34. Cheng, R.C.H.; Amin, N.A.K. Estimating Parameters in Continuous Univariate Distributions with a Shifted Origin. *J. R. Stat. Soc. Ser. B Methodol.* **1983**, *45*, 394–403. [CrossRef]
35. MacDonald, P.D.M. Comment on "An Estimation Procedure for Mixtures of Distributions" by Choi and Bulgren. *J. R. Stat. Soc. Ser. B Methodol.* **1971**, *33*, 326–329. [CrossRef]
36. Anderson, T.W.; Darling, D.A. A test of goodness of fit. *J. Am. Stat. Assoc.* **1954**, *49*, 765–769. [CrossRef]
37. Okorie, I.E.; Akpanta, A.; Ohakwe, J. The exponentiated Gumbel type-2 distribution: properties and application. *Int. J. Math. Math. Sci.* **2016**, *2016*, 5898356. [CrossRef]
38. Mustafa, A.; El-Desouky, B.S.; AL-Garash, S. Weibull generalized exponential distribution. *arXiv* **2016**, arXiv:1606.07378.
39. Adeyemi, A.O.; Adeleke, I.A.; Akarawak, E.E. Lomax gumbel type two distributions with applications to lifetime data. *Int. J. Stat. Appl. Math.* **2022**, *7*, 36–45. [CrossRef]
40. Aarset, M.V. How to identify a bathtub hazard rate. *IEEE Trans. Reliab.* **1987**, *36*, 106–108. [CrossRef]
41. Bekker, A.; Roux, J.J.J.; Mosteit, P.J. A generalization of the compound rayleigh distribution: using a bayesian method on cancer survival times. *Commun. Stat. Theory Methods* **2000**, *29*, 1419–1433. [CrossRef]

entropy

Article

Maximum Entropy-Minimum Residual Model: An Optimum Solution to Comprehensive Evaluation and Multiple Attribute Decision Making

Qi-Yi Tang [1,*] and Yu-Xuan Lin [2,3]

[1] Institute of Insect Sciences, Zhejiang University, Hangzhou 310028, China
[2] Faculty of Science and Technology, BNU-HKBU United International College, Zhuhai 519087, China; yuxuanlin@uic.edu.cn
[3] Guangdong Provincial Key Laboratory of Interdisciplinary Research and Application for Data Science, BNU-HKBU United International College, Zhuhai 519087, China
* Correspondence: qytang@zju.edu.cn; Tel.: +86-571-8694-5271

Abstract: To assess a subject with multiple factors or attributes, a comprehensive evaluation index, or say a composite indicator, is often constructed to make a holistic judgement. The key problem is to assign weights to the factors. There are various weighting methods in the literature, but a gold standard is lacking. Some weighting methods may lead to a trivial weight assignment that is one factor having a weight equal to 1 and the others all zero, while some methods generate a solution contradicting intuitive judgement, or even infeasible to calculate. This paper proposes a new model to generate weights based on the maximum entropy-minimum residual (MEMR) principle, directly estimating the relationship between factor weights and the composite indicator. The MEMR composite indicator extracts the common feature of multiple factors while preserving their diversity. This paper compares the MEMR model with other commonly used weighting methods in various case studies. The MEMR model has more robust, consistent, and interpretable results than others and is suitable for all comprehensive evaluation cases involving quantitative factors. The optimization technique of the proposed MEMR model and the related statistical tests are included as a package in the DPS (data processing system) software V21.05 for the convenience of application in all fields.

Keywords: composite indicator; comprehensive evaluation; entropy; multiple attribute decision making

1. Introduction

Comprehensive evaluation is to assess a subject based on multiple factors or dimensions. It often collaborates with the methods of multiple criteria decision making (MCDM) or multiple attribute decision making (MADM), quantifying and assigning weights to each criterion (or attribute) in order to determine the best decision or choice, providing a holistic judgment. In complex decision-making environments, it facilitates making the optimal decision. Comprehensive evaluation is widely used in emerging strategic fields such as the humanities, environmental protection, technology, diversity, and sustainable development. In the process of constructing the comprehensive evaluation index (CEI), how to reasonably assign weights to the corresponding factors is a key consideration. The weight of each evaluation factor indicates its role and reflects the value orientation of the evaluation subject; it is the core to work out scientific, reasonable, and fair results. Therefore, the weighting method is a key consideration in research on multi-factor comprehensive evaluation. In this regard, ref. [1] systematically reviewed the problems associated with weighting, aggregation, and robustness in CEI construction. In the existing weight assignment methods for CEI, there is no recognized standard. For the same evaluation subject, adopting various comprehensive evaluation methods leads to different ranks and judgments. There is no existing perfect weighting method since each approach has its advantages and limitations. It is an inevitable problem in the field of CEI to be solved.

The handbook published by OECD/EU-JRC in 2008 [2] introduces various weighting methods for CEI calculation, outlining the advantages and disadvantages of each. The lack of a unified weighting method has led some researchers [3,4] to question the rationality and fairness of multi-factor comprehensive evaluation, suggesting that subjectivity is a central defect. In the handbook [2], the authors dedicate a considerable amount of space to the benefit of doubt (BoD) method proposed by [5–7] with reference to the data envelopment analysis (DEA) model as a tool for handling weights in comprehensive evaluation analysis. However, BoD has some serious theoretical problems. For example, some components might be 0 in the weight calculation results, and the extreme situation in which the weight of one factor is not 0 while the weight of others is 0 might arise (i.e., the 0–1 weight problem). The reason for this problem is the loose weight constraints in the original BoD model, resulting in some weight components becoming 0, while others have excessively large weight loads. Since BoD is a weight calculation model that evaluates the relative advantages of evaluation objects through rewards, the weight calculation results can flexibly change based on the information from the evaluation object set, ensuring that each evaluation object receives the optimal score calculation result. However, when a certain factor of an evaluation object stands out too much compared to other evaluation objects, the weight share of that factor may be much higher than other factors, leading to some factors having zero weight. In extreme cases, it may result in a situation where all weights are 0 except for the most salient factor, which is an overly flexible weight phenomenon, also referred to as the overly soft weight phenomenon or the 0–1 weight phenomenon. Specifically, when the number of evaluation objects and factors are close, the frequency of this extreme phenomenon increases. Moreover, BoD models have multiple solutions. In addition, since the weight vectors of each evaluation object in the original BoD model are different, and the sum might not be equal to 1, CEI calculated by BoD is theoretically not comparable.

Especially in China, with the development of the market economy, the existing comprehensive evaluation methods are becoming increasingly inadequate in providing decision-makers with accurate measurements to assess the real situation of economic and social development in various regions under the new circumstances. At the same time, for those evaluation subjects affected by low rankings, if we do not have an objective and standardized comprehensive evaluation system, the evaluated subjects may have reasons to question the fairness and rationality of the evaluation results, which could lead to a reduction in the authority of the comprehensive evaluation. With the rapid growth of available information, CEIs are becoming more widely used. For example, ref. [8] determined more than 400 CEIs for ranking or evaluating countries based on economic, political, social, and environmental factors. Meanwhile, ref. [9] recorded more than 100 CEIs of human progress in a report by the United Nations Development Program. Although these lists are still far from being exhaustive compared to the actual number of applications in use, they provide a good understanding of the growing popularity of CEIs and the increasing demand for data interpretation and integration. However, even if people choose a theoretical framework, invest human and financial resources to collect data, and strive to implement the comprehensive evaluation process flawlessly, there might still be some defects in the evaluation process since there is no "gold standard" for determining factor weight in CEI. Despite such problems, CEIs are widely used by international organizations to measure economic, environmental, and social phenomena, thus serving as highly relevant tools [2].

Comprehensive evaluation or multi attribute decision making is still in a stage of blind exploration. This study aims to address the estimation of factor weights in comprehensive evaluation or MADM by incorporating statistics and informatics. Specifically, it focuses on how to assign scientific, objective, fair, and reasonable weight coefficients to the factors involved in constructing the comprehensive evaluation. The goal is to make a contribution to the methodology of constructing comprehensive evaluation indices. The authors believe that the relationship between the CEI and each evaluation factor, is similar to the relationship between work and energy in physics. The CEI represents the performance of each evaluation factor in comprehensive evaluation, and each evaluation factor is the source of abilities possessed by the CEI. There exists an underlying quantitative functional relationship between the CEI and the individual evaluation factors. In our current study, we establish a specific equation for this underlying function, but we have not yet found a method to solve it. So far, all mathematical approaches to exploring the CEI have not attempted to quantitatively solve this function. Instead, they have explored the correlation between the CEI and the individual evaluation factors from other perspectives. As a result, these non-quantitative methods that deviate from the underlying quantitative function have been in vain.

To address this issue, the author proposes a nonlinear fitting method based on the maximum information entropy [10,11] and the least squares residual, which is similar to weighted regression analysis. This method quantitatively fits the relationship between the CEI and the individual evaluation factors, treating the weight coefficient estimation and indicator fusion as a whole. This approach aims to solve the weights of the individual factors and fundamentally resolve the issues in the modeling process of the CEI. Section 2 specifies the definitions of the proposed maximum entropy-minimum residual model for comprehensive evaluation, and the related statistical tests in the new proposed model. Section 3 provides the definition of min-max normalization that is mainly used as a data preprocessing technique in this paper and gives an illustrative example to elaborate on the optimization results of the new model with DPS software V21.05. Section 4 addresses comparisons of the proposed model with some existing commonly used models in various cases.

2. Maximum Entropy-Minimum Residual Comprehensive Evaluation Index Model

2.1. Comprehensive Evaluation Index Model

Given n samples of p factors, let x_{ij} denote the observation value of the i-th sample from the j-th factor, $i = 1, 2, \cdots, n$, $j = 1, 2, \cdots, p$. From the perspective of statistical models, constructing a multi-factor comprehensive evaluation index, or the so-called composite indicator, $\{y_i\}_{i=1}^{n}$, requires estimating the weight coefficients, w_j, of each factor in the following equation

$$y_i = x_{i1}w_1 + x_{i2}w_2 + \cdots + x_{ip}w_p, \tag{1}$$

where $w_1 + w_2 + \cdots + w_p = 1$, and $w_j \geq 0$. However, since there is no explicit dependent variable (y_i) for reference in the comprehensive evaluation model here, the empirical model proposed by this paper assumes that the composite indicator (y_i) is composed of p factors such that y_i can be considered as the sum of theoretical indicator values from the p factors. Suppose that the j-th factor is assigned a weight w_j, the theoretical indicator value of each factor, also called by theoretical component denoted as C_{ij}, is given by $C_{ij} = y_i w_j$.

The proposed model and the data fitting are based on C_{ij}, where $x_{ij}w_j$ is considered as the observed values of C_{ij}. Therefore, y_i can also be expressed in the form of the sum of its theoretical components,

$$y_i = C_{i1} + C_{i2} + \cdots + C_{ip}. \tag{2}$$

Since the Equations (1) and (2) are equivalent from the left side, it is justified to assume that $x_{ij}w_j$ and C_{ij} are in one-to-one correspondence. Remark that $x_{ij}w_j$ is not necessary to be equal to the true theoretical component C_{ij}. Otherwise, x_{ij} will be exactly equal to y_i, which is not practical. Considering $x_{ij}w_j$ as the observed values of the theoretical components C_{ij}, we can empirically conclude that the closer the two values are, the more representative the CEI becomes.

We define the difference between the observed and the theoretical components as the residual, $\sigma_{ij} = x_{ij}w_j - C_{ij}$, which is considered as a fitted error of the i-th sample of the j-th factor. In a regression model, the parameter estimation is derived from minimizing the residual, or say the root mean square error of y_i, denoted by σ in our case,

$$\sigma = \sqrt{\frac{\sum_{i=1}^{n}\sum_{j=1}^{p}(x_{ij}w_j - C_{ij})^2}{(n-1)p}} = \sqrt{\frac{\sum_{i=1}^{n}\sum_{j=1}^{p}[(x_{ij} - y_i)w_j]^2}{(n-1)p}}. \tag{3}$$

From Equation (3), the residual error σ_{ij} can also be expressed as a weighted difference between the observed value x_{ij} and the theoretical CEI y_i. The larger the weight coefficient of a factor, the greater its impact on the residuals, indicating that the factor is "more important". This approach is essentially a weighted regression analysis process. It is consistent with the principle in multi-factor comprehensive analysis, where a larger weight coefficient for a factor means that the factor is more important. The fitted error term σ_{ij} is assumed independent of other factors, since under ideal circumstances, the component of each individual factor can be considered independent of the other factors in order to measure a specific characteristic of the CEI. The root mean square error of Equation (3) is similar to the decomposition of the sum of squared errors in a regression model, and the corresponding degree of freedom in our case is $(n-1)p$. Equation (3) can be considered as an error function to be minimized when deriving the solution of weights. However, if the weight coefficient of the j-th factor in Equation (3) is equal to one and the weight coefficients of the rest of the factors are zeros, then y_i is equal to the observed value x_{ij} while the residual $y_i - x_{ij}$ is minimized to zero. Obviously, directly minimizing Equation (3) ends up with a trivial solution in which a certain weight is 1 and zero otherwise, making the corresponding factor as the CEI. Although, $\sigma = 0$, in this special case, the resulting CEI is pointless.

2.2. *Maximum Entropy-Minimum Residual (MEMR) Model for Comprehensive Evaluation*

Entropy is a key concept in information theory, as a unit of measurement when quantifying the total amount of information in a dataset. The maximum entropy (ME) principle in [10] provides a method for reasoning from incomplete information. For problems in science, the more information we have, the better the models and theories we can construct. However, for a complex system, such as a multi-factor CEI model, developers never have enough information to unambiguously predict the probability distribution of the weights of individual factors. Indeed, constructing a CEI for such a complex system faces an underdetermined reasoning problem. When the ME principle is adopted by specifying available information as constraints, a model with the least bias can be chosen from all possible models consistent with the information. In establishing a CEI model, since the dimensions of the various indicators are inconsistent, the common approach is to preprocess the data using min-max normalization introduced in Section 3 or other normalization methods so that the normalized values of each factor fall between 0 and 1. We can treat these as ratio values between 0 and 1, representing the probability of a factor's distribution within the evaluation range. ME inference is considered the correct way to estimate an unknown probability distribution given limited information (in the form of moments of the distribution) when entropy defined by [12] is chosen to effectively measure information for the probability distribution of random events [13]. Distributions with higher entropy implicate greater diversity and are more likely to be observed [13]. Thus, ME inference leads to the best probability estimate from the given information, with no need to assume any further knowledge beyond that in a set of constraints. According to ME inference, any other form will be based on nonoptimal inference, either using less information than that available or expressing unjustified bias.

The ME principle is thus adopted in the present study to determine weight coefficients of multiple factors in the construction of a CEI. If each weight coefficient follows a probability distribution for the importance of each factor, the ME form of the probability distribution can be achieved through maximization of Shannon's information entropy, which can be expressed in the following formula containing weight coefficients w_j of all concerned factors,

$$E = -\sum_{j=1}^{p} w_j \log(w_j), \quad (4)$$

in which information entropy is at the maximum when all weight coefficients are equal. When the weight coefficient is equal to 1 for one factor and 0 for each of the other factors, information entropy is at the minimum. This seems to contradict the optimization of a CEI by maximizing information entropy and minimizing residual error according to the ME principle.

The idea of using information entropy for CEI modeling is intuitive, similar to compression regression methods such as LASSO regression, where the optimization function for the CEI model is established in the following form,

$$minf(\sigma, E) = min(\sigma - \lambda E),$$

in which taking different values for λ leads to different optimization results. An appropriate λ may provide a model as required. However, the biggest problem with this approach is how to choose λ. At the same time, the objective function to be optimized is a hybrid because the dimensions of the residuals and information entropy are different. Combining them in the form of a sum or difference as the objective function is inappropriate, since the CEI model essentially aims to optimize the residuals defined by Equation (3). Another possible way to combine residual and entropy is through multiplication or division as

$$minf(\sigma, E) = min(\sigma / E),$$

that simply scales the residuals up or down by several times, which is a linear relationship. The result is the same as optimizing based on the residual σ defined by Equation (3), and it does not yield the desired statistical model. Given that the previous two forms are not suitable for constructing the CEI model, a natural idea is to adopt an exponential function to establish the error function, using the residual σ as the base and information entropy E as the exponent, defined as

$$minf(\sigma, E) = min(\sigma^E). \quad (5)$$

Since the dimensions of all concerned factors are not consistent, data must be properly normalized in advance, such as using the min-max normalization method, in order to construct a CEI or MADM model. The normalized dimension value of each factor is essentially a ratio between 0 and 1, and the resulting residual σ must be less than 1 accordingly, such that the error function value in Equation (5) becomes smaller when the entropy is larger. Therefore, the property of the error function in Equation (5) can be interpreted as the process of minimizing the residual σ within the space of information entropy E. For original data without normalization, each observed value can be divided by the maximum (absolute value) of all observed values to convert it to a ratio between 0 and 1 before the optimization begins. In summary, the maximum entropy-minimum residual (MEMR) comprehensive evaluation index model can be expressed as

$$min_{\{w_j\}_{j=1}^{p}}(\sigma^E),\ s.t. \sum_{j=1}^{p} w_j = 1,\ w_j \geq 0, \tag{6}$$

where w_j, $j = 1, 2, \cdots, p$ with constraint is the optimization variable in this nonlinear regression equation model.

The nonlinear regression Equation (6) with constraints can be solved using a variety of nonlinear optimization methods with constraints. Since convergence speed varies with different optimization algorithms, it may take a long time to achieve the bootstrap sampling estimation of model weight parameters. Thus, it is worthy of searching for an algorithm with stable operation and fast speed. We try to use the sequential unconstrained minimization technique (SUMT) for optimization and obtain optimal results (shown in Section 3). The SUMT optimization algorithm has been included in DPS (data processing system) software package V21.05 [14]. In this paper, a CEI constructed with the proposed MEMR model is called MEMR index, and the corresponding weight coefficient is called MEMR weight. MEMR modeling actually uses least squares techniques to extract the common trends of various factors in the process of building a CEI model or conducting MADM while taking into account all factors (information) as comprehensively as possible. This is highly consistent with the motivation behind conducting comprehensive evaluation or MADM.

2.3. Statistical Tests in Comprehensive Evaluation Index Models

In constructing a CEI, the simplest approach is the equal weighting (EW) model, where all variables are assigned the same weight. If there are p variables, the weight coefficients for all factors are equal to $\frac{1}{p}$. Clearly, in actual comprehensive evaluation and MADM processes, the importance of each evaluation factor is not the same. Here, we use the equal weighting model as a reference (null model) for the CEI model, treating it as a submodel of the MEMR model, and performing statistical tests using a nested model approach. This means we can use statistical testing methods to compare the MEMR model with the EW model, i.e., to test whether the MEMR model can be simplified into the EW model (null hypothesis). The statistical test can be conducted using the F-test. The sum of squared residuals for each model is shown in Table 1, in which

$$RSS(w_{EW}) = \sum_{i=1}^{n}\sum_{j=1}^{p}(\frac{x_{ij} - y_i}{p})^2,\ y_i = \sum_{j=1}^{p}\frac{x_{ij}}{p}, \tag{7}$$

$$RSS(w_{MEMR}) = \sum_{i=1}^{n}\sum_{j=1}^{p}[(x_{ij} - y_i)\cdot w_j]^2,\ y_i = \sum_{j=1}^{p} x_{ij}w_j. \tag{8}$$

Currently, statistical software such as Stata V16.0 and Prism V5.0 have applied analysis of variance (ANOVA) for statistical tests in nested nonlinear models; see [15]. In this paper, based on [16], the F-test statistic is expressed in terms of the sum of squared residuals and serves as a measure of the distance between the EW model and the MEMR model. A larger F-statistic indicates that the two models differ significantly, suggesting that the EW model does not describe the data well due to its equal weight coefficients for all factors.

Therefore, the more general model, MEMR, is more suitable for comprehensive evaluation and MADM. The F-test statistic is a ratio of the last two mean square terms in Table 1, where the numerator is the difference in the variance terms between the two models, divided by the difference in the number of parameters between the models. The denominator is the mean square error of the MEMR model (the full model). The statistical test formula is as follows:

$$F = \frac{\frac{RSS(\hat{w}_{EW}) - RSS(\hat{w}_{MEMR})}{p-1}}{\frac{RSS(\hat{w}_{MEMR})}{(n-1)p}}. \tag{9}$$

The F-test statistic is defined the same way as in linear models. However, unlike in linear models, the F-distribution only holds approximately (it becomes closer as the sample size increases). Based on the F-value and its degrees of freedom, it is not difficult to obtain the significance probability, or p-value. From the F-statistic test, we can conclude that if the statistical test is not significant (for example, using a 0.05 significance level), we can accept the EW model as the CEI model. However, generally speaking, the MEMR model can always improve the effectiveness of comprehensive evaluation or MADM to some extent. If $p < 0.05$, then the EW model may not be suitable as the CEI model, and the MEMR model should be adopted. This is because, in the CEI model, at least one of the weight coefficients is different from the others, making the optimization process meaningful. The weight coefficients generated through optimization significantly improve the closeness of the composite indicator to the observed values compared to the equal weighting coefficients.

Table 1. Analysis of variance in multi-factor comprehensive evaluation index models.

Source of Variation	Sum of Squared Residuals	Degree of Freedom	Mean Square
EW Model	$RSS(w_{EW})$	$np-1$	$\frac{RSS(w_{EW})}{np-1}$
MEMR Model	$RSS(w_{MEMR})$	$(n-1)p$	$\frac{RSS(w_{MEMR})}{(n-1)p}$
EW − MEMR	$RSS(w_{EW}) - RSS(w_{MEMR})$	$p-1$	$\frac{RSS(w_{EW})-RSS(w_{MEMR})}{p-1}$

In addition, we define the model optimization index R as the percentage decrease of the difference in the sum of squared residuals between the EW model and the MEMR model, compared to the sum of squared residuals of the EW model,

$$R = \frac{RSS(\hat{w}_{EW}) - RSS(\hat{w}_{MEMR})}{RSS(\hat{w}_{EW})} \times 100\%. \tag{10}$$

The meaning of R is that, after optimization, it measures the extent to which the CEI model has been improved compared to the null hypothesis, where each factor is assigned an equal weight. This is reflected by the percentage decrease in the sum of squared residuals, or it can be interpreted as the degree to which the goodness of fit has been improved.

Since the MEMR model is a nonlinear model, it is difficult to accurately estimate the standard errors of the weight coefficients. Here, we apply the Bootstrap method for estimation. For the multi-factor MEMR CEI model, a set of weight coefficients can be calculated for each Bootstrap sample. If we draw $n_B = 1000$ Bootstrap samples, we can obtain 1000 sets of weight coefficients.

1. 95% Confidence Interval of Weight Coefficients

Based on these 1000 sets of weight coefficients, the 2.5th percentile and the 97.5lth percentile are calculated to obtain the 95% confidence intervals for each weight coefficient. In case one focuses on the analysis of the impact of the weight coefficients, for a given weight coefficient, if the interval does not include $\frac{1}{p}$, then it can be considered that the influence of this factor is significantly too large or too small. In a comprehensive evaluation, a subset of the weights can be $\frac{1}{p}$, but this does not mean that we have completely equal weights. In this case, it is not appropriate to use equal weight to calculate the composite indicator in a multi-factor comprehensive evaluation.

2. 95% Standard Error of Weight Coefficients and Coefficient of Variation

Based on certain samples drawn using Bootstrap sampling, each having the same sample size as the initial one, and for each sample, the mean and variance of the sample statistics are calculated. For instance, the sample means are denoted by $\bar{x}_1, \bar{x}_2, \cdots, \bar{x}_{n_B}$, and the mean estimation is given by $\hat{\mu} = \sum_{i=1}^{n_B} \frac{\bar{x}_i}{n_B}$. According to the formula, $\sigma^2 = \sum_{i}^{n_B} \frac{(\bar{x}_i - \hat{\mu})^2}{n_B - 1}$, the coefficient of variation for each factor is given by $CV = \hat{\sigma}/\hat{\mu}$.

The DPS V21.05 system calculates the average coefficient of variation for each factor to examine the fluctuation range of the weight coefficients of each factor in the CEI model, as well as the stability of the weight coefficients during the comprehensive evaluation process. Based on the size of the coefficient of variation, models with smaller coefficients of variation are selected from several models as application references.

3. An Example for Optimization of MEMR Model

3.1. Min-Max Normalization

When constructing CEI, many evaluation factors are measured with different units. Sometimes, the factors are considered to be 'good', if a higher value indicates better performance. Otherwise, the factors are considered 'bad', such as 'long-term unemployment' and 'obstruction of daily activities owing to chronic illness,' for which higher values are associated with worse performance. To put all factors on a common dimension, data must be normalized using a rescaling technique. According to a factor that is considered 'good' or 'bad', the following normalization technique is called min-max normalization, which is popularly used for preprocessing data in comprehensive evaluation,

$$x'_{ij} = \begin{cases} \frac{x_{ij} - x_{min\ j}}{x_{max\ j} - x_{min\ j}} & x_{ij} \text{ is a 'good' factor,} \\ \frac{x_{max\ j} - x_{ij}}{x_{max\ j} - x_{min\ j}} & x_{ij} \text{ is a 'bad' factor.} \end{cases} \quad (11)$$

All normalized factors are represented by ratios between 0 and 1, which correspond to the 'worst' and the 'best' performance, respectively. The case studies in this paper adopt the min-max normalization technique for simplicity. The DPS software V21.05 is capable of adopting other normalization techniques.

3.2. An Illustrative Example

For example, the min-max normalization is adopted when conducting a comprehensive evaluation analysis of the average per capita living consumption expenditure level of rural households in different regions of China in 2007 with the original data listed in the following Table 2, downloaded from https://download.csdn.net/download/weixin_42119432/12617871 (accessed on 8 January 2025).

After data normalization using Equation (11), the MEMR model is optimized with a sequential unconstrained minimization technique (SUMT) conducted through DPS software V21.05. The system first outputs the information entropy of the nonlinear MEMR model with constraints with the value of 2.9806, while the logarithm of the objective function is equal to −13.2752 and the residual error $\sigma = 0.0116$, as listed in Table 3. The second part of the results is about the ANOVA table, where the null hypothesis H_0 is that the weight coefficient of the j-th factor is $\frac{1}{p}$, and the alternative hypothesis is that at least one factor j has a weight coefficient unequal to $\frac{1}{p}$. This part of results is interpreted from a statistical perspective in order to test whether there exists a difference among the weight coefficients of factors. If there is no significant difference (do not reject H_0), then an EW model can be used to construct the composite indicator. If the p-value is less than 0.05 (reject H_0), then the composite indicator needs to be calculated by the MEMR weights. In Table 3, p-value is 0.0002, implying that the CEI in this case should be calculated by the estimated weights of the factors instead of equal weights.

Table 2. Average per capita living consumption expenditure of rural households in different regions of China (2007).

Region	Food	Clothing	Housing	HA [1]	TC [2]	EM [3]	HC [4]	Others
Beijing	2132.51	513.44	1023.21	340.15	778.52	870.12	629.56	111.75
Tianjin	1367.75	286.33	674.81	126.74	400.11	312.07	306.19	64.3
Hebei	1025.72	185.68	627.98	140.45	318.19	243.3	188.06	57.4
Shanxi	1033.68	260.88	392.78	120.86	268.75	370.97	170.85	63.81
Inner Mongolia	1280.05	228.4	473.98	117.64	375.58	423.75	281.46	75.29
Liaoning	1334.18	281.19	513.11	142.07	361.77	362.78	265.01	108.05
Jilin	1240.93	227.96	399.11	120.95	337.46	339.77	311.37	87.89
Heilongjiang	1077.34	254.01	691.02	104.99	335.28	312.32	272.49	69.98
Shanghai	3259.48	475.51	2097.21	451.4	883.71	857.47	571.06	249.04
Jiangsu	1968.88	251.29	752.73	228.51	543.97	642.52	263.85	134.41
Zhejiang	2430.6	405.32	1498.5	338.8	782.98	750.69	452.44	142.26
Anhui	1192.57	166.31	479.46	144.23	258.29	283.17	177.04	52.98
Fujian	1870.32	235.61	660.55	184.21	465.4	356.26	174.12	107
Jiangxi	1492.02	147.71	474.49	121.54	277.15	252.78	167.71	61.08
Shandong	1369.2	224.18	682.13	195.99	422.36	424.89	230.84	71.98
Henan	1017.43	189.71	615.62	136.37	269.46	212.36	173.19	62.26
Hubei	1479.04	168.64	434.91	166.25	281.12	284.13	178.77	97.13
Hunan	1675.16	161.79	508.33	152.6	278.78	293.89	219.95	86.88
Guangdong	2087.58	162.33	763.01	163.85	443.24	254.94	199.31	128.06
Guangxi	1378.78	86.9	554.14	112.24	245.97	172.45	149.01	47.98
Hainan	1430.31	86.26	305.9	93.26	248.08	223.98	95.55	73.23
Chongqing	1376	136.34	263.73	138.34	208.69	195.97	168.57	39.06
Sichuan	1435.52	156.65	366.45	142.64	241.49	177.19	174.75	52.56
Guizhou	998.39	99.44	329.64	70.93	154.52	147.31	79.31	34.16
Yunnan	1226.69	112.52	586.07	107.15	216.67	181.73	167.92	38.43
Tibet	1079.83	245	418.83	133.26	156.57	65.39	50	68.74
Shaanxi	941.81	161.08	512.4	106.8	254.74	304.54	222.51	55.71
Gansu	944.14	112.2	295.23	91.4	186.17	208.9	149.82	29.36
Qinghai	1069.04	191.8	359.74	122.17	292.1	135.13	229.28	47.23
Ningxia	1019.35	184.26	450.55	109.27	265.76	192	239.4	68.17
Xinjiang	939.03	218.18	445.02	91.45	234.7	166.27	210.69	45.25

[1] Household Appliance; [2] Transportation and Communication; [3] Entertainment ; [4] Healthcare.

The third part of the output represents the weight coefficients of various factors, which serve as the core and focus of the comprehensive evaluation analysis model. These coefficients reflect both the contribution of each factor to the formation of the CEI and the importance of each factor in the CEI. They are the result of the interaction between individual factors and the CEI, derived under the condition of maximum entropy, minimizing fitting errors while accounting for central tendency, dispersion, and the interrelationships among multiple factors. The second column of the third part of Table 3 is the estimated weight coefficients, where a greater weight indicates that the corresponding factor is more important in comprehensive evaluation. In this case, based on weights, the two factors

'Transportation and Communication' and 'Household Appliance' have the greatest influence on the CEI. The second important factors are 'Others', 'Housing' and 'Food', while the factors such as 'Entertainment' and 'Healthcare' have a mild influence. The sample mean and standard deviation columns are estimated values calculated based on the results of Bootstrap sampling (1000 iterations in this case). The standard deviation here represents the standard error of the weight coefficients under the normality assumption. Using the standard error, the 95% confidence interval can be estimated. The "Median" and "95% Confidence Interval" are estimated based on the percentiles of Bootstrap sampling. Generally, when the 95% confidence interval exceeds $\frac{1}{p}$, the weight coefficient is considered significantly larger; otherwise, the weight coefficient is considered significantly smaller. For example, in this case, the confidence intervals for the weights of the 'Household Appliance' and 'Transportation and Communication' factors are [0.1263, 0.1884] and [0.1350, 0.1826], respectively, both greater than $\frac{1}{p} = 0.125$. Therefore, these two factors can be considered significantly larger in a statistical sense.

Table 3. The summary of MEMR modeling results through DPS software V21.05 with SUMT.

Data Normalization (Min-Max) and Transformation								
log (objective function)			−13.2752					
Residual (σ)			0.011633					
Information entropy (E)			2.980593					
ANOVA table								
Sources of Variation	**SS** [1]	**df** [2]	**Mean square**					
EM model	0.0366	247	0.0001					
MEMR model	0.0325	240	0.0001					
EM − MEMR	0.0041	7	0.0006					
F-value = 4.3389, p-value = 0.0002								
Optimization index = 11.2334%								
Weight coefficients estimated by Bootstrap sampling (1000 times)								
Factors	**Weights**	**Mean**	**Std r** [3]	**Median**	**95% Confidence Interval**			
Food	0.1171	0.1158	0.0071	0.1155	0.0958	0.1392		
Clothing	0.1039	0.1048	0.0102	0.1049	0.0729	0.1369		
Housing	0.1186	0.1181	0.0088	0.1177	0.0879	0.1514		
HA [4]	0.1580	0.1572	0.0101	0.1574	0.1263	0.1884		
TC [5]	0.1612	0.1611	0.0082	0.1615	0.1350	0.1826		
EM [6]	0.1096	0.1097	0.0088	0.1092	0.0793	0.1454		
HC [7]	0.1072	0.1073	0.0075	0.1075	0.0842	0.1345		
Others	0.1245	0.1260	0.0146	0.1248	0.0843	0.1654		
Entropy	2.9806	2.9766	0.0062	2.9769	2.9465	2.9946		
Sample rank and comprehensive evaluation index (CEI)								
Region	**Rank**	**CEI**	**Region**	**Rank**	**CEI**	**Region**	**Rank**	**CEI**
Shanghai	1	0.9782	Hunan	12	0.2279	Sichuan	22	0.1493
Beijing	2	0.7264	Heilongjiang	13	0.2273	Qinghai	23	0.1429
Zhejiang	3	0.7146	Hubei	14	0.2179	Xinjiang	24	0.1225
Jiangsu	4	0.4529	Shanxi	15	0.1851	Guangxi	25	0.1219
Fujian	5	0.3313	Hebei	16	0.1828	Chongqing	26	0.1194
Guangdong	6	0.3205	Jiangxi	17	0.1699	Yunnan	27	0.1133
Shandong	7	0.3	Anhui	18	0.1661	Hainan	28	0.1124
Liaoning	8	0.2837	Henan	19	0.1659	Tibet	29	0.1044
Tianjin	9	0.2751	Ningxia	20	0.1547	Gansu	30	0.0621
Inner Mongolia	10	0.2513	Shaanxi	21	0.1509	Guizhou	31	0.0298
Jilin	11	0.2385						

[1] Sum of Squares; [2] Degrees of Freedom; [3] Standard Deviation; [4] Household Appliance; [5] Transportation and Communication; [6] Entertainment ; [7] Healthcare.

Bootstrap sampling estimation serves two purposes: statistical testing and assessing the sensitivity of each weight coefficient. The smaller the range of the 95% confidence interval based on Bootstrap percentiles, the more robust the weight coefficient of the factor is in evaluating the composite indicator or making multi-attribute decisions. Conversely, a wider confidence interval suggests that the weight coefficient should be treated with more caution when estimating the composite indicator and making decisions. Using Bootstrap simulation sampling, we estimate the standard error of each factor's weight coefficient. To examine the estimation accuracy, we can calculate the mean standard error for all factors, as well as the mean weight coefficient for each factor (equal to $\frac{1}{p}$). Subsequently, we can calculate the coefficients of variation (CV) for the weight coefficients. The CV is typically used to compare the dispersion of different datasets. A larger CV indicates greater variability and higher dispersion, while a smaller CV suggests less variability and lower dispersion. By comparing the CVs of different datasets, we can evaluate their stability and consistency.

Finally, based on the CEI values generated by the maximum entropy-minimum residual model for each sample, we can rank the evaluation indices from highest to lowest to obtain the ranking results for all samples. In this example, the estimated CEIs for each region, ranked from highest to lowest, are listed in the last part of Table 3. Based on the ranking results, a professional interpretation can be made along with a comparison of the positions of the evaluation objects. For example, in this case, Shanghai, Beijing, and Zhejiang rank as the top three, indicating the highest levels of consumption. They are followed by Jiangsu, Fujian, Guangdong, and Shandong, which have slightly lower consumption levels.

4. Comparisons of MEMR Model with Commonly Used Models

4.1. Technical Achievement Index

The original data for the construction of technical achievement index (TAI) by OECD [2] also adopted the min-max normalization, listed in Table A1 of the Appendix A for simplicity. Based on this data set, weight coefficients of eight TAI-based factors computed with the proposed MEMR model are compared with those computed with the methods of equal weighting (EW), principal component analysis (PCA) [17], factor analysis (FA) [18], and standard deviation (SD) [19], and criteria importance through intercriteria correlation (CRITIC) [20]. Through the correlation analysis as shown in Figure 1, only the MEMR weights and the first principal component are highly positively correlated.

PCA is an industry-accepted method to reduce data dimensionality. The example data results show that the trend in the magnitude of the MEMR weights is consistent with the factor loadings of the first principal component in PCA, with a correlation coefficient of 0.8263. This indicates that the MEMR weights are essentially a form of data dimensionality reduction method. The MEMR and PCA weights are mostly negatively correlated with the weight coefficients obtained from other weighting methods. This suggests that, although these weights explain the variation of the evaluation factors, they do not serve the purpose of dimensionality reduction or combining the individual factors into a composite indicator.

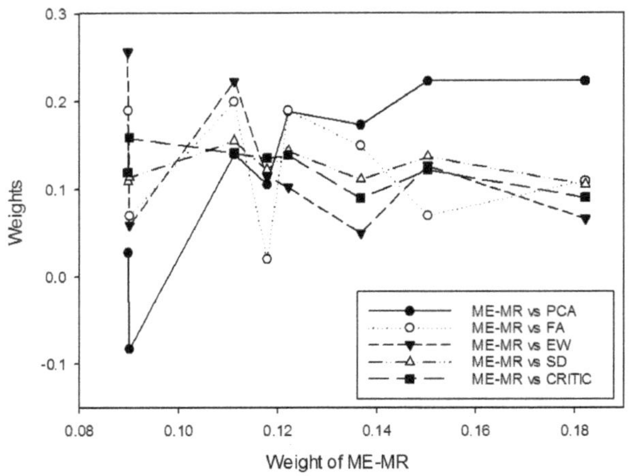

Figure 1. Weight coefficients of various weighting methods for the technological achievement index data.

Here, we also plot the relationships between the composite indicator, factor weights, and normalized values obtained using the MEMR method, the entropy weighting (ET) method [19], the CRITIC method, and the SD method in the form of a line-bubble combination chart as Figure 2. In the chart, the sample identification label (Region) is plotted on the horizontal axis, while the vertical axis represents the CEI values and the normalized values of individual factors, along with the factor weights displayed as bubbles. The diameter of the bubbles is uniformly defined as $0.025 \times \frac{w_j}{w_{max}}$, where w_j is the j-th factor weight coefficient, and w_{max} is the maximum weight coefficient. The chart conveys four main points:

1. Ranking and similarity of evaluation objects: the closer the points are, the more similar the evaluation objects are;
2. Trend of the CEI line: the variation trend of the CEI along the line;
3. Distribution of normalized values of each factor: the positioning of the normalized values of each factor around the CEI line indicates that the more concentrated the values, the better the ranking or evaluation effect;
4. Factor weight coefficients: each factor is represented by a different color, with the size of each bubble indicating the magnitude of the weight coefficient. The larger the weight coefficient, the larger the bubble, and vice versa. This helps identify the distribution trends of different factors and their consistency with the CEI line.

As shown in Figure 2, in the model established using the MEMR method, factors with larger weights are distributed on both sides of the CEI line, while factors with smaller weight coefficients are located farther from the CEI line. The distribution of factor weight magnitudes aligns with the trend of the CEI values. This clearly reflects the representativeness of the CEI for the major factors with larger weight coefficients. However, the ET method, CRITIC method, and SD method do not exhibit a similar trend. This suggests that the methods of estimating factor weights for comprehensive evaluation using entropy weighting, criteria importance through intercriteria correlation, and standard deviation require further consideration. Remark that in the "Handbook on Constructing Composite Indicators" compiled by the OECD/EU-JRC [2], ET and CRITIC weighting methods are not mentioned.

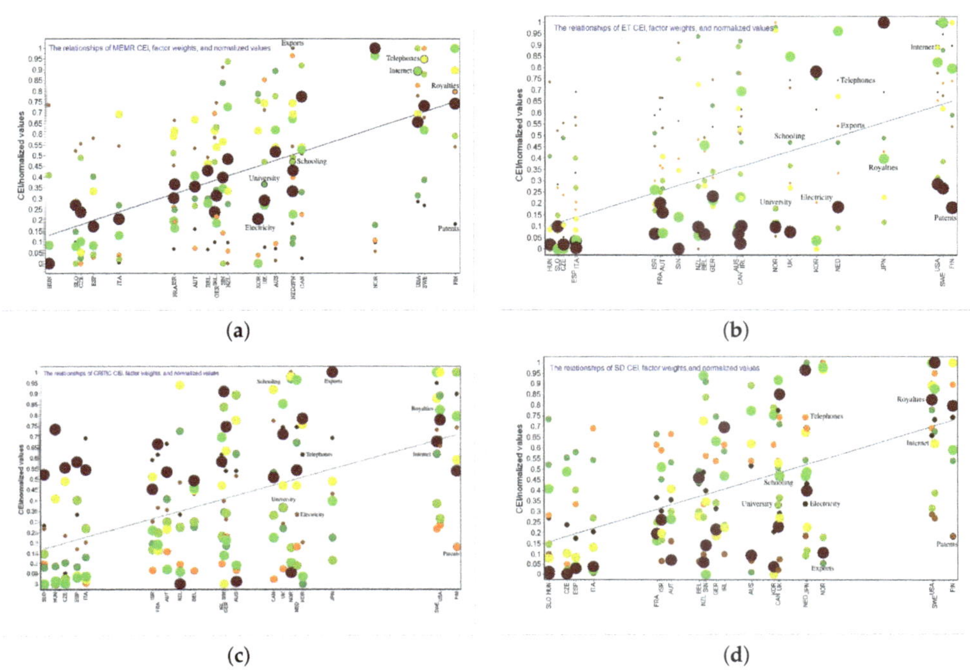

Figure 2. Relationship diagram of composite indicator estimates and factor weights and normalized values for different methods: (**a**) The relationships of MEMR CEI, factor weights, and normalized values. (**b**) The relationships of ET CEI, factor weights, and normalized values. (**c**) The relationships of CRITIC CEI, factor weights, and normalized values. (**d**) The relationships of SD CEI, factor weights, and normalized values.

4.2. Virtual Example Presented by an Orthogonal Table

An orthogonal table provides a virtual dataset comprising 24 orthogonal samples of four factors, each having 2, 3, 4, and 8 levels, respectively, listed in Table A2 of the Appendix A, generated by the DPS software V21.05. All factors have no mutual correlation and hence are independent of one another. In the meanwhile, the importance of the qualitative factors can be intuitively distinguished by the number of levels since more levels imply more information. The original data are normalized with the min-max method. Based on this virtual data set after normalization, the weight estimates of each factor computed by MEMR, ET, SD, CRITIC, and PCA are listed in Table 4.

Table 4. Weight Coefficients of several weighting methods for virtual sample data in the orthogonal table.

Factor	Levels	MEMR	ET	SD	CRITIC	PCA
x_1	2	0.2040	0.3850	0.3109	0.3109	1
x_2	3	0.2469	0.2567	0.2538	0.2538	0
x_3	4	0.2642	0.2082	0.2317	0.2317	0
x_4	8	0.2849	0.1502	0.2035	0.2035	0

The PCA weighting method is used to correct for overlapping information between two or more correlated factors, rather than to measure the theoretical importance of the related indicators. If there is no correlation between the factors, this method should not be used to estimate weights, and in this case, PCA is not suitable for estimation. As the analysis results show, the normalized eigenvector used as the weight coefficient is a 4lth-order identity matrix, with all diagonal elements equal to 1 and all other elements equal to 0. The weight coefficients obtained using the ET method exhibit a trend where the weight coefficient decreases as the number of levels of a factor increases. This contradicts our intuitive analysis of the amount of information contained in the data. Specifically, if we treat each level of a factor as an ordinal variable, variables with more levels should typically have greater information content, providing more potential for analysis and inference. For example, x_4 has 8 levels, which is close to a quantitative indicator, and it should theoretically contain more information, thus having a larger weight in the comprehensive evaluation index. However, the weight coefficient here is less than half that of the two-level factor x_1. Moreover, since the correlation coefficients between the individual factors are zero, the weight results calculated using the CRITIC method are the same as those obtained using the SD method. Their results show a similar trend as the ET method, where the weight coefficient decreases as the number of levels of a factor increases. Therefore, this suggests that the ET, SD, and CRITIC methods, as ways of calculating weight coefficients, need further discussion.

Using the MEMR weights proposed in this paper, the trend shows that the weight coefficient increases as the number of levels of a factor increases. This is consistent with our intuitive understanding that variables with more levels typically contain more information than those with fewer levels. Additionally, with this orthogonal table as an example, if each factor in the orthogonal table adopts a z-score normalization by subtracting the mean and dividing by the standard deviation, then the mean of each factor will be zero, and the standard deviation will be 1. In this case, the weight coefficients of each factor, calculated according to MEMR model Equation (6), will be the same. This further illustrates that orthogonal tables have the characteristics of being uniformly distributed, orderly, and comparable.

4.3. *Example for Comprehensive Development Status of Enterprises*

In order to improve the investment efficiency, a large investment firm intended to evaluate 15 companies with 10 indicators that reflect the enterprise development status [21]. The evaluation results after the min-max normalization are included in Table 5.

Table 5. Normalized data of the comprehensive development status of 15 enterprises.

Enterprise	x_1	x_2	x_3	x_4	x_5	x_6	x_7	x_8	x_9	x_{10}
1	1.0	0.1	0.2	0.3	0.4	0.5	0.6	0.7	0.8	0.9
2	0.9	0.2	0.1	0.2	0.3	0.4	0.5	0.6	0.7	0.8
3	0.8	0.9	0.7	0.1	0.2	0.3	0.4	0.5	0.6	0.7
4	0.7	0.8	0.9	0.3	0.1	0.2	0.3	0.4	0.5	0.6
5	0.6	0.7	0.8	0.9	1.0	0.1	0.2	0.3	0.4	0.5
6	0.5	0.6	0.7	0.8	0.9	1.0	0.1	0.2	0.3	0.4
7	0.4	0.5	0.6	0.7	0.8	0.9	1.0	0.1	0.2	0.3
8	0.3	0.4	0.5	0.6	0.7	0.8	0.9	1.0	0.1	0.2
9	0.2	0.3	0.4	0.5	0.6	0.7	0.8	0.9	0.6	0.1
10	0.1	0.2	0.3	0.4	0.5	0.6	0.7	0.8	0.9	1.0
11	0.8	0.3	0.2	0.5	0.6	0.5	0.8	0.6	0.4	0.7
12	0.9	1.0	0.2	0.5	0.6	0.5	0.8	0.6	0.4	0.7
13	0.8	0.2	1.0	0.6	0.6	0.5	0.8	0.6	0.4	0.7
14	0.8	0.2	0.6	1.0	0.6	0.5	0.8	0.6	0.4	0.7
15	0.8	0.2	0.6	0.2	0.6	0.5	0.8	0.6	1.0	0.7

Ref. [21] used various BoD methods and their improvements to construct weights and calculate the CEI. The corresponding BoD methods and the results of other methods are shown in Table 6.

The non-compensatory BoD method introduced by [6] suffers from a significant 0–1 weight issue and often requires compensation rules of zero weights in the process of weighting. The BoD models without or with weight compensation are referred to as non-compensatory or compensatory BoD. The CEI results of the non-compensatory BoD method for evaluating the comprehensive development status of enterprises are listed in Table 6. From the results, they cannot be used for ranking the enterprises. Ref. [6] gave five weight compensation methods by adding a rigid score compensation constraint to the non-compensatory BoD to address over-flexibility issues. Setting the constraint value to 0.85 as an example of absolute compensation, it is impossible to rank all the concerned companies (Table 6).

Table 6. The comprehensive evaluation indices of 15 enterprises computed with various methods.

Enterprise	Non-Compensatory BoD	Compensatory BoD	Generalized BoD	Two-Set BoD	ABC	EW	MEMR
1	1.0	0.9548	1.0	0.5	1.00	0.55	0.5529
2	1.0	0.9724	1.0	0.5	0.95	0.47	0.4692
3	1.0	0.9985	1.0	1.0	0.90	0.52	0.5007
4	1.0	0.9985	1.0	0.5057	0.85	0.48	0.4604
5	1.0	1.0	1.0	0.5	0.80	0.55	0.5478
6	1.0	0.9985	1.0	0.5	0.75	0.55	0.5573
7	1.0	NULL [1]	1.0	0.6264	0.70	0.55	0.5575
8	1.0	1.0	1.0	0.5	0.65	0.55	0.5634
9	1.0	0.9868	1.0	0.5	0.60	0.51	0.5223
10	1.0	NULL [1]	1.0	0.5	0.55	0.55	0.5621
11	1.0	0.385	0.9938	0.5	0.80	0.54	0.5449
12	1.0	NULL [1]	1.0	0.5	0.90	0.62	0.6111
13	1.0	1.0	1.0	0.5	0.80	0.62	0.6228
14	1.0	1.0	1.0	0.5	0.63	0.62	0.6268
15	1.0	1.0	1.0	0.5	0.80	0.60	0.6020

[1] No solution.

The generalized BoD method [22] relaxes all computational symbols to the general summation operator "$\oplus$" and the general multiplication operator "$\otimes$" by means of a mathematical programming approach with geometric weighting aggregation patterns but is still unable to rank the companies meaningfully. Ref. [23] proposed a concept of "good indices" and "bad indices" from the positive and negative aspects of the two-set BoD weighting method. This approach adds more information to a more discriminative bidirectional composite indicator in the BoD analysis. After the "good" and "bad" indices computed with the two-set BoD method are adjusted with the parameter $\lambda = 0.5$, the resultant composite indicators remain undesirable for ranking the companies (Table 6).

If the importance levels of evaluation factors are known, the method of multi-criteria ABC analysis [24], close to the BoD analysis, can be adopted. Assuming the decreasing importance of each factor for the development status of those companies from left to right, the ABC analysis results in the rankings of the 15 companies from 0.55 to 1 (Table 6). The composite indicators computed with the equal weighting method and the proposed MEMR method range from 0.47 to 0.62 and 0.46 to 0.63 (Table 6), respectively.

From the table, none of the BoD methods are suitable for the comprehensive evaluation of this dataset. A correlation analysis of the CEI computed with the ABC, EW, and MEMR methods shows that the correlation coefficients between the ABC method and the EW method, as well as between the ABC method and the MEMR method, are −0.1694 and −0.2934, respectively, both indicating negative correlations. The correlation coefficient between the MEMR method and the EW method is 0.9801, indicating a high positive correlation. This suggests that the ABC method does not reflect the trend of the composite indicator for each enterprise, whereas the composite indicator obtained through MEMR reflects the overall trend of each enterprise and can better rank the 15 enterprises.

5. Conclusions

Multi-factor comprehensive evaluation is a widely used measurement method, whose results serve as an important auxiliary tool for decision-making. A key problem concerns how to assign weights to each factor when constructing a comprehensive evaluation index. The fair and reasonable calculation of factor weights can provide a reliable foundation for decision-making. An unreasonable indicator, nevertheless, can make it difficult to provide objective evaluation results for decision-making bodies and even result in misleading issues or controversy.

This study proposes an MEMR model based on the maximum entropy–minimum residual principle, directly applying the relationship estimation between multi-factor weights and the composite indicator. Based on the least-squares fitting of the theoretical component and the observed component, the model value of the theoretical component is the closest to the observed value of the actual component. The resulting CEI represents the central tendency and dispersion degree of each factor to the greatest extent, making it the most representative. The optimization process that minimizes the residuals while maximizing the information entropy is a method of extracting the common features of multiple factors or attributes under the premise of retaining as much information as possible. In a sense, this is the process of concentrating on a certain trend based on adopting as many suggestions as possible and synthesizing the common points expressed by each factor, that is, seeking unity while preserving diversity. This aligns with the basic principles of comprehensive evaluation and multiple attribute decision-making.

Our proposed model can reflect the influence of each factor indicator better than the factor weight in the widely used equal weighting method and is closer to the actual meaning expressed by CEI. In the worst case, our model has the same evaluation outcome as the equal weighting method. PCA mainly considers the correlations between each factor. When the correlation coefficient between factors is small, the results of PCA are not very accurate. In addition, there is no standard regarding how many principal components need to be selected. When the number of principal components is different, the comprehensive scores might also be different. In this case, the evaluation object and its stakeholders will question the "rationality" of weight assignment.

The entropy weighting method, standard deviation method, and CRITIC method mainly estimate weight based on the dispersion degree of each factor, without considering the influence of the central tendency of each factor. These weighting methods do not take into account the quantitative relationship between each factor, its weight, and the estimated composite indicator. Instead, they focus more on presenting the data from a certain external characteristic to explain a particular phenomenon. They display data according to certain needs instead of deeply revealing the information contained within the data. There is no standard for when and how to choose these weighting methods, and they are not universally suitable for all comprehensive evaluation processes of quantitative factors.

The problem becomes particularly salient when applying BoD for comprehensive evaluation.

Our proposed maximum entropy-minimum residual composite evaluation analysis modeling technique generates a composite evaluation index through numerical optimization, based on considering as much multi-factor information as possible while refining the central tendency of the factors. In the field of multivariate statistical analysis, the MEMR model employs nonlinear optimization techniques, allowing high-dimensional data to be more effectively mapped to one-dimensional space than principal component analysis. In various scenarios including big data analysis, we can apply the MEMR model for dimensionality reduction analysis of multivariate data.

The MEMR model is a new approach that combines information science and statistics. Accordingly, further theoretical research is needed in the following aspects.

1. Inference and estimation of MEMR model parameters: this includes improving the current nonlinear numerical optimization method and inventing new methods in order to improve the effectiveness and robustness of the optimization process; calculating inference accuracy and the confidence interval of parameter estimation; and further determining how to test the model hypothesis, diagnosing goodness of fit, and determining the rationality of the residual error;
2. Estimation of weight coefficients in a MEMR model with attribute variables;
3. Application to weight estimation in multiple attribute decision making (MADM): in MADM, it is necessary to consider how to evaluate the accuracy of each factor weight estimated by the MEMR model for predicting future data or making new observations;
4. Extensions of the MEMR model: the model can be generalized to the problem involving panel data or time series data; we also need to consider the applications of the MEMR model in different fields, such as medicine, ecology, and finance, and how to customize and improve the model according to the needs of specific fields; how to adjust the model if considering a scenario where the expert defines factor weights in advance.

Author Contributions: Conceptualization, methodology, software, validation, formal analysis, resources, writing—original draft preparation, visualization, supervision, Q.-Y.T.; writing—review and editing, Y.-X.L. All authors have read and agreed to the published version of the manuscript.

Funding: This work was supported by the Hangzhou Ruifeng Information Technology Co., Ltd. We also received funding from the Ministry of Agriculture and Rural Affairs of China as part of the "Crop Disease and Pest Monitoring, Early Warning, and Control Services" project, under government procurement service code A120301.

Institutional Review Board Statement: Not applicable.

Informed Consent Statement: Not applicable.

Data Availability Statement: A part of the dataset utilized in this paper is openly available in CSDN Repository at https://download.csdn.net/download/weixin_42119432/12617871 (accessed on 1 January 2025). Other data are available within the article.

Acknowledgments: The authors thank Ming-Guang Feng, Chuan-Xi Zhang, Zeng-Rong Zhu and Kai-Tai Fang for their advice, comments, and suggestions.

Conflicts of Interest: The authors declare no conflicts of interest. The funders had no role in the design of the study; in the collection, analyses, or interpretation of data; in the writing of the manuscript; or in the decision to publish the results.

Abbreviations

The following abbreviations are used in this manuscript:

MCDM	Multiple criteria decision making
MADM	Multiple attribute decision making
CEI	Comprehensive evaluation index
BoD	Benefit of doubt
DEA	Data envelopment analysis
MEMR	Maximum entropy-minimum residual
ME	Maximum entropy
SUMT	Sequential unconstrained minimization technique
DPS	Data processing system
EW	Equal weighting
CV	Coefficient of variation
TAI	Technical achievement index
PCA	Principal component analysis
FA	Factor analysis
SD	Standard deviation
CRITIC	Criteria importance through intercriteria correlation
ET	Entropy weighting

Appendix A

Table A1. Original data for each factor in the technological achievement index of top 23 countries.

Region	Patents [1]	Royalties [2]	Internet [3]	Exports [4]	Telephones [5]	Electricity [6]	Schooling [7]	University [8]
Finland	187	125.6	200.2	50.7	3.08	4.15	10	27.4
US	289	130	179.1	66.2	3	4.07	12	13.9
Sweden	271	156.6	125.8	59.7	3.1	4.14	11.4	15.3
Japan	994	64.6	49	80.8	3	3.86	9.5	10
Korea	779	9.8	4.8	66.7	2.97	3.65	10.8	23.2
Netherlands	189	151.2	136	50.9	3.02	3.77	9.4	9.5
UK	82	134	57.4	61.9	3.02	3.73	9.4	14.9
Canada	31	38.6	108	48.7	2.94	4.18	11.6	14.2
Australia	75	18.2	125.9	16.2	2.94	3.94	10.9	25.3
Singapore	8	25.5	72.3	74.9	2.95	3.83	7.1	24.2
Germany	235	36.8	41.2	64.2	2.94	3.75	10.2	14.4
Norway	103	20.2	193.6	19	3.12	4.39	11.9	11.2
Ireland	106	110.3	48.6	53.6	2.97	3.68	9.4	12.3
Belgium	72	73.9	58.9	47.6	2.91	3.86	9.3	13.6
New Zealand	103	13	146.7	15.4	2.86	3.91	11.7	13.1
Austria	165	14.8	84.2	50.3	2.99	3.79	8.4	13.6
France	205	33.6	36.4	58.9	2.97	3.8	7.9	12.6
Israel	74	43.6	43.2	45	2.96	3.74	9.6	11
Spain	42	8.6	21	53.4	2.86	3.62	7.3	15.6
Italy	13	9.8	30.4	51	3	3.65	7.2	13
Czech Republic	28	4.2	25	51.7	2.75	3.68	9.5	8.2
Hungary	26	6.2	21.6	63.5	2.73	3.46	9.1	7.7
Slovenia	105	4	20.3	49.5	2.84	3.71	7.1	10.6

[1] Patents granted per 1,000,000 people; [2] US $ per 1000 people; [3] Internet hosts per 1000 people; [4] % exports of high and medium technology products as a share of total goods exports (1999); [5] Telephone lines per 1000 people (log); [6] kWh per capita (log); [7] Mean years of schooling (age 15 and above), which represents the basic education needed to develop cognitive skills; [8] % gross enrollment ratio of tertiary students enrolled in universities.

Table A2. An orthogonal table with 24 runs and 4 factors.

No.	x_1	x_2	x_3	x_4
1	1	1	1	1
2	1	1	2	4
3	2	1	3	3
4	2	1	4	2
5	2	1	1	8
6	2	1	2	5
7	1	1	3	6
8	1	1	4	7
9	1	2	1	2
10	1	2	2	3
11	2	2	3	4
12	2	2	4	1
13	2	2	1	7
14	2	2	2	6
15	1	2	3	5
16	1	2	4	8
17	1	3	1	2
18	1	3	2	3
19	2	3	3	4
20	2	3	4	1
21	2	3	1	7
22	2	3	2	6
23	1	3	3	5
24	1	3	4	8

References

1. Greco, S.; Ishizaka, A.; Tasiou, M.; Torrisi, G. On the methodological framework of composite indices: A review of the issues of weighting, aggregation, and robustness. *Soc. Indic. Res.* **2019**, *141*, 61–94. [CrossRef]
2. Joint Research Centre. *Handbook on Constructing Composite Indicators: Methodology and User Guide*; OECD Publishing: Paris, France, 2008.
3. Sharpe, A. *Literature Review of Frameworks for Macro-Indicators*; Centre for the study of Living Standards: Ottawa, ON, Canada, 2004; Volume 3.
4. Stiglitz, J.E. *Report by the Commission on the Measurement of Economic Performance and Social Progress*; Technical Report; The Commission: Paris, France, 2009.
5. Melyn, W.; Moesen, W. Towards a synthetic indicator of macroeconomic performance: Unequal weighting when limited information is available. *Public Econ. Res. Pap.* **1991**, *1991*, 1–24.
6. Cherchye, L.; Moesen, W.; Rogge, N.; Puyenbroeck, T.V. An introduction to 'benefit of the doubt' composite indicators. *Soc. Indic. Res.* **2007**, *82*, 111–145. [CrossRef]
7. Cherchye, L.; Moesen, W.; Rogge, N.; Puyenbroeck, T.V.; Saisana, M.; Saltelli, A.; Saltelli, A.; Liska, R.; Tarantola, S. Creating composite indicators with DEA and robustness analysis: The case of the Technology Achievement Index. *J. Oper. Res. Soc.* **2008**, *59*, 239–251. [CrossRef]
8. Bandura, R. *Composite Indicators and Rankings: Inventory 2011*; UNDP/ODS Working Paper; United Nations Development Programme, Office of Development Studies: New York, NY, USA, 2011.
9. Yang, L. *An Inventory of Composite Measures of Human Progress*; Occasional Paper on Methodology; United Nations Development Programme: New York, NY, USA, 2014.
10. Jaynes, E.T. Information theory and statistical mechanics. *Phys. Rev.* **1957**, *106*, 620. [CrossRef]
11. Golan, A.; Harte, J. Information theory: A foundation for complexity science. *Proc. Natl. Acad. Sci. USA* **2022**, *119*, e2119089119. [CrossRef]
12. Shannon, C.E. A mathematical theory of communication. *Bell Syst. Tech. J.* **1948**, *27*, 379–423. [CrossRef]
13. Jaynes, E.T. On the rationale of maximum-entropy methods. *Proc. IEEE* **1982**, *70*, 939–952. [CrossRef]
14. Tang, Q.Y.; Zhang, C.X. Data Processing System (DPS) software with experimental design, statistical analysis and data mining developed for use in entomological research. *Insect Sci.* **2013**, *20*, 254–260. [CrossRef] [PubMed]
15. Motulsky, H.; Christopoulos, A. *Fitting Models to Biological Data Using Linear and Nonlinear Regression: A Practical Guide to Curve Fitting*; Oxford University Press: Oxford, UK, 2004.
16. Bates, D.M.; Watts, D.G. *Nonlinear Regression Analysis and Its Applications*; John Wiley & Sons: Hoboken, NJ, USA, 1988.
17. Dunteman, G.H. *Principal Components Analysis*; Sage: Newcastle upon Tyne, UK, 1989; Volume 69.
18. Harman, H.H. *Modern Factor Analysis*; University of Chicago Press: Chicago, IL, USA, 1975.

19. Mukhametzyanov, I. Specific character of objective methods for determining weights of criteria in MCDM problems: Entropy, CRITIC and SD. *Decis. Mak. Appl. Manag. Eng.* **2021**, *4*, 76–105. [CrossRef]
20. Diakoulaki, D.; Mavrotas, G.; Papayannakis, L. Determining objective weights in multiple criteria problems: The critic method. *Comput. Oper. Res.* **1995**, *22*, 763–770. [CrossRef]
21. Su, W. *Comprehensive Evaluation: Basic Theory and Frontier Issues*; Science Press: Beijing, China, 2021. (In Chinese)
22. Rogge, N. Composite indicators as generalized benefit-of-the-doubt weighted averages. *Eur. J. Oper. Res.* **2018**, *267*, 381–392. [CrossRef]
23. Zhou, P.; Ang, B.W.; Poh, K.L. A mathematical programming approach to constructing composite indicators. *Ecol. Econ.* **2007**, *62*, 291–297. [CrossRef]
24. Ng, W.L. A simple classifier for multiple criteria ABC analysis. *Eur. J. Oper. Res.* **2007**, *177*, 344–353. [CrossRef]

entropy

MDPI

Article

Mean Squared Error Representative Points of Pareto Distributions and Their Estimation

Xinyang Li [1] and Xiaoling Peng [2,*]

[1] Faculty of Science and Technology, BNU-HKBU United International College, Zhuhai 519087, China; xinyli@uic.edu.cn

[2] Guangdong Provincial/Zhuhai Key Laboratory of IRADS, BNU-HKBU United International College, Zhuhai 519087, China

* Correspondence: xlpeng@uic.edu.cn

Abstract: Pareto distributions are widely applied in various fields, such as economics, finance, and environmental studies. The modeling of real-world data has created a demand for the discretization of Pareto distributions. In this paper, we propose using mean squared error representative points (MSE-RPs) as the discrete representation of Pareto distributions. We demonstrate the uniqueness and existence of these representative points under certain parameter settings and provide a theoretical k-means algorithm for the computation of MSE-RPs for Pareto I and Pareto II distributions. Furthermore, to enhance the applicability of MSE-RPs, we employ three methodological approaches to estimate the MSE-RPs of Pareto distributions. By analyzing the estimation bias under different parameters and methods, we recommend estimating the distribution parameters first before estimating the MSE-RPS for Pareto I and Pareto II distributions. For Pareto III and Pareto IV distributions, we suggest using the B_q quantiles for MSE-RP estimation. Building on this, we analyze the sources of estimation bias and propose an effective method for determining the number of MSE-RPs based on information gain truncation. Through simulations and real data studies, we demonstrate that the proposed methods for MSE-RP estimation are effective and can be used to fit the empirical distribution function of data accurately.

Keywords: Pareto distributions; MSE-RPs (mean squared error representative points); information gain-based truncation

1. Introduction

The Pareto distribution was originally introduced by the Italian economist Vilfredo Pareto in his seminal work on economics, where it was used as a model for income distribution [1]. Pareto observed that a small proportion of the population tends to control the majority of wealth—a phenomenon commonly referred to as the "80/20 rule", meaning that 20% of people own 80% of the income. Since then, this heavy-tailed distribution has been widely applied in fields such as economics, finance, and risk management [2], particularly for modeling phenomena characterized by significant inequality or extreme outcomes. Examples include modeling stock return distributions [3] and the extreme tails of financial and insurance loss datasets [4]. The classical Pareto distribution, often referred to as the Pareto Type I distribution, is defined by a skewed heavy-tailed model:

$$F_X(x) = 1 - \left(\frac{x}{\sigma}\right)^{-\alpha}, x \geq \sigma > 0, \alpha > 0, \quad (1)$$

https://doi.org/10.3390/e27030249

where $\sigma > 0$ is the scale parameter, typically representing the minimum income in income models, and $\alpha > 0$ is the shape parameter, commonly referred to as the Pareto index. The Pareto index α serves as a measure of inequality, with larger values indicating more equitable distributions. For income analysis, the Pareto index typically fluctuates around 1.5 [5].

While the Pareto Type I distribution performs well in modeling the income of high-income groups, it often fails to capture income distributions across the entire population. To address this limitation, economists and statisticians have extended the Pareto distribution by introducing additional flexibility through the location parameter μ and inequality parameter γ, resulting in the development of Pareto Type II, III, and IV distributions [6]. These generalized Pareto distributions have found broader applications. For instance, the Pareto Type II distribution is used for flood modeling and rainfall analysis [7], the Pareto Type III distribution is commonly applied to earthquake intensity modeling [8], and the Pareto Type IV distribution is employed in insurance risk analysis [9].

In statistical research, most studies on the Pareto family focus on data modeling and statistical inference. A major challenge in statistical inference lies in the complex expressions of the generalized Pareto family. Parameter estimation for the Pareto family often involves significant computational effort due to the lack of closed-form expressions for methods such as moment estimation (ME) and maximum likelihood estimation (MLE). Additionally, there has been a lot of research focus on the performance of parameter estimation in small samples and the robustness of these estimates [10–12]. In practical data modeling, it is often necessary to discretize continuous data into discrete models while retaining the desirable properties of continuous distributions. For example, Ghosh [13] proposed a discrete version of the Pareto IV distribution derived from rounding continuous random variables to improve the accuracy of lifetime modeling.

In this paper, we focus on the discretization of the Pareto family under the minimum mean squared error (MSE). In statistics, for a given continuous distribution, we can identify optimal discrete approximations, referred to as representative points (RPs), based on different kinds of errors. Different error metrics yield different types of RPs, such as mean squared error representative points (MSE-RPs) [14], Monte Carlo representative points (MC-RPs) [15], and quasi-Monte Carlo representative points (QMC-RPs) [16]. Among these, MSE-RPs are the most widely used, as they demonstrate superior performance over other RPs in distribution fitting [15].

MSE-RPs were initially applied to optimize signal transmission [17]. Since signal distortion in transmission is defined as the expected squared error between the quantizer input and output, which aligns with the MSE-RP criterion, Max successfully applied it to minimize signal distortion using quantizers with fixed output levels [18]. Fang and He [14] further advanced the computation and applications of MSE-RPs. Subsequently, MSE-RPs have been widely studied and applied in various fields, including clothing standardization [14], determining optimal sizes and shapes for protective masks [19], signal and image processing, information theory [20], psychiatric classification [21], statistical inference using resampling techniques [22], and reducing variance in one-dimensional Monte Carlo estimations [23]. They have also been utilized in parameter estimation, such as using MSE-RPs from the gamma distribution as standard samples to improve parameter estimation accuracy [24].

The majority of existing studies on MSE-RPs have focused on univariate continuous distributions, such as normal, exponential, gamma, Weibull, logistic, and mixed normal distributions. However, no studies have been conducted on MSE-RPs derived from Pareto distributions. Owing to the complexity of Pareto density functions, the study of MSE-RP generation and estimation presents significant challenges. Current studies propose two main approaches to generate MSE-RPs for continuous distributions. The first approach relies on the self-consistency property shared by MSE-RPs and k-means cluster centers, which has led to the development of k-means-based algorithms for generating MSE-RPs. This method was initially proposed by Lloyd [25] and Max [18], and is referred to as the Lloyd I algorithm, specifically designed for univariate continuous distributions. To mitigate the impact of initial values and training sets on MSE-RPs, Linde et al. [26] proposed an iterative algorithm, referred to as the LBG algorithm. Fang et al. [27] later developed an enhanced version of the LBG algorithm, employing number-theoretic methods to generate initial points and training sets, which is referred to as the NTLBG algorithm. The second approach derives from the definition of MSE-RPs, with the objective of finding a discrete distribution that minimizes the MSE between it and the density function. This involves solving a series of equations for obtaining the MSE-RPs, a method referred to as the Fang–He algorithm [14]. Compared to k-means based methods, the Fang–He algorithm offers greater accuracy in the computation of MSE-RPs. However, it requires verifying the convergence of the algorithm, which needs to be addressed separately for each specific distribution.

In practical applications, it is often necessary to optimally discretize continuous data, which involves estimating the MSE-RPs of the underlying continuous distribution that the data follow. Tarpey [28] proposed four methods for estimating the MSE-RPs of univariate continuous distributions: maximum likelihood estimation, semi-parametric estimation, quantile estimation, and the k-means algorithm. Subsequent research has expanded these methods. For instance, Matsuura et al. [29] developed an optimal estimation approach for the t-distribution and extended it to the location–scale family and multivariate distributions. In the case of the Pareto distribution, we primarily study the latter two methods for estimating MSE-RPs.

The Pareto distribution is a right-skewed distribution, where the estimation bias of the quantiles at the tail is relatively large. Consequently, when using the quantile method to estimate the MSE-RPs located in the tail, the bias will also be significant. Similarly, due to the smaller number of samples in the tail, the k-means method also introduces substantial bias. The inaccurate estimation of MSE-RPs in the tail increases the bias of the overall estimate. In fact, the amount of information contained in the MSE-RPs at the tail is very limited. This information can be quantified using information gain (IG), which has been applied to evaluate the information content of MSE-RPs in mixed normal distributions [30]. Based on this, we introduce a truncation method based on IG to determine the sufficient number of MSE-RPs. This approach aims to reduce the estimation bias while preserving as much information as possible in the MSE-RPs.

In conclusion, our study focus on the generation and estimation of MSE-RPs for the four types of Pareto distributions. We examine the properties of MSE-RPs for Pareto distributions and propose a reliable algorithm for their generation based on the properties. In addition, simulation results reveal that existing methods for estimating MSE-RPs suffer from significant bias when applied to skewed and heavy-tailed distributions. To address this issue, we introduce the innovative concept of IG-truncated representative points. This approach also provides a new perspective for estimating MSE-RPs for other heavy-tailed distributions.

The structure of this paper is as follows: Section 2 introduces the fundamentals of the Pareto family. Section 3 presents the MSE-RPs of Pareto distributions, including their properties, computation methods, and results. Section 4 compares different methods for estimating the MSE-RPs of Pareto distributions and proposes an IG-based truncation method for selecting the number of MSE-RPs. In Section 5, a real dataset is analyzed in order to illustrate the proposed methods. Finally, this paper is concluded in Section 6.

2. Preliminaries of Pareto Distributions

2.1. Four Types of Pareto Distributions

The two-parameter Pareto distribution was first introduced by Vilfredo Pareto, and its cumulative distribution function (CDF) is given in Equation (1). This distribution is also known as the Pareto Type I distribution, denoted as $X \sim P(I)(\sigma, \alpha)$.

Building upon this, Pareto proposed two additional variations. The Pareto Type II distribution, also known as the Lomax distribution, is a three-parameter distribution derived from the analysis of business failure data [31]. Its CDF is given by

$$F_X(x) = 1 - \left(1 + \frac{x - \mu}{\sigma}\right)^{-\alpha}, x \geq \mu, \sigma, \alpha > 0, \tag{2}$$

where μ is the location parameter, generally assumed to be non-negative. Additionally, $\alpha > 1$ is required to ensure a finite expected value. This distribution is denoted as $P(II)(\mu, \sigma, \alpha)$.

The Pareto Type III distribution is another three-parameter distribution, and its CDF is defined as follows:

$$F_X(x) = 1 - \left(1 + \left(\frac{x - \mu}{\sigma}\right)^{\frac{1}{\gamma}}\right)^{-1}, x > \mu, \sigma, \gamma > 0, \tag{3}$$

denoted as $P(III)(\mu, \sigma, \gamma)$. When $\mu = 0$ and $\gamma \leq 1$, the parameter γ represents the Gini index for inequality.

In 1983, Arnold introduced the Pareto Type IV distribution, also referred to as the Burr distribution. Its CDF is expressed as follows:

$$F_X(x) = 1 - \left(1 + \left(\frac{x - \mu}{\sigma}\right)^{\frac{1}{\gamma}}\right)^{-\alpha}, x \geq \mu, \sigma, \gamma, \alpha > 0, \tag{4}$$

denoted as $Pareto(IV)(\mu, \sigma, \gamma, \alpha)$.

The four types of Pareto distributions are not entirely independent and can be transformed into one another by adjusting the parameters. Specifically, Pareto(I), Pareto(II), and Pareto(III) distributions are special cases of the Pareto(IV) distribution. These relationships are expressed as follows:

$$\begin{aligned} P(I)(\sigma, \alpha) &= P(IV)(\sigma, \sigma, 1, \alpha), \\ P(II)(\mu, \sigma, \alpha) &= P(IV)(\mu, \sigma, 1, \alpha), \\ P(III)(\mu, \sigma, \gamma) &= P(IV)(\mu, \sigma, \gamma, 1). \end{aligned} \tag{5}$$

By modifying the parameters of the Pareto IV distribution, the other three types can be derived. Thus, Pareto I, II, and III can all be viewed as special cases of the Pareto IV distribution.

In its early development, the Pareto distribution was considered a specific form of the exponential distribution, as it can be transformed into an exponential distribution. If $U \sim \Gamma(1,1)$ is a standard exponential random variable, then $X = \sigma e^{\frac{U}{\alpha}} \sim P(I)(\sigma, \alpha)$ and $Y = \mu + \sigma\left(e^{\frac{U}{\alpha}} - 1\right) \sim P(II)(\mu, \sigma, \alpha)$.

Furthermore, all four types of Pareto distributions can be transformed into their standard forms by adjusting their parameters. For $k > 0$ and $\gamma > 0$, the following hold:

- If $X \sim P(I)(1, \alpha)$, then
$$Z = \sigma X^{1/k} \sim P(I)(\sigma, k\alpha). \tag{6}$$

- If $X \sim P(II)(0,1,\alpha)$, then

$$Z = \mu - \sigma + \sigma(1+X)^{1/k} \sim P(II)(\mu,\sigma,k\alpha). \tag{7}$$

- If $X \sim P(III)(0,1,1)$, then

$$Z = \mu + \sigma X^{\gamma} \sim P(III)(\mu,\sigma,\gamma). \tag{8}$$

- If $X \sim P(IV)(0,1,1,\alpha)$, then

$$Z = \mu + \sigma\left[(1+X)^{1/k} - 1\right]^{\gamma} \sim P(IV)(\mu,\sigma,\gamma,k\alpha). \tag{9}$$

2.2. Parameter Estimation of Pareto Distributions

Although numerous studies have explored parameter estimation for Pareto distributions, most focus on the Pareto Type I distribution due to its simplicity, widespread use, and interpretability. Here, we divide the discussion into two parts: parameter estimation for the Pareto Type I distribution and for the Pareto Type II–IV distributions.

1. Pareto Type I Distribution:
    (a) Maximum Likelihood Estimation (MLE): Assume a sample $X_1,\ldots,X_n$ is drawn from $P(I)(\sigma,\alpha)$, and let $X_{(n,1)} < \cdots < X_{(n,n)}$ denote the order statistics. The likelihood function is given by

    $$L(\alpha,\sigma \mid X_1,\ldots,X_n) = \prod_{i=1}^{n} \frac{\alpha\sigma^{\alpha}}{X_i^{\alpha+1}} I(\sigma \le X_{(n,1)}). \tag{10}$$

    When α is known, the likelihood function is a decreasing function of σ. Thus, the MLE of σ is

    $$\hat{\sigma}_{ML} = X_{(n,1)}. \tag{11}$$

    Taking the logarithm of the likelihood function and differentiating with respect to α yields

    $$\hat{\alpha}_{ML} = \frac{n}{\sum_{i=1}^{n}\log(X_i/\hat{\sigma}_{ML})}. \tag{12}$$

    While MLE is asymptotically consistent, normal, and efficient, it is not the minimum variance unbiased estimator (MVUE). The MVUE for this distribution is given by

    $$\hat{\sigma}^{U} = \left[1-(n-1)^{-1}\hat{\alpha}_{ML}^{-1}\right]\hat{\sigma}_{ML}, \quad \hat{\alpha}^{U} = \frac{n-2}{n}\hat{\alpha}_{ML}. \tag{13}$$

    (b) Moment Estimation (ME): For a Pareto Type I distribution with $\alpha > 1$, the first moment is

    $$E(X) = \frac{\alpha\sigma}{\alpha-1}, \quad \alpha > 1. \tag{14}$$

    Using the first moment, the method of moments estimators are as follows:

    $$\hat{\alpha}_{ME} = \frac{n\overline{X} - X_{(n,1)}}{n(\overline{X} - X_{(n,1)})}, \quad \hat{\sigma}_{ME} = \left(1 - \frac{1}{n\hat{\alpha}_{ME}}\right)X_{(n,1)}. \tag{15}$$

    While $\hat{\alpha}_{ME}$ requires $\alpha > 1$, $\hat{\sigma}_{ME}$ does not rely on this condition, as it is derived from the CDF of $X_{(n,1)}$ [10]. Simulations by Lu and Tao [32] indicate that ME performs better than MLE for estimating σ, provided the estimation of σ is independent of α.
2. Pareto Type II–IV Distributions:

(a) Maximum Likelihood Estimation (MLE): For simplicity, we focus on the Pareto Type IV distribution, as Pareto Types II and III are special cases (see Equation (5)). The likelihood function for a sample $X_1, \dots, X_n$ from $P(IV)(\mu, \sigma, \gamma, \alpha)$ is

$$\begin{aligned} L(\mu,\sigma,\gamma,\alpha \mid X_1,\dots,X_n) = &\left(\frac{1}{\gamma}-1\right)\sum_{i=1}^{n}\log\left(\frac{X_i-\mu}{\sigma}\right) \\ &-(\alpha+1)\sum_{i=1}^{n}\log\left(1+\left(\frac{X_i-\mu}{\sigma}\right)^{1/\gamma}\right) \\ &-n\log\gamma - n\log\sigma + n\log\alpha. \end{aligned} \tag{16}$$

The order statistic $X_{(n,1)}$ serves as a consistent estimator of μ. Once μ is estimated, the problem can be reduced to estimating the parameters of $P(IV)(0, \sigma, \gamma, \alpha)$ using the remaining $n-1$ samples, $X_{(n,2)}, \dots, X_{(n,n)}$. Taking partial derivatives of the log-likelihood function with respect to σ, γ, and α yields

$$\begin{aligned} \frac{\partial \log L}{\partial \sigma} &= \frac{\alpha(n-1)}{\gamma\sigma} - \frac{\alpha+1}{\gamma\sigma}\sum_{i=1}^{n-1}\frac{1}{1+(X_i/\sigma)^{1/\gamma}} = 0, \\ \frac{\partial \log L}{\partial \gamma} &= \frac{\alpha}{\gamma^2}\sum_{i=1}^{n-1}\log\left(\frac{X_i}{\sigma}\right) - \frac{\alpha+1}{\gamma^2}\sum_{i=1}^{n-1}\frac{\log(X_i/\sigma)}{1+(X_i/\sigma)^{1/\gamma}} - \frac{n-1}{\gamma} = 0, \\ \frac{\partial \log L}{\partial \alpha} &= -\sum_{i=1}^{n-1}\log\left(1+\left(\frac{X_i}{\sigma}\right)^{1/\gamma}\right) + \frac{n-1}{\alpha} = 0. \end{aligned} \tag{17}$$

Solving these equations yields the MLEs for $P(IV)(0, \sigma, \gamma, \alpha)$.

(b) Moment Estimation (ME): Direct computation of moments for Pareto distributions is challenging. Arnold proposed a method based on constructing a statistic relying on the Gamma distribution [6]. Define

$$X = \mu + \sigma\left(\frac{U_1}{U_2}\right)^{\gamma} \sim P(IV)(\mu, \sigma, \gamma, \alpha), \tag{18}$$

where $U_1 \sim \Gamma(1,1)$ and $U_2 \sim \Gamma(\alpha, 1)$ are independent. Using the moments of the Gamma distribution, the δ-th moment of X is

$$E(X^{\delta}) = \sigma^{\delta}\frac{\Gamma(1+\delta\gamma)\Gamma(\alpha-\delta\gamma)}{\Gamma(\alpha)}, \quad -\frac{1}{\gamma} < \delta < \frac{\alpha}{\gamma}. \tag{19}$$

By constructing equations from these moments and using $X_{(n,1)}$ as a consistent estimator of μ, the moment estimators for Pareto Type IV distributions can be obtained. However, the existence of moments depends on the parameter conditions.

3. MSE-RPs of Pareto Distributions

3.1. Definition and Properties of MSE-RPs

Given a continuous random variable $\mathbf{X} \sim F(\mathbf{x})$, a set of points $\{\mathbf{y}_i \in \mathbb{R}^d, i \in \{1, \dots, m\}\}$ and their associated probabilities form the MSE-RPs of $F(x)$ if and only if the following condition is satisfied:

$$E[d^2(\mathbf{x}|\mathbf{y}_1, \dots, \mathbf{y}_m)] = \min_{\substack{\xi_i \in \mathbb{R}^d \\ i=1,\dots,m}} E[d^2(\mathbf{x}|\xi_1, \dots, \xi_m)], \tag{20}$$

where

$$d^2(\mathbf{x}|\boldsymbol{\xi}_1,\ldots,\boldsymbol{\xi}_m) = \min_{j\in\{1,\ldots,m\}} \|\mathbf{x}-\boldsymbol{\xi}_j\| \tag{21}$$

represents the minimum ℓ_2-norm distance between $\mathbf{x}$ and $\boldsymbol{\xi}_j$, $j \in \{1,\ldots,m\}$.

The probability of $\mathbf{y}_i \in \mathbb{R}^d$ is given by $P(\mathbf{y}_i) = P(\mathbf{X} \mid \mathbf{X} \in V_i)$, where

$$V_i = \{\mathbf{x} \in \mathbb{R}^d \mid (\mathbf{x}-\mathbf{y}_i)'(\mathbf{x}-\mathbf{y}_i) \leqslant (\mathbf{x}-\mathbf{y}_j)'(\mathbf{x}-\mathbf{y}_j),\ \forall i \neq j\},\ i \in \{1,\ldots,m\}. \tag{22}$$

MSE-RPs essentially represent the discretization of a continuous distribution. Through $\mathbf{y}_i$ and their associated probabilities, the support of the continuous distribution is divided into m adjacent and non-overlapping regions, known as Voronoi partitions. For each partition V_i, its center $\mathbf{y}_i$ satisfies

$$E[\mathbf{X} \mid \mathbf{X} \in V_i] = \mathbf{y}_i, \quad i = 1,\ldots,m. \tag{23}$$

These centers are also referred to as self-consistent points. Tarpey and Flury [33] proved that the set of self-consistent points minimizing the MSE is precisely the set of MSE-RPs.

For one-dimensional continuous distributions, MSE-RPs can be arranged as $y_1 < y_2 < \cdots < y_m$. In this case, the probability corresponding to y_i is given by

$$P_m(y_i) = \int_{M_i}^{M_{i+1}} f(x)\,dx, \quad i = 1,\ldots,m, \tag{24}$$

where $M_1 = F^{-1}(0)$, $M_i = \frac{y_{i-1}+y_i}{2}$, $i = 2,\ldots,m$, and $M_{m+1} = F^{-1}(1)$.

For location–scale distributions with standard forms, it suffices to study their MSE-RPs in the standard case. These standard MSE-RPs can then be extended to the full parameter space using the location–scale transformation properties of MSE-RPs proposed by Zoppè [34]. Since the Pareto Type IV distribution belongs to the location–scale family and Pareto Types I-III are special cases of it, we focus on the MSE-RPs of $P(IV)(0,1,\gamma,\alpha)$. This leads to the following corollary.

Corollary 1. *If $\{y_i, i = 1,\ldots,m\}$ are the m MSE-RPs of $P(IV)(0,1,\gamma,\alpha)$, then $\{z_i = \sigma y_i + \mu, i = 1,\ldots,m\}$ are the m MSE-RPs of $P(IV)(\mu,\sigma,\gamma,\alpha)$.*

3.2. Existence and Uniqueness

The existence of MSE-RPs for a continuous distribution requires that its first two moments exist [35]. For Pareto distributions, the conditions for the existence of the second moment are as follows:

$$\begin{aligned} P(I)(\sigma,\alpha):&\quad \alpha > 2, \\ P(II)(\mu,\sigma,\alpha):&\quad \alpha > 2, \\ P(III)(\mu,\sigma,\gamma):&\quad 0 < \gamma < \frac{1}{2}, \\ P(IV)(\mu,\sigma,\gamma,\alpha):&\quad \frac{\alpha}{\gamma} > 2. \end{aligned} \tag{25}$$

If the parameters of a Pareto distribution do not satisfy the above conditions, its MSE-RPs do not exist.

Next, we examine the shape of the density function. According to the theorem by Trushkin [36], if the density function $f(x)$ of a continuous distribution is unimodal and log-concave, the MSE-RPs of the distribution are unique. The density function of $P(IV)(0,1,\gamma,\alpha)$ is unimodal, and we provide the following lemma regarding its shape.

Lemma 1. *Let $x \sim P(IV)(0,1,\gamma,\alpha)$, with $\frac{1}{\gamma} > 1$. Define a random variable $z = \frac{x^{1/\gamma}}{1+x^{1/\gamma}}, 0 < z < 1$. Then, there exists a z_2^* given by*

$$z_2^* = \frac{(\alpha+1)\left(\frac{1}{\gamma}-1\right) + \sqrt{(\alpha+1)^2\left(\frac{1}{\gamma}-1\right)^2 + 4(\alpha+1)\left(\frac{1}{\gamma}-1\right)}}{2(\alpha+1)/\gamma}, \tag{26}$$

such that when $z \in (0, z_2^*)$, the density function of $P(IV)(0,1,\gamma,\alpha)$ is log-concave. Moreover, as $\alpha \to +\infty$, $z_2^* \to 1-\gamma$.

We prove that the density function is log-concave by demonstrating that its logarithmic first derivative is a strictly decreasing function. The detailed proof is provided in Appendix A. Using this theorem, we establish the existence and uniqueness of the MSE-RPs for the Pareto IV distribution under the condition $\frac{1}{\gamma} > 1$.

For other parameter settings where the density function is not log-concave, we rely on proving the uniqueness of the solutions to the system of equations to demonstrate the uniqueness of the MSE-RPs. This approach was proposed by Fang and He [14] in their proof of the uniqueness of MSE-RPs for the normal distribution. The method involves showing that the equations derived from setting the first derivative of (20) to zero have a unique solution.

By taking the partial derivative of (20), we obtain

$$\frac{\partial E[d^2(x \mid y_1, \ldots, y_m)]}{\partial y_i} = 0, \quad i = 1, \ldots, m, \tag{27}$$

which simplifies to the following system of equations:

$$L_i = \int_{M_i}^{M_{i+1}} (x - y_i) f(x)\, dx = 0, \quad i = 1, \ldots, m. \tag{28}$$

For $i = 1, \ldots, m-1$, taking the partial derivative of L_i with respect to y_{i+1} gives

$$\frac{\partial L_i}{\partial y_{i+1}} = \frac{1}{2} f(M_{i+1})(M_{i+1} - y_i) > 0, \quad i = 1, \ldots, m-1. \tag{29}$$

Similarly, for L_m, taking the partial derivative with respect to y_m yields

$$\frac{\partial L_m}{\partial y_m} = \frac{1}{2} f(M_i)(-M_m + y_m) < 0. \tag{30}$$

From (29) and (30), it can be seen that for the i-th equation, given that $y_{j,j<i+1}$ are known, the equation has a unique solution for y_{i+1}. When solving the system of equations, an initial value is typically assigned to y_1, and the values are sequentially substituted into the equations to solve for subsequent variables. For $m-1$ unknowns, there are m equations, with the last two equations both involving y_m. By iteratively comparing the solutions of the last two equations for y_m, the system converges to a unique solution when the two solutions are equal.

Next, we analyze the existence conditions for solutions to the system of Equations (29) and (30) for $P(IV)(0,1,\gamma,\alpha)$. It is known that L_i is a monotonic function of y_{i+1}, where $y_{i+1} > 0$. The condition for the existence of a solution to $L_i = 0$ is

$$L_i(y_{i+1} \to y_i) * L_i(y_{i+1} \to +\infty) < 0. \tag{31}$$

Theorem 1. *For the Pareto distribution $P(IV)(0,1,\gamma,\alpha)$, the system of Equation (29) has a unique solution when $y_1 < E(X)$ and $\{y_i < \frac{E(X)-\sum_{j=1}^{i-1} y_j}{1-F(M_i)}, i = 2,\ldots,m-1\}$.*

The proof is provided in Appendix A.

3.3. Generation of MSE-RPs

From the definition of MSE-RPs, it can be seen that solving for MSE-RPs is essentially an optimization problem concerning (20). The conditions for the existence of a solution to this optimization problem are strict, and it may not be possible to derive explicit solutions for MSE-RPs by taking partial derivatives of the objective function. To address this issue, Fang and He [14] proposed an iterative method for solving a system of nonlinear Equation (28). Alternatively, MSE-RPs can also be obtained by leveraging their property as a set of self-consistent points that minimize the mean squared error (MSE). Since the centroids of the k-means algorithm are also self-consistent points, when MSE-RPs exist and are unique, k-means can be used to find the centroids, with the set of centroids that minimizes the MSE being the MSE-RPs. This method is efficient and fast but requires multiple iterations until the results stabilize and may converge to a local minimum.

To address the drawbacks of these methods, Xu et al. [37] proposed a k-means method based on the special properties of MSE-RPs for exponential distributions. This method avoids solving large systems of nonlinear equations and prevents k-means from converging to local minima. Inspired by this, we propose a similar method for generating MSE-RPs for Pareto distributions.

For Pareto I and II distributions, substituting their density functions into the last equation in (28) and simplifying yields

$$\begin{aligned} P(I)(1,\alpha) :& \frac{\alpha}{-\alpha+1}x^{-\alpha+1} + y_m x^{-\alpha}\Big|_{(y_{m-1}+y_m)/2}^{+\infty} = 0. \\ P(II)(0,1,\alpha) :& \frac{\alpha}{-\alpha+1}(1+x)^{-\alpha+1} + (1+y_m)(1+x)^{-\alpha}\Big|_{(y_{m-1}+y_m)/2}^{+\infty} = 0. \end{aligned} \tag{32}$$

Simplifying further, we obtain

$$\begin{aligned} P(I)(1,\alpha) :& \alpha y_{m-1} + (2-\alpha)y_m = 0. \\ P(II)(0,1,\alpha) :& \alpha y_{m-1} + 2 + (2-\alpha)y_m = 0. \end{aligned} \tag{33}$$

These equations describe the relationship between the last two points in a set of MSE-RPs for Pareto I and II distributions, leading to the following theorems.

Theorem 2. *Suppose $y_1 < y_2 < \ldots < y_m$ are the m MSE-RPs of a Pareto distribution $P(I)(1,\alpha|\alpha > 2)$. Then, the following relationship holds for y_{m-1} and y_m:*

$$y_m = \frac{\alpha y_{m-1}}{\alpha - 2}. \tag{34}$$

Theorem 3. *Suppose $y_1 < y_2 < \ldots < y_m$ are the m MSE-RPs of a Pareto distribution $P(II)(0,1,\alpha|\alpha > 2)$. Then, the following relationship holds for y_{m-1} and y_m:*

$$y_m = \frac{\alpha y_{m-1} + 2}{\alpha - 2}. \tag{35}$$

Unfortunately, for Pareto III and IV distributions, no similar theorems exist. Therefore, we propose the following Algorithm 1 for Pareto I and II distributions.

Algorithm 1: Theoretical k-means algorithm for Pareto I and II distributions

Step 1: For a given pdf $p(x)$, the number of MSE-RPs m, initial iteration $t = 0$, and tolerance ϵ, input an initial set of number-theoretic methods representative points (NTM-RPs) [16] $y_1^{(t)} < y_2^{(t)} < \ldots < y_m^{(t)}$. Define a partition of $\mathbb{R}$ as:

$$I_i^{(t)} = \left(a_i^{(t)}, a_{i+1}^{(t)}\right],\ i = 1, \ldots, m-1,\ I_m^{(t)} = \left(a_{m-1}^{(t)}, a_m^{(t)}\right),$$

where

$$a_1^{(t)} = -\infty, \quad a_i^{(t)} = \frac{y_{i-1}^{(t)} + y_i^{(t)}}{2},\ i = 2, \ldots, m, \quad a_m^{(t)} = \infty.$$

Step 2: Calculate probabilities:

$$p_j^{(t)} = \int_{I_j^{(t)}} p(x)\,dx,\ j = 1, \ldots, m;$$

Step 3: Calculate conditional means:

For $j = 1, \ldots, m-1$:

$$y_j^{(t+1)} = \frac{\int_{I_j^{(t)}} x p(x)\,dx}{\int_{I_j^{(t)}} p(x)\,dx} = \frac{\int_{I_j^{(t)}} x p(x)\,dx}{p_j^{(t)}},\ j = 1, \ldots, m-1.$$

For $P(I)(1, \alpha)$:

$$y_m^{(t+1)} = \frac{\alpha}{\alpha - 2} y_{m-1}^{(t+1)}.$$

For $P(II)(0, 1, \alpha)$:

$$y_m^{(t+1)} = \frac{\alpha y_{m-1}^{(t+1)} + 2}{\alpha - 2}.$$

Step 4: Sort $\{y_1^{(t+1)}, \ldots, y_m^{(t+1)}\}$ from smallest to largest.

Step 5: Calculate $|y_m^{(t+1)} - b|$, where

$$b = \frac{\int_{I_m^{(t)}} x p(x)\,dx}{p_m^{(t)}}.$$

Step 6: If $|y_m^{(t+1)} - b| < \epsilon$, the process stops, and $\{y_j^{(t)}\}$ are delivered as the MSE-RPs of the distribution with probabilities $\{p_j^{(t)}\}$. Otherwise, let $t := t + 1$ and return to Step 1.

This method not only guarantees that the points obtained are MSE-RPs by leveraging Theorems 2 and 3, but also significantly improves convergence speed by replacing the computation of y_m.

For Pareto III and IV distributions, solving (28) directly is challenging due to the presence of terms such as $x^{1/\gamma}, x^{2/\gamma}, \ldots, x^{(\gamma-1)/\gamma}$ and $\ln(1 + x^{1/\gamma})$, which make the equations complex and computationally expensive. Thus, we also adopt the k-means method (Algorithm 2) for obtaining MSE-RPs for these distributions [38].

Algorithm 2: Parametric k-means algorithm

Step 1: For a given pdf $p(x)$, the number of MSE-RPs m, and initial iteration $t = 0$, input an initial set of points $y_1^{(t)} < y_2^{(t)} < \ldots < y_m^{(t)}$. Define a partition of $\mathbb{R}$ as:

$$I_i^{(t)} = \left(a_i^{(t)}, a_{i+1}^{(t)}\right],\ i = 1, \ldots, m-1,\ I_m^{(t)} = \left(a_{m-1}^{(t)}, a_m^{(t)}\right),$$

where:

$$a_1^{(t)} = -\infty,\ a_i^{(t)} = \frac{y_{i-1}^{(t)} + y_i^{(t)}}{2},\ i = 2, \ldots, m,\ a_m^{(t)} = \infty.$$

Step 2: Calculate probabilities:

$$p_j^{(t)} = \int_{I_j^{(t)}} p(x)dx,\ j = 1, \ldots, m;$$

Step 3: Calculate conditional means:

$$y_j^{(t+1)} = \frac{\int_{I_j^{(t)}} xp(x)dx}{\int_{I_j^{(t)}} p(x)dx} = \frac{\int_{I_j^{(t)}} xp(x)dx}{p_j^{(t)}}, j = 1, \cdots, m.$$

Step 4: If $\{y_j^{(t)}\}$ and $\{y_j^{(t+1)}\}$ are identical, the process stops, and $\{y_j^{(t)}\}$ are delivered as the MSE-RPs of the distribution with probabilities $\{p_j^{(t)}\}$. Otherwise, let $t := t + 1$ and return to Step 1.

Using the parametric k-means method is highly effective for calculating MSE-RPs. However, this method cannot guarantee that the output is always the MSE-RPs and may instead converge to other sets of self-consistent points, as pointed out by Stampfer and Stadlober [38]. Therefore, we maximize the sample size for each calculation and select the set of points with the smallest MSE until the results stabilize. Since calculating MSE-RPs for Pareto III and IV distributions is slow, we provide up to 31 MSE-RPs and their corresponding probabilities for reference in Appendix B.

4. Estimation of MSE-RPs from Pareto Distributions

Currently, methods for estimating MSE-RPs from a sample can be categorized into three types based on whether the underlying distribution type and parameters are known:

1. The first type requires knowledge of the distribution type. After estimating the distribution parameters, the MSE-RPs are computed directly from the estimated distribution.
2. The second type also requires knowledge of the distribution type but does not involve parameter estimation. Instead, it estimates MSE-RPs by locating the sample quantiles corresponding to the positions of MSE-RPs. This method is limited to distributions with location–scale properties.
3. The third type does not require any prior information about the distribution. It directly estimates MSE-RPs from the sample by leveraging the property that k-means cluster centers are also self-consistent points. MSE-RPs are estimated as the centers of clusters formed by classifying the sample.

For the first type of method, estimating MSE-RPs for Pareto distributions, faces challenges regardless of whether the method of ME or MLE is used. The ME method requires the existence of moments, while the MLE method is computationally complex, making it difficult to achieve accurate results. Therefore, in the simulations presented in this paper, we estimate MSE-RPs under the assumption that the parameters γ and α are known, and only μ and σ are estimated. Specifically, our estimates are as follows:

- For a sample following $P(I)(\hat{\sigma}, \alpha)$, the MSE-RPs are estimated as

$$\hat{\mathbf{y}} = \hat{\sigma}\mathbf{y},$$

  where $\mathbf{y}$ are the MSE-RPs of $P(I)(1, \alpha)$.
- For a sample following $P(IV)(\hat{\mu}, \hat{\sigma}, \gamma, \alpha)$, the MSE-RPs are estimated as

$$\hat{\mathbf{y}} = \hat{\sigma}\mathbf{y} + \hat{\mu},$$

  where $\mathbf{y}$ are the MSE-RPs of $P(IV)(0, 1, \gamma, \alpha)$.

The second type of method views MSE-RPs as specific quantiles of the distribution. For distributions with location–scale properties, the positions of quantiles remain unchanged under parameter transformation. Thus, the MSE-RPs can be estimated by determining their corresponding quantile positions in the standard distribution and then estimating these quantiles in the sample. The steps are as follows:

1. Compute the MSE-RPs $y_1, \ldots, y_m$ of the continuous distribution $F(x)$.
2. Compute the positions q_i of y_i in the standard distribution $F(x)$:

$$q_i = \int_{-\infty}^{y_i} f(x)\, dx, \quad i = 1, \ldots, m.$$

3. In an independent and identically distributed sample $S_1, \ldots, S_n$, estimate the sample quantiles $Q(q_i)$ for $i = 1, \ldots, m$, which serve as the estimated MSE-RPs for the sample.

The accuracy of this method depends heavily on the choice of the quantile estimation method. Different distributions have unique characteristics, and the optimal method for quantile estimation may vary. Since the Pareto distribution is a heavy-tailed distribution, we consider the following four quantile estimation methods, which are known to perform well in the tails of distributions. Consider estimating the quantile $Q(q)$; the sample size is n and $X(i)$ is the i-th order statistic of the sample:

- HD_q quantile estimator [39]:

$$HD_q = \sum_{i=1}^{n} \left[\int_{i-1/n}^{i/n} \frac{\Gamma(n+1)}{\Gamma((n+1)q)\Gamma((n+1)p)} t^{(n+1)q-1}(1-t)^{(n+1)p-1}\, dt \right] X_{(i)}, \quad p = 1 - q. \tag{36}$$

- B_q quantile estimator [40]:

$$B_q = \sum_{i=1}^{n} \left[n^{-1} \cdot \frac{\Gamma(n+1)}{\Gamma(i)\Gamma(n-i+1)} q^{i-1}(1-q)^{n-i} \right] X_{(i)}. \tag{37}$$

- Q_j quantile estimator [41]:
  1. Choose an increasing sequence of proportions $\{q_0, q_1, \cdots, q_{m-1}, q_m\}$, where $q_0 = 0$ and $q_m = 1$, with $m \leq n$ corresponding to the cumulative probabilities of each quantile.
  2. Estimate the quantiles as follows:

$$Q_j = X_{(I_j^-)} + \left(X_{(I_j^+)} - X_{(I_j^-)} \right)\left(I_j - I_j^- \right), \quad j = 1, \ldots, (m-1). \tag{38}$$

  $I_j = q_j n + 1/2$, I_j^- is the largest integer less than or equal to I_j, and I_j^+ is the smallest integer greater than or equal to I_j.

- NO quantile estimator [42]:

$$
\begin{aligned}
NO_q = & (B(0;n,q)2q + B(1;n,q)q)X_{(1)} + B(0;n,q)(2-3q)X_{(2)} - B(0;n,q)(1-q)X_{(3)} \\
& + \sum_{i=1}^{n-2}(B(i;n,q)(1-q) + B(i+1;n,q)q)X_{(i+1)} \\
& - B(n;n,q)qX_{(n-2)} + B(n;n,q)(3q-1)X_{(n-1)} \\
& + (B(n-1;n,q)(1-q) + B(n;n,q)(2-2q))X_{(n)}.
\end{aligned} \tag{39}
$$

$B(i;n,q)$ is the binomial probability and q is the probability of success.

The first two methods are modifications of kernel-based quantile estimation methods, optimized by selecting the best bandwidth under various conditions. The last two methods adjust sample quantiles based on order statistics.

We apply these methods to estimate the MSE-RPs for $P(I)(1,5)$, $P(II)(0,1,5)$, $P(III)(0,1,0.2)$, and $P(IV)(0,1,0.1,0.5)$, and three sample sizes. Each method is tested through 1000 simulations, and the bias is reported in Table 1. Here, n represents the sample size, m represents the number of MSE-RPs, and the bias is calculated as follows:

$$ac = \text{average}\left(\left|\widehat{\text{RPs}} - \text{RPs}\right|\right).$$

Table 1. Comparison of mean absolute bias from 1000 simulations in MSE-RP estimation based on sample sizes ($n = 20, 50, 100$) and the number of MSE-RPs ($m = 5, 10, 17$) for four types of Pareto distributions using different methods.

				$P(I)(1,5)$				
		k-means	HD_q	B_q	Q_j	NO	MLE	ME
n = 20	m = 5	0.6244	0.7308	0.5248	0.5949	0.5831	**0.0215**	0.0926
	m = 10	1.1965	1.3143	0.9585	0.9729	1.0274	**0.0260**	0.1136
n = 50	m = 5	0.4999	0.4832	0.4027	0.4299	0.4524	**0.0084**	0.0588
	m = 10	1.0495	1.1282	0.8115	0.8270	0.8827	**0.0098**	0.0734
	m = 17	1.5442	1.4437	1.1951	1.2309	1.2693	**0.0122**	0.0830
n = 100	m = 5	0.4330	0.3619	0.3340	0.4179	0.3675	**0.0040**	0.0403
	m = 10	0.9402	0.9950	0.7154	0.7582	0.7707	**0.0005**	0.0165
	m = 17	1.4375	1.3352	1.0844	1.1220	1.1584	**0.0061**	0.0582
				$P(II)(0,1,5)$				
		k-means	HD_q	B_q	Q_j	NO	MLE	ME
n = 20	m = 5	0.6327	0.6391	0.5318	0.5909	0.5881	0.3004	**0.2449**
	m = 10	1.2019	1.1455	0.9519	0.9672	1.0334	0.4343	**0.3501**
n = 50	m = 5	0.5001	0.4517	0.4005	0.4242	0.4579	0.1676	**0.1480**
	m = 10	1.0482	1.0016	0.8047	0.8201	0.8769	0.2341	**0.2215**
	m = 17	1.2133	1.2449	0.9206	0.9530	0.9812	0.3084	**0.2775**
n = 100	m = 5	0.4191	0.3445	0.3212	0.4027	0.3611	0.1116	**0.1074**
	m = 10	0.9367	0.8971	0.7084	0.7551	0.7698	0.1646	**0.1542**
	m = 17	1.1286	1.1215	0.8195	0.8511	0.8836	0.2091	**0.1985**

Table 1. *Cont.*

		$P(III)(0,1,0.2)$						
		k-means	HD_q	B_q	Q_j	NO	MLE	ME
n = 20	m = 5	0.4507	0.3973	**0.3499**	0.3798	0.3850	0.4682	0.5153
	m = 10	0.8443	0.8867	0.6548	0.6767	0.7055	**0.4795**	0.5273
n = 50	m = 5	0.3491	0.2579	**0.2463**	0.2586	0.2781	0.4039	0.4199
	m = 10	0.7155	0.7263	0.5196	0.5378	0.5706	**0.4092**	0.4314
	m = 17	1.0939	1.0846	0.8075	0.8303	0.8636	**0.4078**	0.4300
n = 100	m = 5	0.3079	0.1938	**0.1867**	0.1975	0.2059	0.4682	0.5153
	m = 10	0.6184	0.6178	0.4380	0.4727	0.4813	**0.3542**	0.3651
	m = 17	0.9937	0.9762	0.7107	0.7345	0.7623	**0.3617**	0.3726
		$P(IV)(0,1,0.1,0.5)$						
		k-means	HD_q	B_q	Q_j	NO	MLE	ME
n = 20	m = 5	0.5168	0.5184	**0.4140**	0.4325	0.4533	0.7317	0.7478
	m = 10	0.9466	1.0216	**0.7395**	0.7775	0.8026	0.7453	0.7638
n = 50	m = 5	0.4065	0.3319	**0.3038**	0.3693	0.3374	0.6847	0.6920
	m = 10	0.8222	0.8568	**0.6170**	0.6563	0.6682	0.6844	0.6917
	m = 17	1.0939	1.0846	0.8075	0.8303	0.8636	**0.6726**	0.6849
n = 100	m = 5	0.3566	0.2479	**0.2382**	0.2404	0.2641	0.6376	0.6418
	m = 10	0.7219	0.7425	**0.5237**	0.5565	0.5741	0.6381	0.6431
	m = 17	0.9937	0.9762	0.7107	0.7345	0.7623	**0.6412**	0.6470

The bold numbers in Table 1 indicate the minimum bias in each row. We analyze the impact of sample size, the number of MSE-RPs, the type of Pareto distribution, and parameter values on the accuracy of representative point estimation. From Table 1, it can be observed that, for fixed parameter values and a fixed number of MSE-RPs, the estimation bias decreases as the sample size increases. Conversely, as the number of MSE-RPs increases, the estimation bias increases for both quantile-based methods and the k-means method. However, the bias remains nearly unchanged for parameter-based estimation methods. This is because increasing the number of MSE-RPs does not introduce new estimators, ensuring that the estimation remains highly stable.

The type of Pareto distribution also significantly affects the bias of estimation methods in Table 1, mainly due to differences in distribution complexity and tail behavior. For Pareto I and II distributions, parameter-based estimation methods perform the best, as parameter estimation is relatively straightforward. However, for Pareto III and IV distributions, which introduce additional parameters, solving the nonlinear Equation (17) often results in convergence issues or requires large sample sizes, leading to increased bias. In contrast, the B_q method utilizes quantile positions, which are more robust to heavy tails. The flexibility of Pareto III/IV in modeling the tail behavior aligns well with quantile-based estimation, thus reducing sensitivity to parameter misestimation.

The impact of parameters on MSE-RP estimation primarily manifests in the tail region. Smaller values of γ and α increase the difficulty of estimating μ, which relies heavily on the sample minimum. This, in turn, exacerbates the bias of parameter-based estimation methods. However, the B_q method remains relatively stable, particularly for Pareto III and IV distributions, where the tail dominates. The B_q method effectively captures the critical regions, improving the accuracy of MSE-RP estimation.

Furthermore, we analyze the sources of bias in quantile-based estimation. To investigate how different methods estimate MSE-RPs across various positions in the distribution, we plot the estimation results for $m = 10$ MSE-RPs of $P(I)(1,5)$ in Figure 1.

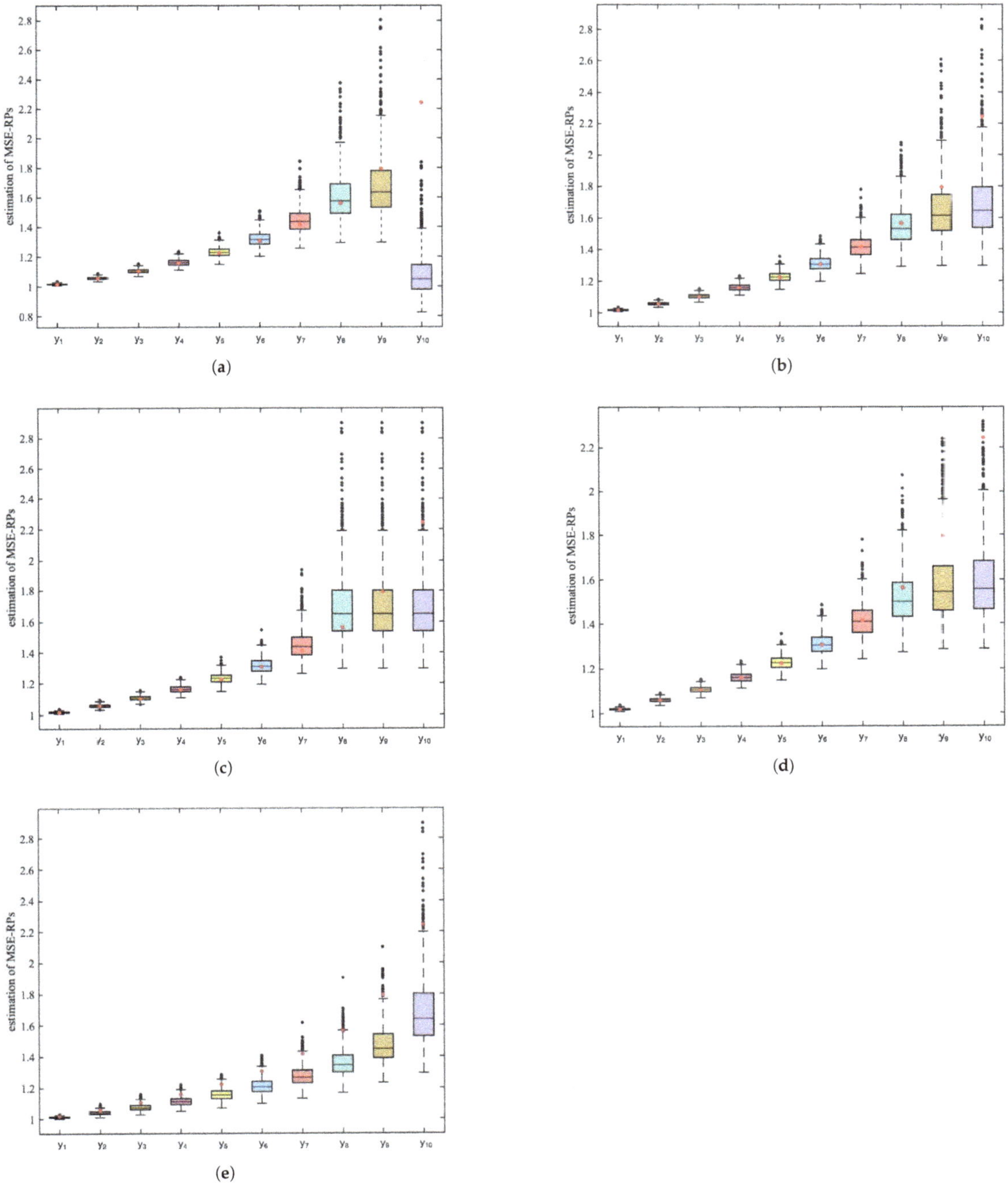

Figure 1. Box-plots of estimations of $m = 10$ MSE-RPs from $P(I)(1,5)$. (**a**) Description of the box-plots estimated for each representative point using the HD_q quantile estimator. (**b**) Description of the box-plots estimated for each representative point using the B_q quantile estimator. (**c**) Description of the box-plots estimated for each representative point using the Q_j quantile estimator. (**d**) Description of the box-plots estimated for each representative point using the NO quantile estimator. (**e**) Description of the box-plots estimated for each representative point using the k-means method.

In Figure 1, the red dots represent the true values of the MSE-RPs. From the boxplots, it can be observed that for the k-means and B_q methods, the estimation bias exhibits increasing fluctuation as the MSE-RPs move farther away from the mean of the Pareto distribution. Meanwhile, the Q_j method shows low sensitivity to the estimation of MSE-RPs in the tail. The HD_q method has a significant estimation bias for the last representative point, and the NO method exhibits a large overall bias with noticeable increases in fluctuation.

Therefore, considering all factors, the B_q method is the most stable and accurate method for estimating the MSE-RPs of the Pareto distribution when γ and α are small. However, by examining the MSE-RPs and their corresponding probabilities, it can be observed that as the number of MSE-RPs increases, the probability associated with the tail MSE-RPs becomes significantly smaller, while their corresponding values become exceedingly large. Estimating these tail MSE-RPs notably increases the overall estimation bias.

Li et al. [30] previously proposed a method to measure the information gain (IG) of MSE-RPs, similar to the variance ratio used in principal component analysis. The range of IG is from 0 to 1, and the calculation formula is as follows:

$$IG = 1 - \frac{MSE(y_1, \ldots, y_k \mid x)}{\mathrm{var}(x)}, \tag{40}$$

where $k \leq m$ is the number of MSE-RPs used in calculating the IG. We can use the same IG function to calculate the number of MSE-RPs and their corresponding coverage under different levels of information gain. See Appendix C for details.

By calculating the information gain, we find that for the Pareto distribution, as the number of MSE-RPs increases, the information gain for the tail MSE-RPs becomes very small. For example, for the $P(I)(1,5)$ distribution, when $m = 17$, the first 12 MSE-RPs account for 90% of the information. We re-estimate the MSE-RPs for the above distributions with $m = 17$ under different IG proportions, and the results are presented in Table 2.

Table 2. Comparison of mean absolute bias from 1000 simulations in MSE-RP estimation at three levels of IG with $m = 17$.

		k-means	HD_q	B_q	Q_j	NO	MLE	ME
$P(I)(1,5)$								
$90\% \leq IG \leq 95\%$	n = 100	0.3677	0.1373	0.1145	0.1796	0.1147	**0.0033**	0.0321
	n = 50	0.4245	0.1725	0.1534	0.2062	0.1583	**0.0067**	0.0458
$95\% \leq IG \leq 98\%$	n = 100	0.5693	0.2572	0.2333	0.2898	0.2552	**0.0039**	0.0375
	n = 50	0.6434	0.3426	0.3029	0.3466	0.3294	**0.0079**	0.0535
$98\% \leq IG$	n = 100	0.9768	0.8248	0.5915	0.6400	0.6532	**0.0049**	0.0475
	n = 50	1.0733	0.9683	0.6977	0.7355	0.7558	**0.0100**	0.0678
$P(II)(0,1,5)$								
		k-means	HD_q	B_q	Q_j	NO	MLE	ME
$90\% \leq IG \leq 95\%$	n = 100	0.3684	0.1347	0.1172	0.1723	0.1195	0.0671	**0.0643**
	n = 50	0.4244	0.1773	0.1577	0.2112	0.1644	0.0988	**0.0901**
$95\% \leq IG \leq 98\%$	n = 100	0.5708	0.2581	0.2412	0.2879	0.2645	0.0966	**0.0922**
	n = 50	0.6430	0.3354	0.3053	0.3492	0.3367	0.1424	**0.1290**
$98\% \leq IG$	n = 100	0.9805	0.7551	0.6055	0.6455	0.6630	0.1512	**0.1438**
	n = 50	1.0725	0.8693	0.7017	0.7396	0.7624	0.2229	**0.2011**

Table 2. *Cont.*

		k-means	HD_q	B_q	Q_j	NO	MLE	ME
$P(III)(0,1,0.2)$								
$90\% \leq IG \leq 95\%$	n = 100	0.3074	0.1055	**0.0920**	0.1225	0.0921	0.3624	0.3682
	n = 50	0.3525	0.1324	**0.1213**	0.1539	0.1268	0.4078	0.4206
$95\% \leq IG \leq 98\%$	n = 100	0.3817	0.1469	**0.1331**	0.1638	0.1382	0.3618	0.3682
	n = 50	0.4363	0.1820	**0.1723**	0.2013	0.1866	0.4065	0.4207
$98\% \leq IG$	n = 100	0.6628	0.4709	0.3625	0.3878	0.3964	**0.3604**	0.3689
	n = 50	0.7429	0.5813	0.4387	0.4629	0.4809	**0.4045**	0.4227
$P(IV)(0,1,0.1,0.5)$								
		k-means	HD_q	B_q	Q_j	NO	MLE	ME
$90\% \leq IG \leq 95\%$	n = 100	0.3424	0.1203	**0.1061**	0.1497	0.1094	0.6424	0.6457
	n = 50	0.3816	0.1615	**0.1454**	0.1898	0.1527	0.6781	0.6850
$95\% \leq IG \leq 98\%$	n = 100	0.4310	0.1691	**0.1563**	0.1964	0.1694	0.6422	0.6459
	n = 50	0.4785	0.2248	**0.2082**	0.2486	0.2257	0.6773	0.6848
$98\% \leq IG$	n = 100	0.7559	0.5726	**0.4279**	0.4615	0.4746	0.6417	0.6464
	n = 50	0.8246	0.7006	**0.5137**	0.5482	0.5595	0.6748	0.6844

The bold numbers in Table 2 indicate the minimum bias in each row. From the comparison between Tables 1 and 2, it can be observed that sacrificing a small amount of information gain can significantly improve the accuracy of representative point estimation. Furthermore, when the parameters γ and α are small, the B_q quantile method provides relatively accurate and stable estimates.

The IG truncation method dynamically determines the number of MSE-RPs required to achieve a specified IG level. This process focuses on selecting the most informative points while discarding tail points, which, although having high estimation bias, contribute little to the overall information. As a result, the outcomes presented in Table 2 can be considered robust to the choice of m.

In practical applications, the number of MSE-RPs needed can be determined by referring to Appendix C, which provides the number of MSE-RPs corresponding to different levels of IG and their coverage regions.

5. Real Data Study

5.1. Case I

We utilize commonly used Pareto I distribution data, which are taken from the appendix of Brazauskas' study [43]. These data were also used by Kim et al. to demonstrate the best parameter estimator for the Pareto I distribution [44]. Therefore, we can directly use the estimated parameters of this dataset from their paper. The study indicates that the data follow a $P(I)(497.085, 1.2078)$ distribution, for which MSE-RPs do not exist.

Using the properties of the Pareto distribution discussed in Section 2 and Formula (6), this dataset can be approximately transformed into data following a $P(I)(1,5)$ distribution, enabling the estimation of MSE-RPs. Since Formula (6) is an affine transformation that preserves the information content, no significant loss of information occurs during this process. To verify whether the data follow the distribution we mentioned, we performed a KS-test on both the transformed and original data, and the results were consistent. The p-value was 0.8943, and the KS statistic was 0.0472. Therefore, we believe the data follow the distribution mentioned above, and there is no loss of information before or after the transformation.

The transformed data are observed to have a distribution range of $(1.0014, 3.0836)$. Referring to the IG coverage tables provided in Appendix C, we perform the following estimations:

- For $90\% \leq IG \leq 95\%$, we first estimate $m = 7$ MSE-RPs and select the first 6 MSE-RPs as those providing valid information.
- For $95\% \leq IG \leq 98\%$, we first estimate $m = 18$ MSE-RPs and select the first 14 MSE-RPs as those providing valid information.

We compare the fit of the data using MSE-RPs estimated using different methods.

From Figure 2, it can be observed that as IG increases, the empirical distribution fitted using MSE-RPs becomes closer to the true distribution. Furthermore, apart from the MSE-RPs estimated using the k-means method, which exhibit significant bias, the MSE-RPs estimated using the other three methods show no noticeable differences in the fitting process.

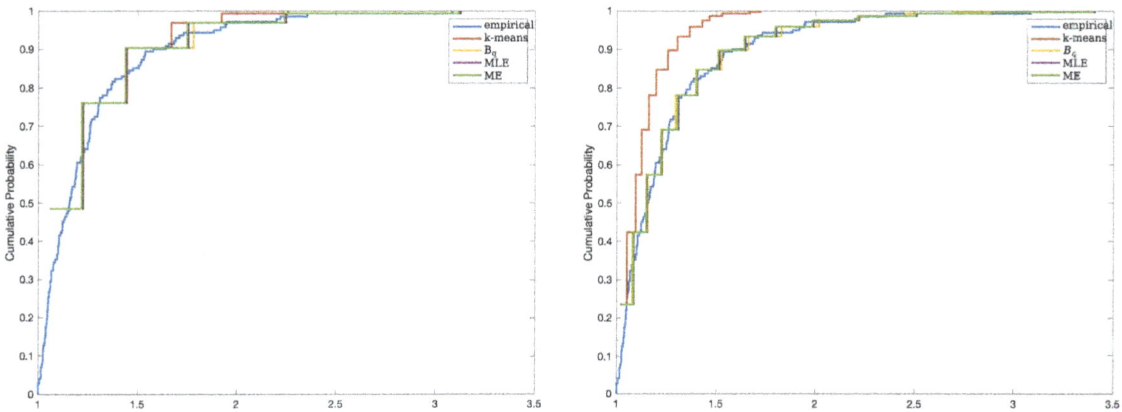

(**a**) (**b**)

Figure 2. Case I data fitting $P(I)(1,5)$ using MSE-RPs estimated using different methods. (**a**) Description of using MSE-RPs containing $90\% \leq IG \leq 95\%$. (**b**) Description of using MSE-RPs containing $95\% \leq IG \leq 98\%$.

5.2. Case II

Next, we estimate MSE-RPs for real data from a Pareto IV distribution. The data were obtained from testing the unit stress voltage of miniature light bulbs [45]. According to the literature, the data follow a $P(IV)(0, 95.6575, 0.3631, 6.0973)$ distribution. Using the properties of the Pareto distribution and Formula (9), the data are transformed to correspond to a $P(IV)(0, 1, 0.1, 0.5)$ distribution. Since Formula (9) is also an affine transformation that preserves the information content, no significant loss of information occurs during this process. In order to confirm that the data follow the distribution we specified, we conducted a KS-test on both the original and transformed data. The results were consistent, with a p-value of 0.2004 and a KS statistic of 0.0957. So we conclude that the data follow the mentioned distribution, and the transformation process does not result in any loss of information.

The transformed data are observed to have a distribution range of $(0.1187, 1.9827)$. Referring to the IG coverage tables provided in Appendix C, we perform the following estimations:

- For $90\% \leq IG \leq 95\%$, we first estimate $m = 11$ MSE-RPs and select the first 9 MSE-RPs as those providing valid information.
- For $95\% \leq IG \leq 98\%$, we first estimate $m = 20$ MSE-RPs and select the first 16 MSE-RPs as those providing valid information.

We compare the fit of the data distribution using MSE-RPs estimated using different methods.

From Figure 3, it can be observed that, similarly, as IG increases, the empirical distribution fitted using MSE-RPs becomes closer to the true distribution. However, unlike Case I, in Case II, the MSE-RPs estimated using the B_q method result in a closer fit to the true distribution in terms of empirical distribution, while the other three methods exhibit larger biases.

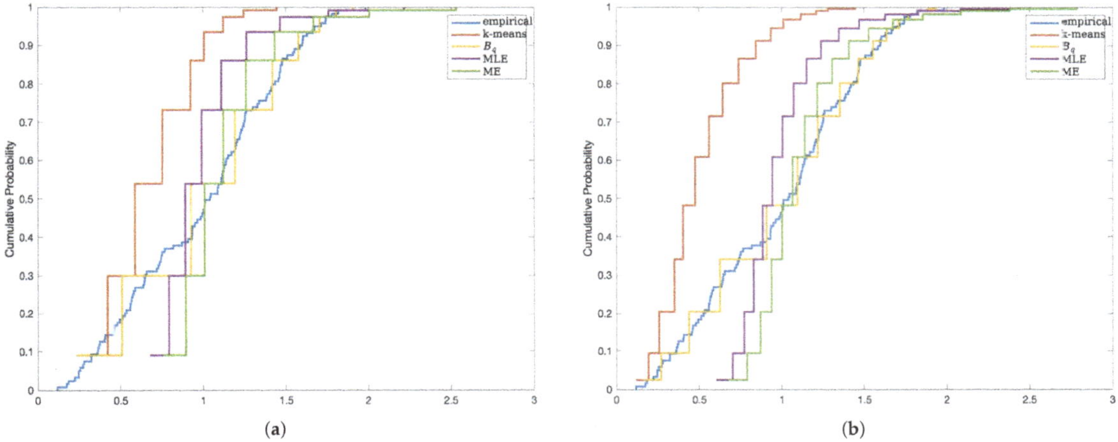

Figure 3. Case II data fitting $P(IV)(0,1,0.1,0.5)$ using MSE-RPs estimated using different methods. (**a**) Description of using MSE-RPs containing $90\% \le IG \le 95\%$. (**b**) Description of using MSE-RPs containing $95\% \le IG \le 98\%$.

6. Conclusions

This paper primarily investigates the MSE-RPs of Pareto distributions and their estimation. We provided the uniqueness conditions for MSE-RPs and derived the corresponding unique intervals. For the computation of MSE-RPs of Pareto I and II distributions, we proposed an improved parametric k-means method.

For the estimation of MSE-RPs, we compared three categories of methods: the k-means method, the quantile-based estimation method, and methods that first estimate the parameters and then estimate the MSE-RPs. Based on simulations, we found that the k-means method is unsuitable for estimating MSE-RPs of Pareto distributions. The MLE-based parameter estimation method has the smallest bias when estimating MSE-RPs of Pareto I distributions, while the ME-based parameter estimation method performs best for Pareto II distributions. As the parameters γ and α decrease, the bias when using the B_q quantile method to estimate MSE-RPs becomes minimal.

Since the tail MSE-RPs of Pareto distributions contribute significant bias while having very low probabilities, we propose using the IG function to calculate the information content of MSE-RPs. We also provide the number of MSE-RPs required for three levels of IG and their corresponding covered ranges to help select an appropriate number of MSE-RPs in practical analyses. Simulation results demonstrate that sacrificing a small amount of information gain can significantly improve the accuracy of representative point estimation.

Additionally, we applied the proposed methods to estimate MSE-RPs for real data from two different distributions. Using different IG intervals, we estimated MSE-RPs for the data and used them to fit the empirical distribution functions of the real data. These results were consistent with the simulation findings.

In conclusion, this paper studies the MSE-RPs of Pareto distributions and their estimation methods, analyzes the bias characteristics of representative point estimation, and proposes an IG-based optimization method for selecting MSE-RPs. The effectiveness and applicability of the proposed method were validated through simulations and real data studies.

Author Contributions: Conceptualization and writing—review and editing, X.P.; methodology and software, X.L.; software and writing—original draft preparation, X.L. All authors have read and agreed to the published version of the manuscript.

Funding: This research was supported in part by the National Key R & D Program of China (No. 2022YFC3600300) and in part by Guangdong Provincial Key Laboratory of IRADS (2022B1212010006).

Institutional Review Board Statement: Not applicable.

Informed Consent Statement: Not applicable.

Data Availability Statement: The data used in Case I were obtained from Table A2 in the Appendix of Reference [43]. The data used in Case II were obtained from Table 1 in Section 6 of reference [13]. Further details about the data sources can be found in the cited references. No new data were created in this study.

Acknowledgments: We would like to express our heartfelt gratitude to Zhou Yongdao for his invaluable suggestions, which greatly contributed to the improvement of this work.

Conflicts of Interest: The authors declare no conflicts of interest. The funders had no role in the design of the study; in the collection, analyses, or interpretation of data; in the writing of the manuscript; or in the decision to publish the results.

Appendix A. Proof

Appendix A.1

Proof of Lemma 1. Taking the logarithm of the density function of $P(IV)(0,1,\gamma,\alpha)$, we have

$$g(x) = \log f(x) = \log \alpha + \log \gamma - (\alpha+1)\log(1+x^{\frac{1}{\gamma}}) + \left(\frac{1}{\gamma}-1\right)\log x. \quad \text{(A1)}$$

By taking the second derivative of $g(x)$, we obtain

$$\frac{\partial^2 g(x)}{\partial x^2} = \frac{1}{x^2}\left[\frac{(\alpha+1)}{\gamma^2}\left(\frac{x^{1/\gamma}}{1+x^{1/\gamma}}\right)^2 - \frac{(\alpha+1)}{\gamma}\left(\frac{1}{\gamma}-1\right)\left(\frac{x^{1/\gamma}}{1+x^{1/\gamma}}\right) - \left(\frac{1}{\gamma}-1\right)\right]. \quad \text{(A2)}$$

From (A2), it is evident that when $\frac{1}{\gamma}-1 \leq 0$, we have $\frac{\partial^2 g(x)}{\partial x^2} \geq 0$, which implies the function is not log-concave. Therefore, it is required that $\frac{1}{\gamma} > 1$.

Let $z = \frac{x^{1/\gamma}}{1+x^{1/\gamma}}$, $0 < z < 1$, then

$$h(z) = \frac{(\alpha+1)}{\gamma^2}z^2 - \frac{(\alpha+1)}{\gamma}\left(\frac{1}{\gamma}-1\right)z - \left(\frac{1}{\gamma}-1\right). \quad \text{(A3)}$$

It is clear that $h(z)$ is an upward-opening parabola, and z is an increasing function of x. The two roots of $h(z) = 0$ are as follows:

$$\begin{aligned} z_1^* &= \frac{(\alpha+1)\left(\frac{1}{\gamma}-1\right) - \sqrt{(\alpha+1)^2\left(\frac{1}{\gamma}-1\right)^2 + 4(\alpha+1)\left(\frac{1}{\gamma}-1\right)}}{2(\alpha+1)/\gamma}, \\ z_2^* &= \frac{(\alpha+1)\left(\frac{1}{\gamma}-1\right) + \sqrt{(\alpha+1)^2\left(\frac{1}{\gamma}-1\right)^2 + 4(\alpha+1)\left(\frac{1}{\gamma}-1\right)}}{2(\alpha+1)/\gamma}. \end{aligned} \tag{A4}$$

Clearly, $z_1^* < 0$ and $z_2^* > 0$. Next, we examine whether z_2^* is within the range of z:

$$z_2^* - 1 = -\frac{1}{2}(1+\gamma) + \frac{1}{2}\sqrt{(1-\gamma)^2 + \frac{4(\gamma-\gamma^2)}{(\alpha+1)}}. \tag{A5}$$

To determine whether $z_2^* > 1$ or $z_2^* < 1$, we square both parts of (A5) and subtract the squares. Since

$$(1-\gamma)^2 + \frac{4(\gamma-\gamma^2)}{(\alpha+1)} - (1+\gamma)^2 = \frac{-4\gamma\alpha - 4\gamma^2}{\alpha+1} < 0, \tag{A6}$$

it follows that $z_2^* < 1$. Therefore, when $\frac{1}{\gamma} > 1$, and z lies within $(0, z_2^*)$, the density function of $P(IV)(0,1,\gamma,\alpha)$ is log-concave, which guarantees the uniqueness of the MSE-RPs. Furthermore, as $\alpha \to +\infty$, $z_2^* \to 1-\gamma$. □

Appendix A.2

Proof of Theorem 1. Let

$$G(y_{i+1}) = M_{i+1}F(M_{i+1}) - M_iF(M_i) - \int_{M_i}^{M_{i+1}} F(x)dx - y_i(F(M_{i+1}) - F(M_i)), \tag{A7}$$

where $M_1 = F^{-1}(0)$, $M_i = \frac{y_{i-1}+y_i}{2}$, $i = 2, \ldots, m$, and $M_{m+1} = F^{-1}(1)$.

To prove that the equation has a solution, for $i = 1, \ldots, m-1$, we need to show that $G(y_{i+1} = y_i) < 0$ and $\lim_{y_{i+1}\to+\infty} G(y_{i+1}) > 0$. For $i = m$, we need to show that $G(y_{i+1} = y_i) > 0$ and $\lim_{y_{i+1}\to+\infty} G(y_{i+1}) < 0$.

1. Case I: For $i = 1, \ldots, m-1$,

$$G(y_{i+1} = y_i) = (y_i - M_i)F(M_i) - \int_{M_i}^{y_i} F(x)dx. \tag{A8}$$

By the mean value theorem, there exists $\eta \in (M_i, y_i)$ such that $\int_{M_i}^{y_i} F(x)dx = (y_i - M_i)F(\eta)$. Therefore, $G(y_{i+1} = y_i) < 0$.

$$\lim_{y_{i+1}\to+\infty} G(y_{i+1}) = \lim_{M_{i+1}\to+\infty} (y_i - M_i)F(M_i) + (M_{i+1} - y_i)F(M_{i+1}) - \int_{M_i}^{M_{i+1}} F(x)dx. \tag{A9}$$

Substituting $F(x) = 1 - (1 + x^{1/\gamma})^{-\alpha}$, we have

$$\begin{aligned} h(y_i) = \lim_{y_{i+1}\to+\infty} G(y_{i+1}) &= (y_i - M_i)(F(M_i) - 1) + \int_{M_i}^{+\infty} (1 - F(x))dx \\ &= y_i(F(M_i) - 1) + \int_{M_i}^{+\infty} xf(x)dx, \end{aligned} \tag{A10}$$

where the last equality holds because, when $\frac{\alpha}{\gamma} > 2$,

$$\lim_{x \to +\infty} x(F(x) - 1) = \lim_{x \to +\infty} x^{1-\frac{\alpha}{\gamma}} = 0. \tag{A11}$$

For $i = 1$,

$$h(y_1) = -y_1 + \int_0^{+\infty} xf(x)dx = E(X) - y_1. \tag{A12}$$

Thus, when $y_1 < E(X)$, $h(y_1) > 0$, which ensures the existence of a solution.
For $i = 2, \dots, m-1$,

$$\begin{aligned} h(y_i) &= y_i(F(M_i) - 1) + \int_0^{+\infty} xf(x)dx - \sum_{j=1}^{i-1} \int_{M_j}^{M_{j+1}} xf(x)dx \\ &= y_i(F(M_i) - 1) + E(X) - \sum_{j=1}^{i-1} y_j. \end{aligned} \tag{A13}$$

Thus, when $y_i < \frac{E(X) - \sum_{j=1}^{i-1} y_j}{1 - F(M_i)}$, $h(y_i) > 0$, and the equation has a solution.

2. Case II: For $i = m$

$$G(y_m = y_{m-1}) = \lim_{N \to +\infty} (N - y_{m-1})F(N) - \int_{y_{m-1}}^{N} F(x)dx. \tag{A14}$$

By the mean value theorem, there exists $\eta \in (y_{m-1}, N)$ such that $\int_{y_{m-1}}^{N} F(x)dx = (N - y_{m-1})F(\eta)$. Thus, $G(y_m = y_{m-1}) > 0$.

$$\lim_{y_m \to +\infty} G(y_m) = \lim_{M_{m+1} \to +\infty} -y_m(F(M_{m+1}) - F(M_m)) < 0. \tag{A15}$$

□

Appendix B. MSE-RPs of Pareto III and IV Distributions

Table A1. The points of MSE-RPs from $P(III)(0,1,0.2)$.

	MSE	RP1	RP2	RP3	RP4	RP5	RP6	RP7	RP8	RP9	RP10	RP11	RP12	RP13	RP14	RP15	RP16
m = 2	0.081005705	0.893248503	1.624569032														
m = 3	0.046924	0.792100	1.264540	2.150314													
m = 4	0.030749	0.722458	1.095883	1.588422	2.665352												
m = 5	0.021748	0.670249	0.990624	1.343028	1.899748	3.175156											
m = 6	0.016210	0.629031	0.915762	1.198240	1.573247	2.206232	3.681976										
m = 7	0.012554	0.595321	0.858417	1.099461	1.385825	1.796710	2.510388	4.186923									
m = 8	0.010013	0.567032	0.812355	1.026063	1.261175	1.564830	2.016989	2.813247	4.690613								
m = 9	0.008174	0.542819	0.774120	0.968406	1.170558	1.412900	1.739604	2.235580	3.115306	5.193419							
m = 10	0.006800	0.521766	0.741610	0.921328	1.100659	1.304042	1.559465	1.912082	2.453194	3.416831	5.695577						
m = 11	0.005746	0.503227	0.713457	0.881789	1.044432	1.221182	1.431611	1.703127	2.083222	2.670200	3.717980	6.197247					
m = 12	0.004920	0.486728	0.688722	0.847862	0.997781	1.155313	1.335200	1.555742	1.845052	2.253536	2.886806	4.018854	6.698539				
m = 13	0.004260	0.471912	0.666734	0.818261	0.958149	1.101222	1.259236	1.445329	1.677757	1.985886	2.423314	3.103136	4.319518	7.199533			
m = 14	0.003725	0.458507	0.646998	0.792087	0.923850	1.055678	1.197364	1.358900	1.553005	1.798412	2.126004	2.592731	3.319267	4.620018	7.700288		
m = 15	0.003285	0.446297	0.629138	0.768688	0.893721	1.016564	1.145654	1.288950	1.455822	1.659071	1.918161	2.265638	2.761895	3.535249	4.920388	8.200847	
m = 16	0.002918	0.435111	0.612864	0.747579	0.866934	0.982432	1.101539	1.230836	1.377547	1.550909	1.764044	2.037287	2.404934	2.930878	3.751119	5.220652	8.701244
m = 17	0.002610	0.424810	0.597944	0.728389	0.842877	0.952257	1.063273	1.181533	1.312824	1.464112	1.644728	1.868254	2.155975	2.543988	3.099726	3.966900	5.520828
m = 18	0.002348	0.415283	0.584195	0.710828	0.821087	0.925287	1.029620	1.138984	1.258163	1.392609	1.549251	1.737649	1.971919	2.274345	2.682864	3.268472	4.182610
m = 19	0.002124	0.406433	0.571465	0.694667	0.801208	0.900961	0.999682	1.101739	1.211192	1.332442	1.470827	1.633366	1.829920	2.075187	2.392483	2.821608	3.437139
m = 20	0.001930	0.398184	0.559631	0.679718	0.782960	0.878848	0.972791	1.068747	1.170240	1.280923	1.405031	1.547906	1.716732	1.921712	2.178159	2.510446	2.960250
m = 21	0.001762	0.390469	0.548588	0.665831	0.766116	0.858610	0.948434	1.039225	1.134101	1.236160	1.348856	1.476378	1.624142	1.799537	2.013145	2.280909	2.628276
m = 22	0.001614	0.383232	0.538250	0.652880	0.750496	0.839981	0.926216	1.012580	1.101874	1.196783	1.300186	1.415454	1.546794	1.699742	1.881919	2.104304	2.383489
m = 23	0.001485	0.376424	0.528543	0.640759	0.735950	0.822744	0.905821	0.988349	1.072880	1.161777	1.257491	1.362796	1.481044	1.616503	1.774855	1.963975	2.195251
m = 24	0.001370	0.370003	0.519402	0.629380	0.722352	0.806724	0.886999	0.966171	1.046591	1.130371	1.219635	1.316709	1.424326	1.545859	1.685666	1.849592	2.045778
m = 25	0.001269	0.363935	0.510773	0.618665	0.709599	0.791774	0.869544	0.945754	1.022593	1.101971	1.185757	1.275939	1.374784	1.485021	1.610073	1.754403	1.924033
m = 26	0.001178	0.358186	0.502610	0.608552	0.697601	0.777774	0.853287	0.926865	1.000556	1.076111	1.155196	1.239534	1.331043	1.431969	1.545062	1.673812	1.822802
m = 27	0.001097	0.352729	0.494869	0.598982	0.686283	0.764620	0.838090	0.909309	0.980212	1.052419	1.127429	1.206762	1.292060	1.385207	1.488451	1.604584	1.737175
m = 28	0.001023	0.347541	0.487516	0.589908	0.675580	0.752225	0.823833	0.892927	0.961344	1.030594	1.102044	1.177046	1.257031	1.343599	1.438623	1.544373	1.663692
m = 29	0.000957	0.342599	0.480518	0.581285	0.665436	0.740515	0.810419	0.877586	0.943772	1.010392	1.078707	1.149931	1.225327	1.306273	1.394351	1.491441	1.599845
m = 30	0.000897	0.337883	0.473846	0.573078	0.655800	0.729425	0.797761	0.863172	0.927344	0.991612	1.057145	1.125049	1.196447	1.272543	1.354691	1.444469	1.543774
m = 31	0.000843	0.333378	0.467476	0.565251	0.646630	0.718899	0.785786	0.849591	0.911934	0.974085	1.037136	1.102100	1.169989	1.241865	1.318901	1.402441	1.494069
		RP17	RP18	RP19	RP20	RP21	RP22	RP23	RP24	RP25	RP26	RP27	RP28	RP29	RP30	RP31	
m = 17		9.201507															
m = 18		5.820932	9.701655														
m = 19		4.398262	6.120974	10.201706													
m = 20		3.605744	4.613867	6.420963	10.701674												
m = 21		3.098813	3.774299	4.829431	6.720907	11.201569											
m = 22		2.746003	3.237314	3.942814	5.044962	7.020812	11.701401										
m = 23		2.485936	2.863649	3.375766	4.111295	5.260464	7.320682	12.201178									
m = 24		2.286034	2.588279	2.981231	3.514177	4.279747	5.475941	7.620523	12.700906								
m = 25		2.127382	2.376686	2.690539	3.098762	3.652556	4.448176	5.691397	7.920337	13.200591							
m = 26		1.998240	2.208827	2.467235	2.792733	3.216251	3.790908	4.616585	5.906833	8.220127	13.700237						
m = 27		1.890933	2.072259	2.290146	2.557699	2.894874	3.333705	3.929236	4.784977	6.122252	8.519896	14.199850					
m = 28		1.800235	1.958847	2.146128	2.371361	2.648096	2.996970	3.451131	4.067546	4.953354	6.337657	8.819647	14.699431				
m = 29		1.722464	1.863050	2.026586	2.219873	2.452493	2.738437	3.099030	3.568534	4.205839	5.121717	6.553048	9.119380	15.198984			
m = 30		1.654949	1.780963	1.925665	2.094181	2.293518	2.533556	2.828733	3.201060	3.685917	4.344118	5.290069	6.768427	9.419099	15.698512		
m = 31		1.595710	1.709754	1.839238	1.988116	2.161658	2.367080	2.614562	2.918990	3.303065	3.803283	4.482385	5.458410	6.983796	9.718803	16.198018	

Table A2. The corresponding probabilities of MSE-RPs from $P(III)(0,1,0.2)$.

	P1	P2	P3	P4	P5	P6	P7	P8	P9	P10	P11	P12	P13	P14	P15	P16
m = 2	0.759735	0.240265														
m = 3	0.534851	0.400680	0.064469													
m = 4	0.383170	0.430096	0.164274	0.022460												
m = 5	0.283123	0.400708	0.234239	0.072513	0.009417											
m = 6	0.215635	0.353219	0.267478	0.123827	0.035341	0.004501										
m = 7	0.168676	0.304742	0.274248	0.163070	0.068132	0.018763	0.002369									
m = 8	0.134990	0.261237	0.265497	0.187507	0.099284	0.039460	0.010681	0.001343								
m = 9	0.110152	0.224090	0.248945	0.199247	0.124372	0.061963	0.023989	0.006435	0.000807							
m = 10	0.091389	0.192998	0.229277	0.201662	0.142152	0.082844	0.039889	0.015218	0.004061	0.000509						
m = 11	0.076910	0.167141	0.209103	0.197859	0.153120	0.100258	0.056114	0.026481	0.010016	0.002665	0.000334					
m = 12	0.065529	0.145634	0.189765	0.190239	0.158475	0.113563	0.071070	0.038801	0.018086	0.006804	0.001807	0.000226				
m = 13	0.056437	0.127683	0.171881	0.180501	0.159545	0.122862	0.083860	0.050991	0.027400	0.012671	0.004751	0.001260	0.000158			
m = 14	0.049069	0.112623	0.155667	0.169784	0.157524	0.128628	0.094123	0.062225	0.037124	0.019742	0.009082	0.003398	0.000901	0.000113		
m = 15	0.043020	0.099912	0.141131	0.158819	0.153385	0.131472	0.101855	0.072015	0.046592	0.027443	0.014491	0.006643	0.002482	0.000658	0.000082	
m = 16	0.038000	0.089119	0.128177	0.148056	0.147879	0.132010	0.107256	0.080146	0.055336	0.035269	0.020590	0.010819	0.004948	0.001846	0.000489	0.000061
m = 17	0.033789	0.079895	0.116667	0.137757	0.141558	0.130792	0.110628	0.086584	0.063072	0.042822	0.027006	0.015667	0.008203	0.003745	0.001397	0.000370
m = 18	0.030226	0.071967	0.106447	0.128061	0.134823	0.128287	0.112300	0.091421	0.069659	0.049821	0.033418	0.020915	0.012078	0.006309	0.002877	0.001072
m = 19	0.027186	0.065111	0.097369	0.119031	0.127952	0.124871	0.112592	0.094810	0.075065	0.056086	0.039578	0.026313	0.016376	0.009426	0.004914	0.002239
m = 20	0.024573	0.059150	0.089294	0.110677	0.121135	0.120843	0.111794	0.096937	0.079329	0.061526	0.045305	0.031651	0.020904	0.012956	0.007438	0.003873
m = 21	0.022311	0.053941	0.082098	0.102986	0.114497	0.116431	0.110156	0.097993	0.082534	0.066110	0.050483	0.036766	0.025493	0.016753	0.010350	0.005931
m = 22	0.020340	0.049365	0.075671	0.095923	0.108119	0.111808	0.107889	0.098159	0.084788	0.069855	0.055047	0.041539	0.030000	0.020681	0.013539	0.008344
m = 23	0.018614	0.045327	0.069918	0.089448	0.102046	0.107104	0.105165	0.097603	0.086209	0.072807	0.058973	0.045890	0.034313	0.024620	0.016897	0.011029
m = 24	0.017095	0.041749	0.064753	0.083516	0.096301	0.102411	0.102124	0.096470	0.086912	0.075030	0.062267	0.049773	0.038352	0.028472	0.020325	0.013901
m = 25	0.015750	0.038564	0.060106	0.078082	0.090894	0.097797	0.098876	0.094886	0.087009	0.076599	0.064954	0.053168	0.042059	0.032157	0.023738	0.016878
m = 26	0.014554	0.035719	0.055913	0.073103	0.085820	0.093308	0.095508	0.092958	0.086603	0.077590	0.067074	0.056075	0.045401	0.035618	0.027065	0.019889
m = 27	0.013487	0.033168	0.052121	0.068536	0.081071	0.088974	0.092087	0.090774	0.085784	0.078079	0.068674	0.058509	0.048362	0.038815	0.030249	0.022871
m = 28	0.012530	0.030872	0.048682	0.064345	0.076633	0.084816	0.088665	0.088409	0.084632	0.078136	0.069806	0.060495	0.050940	0.041722	0.033249	0.025772
m = 29	0.011670	0.028800	0.045557	0.060493	0.072490	0.080843	0.085279	0.085920	0.083216	0.077828	0.070522	0.062064	0.053143	0.044325	0.036033	0.028550
m = 30	0.010893	0.026924	0.042709	0.056949	0.068624	0.077062	0.081958	0.083358	0.081595	0.077215	0.070873	0.063251	0.054986	0.046622	0.038584	0.031175
m = 31	0.010190	0.025220	0.040108	0.053685	0.065017	0.073471	0.078724	0.080759	0.079820	0.076349	0.070906	0.064092	0.056492	0.048617	0.040889	0.033622

	P17	P18	P19	P20	P21	P22	P23	P24	P25	P26	P27	P28	P29	P30	P31
m = 17	0.000046														
m = 18	0.000284	0.000036													
m = 19	0.000834	0.000221	0.000028												
m = 20	0.001763	0.000657	0.000174	0.000022											
m = 21	0.003085	0.001404	0.000523	0.000138	0.000017										
m = 22	0.004775	0.002482	0.001129	0.000420	0.000111	0.000014									
m = 23	0.006785	0.003878	0.002014	0.000916	0.000341	0.000090	0.000011								
m = 24	0.009052	0.005561	0.003176	0.001649	0.000749	0.000279	0.000074	0.000009							
m = 25	0.011511	0.007483	0.004591	0.002620	0.001360	0.000618	0.000230	0.000061	0.000008						
m = 26	0.014097	0.009593	0.006227	0.003817	0.002177	0.001130	0.000513	0.000191	0.000051	0.000006					
m = 27	0.016747	0.011839	0.008042	0.005214	0.003194	0.001821	0.000944	0.000429	0.000160	0.000042	0.000005				
m = 28	0.019408	0.014169	0.009996	0.006781	0.004392	0.002689	0.001532	0.000795	0.000361	0.000134	0.000036	0.000004			
m = 29	0.022033	0.016538	0.012045	0.008483	0.005748	0.003720	0.002276	0.001297	0.000672	0.000305	0.000114	0.000030	0.000004		
m = 30	0.024584	0.018904	0.014151	0.010287	0.007234	0.004897	0.003167	0.001937	0.001104	0.000572	0.000260	0.000097	0.000026	0.000003	
m = 31	0.027029	0.021231	0.016277	0.012158	0.008823	0.006198	0.004192	0.002710	0.001657	0.000944	0.000489	0.000222	0.000083	0.000022	0.000003

Table A3. The points of MSE-RPs from $P(IV)(0, 1, 0.1, 0.5)$.

	MSE	RP1	RP2	RP3	RP4	RP5	RP6	RP7	RP8	RP9	RP10	RP11	RP12	RP13	RP14	RP15	RP16
m = 2	0.060997	1.073328	1.797978														
m = 3	0.035699	1.001741	1.421058	2.369184													
m = 4	0.023552	0.950106	1.259380	1.756498	2.927609												
m = 5	0.016738	0.909934	1.165271	1.499730	2.087874	3.479813											
m = 6	0.012520	0.877230	1.101445	1.355579	1.736728	2.417078	4.028470										
m = 7	0.009724	0.849773	1.053992	1.261844	1.541057	1.972432	2.744937	4.574898									
m = 8	0.007773	0.826198	1.016533	1.195035	1.415336	1.725089	2.207414	3.071896	5.119828								
m = 9	0.006357	0.805607	0.985714	1.144306	1.327099	1.566758	1.908503	2.441918	3.398221	5.663702							
m = 10	0.005296	0.787374	0.959595	1.103973	1.261260	1.456271	1.717401	2.091572	2.676082	3.724081	6.206803						
m = 11	0.004481	0.771051	0.936964	1.070775	1.209858	1.374446	1.584345	1.867679	2.274413	2.909991	4.049591	6.749318					
m = 12	0.003841	0.756303	0.917022	1.042710	1.168304	1.311128	1.486132	1.711938	2.017753	2.457091	3.143704	4.374829	7.291381				
m = 13	0.003329	0.742874	0.899212	1.018482	1.133771	1.260437	1.410459	1.597154	1.839288	2.167695	2.639643	3.377263	4.699852	7.833086			
m = 14	0.002913	0.730564	0.883135	0.997212	1.104427	1.218740	1.350190	1.508903	1.707853	1.966500	2.317542	2.822096	3.610697	5.024702	8.374504		
m = 15	0.002571	0.719216	0.868495	0.978282	1.079037	1.183673	1.300901	1.438808	1.606909	1.818377	2.093623	2.467316	3.004468	3.844030	5.349412	8.915686	
m = 16	0.002286	0.708702	0.855064	0.961247	1.056733	1.153635	1.259709	1.381673	1.526852	1.704682	1.928799	2.220684	2.617033	3.186775	4.077279	5.674005	9.456674
m = 17	0.002045	0.698916	0.842665	0.945772	1.036893	1.127505	1.224656	1.334104	1.461720	1.614588	1.802324	2.039155	2.347697	2.766704	3.369027	4.310458	5.998500
m = 18	0.001841	0.689774	0.831159	0.931604	1.019055	1.104474	1.194366	1.293790	1.407615	1.541370	1.702149	1.899885	2.149465	2.474674	2.916335	3.551232	4.543578
m = 19	0.001666	0.681201	0.820431	0.918545	1.002873	1.083947	1.167846	1.259107	1.361880	1.480630	1.620792	1.789607	1.997395	2.259742	2.601620	3.065934	3.733397
m = 20	0.001515	0.673137	0.810387	0.906441	0.988078	1.065474	1.144362	1.228880	1.322646	1.429371	1.553357	1.700079	1.877000	2.094869	2.369992	2.728541	3.215504
m = 21	0.001383	0.665531	0.800951	0.895164	0.974460	1.048709	1.123361	1.202238	1.288558	1.385480	1.496506	1.625910	1.779281	1.964349	2.192316	2.480221	2.855441
m = 22	0.001268	0.658336	0.792057	0.884612	0.961854	1.033383	1.104417	1.178524	1.258612	1.347425	1.447886	1.563423	1.698354	1.858430	2.051670	2.289743	2.590433
m = 23	0.001167	0.651516	0.783649	0.874702	0.950123	1.019283	1.087199	1.157233	1.232046	1.314068	1.405790	1.510027	1.630204	1.770730	1.937543	2.138968	2.387155
m = 24	0.001077	0.645035	0.775682	0.865362	0.939159	1.006237	1.071444	1.137969	1.208276	1.284548	1.368948	1.463838	1.571998	1.696896	1.843059	2.016630	2.226251
m = 25	0.000997	0.638865	0.768113	0.856532	0.928870	0.994106	1.056942	1.120420	1.186845	1.258201	1.336399	1.423458	1.521682	1.633859	1.763530	1.915357	2.095698
m = 26	0.000926	0.632979	0.760907	0.848163	0.919180	0.982776	1.043521	1.104335	1.167389	1.234508	1.307402	1.387827	1.477726	1.579390	1.695647	1.830124	1.987632
m = 27	0.000862	0.627356	0.754034	0.840210	0.910026	0.972151	1.031042	1.089511	1.149617	1.213056	1.281375	1.356125	1.438973	1.531833	1.637009	1.757384	1.896690
m = 28	0.000805	0.621974	0.747467	0.832636	0.901354	0.962153	1.019389	1.075782	1.133294	1.193513	1.257857	1.327710	1.404526	1.489929	1.585829	1.694564	1.819087
m = 29	0.000753	0.616815	0.741181	0.825408	0.893117	0.952714	1.008465	1.063009	1.118225	1.175611	1.236477	1.302073	1.373683	1.452707	1.540754	1.639750	1.752077
m = 30	0.000706	0.611864	0.735154	0.818497	0.885274	0.943778	0.998189	1.051078	1.104251	1.159129	1.216933	1.278803	1.345886	1.419405	1.500735	1.591488	1.693618
m = 31	0.000663	0.607106	0.729369	0.811879	0.877792	0.935294	0.988493	1.039892	1.091239	1.143885	1.198977	1.257566	1.320686	1.389417	1.464951	1.548656	1.642158

		RP17	RP18	RP19	RP20	RP21	RP22	RP23	RP24	RP25	RP26	RP27	RP28	RP29	RP30	RP31
m = 17		9.997500														
m = 18		6.322913	10.538188													
m = 19		4.776647	6.647255	11.078759												
m = 20		3.915529	5.009672	6.971538	11.619229											
m = 21		3.365050	4.097631	5.242661	7.295767	12.159612										
m = 22		2.982322	3.514574	4.279707	5.475616	7.619951	12.699919									
m = 23		2.700629	3.109187	3.664081	4.461761	5.708542	7.944095	13.240159								
m = 24		2.484553	2.810813	3.236039	3.813570	4.643795	5.941443	8.268204	13.780340							
m = 25		2.313520	2.581941	2.920986	3.362877	3.963046	4.825811	6.174322	8.592281	14.320469						
m = 26		2.174753	2.400779	2.679319	3.031149	3.489705	4.112508	5.007812	6.407180	8.916331	14.860551					
m = 27		2.059891	2.253796	2.488030	2.776688	3.141303	3.616523	4.261959	5.189799	6.640021	9.240355	15.400592				
m = 28		1.963236	2.132138	2.332832	2.575273	2.874051	3.251450	3.743332	4.411400	5.371773	6.872845	9.564357	15.940596			
m = 29		1.880765	2.029768	2.204376	2.411860	2.662510	2.971407	3.361589	3.870134	4.560831	5.553736	7.105655	9.888339	16.480566		
m = 30		1.809559	1.942425	2.096288	2.276606	2.490882	2.749742	3.068757	3.471722	3.996928	4.710254	5.735688	7.338452	10.212303	17.020505	
m = 31		1.747447	1.867019	2.004072	2.162801	2.348830	2.569899	2.836968	3.166103	3.581850	4.123715	4.859669	5.917632	7.571237	10.536250	17.560417

Table A4. The corresponding probabilities of MSE-RPs from $P(IV)(0,1,0.1,5)$.

	P1	P2	P3	P4	P5	P6	P7	P8	P9	P10	P11	P12	P13	P14	P15	P16
m = 2	0.838195	0.161805														
m = 3	0.642074	0.317052	0.040874													
m = 4	0.480670	0.392115	0.113025	0.014190												
m = 5	0.360663	0.407760	0.177812	0.047784	0.005981											
m = 6	0.274208	0.389276	0.224062	0.086585	0.022992	0.002876										
m = 7	0.212063	0.354907	0.251141	0.122229	0.045963	0.012174	0.001523									
m = 8	0.166921	0.315534	0.262271	0.151081	0.070187	0.026203	0.006935	0.000868								
m = 9	0.133615	0.276854	0.261638	0.172141	0.092750	0.042471	0.015821	0.004186	0.000524							
m = 10	0.108618	0.241452	0.253125	0.185756	0.112147	0.059021	0.026891	0.010010	0.002649	0.000331						
m = 11	0.089537	0.210216	0.239839	0.192916	0.127760	0.074591	0.038905	0.017693	0.006584	0.001742	0.000218					
m = 12	0.074738	0.183188	0.224055	0.194845	0.139506	0.088447	0.050925	0.026464	0.012025	0.004474	0.001184	0.000148				
m = 13	0.063088	0.160034	0.207328	0.192766	0.147618	0.100223	0.062318	0.035661	0.018502	0.008404	0.003127	0.000827	0.000103			
m = 14	0.053791	0.140284	0.190660	0.187775	0.152501	0.109792	0.072685	0.044785	0.025555	0.013248	0.006017	0.002239	0.000592	0.000074		
m = 15	0.046280	0.123453	0.174657	0.180790	0.154634	0.117189	0.081801	0.053484	0.032807	0.018694	0.009688	0.004400	0.001637	0.000433	0.000054	
m = 16	0.040143	0.109092	0.159650	0.172542	0.154509	0.122550	0.089560	0.061522	0.039968	0.024460	0.013928	0.007216	0.003277	0.001219	0.000323	0.000040
m = 17	0.035076	0.096807	0.145794	0.163592	0.152594	0.126068	0.095944	0.068755	0.046827	0.030318	0.018532	0.010548	0.005465	0.002482	0.000923	0.000244
m = 18	0.030853	0.086264	0.133131	0.154354	0.149307	0.127969	0.100994	0.075103	0.053237	0.036087	0.023321	0.014245	0.008106	0.004200	0.001907	0.000709
m = 19	0.027304	0.077181	0.121636	0.145122	0.145009	0.128487	0.104790	0.080538	0.059101	0.041635	0.028147	0.018170	0.011095	0.006313	0.003270	0.001485
m = 20	0.024297	0.069324	0.111245	0.136102	0.140002	0.127850	0.107438	0.085064	0.064361	0.046864	0.032894	0.022203	0.014324	0.008744	0.004975	0.002577
m = 21	0.021732	0.062501	0.101876	0.127425	0.134531	0.126271	0.109056	0.088715	0.068988	0.051707	0.037474	0.026246	0.017699	0.011414	0.006967	0.003964
m = 22	0.019528	0.056550	0.093438	0.119175	0.128793	0.123942	0.109770	0.091541	0.072976	0.056121	0.041819	0.030220	0.021138	0.014246	0.009185	0.005606
m = 23	0.017623	0.051339	0.085843	0.111396	0.122939	0.121033	0.109703	0.093602	0.076335	0.060081	0.045882	0.034065	0.024573	0.017173	0.011570	0.007458
m = 24	0.015968	0.046758	0.079004	0.104106	0.117084	0.117689	0.108972	0.094969	0.079090	0.063578	0.049631	0.037732	0.027949	0.020138	0.014066	0.009474
m = 25	0.014521	0.042715	0.072840	0.097304	0.111316	0.114035	0.107689	0.095714	0.081273	0.066613	0.053045	0.041188	0.031222	0.023092	0.016626	0.011609
m = 26	0.013251	0.039135	0.067280	0.090980	0.105695	0.110173	0.105952	0.095908	0.082923	0.069196	0.056115	0.044407	0.034359	0.025995	0.019207	0.013822
m = 27	0.012130	0.035952	0.062257	0.085113	0.100266	0.106189	0.103853	0.095622	0.084081	0.071344	0.058836	0.047373	0.037332	0.028816	0.021773	0.016077
m = 28	0.011138	0.033114	0.057713	0.079678	0.095057	0.102148	0.101470	0.094922	0.084794	0.073080	0.061214	0.050076	0.040123	0.031528	0.024297	0.018343
m = 29	0.010255	0.030574	0.053595	0.074649	0.090085	0.098107	0.098871	0.093872	0.085106	0.074430	0.063257	0.052513	0.042719	0.034113	0.026753	0.020594
m = 30	0.009467	0.028295	0.049856	0.069998	0.085359	0.094107	0.096116	0.092527	0.085060	0.075419	0.064978	0.054684	0.045111	0.036555	0.029122	0.022807
m = 31	0.008761	0.026243	0.046457	0.065697	0.080880	0.090180	0.093254	0.090941	0.084700	0.076079	0.066391	0.056592	0.047295	0.038843	0.031389	0.024964

	P17	P18	P19	P20	P21	P22	P23	P24	P25	P26	P27	P28	P29	P30	P31
m = 17	0.000031														
m = 18	0.000188	0.000023													
m = 19	0.000552	0.000146	0.000018												
m = 20	0.001170	0.000435	0.000115	0.000014											
m = 21	0.002053	0.000932	0.000347	0.000092	0.000011										
m = 22	0.003189	0.001652	0.000750	0.000279	0.000074	0.000009									
m = 23	0.004552	0.002590	0.001341	0.000609	0.000227	0.000060	0.000008								
m = 24	0.006107	0.003727	0.002120	0.001098	0.000499	0.000186	0.000049	0.000006							
m = 25	0.007818	0.005039	0.003075	0.001749	0.000906	0.000412	0.000153	0.000041	0.000005						
m = 26	0.009649	0.006497	0.004188	0.002556	0.001454	0.000753	0.000342	0.000127	0.000034	0.000004					
m = 27	0.011565	0.008072	0.005435	0.003503	0.002138	0.001216	0.000630	0.000286	0.000106	0.000028	0.000004				
m = 28	0.013537	0.009736	0.006795	0.004575	0.002949	0.001799	0.001024	0.000530	0.000241	0.000090	0.000024	0.000003			
m = 29	0.015538	0.011463	0.008244	0.005753	0.003873	0.002496	0.001523	0.000867	0.000449	0.000204	0.000076	0.000020	0.000003		
m = 30	0.017543	0.013230	0.009759	0.007017	0.004897	0.003297	0.002125	0.001297	0.000738	0.000382	0.000174	0.000065	0.000017	0.000002	
m = 31	0.019532	0.015015	0.011321	0.008349	0.006003	0.004189	0.002820	0.001818	0.001109	0.000631	0.000327	0.000148	0.000055	0.000015	0.000002

Appendix C. Information Gain and Related Covered Range

Table A5. The IG from different numbers of MSE-RPs of $P(I)(1,5)$ and related covered range.

Number of MSE-RPs	IG	Covered Number of MSE-RPs	Covered Range
m = 6	$90\% \leq IG \leq 95\%$	6	$(1, 4.557853)$
m = 7	$90\% \leq IG \leq 95\%$	6	$(1, 3.122798)$
m = 8	$90\% \leq IG \leq 95\%$	7	$(1, 3.510284)$
	$95\% \leq IG \leq 98\%$	8	$(1, 5.850473)$
m = 9	$90\% \leq IG \leq 95\%$	7	$(1, 2.800594)$
	$95\% \leq IG \leq 98\%$	9	$(1, 6.495583)$
m = 10	$90\% \leq IG \leq 95\%$	8	$(1, 3.078516)$
	$95\% \leq IG \leq 98\%$	9	$(1, 4.284110)$
m = 11	$90\% \leq IG \leq 95\%$	9	$(1, 3.356274)$
	$95\% \leq IG \leq 98\%$	10	$(1, 4.670642)$
m = 12	$90\% \leq IG \leq 95\%$	9	$(1, 2.840237)$
	$95\% \leq IG \leq 98\%$	11	$(1, 5.056998)$
m = 13	$90\% \leq IG \leq 95\%$	10	$(1, 3.057155)$
	$95\% \leq IG \leq 98\%$	11	$(1, 3.911437)$
	$98\% \leq IG \leq 99\%$	13	$(1, 9.072026)$
m = 14	$90\% \leq IG \leq 95\%$	10	$(1, 2.688677)$
	$95\% \leq IG \leq 98\%$	12	$(1, 4.188889)$
	$98\% \leq IG \leq 99\%$	14	$(1, 9.715537)$
m = 15	$90\% \leq IG \leq 95\%$	11	$(1, 2.866721)$
	$95\% \leq IG \leq 98\%$	12	$(1, 3.490814)$
	$98\% \leq IG \leq 99\%$	14	$(1, 6.215339)$
m = 16	$90\% \leq IG \leq 95\%$	12	$(1, 3.044731)$
	$95\% \leq IG \leq 98\%$	13	$(1, 3.707577)$
	$98\% \leq IG \leq 99\%$	15	$(1, 6.601282)$
m = 17	$90\% \leq IG \leq 95\%$	12	$(1, 2.734661)$
	$95\% \leq IG \leq 98\%$	14	$(1, 3.924305)$
	$98\% \leq IG \leq 99\%$	16	$(1, 6.987163)$
m = 18	$90\% \leq IG \leq 95\%$	13	$(1, 2.885668)$
	$95\% \leq IG \leq 98\%$	14	$(1, 3.400669)$
	$98\% \leq IG \leq 99\%$	16	$(1, 5.298153)$
m = 19	$90\% \leq IG \leq 95\%$	13	$(1, 2.637633)$
	$95\% \leq IG \leq 98\%$	15	$(1, 3.578605)$
	$98\% \leq IG \leq 99\%$	17	$(1, 5.575373)$
	$99\% \leq IG$	19	$(1, 12.93129)$
m = 20	$90\% \leq IG \leq 95\%$	14	$(1, 2.768771)$
	$95\% \leq IG \leq 98\%$	16	$(1, 3.756524)$
	$98\% \leq IG \leq 99\%$	18	$(1, 5.852566)$
	$99\% \leq IG$	20	$(1, 13.574203)$

Table A6. The IG from different numbers of MSE-RPs of $P(III)(0,1,0.2)$ and related covered range.

Number of MSE-RPs	IG	Covered Number of MSE-RPs	Covered Range
m = 7	$90\% \leq IG \leq 95\%$	7	(0, 4.186923)
m = 8	$90\% \leq IG \leq 95\%$	7	(0, 2.813247)
m = 9	$90\% \leq IG \leq 95\%$	8	(0, 3.115306)
	$95\% \leq IG \leq 98\%$	9	(0, 5.193419)
m = 10	$90\% \leq IG \leq 95\%$	8	(0, 2.453194)
	$95\% \leq IG \leq 98\%$	10	(0, 5.695577)
m = 11	$90\% \leq IG \leq 95\%$	9	(0,2.670200)
	$95\% \leq IG \leq 98\%$	10	(0,3.717980)
m = 12	$90\% \leq IG \leq 95\%$	9	(0, 2.253536)
	$95\% \leq IG \leq 98\%$	11	(0, 4.018854)
m = 13	$90\% \leq IG \leq 95\%$	10	(0, 2.423314)
	$95\% \leq IG \leq 98\%$	12	(0, 4.319518)
m = 14	$90\% \leq IG \leq 95\%$	11	(0, 2.592731)
	$95\% \leq IG \leq 98\%$	12	(0, 3.319267)
m = 15	$90\% \leq IG \leq 95\%$	11	(0, 2.265638)
	$95\% \leq IG \leq 98\%$	13	(0, 3.535249)
	$98\% \leq IG \leq 99\%$	15	(0, 8.200847)
m = 16	$90\% \leq IG \leq 95\%$	12	(0, 2.404934)
	$95\% \leq IG \leq 98\%$	14	(0, 3.751119)
	$98\% \leq IG \leq 99\%$	16	(0, 8.701244)
m = 17	$90\% \leq IG \leq 95\%$	13	(0, 2.543988)
	$95\% \leq IG \leq 98\%$	14	(0, 3.099726)
	$98\% \leq IG \leq 99\%$	16	(0, 5.520828)
m = 18	$90\% \leq IG \leq 95\%$	13	(0, 2.274345)
	$95\% \leq IG \leq 98\%$	15	(0, 2.682864)
	$98\% \leq IG \leq 99\%$	17	(0, 4.182610)
m = 19	$90\% \leq IG \leq 95\%$	14	(0, 2.392483)
	$95\% \leq IG \leq 98\%$	16	(0, 3.437139)
	$98\% \leq IG \leq 99\%$	18	(0, 6.120974)
m = 20	$90\% \leq IG \leq 95\%$	14	(0, 2.178159)
	$95\% \leq IG \leq 98\%$	16	(0, 2.960250)
	$98\% \leq IG \leq 99\%$	18	(0, 4.613867)
m = 21	$90\% \leq IG \leq 95\%$	15	(0, 2.280909)
	$95\% \leq IG \leq 98\%$	17	(0, 3.098813)
	$98\% \leq IG \leq 99\%$	19	(0, 4.829431)
	$99\% \leq IG$	21	(0, 11.201569)

Table A7. The IG from different numbers of MSE-RPs of $P(IV)(0,1,0.1,0.5)$ and related covered range.

Number of MSE-RPs	IG	Covered Number of MSE-RPs	Covered Range
m = 7	$90\% \leq IG \leq 95\%$	7	$(0, 4.574898)$
m = 8	$90\% \leq IG \leq 95\%$	7	$(0, 3.071896)$
m = 9	$90\% \leq IG \leq 95\%$	8	$(0, 3.398221)$
	$95\% \leq IG \leq 98\%$	9	$(0, 5.663702)$
m = 10	$90\% \leq IG \leq 95\%$	8	$(0, 2.676082)$
	$95\% \leq IG \leq 98\%$	10	$(0, 6.206803)$
m = 11	$90\% \leq IG \leq 95\%$	9	$(0, 2.909991)$
	$95\% \leq IG \leq 98\%$	10	$(0, 4.049591)$
m = 12	$90\% \leq IG \leq 95\%$	10	$(0, 3.143704)$
	$95\% \leq IG \leq 98\%$	11	$(0, 4.374829)$
m = 13	$90\% \leq IG \leq 95\%$	10	$(0, 2.639643)$
	$95\% \leq IG \leq 98\%$	12	$(0, 4.699852)$
m = 14	$90\% \leq IG \leq 95\%$	11	$(0, 2.822096)$
	$95\% \leq IG \leq 98\%$	12	$(0, 3.610697)$
m = 15	$90\% \leq IG \leq 95\%$	11	$(0, 2.467316)$
	$95\% \leq IG \leq 98\%$	13	$(0, 3.844030)$
	$98\% \leq IG \leq 99\%$	15	$(0, 8.915686)$
m = 16	$90\% \leq IG \leq 95\%$	12	$(0, 2.617033)$
	$95\% \leq IG \leq 98\%$	14	$(0, 4.077279)$
	$98\% \leq IG \leq 99\%$	16	$(0, 9.456674)$
m = 17	$90\% \leq IG \leq 95\%$	13	$(0, 2.766704)$
	$95\% \leq IG \leq 98\%$	14	$(0, 3.369027)$
	$98\% \leq IG \leq 99\%$	16	$(0, 5.998500)$
m = 18	$90\% \leq IG \leq 95\%$	13	$(0, 2.474674)$
	$95\% \leq IG \leq 98\%$	15	$(0, 3.551232)$
	$98\% \leq IG \leq 99\%$	17	$(0, 6.322913)$
m = 19	$90\% \leq IG \leq 95\%$	14	$(0, 2.601620)$
	$95\% \leq IG \leq 98\%$	16	$(0, 3.733397)$
	$98\% \leq IG \leq 99\%$	18	$(0, 6.647255)$
m = 20	$90\% \leq IG \leq 95\%$	15	$(0, 2.728541)$
	$95\% \leq IG \leq 98\%$	16	$(0, 3.215504)$
	$98\% \leq IG \leq 99\%$	18	$(0, 5.009672)$
m = 21	$90\% \leq IG \leq 95\%$	15	$(0, 2.480221)$
	$95\% \leq IG \leq 98\%$	17	$(0, 3.365050)$
	$98\% \leq IG \leq 99\%$	19	$(0, 5.242661)$
m = 22	$90\% \leq IG \leq 95\%$	16	$(0, 2.590433)$
	$95\% \leq IG \leq 98\%$	18	$(0, 3.514574)$
	$98\% \leq IG \leq 99\%$	20	$(0, 5.475616)$
	$99\% \leq IG$	22	$(0, 12.699919)$

References

1. Pareto, V. *Cours d'Économie Politique*; Librairie Droz: Geneva, Switzerland, 1964; Volume 1.
2. Kleiber, C. *Statistical Size Distributions in Economics and Actuarial Sciences*; John Wiley & Sons, Inc.: Hoboken, NJ, USA, 2003.
3. Coronel-Brizio, H.F.; Hernandez-Montoya, A.R. On fitting the Pareto–Levy distribution to stock market index data: Selecting a suitable cutoff value. *Phys. A Stat. Mech. Its Appl.* **2005**, *354*, 437–449. [CrossRef]
4. Embrechts, P.; Kluppelberg, C.; Mikosch, T. Modelling extremal events. *Br. Actuar. J.* **1999**, *5*, 465.
5. Bartlett, M.S. Properties of sufficiency and statistical tests. *Proc. R. Soc. Lond. Ser. A-Math. Phys. Sci.* **1937**, *160*, 268–282.

6. Arnold, B.C. Pareto and generalized Pareto distributions. In *Modeling Income Distributions and Lorenz Curves*; Springer: Berlin/Heidelberg, Germany, 2008; pp. 119–145.
7. Van Montfort, M.A.J.; Witter, J.V. The generalized Pareto distribution applied to rainfall depths. *Hydrol. Sci. J.* **1986**, *31*, 151–162. [CrossRef]
8. Kagan, Y.Y. Earthquake size distribution and earthquake insurance. *Commun. Stat. Stoch. Model.* **1997**, *13*, 775–797. [CrossRef]
9. Khu, S.T.; Madsen, H. Multiobjective calibration with Pareto preference ordering: An application to rainfall-runoff model calibration. *Water Resour. Res.* **2005**, *41*, W03004. [CrossRef]
10. Quandt, R.E. Old and mew methods of estimation and the pareto distribution. *Metrika* **1966**, *10*, 55–82. [CrossRef]
11. Brazauskas, V.; Serfling, R. Robust estimation of tail parameters for two-parameter Pareto and exponential models via generalized quantile statistics. *Extremes* **2000**, *3*, 231–249. [CrossRef]
12. Brazauskas, V.; Serfling, R. Small sample performance of robust estimators of tail parameters for Pareto and exponential models. *J. Stat. Comput. Simul.* **2001**, *70*, 1–19. [CrossRef]
13. Ghosh, I. A new discrete pareto type (IV) model: Theory, properties and applications. *J. Stat. Distrib. Appl.* **2020**, *7*, 3. [CrossRef]
14. Fang, K.T.; He, S.D. *The Problem of Selecting a Given Number of Representative Points in a Normal Population and a Generalized Mills' Ratio*; Department of Statistic Stanford University: Stanford, CA, USA, 1982.
15. Yang, J.; He, P.; Fang, K.T. Three kinds of discrete approximations of statistical multivariate distributions and their applications. *J. Multivar. Anal.* **2022**, *188*, 104829. [CrossRef]
16. Niederreiter, H. *Random Number Generation and Quasi-Monte Carlo Methods*; SIAM: Pennsylvania, PA, USA, 1992.
17. Pagès, G. Introduction to Vector Quantization and Its Applications for Numerics. *ESAIM Proc. Surv.* **2015**, *48*, 29–79. [CrossRef]
18. Max, J. Quantizing for Minimum Distortion. *IRE Trans. Inf. Theory* **1960**, *6*, 7–12. [CrossRef]
19. Flury, B. Principal Points. *Biometrika* **1990**, *77*, 33–41. [CrossRef]
20. Gersho, A.; Gary, R. *Vector Quantization and Signal Compression*; Kluwer Academic Publishers: Boston, MA, USA, 1992.
21. Tarpey, T.; Petkova, E. Principal Point Classification: Applications to Differentiating Drug and Placebo Responses in Longitudinal Studies. *J. Stat. Plan. Inference* **2010**, *140*, 539–550. [CrossRef]
22. Fang, K.; Zhou, M.; Wang, W. Applications of the Representative Points in Statistical Simulations. *Sci. China Math.* **2014**, *57*, 2609–2620. [CrossRef]
23. Lemaire, V.; Montes, T.; Pagès, G. New Weak Error Bounds and Expansions for Optimal Quantization. *J. Comput. Appl. Math.* **2020**, *371*, 112670. [CrossRef]
24. Ke, X.; Wang, S.R.; Zhou, M.; Ye, H.J. New approaches on parameter estimation of the gamma distribution. *Mathematics* **2023**, *11*, 927. [CrossRef]
25. Lloyd, S. Least squares quantization in PCM. *IEEE Trans. Inf. Theory* **1982**, *28*, 129–137. [CrossRef]
26. Linde, Y.; Buzo, A.; Gray, R. An algorithm for vector quantizer design. *IEEE Trans. Commun.* **1980**, *28*, 84–95. [CrossRef]
27. Fang, K.T.; Wang, Y.; Bentler, P.M. Some applications of number-theoretic methods in statistics. *Stat. Sci.* **1994**, *9*, 416–428. [CrossRef]
28. Tarpey, T. Estimating principal points of univariate distributions. *J. Appl. Stat.* **1997**, *24*, 499–512. [CrossRef]
29. Matsuura, S.; Tarpey, T. Optimal principal points estimators of multivariate distributions of location-scale and location-scale-rotation families. *Stat. Pap.* **2020**, *61*, 1629–1643. [CrossRef]
30. Li, Y.N.; Fang, K.T.; He, P.; Peng, H. Representative points from a mixture of two normal distributions. *Mathematics* **2022**, *10*, 3952. [CrossRef]
31. Lomax, K.S. Business failures: Another example of the analysis of failure data. *J. Am. Stat. Assoc.* **1954**, *49*, 847–852. [CrossRef]
32. Lu, H.L.; Tao, S.H. The estimation of Pareto distribution by a weighted least square method. *Qual. Quant.* **2007**, *41*, 913–926. [CrossRef]
33. Tarpey, T.; Flury, B. Self-consistency: A fundamental concept in statistics. *Stat. Sci.* **1996**, *11*, 229–243. [CrossRef]
34. Zoppè, A. Principal points of univariate continuous distributions. *Stat. Comput.* **1995**, *5*, 127–132. [CrossRef]
35. Fang, K.; Pan, J. A Review of Representative Points of Statistical Distributions and Their Applications. *Mathematics* **2023**, *11*, 2930. [CrossRef]
36. Trushkin, A. Sufficient conditions for uniqueness of a locally optimal quantizer for a class of convex error weighting functions. *IEEE Trans. Inf. Theory* **1982**, *28*, 187–198. [CrossRef]
37. Xu, L.H.; Fang, K.T.; He, P. Properties and generation of representative points of the exponential distribution. In *Statistical Papers*; Springer: Berlin/Heidelberg, Germany, 2022; pp. 1–27.
38. Stampfer, E.; Stadlober, E. Methods for estimating principal points. *Commun. Stat.-Simul. Comput.* **2002**, *31*, 261–277. [CrossRef]
39. Harrell, F.E.; Davis, C.E. A new distribution-free quantile estimator. *Biometrika* **1982**, *69*, 635–640. [CrossRef]
40. Brewer, K.R.W. Likelihood based estimation of quantiles and density estimation. 1986, *Unpublished manuscript*.
41. Heathcote, A.; Brown, S.; Mewhort, D.J.K. Quantile maximum likelihood estimation of response time distributions. *Psychon. Bull. Rev.* **2002**, *9*, 394–401. [CrossRef] [PubMed]

42. Navruz, G.; Özdemir, A.F. A new quantile estimator with weights based on a subsampling approach. *Br. J. Math. Stat. Psychol.* **2020**, *73*, 506–521. [CrossRef]
43. Brazauskas, V.; Serfling, R. Favorable estimators for fitting Pareto models: A study using goodness-of-fit measures with actual data. *ASTIN Bull. J. IAA* **2003**, *33*, 365–381. [CrossRef]
44. Kim, J.H.T.; Ahn, S.; Ahn, S. Parameter estimation of the Pareto distribution using a pivotal quantity. *J. Korean Stat. Soc.* **2017**, *46*, 438–450. [CrossRef]
45. Abd El-Raheem, A.M.; Abu-Moussa, M.H.; Mohie El-Din, M.M.; Hafez, E.H. Accelerated life tests under Pareto-IV lifetime distribution: Real data application and simulation study. *Mathematics* **2020**, *8*, 1786. [CrossRef]

entropy

MDPI

Article

An Aliasing Measure of Factor Effects in Three-Level Regular Designs

Qiuying Chen, Zhiming Li * and Zhi Li

College of Mathematics and System Science, Xinjiang University, Urumqi 830017, China; 107552300624@stu.xju.edu.cn (Q.C.); lizhi@xju.edu.cn (Z.L.)
* Correspondence: zmli@xju.edu.cn

Abstract

For three-level regular designs, the confounding from the perspectives of both factor and component effects leads to different results. The aliasing properties of factor effects are more significant than the latter in the experimental model. In this paper, a new three-level aliasing pattern is proposed to evaluate the degree of aliasing among different factors. Based on the classification pattern, a new criterion is introduced for choosing optimal three-level regular designs. Then, we analyze the relationship between the criterion and the existing criteria, including general minimum lower-order confounding, entropy, minimum aberration, and clear effects. The results show that the classification patterns of other criteria can be expressed as functions of our proposed pattern. Further, an aliasing algorithm is provided, and all 27-run, some of the 81-run, and 243-run three-level designs are listed in tables and compared with the rankings under other criteria. A real example is provided to illustrate the proposed methods.

Keywords: regular design; optimal criterion; aliasing information; algorithm

1. Introduction

Regular designs are widely applied in agriculture, industry, and other fields. The selection of optimal regular designs for improving yield and shortening testing cycles has garnered attention in theoretical and practical fields. Several criteria have been established for the selection of optimal designs. The first criterion is the maximum resolution (MR) criterion introduced by Box and Hunter [1], which selects designs with higher resolutions. The second one, proposed by Fries and Hunter [2], is the minimum aberration (MA) criterion, which is based on the word-length pattern (WLP). The third criterion, based on the definition of clear effects, was proposed by Wu and Chen [3], which selects designs with the maximum number of clear main effects and two-factor interactions (2fis) [4]. More details of the above criteria can be found in Mukerjee and Wu [5] and Wu and Hamada [6]. Zhang and Wang [7] proved the entropy optimality of orthogonal designs. The characterization of confounding information under these criteria varies, leading to the selection of different optimal designs.

To reveal the essence of the aforementioned criteria, Zhang et al. [8] introduced an aliased effect-number pattern (AENP) for two-level designs. Based on AENP, a general minimum lower-order confounding (GMC) criterion is proposed to evaluate two-level regular designs. Zhang and Mukerjee [9] studied the properties of s-level GMC designs via complementary sets. Li et al. [10] introduced the aliased component-number pattern (ACNP) and proposed a three-level GMC criterion. Li et al. [11] proved that classification

https://doi.org/10.3390/e27070680

patterns for MR, MA, and CE can be represented by the ACNP. In this sense, the GMC criterion is more informative and elaborate than other criteria. Up to now, there have been many achievements for three-level GMC designs [12,13]. However, the classification patterns of all the above results are based on the component properties of designs. Unlike the two-level case, the interpretability of component confounding is limited in higher-level designs. It is not easy to distinguish between factor aliasing effectively. Furthermore, the number of components increases exponentially, significantly raising computational complexity. The nonlinear relationships between component effects may introduce unnecessary complexity in modeling [6].

In a practical model, the aliasing between factors with three levels is often more critical to optimize experimental conditions (Jaynes et al. [14], Suriyaamporn et al. [15], and Nieweś [16]). Guo et al. [17] and Cheng et al. [18] screened the optimal process conditions through three-level orthogonal designs and validated the selected results using the entropy weight method. So far, the study of higher-level factor aliasing remains unfulfilled for regular designs with three levels. It is difficult for the existing results to express the aliasing among factor effects. Motivated by the analysis above, we focus on studying three-level factor aliasing. From a factor-based perspective, the aliasing measure aims to reduce computational complexity, make the results easier to interpret, and enhance the practical value for modeling applications. Thus, the main contributions and innovations of our work focus on the following aspects:

(i) A factor aliasing pattern is first proposed to describe the aliasing information of three-level regular designs, and a new criterion is introduced based on the pattern. For the two-level design, the pattern is equivalent to the AENP. However, it differs from the ACNP of three-level designs because of the relationship between factor and component effects.

(ii) We analyze the relationship between the proposed and existing patterns to reveal the essential characteristics of various confounding and alias relations.

(iii) Based on the proposed criterion, we propose an aliasing algorithm of lower-order factors to choose optimal designs. Compared with other criteria, tables list all 27-, some 81-, and 243-run optimal designs.

The main structure of this paper is organized as follows. Section 2 introduces a new measure for describing factor aliasing, known as the aliased factor-number pattern (AFNP) for three-level regular designs, along with a criterion for general minimizing lower-order aliasing based on factor effect (GMAF), which utilizes the AFNP. The relationship between the new criterion and the GMC, entropy, MA, and CE criteria is discussed in Section 3. Section 4 presents an aliasing algorithm of the GMAF criteria and a catalog of the optimal designs for all 27- and some 81- and 243-run designs of resolution IV or higher. Section 5 provides an example to illustrate the application of the new criterion. Section 6 offers a brief conclusion.

2. Some Basic Concepts

We first review some basic concepts of three-level designs. Let n and m be two positive integers with $n > m$. Define $q = n - m$ and $N = 3^q$. The numbers $1, 2, \ldots, q$ correspond to q independent columns. A $3^{(N-1)/2-((N-1)/2-q)}$ saturated design H_q is determined by the following recursive process:

$$H_1 = \{1\}, \quad H_r = \{H_{r-1}, r, rH_{r-1}, r^2 H_{r-1}\}, \quad r = 2, \ldots, q,$$

where $r^i H_{r-1} = \{r^i d : d \in H_{r-1}\}$ for $r = 2, \ldots, q$ and $i = 1, 2$. Here, the operation rd is the element-wise addition modulo 3 over the Galois field of order 3, denoted as $GF(3)$. Thus, $H_q = \{H_{q-1}, q, qH_{q-1}, q^2 H_{q-1}\}$. A 3^{n-m} design with n factors $d_1, \ldots, d_n$, each having three levels, is constructed by q independent columns $1, \ldots, q$ and m additional columns generated from the three-level saturated design H_q. We call $d_{l_1} \times d_{l_2} \times \cdots \times d_{li} (1 \le i, l_i \le n)$ an i-order factor interaction ($i$fi) of the design, corresponding to 2^{i-1} orthogonal factor-interaction components (fics). In particular, d_i is the main effect, and $d_{l_1} \times d_{l_2}$ means a 2fi.

Consider a 3^{4-1} design $D = \{1, 2, 3, 123\}$ with the defining relation $I = 1234^2$. Suppose that third- and higher-order interactions are negligible. By multiplying both sides of $I = 1234^2$ by main effect and 2fic, we have $12 = 34^2, 13 = 24^2$ and $23 = 14^2$. It is evident that no main effects are aliased with other main effects or 2fics, and six 2fics are confounded with one other 2fic. Suppose any component of a factor effect is confounded with a component of another factor. In that case, the factor is aliased with the corresponding factor, and the symbol "$\approx$" denotes that two factors are aliased. Thus, 2fis $1 \times 2, 1 \times 3, 1 \times 4, 2 \times 3, 2 \times 4, 3 \times 4$ are aliased with one other two-factor interaction, denoted by $1 \times 2 \approx 3 \times 4, 1 \times 3 \approx 2 \times 4, 2 \times 3 \approx 1 \times 4$. In this example, the confounding relationship between component and factor effects is one-to-one. However, this is a special case. In most three-level designs, the confounding relationships between the two are not necessarily one-to-one. For example, consider another 3^{5-2} design $D = \{1, 2, 3, 123, 12^2\}$ with the defining relation $I = 1234^2 = 12^25^2 = 13^245 = 23^245^2$. We have $12 = 34^2 = 15 = 25^2$, $12^2 = 5$, $13 = 24^2$, and $13^2 = 45$. Thus, 2fis $1 \times 2 \approx 3 \times 4 \approx 1 \times 5 \approx 2 \times 5 \approx 5$, and $1 \times 3 \approx 2 \times 4 \approx 4 \times 5$. Note that in the aliasing relationship denoted by $\approx$, transitivity does not hold. Using the aforementioned aliasing relationships as an example, 1×2 is aliased with three 2fis: 3×4, 1×5, 2×5, and one main effect 5. However, it cannot be inferred that the 2fi 3×4 is aliased with 1×5, 2×5, or the main effect 5.

Next, we introduce a new classification pattern to describe the aliasing relationships among various factor effects in three-level designs. In the orthogonal component system, a $j$fi consists of 2^{j-1} mutually orthogonal $j$fics. Thus, an $i$fi is aliased with at most one component of a $j$fi, while the remaining $i$fics are not aliased with this $j$fi. Denote $K_j = \binom{n}{j}$. An $i$fi is aliased with at most K_j $j$fis. For $0 \le i, j \le n$ and $0 \le k \le K_j$, let ${}^{\#}_{i}A_j^{(k)}$ be the number of $i$fis aliased with k $j$fis. The set $\{{}^{\#}_{i}A_j^{(k)}, i, j = 0, 1, 2, \ldots, n; k = 0, 1, 2, \ldots, K_j\}$ is used to measure the aliasing degrees between various factor effects of any three-level designs. The larger k is, the more severe the aliasing in the set. Given the fixed value (i, j), ${}^{\#}_{i}A_j^{(k)} (k = 0, 1, \ldots, K_j)$ are arranged according to the aliasing severity, and denote ${}^{\#}_{i}A_j = ({}^{\#}_{i}A_j^{(0)}, {}^{\#}_{i}A_j^{(1)}, \ldots, {}^{\#}_{i}A_j^{(K_j)})$ for $0 \le i, j \le n$.

Based on the effect hierarchy principle, we introduce a factorial effect hierarchy principle (FEHP): (i) A lower-order factor effect is likely more important than a higher-order one, and (ii) factor effects of the same order are equally important. For any (i, j) and (s, t), the sorting rules are based on the FEHP: (i) If $\max\{i, j\} < \max\{s, t\}$, then ${}^{\#}_{i}A_j$ is ranked before ${}^{\#}_{s}A_t$. (ii) If $\max\{i, j\} = \max\{s, t\}$ and $i < s$, then ${}^{\#}_{i}A_j$ is ranked before ${}^{\#}_{s}A_t$. (iii) If $\max\{i, j\} = \max\{s, t\}$ and $i = s$, $j < t$, then ${}^{\#}_{i}A_j$ is ranked before ${}^{\#}_{s}A_t$. Note that the 0th-order effect is the grand mean. For $i \ge 2$, we have ${}^{\#}_{i}A_0 = (\binom{n}{i} - A_i, A_i)$ and ${}^{\#}_{0}A_i = (0^{A_i}, 1)$, where A_i is the number of $i$fics aliased with the grand mean. We use 0^s to denote s successive zero components; the tail part is cut hereafter if it has a tail with successive zero components. Since ${}^{\#}_{i}A_0$ is determined from the preceding ${}^{\#}_{0}A_i$, ${}^{\#}_{i}A_0$ is ignored in the ranking process. According to the above ranking rules, we obtain a new sequence as follows:

$$^{\#}A = ({}^{\#}_{1}A_2, {}^{\#}_{2}A_1, {}^{\#}_{2}A_2, {}^{\#}_{0}A_3, {}^{\#}_{1}A_3, {}^{\#}_{2}A_3, {}^{\#}_{3}A_1, {}^{\#}_{3}A_2, {}^{\#}_{3}A_3, \ldots), \tag{1}$$

called the aliased factor-number pattern (AFNP) of a three-level design. For the abovementioned 3^{5-2} design, we have $({}^{\#}_{1}A_2; {}^{\#}_{2}A_1; {}^{\#}_{2}A_2) = $ (2,3;7,3;0,0,6,4). Based on the definition of factor aliasing, the relationship $\sum_{k=1}^{2} k\,{}_2^{\#}A_1^{(k)} = \sum_{k=1}^{K_2} k\,{}_1^{\#}A_2^{(k)}$ holds. Thus, in analyzing the aliasing between main effects and 2fis, only ${}_1^{\#}A_2$ needs to be considered.

One of the main objectives of experimental design is to estimate as many factor effects as possible, particularly lower-order factor effects, such as main effects and 2fis. Therefore, a good design should minimize aliasing among lower-order factor effects and sequentially maximize the elements in ${}^{\#}A$. Based on the AFNP, we propose a new optimal criterion as follows.

Definition 1. *Let ${}^{\#}A_l$ be the l-th component of ${}^{\#}A$ and ${}^{\#}A(D_i)(i = 1,2)$ be the AFNPs of designs $D_i(i = 1,2)$. Suppose that ${}^{\#}A_l$ is the first element such that ${}^{\#}A(D_1)$ and ${}^{\#}A(D_2)$ are different. If ${}^{\#}A_l(D_1) > {}^{\#}A_l(D_2)$, then D_1 has less general lower-order aliasing based on factor effect (GLOAF) than D_2. A design D is said to have general minimum lower-order aliasing based on factor effects (GMLOAF, or GMAF for short) if no other design has less GLOAF than D, and such a design is a GMAF design.*

Example 1. *Consider three 3^{8-4} designs $D_i(i = 1,2,3)$. Table 1 shows the elements ${}_i^{\#}A_j(i, j = 1,2)$ of their AFNPs. Thus, the optimal ordering of the designs under the GMAF criterion is D_1, D_2, D_3, whereas the ordering changes to D_3, D_2, D_1 under the GMC criterion. This indicates that the ranking results of designs vary significantly under different optimal criteria. The designs selected based on the GMAF criterion minimize aliasing among lower-order factor effects. Unlike the GMC criterion, which evaluates confounding at the components of a factor, GMAF considers the factor as a whole, thereby reducing computational complexity and improving the efficiency of identifying optimal factor combinations.*

Table 1. Some ${}_i^{\#}A_j$'s of designs $D_i(i = 1,2,3)$ for $i, j = 1,2$.

Design	D_1		D_2		D_3	
${}_i^{\#}A_j$	$j = 1$	$j = 2$	$j = 1$	$j = 2$	$j = 1$	$j = 2$
$i = 1$	-	8	-	8	-	8
$i = 2$	28	0, 0, 24, 4	28	0, 0, 18, 10	28	0, 0, 12, 16

Under the assumption that all three-order or higher-order effects are negligible, we only analyze two elements ${}_1^{\#}A_2(D)$ and ${}_2^{\#}A_2(D)$ of the AFNP. Let F_q be a set of all possible pairwise combinations of elements in H_q, with its explicit structure:

$$F_q = \{a \times b \mid a, b \in H_q, a \neq b\}.$$

For instance, $F_2 = \{1 \times 2,\ 1 \times (12),\ 1 \times (12^2),\ 2 \times (12),\ 2 \times (12^2),\ (12) \times (12^2)\}$. Note that the number of elements in H_q is given by $(3^m - 1)/2$, and the number of elements in F_q is $\binom{(3^m-1)/2}{2}$. Let $\widetilde{D}$ denote the factor structure of D. In a three-level design D, the number of 2fis aliased with $\eta \in \widetilde{D} \cup F_q$ is defined as:

$$E_2(D, \eta) = \#\{(d_1, d_2) : d_1 \times d_2 \approx \eta,\ d_1, d_2 \in D\},$$

where $d_1 \times d_2$ represents the corresponding two-factor interaction. Thus, the following expressions of ${}_1^{\#}A_2$ and ${}_2^{\#}A_2$ are derived by

$${}_1^{\#}A_2^{(k)}(D) = \#\{\eta : \eta \in \widetilde{D},\ E_2(D, \eta) = k\},\quad {}_2^{\#}A_2^{(k)}(D) = \#\{\eta : \eta \in F_q,\ E_2(D, \eta) = k + 1\} \quad (2)$$

for $0 \leq k \leq K_2$.

Example 2. *Consider a 3^{5-2} design $D_4 = \{1, 2, 3, 123, 12\}$, with its factor structure $\widetilde{D}_4 = \{1, 2, 3, 1 \times 2 \times 3, 1 \times 2\}$. The confounding relationships between main effects and 2fics are given as follows:*

$$1 = 25^2, \quad 2 = 15^2, \quad 3 = 45^2, \quad 4 = 35, \quad 5 = 12 = 34^2,$$
$$13 = 24^2, \quad 23 = 14^2, \quad 25 = 12^2 = 15, \quad 35^2 = 45 = 34.$$

We first calculate the values of ${}_1^{\#}A_2^{(k)}$ for $\eta \in \widetilde{D}$ by the definition of $E_2(D, \eta)$. For $\eta \in \widetilde{D}$, we have:

$$E_2(D, \eta) = \begin{cases} 1, & \eta \in \{1,\ 2,\ 3,\ 1 \times 2 \times 3\}, \\ 2, & \eta = 1 \times 2. \end{cases}$$

Thus, ${}_1^{\#}A_2^{(1)}(D_4) = \#\{\eta : \eta \in \widetilde{D}_4, E_2(D_4, \eta) = 1\} = 4$, ${}_1^{\#}A_2^{(2)}(D_4) = \#\{\eta : \eta \in \widetilde{D}_4, E_2(D_4, \eta) = 2\} = 1$. For all other k, ${}_1^{\#}A_2^{(k)}(D_4) = 0$. Then, ${}_1^{\#}A_2(D_4) = (0, 4, 1)$. For $\eta \in F_3$, we have:

$$E_2(D, \eta) = \begin{cases} 2, & \eta \in \{1 \times 3,\ 1 \times (123),\ 2 \times 3,\ 2 \times (123)\}, \\ 3, & \eta \in \{1 \times (12),\ 2 \times (12),\ 3 \times (12),\ (123) \times (12)\}, \\ 4, & \eta \in \{1 \times 2,\ 3 \times (123)\}. \end{cases}$$

Hence, ${}_2^{\#}A_2^{(1)}(D_4) = \#\{\eta : \eta \in F_3, E_2(D_4, \eta) = 2\} = 4$, ${}_2^{\#}A_2^{(2)}(D_4) = \#\{\eta : \eta \in F_3, E_2(D_4, \eta) = 3\} = 4$, and ${}_2^{\#}A_2^{(3)}(D_4) = 2$. For all other k, ${}_2^{\#}A_2^{(k)}(D_4) = 0$. Therefore, ${}_2^{\#}A_2(D_4) = (0, 4, 4, 2)$.

3. Relationship with the Existing Criteria

3.1. Relationship with GMC Criterion

We review the GMC criterion proposed by Li et al. [10] for selecting optimal three-level designs. For $1 \le i, j \le n$, let ${}_i^{\#}C_j^{(k)}$ be the number of ith-order effects confounded with k jth-order effects. Denote ${}_i^{\#}C_j = ({}_i^{\#}C_j^{(0)}, {}_i^{\#}C_j^{(1)}, \ldots, {}_i^{\#}C_j^{(K_j)})$ for $0 \le i, j \le n$ and $K_j = \binom{n}{j}$. We call the simplified sequence

$${}^{\#}C = ({}_1^{\#}C_2, {}_2^{\#}C_2, {}_1^{\#}C_3, {}_2^{\#}C_3, {}_3^{\#}C_2, {}_3^{\#}C_3, \cdots),$$

the ACNP of the design. A design that sequentially maximizes ${}^{\#}C$ is called a GMC design. Following Li et al. [10], for a 3^{n-m} design D, $B_2(D, \gamma)$ is the number of 2fics in D, confounded with $\gamma (\in H_q)$, and defined as follows:

$$B_2(D, \gamma) = \#\{(d_1, d_2) : d_1 d_2 = \gamma \text{ or } d_1 d_2^2 = \gamma,\ d_1, d_2 \in D\}.$$

Further, ${}_1^{\#}C_2$ and ${}_2^{\#}C_2$ are expressed as:

$${}_1^{\#}C_2^{(k)}(D) = \#\{\gamma : \gamma \in D,\ B_2(D, \gamma) = k\},$$
$${}_2^{\#}C_2^{(k)}(D) = (k+1)\#\{\gamma : \gamma \in H_q,\ B_2(D, \gamma) = k+1\}.$$

Since every main effect only corresponds to a component, it follows that:

$$\#\{\gamma : \gamma \in D,\ B_2(D, \gamma) = k\} = \#\{\eta : \eta \in \widetilde{D},\ E_2(D, \eta) = k\}.$$

That is to say, ${}_1^{\#}C_2^{(k)}(D) = {}_1^{\#}A_2^{(k)}(D)$ always holds. More generally, ${}_1^{\#}C_j^{(k)}(D) = {}_1^{\#}A_j^{(k)}(D)$ for any $0 \le j \le n$.

Based on the GMAF criterion, we analyze the relationship between the AFNP and the ACNP. If an $i$fi is aliased with k $j$fis, let k_t represent the degree of confounding between the t-th component of the $i$fi and $j$fics, where $t = 1, 2, \ldots, 2^{i-1}$. It holds that $\sum_{t=1}^{2^{i-1}} k_t = k$. In the case of 2fis, each 2fi generates two components. Thus, for a 3^{n-m} design, the value of ${}_2^{\#}A_2^{(k)}(D)$ represents the number of $\eta \in F_q$ that are aliased with $k+1$ 2fis, and is defined as

$$ {}_2^{\#}A_2^{(k)}(D) = \#\{\eta : \eta \in F_q,\ E_2(D,\eta) = k_1 + k_2 + 1\} $$

with $k_1 + k_2 = k$. The terms k_1 and k_2 indicate the degrees to which the two 2fics of a given 2fi are confounded with other 2fics, and their sum reflects the overall degree of aliasing of the 2fi. Consequently, for each component, we have:

$$ {}_2^{\#}C_2^{(k_1)}(D) = (k_1+1)\#\{\gamma : \gamma \in H_q,\ B_2(D,\gamma) = k_1 + 1\}, $$
$$ {}_2^{\#}C_2^{(k_2)}(D) = (k_2+1)\#\{\gamma : \gamma \in H_q,\ B_2(D,\gamma) = k_2 + 1\}. $$

In the case that $i$fi and $j$fi are aliased, if the 2^{i-1} $i$fics within $i$fi contain only one $i$fic that is confounded with $j$fic, the component confounding and factor aliasing can be considered to have a one-to-one relationship. In this specific scenario, the AFNP and the ACNP are equivalent, that is, ${}_i^{\#}C_j^{(k)} = {}_i^{\#}A_j^{(k)} (i, j = 1, \ldots, n)$. Next, we will analyze the relationship between the lower-order AFNP and ACNP in general cases.

Theorem 1. *For a 3^{n-m} regular design with resolution $R \geq III$, the following results hold.*

(a) For $k = 0$, we have ${}_2^{\#}C_2^{(0)} - 2{}_2^{\#}A_2^{(0)} = \#\{\eta : \eta \in F_q,\ E_2(D,\eta) = k_2 + 1,\ k_2 \geq 1\}$.

(b) If ${}_2^{\#}C_2^{(k)} > {}_2^{\#}A_2^{(k)}$ for $k \geq 1$, then

$$ \begin{aligned} {}_2^{\#}C_2^{(k)} - {}_2^{\#}A_2^{(k)} =& \#\{\eta : \eta \in F_q,\ E_2(D,\eta) = k + k_2 + 1,\ 1 \leq k_2 \neq k\} \\ &+ 2\#\{\eta : \eta \in F_q,\ E_2(D,\eta) = 2k + 1,\ k_1 = k_2 = k\}. \end{aligned} $$

(c) If ${}_2^{\#}C_2^{(k)} < {}_2^{\#}A_2^{(k)}$ for $k \geq 2$, then

$$ {}_2^{\#}A_2^{(k)} - {}_2^{\#}C_2^{(k)} = \#\{\eta : \eta \in F_q,\ E_2(D,\eta) = k_1 + k_2 + 1,\ k_1 + k_2 = k,\ k_1, k_2 > 0\} $$

Proof. (a) According to the definition of factor aliasing, if a 2fi is not aliased with other 2fis, its components are also not confounded with any other 2fics. However, a 2fi may have one component confounded with other 2fics while the other remains unconfounded. This scenario leads to the inequality ${}_2^{\#}C_2^{(0)} \geq {}_2^{\#}A_2^{(0)}$.

To quantify this phenomenon, we use ${}_2^{\#}C_2^{(0)} - 2{}_2^{\#}A_2^{(0)}$ to represent the number of 2fics within 2fis that are aliased with other 2fis but, at the same time, are not themselves confounded with any other 2fics. For such 2fis, there exists exactly one 2fic that is not confounded with any other 2fics. Without loss of generality, assume that the first 2fic of such a 2fi is unconfounded with other 2fics, i.e., let $k_1 = 0$. Under this assumption, the number of 2fics satisfying the above description can be expressed as:

$$ {}_2^{\#}C_2^{(0)} - 2{}_2^{\#}A_2^{(0)} = \#\{\eta : \eta \in F_q,\ E_2(D,\eta) = k_2 + 1,\ k_2 \geq 1\}. $$

(b) In the case of 2fis aliased with k other 2fis, if one of the two 2fic components of the 2fi is confounded with k other 2fics while the other 2fic is not confounded with any other 2fics, then ${}_2^{\#}C_2^{(k)} = {}_2^{\#}A_2^{(k)}$.

If a 2fi is aliased with other 2fis to a degree strictly greater than k, two particular 2fics involving this 2fi can be identified. One of these 2fics is confounded with exactly k other

2fics, while the other, although also confounded with this 2fic, has a confounding degree with other 2fics that is not equal to k. The number of such 2fics is expressed as:

$$\#\{\eta : \eta \in F_q,\ E_2(D,\eta) = k + k_2 + 1,\ 1 \leq k_2 \neq k\}.$$

On the other hand, if both 2fics of the 2fi are confounded with k other 2fics, the difference value of ${}_2^{\#}C_2^{(k)} - {}_2^{\#}A_2^{(k)}$ reflects the number of 2fics within 2fis whose aliasing degree is $2k$. These 2fics are also confounded with k other 2fics. The number of 2fics satisfying this condition can be expressed as:

$$2\#\{\eta : \eta \in F_q,\ E_2(D,\eta) = 2k + 1,\ k_1 = k_2 = k\}.$$

Therefore, when ${}_2^{\#}C_2^{(k)} > {}_2^{\#}A_2^{(k)}$, the corresponding difference equals the total number of 2fics within 2fis aliased with more than k other 2fis, where the degree of confounding with 2fics is k. This total number can be expressed as:

$$\begin{aligned}{}_2^{\#}C_2^{(k)} - {}_2^{\#}A_2^{(k)} = &\#\{\eta : \eta \in F_q,\ E_2(D,\eta) = k + k_2 + 1,\ 1 \leq k_2 \neq k\}\\ &+ 2\#\{\eta : \eta \in F_q,\ E_2(D,\eta) = 2k + 1,\ k_1 = k_2 = k\}.\end{aligned}$$

In this scenario, at least one 2fic must be confounded with k other 2fics. Thus, $k \geq 1$.

(c) When ${}_2^{\#}C_2^{(k)} < {}_2^{\#}A_2^{(k)}$, the aliasing degree k can be achieved in multiple ways. If a 2fi has only one 2fic confounded with k other 2fics, while the remaining 2fic is not confounded with any other 2fi, then the aliasing degree k is entirely determined by this single component. In this scenario, the factor aliasing and component confounding correspond individually.

When at least two components determine the aliasing degree k, the difference value of ${}_2^{\#}A_2^{(k)} - {}_2^{\#}C_2^{(k)}$ represents a situation that, among the 2fis aliased with k other 2fis, the degree k is jointly determined by exactly two 2fics. The number of 2fis fitting this description can be expressed as:

$${}_2^{\#}A_2^{(k)} - {}_2^{\#}C_2^{(k)} = \#\{\eta : \eta \in F_q,\ E_2(D,\eta) = k_1 + k_2 + 1,\ k_1 + k_2 = k,\ k_1, k_2 > 0\}.$$

Note that the aliasing degree k can only be determined by a single component when $k = 1$. Therefore, the situation ${}_i^{\#}C_j^{(1)} \geq {}_i^{\#}A_j^{(1)}$ can only occur when $k \geq 2$. □

We provide an example to illustrate Theorem 1.

Example 3. *Consider a 3^{6-2} design $D_5 = \{1, 2, 3, 4, 1234, 12^23\}$. Based on the AFNP and ACNP, its lower-order aliasing indices are $({}_1^{\#}A_2; {}_2^{\#}A_2) = (6; 4, 10, 1)$ and ${}_2^{\#}C_2 = (18, 12)$. The specific confounding patterns of the 2fics are as follows:*

$$13 = 26, 23^2 = 16^2, 24^2 = 56^2, 26^2 = 45^2, 46 = 25, 36^2 = 12^2, 56^2 = 24.$$

According to Theorem 1, ${}_2^{\#}C_2^{(0)} - 2{}_2^{\#}A_2^{(0)} = 10$. Thus, there are 10 2fis with two components, one of which is confounded with the other 2fics, and the other is not. These 2fis are $1 \times 2, 1 \times 3, 1 \times 6, 2 \times 3, 2 \times 4, 2 \times 5, 3 \times 6, 4 \times 5, 4 \times 6, 5 \times 6$. From ${}_2^{\#}C_2^{(1)} - {}_2^{\#}A_2^{(1)} = 2$, it can be concluded that among the 2fis aliased with at least one other 2fi, two of their components, 26 and 26^2, are each confounded with one other 2fic. Finally, from ${}_2^{\#}A_2^{(2)} - {}_2^{\#}C_2^{(2)} = 1$, it follows that there exists a 2fi aliased with two other 2fis, and its aliasing degree is determined by two components. The 2fi satisfying this case is 2×6.

The definitions of the GMAF and GMC criteria clearly show that the GMAF criterion imposes stricter requirements for optimal designs than the GMC criterion. The GMAF criterion focuses on the overall aliasing of factor effects rather than the factor effect components.

3.2. Relationship with Entropy

To adapt to the entropy formulation, in a 3^{n-m} design, denote the factors as $d_1, d_2, \ldots, d_n$, where $d_1, \ldots, d_{n-m}$ represent independent factors (i.e., independent columns), and the remaining $d_{n-m+1}, \ldots, d_n$ are generator factors (i.e., additional columns). We employ entropy to measure factor uncertainty. Let $\mathcal{F}$ denote all possible combinations of factor values, and $p(d)$ represent the estimated probability of occurrence for a particular combination $d \in \mathcal{F}$ [17,18]. The entropy of the design matrix is defined as

$$H(\mathbf{d}) = -\sum_{d \in \mathcal{F}} p(d) \log p(d).$$

In fractional factorial designs, to assess the degree of aliasing among factors, we focus on the conditional entropy of generators with respect to other factors, such as $H(d_i | d_1, \ldots, d_{i-1}, d_{i+1}, \ldots, d_m)$. Lower conditional entropy indicates stronger dependence of the factor on other generators, implying more severe aliasing. Specifically, if a factor is a function of other generators, its conditional entropy equals zero, indicating aliasing. Conversely, higher conditional entropy suggests that the factor retains uncertainty given other factors, indicating less aliasing.

Example 4. *Consider two 3^{5-1} designs: $D = \{d_1, d_2, d_3, d_4, d_5 = d_1 d_2\}$ and $D' = \{d_1, d_2, d_3, d_4, d_5 = d_1 d_2 d_3\}$, where d_5 is the only generated factor. In design D, the conditional entropy $H(d_5 | d_1, d_2) = 0$, indicating that d_5 is fully determined by d_1 and d_2, and thus entirely confounded with them. In contrast, for D', although $H(d_5 | d_1, d_2, d_3) = 0$, it holds that $H(d_5 | d_1, d_2) > 0$, meaning that d_5 retains some uncertainty given only d_1 and d_2. This implies that design D' has a lower degree of aliasing compared to D.*

Therefore, for a fixed number of factors n and generators m with the same number of levels, we can compare the conditional entropies associated with generators across designs to evaluate the confounding severity. Specifically, under the same conditions, a larger conditional entropy indicates lower confounding among factors and higher resolution. Consequently, the designs selected based on the conditional entropy criterion yield the same results as those obtained under the MR criterion. However, the conditional entropy criterion exhibits an inherent limitation; it cannot differentiate among multiple designs with same resolution. Based on Definition 1, we can directly obtain the following theorem.

Theorem 2. *A GMAF 3^{n-m} design must have maximum resolution among all 3^{n-m} designs, and exhibit the minimum factor aliasing among all 3^{n-m} designs with the same conditional entropy.*

According to this theorem, the GMAF criterion overcomes the inherent limitations of the conditional entropy criterion. GMAF designs not only satisfy the maximum resolution criterion, but also minimize factor aliasing among all designs with the same conditional entropy. This provides a more precise discrimination for comparing designs with the same conditional entropy.

3.3. Relationship with MA Criterion

For a 3^{n-m} design, the set of all possible products of the m words generates a defining contrast subgroup G. Let A_i $(i = 1, \ldots, n)$ denote the number of words of length i in G. The vector $W = (A_1, A_2, \ldots, A_n)$ is called the WLP. A design sequentially minimizing the vector W is considered an MA design. To study the relationship between the GMAF and MA criteria, we investigate the relationship between the WLP and the AFNP as the cores of MA and GMAF criteria, respectively.

Theorem 3. *For a 3^{n-m} regular design with a resolution $R \geq III$, we have:*

$$A_i = \frac{1}{i}\sum_{k=1}^{K_{i-1}} k{}_1^{\#}A_{i-1}^{(k)} - 2\left(\frac{n+2-i}{i}\right)A_{i-2} - \left(\frac{i-1}{i}\right)A_{i-1}$$
$$= \frac{1}{i}\sum_{k=1}^{2^{i-2}} k{}_{i-1}^{\#}A_1^{(k)} - 2\left(\frac{n+2-i}{i}\right)A_{i-2} - \left(\frac{i-1}{i}\right)A_{i-1}, \quad i \geq 3.$$

Proof. If $i \geq 3$, it is known from Zhang and Mukerjee [9] that:

$$\sum_{k=1}^{K_{i-1}} k{}_1^{\#}C_{i-1}^{(k)} = 2(n-i+2)A_{i-2} + (i-1)A_{i-1} + iA_i.$$

Since ${}_1^{\#}C_{i-1}^{(k)} = {}_1^{\#}A_{i-1}^{(k)}$, then by keeping iA_i on the right-hand side, we have:

$$iA_i = \sum_{k=1}^{K_{i-1}} k{}_1^{\#}A_{i-1}^{(k)} - 2(n-i+2)A_{i-2} - (i-1)A_{i-1}.$$

Dividing both sides by i yields:

$$A_i = \frac{1}{i}\sum_{k=1}^{K_{i-1}} k{}_1^{\#}A_{i-1}^{(k)} - 2\left(\frac{n+2-i}{i}\right)A_{i-2} - \left(\frac{i-1}{i}\right)A_{i-1}.$$

By rearranging this equation, the value of A_i can be expressed as a weighted sum of $\sum_{k=1}^{K_{i-1}} k{}_1^{\#}A_{i-1}^{(k)}$, A_{i-2}, and A_{i-1}. Moreover, since the resolution $R \geq$ III, the main effects are not aliased with other main effects, and the following equivalence holds: $\sum_{k=1}^{K_{i-1}} k{}_1^{\#}A_{i-1}^{(k)} = \sum_{k=1}^{2^{i-2}} k{}_{i-1}^{\#}A_1^{(k)}$. In particular, it follows that $A_1 = A_2 = 0$ when $R \geq$ III. □

Through calculations, the relationship between the three-level WLP and AFNP is derived as follows:

$$A_3 = \frac{1}{3}\sum_{k=1}^{K_2} k{}_1^{\#}A_2^{(k)} = \frac{1}{3}\sum_{k=1}^{2} k{}_2^{\#}A_1^{(k)},$$
$$A_4 = \frac{1}{4}\sum_{k=1}^{K_3} k{}_1^{\#}A_3^{(k)} - \frac{3}{4}A_3 = \frac{1}{4}\sum_{k=1}^{2^2} k{}_3^{\#}A_1^{(k)} - \frac{3}{4}A_3 = \frac{1}{4}\sum_{k=1}^{K_3} k{}_1^{\#}A_3^{(k)} - \frac{1}{4}\sum_{k=1}^{K_2} k{}_1^{\#}A_2^{(k)},$$
$$A_5 = \frac{1}{5}\sum_{k=1}^{K_4} k{}_1^{\#}A_4^{(k)} - 2\left(\frac{n-3}{5}\right)A_3 - \frac{4}{5}A_4 = \frac{1}{5}\sum_{k=1}^{2^3} k{}_4^{\#}A_1^{(k)} - 2\left(\frac{n-3}{5}\right)A_3 - \frac{4}{5}A_4$$
$$= \frac{1}{5}\sum_{k=1}^{K_4} k{}_1^{\#}A_4^{(k)} - \frac{1}{5}\sum_{k=1}^{K_3} k{}_1^{\#}A_3^{(k)} + \frac{9-2n}{15}\sum_{k=1}^{K_2} k{}_1^{\#}A_2^{(k)}.$$

For example, a 3^{5-2} design $D_6 = \{1, 2, 3, 12, 12^2\}$ have ${}_2^{\#}A_1 = (4, 0, 6)$. Hence, $A_3 = \frac{1}{3}\sum_{k=1}^{2} k{}_2^{\#}A_1^{(k)} = 4$.

Note that a design includes k *i*fics from the same *i*fi in its independent defining relation, which necessarily results in ${}_i^{\#}A_1^{(k)} \neq 0$ when $k \geq 2$. Based on the WLP, the designs with different WLPs may have different AFNPs. Minimizing the WLP sequentially is equivalent to maximizing $\{{}_i^{\#}A_0, i = 3, \ldots, n\}$ or $\{{}_0^{\#}A_i, i = 3, \ldots, n\}$ sequentially. However, the different AFNPs may have the same WLP.

Example 5. *Consider the two* 3^{13-8} *designs:*

$$D_7 = \{1,\ 2,\ 3,\ 4,\ 5,\ 12345,\ 12^23^24,\ 12^24^25,\ 23^24^25,\ 123^25^2,\ 12^23,\ 124,\ 125\},$$
$$D_8 = \{1,\ 2,\ 3,\ 4,\ 5,\ 12345,\ 12^23^24,\ 12^24^25,\ 23^24^25,\ 123^25^2,\ 12^23,\ 124,\ 13^245\}.$$

The AFNPs of designs D_7 and D_8 are different. In particular, they first differ at ${}^{\#}_{2}A_2^{(1)}(D_7) = 5$ and ${}^{\#}_{2}A_2^{(1)}(D_8) = 3$. However, they share the same $W = (A_3,\ A_4,\ A_5,\ A_6) = (0,\ 24,\ 108,\ 207)$.

Consequently, the AFNP is a more refined pattern than the WLP since the WLP is only related to the elements $\{{}^{\#}_{i}A_0^{(1)},\ i = 1, 2, \ldots, n\}$ of the AFNP. Consider two design:

$$D: I = 123456^2 = 12^23^247^2 = 12^24^258^2 = 12^23^29^2 = 13^25^2t_0^2 = 134^2t_1^2 = 23^24^2t_2^2,$$
$$D': I = 123456^2 = 12^23^247^2 = 12^24^258^2 = 23^24^259^2 = 123^25^2t_0^2 = 12^23t_1^2 = 124t_2^2,$$

where t_0, t_1, t_2 represent factors 10, 11, and 12, respectively. Under the MA criterion, the design D is better than D'. However, according to the GMAF criterion, the design D' is optimal. Since the MA criterion uses only part of the information in the AFNP, the optimal design under the MA criterion is not as good as that obtained by the GMAF criterion.

3.4. Relationship with CE Criterion

For a three-lever design, a main effect or 2fi is called clear if it is not aliased with other main effects or 2fis. We study the relationship between the CE and GMAF criteria by calculating the number of clear effects using the AFNP. Let C_1, C_2, and CC be the number of clear main effects, clear 2fis, and clear 2fics, respectively.

Theorem 4. *For any three-level design with resolution III or higher, we have:*

$$C_1 = {}^{\#}_{1}A_2^{(0)}, \quad C_2 = {}^{\#}_{2}A_2^{(0)}.$$

Proof. For three-level designs with resolution III or higher, any main effect is not aliased with other main effects. The ${}^{\#}_{1}A_2^{(0)}$ is just the number of main effects that are aliased with neither any main effect nor any 2fi, that is, $C_1 = {}^{\#}_{1}A_2^{(0)}$.

Consider a 2fi $A \times B$, with its two 2fics AB and AB^2 not confounded with any other 2fics. Suppose AB or AB^2 is confounded with a main effect. In a defining word of length 3, if AB or AB^2 is confounded with a main effect, the defining word must include both factors A and B. This would inevitably lead to AB or AB^2 being confounded with other 2fics, contradicting the initial assumption. Therefore, if the two components of a 2fi are not confounded with any other 2fics, then the 2fi is clear. Based on the definition of ${}^{\#}_{2}A_2^{(0)}$, it represents the number of 2fis that are not aliased with any other 2fis. Thus, $C_2 = {}^{\#}_{2}A_2^{(0)}$. □

Therefore, in the factor aliasing of three-level designs, the CE criterion selects designs that sequentially maximize C_1 and C_2. According to the definitions of clear 2fis and clear 2fics, the difference value between CC and C_2 represents the number of 2fics within 2fis aliased with other 2fis but not with any other 2fics. Specifically, this relationship can be expressed as:

$$CC - 2C_2 = {}^{\#}_{2}C_2^{(0)} - {}^{\#}_{1}C_2^{(1)} - 2{}^{\#}_{2}A_2^{(0)}.$$

The inequality $CC - 2C_2 \geq 0$ implies that, in general, the number of clear 2fics is greater than or equal to the number of clear 2fis. This follows from the fact that a 2fi is considered clear only if both of its 2fics are clear. Therefore, the criterion for a clear 2fi is inherently more stringent than that for individual components. From a design perspective, the stricter requirement for clarity in factor effects better aligns with the practical need to accurately identify significant factor effects in experimental settings.

The following results are obtained based on Theorems 1 and 3 in Ai and Zhang [19].

Theorem 5. *(i) If $n \leq (3^{q-1}-1)/2+1$, a 3^{n-m} design with sequentially maximizing $^{\#}_{1}A_2^{(0)}$ and $^{\#}_{2}A_2^{(0)}$ is an optimal design under CE criterion.*

(ii) If there exists an optimal 3^{n-m} design with resolution IV under the CE criterion, then the GMAF design must be the best one among all optimal designs under the CE criterion, where the meaning of 'best' is under the comparison in Definition 1 of the GMAF criterion.

However, the CE criterion cannot distinguish designs with the same number of clear main effects and 2fis, while the GMAF criterion can. The following example illustrates this point.

Example 6. *Consider the type of 3^{7-3} designs. According to Xu [20], there are 19 non-isomorphic designs. Under the CE criterion, the optimal designs are $D = \{1,2,3,4,134^2,12^23,13^24\}$ and $D' = \{1,2,3,4,1234,12^23,12^24\}$. Both designs have 7 clear main effects and no clear 2fis. However, $^{\#}_{2}A_2(D) = (0,12,9)$, and $^{\#}_{2}A_2(D') = (0,6,15)$. Under the GMAF criterion, the design D is better than the design D'. It can be concluded that the optimal design under the GMAF criterion represents the best-performing design among all optimal designs under the CE criterion.*

4. Aliasing Algorithm of Lower-Order Factors

Factor aliasing patterns are crucial in selecting optimal designs, especially in aliasing lower-order factors. This section mainly introduces some algorithms to calculate the lower-order factor aliasing. The algorithm is based on defined contrast subgroups. It includes the following three steps: (i) generate a design matrix from a saturated design, (ii) construct the defining contrast subgroup matrix, and (iii) calculate the low-order factor aliasing values of the design. The specific implementation code is available in the supplementary materials.

4.1. Generate Design Matrix

Let $M(D)$ be the design matrix of a 3^{n-m} design D. The matrix $M(D)$ is generated from the corresponding saturated design H_q, which each component is expressed as $(b_1, b_2, \ldots, b_q)'$, where $b_i \in GF(3)$ and $b_1, b_2, \ldots, b_q$ are not all zero. Proportional components are considered equivalent. A vector $b = (b_1, \ldots, b_n)'$ can be denoted as $1^{b_1}2^{b_2}\cdots n^{b_n}$, with the convention that i^{b_i} is omitted for $b_i = 0$. For example, in H_3, 12 corresponds to the vector $(1,1,0)$, while in H_4, it is represented as $(1,1,0,0)$. In the following, we present an algorithm for generating the design matrix.

Example 7. *Consider a 3^{5-2} design with index set $D = \{1,2,5,8,4\}$. The design matrix $M(D)$ is constructed by extracting columns 1, 2, 5, 8, and 4 from the saturated design matrix H_3. Using Algorithm 1, we obtain:*

$$H_3 = \begin{bmatrix} 1 & 0 & 1 & 1 & 0 & 1 & 0 & 1 & 1 & 1 & 0 & 1 & 1 \\ 0 & 1 & 1 & 2 & 0 & 0 & 1 & 1 & 2 & 0 & 1 & 1 & 2 \\ 0 & 0 & 0 & 0 & 1 & 1 & 1 & 1 & 1 & 2 & 2 & 2 & 2 \end{bmatrix}, \quad M(D) = \begin{bmatrix} 1 & 0 & 0 & 1 & 1 \\ 0 & 1 & 0 & 1 & 2 \\ 0 & 0 & 1 & 1 & 0 \end{bmatrix}.$$

The saturated matrix H_3 has 13 columns, each of which can be represented as a component. The first and second columns of H_3 are independent components. Using addition modulo 3 over $GF(3)$, the interaction of the first and second columns produces two components, 12 and 12^2, represented by the third and fourth columns of H_3, respectively.

According to the design column index set $D = \{1, 2, 5, 8, 4\}$, the 1st, 2nd, 5th, 8th, and 4th columns are selected from H_3 to form the design matrix $M(D)$.

Algorithm 1: Generate design matrix $M(D)$

Input:

q: Number of independent columns in the design.

D: Index set of design columns.

Output:

Design matrix $M(D)$.

```
Initialize the identity element H_1, of length q, with the first row as 1 and all other
  rows as 0;
Initialize H_q as the identity matrix H_1;
Generate the columns of H_q;
for i = 2 → q do
    Define the column vector r with the rth row to 1 and all other rows to 0;
    Save the current H_q;
    Extend H_q by adding the results of r, rH_{q-1}, and r^2 H_{q-1} under modulo 3
      addition;
end
Generate the design matrix M(D) by extracting the elements from H_q at the
  positions specified by the index set D.
```

4.2. Construct Defining Contrast Matrix

Through Algorithm 1, we can obtain the additional column matrix F from the design matrix $M(D)$. Next, we calculate the defining contrast matrix $M(G)$ under modulo 3 addition in Algorithm 2.

Algorithm 2: Construct defining contrast matrix $M(G)$

Input:

m: Number of additional columns in the design.

$M(D)$: Design matrix.

Output:

Defining contrast matrix $M(G)$.

```
Generate the additional column matrix F, with n rows and m columns;
Initialize M(G) as F ;
for i = 1 → m do
    Update M(G) to include all possible products of the m independent defining
      columns;
    Expand M(G) to include its equivalent matrix under modulo 3 addition.
end
```

In Example 7, the two columns of F represent 1234^2 and 12^25^5. Subsequently, we construct a defining contrast matrix $M(G)$ under modulo 3 addition, which contains eight elements, including the modulo 3 equivalent components for each element.

$$F = \begin{bmatrix} 1 & 1 \\ 1 & 2 \\ 1 & 0 \\ 2 & 0 \\ 0 & 2 \end{bmatrix}, \quad M(G) = \begin{bmatrix} 1 & 1 & 2 & 0 & 0 & 1 & 2 & 2 \\ 1 & 2 & 0 & 2 & 1 & 0 & 2 & 1 \\ 1 & 0 & 1 & 1 & 2 & 2 & 2 & 0 \\ 2 & 0 & 2 & 2 & 1 & 1 & 1 & 0 \\ 0 & 2 & 2 & 1 & 2 & 1 & 0 & 1 \end{bmatrix}.$$

4.3. Calculate the Lower-Order Factor Aliasing

Based on the FEHP, lower-order factor effects are more important than high-order ones. An algorithm is used to calculate $^{\#}_{1}A_2$ and $^{\#}_{2}A_2$ for any 3^{n-m} design D. These results are instrumental in identifying GMAF designs. The detailed steps of the algorithm are outlined below.

Algorithm 3 provides a method for calculating lower-order factor aliasing based on the defining contrast matrix $M(G)$. For Example 7, we first generate the corresponding 2fic matrix $B(5)$ as follows:

$$B(5) = \begin{bmatrix} 1 & 1 & 1 & 1 & 1 & 1 & 1 & 1 & 0 & 0 & 0 & 0 & 0 & 0 & 0 & 0 & 0 & 0 & 0 & 0 \\ 1 & 2 & 0 & 0 & 0 & 0 & 0 & 0 & 1 & 1 & 1 & 1 & 1 & 1 & 0 & 0 & 0 & 0 & 0 & 0 \\ 0 & 0 & 1 & 2 & 0 & 0 & 0 & 0 & 1 & 2 & 0 & 0 & 0 & 0 & 1 & 1 & 1 & 1 & 0 & 0 \\ 0 & 0 & 0 & 0 & 1 & 2 & 0 & 0 & 0 & 0 & 1 & 2 & 2 & 0 & 1 & 2 & 0 & 0 & 1 & 1 \\ 0 & 0 & 0 & 0 & 0 & 0 & 1 & 2 & 0 & 0 & 0 & 0 & 0 & 2 & 0 & 0 & 2 & 2 & 1 & 2 \end{bmatrix}.$$

The elements in the $B_{split}(5)$ are written as follows:

$$B_1 = \{(1,1,0,0,0)', (1,2,0,0,0)'\}, \ldots, B_{10} = \{(0,0,0,1,1)', (0,0,0,1,2)'\}.$$

Algorithm 3: Calculate $^{\#}_{1}A_2$ and $^{\#}_{2}A_2$

Input:

n: Number of independent columns in the design.

$M(G)$: Defining contrast matrix.

Output:

Values of $^{\#}_{1}A_2^{(k)}$ and $^{\#}_{2}A_2^{(k)}$.

1 Generate an n-order identity matrix I_n, where each column is a standard basis vector e_i ;

2 **for** $i = 1 \to n$ **do**

3   Compute all 2fics sequentially and store them in matrix $B(n)$;

4   Define TwoFIC(n) as the set containing $B(n)$ and its equivalent matrices under modulo 3 addition;

5   Partition $B(n)$ with a step size of 2 and denote the result as $B_{\text{split}}(n)$, with each partitioned submatrix denoted by B_i;

6 **end**

7 To compute $^{\#}_{1}A_2^{(k)}$: Perform the Kronecker product of the standard basis vector e_i with each column of the matrix $M(G)$. Count the number of e_i whose resulting matrices contain exactly k columns identical to those in $TwoFIC(n)$. This count is the value of $^{\#}_{1}A_2^{(k)}$.

8 To compute $^{\#}_{2}A_2^{(k)}$: Perform the Kronecker product of the vector B_i with each column of the matrix $M(G)$. Count the number of B_i whose resulting matrices contain exactly k columns identical to those in $TwoFIC(n)$. This count is the value of $^{\#}_{2}A_2^{(k)}$.

Subsequently, each e_i $(i = 1, 2, \ldots, 5)$ and B_i $(i = 1, 2, \ldots, 10)$ is combined with the columns of $M(G)$ under addition modulo 3 over $GF(3)$ to perform the Kronecker product. The result is $^{\#}_{1}A_2 = (2, 3)$, indicating that two main effects are not aliased with any 2fi, and the remaining three main effects are each aliased with one other 2fi. Among the 10 2fis, six are aliased with two other 2fis, and the remaining four are aliased with three other 2fis, represented as $^{\#}_{2}A_2 = (0, 0, 6, 4)$.

4.4. A Catalog of Three-Level Designs with Lower-Order AFNP

Based on the aforementioned aliasing algorithm, the lower-order AFNP of all the 27-, 81-run designs with factor numbers $n = 5, \ldots, 20$, and 243-run designs with resolution IV or higher are listed in Tables 2–4. For a design 3^{n-m}, denoted as $n - m.i$, we only list the additional columns (abbreviated as add. columns), where i indicates the ranking of the design under the GMAF criterion. Here, the $n - m.1$ design is always the GMAF design. The first column of the table represents the selected design, and the second column represents the positions in the Yates order. The table also includes $W = (A_3, A_4, A_5, A_6)$, C_1, C_2, CC, and the two primary components ${}^{\#}_{1}A_2$ and ${}^{\#}_{2}A_2$ of the AFNP, along with the two primary components ${}^{\#}_{1}C_2$ and ${}^{\#}_{2}C_2$ of the ACNP. The designs are ranked under the GMC and MA criteria at the end.

Table 2 presents all 27-run designs. The results show that each GMAF design is also a GMC and MA design, with equal rankings under both GMAF and GMC criteria. This indicates that the GMAF designs with 27 runs retain the advantageous properties of both GMC designs and MA designs. Moreover, the rankings of designs 5-2.2 and 5-2.3 under the GMC and MA criteria are 2, 3, and 3, 2, respectively. Similarly, for designs 6-3.3 and 6-3.4, the rankings under the GMC and MA criteria are 3, 4, and 4, 3, respectively. The rankings of the remaining 23 designs are consistent under the GMAF, GMC, and MA criteria.

Table 2. Complete catalog of 27-run designs under MA, CE, and GMAF criteria.

Design	Add. Columns	WLP	Cs			AFNP and ACNP			Order
		$A_3, \ldots, A_6$	C_1	C_2	CC	${}^{\#}_{1}A_2$ (${}^{\#}_{1}C_2$)	${}^{\#}_{2}A_2$	${}^{\#}_{2}C_2$	G;M
4-1.1	8	0 1	4	0	6	4	0,6	6,6	1;1
4-1.2	3	1 0	1	3	6	1,3	3,0,3	9,0,3	2;2
5-2.1	8 4	1 3 0	2	0	1	2,3	0,0,6,4	4,12,4	1;1
5-2.2	3 4	4 0 0	1	4	8	$1,0^2,4$	4,0,0,0,6	8,0,12	2;3
5-2.3	8 3	2 1 1	0	0	4	0,4,1	0,4,4,2	8,6,6	3;2
6-3.1	8 4 12	2 9 0 2	0	0	0	0,6	$0^4,9,6$	6,0,18,0,0,6	1;1
6-3.2	8 4 6	3 6 3 1	0	0	0	0,3,3	0,0,0,6,9	3,12,3,12	2;2
6-3.3	8 4 3	5 3 3 2	0	0	0	0,2,0,3,1	0,0,8,0,3,4	2,12,12,4	3;4
6-3.4	8 3 6	4 3 6 0	0	0	0	$0^2,6$	0,0,3,12	0,18,12	4;3
7-4.1	8 4 12 6	5 1 5 9 8	0	0	0	$0^2,6,1$	$0^5,6,15$	0,12,9,0,15.6	1;1
7-4.2	8 4 6 7	6 11 15 4	0	0	0	$0^2,3,4$	$0^4,6,12,3$	0,6,12,24	2;2
7-4.3	8 4 6 3	7 10 12 9	0	0	0	$0^2,3,1,3$	$0^4,9,6,6$	0,6,12,24	3;3
7-4.4	8 4 12 3	8 9 9 14	0	0	0	$0^3,6,0^2,1$	$0^4,15,0,0,6$	0,0,36,0,0.6	4;4
8-5.1	8 4 12 6 11	8 30 24 32	0	0	0	$0^3,8$	$0^8,24,4$	0,0,24,4,0,0,28	1;1
8-5.2	8 4 12 6 7	10 23 32 30	0	0	0	$0^3,4,2,2$	$0^6,9,8,11$	0,0,12,8,30,6	2;2
8-5.3	8 4 12 6 3	11 21 30 38	0	0	0	$0^3,1,6,0,1$	$0^6,10,12,6$	0,0,3,32,15,6	3;3
9-6.1	8 4 12 6 11 13	12 54 54 96	0	0	0	$0^4,9$	$0^{11},36$	$0^3,36,0^4,36$	1;1
9-6.2	8 4 12 6 11 3	15 42 69 96	0	0	0	$0^4,2,6,0,1$	$0^8,8,6,18,11$	$0^3,8,30,6.28$	2;2
9-6.3	8 4 12 6 7 3	16 39 69 106	0	0	0	$0^4,0,6,3$	$0^8,3,24,9$	$0^4,30,42$	3;3
10-7.1	8 4 12 6 11 13 3	21 72 135 240	0	0	0	$0^6,9,0^2,1$	$0^{10},9,36$	$0^5,54,0,0,36$	1;1
10-7.2	8 4 12 6 11 3 7	22 68 138 250	0	0	0	$0^6,4,6$	$0^{11},12,24,6,3$	$0^5,24,42,24$	2;2

For 81-run designs, there can be up to 40 columns. Table 3 lists the WLP, the number of clear main effects and clear 2fis, the AFNP, and the ACNP of some 81-run designs. As Xu [20] noted, any 27-run design can be considered a degenerate 81-run design. The number of non-isomorphic designs for $n = 21, \ldots, 35$ is equal to the number of non-isomorphic designs for $n = 5, \ldots, 19$. Thus, only 81-run designs with $m = 5, \ldots, 20$ are listed. It can be observed that the GMAF designs for the 81-run are not necessarily GMC or MA designs. The results are summarized as follows. In the 81-run designs, among the optimal designs selected under the GMAF criterion: (i) Only designs 7-3.1 and 8-4.1 are not optimal under the GMC criterion, while the remaining designs are optimal under both the GMAF and GMC criteria. (ii) Only designs 12-8.1, 13-9.1, 14-10.1, 15-11.1, and 16-12.1 are not optimal under the MA criterion, while the remaining designs are optimal under both the GMAF and MA criteria.

Table 3. Selected 81-run designs for 5-20 columns under MA, CE, and GMAF criteria.

Design	Add. Columns	WLP	Cs			AFNP and ACNP			Order
		$A_3, \ldots, A_6$	C_1	C_2	CC	${}^{\#}_{1}A_2$ $({}^{\#}_{1}C_2)$	${}^{\#}_{2}A_2$	${}^{\#}_{2}C_2$	G;M
5-1.1	22	0 0 1	5	10	20	5	10	20	1;1
6-2.1	22 9	0 2 2 0	6	4	18	6	4,10,1	18,12	1;1
7-3.1	22 9 24	0 5 6 1	7	0	15	7	0,12,9	15,24,3	2;1
7-3.2	22 9 18	0 6 3 4	7	0	18	7	0,6,15	18,12,12	1;2
8-4.1	22 9 24 31	0 10 16 4	8	0	8	8	0,0,24,4	8,36,12	3;1
8-4.2	22 9 24 25	0 11 12 10	8	0	16	8	0,0,18,10	16,18,18,4	2;2
8-4.3	22 9 18 38	0 12 8 16	8	0	16	8	0,0,12,16	16,24,0,16	1;3
9-5.1	22 9 24 31 34	0 18 36 12	9	0	0	9	0^3,36	0,36,36	1;1
10-6.1	22 9 24 31 34 39	0 30 72 30	10	0	0	10	0^4,45	0,0,90	1;1
11-7.1	22 9 24 31 34 39 3	3 42 111 132	4	0	0	4,6,0,1	0^3,18 24,13	6,0,57 32,15	1;1
12-8.1	22 9 24 31 3 13 6 7	8 73 124 364	4	0	4	4,0,0,8	0^4,24,8 0,6,12,14,2	4,2,48,44 0^3,16,18	1;72
12-8.85	22 9 24 31 3 25 13 37	4 72 144 354	0	0	0	0,12	0^6,36,12 12,0,6	12,0,18,72 0,12,0^2,18	86;1
13-9.1	22 9 24 31 3 13 6 7 12	12 109 198 672	4	0	4	4,0^3,9	0^6,36,0^3 6,0,18,18	4,2,0,108 0^5,20,22	1;209
13-9.56	22 9 24 31 3 25 13 37 6	7 102 219 690	0	0	0	0,6,6,1	0^7,24,22 18,9,2,3	6,12,18,24,60, 0,0,16,9,11	56;1
14-10.1	22 9 24 31 3 25 13 6 7 12	13 147 315 1200	2	0	1	2,3,0,0,9	0^8,45,0,0 6,4,27,0,9	4,6,0,36,90 0^5,33,0,13	1;46
14-10.374	22 9 24 31 3 25 13 37 6 18	10 140 334 1236	0	0	0	0,0,12,2	0^8,13,24 20,28,6	0,24,18,0,50 48,0^3,20,22	375;1
15-11.1	22 9 24 31 3 25 13 37 6 7 12	14 198 486 2009	0	0	0	0,6,0,0,9	0^{10},54,0 0,9,33,0,0,9	6,0,9,36,0,108 0^5,36,0,0,15	1;2
15-11.131	22 9 24 31 3 25 13 37 6 18 7	13 192 495 2055	0	0	0	0,0,6,9	0^{10},30 24,8,33,9,1	0,12,33,4,0, 84,28,0^4,36,13	131;1
16-12.1	22 9 24 31 3 25 13 37 6 18 7 12	17 258 711 3275	0	0	0	0,0,6,1,9	0^{12},63,0 6,15,27,9	0,12,9,36,0,0 126,0^6,42,15	1;2
16-12.531	22 9 24 31 3 25 13 37 6 18 7 35	16 256 720 3288	0	0	0	0,0,0,16	0^{12},48 16,0,48,8	0,0,48,8,0,0 112,16,0^5,56	531;1
17-13.1	22 9 24 31 3 25 13 37 6 18 7 35 12	20 336 1014 5072	0	0	0	0^3,8,9	0^{14},72,0 0,24,40	0,0,24,40,0^3 144,0^7,64	1;1
18-14.1	22 9 24 31 3 25 13 37 6 18 7 35 12 38	24 432 1404 7608	0	0	0	0^4,18	0^{16}, 81,0, 0,0,72	0^3,72,0^4 162, 0^8,72	1;1
19-15.1	22 9 24 31 3 25 13 37 6 18 7 35 12 38 15	33 504 2052 10884	0	0	0	0^5,18,0^3,1	0^{14},18,0^3 81,0,0,72	0^4,90,0^3,81 0,99,0^6,72	1;1
20-16.1	22 9 24 31 3 25 13 37 6 18 7 35 12 38 15 16	42 603 2808 15537	0	0	0	0^6,18,0,0,2	0^{17},36,0,0,72 9,54,18,0^3,1	0^5,108,0,0,72,10 0^2,117,0^4,54,19	1;1

For 243-run designs, there can be a maximum of 121 columns. Table 4 lists some 243-run designs. Following Xu [20], each 243-run design with a resolution of at least IV has a maximum of 20 columns. We only list 243-run designs with $n = 6, \ldots, 20$. It can be observed that in the 243-run designs, when the number of independent columns is fewer than 7, designs 6-1.1, 7-2.1, 8-3.1, 9-4.1, 10-5.1, and 11-6.1 are optimal under the GMAF, GMC, and MA criteria. However, when the number of independent columns exceeds 7, designs 13-8.1, 14-9.1, 15-10.1, 16-11.1, 17-12.1, 18-13.1, 19-14.1, and 20-15.1 are optimal only under the GMAF criterion.

Table 4. Selected 243-run designs with resolution IV or higher under MA, CE, and GMAF criteria.

Design	Add. Columns	WLP	Cs			AFNP and ACNP			Order
		$A_3, \ldots, A_6$	C_1	C_2	CC	$^{\#}_{1}A_2$ $(^{\#}_{1}C_2)$	$^{\#}_{2}A_2$	$^{\#}_{2}C_2$	G;M
6-1.1	63	0 0 0 1	6	15	30	6	15	30	1;1
7-2.1	63 27	0 0 3 1	7	21	42	7	21	42	1;1
8-3.1	63 27 72	0 0 8 4	8	28	56	8	28	56	1;1
9-4.1	63 27 72 79	0 0 18 12	9	36	72	9	36	72	1;1
10-5.1	63 27 72 79 93	0 0 36 30	10	45	90	10	45	90	1;1
11-6.1	63 27 72 79 93 114	0 0 66 66	11	55	110	11	55	110	1;1
12-7.1	63 27 72 12 91 33 38	0 15 72 126	12	16	60	12	16,20,24 2,4	60,54,18	1;4
12-7.2	63 27 72 79 93 9 17	0 14 74 110	12	14	57	12	14,26,20,6	57,66,9	6;1
13-8.1	63 27 72 79 93 9 17 21	0 25 108 201	13	8	45	13	8,17,28, 23,2	45,72,39	299;27
13-8.58	63 27 72 79 9 44 57 39	0 24 105 222	13	4	42	13	4,23,33 17,1	42,84,30	640;1
13-8.1270	63 27 45 97 9 105 20 100	0 34 75 216	13	0	60	13	0,12,24 24,18	60,24 36,36	1;1398
14-9.1	63 27 72 12 91 33 38 44 50	0 38 152 402	14	8	40	14	8,0,48 10,24,0,1	40,82,39 16,5	452;76
14-9.224	63 27 72 79 9 44 57 39 65	0 36 155 390	14	1	33	14	1,13,37 31,9	33,90,51,8	1387;1
14-9.2019	63 27 44 9 104 21 17 89 48	0 54 100 396	14	0	52	14	0,0,4,48 24,14,1	52,26,39 40,25	1;2019
15-10.1	63 27 72 12 66 44 36 30 21 20	0 62 221 576	15	2	33	15	2,7,15,20 36,19,6	33,38,93 36,10	601;1612
15-10.1466	63 27 72 79 93 9 17 44 74 117	0 50 231 635	15	0	15	15	0,0,40 40,25	15,100,90 0,5	1771;1
15-10.1778	63 27 44 9 104 21 17 89 33 48	0 72 162 640	15	0	54	15	0^3,18 72,0,15	54,18,45 48,45	1;1777
16-11.1	63 27 72 79 9 44 57 65 21 87 109	0 80 312 964	16	0	28	16	0,6,12,18 42,24,18	28,44,108 20,40	233;827
16-11.364	63 27 72 79 9 44 57 39 65 73 21	0 70 334 974	16	0	13	16	0,0,18,48 35,15,3,1	13,88 90,44,5	997;1
16-11.1019	63 27 44 9 104 21 17 89 33 39 48	0 95 252 991	16	0	60	16	0^4,60 45,0,15	60,0,45 60,75	1;1018
17-12.1	63 27 72 79 9 44 57 39 89 21 101 118	0 101 441 1531	17	0	15	17	0,0,12,24 21,54,19,6	15,72,75 68,30,12	210;209
17-12.274	63 27 72 79 93 9 17 44 74 117 21 48	0 95 450 1561	17	0	9	17	0^3,30 59,38,9	9,48,144 64,0,0,7	327;1
17-12.330	63 27 72 12 102 44 66 54 70 20 87 38	0 106 393 1660	17	0	24	17	0^3,13 49,47,23,4	24,66,66 56,30,30	1;312
18-13.1	63 27 72 79 9 44 57 39 89 21 113 101 118	0 128 606 2344	18	0	4	18	0^3,24,36 24,54,12,3	4,84,69 88,30,24,7	87;38
18-13.5	63 27 72 79 9 44 57 54 21 87 74 109 65	0 134 594 2296	18	0	20	18	0^3,18,30 24,60,18,3	20,36,84, 92,60,0,14	1;78
18-13.78	63 27 72 79 93 9 17 44 74 117 21 48 101	0 123 618 2352	18	0	8	18	0^4,58 72,15,8	8,22,144 124,0^3,8	79;1
19-14.1	63 27 72 79 93 9 17 44 21 101 113 33 39 116	0 168 819 3318	19	0	9	19	0^4,45 36,0,72,18	9,18,117,108 45,36,0,0,9	7;18
19-14.17	63 27 72 79 93 9 17 44 74 117 21 48 101 109	0 156 837 3444	19	0	9	19	0^5,108 54,0,9	9,0,108 216, 0^4,9	15;1
19-14.20	63 27 72 8 52 70 56 38 104 54 17 36 47 85	0 180 720 3570	19	0	9	19	0^6,126 36,9	9,36,126 0,90,72,0,0,9	1;20
20-15.1	63 27 72 79 93 9 17 44 21 101 113 33 39 116 118	0 210 1092 4740	20	0	10	20	0^5,90,0 0,90,10	10,0,90,180 0,90,0^3,10	4;7
20-15.7	63 27 72 79 93 9 17 44 74 117 21 48 101 109 113	0 195 1116 4920	20	0	10	20	0^6,180 0,0,10	10,0,0 360,0^5,10	8;1
20-15.9	63 27 72 8 52 70 56 38 104 54 17 36 47 85 102	0 225 960 5100	20	0	10	20	0^7,180 0,10	10,0,180,0,0 180,0^3,10	1;9

5. A Real Example

This section provides a seatbelt experiment to illustrate the effectiveness of the AFNP and the GMAF criterion [6]. In the study, we mainly investigate the aliasing properties of four factors on the pull strength of truck seat belts. The four factors are hydraulic pressure of crimping (1), die flat middle setting (2), length of crimp (3), and anchor lot (4), with each factor at three levels.

Since three-level regular designs are run size economy, we try to select an optimal 3^{4-1} design under the GMAF and other criteria. For 3^{4-1} designs, there are only two non-isomorphic 3^{4-1} designs $D_1 = \{1,2,3,12\}$ and $D_2 = \{1,2,3,123\}$, determined by the defining relations $4 = 12$ and $4 = 123$, respectively. The set $\widetilde{D}_i (i = 1,2)$ is the factor structure of $D_i (i = 1,2)$. By calculation, we obtain the confounded relations between the main effects and 2fics of the design D_1 as follows:

$$1 = 24^2, 2 = 14^2, 4 = 12, 14 = 12^2 = 24.$$

For $\eta \in \widetilde{D}_1 \cup F_3$, we have:

$$E_2(D_1, \eta) = \begin{cases} 0, & \text{if } \eta = 3, \\ 1, & \text{if } \eta \in \{1, 2, 1 \times 2\}. \end{cases} \quad E_2(D_1, \eta) = \begin{cases} 1, & \text{if } \eta \in \{1 \times 3, 2 \times 3, 3 \times (12)\}, \\ 3, & \text{if } \eta \in \{1 \times 2, 1 \times (12), 2 \times (12)\}. \end{cases}$$

From (2), it yields that $({}^{\#}_{1}A_2(D_1); {}^{\#}_{2}A_2(D_1)) = (1,3;3,0,3)$. Similarly, $E_2(D_2, \eta) = 0$ when $\eta \in \widetilde{D}_2$. For $\eta \in \{1 \times 2, 1 \times 3, 1 \times (12), 2 \times 3, 2 \times (123), 3 \times (123)\} \subset F_3$, we have $E_2(D_2, \eta) = 2$. Thus, $({}^{\#}_{1}A_2(D_2); {}^{\#}_{2}A_2(D_2)) = (4;0,6)$. We observe that ${}^{\#}_{1}A_2$ is the first element, which makes ${}^{\#}A(D_1) \neq {}^{\#}A(D_2)$. Thus, the design D_2 is a GMAF design.

Under the GMC criterion, we need to calculate ${}^{\#}_{1}C_2$ and ${}^{\#}_{2}C_2$. Based on the relationship of the AFNP and ACNP, we have ${}^{\#}_{1}C_2(D_i) = {}^{\#}_{1}A_2(D_i), i = 1,2$. That is to say, ${}^{\#}_{1}C_2(D_1) = (1,3)$, and ${}^{\#}_{1}C_2(D_2) = (4,0)$. According to Theorem 1, we have

$$\begin{aligned} {}^{\#}_{2}C_2^{(0)}(D_1) =& 2{}^{\#}_{2}A_2^{(0)} + \#\{\eta : \eta \in F_3, E_2(D_1, \eta) = k_2 + 1, k_2 \geq 1\} = 9, \\ {}^{\#}_{2}C_2^{(1)}(D_1) =& \#\{\eta : \eta \in F_3, E_2(D_1, \eta) = 1 + k_2 + 1, k_2 \neq 1\} \\ &+ 2\#\{\eta : \eta \in F_3, E_2(D_1, \eta) = 2 + 1, k_1 = k_2 = 1\} = 0, \\ {}^{\#}_{2}C_2^{(2)}(D_1) =& \#\{\eta : \eta \in F_3, E_2(D_1, \eta) = 2 + k_2 + 1, k_2 \neq 2\} \\ &+ 2\#\{\eta : \eta \in F_3, E_2(D_1, \eta) = 4 + 1, k_1 = k_2 = 2\} = 3. \end{aligned}$$

For any other $k, {}^{\#}_{2}C_2^{(k)}(D_1) = 0$. Hence, we have ${}^{\#}_{2}C_2(D_1) = (9,0,3)$. Similarly, for the design D_2, we have ${}^{\#}_{2}C_2(D_2) = (6,6)$. Then, the design D_2 is also a GMC design.

To compare the WLP and the number of clear factors between the two designs, it can be derived from Theorem 3 that:

$$A_3(D_1) = \frac{1}{3}\sum_{k=1}^{K_2} k\,{}^{\#}_{1}A_2^{(k)}(D_1) = 1; \quad A_4 = \frac{1}{4}\sum_{k=1}^{K_3} k\,{}^{\#}_{1}A_3^{(k)}(D_1) - \frac{1}{4}\sum_{k=1}^{K_2} k\,{}^{\#}_{1}A_2^{(k)}(D_1) = 0,$$

$$A_3(D_2) = \frac{1}{3}\sum_{k=1}^{K_2} k\,{}^{\#}_{1}A_2^{(k)}(D_2) = 0; \quad A_4 = \frac{1}{4}\sum_{k=1}^{K_3} k\,{}^{\#}_{1}A_3^{(k)}(D_2) - \frac{1}{4}\sum_{k=1}^{K_2} k\,{}^{\#}_{1}A_2^{(k)}(D_2) = 1.$$

According to Theorem 4, we have $C_1(D_1) = {}^{\#}_{1}A_2^{(0)}(D_1) = 1$, $C_2(D_1) = {}^{\#}_{2}A_2^{(0)}(D_1) = 3$, $C_1(D_1) = {}^{\#}_{1}A_2^{(0)}(D_2) = 4$, and $C_2(D_2) = {}^{\#}_{2}A_2^{(0)}(D_2) = 0$.

Consider the two 3^{n-m} designs described above: design $D_1 = \{d_1, d_2, d_3, d_4 = d_1 d_2\}$, where factor d_4 is determined by d_1 and d_2, and design $D_2 = \{d_1, d_2, d_3, d_4 = d_1 d_2 d_3\}$, where factor d_4 is determined by d_1, d_2, and d_3. In both designs, the individual entropies of the first three factors d_1, d_2, d_3 are approximately $H(d_i) \approx 0.918$ bits (corresponding to the case where, among three levels, one level appears once and another appears twice), indicating a relatively balanced level distribution. We examine the conditional entropy of factor d_4 to reveal its aliasing relationships with other factors. In design D_1, since $d_4 = d_1 d_2$, its conditional entropy satisfies $H(d_4|d_1, d_2) = 0$. This means that once d_1 and d_2 are given, the value of d_4 is completely determined with no remaining uncertainty, indicating that d_4 is confounded with d_1 and d_2. In design D_2, where $d_4 = d_1d_2d_3$, we have $H(d_4|d_1, d_2, d_3) = 0$. However, the key difference is that $H(d_4|d_1, d_2) > 0$. This indicates that when only d_1 and d_2 are known, d_4 retains some uncertainty. Therefore, $H(d_4|d_1, d_2)(D_2) > H(d_4|d_1, d_2)(D_1)$, demonstrating that design D_2 has less aliasing compared to design D_1, which aligns with the difference in design resolution.

The entropy analysis confirms the validity of the selected designs. Moreover, design D_2 is better than design D_1 under the MA, CE, GMC, and GMAF criteria. Thus, design D_2 should be selected for the experiment, with factors *A*–*D* assigned to its four columns. The WLP, along with C_1 and C_2, is the core of the MA and CE criteria, and all are functions of the AFNP, which offers more comprehensive information on factor aliasing compared to the WLP and C_1, C_2. Additionally, the GMAF criterion retains the advantages of GMC, MA, and CE criteria while measuring aliasing from the factors' perspective, thereby reducing computational complexity. This indicates that the GMAF criterion is practical and applicable for optimizing and selecting experimental designs.

6. Conclusions

This paper introduces the AFNP, which mainly uses three-level regular designs, and proposes the GMAF criterion. The AFNP's main advantage embodies several aspects. First, the classification pattern contains all aliasing information between various factors of any three-level design. Based on the FEHP, assuming higher-order interactions can be ignored, $E_2(D, \eta)$ is defined to represent the number of 2fis aliased with η in a design D. For different values of η within the set D or F_q, $E_2(D, \eta)$ is used to represent both ${}^{\#}_{1}A_2^{(k)}$ and ${}^{\#}_{2}A_2^{(k)}$, which facilitates the establishment of relationships between the GMAF criterion and other criteria. For instance, Theorem 1 demonstrates the quantitative relationship between ${}^{\#}_{2}A_2^{(k)}$ and ${}^{\#}_{2}C_2^{(k)}$, establishing the connection between the GMAF and GMC criteria. Theorem 2 shows that the GMAF criterion overcomes the limitation of the conditional entropy criterion in evaluating designs with the same conditional entropy. Theorems 3 and 4 separately explore the relationships of the GMAF criterion with the MA and CE criteria. The MA criterion utilizes information from $\{{}^{\#}_{i}A_j^{(k)} \mid i, j = 0, 1, \ldots, n, k = 1, \ldots, K_j\}$, whereas the CE criterion relies solely on $\{{}^{\#}_{i}A_j^{(0)} \mid i, j = 0, 1, \ldots, n\}$. The GMAF criterion provides a more precise method for selecting designs. It overcomes the limitation of the MA criterion, which becomes inapplicable when the WLPs are identical. It outperforms the CE criterion by distinguishing optimal designs when the C_1 and C_2 parameters are equal. The results show that the core of other criteria is the specific functions of the AFNP. Then, an algorithm based on the definition of contrast subgroups is proposed to calculate lower-order factor aliasing, enabling the search for GMAF designs. The tables show catalogs of all 27-run designs, selected 81-run designs, and 243-run designs with resolutions higher than IV under the GMAF criterion. Finally, using the seatbelt experiment as an example, it is demonstrated that the GMAF criterion is practical and effective in its application.

This paper only focuses on the AFNP and GMAF criteria of three-level designs. The criterion can be extended to higher-level regular, blocked, and mixed-level designs. Additionally, how to construct a GMAF design needs to be further investigated, which is more complex than the topics discussed here and remains an open problem.

Supplementary Materials: The following supporting information can be downloaded at: https://www.mdpi.com/article/10.3390/e27070680/s1.

Author Contributions: Q.C.: Writing—original draft. Z.L. (Zhiming Li): Supervision, Funding acquisition, Writing—review and editing. Z.L. (Zhi Li): Writing—review and editing. All authors have read and agreed to the published version of the manuscript.

Funding: This work is supported by the Central Guidance for Local Science and Technology Development Fund (Grant No. ZYYD2025ZY20).

Institutional Review Board Statement: Not applicable.

Data Availability Statement: The original contributions presented in this study are included in the article/Supplementary Material. Further inquiries can be directed to the corresponding author(s).

Conflicts of Interest: The authors declare no conflicts of interest.

References

1. Box, G.E.P.; Hunter, J.S. The 2^{k-p} fractional factorial designs. *Technometrics* **1961**, *3*, 311–351.
2. Fries, A.; Hunter, W.G. Minimum aberration 2^{k-p} designs. *Technometrics* **1980**, *22*, 601–608.
3. Wu, C.F.J.; Chen, Y.Y. A graph-aided method for planning two-level experiments when certain interactions are important. *Technometrics* **1992**, *34*, 162–175. [CrossRef]
4. Wu, H.Q.; Wu, C.F.J. Clear two-factor interactions and minimum aberration. *Ann. Stat.* **2002**, *30*, 1496–1511. [CrossRef]
5. Mukerjee, R.; Wu, C.F.J. *A Modern Theory of Factorial Design*; Springer: New York, NY, USA, 2007.
6. Wu, C.F.J.; Hamada, M. *Experiments: Planning, Analysis, and Optimization*; John Wiley & Sons: Hoboken, NJ, USA, 2011.
7. Zhang, Z.M.; Wang, C.Y. Entropy optimality of orthogonal designs. *Chin. J. Oper. Res.* **1983**, *2*, 61–62, 69.
8. Zhang, R.C.; Li, P.; Zhao, S.L.; Ai, M.Y. A general minimum lower-order confounding criterion for two-level regular designs. *Stat. Sin.* **2008**, *18*, 1689–1705.
9. Zhang, R.C.; Mukerjee, R. Characterization of general minimum lower order confounding via complementary sets. *Stat. Sin.* **2009**, *19*, 363–375.
10. Li, Z.M.; Zhang, T.F.; Zhang, R.C. Three-level regular designs with general minimum lower-order confounding. *Can. J. Stat.* **2013**, *41*, 192–210. [CrossRef]
11. Li, Z.M.; Zhao, S.L.; Zhang, R.C. On general minimum lower order confounding criterion for *s*-level regular designs. *Stat. Probab. Lett.* **2015**, *99*, 202–209. [CrossRef]
12. Huang, Z.Y.; Li, Z.M.; Zhang, G.; Chen, T. Lower-order confounding information of inverse Yates-order designs with three levels. *Metrika* **2023**, *86*, 239–259. [CrossRef]
13. Zhang, T.F.; Duan, Y.X.; Zhao, S.L.; Li, Z.M. Construction of three-level factorial designs with general minimum lower-order confounding via resolution IV designs. *Metrika* **2024**, *87*, 1–9. [CrossRef]
14. Jaynes, J.; Ding, X.T.; Xu, H.Q.; Wong, W.K.; Ho, C.M. Application of fractional factorial designs to study drug combinations. *Stat. Med.* **2013**, *32*, 307–318. [CrossRef] [PubMed]
15. Suriyaamporn, P.; Sukma, M.; Rangsimawong, W. Design and investigation of optimal dissolving polymeric microneedles for ocular application by using three-level factorial design. *Key Eng. Mater.* **2022**, *914*, 63–68. [CrossRef]
16. Niewés, D. Modelling of humic acids extraction process assisted by low-intensity ultrasound with the use of three-level fractional factorial design. *Korean J. Chem. Eng.* **2024**, *41*, 681–695. [CrossRef]
17. Guo, J.J.; Shi, Y.L.; Li, S.; Yang, Z.J.; Yang, X.J.; Duan, G.J.; Tian, Y.H.; Li, Y.F. Process optimization of stir-frying with yellow Wine for glycyrrhiza Based on orthogonal design and entropy weight combined with TOPSIS Method. *Lishizhen Med. Mater. Medica Res.* **2024**, *35*, 1639–1642.
18. Cheng, Y.J.; Wen, S.; Deng, Y.F.; Liu, Q.Z.; Lin, R.K.; Li, L.; Wei, M. Optimization of the processing technology of beads of asini corii colla by orthogonal experimental design and entropy teight-TOPSIS method. *Mod. Chin. Med.* **2023**, *25*, 361–368.
19. Ai, M.Y.; Zhang, R.C. s^{n-m} designs containing clear main effects or clear two-factor interactions. *Stat. Probab. Lett.* **2004**, *69*, 151–160. [CrossRef]
20. Xu, H.Q. A catalogue of three-level regular fractional factorial designs. *Metrika* **2005**, *62*, 259–281. [CrossRef]

entropy

MDPI

Article

Two-Level Regular Designs for Baseline Parameterization

Shengli Zhao [1,*] and Mengru Qin [2]

[1] School of Statistics and Data Science, Qufu Normal University, Qufu 273165, China
[2] Zaozhuang No.2 Middle School, Zaozhuang 277000, China
* Correspondence: zhaoshengli@qfnu.edu.cn

Abstract

This paper considers two-level regular fractional factorial designs for baseline parameterization. Some new results that reveal relationships between the K-values and word length pattern are developed. The new results help find two-level regular fractional factorial designs that are likely to be optimal under the K-aberration criterion. Illustrative examples are included to demonstrate this point.

Keywords: baseline parameterization; K-aberration; two-level regular design; word length pattern

1. Introduction

The application of experimental design in information theory is primarily reflected in optimizing experimental schemes to maximize information acquisition efficiency while minimizing uncertainty. The core concepts of information theory, such as entropy, provide quantitative tools for experimental design. For example, in the field of communications, experimental design can optimize channel coding schemes, thereby improving transmission reliability. Additionally, in machine learning feature selection, experimental design based on information entropy can identify the most discriminative feature subsets, reducing model complexity and enhancing classification accuracy. The integration of experimental design and information theory enables a systematic approach to solving key challenges in information acquisition, processing, and optimization, offering theoretical guidance for engineering and scientific experiments. Bose explored the interplay between statistical experimental design and information-theoretic concepts, discussing how to construct designs that maximize informational yield from data [1]. His work established parallels between statistical efficiency (particularly variance minimization in parameter estimates) and information-theoretic principles.

Factorial designs have a wide application in various fields. The baseline parameterization (BP) model and the orthogonal parameterization (OP) model are two of the most used models in the analysis of experimental data. The BP model is a linear model based on baseline constraints while the OP model is based on zero-sum constraints. There are numerous research findings under the OP model. For details, please refer to [2,3] and the references therein. BP is quite a natural option for modeling the experiments with each factor having a null state or baseline level. For example, in toxicology experiments [4], each binary factor represents the presence or absence of a particular toxin. Scientists consider the absence of all toxins to be the natural reference for the possible presence of some toxins. In such experiments, the status of the absence of a toxin can be naturally regarded as a baseline level. Another practical example is introduced by Glonek and Solomon [5] in a leukemic mice experiment. The authors presented two binary components that stand for sample and time, respectively. A natural baseline level is the condition of the non-leukemic line for one factor and time zero for another factor. For a broader interpretation of BP, one is referred to [6,7].

In recent years, choosing efficient designs under BP has raised considerable attention from researchers. The D-optimality and A-optimality are two commonly used efficiency criteria for selecting optimal experimental designs under the main effect model. From an information perspective, they aim to maximize the information content of the experimental data or minimize the variance of parameter estimates. Mukerjee and Tang [7] highlighted the A-optimality of two-level orthogonal arrays for BP when the interaction effects are all absent. Mukerjee and Huda [8] applied approximate theory together with discretization procedures to find designs that have high A-efficiencies and are robust to model misspecification. Liu et al. [9] employed the D-optimality criterion to find designs under BP that are both efficient and robust.

For situations where the interaction effects are present, the experimenter usually concerns the bias caused by interaction effects in estimating the main effects. Karunanayaka and Tang [10] proposed to add runs to one-factor-at-a-time designs for generating compromise designs that are competitive under both the efficiency criterion and the bias criterion. Mukerjee and Tang [7] proposed an optimality criterion, the K-aberration criterion, which quantifies the bias for two-level designs. Under the K-aberration criterion, a few works on designs for BP emerged. Li et al. [11] proposed an efficient incomplete search algorithm for finding nearly optimal designs and tabulated some 20-run (nearly) optimal two-level designs. Miller and Tang [12] focused on identifying efficient two-level regular designs through bridging the K-values and word length pattern. Mukerjee and Tang [13] developed certain rank conditions which, in conjunction with the idea of the minimum moment aberration and recursive set, help alleviate the burden of finding optimal two-level regular designs. Lin and Yang [14] considered finding multistratum designs for BP by using the coordinate-exchange algorithm. Li et al. [15] further proposed a theoretical construction method of compromise designs. Chen et al. [16] considered the situations where some two-factor interactions are also of interest in addition to the main effects and proposed an algorithm for searching optimal designs under their proposed minimum aberration criterion. Sun and Tang [17] investigated the linear relationship between the effects under BP and those under OP and explored its applications to design construction under BP in terms of estimability, optimality, and robustness. Yan and Zhao [18,19] put forward a minimum aberration criterion for three-level designs for BP and found some optimal designs using their proposed construction algorithm.

This paper focuses on two-level regular designs under the K-aberration. Though the two-level nonregular designs may outperform the regular ones in some cases, there is a compelling reason for considering two-level regular designs as has been justified in [13]: the results on two-level regular designs serve as a benchmark for evaluating further work on nonregular ones that have to be compared. Given the importance of the two-level regular designs for BP, we endeavor to make further progress on bridging the K-values and word length pattern and analytically calculate the quantities for two-level regular designs with a higher resolution based on the results in [13]. Such new progress has the following advantages: (i) it can help screen out the candidate designs that are not likely to be K-aberration optimal and thus can yield a further simplification of the search algorithm in [13]; (ii) it is capable of finding two-level regular designs that have better or even optimal K-aberration characteristics than those identified by the results in [13]. Illustrative examples are given to demonstrate these points.

The rest of this paper is organized as follows. Section 2 introduces some necessary notation and elementary knowledge of BP and the word length pattern. Section 3 presents the main results of this paper. Applications of the theoretical results are included in Section 4. The concluding remarks are given in Section 5.

2. Preliminaries

Consider an experiment with n factors each at two levels. A full design includes 2^n runs that correspond to 2^n level combinations of the n factors. Suppose only a 2^{-m} fraction of the full design can be carried out for economic reasons. This paper considers the regular fraction of the full design. Let 2^{n-m} denote a two-level regular fractional factorial design D with $N = 2^{n-m}$ runs and n columns, with each column at two levels 0 and 1; such a design can be obtained as follows: Let $q = n - m$. Define the $N \times (N-1)$ matrix

$$H_q = (1, 2, 12, 3, 13, \ldots, q, 1q, \ldots, 12\cdots q), \tag{1}$$

with columns arranged in Yates order, where

$$\begin{aligned} 1 &= (0,1,0,1,\ldots,0,1,0,1)'_{2^q}, \\ 2 &= (0,0,1,1,\ldots,0,0,1,1)'_{2^q}, \\ &\cdots \\ q &= (0,\ldots,0,1,\ldots,1)'_{2^q} \end{aligned}$$

are q independent columns, and the other columns are obtained by taking the component-wise sum (modulo 2) of the independent ones, and say $12 = (0,1,1,0,\ldots,0,1,1,0)'_{2^q}$. A regular 2^{n-m} design D can be obtained by selecting n columns of H_q such that q are independent and the other $m(= n-q)$ columns are component-wise sums (modulo 2) of the q independent ones. Clearly, the design D is an $N \times n$ submatrix of H_q.

For a regular 2^{n-m} design D, we regard it as a set with elements being the n columns of D and denote still the set as D without causing confusion. Let $\omega_s = \{g_1, \ldots, g_s\}$ denote a subset of s columns of D and $\Omega^s(D)$ denote the collection of all the possible ω_s, where $s \leq n$. For ease of presentation, Ω^s is sometimes used instead of $\Omega^s(D)$ without causing confusion. Then for any $\omega \in \Omega^s(D)$, ω is also an $N \times s$ submatrix of D. Note that each row of ω is an s-tuple with entries of 0 or 1; we call it a binary s-tuple. Let $\alpha(\omega)$ be the number of times that the s-tuple $11\cdots1$ occurs in the submatrix ω. For a regular 2^{n-m} design D, let K_s denote the total bias to the main effects estimations caused by all the s-factor interaction effects. Mukerjee and Tang [7] proved that

$$K_s = (4/N^2)(sT_{1s} + T_{2s}), \tag{2}$$

where

$$T_{1s} = \sum_{\omega_s \in \Omega^s(D)} (\alpha(\omega_s))^2, \tag{3}$$

$$T_{2s} = \sum_{\omega_{s+1} \in \Omega^{s+1}(D)} \sum_{\omega_s \in \Omega^s(\omega_{s+1})} (2\alpha(\omega_{s+1}) - \alpha(\omega_s))^2,$$

and $\Omega^s(\omega_{s+1})$ denotes the collection of all the possible $\omega_s \subset \omega_{s+1}$ for given $\omega_{s+1} \in \Omega^{s+1}(D)$. Formula (2) applies to any two-level designs not just the regular ones. For more details of the K-aberration, one is referred to [7]. A two-level orthogonal array is K-aberration optimal if it sequentially minimizes the following sequence:

$$(K_2, K_3, \ldots, K_m) \tag{4}$$

among all the two-level designs, given the run size and the number of columns.

The word length pattern (WLP) is a concept proposed for the designs under OP. With a slight modification, such a concept can also be applied to the two-level regular designs under BP as follows: For the original definition of WLP under OP, one is referred to [20]. For any regular 2^{n-m} baseline design D, denote $\psi(\omega_k)$ as the sum of the components of the vector $g_1 + \cdots + g_k$ (modulo 2), where $\omega_k = \{g_1, \ldots, g_k\} \in \Omega^k(D)$. Define

$$J_k(\omega_k) = |2\psi(\omega_k) - N|.$$

If the k columns in ω_k satisfy $g_1 + \cdots + g_k$ (modulo 2)$= 1_N$ or 0_N, then we have $\psi(\omega_k) = N$ or 0, which leads to $J_k(\omega_k) = N$ and the k columns correspond to a defining word, where 1_N and 0_N denote the N-vectors with all components being 1 or 0, respectively. If the k columns in ω_k do not correspond to a defining word, then these columns must be independent of each other. This means that all of the binary k-tuples appear equally often as rows in ω_k, which leads to $J_k(\omega_k) = 0$. Let $A_k(D) = \sum_{\omega_k \in \Omega^k(D)} J_k(\omega_k)/N$, then $A_k(D)$ is the number of defining words of length k of the regular design D. For a given two-level regular design, we call the corresponding sequence

$$(A_3, A_4, A_5, \ldots, A_n), \tag{5}$$

as its word length pattern and t as its resolution, if the first nonzero element in Sequence (5) is A_t, where $3 \leq t \leq n$.

With the primary knowledge above, the next section builds connections between Sequences (4) and (5).

3. Main Results

Note that both Sequences (4) and (5) are closely related to the collection ω of a regular 2^{n-m} design. Recalling the definition of T_{1s} in (3), when an s-column collection ω_s contains no defining word, all of the binary s-tuples appear exactly $N/2^s$ times in ω_s, which means that such an ω_s contributes $N/2^s$ to T_{1s}. When an s-column collection ω_s contains some defining words, i.e., the columns in ω_s form some defining words, the analyses for the contribution to T_{1s} caused by such an ω_s become complex. Similar analyses are also required when considering T_{2s}. Therefore, it is necessary to investigate the possible cases of a given collection ω_s containing defining words, so as to calculate K_s. Suppose a regular 2^{n-m} design has a resolution of t. Lemma 1 presents the maximum number of defining words in each of its $(t+2)$-column collections ω_{t+2}.

Lemma 1. *Suppose D is a regular 2^{n-m} design of resolution t and $\omega_{t+2} \in \Omega^{t+2}(D)$. Then*

(i) *ω_{t+2} contains at most two independent defining words for $t = 3, 4$;*

(ii) *ω_{t+2} contains at most one defining word for $t \geq 5$,*

where $t + 2 \leq n$.

Proof. (i) For $t = 3$, denote $\omega_5 = \{g_1, g_2, g_3, g_4, g_5\}$. If ω_5 contains three independent defining words W_1, W_2, and W_3, then W_1, W_2, and W_3 generate another four defining words W_1W_2, W_1W_3, W_2W_3, and $W_1W_2W_3$. These seven defining words contain at least 21 letters (columns) since each defining word contains at least $t(= 3)$ letters. Note that a letter appears at most four times among the seven defining words. Then the seven defining words contain no more than 20 letters since there are only five columns in ω_5. This contradiction shows the validity of (i) for $t = 3$. For $t = 4$, the proof is similar.

(ii) If ω_{t+2} contains two defining words W_1 and W_2 with the length t_1 and t_2, respectively, then W_1 and W_2 have at least $t_1 + t_2 - (t+2)$ common letters. Since $t_1 \geq t$ and

$t_2 \geq t$, the length of the defining word W_1W_2 is at most $(t_1 + t_2) - 2[t_1 + t_2 - (t+2)] \leq 4$, which contradicts $t \geq 5$. This completes the proof of (ii). □

Before proceeding to the main results of this section, we first introduce a lemma that is a refinement of the results from [12,21].

Lemma 2. *Denote $g_1, g_2, \ldots, g_i, g_{i+1}, \ldots, g_j$ as j columns from a regular 2^{n-m} design D of resolution t. Suppose, among these j columns, only the first i ones correspond a defining word, i.e., $g_1 + g_2 + \cdots + g_i (\text{modulo } 2) = 0_N$ or 1_N. Then, we have the following:*

- (i) *The rows in the i-column matrix $(g_1, g_2, \ldots, g_i)$ must consist of $N/2^{i-1}$ copies of a half replicate of the full 2^i factorial design;*
- (ii) *Furthermore, in matrix $(g_1, g_2, \ldots, g_i, g_{i+1}, \ldots, g_j)$, for the $N/2^{i-1}$ copies of each distinct row of matrix $(g_1, g_2, \ldots, g_i)$, all the 2^{j-i} distinct rows of matrix $(g_{i+1}, \ldots, g_j)$ appear equally $N/2^{j-1}$ times,*

where $3 \leq t \leq i < j \leq n$.

In (i) of Lemma 2, the half replicate of the full 2^i factorial design that the i-column matrix $(g_1, g_2, \ldots, g_i)$ contains depends on whether $g_1 + g_2 + \cdots + g_i = 0_N$ or 1_N (modulo 2). This is addressed in detail in Remark 1.

Remark 1. In Lemma 2, if $g_1 + g_2 + \cdots + g_i = 0_N$ (modulo 2), then all the possible i-tuples that contain an even number of ones appear $N/2^{i-1}$ times in the i-column matrix $(g_1, g_2, \ldots, g_i)$. If $g_1 + g_2 + \cdots + g_i = 1_N$ (modulo 2), then all the possible i-tuples that contain an odd number of ones appear $N/2^{i-1}$ times in the i-column matrix $(g_1, g_2, \ldots, g_i)$.

For a defining word W, let $\phi(W)$ denote the vector generated by taking component-wise sums (modulo 2) of the columns in the defining word. Then, $\phi = 0_N$ or 1_N. Denote A_i^0 and A_i^1 as the numbers of length i defining words with $\phi = 0_N$ and 1_N, respectively, where $i = 3, 4, \ldots, n$. Clearly, $A_i^0 + A_i^1 = A_i$. Denote $A_4^{0,0}$ as the number of pairs of length four defining words that have two common columns and $\phi = 0_N$, and $A_4^{1,1}$ as the number of pairs of length four defining words that have two common columns and $\phi = 1_N$. Theorem 1 builds the bridge between K_{t+1} and the WLP for $t = 4$.

Theorem 1. *Suppose D is a regular 2^{n-m} design with resolution $t = 4$, then*

$$\begin{aligned} K_5 &= (1/16)^2\left[5\binom{n}{5} + (n-4)(2n-15)A_4 + 20(n-4)A_4^0 - 4A_4^{0,0} - 8A_4^{1,1}\right] \\ &\quad + (1/16)^2\left[5(n-6)A_5 + 20A_5^1 + 6A_6\right]. \end{aligned} \tag{6}$$

Proof. We calculate T_{15} and T_{25}, separately. For T_{15}, suppose $\omega_5 = \{g_1, g_2, g_3, g_4, g_5\} \in \Omega^5(D)$. Since D has resolution 4, ω_5 contains at most one defining word. There are five scenarios as follows:

- (a1) ω_5 contains one length-four defining word W with $\phi(W) = 0_N$;
- (a2) ω_5 contains one length-four defining word W with $\phi(W) = 1_N$;
- (a3) ω_5 contains one length-five defining word W with $\phi(W) = 0_N$;
- (a4) ω_5 contains one length-five defining word W with $\phi(W) = 1_N$;
- (a5) The five columns in ω_5 are independent of each other.

For (a1), suppose the defining word is $g_1 + g_2 + g_3 + g_4 = 0_N$ (modulo 2) without loss of generality. According to Lemma 2 (i) and Remark 1, the rows that consist of four ones appear $N/2^3$ times in the four-column matrix (g_1, g_2, g_3, g_4). Therefore, the columns of entire ones appear $N/2^4$ times in the five-column matrix $(g_1, g_2, g_3, g_4, g_5)$, i.e., $\alpha(\omega_5) = N/16$.

For (a2), suppose the defining word is $g_1 + g_2 + g_3 + g_4 = 1_N$ (modulo 2) without loss of generality. According to Lemma 2 (i) and Remark 1, the four-column matrix (g_1, g_2, g_3, g_4) contains only rows that consist of an odd number of ones. This implies that none of the rows in matrix $(g_1, g_2, g_3, g_4, g_5)$ contains entire ones, i.e., $\alpha(\omega_5) = 0$.

With similar arguments to (a1) and (a2), we can obtain $\alpha(\omega_5) = 0$ and $\alpha(\omega_5) = N/16$ for (a3) and (a4), respectively. It is obvious that $\alpha(\omega_5) = N/32$ for (a5). The number of ω_5s belonging to (a1)–(a5) are $(n-4)A_4^0$, $(n-4)A_4^1$, A_5^0, A_5^1, and $\binom{n}{5} - (n-4)A_4^0 - (n-4)A_4^1 - A_5^0 - A_5^1$, respectively. With the analysis above, it yields that

$$T_{15} = (N/16)^2(n-4)A_4^0 + (N/16)^2 A_5^1 + (N/32)^2\left[\binom{n}{5} - (n-4)A_4 - A_5\right]. \tag{7}$$

Now, we consider calculating T_{25}. According to Lemma 1 (i) for $t = 4$, there are nine possibilities for $\omega_6 \in \Omega^6(D)$:

(b1) ω_6 contains two independent defining words W_1 and W_2, which generate the third defining word $W_3 = W_1W_2$. Each of the three defining words has a length of four, one has $\phi = 0_N$ and the other two have $\phi = 1_N$;
(b2) ω_6 contains two independent defining words W_1 and W_2, which generate the third defining word $W_3 = W_1W_2$. Each of the three defining words has a length of four and $\phi = 0_N$;
(b3) ω_6 contains only one defining word with a length of four and $\phi = 0_N$;
(b4) ω_6 contains only one defining word with a length of four and $\phi = 1_N$;
(b5) ω_6 contains only one defining word with a length of five and $\phi = 0_N$;
(b6) ω_6 contains only one defining word with a length of five and $\phi = 1_N$;
(b7) ω_6 contains only one defining word with a length of six and $\phi = 0_N$;
(b8) ω_6 contains only one defining word with a length of six and $\phi = 1_N$;
(b9) The six columns in ω_6 are independent of each other.

For (b1)–(b9), denote ω_5 as any five-column subset of ω_6, i.e., $\omega_5 \in \Omega^5(\omega_6)$. Now we proceed to investigate the values of $2\alpha(\omega_6) - \alpha(\omega_5)$ and the number of ω_6s in each of the cases for (b1)–(b9).

For (b1), since there is a length-four defining word, say W_1, with $\phi(W_1) = 1_N$ in ω_6, none of the rows in the matrix consisting of the columns involved in W_1 contains entire ones and thus $\alpha(\omega_6) = 0$. With careful checking, each $\omega_5 \in \Omega^5(\omega_6)$ must contain only one defining word, say W, which has a length of four with either $\phi(W) = 0_N$ or 1_N. For the ω_5s of the former case, we have $\alpha(\omega_5) = N/2^4$ and there are two such ω_5s in $\Omega^5(\omega_6)$. For the ω_5s of the latter case, we have $\alpha(\omega_5) = 0$ and there are four such ω_5s in $\Omega^5(\omega_6)$. Note that the ω_6 in (b1) contains a pair of length-four defining words that have two columns in common and their $\phi = 1_N$. Recalling the meaning of $A_4^{1,1}$, we conclude that the number of ω_6s belonging to (b1) is $A_4^{1,1}$.

For (b2), since ω_6 contains three length-four defining words and each of which has $\phi = 0_N$, we have $\alpha(\omega_6) = N/2^5$ according to Lemma 2 (ii). Note that each $\omega_5 \in \Omega^5(\omega_6)$ must contain one of these three defining words. From Lemma 2 (ii), we have $\alpha(\omega_5) = N/2^4$ for each $\omega_5 \in \Omega^5(\omega_6)$ and there are six such ω_5s in $\Omega^5(\omega_6)$. Note that there are three pairs of length-four defining words in ω_6 and each pair has two columns in common. Thus, it has totally $A_4^{0,0}/3$ ω_6s in (b2).

For (b3), it is easy to obtain that $\alpha(\omega_6) = N/2^5$. Each $\omega_5 \in \Omega^5(\omega_6)$ contains either a length-four defining word with $\phi = 0_N$ or five independent columns. For the ω_5s of the former case, we have $\alpha(\omega_5) = N/2^4$ and there are two such ω_5s in $\Omega^5(\omega_6)$. For the ω_5s of the latter case, we have $\alpha(\omega_5) = N/2^5$ and there are four such ω_5s in $\Omega^5(\omega_6)$. Now we investigate the number of ω_6s that belong to (b3). The four columns of each of the A_4^0 defining words jointed with any two of the remaining $n-4$ columns of D induce an $\omega_6 \in \Omega^6(D)$. Notably, the three defining words in each ω_6 of case (b2) induce exactly the ω_6 itself. Similarly, the ω_6 in case (b1) can be induced by the length-four defining word with $\phi = 0_N$ in it. Therefore, the number of ω_6s in case (b3) is $\binom{n-4}{2}A_4^0 - A_4^{0,0} - 2A_4^{1,1}$.

For (b4), we have $\alpha(\omega_6) = 0$ as there is a length-four defining word with $\phi = 1_N$. With a similar analysis to (b3), among the six ω_5s in $\Omega^5(\omega_6)$, two of them have $\alpha(\omega_5) = 0$ and four of them have $\alpha(\omega_5) = N/2^5$, depending on whether the ω_5 contains a length-four defining word with $\phi = 1_N$ or not. The four columns of each of the A_4^1 defining words jointed with any two of the remaining $n-4$ columns of D induce an ω_6 in $\Omega^6(D)$. One thing to note is that the two length-four defining words with $\phi = 1_N$ in each ω_6 of case (b1) induce exactly the ω_6 itself. The number of ω_6s belonging to (b4) is $\binom{n-4}{2}A_4^1 - 2A_4^{1,1}$.

For cases (b5)–(b8), the results on the values of $\alpha(\omega_6)$s, the number of ω_6s belonging to each case, the values of $\alpha(\omega_5)$s, and the number of ω_5s in each $\Omega^5(\omega_6)$, which have the same values of $\alpha(\omega_5)$s, are straightforward. These results are summarized in Table 1 along with those for cases (b1)–(b4), where the notation n_{ω_5} represents the number of $\alpha(\omega_5)$s of each value. Note that each ω_6 in (b9) has $\alpha(\omega_6) = N/2^6$ and $\alpha(\omega_5) = N/2^5$ for each $\omega_5 \in \Omega^5(\omega_6)$; this results in $2\alpha(\omega_6) - \alpha(\omega_5) = 0$. Therefore, there is no need to consider case (b9) when calculating T_{25}.

Table 1. $\alpha(\omega_6)$ and $\alpha(\omega_5)$ for calculating T_{25} in Theorem 1.

Scenario	$\alpha(\omega_6)$	$\alpha(\omega_5) : n_{\omega_5}$	n_{ω_6}
(b1)	0	$N/16 : 2$ and $0 : 4$	$A_4^{1,1}$
(b2)	$N/32$	$N/16 : 6$	$A_4^{0,0}/3$
(b3)	$N/32$	$N/16 : 2$ and $N/32 : 4$	$\binom{n-4}{2}A_4^0 - A_4^{0,0} - 2A_4^{1,1}$
(b4)	0	$0 : 2$ and $N/32 : 4$	$\binom{n-4}{2}A_4^1 - 2A_4^{1,1}$
(b5)	0	$N/32 : 5$ and $0 : 1$	$(n-5)A_5^0$
(b6)	$N/32$	$N/32 : 5$ and $N/16 : 1$	$(n-5)A_5^1$
(b7)	$N/32$	$N/32 : 6$	A_6^0
(b8)	0	$N/32 : 6$	A_6^1

n_{ω_5}: the number of $\alpha(\omega_5)$s of each value for ω_6. n_{ω_6}: the number of ω_6s in (b1)–(b8).

With Table 1, it is obtained that

$$T_{25} = (N/32)^2 \left[4\binom{n-4}{2}A_4 - 4A_4^{0,0} - 8A_4^{1,1} + 5(n-5)A_5 + 6A_6\right]. \quad (8)$$

With Equations (7) and (8), we obtain

$$\begin{aligned} K_5 &= (4/N^2)(5T_{15} + T_{25}) \\ &= (1/16)^2\left[5\binom{n}{5} + (n-4)(2n-15)A_4 + 20(n-4)A_4^0 - 4A_4^{0,0} - 8A_4^{1,1}\right] \\ &\quad +(1/16)^2\left[5(n-6)A_5 + 20A_5^1 + 6A_6\right]. \end{aligned}$$

This completes the proof. □

Theorem 2 below builds the relationship between K_{t+1} and the WLP for $t \geq 5$.

Theorem 2. *Suppose D is a regular 2^{n-m} design with resolution $t \geq 5$, then*

$$
\begin{aligned}
K_{t+1} &= (1/2^{2t})\left[4(t+1)(n-t)A_t^1 + 4(t+1)A_{t+1}^0 + \left(t\binom{n-t}{2} - (t+1)(n-t)\right)A_t\right] \\
&\quad +(1/2^{2t})\left[(t+1)(n-t-2)A_{t+1} + (t+2)A_{t+2} + (t+1)\binom{n}{t+1}\right]
\end{aligned}
$$

for an odd $t \geq 5$, and

$$
\begin{aligned}
K_{t+1} &= (1/2^{2t})\left[4(t+1)(n-t)A_t^0 + 4(t+1)A_{t+1}^1 + \left(t\binom{n-t}{2} - (t+1)(n-t)\right)A_t\right] \\
&\quad +(1/2^{2t})\left[(t+1)(n-t-2)A_{t+1} + (t+2)A_{t+2} + (t+1)\binom{n}{t+1}\right]
\end{aligned}
$$

for an even $t \geq 5$.

Proof. To calculate T_{1s} in (2) for $s = t+1$, consider five possibilities for $\omega_{t+1} \in \Omega^{t+1}(D)$:
(c1) ω_{t+1} contains only one defining word with length t and $\phi = 0_N$;
(c2) ω_{t+1} contains only one defining word with length t and $\phi = 1_N$;
(c3) ω_{t+1} contains only one defining word with length $t+1$ and $\phi = 0_N$;
(c4) ω_{t+1} contains only one defining word with length $t+1$ and $\phi = 1_N$;
(c5) ω_{t+1} consists of $t+1$ columns that are independent of each other.
With similar analyses to Theorem 1 , we have Tables 2 and 3 for calculating $T_{1(t+1)}$ for an odd and even $t \geq 5$, respectively. With Tables 2 and 3, we obtain that

$$T_{1(t+1)} = (N/2^{t+1})^2\left[4(n-t)A_t^1 + 4A_{t+1}^0 + \binom{n}{t+1} - (n-t)A_t - A_{t+1}\right] \tag{9}$$

for an odd $t \geq 5$, and

$$T_{1(t+1)} = (N/2^{t+1})^2\left[4(n-t)A_t^0 + 4A_{t+1}^1 + \binom{n}{t+1} - (n-t)A_t - A_{t+1}\right] \tag{10}$$

for an even $t \geq 5$.

Table 2. $\alpha(\omega_{t+1})$ for calculating $T_{1(t+1)}$ for an odd $t \geq 5$ in Theorem 2.

	$\alpha(\omega_{t+1})$	$n_{\omega_{t+1}}$
(c1)	0	$(n-t)A_t^0$
(c2)	$N/2^t$	$(n-t)A_t^1$
(c3)	$N/2^t$	A_{t+1}^0
(c4)	0	A_{t+1}^1
(c5)	$N/2^{t+1}$	$\binom{n}{t+1} - (n-t)A_t - A_{t+1}$

$n_{\omega_{t+1}}$: the number of ω_{t+1}s in (c1)–(c5).

Table 3. $\alpha(\omega_{t+1})$ for calculating $T_{1(t+1)}$ for an even $t \geq 5$ in Theorem 2.

	$\alpha(\omega_{t+1})$	$n_{\omega_{t+1}}$
(c1)	$N/2^t$	$(n-t)A_t^0$
(c2)	0	$(n-t)A_t^1$
(c3)	0	A_{t+1}^0
(c4)	$N/2^t$	A_{t+1}^1
(c5)	$N/2^{t+1}$	$\binom{n}{t+1} - (n-t)A_t - A_{t+1}$

$n_{\omega_{t+1}}$: the number of ω_{t+1}s in (c1)–(c5).

Considering $T_{2(t+1)}$, there are seven possibilities for $\omega_{t+2} \in \Omega^{t+2}(D)$:

(d1) ω_{t+2} contains only one defining word and its length is t with $\phi = 0_N$;
(d2) ω_{t+2} contains only one defining word and its length is t with $\phi = 1_N$;
(d3) ω_{t+2} contains only one defining word and its length is $t+1$ with $\phi = 0_N$;
(d4) ω_{t+2} contains only one defining word and its length is $t+1$ with $\phi = 1_N$;
(d5) ω_{t+2} contains only one defining word and its length is $t+2$ with $\phi = 0_N$;
(d6) ω_{t+2} contains only one defining word and its length is $t+2$ with $\phi = 1_N$;
(d7) ω_{t+2} consists of $t+2$ columns that are independent of each other.

With similar analyses to Theorem 1, we have Tables 4 and 5 for calculating $T_{2(t+1)}$ for an odd and even $t \geq 5$, respectively. Note that each ω_{t+2} in (d7) has $\alpha(\omega_{t+2}) = N/2^{t+2}$ and $\alpha(\omega_{t+1}) = N/2^{t+1}$ for each $\omega_{t+1} \in \Omega^{t+1}(\omega_{t+2})$; this results in $2\alpha(\omega_{t+2}) - \alpha(\omega_{t+1}) = 0$. Therefore, there is no need to consider case (d7) when calculating $T_{2(t+1)}$.

Table 4. $\alpha(\omega_{t+2})$ and $\alpha(\omega_{t+1})$ for calculating $T_{2(t+1)}$ for an odd $t \geq 5$ in Theorem 2.

	$\alpha(\omega_{t+2})$	$\alpha(\omega_{t+1}) : n_{\omega_{t+1}}$	$n_{\omega_{t+2}}$
(d1)	0	$N/2^{t+1} : t$ or $0 : 2$	$\binom{n-t}{2}A_t^0$
(d2)	$N/2^{t+1}$	$N/2^{t+1} : t$ or $N/2^t : 2$	$\binom{n-t}{2}A_t^1$
(d3)	$N/2^{t+1}$	$N/2^{t+1} : (t+1)$ or $N/2^t : 1$	$(n-t-1)A_{t+1}^0$
(d4)	0	$N/2^{t+1} : (t+1)$ or $0 : 1$	$(n-t-1)A_{t+1}^1$
(d5)	0	$N/2^{t+1} : (t+2)$	A_{t+2}^0
(d6)	$N/2^{t+1}$	$N/2^{t+1} : (t+2)$	A_{t+2}^1

$n_{\omega_{t+1}}$: the number of $\alpha(\omega_{t+1})$s of each value for ω_{t+2}. $n_{\omega_{t+2}}$: the number of ω_{t+2}s in (d1)–(d6).

Table 5. $\alpha(\omega_{t+2})$ and $\alpha(\omega_{t+1})$ for calculating $T_{2(t+1)}$ for an even $t \geq 5$ in Theorem 2

	$\alpha(\omega_{t+2})$	$\alpha(\omega_{t+1}) : n_{\omega_{t+1}}$	$n_{\omega_{t+2}}$
(d1)	$N/2^{t+1}$	$N/2^t : 2$ or $N/2^{t+1} : t$	$\binom{n-t}{2}A_t^0$
(d2)	0	$N/2^{t+1} : t$ or $0 : 2$	$\binom{n-t}{2}A_t^1$
(d3)	0	$N/2^{t+1} : (t+1)$ or $0 : 1$	$(n-t-1)A_{t+1}^0$
(d4)	$N/2^{t+1}$	$N/2^{t+1} : (t+1)$ or $N/2^t : 1$	$(n-t-1)A_{t+1}^1$
(d5)	$N/2^{t+1}$	$N/2^{t+1} : (t+2)$	A_{t+2}^0
(d6)	0	$N/2^{t+1} : (t+2)$	A_{t+2}^1

$n_{\omega_{t+1}}$: the number of $\alpha(\omega_{t+1})$s of each value for ω_{t+2}. $n_{\omega_{t+2}}$: the number of ω_{t+2}s in (d1)–(d6).

With Tables 4 and 5, we obtain that

$$T_{2(t+1)} = (N/2^{t+1})^2\left[t\binom{n-t}{2}A_t + (t+1)(n-t-1)A_{t+1} + (t+2)A_{t+2}\right] \tag{11}$$

for both an odd and even $t \geq 5$.

With Equations (9)–(11), we have

$$\begin{aligned} K_{t+1} &= (4/N^2)[(t+1)T_{1(t+1)} + T_{2(t+1)}] \\ &= (1/2^{2t})\left[4(t+1)(n-t)A_t^1 + 4(t+1)A_{t+1}^0 + \left(t\binom{n-t}{2} - (t+1)(n-t)\right)A_t\right] \\ &\quad +(1/2^{2t})\left[(t+1)(n-t-2)A_{t+1} + (t+2)A_{t+2} + (t+1)\binom{n}{t+1}\right] \end{aligned}$$

for an odd $t \geq 5$, and

$$\begin{aligned} K_{t+1} &= (4/N^2)[(t+1)T_{1(t+1)} + T_{2(t+1)}[\\ &= (1/2^{2t})\left[4(t+1)(n-t)A_t^0 + 4(t+1)A_{t+1}^1 + \left(t\binom{n-t}{2} - (t+1)(n-t)\right)A_t\right] \\ &\quad +(1/2^{2t})\left[(t+1)(n-t-2)A_{t+1} + (t+2)A_{t+2} + (t+1)\binom{n}{t+1}\right] \end{aligned}$$

for an even $t \geq 5$. This completes the proof. □

Remark 2. Theorems 1 and 2 establish relationships between the K-aberration and WLP that are further developments based on the work in [12]. Theorems 1 and 2 help narrow down the choice of finding optimal regular 2^{n-m} designs. Moreover, for some situations, Theorems 1 and 2 are capable of identifying the optimal ones. This point will be demonstrated in Section 4.

4. Applications

It is worth noting that the concept of isomorphism for the designs under BP is different from that under OP. Under OP, two designs are called isomorphic if one can be obtained from the other by column-permuting, row-permuting, or symbol-switching. However, the symbols of the two-level designs are not interchangeable under BP. Hence, two designs are called isomorphic under BP if one can be obtained from the other by column-permuting or row-permuting. Hereafter, we use the terms OP regular 2^{n-m} designs versus BP regular 2^{n-m} designs as discriminations. Clearly, switching symbols of some columns of OP regular 2^{n-m} designs may result in nonisomorphic BP designs. In the following, we illustrate how to find BP regular 2^{n-m} designs that have desirable K-aberration characteristics by using the catalogs of nonisomorphic OP regular 2^{n-m} designs displayed in [22].

Consider finding desirable BP regular 2^{16-10} designs under K-aberration. By checking the catalogs of nonisomorphic OP designs displayed in [22], all the OP regular 2^{16-10} designs have a resolution of either $t = 3$ or 4. According to Theorem 1 in [12], any OP regular 2^{16-10} design with a resolution of $t = 4$ has a smaller K_2 than those with a resolution of $t = 3$, noting that $K_2 = 2\binom{n}{2}(1/2^{4-2}) = 60$ for $t = 4$ and $K_2 = (1/2^{2t-4})\left[(t-1)\binom{n}{t-1} + tA_t\right] = 60 + 3A_3/4$ for $t = 3$. Among the OP regular 2^{16-10} designs of resolution $t = 4$, the designs with the minimum A_4 have a smaller K_3 according to Theorem 1 (b) in [12]. According to [22], the unique OP regular 2^{16-10} design with the minimum A_4, denoted as D_0, is determined by the following ten independent defining words: $g_1g_2g_3g_4g_5g_7$, $g_1g_2g_3g_6g_8$, $g_1g_4g_6g_9$, $g_1g_2g_5g_6g_{10}$, $g_1g_3g_4g_{11}$, $g_1g_3g_5g_{12}$, $g_1g_2g_4g_{13}$, $g_3g_5g_6g_{14}$, $g_2g_4g_5g_6g_{15}$, and $g_2g_3g_5g_{16}$, where $g_1, \ldots, g_6$ are the 1st, 2nd, 2^2th, ..., 2^5th columns of the matrix H_q in (1) with $q = 6$. The ϕs of these ten defining words equaling to 0_N or 1_N determines 2^{10} BP regular designs that may have different K-aberration performances. According to Theorem 2 of [12], among the 2^{10} BP designs, those with the minimum A_4^0 have a smaller K_4. For example, the following two BP regular 2^{16-10} designs D_1 and D_2 have the minimum $A_4^0 = 17$, which results in the minimum $K_4 = 153.8906$:

Although D_1 and D_2 have the same value of K_4, they can be discriminated with respect to K_5 by applying Theorem 1. Compared to D_1, D_2 has the same $A_4^{0,0}$ and $A_4^{1,1}$ but a smaller A_5^1 than D_1. This means that D_2 has a smaller K_5 than D_1 according to Theorem 1. As a confirmation, we calculate the K_s values of the previously stated 2^{10} BP regular 2^{16-10} designs, and it transpires that D_2 is one of the K-aberration optimal BP regular 2^{10-6} designs.

$$
\begin{aligned}
D_1: \quad & \phi(g_1g_2g_3g_4g_5g_7) = 1_N, && \phi(g_1g_2g_3g_6g_8) = 0_N, && \phi(g_1g_4g_6g_9) = 1_N, \\
& \phi(g_1g_2g_5g_6g_{10}) = 1_N, && \phi(g_1g_3g_4g_{11}) = 1_N, && \phi(g_1g_3g_5g_{12}) = 0_N, \\
& \phi(g_1g_2g_4g_{13}) = 0_N, && \phi(g_3g_5g_6g_{14}) = 1_N, && \phi(g_2g_4g_5g_6g_{15}) = 0_N, \\
& \phi(g_2g_3g_5g_{16}) = 1_N. \\
D_2: \quad & \phi(g_1g_2g_3g_4g_5g_7) = 1_N, && \phi(g_1g_2g_3g_6g_8) = 0_N, && \phi(g_1g_4g_6g_9) = 1_N, \\
& \phi(g_1g_2g_5g_6g_{10}) = 1_N, && \phi(g_1g_3g_4g_{11}) = 1_N, && \phi(g_1g_3g_5g_{12}) = 0_N, \\
& \phi(g_1g_2g_4g_{13}) = 0_N, && \phi(g_3g_5g_6g_{14}) = 0_N, && \phi(g_2g_4g_5g_6g_{15}) = 0_N, \\
& \phi(g_2g_3g_5g_{16}) = 1_N.
\end{aligned}
$$

Here is an example of the application of Theorem 2. Consider finding BP regular 2^{10-3} designs that have desirable K-aberration characteristics. By checking the catalogs of nonisomorphic OP regular 2^{10-3} designs provided in [22], we only need to consider the OP regular 2^{10-3} design, denoted as D_3, determined by the independent defining words $g_1g_2g_3g_4g_5g_8$, $g_1g_2g_4g_6g_9$, and $g_1g_2g_3g_6g_7g_{10}$, since it has $A_4 = 0$ and the minimum A_5 among all the nonisomorphic regular 2^{10-3} designs, where g_i is the 2^{i-1}th column of the matrix H_q in (1) with $q = 7$, $i = 1, \ldots, 7$. There are 2^3 BP regular 2^{10-3} designs associated with D_3 depending on whether the previously mentioned three defining words are equal to 0_N or 1_N. Among these regular BP 2^{10-3} designs, those with the minimum A_5^0 have the minimum K_5 according to Theorem 2 of [12]. For example, the regular BP 2^{10-3} design, denoted as D_4, which is determined by the defining words $g_1g_2g_3g_4g_5g_8 = 0_N$, $g_1g_2g_4g_6g_9 = 0_N$, and $g_1g_2g_3g_6g_7g_{10} = 0_N$, has the minimum $A_5^0 = 3$ and then the minimum $K_5 = 5.227$. At the same time, D_4 has the minimum $A_6^0 = 3$, which indicates that D_4 has the minimum K_6 according to Theorem 2. As a confirmation, we calculate the K_s values of all the 2^3 BP regular designs and find that D_4 is one of the K-aberration optimal BP regular 2^{10-3} designs.

The two examples above show that Theorems 1 and 2 can help to filter or select designs. Take Theorem 1 as an example. When the experimenters need to compare 2^{n-m} designs with resolution 4, they can firstly calculate A_4, A_4^0, $A_4^{0,0}$, $A_4^{1,1}$, A_5, A_5^1, and A_6 according to the defining words of the designs and then K_5 according to Theorem 1. Clearly, this is time-saving compared with calculating K_5 among the 2^{10} designs.

The results of Theorems 1 and 2 establish a relation between the K-values and word length pattern of a design. To facilitate practitioners in other fields applying the methods, the following algorithm is provided based on Theorem 1. The algorithm (Algorithm 1) can be directly extended if Theorem 2 is required.

Algorithm 1: For a given n and m, consider a 2^{n-m} design D with resolution 4.

Step 1. List all the defining words of D.
Step 2. Calculate A_4, A_4^0, $A_4^{0,0}$, $A_4^{1,1}$, A_5, A_5^1, and A_6 according to the defining words.
Step 3. Calculate K_5 using (6) directively.

Here, we would like to point out that, to calculate the defining words of D, one should refer to [20].

5. Concluding Remarks

In experiments with each factor having a null state or baseline level, the BP model has quite a natural explanation. Then, finding the optimal fractional factorial designs under BP becomes important. However, the number of nonisomorphic designs under BP is much larger than that under OP, which makes it intricate for us in finding the optimal designs. Together with the results in [12], the present work helps narrow down the choice of finding the optimal regular 2^{n-m} designs through bridging the K-values and WLP. Nonregular designs are commonly used in various experiments due to their flexibility of the run size. Therefore, further study that focuses on finding the optimal nonregular designs under BP is deserved. However, just like the regular designs, it is also intricate in finding the optimal nonregular designs under BP. An algorithm reducing the candidates of the optimal designs would be very useful.

Author Contributions: Conceptualization, S.Z.; methodology, S.Z. and M.Q.; writing—original draft preparation, M.Q.; writing—review and editing, S.Z.; funding acquisition, S.Z. All authors have read and agreed to the published version of the manuscript.

Funding: This research was funded by the National Natural Science Foundation of China, grant number 12171277.

Institutional Review Board Statement: Not applicable.

Data Availability Statement: No new data were created or analyzed in this study. Data sharing is not applicable to this article.

Conflicts of Interest: The authors declare no conflicts of interest.

References

1. Bose, R.C. On some connections between the design of experiments and information theory. *Bull. Inst. Internat. Statist.* **1961**, *38*, 257–271.
2. Cheng, C.-S.; Tang, B. *Theory of Nonregular Factorial Designs*; CRC Press: Boca Raton, FL, USA, 2025.
3. Dey, A.; Mukerjee, R. *Fractional Factorial Plans*; Wiley: New York, NY, USA, 2009.
4. Kerr, K.F. Efficient 2^k factorial designs for blocks of size 2 with microarray applications. *J. Qual. Technol.* **2006**, *38*, 309–318. [CrossRef]
5. Glonek, G.F.V.; Solomon, P.J. Factorial and time course designs for cDNA microarray experiments. *Biostatistics* **2004**, *5*, 89–111. [CrossRef] [PubMed]
6. Banerjee, T.; Mukerjee, R. Optimal factorial designs for cDNA microarray experiments. *Ann. Appl. Statist.* **2008**, *2*, 366–385. [CrossRef]
7. Mukerjee, R.; Tang, B. Optimal fractions of two-level factorials under a baseline parameterization. *Biometrika* **2012**, *99*, 71–84. [CrossRef]
8. Mukerjee, R.; Huda, S. Approximate theory-aided robust efficient factorial fractions under baseline parametrization. *Ann. Inst. Statist. Math.* **2016**, *68*, 787–803. [CrossRef]
9. Liu, Y.; Ren, M.; Zhao, S.L. Robust and efficient factorial designs under baseline parametrization. *Commun. Statist. Theory Methods* **2025**, *54*, 1868–1879. [CrossRef]
10. Karunanayaka, R.C.; Tang, B. Compromise designs under baseline parameterization. *J. Statist. Plann. Inference* **2017**, *190*, 32–38. [CrossRef]
11. Li, P.; Miller, A.; Tang, B. Algorithmic search for baseline minimum aberration designs. *J. Statist. Plann. Inference* **2014**, *149*, 172–182. [CrossRef]
12. Miller, A.; Tang, B. Using regular fractions of two-level designs to find baseline designs. *Statist. Sinica* **2016**, *26*, 745–759. [CrossRef]
13. Mukerjee, R.; Tang, B. Optimal two-level regular designs under baseline parametrization via cosets and minimum moment aberration. *Statist. Sinica* **2016**, *26*, 1001–1019. [CrossRef]
14. Lin, C.Y.; Yang, P. Robust multistratum baseline design. *Comput. Statist. Data Anal.* **2018**, *118*, 98–111. [CrossRef]
15. Li, W.; Liu, M.Q.; Tang, B. A systematic construction of compromise designs under baseline parameterization. *J. Statist. Plann. Inference* **2022**, *219*, 33–42. [CrossRef]
16. Chen, A.; Sun, C.Y.; Tang, B. Selecting baseline designs using a minimum aberration criterion when some two-factor interactions are important. *Statist. Theory Relat. Fields* **2021**, *5*, 95–101. [CrossRef]
17. Sun, C.Y.; Tang, B. Relationship between orthogonal and baseline parameterizations and its application to design constructions. *Statist. Sinica* **2022**, *32*, 239–250. [CrossRef]
18. Yan, Z.H.; Zhao, S.L. Optimal fractions of three-level factorials under a baseline parameterization. *Statist. Probab. Lett.* **2023**, *202*, 109902. [CrossRef]
19. Yan, Z.H.; Zhao, S.L. Optimal s-level fractional factorial designs under baseline parameterization. *J. Statist. Plann. Inference* **2025**, *236*, 106242. [CrossRef]

20. Fries, A.; Hunter, W.G. Minimum aberration 2^{k-p} designs. *Technometrics* **1980**, *22*, 601–608.
21. Deng, L.-Y.; Tang, B. Generalized resolution and minimum aberration criteria for Plackett-Burman and other nonregular factorial designs. *Statist. Sin.* **1999**, *9*, 1071–1082.
22. Xu, H. Algorithmic Construction of Efficient Fractional Factorial Designs with Large Run Sizes. Available online: http://www.stat.ucla.edu/~hqxu/pub/ffd2r/ (accessed on 30 March 2025).

entropy

MDPI

Article

Federated Semi-Supervised Learning with Uniform Random and Lattice-Based Client Sampling

Mei Zhang [1] and Feng Yang [2,*]

[1] School of Mathematics, Southwest Minzu University, Chengdu 610225, China; zhangmei150320@163.com
[2] School of Mathematical Sciences, Sichuan Normal University, Chengdu 610066, China
* Correspondence: yangfeng@sicnu.edu.cn

Abstract

Federated semi-supervised learning (Fed-SSL) has emerged as a powerful framework that leverages both labeled and unlabeled data distributed across clients. To reduce communication overhead, real-world deployments often adopt partial client participation, where only a subset of clients is selected in each round. However, under non-i.i.d. data distributions, the choice of client sampling strategy becomes critical, as it significantly affects training stability and final model performance. To address this challenge, we propose a novel federated averaging semi-supervised learning algorithm, called FedAvg-SSL, that considers two sampling approaches, uniform random sampling (standard Monte Carlo) and a structured lattice-based sampling, inspired by quasi-Monte Carlo (QMC) techniques, which ensures more balanced client participation through structured deterministic selection. On the client side, each selected participant alternates between updating the global model and refining the pseudo-label model using local data. We provide a rigorous convergence analysis, showing that FedAvg-SSL achieves a sublinear convergence rate with linear speedup. Extensive experiments not only validate our theoretical findings but also demonstrate the advantages of lattice-based sampling in federated learning, offering insights into the interplay among algorithm performance, client participation rates, local update steps, and sampling strategies.

Keywords: federated semi-supervised learning; convergence rate; linear speedup; quasi-Monte Carlo techniques; partial client participation

1. Introduction

1.1. Background

With the exponential growth of decentralized data generated by devices such as smartphones, federated learning (FL) [1,2] provides a framework for training high-quality shared global models while preserving data privacy. However, compared with the decentralized optimization [3,4], FL gives rise to significant challenges, particularly in terms of communication efficiency and client availability. To address these challenges, various FL algorithms have been developed [2], with federated averaging (FedAvg) [1] being one of the most widely used. FedAvg works by randomly selecting a subset of clients, performing local stochastic gradient descent (SGD) [5] on the selected clients, and aggregating the resulting models at the server [6]. Numerous studies have analyzed the convergence of FedAvg [7] and have proposed its variations [8–10], particularly in scenarios with partial client participation.

Existing federated learning approaches [11,12] commonly assume a supervised learning setup, where local private data is fully labeled. However, data labeling is often expensive and time-consuming, while unlabeled data is readily available in abundance. This drives us to effectively leverage these massive, distributed pools of unlabeled data to enhance federated learning. A straightforward approach might be to apply semi-supervised learning (SSL) techniques [13–15] to handle unlabeled data, while using traditional federated learning algorithms to aggregate the learned weights.

1.2. Related Works

Semi-Supervised Learning. Numerous studies have explored centralized semi-supervised learning. One prominent approach is pseudo-labeling [16], which generates one-hot labels from highly confident predictions on unlabeled data and uses these labels as training targets with a standard cross-entropy loss. Another major category of SSL methods involves consistency regularization. These methods, such as the ladder network [17], the Π model [18], the mean teacher [19], virtual adversarial training (VAT) [20,21], and MixMatch [22], assume that the class semantics remain invariant under transformations of the input instances. To leverage this assumption, they enforce the model's predictions to be consistent across different perturbations of the input data. Notably, Du et al. [23] further advanced this direction by proposing label propagation for imbalanced multi-label classification, and Ref. [24] developed specialized augmentation strategies for semi-supervised medical image segmentation.

Federated Semi-Supervised Learning. Federated semi-supervised learning (Fed-SSL) [25] extends traditional federated learning to scenarios characterized by limited labeled data and abundant distributed unlabeled data. Notable methods in this area include FedSem [26], which trains a global model on labeled data and incorporates unlabeled data using pseudo-labeling. Jeong et al. [27] introduced an inter-client consistency loss to align predictions across clients, enhancing the utilization of unlabeled data. Recently, Wang et al. [28] proposed a personalized Fed-SSL framework that leverages adaptive variance reduction and normalized aggregation to address client heterogeneity and improve convergence. Similarly, Liang et al. [29] developed RSCFed, which constructs multiple sub-consensus models by randomly sampling clients and then aggregates these sub-consensus models into the global model for improved reliability and performance. Ref. [30] proposed a two-stage sampling method that uses the predicted distribution changes of samples after different data augmentations.

Partial Client Participation. In federated learning (FL), clients may randomly join or leave the system, leading to a stochastic and time-varying set of active participants across communication rounds. For FL with non-i.i.d. datasets and partial client participation [31], several advancements have been made. Yang et al. [7] established a linear speedup in the convergence of FedAvg under partial client participation. Wang et al. [11] provided a unified convergence analysis for FL with arbitrary client participation, and Wang et al. [32] proposed FedAU, which adaptively weights client updates using online estimates of optimal weights without requiring prior knowledge of participation statistics. Ref. [33] considered a variance reduction algorithm applied at the server that eliminates error due to partial client participation.

Despite these efforts, most convergence analyses focus solely on traditional FL. In the context of federated semi-supervised learning, especially with non-i.i.d. datasets and partial client participation, the convergence behavior remains underexplored. A fundamental question arises: Can an algorithm in Fed-SSL still achieve the same linear speedup for convergence under non-i.i.d. data distributions and varying degrees of client participation?

Addressing this challenge is crucial for extending the theoretical foundations of Fed-SSL and ensuring its robustness in practical applications.

Quasi-Monte Carlo Methods in Subsampling. The challenge of partial client participation in FL shares similarities with high-dimensional numerical integration. Quasi-Monte Carlo (QMC) methods [34], rooted in number-theoretic techniques [35], address this by constructing low-discrepancy sequences that achieve superior uniformity in sample distribution—akin to the uniform design in experimental design theory. Zhang et al. [36] and Zhou et al. [37] proposed an efficient model-free subsampling method based on uniform design, which generates representative subdata from the original dataset. This inspires us to similarly employ quasi-Monte Carlo approaches to address the partial client participation.

1.3. Contributions

In this paper, we tackle the federated semi-supervised learning problem with partial client participation, which introduces significant complexity compared to traditional federated optimization problems. Specifically, Fed-SSL involves two sets of optimization variables: the global model and the pseudo-labels, along with the added challenge of constraints. As a result, proving the convergence of algorithms for this problem is notably more difficult.

The main contributions of this paper are as follows:

- We propose an efficient federated learning algorithm, FedAvg-SSL, which incorporates partial client participation and alternates between updating the global model and refining pseudo-labels on local clients. The algorithm supports both uniform random sampling and a more structured lattice-based sampling strategy at the server side. While uniform sampling ensures simplicity and unbiased selection, the lattice-based approach offers more balanced client participation, which improves model stability under non-i.i.d. data.
- We establish a rigorous convergence analysis for FedAvg-SSL, demonstrating a sublinear convergence rate and linear speedup under partial client participation.
- Experimental results validate the performance of the proposed algorithm, showing its consistency with theoretical findings and illustrating the relationship between algorithm performance, the number of participating clients, and the number of local steps.

1.4. Organization

The rest of the paper is organized as follows. Section 2 introduces the federated SSL optimization problem. In Section 3, we present an efficient federated SSL algorithm that incorporates partial client participation via both uniform random sampling and a more structured lattice-based sampling strategy at the server side. In addition, the proposed algorithm alternates between updating the global model and refining pseudo-labels on local clients.

Section 4 provides a convergence rate analysis of the proposed algorithm. In Section 5, we discuss the practical implications of our results. Finally, we conclude in Section 6, with all proofs deferred to the appendix.

2. Problem Formulation

Consider a FL setting with a server and K distributed clients. We assume that both labeled data $\mathcal{L}$ and unlabeled data $\mathcal{U}$ are distributed across these K clients. Specifically, for each client k, the local dataset $\mathcal{D}_k$ consists of both labeled and unlabeled data, i.e.,

$$\mathcal{D}_k = \mathcal{L}_k \cup \mathcal{U}_k,$$

where $\mathcal{L}_k = \{(x_{k,i}, y_{k,i}), i = 1, \ldots, N_k\}$ is the local labeled dataset and $\mathcal{U}_k = \{u_{k,i}, i = 1, \ldots, M_k\}$ is the local unlabeled dataset. Here, $x_{k,i}$ is the i-th labeled sample for the k-th client with the corresponding label $y_{k,i} \in \mathbb{R}^C$, which is a one-hot vector representing the true class label, and C is the number of classes. Similarly, $u_{k,i}$ is the i-th unlabeled sample for the k-th client. The datasets $\mathcal{D}_k$, for $k \in [K] \triangleq \{1, \ldots, K\}$, are assumed to be non-overlapping. Additionally, N_k and M_k denote the number of labeled and unlabeled samples, respectively, for client k.

Let $\hat{\mathbf{y}} = \{\hat{\mathbf{y}}_1, \ldots, \hat{\mathbf{y}}_K\}$ denote the collection of pseudo-labels across all clients, where $\hat{\mathbf{y}}_k = \{\hat{y}_{k,1}, \ldots, \hat{y}_{k,M_k}\}$ represents the set of pseudo-labels for the k-th client. Each pseudo-label $\hat{y}_{k,i} \in \mathbb{R}^C$ belongs to the feasible set $\mathcal{Y}_k = \{\hat{\mathbf{y}}_k \mid e^\top \hat{y}_{k,i} = 1,\ \hat{y}_{k,i} \geq 0, i \in [M_k]\}$, ensuring proper probability distributions. Following [38], we formulate the Fed-SSL optimization problem as follows:

$$\min_{\theta, \hat{\mathbf{y}}} \ F(\theta, \hat{\mathbf{y}}) \triangleq \frac{1}{K} \sum_{k=1}^{K} \Big[\underbrace{\ell_k(\theta, \hat{\mathbf{y}}_k) + \alpha_1 r_1(\hat{\mathbf{y}}_k)}_{\triangleq F_k(\theta, \hat{\mathbf{y}}_k)} \Big] \tag{1a}$$

$$\text{s.t. } \hat{\mathbf{y}}_k \in \mathcal{Y}_k,\ k \in [K]. \tag{1b}$$

The loss function for each client consists of two components: a supervised loss on labeled data and a pseudo-labeled loss on unlabeled data, defined as follows: $\ell_k(\theta, \hat{\mathbf{y}}_k) = L_{\text{CE}}(\theta; \mathcal{L}_k) + \alpha_0 L_{\text{CE}}(\theta; \mathcal{U}_k, \hat{\mathbf{y}}_k)$ where the cross-entropy loss is given by the following:

$$L_{\text{CE}}(\theta; \mathcal{L}) = -\frac{1}{N} \sum_{i=1}^{N} \Big\langle y_i, \log\big(f_\theta(x_i)\big) \Big\rangle.$$

To prevent overconfident pseudo-labels, we introduce a regularization term $r_1(\hat{\mathbf{y}}_k)$:

$$r_1(\hat{\mathbf{y}}_k) = \frac{1}{M_k} \sum_{i=1}^{M_k} \text{KL}(\hat{y}_{k,i}, \mathbf{u}), \tag{2}$$

where $\mathbf{u} = [\frac{1}{C}, \ldots, \frac{1}{C}] \in \mathbb{R}^C$ represents a uniform distribution, and $\text{KL}(\cdot,\cdot)$ denotes the Kullback–Leibler divergence.

The optimization problem in (1) presents two main challenges: (a) it involves two groups of variables (θ and $\hat{\mathbf{y}}$), and (b) the pseudo-labels must satisfy probability simplex constraints. These characteristics naturally suggest an alternating optimization approach for updating these variables.

3. FedAvg-SSL Algorithm

In this section, we propose the FedAvg semi-supervised learning (FedAvg-SSL) algorithm as a solution approach to the optimization problem formulated in (1).

The FedAvg-SSL framework operates under the standard federated learning paradigm, where a central server coordinates training across K distributed clients. In each communication round t, the server selects a subset of clients $\mathcal{S}^t \subseteq \mathcal{K} = \{1, 2, \ldots, K\}$ of fixed size M to participate in model updates. When $M = K$, all clients are involved in every round. In this section, we explore two distinct strategies for determining the active client subset $\mathcal{S}^t$ at each round t.

3.1. Random Sampling Method

The random sampling method in federated learning selects clients for each round independently and uniformly from the entire client. Let $\mathcal{K} = \{1, 2, \ldots, K\}$ be the set of all clients. For each iteration $t \in \{0, 1, \ldots, T-1\}$, we select a subset of clients $\mathcal{S}^t$ via uniform random sampling without replacement from set $\mathcal{K}$ with size M; then, the probability of any client being selected in a round is

$$P(i \in \mathcal{S}^t) = \frac{M}{K}, \forall\, i = 1, \ldots, K.$$

Although each client has the same probability of being selected in each round, the random sampling method can lead to uneven client participation where some clients might be selected multiple times while others might never be selected, especially when the number of communication rounds is limited.

3.2. Lattice-Based Sampling Method

To improve participation uniformity, we propose a lattice-based sampling method that leverages a uniform design to construct a deterministic selection matrix. This method aims to ensure that all clients are sampled more evenly across communication rounds.

Let T be the number of total rounds and M be the number of clients selected per round. Typically, the selected subset size M is a divisor of the total client number K. Let $q = K/M$, then the set of all clients $\mathcal{K} = \{1, 2, \ldots, K\}$ could be divided into M groups with q clients in each group: $\{1, 2, \ldots, q\}, \{q+1, q+2, \ldots, 2q\}, \ldots, \{(M-1)q+1, (M-1)q+2, \ldots, K\}$. Our selection strategy requires choosing exactly one client from each of M predefined groups, resulting in M selected clients per round. It is noticed that each group contains q distinct clients, which naturally evokes the concept of q-level uniform designs in experimental design theory. The uniform designs always have a good space-filling property on the experimental domain. We treat the M groups, each containing q distinct clients, as the value ranges for M factors in the experimental design framework. To ensure that all clients are sampled more evenly across T rounds, we perform sampling according to the rows of the uniform design.

Let $U = U_T(q^M)$ denote a uniform design comprising T runs for M factors, each having q levels, such that we

(1) Let $U(t, k) \in \{1, 2, \ldots, q\}$ denote the element in the t-th row and k-th column of the matrix U for all $t = 0, \ldots, T-1, k = 1, \ldots, K$;
(2) Each level appears equally often in every column.

To obtain a uniform design $U = U_T(q^M)$, the first method is finding designs straightforwardly from the library of uniform designs given by [39], which does not require any calculations. If there is no such design in the library, two other methods can be used to construct such a design. Let $k(T) = \phi(T)/2 + 1$, where $\phi(\cdot)$ is the Euler function. If $M < k(T+1)$, the leave-one-out good lattice point method combined with pseudo-level transformations [40] can be used to construct a nearly uniform design. For the other cases, we can use the R package UniDOE (proposed by [41]) on R version 3.4.1 to search for a nearly uniform design. Actually, the UniDOE package can be used to search for a nearly uniform design for arbitrary T, M. However, the UniDOE package is a little slower than the leave-one-out good lattice point method in general; then, we recommend to use the former only when $M \geq k(T+1)$.

Based on the uniform design U, the sampling design D is obtained by a deterministic offset

$$D(t, k) = U(t, k) + (k-1)q, \ \forall\, t = 0, \ldots, T-1, \ \forall\, k = 1, \ldots, K. \tag{3}$$

Then, all elements of the sampling design D are the actual client IDs. At each communication round t, one row of the matrix D is selected (either sequentially or randomly without replacement), and the resulting client indices form the active set $\mathcal{S}^t$.

This lattice-based scheme systematically spreads participation over time, significantly reducing the risk of client over-sampling or under-sampling (see Figure 1). As a result, it is particularly advantageous in federated semi-supervised learning scenarios, where balanced exposure to heterogeneous client data is crucial for effective model generalization.

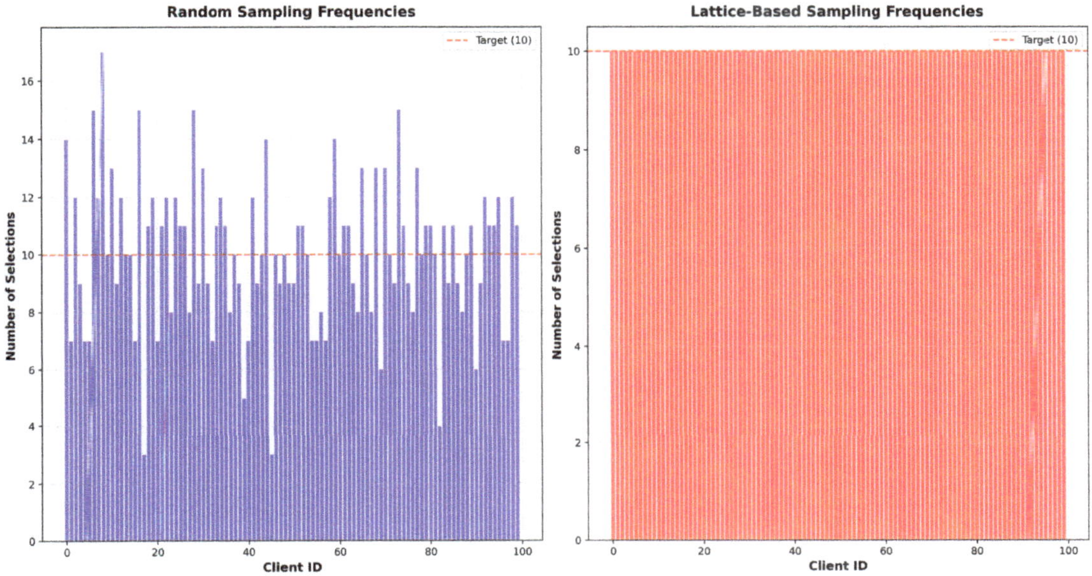

Figure 1. A toy example of our client selection procedure where we sequentially select 10 clients from 100 clients in total over 100 communication rounds. The red dashed line indicates the mean selection count (10) in the non-sampling scheme. The left subplot shows the random sampling pattern where some clients might be selected multiple times (blue bars) while others might be rarely selected, while the right subplot demonstrates our lattice-based sampling method that ensures each client is selected exactly 10 times (red bars) with a systematic and balanced distribution.

3.3. The Proposed Federated SSL Algorithm

In this subsection, we present the proposed Fed-SHVR algorithm for solving problem (1), and its detailed pseudo code is presented in Algorithms 1 and 2. Since the considered problem (1) involves two blocks of variables θ and $\hat{\mathbf{y}}$, we propose to train a global model for (1) in a novel way that combines an alternatively updating strategy with the local SGD algorithm.

Specifically, for each communication round, our algorithm has two parts: one is the client update and the other is the server update.

Client Side. After the server broadcasts the current global model θ^t to all active clients in $\mathcal{S}^t$, each active client k first updates its pseudo-labels by solving the following optimization problem:

$$\hat{\mathbf{y}}_k^{t+1} = \arg\min_{\hat{\mathbf{y}}_k} \alpha_0 L_{\mathrm{CE}}(\theta^t; u_k, \hat{\mathbf{y}}_k) + \alpha_1 r_1(\hat{\mathbf{y}}_k) \tag{4a}$$

$$\text{s.t. } \hat{\mathbf{y}}_k \in \mathcal{Y}_k. \tag{4b}$$

Following [38], this optimization problem admits a closed-form solution:

$$[\hat{y}_{k,i}^{t+1}]_j = \frac{[f_{\theta^t}(u_{k,i})]_j^{\frac{\alpha_Q}{\alpha_1}}}{\sum_{j=1}^{C}[f_{\theta^t}(u_{k,i})]_j^{\frac{\alpha_Q}{\alpha_1}}}, j = 1, \ldots, C, \tag{5}$$

where $[\hat{y}_{k,i}]_j$ denotes the j-th entry of $\hat{y}_{k,i}$. After updating the pseudo-labels, each client performs local model updates:

- Samples mini-batches of labeled data ξ_k and unlabeled data ζ_k uniformly at random from $\mathcal{L}_k$ and $\mathcal{U}_k$, respectively.
- Computes the stochastic gradient of the local loss function

$$g_k(\theta_k, \hat{\mathbf{y}}_k) := \nabla_\theta F_k(\theta_k, \hat{\mathbf{y}}_k; \xi_k, \zeta_k). \tag{6}$$

- Updates its local model copy θ_k using SGD.

Server Side. Each active client transmits its updated local model $\theta_{k,Q}$ back to the server, which aggregates these updates to compute the new global model θ^{t+1} via (7).

Algorithm 1 `FedAvg SSL` `[Server]`

Input: initial model parameters θ^0.
for communication round $t = 0$ **to** $T-1$ **do**
  Sample clients $\mathcal{S}^t$ uniformly randomly so that $|\mathcal{S}^t| = M$, or according to the sampling design D obtained by (3).
  for each client $k \in \mathcal{S}^t$ **in parallel do**
    Send θ^t to client k.
    Receive θ_k^{t+1} from client k via Algorithm 2.
  end for
  Update global model

$$\theta^{t+1} = (1-\eta_\theta)\theta^t + \frac{\eta_\theta}{M}\sum_{k\in\mathcal{S}^t}\theta_k^{t+1}. \tag{7}$$

end for

Algorithm 2 `FedAvg SSL` `[Client]`

Receive θ^t from the server.
Update pseudo-label $\hat{\mathbf{y}}_k^{t+1}$ from (5).
Initialize $\theta_{k,0}^t = \theta^t$.
for $q = 0, \ldots, Q-1$ **do**
  Select data $\xi_{k,q}^t$ and $\zeta_{k,q}^t$ uniformly at random from $\mathcal{L}_k$ and $\mathcal{U}_k$.
  Update local client model

$$\theta_{k,q+1}^t = \theta_{k,q}^t - \eta_g g_k(\theta_{k,q}^t, \hat{\mathbf{y}}_k^{t+1}). \tag{8}$$

end for
Set $\theta_k^{t+1} = \theta_{k,Q}^t$.
Send θ_k^{t+1} back to the server.

4. Convergence Analysis with Partial Client Participation

In this section, we establish the convergence properties of FedAvg-SSL when only a subset of clients updates their variables per outer loop.

4.1. Assumptions

We first make some standard assumptions.

Assumption 1. *The regularization term $r_1(\hat{\mathbf{y}})$ is a continuously differentiable function. Furthermore, $r_1(\hat{\mathbf{y}})$ is μ-strongly convex, where $\mu > 0$. Specifically, for any $\hat{\mathbf{y}}_1, \hat{\mathbf{y}}_2 \in \mathcal{Y}_k$, the following inequality holds:*

$$r_1(\hat{\mathbf{y}}_1) - r_1(\hat{\mathbf{y}}_2) - \langle \nabla r_1(\hat{\mathbf{y}}_2), \hat{\mathbf{y}}_1 - \hat{\mathbf{y}}_2 \rangle \geq \frac{\mu}{2} \|\hat{\mathbf{y}}_1 - \hat{\mathbf{y}}_2\|^2. \tag{9}$$

The regularization term $r_1(\hat{\mathbf{y}}_k)$ defined in (2) is strongly convex over the probabilistic simplex $\mathcal{Y}_k$ (see [42], Definition 2 and Example 2). However, it is important to note that the objective function $F_k(\theta, \hat{\mathbf{y}}_k)$ in (1a) is not jointly convex with respect to $(\theta, \hat{\mathbf{y}})$.

Assumption 2. *The local cost $F_k(\theta, \hat{\mathbf{y}}_k)$ is L-smooth (possibly non-convex) with respect to $(\theta, \hat{\mathbf{y}}_k)$ for $k \in [K]$, i.e.,*

$$\|\nabla_\theta F_k(\theta, \hat{\mathbf{y}}_k) - \nabla_\theta F_k(\theta', \hat{\mathbf{y}}'_k)\| \leq L\sqrt{\|\theta - \theta'\|^2 + \|\hat{\mathbf{y}}_k - \hat{\mathbf{y}}'_k\|^2}, \tag{10}$$

for all θ, θ' and $\hat{\mathbf{y}}_k, \hat{\mathbf{y}}'_k \in \mathcal{Y}_k$.

Assumption 3. *Given $\hat{\mathbf{y}}_k$, for any $k \in [K]$, the stochastic gradient is unbiased for any θ. Specifically, the following conditions hold:*

$$\mathbb{E}[g_k(\theta_k, \hat{\mathbf{y}}_k)] = \nabla_\theta F_k(\theta_k, \hat{\mathbf{y}}_k), \tag{11}$$

$$\mathbb{E}[\|g_k(\theta_k, \hat{\mathbf{y}}_k) - \nabla_\theta F_k(\theta_k, \hat{\mathbf{y}}_k)\|^2] \leq \sigma_\theta^2, \tag{12}$$

where σ_θ represents the noise variance, and $\mathbb{E}$ denotes the expectation with respect to all random variables $\{\xi_k, \zeta_k\}$.

Assumption 4 (Bounded Gradient Dissimilarity). *There exists a constant $\sigma_G > 0$ such that for any θ and $\hat{\mathbf{y}}$, the following inequality holds:*

$$\frac{1}{K}\sum_{k=1}^{K} \|\nabla_\theta F_k(\theta, \hat{\mathbf{y}}_k) - \nabla_\theta F(\theta, \hat{\mathbf{y}})\|^2 \leq \sigma_G^2. \tag{13}$$

Assumptions 2 and 3 are standard in first-order stochastic algorithms, while Assumption 4 constrains the data heterogeneity by bounding the gradient dissimilarity between different clients, which is commonly used in [7,11,28].

4.2. Convergence Analysis of FedAvg-SSL

From (7) and (8), the update for the global model across consecutive outer loops is given by

$$\theta^{t+1} - \theta^t = \frac{\eta_\theta}{M}\sum_{k \in \mathcal{S}^t} (\theta_k^{t+1} - \theta^t) = -\frac{\eta}{M}\sum_{k,q} \mathbb{I}_{k \in \mathcal{S}^t} g_k(\theta_{k,q}^t, \hat{\mathbf{y}}_k^{t+1}), \tag{14}$$

where $\eta = \eta_\theta \gamma_\theta$ and $\mathbb{I}_{k \in \mathcal{S}^t}$ denote the characteristic function of the set $\mathcal{S}^t$, representing the subset of clients participating in the current round.

A critical challenge arises because the right-hand side of the above equation does not provide an unbiased estimation of the full gradient. Specifically, we have

$$\frac{1}{M}\sum_{k,q} \mathbb{E}[\mathbb{I}_{k \in \mathcal{S}^t} g_k(\theta_{k,q}^t, \hat{\mathbf{y}}_k^{t+1})] \neq \nabla F(\theta, \mathbf{y}^{t+1}), \tag{15}$$

where $\nabla F(\theta, \mathbf{y}^{t+1})$ is the gradient of the full objective function.

This discrepancy stems from the stochastic nature of partial client participation, as only a subset of clients $\mathcal{S}^t$ is actively involved in each communication round. Consequently, the aggregated gradient $\frac{1}{M}\sum_{k,q}\mathbb{I}_{k\in\mathcal{S}^t}g_k$ introduces bias, which complicates the convergence analysis. Specifically, controlling this bias becomes essential to establish rigorous convergence guarantees for FedAvg-SSL under partial client participation.

Before we show the convergence, let us first define the following optimality gap:

$$g_t \triangleq \mathbb{E}[\|\nabla_\theta F(\theta^t, \hat{\mathbf{y}}^{t+1})\|^2] + \frac{1}{K}\sum_{k=1}^{K}\mathbb{E}[\|\hat{\mathbf{y}}_k^{t+1} - \hat{\mathbf{y}}_k^t\|^2]. \tag{16}$$

which measures how far an iteration point is away from the stationary point. From the definition, we know $g_t \geq 0$. If $g_t = 0$, the iterate $\{\theta^t, \hat{\mathbf{y}}^t\}$ will be a stationary point of problem (1). According to (16), we have

$$\nabla_\theta F(\theta^t, \hat{\mathbf{y}}^t) = 0,\ \hat{\mathbf{y}}_k^{t+1} - \hat{\mathbf{y}}_k^t = 0. \tag{17}$$

Since $\hat{y}_k^{t+1}$ is the optimal solution of $F_k(\theta^t, \hat{\mathbf{y}})$, from the first order optimality condition, we get

$$\langle \nabla_{\hat{\mathbf{y}}_k} F_k(\theta^t, \hat{\mathbf{y}}_k^{t+1}), \hat{\mathbf{y}}_k - \hat{\mathbf{y}}_k^{t+1}\rangle \geq 0,\ \text{for}\ \forall\, \hat{\mathbf{y}}_k \in \mathcal{Y}_k. \tag{18}$$

Combing (17) and (18), for $\forall\, \theta, \hat{\mathbf{y}}_k \in \mathcal{Y}_k$, we have

$$\langle \nabla_\theta F(\theta^t, \hat{\mathbf{y}}^t), \theta - \theta^t\rangle + \sum_{k=1}^{K}\langle \nabla_{\hat{\mathbf{y}}_k} F_k(\theta^t, \hat{\mathbf{y}}_k^t), \hat{\mathbf{y}}_k - \hat{\mathbf{y}}_k^t\rangle \geq 0.$$

The above inequality implies that $\{\theta^t, \hat{\mathbf{y}}^t\}$ is a stationary point to problem (1).

Theorem 1. *If $\eta_g^2 \leq \frac{1}{64Q(Q-1)L^2}$ and $\eta := \eta_g\eta_\theta \leq \frac{M(K-1)}{(3+12Q)QL(K-M)}$, we have that the sequence $\{\theta^t, \hat{\mathbf{y}}^t\}$ generated by Algorithm 1 satisfies*

$$\frac{1}{T}\sum_{t=0}^{T-1} g_t \leq \frac{4\mathbb{E}[F(\theta^0, \hat{\mathbf{y}}^0)]}{\eta QT} + \eta_g^2 B_1 + 4\eta\eta_g^2 B_2 + 4\eta B_3, \tag{19}$$

where

$$B_1 = L^2(Q(Q-1))\sigma_G^2 + 2L^2(Q-1)\sigma_\theta^2, \tag{20}$$

$$B_2 = \frac{24Q^3L^3(K-M)}{M(K-1)}\sigma_G^2 + \frac{6Q(Q-1)L^3(K-M)}{M(K-1)}\sigma_\theta^2, \tag{21}$$

$$B_3 = \frac{3LQ(K-M)}{2M(K-1)}\sigma_G^2 + \frac{L}{2M}\sigma_\theta^2. \tag{22}$$

Proof. See Appendix A. □

Remark 1. *Theorem 1 provides an explicit upper bound on the optimality gap, which offers useful insights into how several key factors influence the convergence behavior of the proposed FedAvg-SSL algorithm:*

- *Number of participating clients (M): When all clients participate in each round, i.e., $M = K$, the term B_2 in the bound becomes zero. As a result, the convergence rate improves, demonstrating the benefit of increased client participation.*

- *Number of local steps (Q): As Q increases, the accumulated local update noise can affect convergence. Theorem 1 suggests that in such cases, the global and local learning rates η and η_g should be chosen smaller to maintain stability and ensure convergence.*

  These observations provide practical guidance for selecting different parameters in FedAvg-SSL.

With appropriate step sizes, we can derive the following corollary.

Corollary 1. *Let $\eta_g = \frac{1}{\sqrt{TQL}}$ and $\eta = \frac{\sqrt{M}}{\sqrt{TQL}}$; the convergence rate of the FedAvg-SSL algorithm under partial client participation is given by*

$$\min_{t=0,\ldots,T-1} g_t \leq \mathcal{O}\left(\frac{1}{\sqrt{MTQ}} + \frac{1}{T}\right). \tag{23}$$

Remark 2. *Corollary 1 demonstrates that the required number of outer loop iterations T to achieve an ϵ-solution decreases linearly as M increases. This phenomenon is commonly referred to as linear speedup with respect to M. To the best of our knowledge, this is the first work to establish the linear speedup of a federated semi-supervised learning algorithm.*

5. Simulation Results

We conducted extensive experiments on the MNIST dataset to evaluate the effectiveness of our proposed federated semi-supervised learning approach. The experiments were implemented using PyTorch version 1.8 on a CUDA-enabled GPU, utilizing the MNIST dataset which contains 60,000 training images and 10,000 test images of handwritten digits.

To simulate a realistic federated learning scenario, we configured our system with 100 clients ($K = 100$) and implemented a partial participation strategy where only 10% of clients (10 clients) participate in each federation round. The dataset was divided into labeled and unlabeled portions, with 30% of the data being labeled and the remaining 70% unlabeled. We investigated two distinct data distribution scenarios:

- IID Setting: The training data is randomly and uniformly distributed across clients, ensuring each client receives approximately equal amounts of both labeled and unlabeled samples. This setting serves as our baseline distribution.
- Non-IID Setting: Labeled data is randomly shuffled and split into twice as many shards as there are clients, with each client randomly assigned two unique shards. This ensures that each client receives a distinct, non-overlapping subset of the labeled data, with each shard containing a random mix of classes. The unlabeled data is distributed using a Dirichlet distribution ($\alpha = 0.01$) to further enhance the non-IID nature of the data across clients.

For our model architecture, we employed a simple multi-layer perceptron (MLP) with one hidden layer containing 256 units and ReLU activations. The training process utilized a mini-batch size of 32 for both labeled and unlabeled data, with learning rates set to $\eta_g = \eta_\theta = 0.01$. Each participating client performed 10 local epochs during their training phase.

Impact of hyperparameters α_0 and α_1. The hyperparameter α_0 controls the model's reliance on the unlabeled data during training. To prevent the model from prematurely overfitting to noisy pseudo-labels, we adopt a gradually increasing schedule for α_0, inspired by the work in [16]. Specifically, we define

$$\alpha_0 = \begin{cases} \exp\left(-5\left(1 - \frac{t}{T_1}\right)^2\right), & \text{if } t < T_1 \\ 1, & \text{if } t \geq T_1. \end{cases}$$

The second hyperparameter, α_1, serves as a regularization weight in the pseudo-label refinement process. It controls the entropy of the pseudo-labels: smaller values encourage confident (i.e., lower-entropy) predictions, while larger values encourage more conservative updates by penalizing overconfidence. Thus, tuning α_1 balances the trade-off between exploration and exploitation of pseudo-labels.

To investigate the impact of these hyperparameters, we conduct a sensitivity analysis and summarize the results in the table below. The test accuracy is evaluated under different combinations of T_1 and α_1 in the non-IID setting. As shown in Table 1, the highest accuracy of 97.5% occurs when $T_1 = 10$ and $\alpha_1 = 0.5$, outperforming other configurations. Based on these results, we adopt this parameter configuration for all subsequent experiments. Figure 2 further illustrates the effects of these parameters on training dynamics.

Table 1. Test accuracy of the proposed algorithm by using different parameters α_1 and α_2 on the non-IID case.

	$T_1 = 10$	$T_1 = 50$
$\alpha_1 = 0$	96.91%	97.21%
$\alpha_1 = 0.5$	**97.5%**	96.89%
$\alpha_1 = 1$	96.71%	96.76%

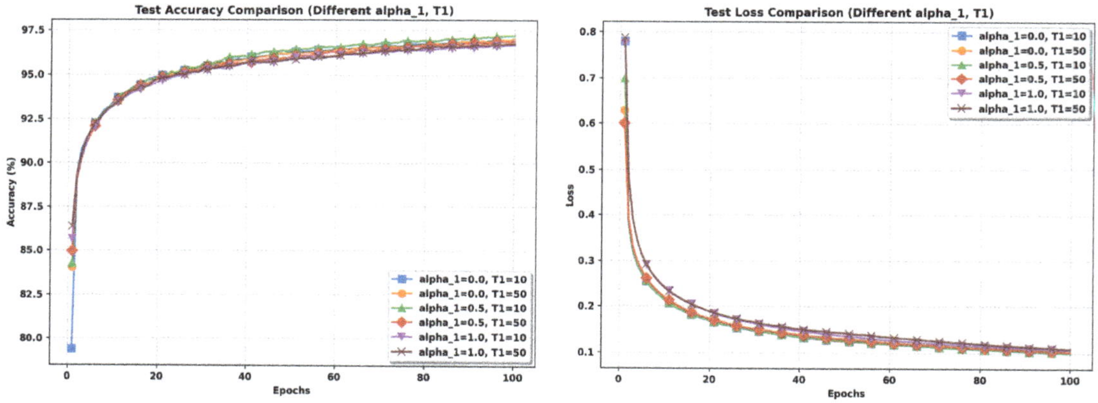

(a) (b)

Figure 2. Performance comparison of FedAvg-SSL approaches under different parameter settings. (**a**) Test Accuracy Comparison. (**b**) Test Loss Comparison.

Impact of non-IID datasets. As illustrated in Figure 3a, we present comprehensive experimental results comparing the performance of federated semi-supervised learning under both IID and non-IID data distributions. The test accuracy curves in Figure 3a demonstrates that the non-IID data distribution significantly impacts the model's convergence and final performance. Under the IID setting with SSL, the model achieves the highest accuracy of approximately 83%, while the same approach under non-IID conditions reaches only 78%, indicating a clear performance degradation due to data heterogeneity.

A key observation from the loss curves in Figure 3b is that the non-IID data distribution notably slows down the convergence rate. The IID+SSL configuration shows the fastest convergence and reaches the lowest loss value of approximately 1.15, while its non-IID counterpart maintains a consistently higher loss of around 1.4. This pattern aligns with theoretical expectations that higher degrees of data heterogeneity lead to slower convergence and higher final loss values.

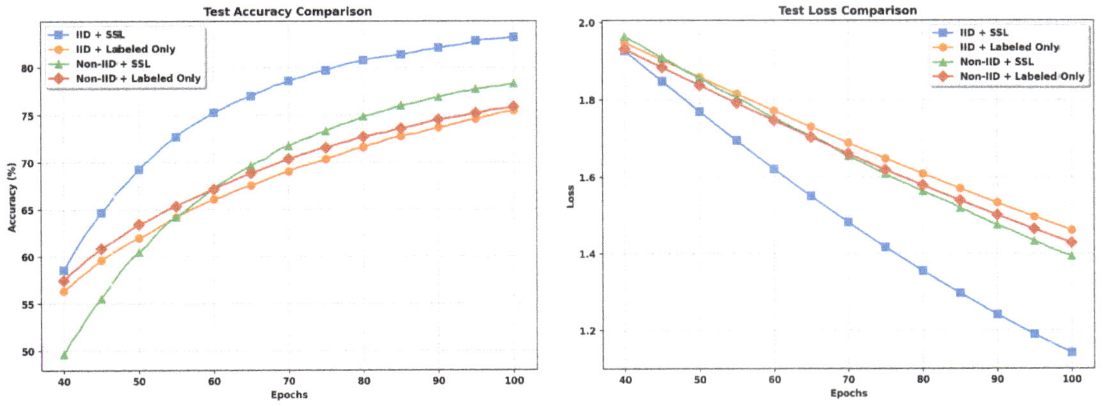

(a) (b)

Figure 3. Performance comparison of federated learning approaches under different data distribution settings. The results show the superiority of SSL methods over supervised-only approaches in both IID and non-IID scenarios. (**a**) Test Accuracy Comparison. (**b**) Test Loss Comparison.

Furthermore, the impact of non-IID data is evident in both SSL and supervised-only approaches, though with varying degrees. The performance gap between IID and non-IID settings is more pronounced in the SSL approach (5% difference) compared to the supervised-only setting (1% difference). This observation suggests that while SSL techniques can effectively leverage unlabeled data, their benefits are somewhat diminished under non-IID conditions, highlighting the fundamental challenges that data heterogeneity poses in federated learning scenarios.

Impact of label ratios. To investigate how the proportion of labeled data affects model performance, we conducted experiments with varying label ratios. Figure 4 presents the test accuracy and loss curves for different label ratios ranging from 0.1 to 0.9.

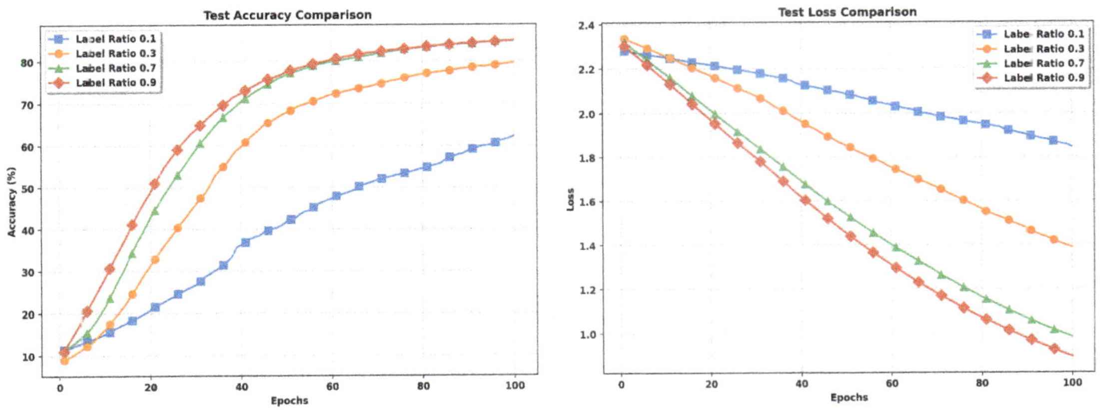

(a) (b)

Figure 4. Performance comparison with different label ratios (0.1, 0.3, 0.7, and 0.9) under non-IID settings. Higher label ratios generally lead to better performance and faster convergence. (**a**) Test Accuracy with Different Label Ratios. (**b**) Test Loss with Different Label Ratios.

Figure 4a demonstrates a clear correlation between label ratio and model performance. With a high label ratio of 0.9, the model achieves the best performance, reaching approximately an 85% accuracy after 100 epochs. The convergence is also notably faster, showing steep improvement in the early stages (20–40 epochs). In contrast, with only 10% labeled data (ratio 0.1), the model struggles significantly, achieving only about 62% accuracy and showing much slower convergence throughout the training process. The loss curves in Figure 4b further reinforce these findings. Models trained with higher label ratios (0.7 and 0.9) demonstrate more efficient optimization, reaching lower loss values (around 0.9–1.0) and showing steeper descent curves.

Impact of Local Training Steps. To validate Theorem 1 and investigate the effect of local training steps on Fed-SSL's performance under non-IID settings, we conducted experiments with varying numbers of local steps (5, 10, 20, and 30). Figure 5 presents the experimental results.

The experimental results strongly align with our theoretical analysis in Theorem 1 regarding the convergence of Fed-SSL. As shown in Figure 5a, increasing the number of local steps significantly improves both convergence speed and final model performance. With 30 local steps, the model achieves the highest accuracy of approximately 85% and demonstrates the fastest convergence rate, particularly during the early stages (20–40 communication rounds). In contrast, with only five local steps, the model shows slower convergence and reaches a lower final accuracy of about 73%.

The loss curves in Figure 5b further validate our theoretical findings. Models trained with more local steps (20 and 30) exhibit more efficient optimization trajectories, achieving lower final loss values (around 0.9–1.0) and showing steeper descent curves. This observation is consistent with Theorem 1, which suggests that increasing local training steps can enhance convergence stability and final performance, provided the learning rate is properly chosen.

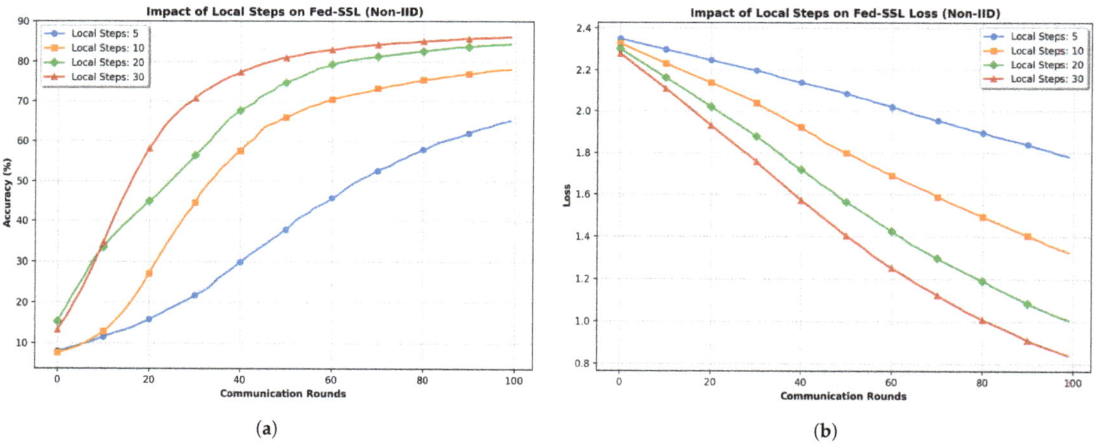

Figure 5. Impact of local training steps on Fed-SSL performance under non-IID settings. Increasing local steps leads to faster convergence and better final performance, consistent with Theorem 1. (**a**) Test Accuracy with Different Local Steps. (**b**) Test Loss with Different Local Steps.

Impact of Client Number. As shown in Figure 6, we compare the test accuracy and loss curves among three different participation rates: full worker participation ($K = 100$) and partial worker participation ($M = 30$ and $M = 10$) under the same hyperparameter settings. The results demonstrate that full worker participation consistently outperforms partial participation scenarios, achieving approximately 83% accuracy compared to 82.5% and 82% for 10% and 30% participation rates, respectively. This performance gap can be attributed to the additional randomness introduced by partial worker participation, resulting in slower convergence rates as evidenced by the more gradual slopes of both accuracy and loss curves.

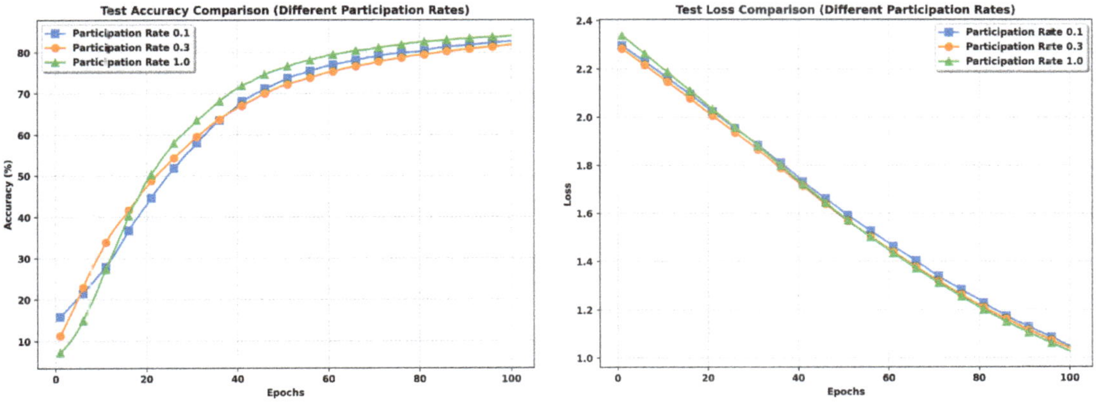

(a) (b)

Figure 6. Performance comparison of FedSSL with different participation rates under non-IID setting. (**a**) Test Accuracy with Different Numbers of Clients. (**b**) Test Loss with Different Numbers of Clients.

This phenomenon is particularly pronounced in our non-IID setting, where system heterogeneity plays a crucial role. Full worker participation effectively neutralizes this heterogeneity in each communication round by incorporating updates from all clients. In contrast, partial participation struggles to maintain this balance, as the selected subset of workers may not adequately represent the overall data distribution. For instance, with only 10 or 30 active workers, the available training data might cover only a subset of the MNIST dataset's 10 digit classes, leading to biased model updates. This effect is clearly visible in both the accuracy and loss trajectories, where partial participation schemes exhibit consistently inferior performance throughout the training process.

Impact of Sampling Strategies. As shown in Figure 7, the lattice-based sampling consistently outperforms random sampling in both test accuracy and test loss. The reason may be that the lattice-based sampling method ensures that all clients contribute equally across communication rounds, effectively mitigating the bias introduced by data heterogeneity. In contrast, random sampling may result in some clients being over- or under-represented, leading to less representative model updates (see Figure 1).

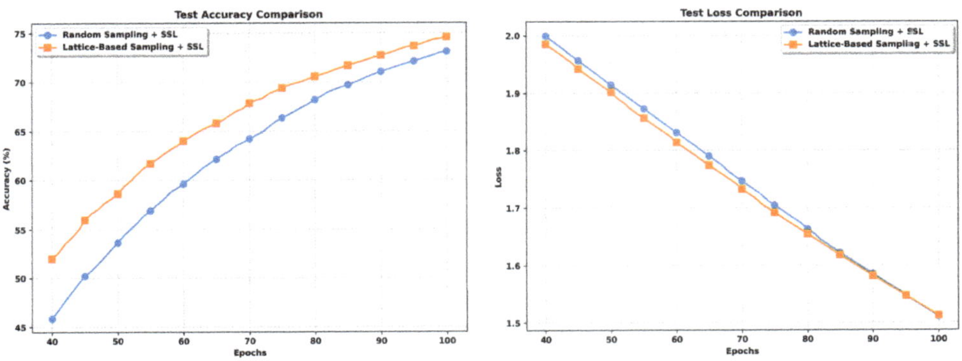

(a) (b)

Figure 7. Performance comparison of FedSSL with different sampling strategies under non-IID setting. (**a**) Test Accuracy with Different Sampling Strategies. (**b**) Test Loss with Different Sampling Strategies.

6. Conclusions

In this paper, we propose an efficient FedAvg-SSL algorithm that alternately updates model parameters and pseudo-labels in non-IID federated settings for general non-convex optimization. To address the challenge of partial client participation, we introduce and compare two sampling strategies—uniform random sampling and lattice-based sampling—at the server side. The lattice-based method is shown to enhance participation balance and reduce selection variance across communication rounds. We provide a rigorous theoretical analysis demonstrating that FedAvg-SSL achieves a sublinear convergence rate with linear speedup under partial participation. Extensive experiments on the MNIST dataset support our theoretical claims and offer practical insights into how sampling strategy, participation rate, and local update steps jointly influence learning performance. These results provide valuable guidance for the design of efficient and robust federated semi-supervised learning systems. In future work, we plan to explore fairness-aware QMC-based client selection strategies, building on insights from [43], to ensure more equitable participation and performance across clients.

Author Contributions: Conceptualization, M.Z. and F.Y.; methodology, M.Z. and F.Y.; writing—original draft preparation, M.Z.; writing—review and editing, M.Z. and F.Y.; supervision, F.Y.; funding acquisition, M.Z. and F.Y. All authors have read and agreed to the published version of the manuscript.

Funding: This research was funded by the National Natural Science Foundation of China (No. 12301321, 12101435), the Fundamental Research Funds for the Central Universities at Southwest Minzu University (No. ZYN2024203), and the Research Foundation of Sichuan Normal University (No. pt12101435, ky20200919).

Institutional Review Board Statement: Not applicable.

Data Availability Statement: The data presented in this study are available on request from the first author.

Acknowledgments: The authors would like to thank Yongdao Zhou for his valuable comments.

Conflicts of Interest: The authors declare no conflicts of interest.

Appendix A. Proof of Theorem 1

For ease of presentation, we first show some important lemmas about the descent of the objective.

Appendix A.1. Some Auxiliary Lemmas

The following lemma bounds the change in function value across consecutive outer loops for FedAvg-SSL with partial client participation.

Lemma A1. *Under Assumptions 1 and 2, it holds that*

$$\begin{aligned}\mathbb{E}[F(\theta^{t+1},\hat{\mathbf{y}}^{t+1})]-\mathbb{E}[F(\theta^{t},\hat{\mathbf{y}}^{t})] \leq &\mathbb{E}[\langle\nabla_{\theta}F(\theta^{t},\hat{\mathbf{y}}^{t+1}),\theta^{t+1}-\theta^{t}\rangle]+\frac{L}{2}\mathbb{E}[\|\theta^{t+1}-\theta^{t}\|^{2}]\\ &-\frac{\mu\alpha_1}{2K}\sum_{k=1}^{K}\mathbb{E}[\|\hat{\mathbf{y}}_k^{t}-\hat{\mathbf{y}}_k^{t+1}\|^{2}].\end{aligned} \tag{A1}$$

Proof. Firstly, we can establish the following equality:

$$F_k(\theta^{t+1},\hat{\mathbf{y}}_k^{t+1})-F_k(\theta^{t},\hat{\mathbf{y}}_k^{t})=F_k(\theta^{t+1},\hat{\mathbf{y}}_k^{t+1})-F_k(\theta^{t},\hat{\mathbf{y}}_k^{t+1})+F_k(\theta^{t},\hat{\mathbf{y}}_k^{t+1})-F_k(\theta^{t},\hat{\mathbf{y}}_k^{t}). \tag{A2}$$

Since each client F_k has Lipschitz continuous gradients with respect to $(\theta, \hat{\mathbf{y}}_k)$ by Assumption 2, we have

$$F_k(\theta^{t+1}, \hat{\mathbf{y}}_k^{t+1}) - F_k(\theta^t, \hat{\mathbf{y}}_k^{t+1}) \leq \langle \nabla_\theta F_k(\theta^t, \hat{\mathbf{y}}_k^{t+1}), \theta^{t+1} - \theta^t \rangle + \frac{L}{2} \|\theta^{t+1} - \theta^t\|^2. \tag{A3}$$

According to (1a), we have

$$F_k(\theta^t, \hat{\mathbf{y}}_k^{t+1}) - F_k(\theta^t, \hat{\mathbf{y}}_k^t) = \alpha_0 [L_{\text{CE}}(\theta^t; \hat{\mathbf{y}}_k^{t+1}) - L_{\text{CE}}(\theta^t; \hat{\mathbf{y}}_k^t)] + \alpha_1 [r_1(\hat{\mathbf{y}}_k^{t+1}) - r_1(\hat{\mathbf{y}}_k^t)]. \tag{A4}$$

Since $L_{\text{CE}}(\theta; u_k, \hat{\mathbf{y}}_k)$ is a linear function with respect to $\hat{\mathbf{y}}_k$, and $r_1(\hat{\mathbf{y}}_k)$ is a strongly convex function about $\hat{\mathbf{y}}_k$, using Assumption 1, we have

$$\begin{aligned} &\alpha_0 L_{\text{CE}}(\theta^t; u_k, \hat{\mathbf{y}}_k^t) + \alpha_1 r_1(\hat{\mathbf{y}}_k^t) - \alpha_0 L_{\text{CE}}(\theta^t; u_k, \hat{\mathbf{y}}_k^{t+1}) - \alpha_1 r_1(\hat{\mathbf{y}}_k^{t+1}) \\ &\geq \langle \alpha_0 \nabla_{\mathbf{y}_k} L_{\text{CE}}(\theta^t; u_k, \hat{\mathbf{y}}_k^{t+1}) + \alpha_1 \nabla_{\mathbf{y}_k} r_1(\hat{\mathbf{y}}_k^{t+1}), \hat{\mathbf{y}}_k^t - \hat{\mathbf{y}}_k^{t+1} \rangle + \frac{\mu \alpha_1}{2} \|\hat{\mathbf{y}}_k^t - \hat{\mathbf{y}}_k^{t+1}\|^2. \end{aligned} \tag{A5}$$

In (4), we see that $\hat{\mathbf{y}}_k^{t+1}$ is the optimal solution. Using the first-order condition implies

$$\langle \alpha_0 \nabla_{\mathbf{y}_k} L_{\text{CE}}(\theta^t; u_k, \hat{\mathbf{y}}_k^{t+1}) + \alpha_1 \nabla_{\mathbf{y}_k} r_1(\hat{\mathbf{y}}_k^{t+1}), \hat{\mathbf{y}}_k^t - \hat{\mathbf{y}}_k^{t+1} \rangle \geq 0. \tag{A6}$$

Substituting (A6) into (A5) and (A4) gives rise to

$$F_k(\theta^t, \hat{\mathbf{y}}_k^{t+1}) - F_k(\theta^t, \hat{\mathbf{y}}_k^t)) \leq -\frac{\mu \alpha_1}{2} \|\hat{\mathbf{y}}_k^t - \hat{\mathbf{y}}_k^{t+1}\|^2. \tag{A7}$$

Finally, we combine (A3) and (A4) to obtain the final result of this lemma by considering the relationship $F(\theta, \hat{\mathbf{y}}) = \frac{1}{K} \sum_{k=1}^K F_k(\theta, \hat{\mathbf{y}}_k)$ and taking the expected value. □

Lemma A2. *Under Assumptions 1 and 2, it holds that*

$$\begin{aligned} \mathbb{E}[\langle \nabla_\theta F(\theta^t, \hat{\mathbf{y}}^{t+1}), \theta^{t+1} - \theta^t \rangle] \leq &-\frac{\eta Q}{2} \mathbb{E}[\|\nabla_\theta F(\theta^t, \hat{\mathbf{y}}^{t+1})\|^2] + \frac{\eta L^2}{2K} \sum_{k,q} \mathbb{E}[\|\theta^t - \theta_{k,q}^t\|^2] \\ &- \frac{\eta}{2K^2 Q} \mathbb{E}[\| \sum_{k,q} \nabla_\theta F_k(\theta_{k,q}^t, \hat{\mathbf{y}}_k^{t+1})\|^2], \end{aligned} \tag{A8}$$

where $\eta = \eta_\theta \eta_g$.

Proof. In order to bound the above error, we need to introduce the following two σ-algebras as follows:

$$\begin{aligned} \mathcal{F}^t &:= \sigma\Big(\{\xi_{k,q}^t, \zeta_{k,q}^t, \mathcal{S}^r : k \in [K], 0 \leq q \leq Q-1, 0 \leq t \leq t-1\}\Big), \\ \mathcal{F}_{k,q}^t &:= \sigma\Big(\mathcal{F}^t \cup \mathcal{S}^t \cup \{\xi_{k,l}^t, \zeta_{k,l}^t : l \leq q\} \cup \{\xi_{j,l}^t, \zeta_{j,l}^t : j \leq k-1, l \leq Q-1\}\Big). \end{aligned}$$

Thus, it holds that

$$\begin{aligned} \mathbb{E}[\langle \nabla_\theta F(\theta^t, \hat{\mathbf{y}}^{t+1}), \theta^{t+1} - \theta^t \rangle] &= \mathbb{E}[\langle \nabla_\theta F(\theta^t, \hat{\mathbf{y}}^{t+1}), -\frac{\eta_\theta \eta_g}{M} \sum_{k,q} \mathbb{I}_{k \in \mathcal{S}^t} g_k(\theta_{k,q}^t, \hat{\mathbf{y}}_k^{t+1}) \rangle] \\ &= -\frac{\eta_\theta \eta_g}{M} \sum_{k,q} \mathbb{E}\Big[\mathbb{E}[\langle \nabla_\theta F(\theta^t, \hat{\mathbf{y}}^{t+1}), \mathbb{I}_{k \in \mathcal{S}^t} g_k(\theta_{k,q}^t, \hat{\mathbf{y}}_k^{t+1}) \rangle] | \mathcal{F}_{k,q-1}^t\Big] \end{aligned}$$

where the last equality is due to the tower property of conditional expectation. Since $\mathbb{I}_{k \in \mathcal{S}^t}$ and $g_k(\theta_{k,q-1}^t, \hat{\mathbf{y}}_k^{t+1})$ are $\mathcal{F}_{k,q-1}^t$-measurable, we have that

$$
\begin{aligned}
\mathbb{E}[\langle \nabla_\theta F(\theta^t, \hat{\mathbf{y}}^{t+1}), \theta^{t+1} - \theta^t \rangle] &= \mathbb{E}[\langle \nabla_\theta F(\theta^t, \hat{\mathbf{y}}^{t+1}), -\frac{\eta_\theta \eta_g}{M} \sum_{k,q} \mathbb{I}_{k \in \mathcal{S}^t} g_k(\theta^t_{k,q}, \hat{\mathbf{y}}^{t+1}_k) \rangle] \\
&= -\frac{\eta_\theta \eta_g}{M} \sum_{k,q} \mathbb{E}\Big[\langle \nabla_\theta F(\theta^t, \hat{\mathbf{y}}^{t+1}), \mathbb{I}_{k \in \mathcal{S}^t} \mathbb{E}[g_k(\theta^t_{k,q}, \hat{\mathbf{y}}^{t+1}_k)] \rangle \Big] \\
&= -\frac{\eta_\theta \eta_g}{K} \sum_{k,q} \mathbb{E}[\langle \nabla_\theta F(\theta^t, \hat{\mathbf{y}}^{t+1}), \nabla_\theta F_k(\theta^t_{k,q}, \hat{\mathbf{y}}^{t+1}_k) \rangle], \qquad \text{(A9)}
\end{aligned}
$$

where the last equality is due to (11), and we sample clients $\mathcal{S}^t$ uniformly randomly, which leads to $\mathbb{E}[\mathbb{I}_{k \in \mathcal{S}^t}] = \frac{M}{K}$. Based on the common equality $-\langle a, b \rangle = \frac{1}{2}[\|a - b\|^2 - \|a\|^2 - \|b\|^2]$, we know

$$
\begin{aligned}
&\mathbb{E}[\langle \nabla_\theta F(\theta^t, \hat{\mathbf{y}}^{t+1}), \theta^{t+1} - \theta^t \rangle] \\
&= -\eta Q \mathbb{E}[\langle \nabla_\theta F(\theta^t, \hat{\mathbf{y}}^{t+1}), \sum_{k,q} \frac{1}{KQ} \nabla_\theta F_k(\theta^t_{k,q}, \hat{\mathbf{y}}^{t+1}_k) \rangle] \\
&= -\frac{\eta Q}{2} \left[\mathbb{E}[\|\nabla_\theta F(\theta^t, \hat{\mathbf{y}}^{t+1})\|^2] + \mathbb{E}[\| \sum_{k,q} \frac{1}{KQ} \nabla_\theta F_k(\theta^t_{k,q}, \hat{\mathbf{y}}^{t+1}_k) \|^2] \right] \\
&\quad + \frac{\eta Q}{2} \mathbb{E}[\|\nabla_\theta F(\theta^t, \hat{\mathbf{y}}^{t+1}) - \sum_{k,q} \frac{1}{KQ} \nabla_\theta F_k(\theta^t_{k,q}, \hat{\mathbf{y}}^{t+1}_k)\|^2]. \qquad \text{(A10)}
\end{aligned}
$$

Note that

$$
\nabla_\theta F(\theta^t, \hat{\mathbf{y}}^{t+1}) = \sum_{k,q} \frac{1}{KQ} \nabla_\theta F_k(\theta^t, \hat{\mathbf{y}}^{t+1}_k),
$$

We get

$$
\mathbb{E}[\|\nabla_\theta F(\theta^t, \hat{\mathbf{y}}^{t+1}) - \sum_{k,q} \frac{1}{KQ} \nabla_\theta F_k(\theta^t_{k,q-1}, \hat{\mathbf{y}}^{t+1}_k)\|^2] \leq \frac{L^2}{KQ} \sum_{k,q} \mathbb{E}[\|\theta^t - \theta^t_{k,q}\|^2], \qquad \text{(A11)}
$$

where the inequality is due to the convexity of $\|\cdot\|^2$ and the L-smooth assumption (10). Substituting (A11) into (A10), we obtain the final result. □

Lemma A3. *Let $\eta = \eta_\theta \eta_g$, under Assumptions 2–4, it holds that*

$$
\begin{aligned}
&\mathbb{E}[\|\theta^{t+1} - \theta^t\|^2] \\
&\leq \frac{\eta^2 (K - M)}{MK(K-1)} \left(3KQ^2 \mathbb{E}[\|\nabla_\theta F(\theta^t, \hat{\mathbf{y}}^{t+1})\|^2] + 3KQ^2 \sigma_G^2 + 3QL^2 \sum_{k,q} \mathbb{E}[\|\theta^t - \theta^t_{k,q}\|^2] \right) \\
&\quad + \frac{\eta^2 (M-1)}{MK(K-1)} \mathbb{E}[\| \sum_{k,q} \nabla_\theta F_k(\theta^t_{k,q}, \hat{\mathbf{y}}^{t+1}_k)\|^2] + \frac{\eta^2 Q \sigma_\theta^2}{M}. \qquad \text{(A12)}
\end{aligned}
$$

Proof. By using Assumption 3 and equation (14), we have

$$
\begin{aligned}
\mathbb{E}[\|\theta^{t+1} - \theta^t\|^2] &= \mathbb{E}[\| \frac{\eta}{M} \sum_{k,q} \mathbb{I}_{k \in \mathcal{S}^t} g_k(\theta^t_{k,q}, \hat{\mathbf{y}}^{t+1}_k)\|^2] \\
&\leq \frac{\eta^2}{M^2} \mathbb{E}[\| \sum_{k,q} \mathbb{I}_{k \in \mathcal{S}^t} \nabla_\theta F_k(\theta^t_{k,q}, \hat{\mathbf{y}}^{t+1}_k)\|^2] + \frac{\eta^2 Q \sigma_\theta^2}{M}. \qquad \text{(A13)}
\end{aligned}
$$

Let $\mathbf{t}_k = \sum_{q=0}^{Q-1} \nabla_\theta F_k(\theta^t_{k,q}, \hat{\mathbf{y}}^{t+1}_k)$. Using this definition and expanding the squared norm, we have

$$\mathbb{E}[\|\sum_{k,q}\mathbb{I}_{k\in\mathcal{S}^t}\nabla_\theta F_k(\theta_{k,q}^t,\hat{\mathbf{y}}_k^{t+1})\|^2] = \mathbb{E}[\|\sum_{k=1}^{K}\mathbb{I}_{k\in\mathcal{S}^t}\mathbf{t}_k\|^2] = \sum_{i,j}\mathbb{E}[\mathbb{I}_{i\in\mathcal{S}^t}\mathbb{I}_{j\in\mathcal{S}^t}\langle\mathbf{t}_i,\mathbf{t}_j\rangle]. \tag{A14}$$

For the case where $i = j$, noting that $\mathbb{I}_{i\in\mathcal{S}^t}$ is an indicator function and $\mathbb{P}(i \in \mathcal{S}^t) = \frac{M}{K}$, we have

$$\mathbb{E}[\mathbb{I}_{i\in\mathcal{S}^t}\mathbb{I}_{j\in\mathcal{S}^t}\langle\mathbf{t}_i,\mathbf{t}_j\rangle] = \mathbb{E}[\mathbb{I}_{i\in\mathcal{S}^t}]\|\mathbf{t}_i\|^2 = \frac{M}{K}\mathbb{E}[\|\mathbf{t}_i\|^2].$$

For the case where $i \neq j$, considering the probability of selecting two distinct clients from K total clients, we obtain

$$\mathbb{E}[\mathbb{I}_{i\in\mathcal{S}^t}\mathbb{I}_{j\in\mathcal{S}^t}\langle\mathbf{t}_i,\mathbf{t}_j\rangle] = \frac{M(M-1)}{K(K-1)}\mathbb{E}[\langle\mathbf{t}_i,\mathbf{t}_j\rangle].$$

Then, we derive that

$$\begin{aligned}\mathbb{E}[\|\sum_{k=1}^{K}\mathbb{I}_{k\in\mathcal{S}^t}\mathbf{t}_k\|^2] &= \frac{M}{K}\sum_{i=1}^{K}\|\mathbf{t}_i\|^2 + \frac{M(M-1)}{K(K-1)}\sum_{i\neq j}\langle\mathbf{t}_i,\mathbf{t}_j\rangle \\ &= \frac{M^2}{K}\sum_{i=1}^{K}\|\mathbf{t}_i\|^2 - \frac{M(M-1)}{2K(K-1)}\sum_{i\neq j}\|\mathbf{t}_i - \mathbf{t}_j\|^2,\end{aligned} \tag{A15}$$

where the last equality is due to the fact that $\langle a,b\rangle = \frac{1}{2}[\|a\|^2 + \|b\|^2 - \|a-b\|^2]$. Similarity,

$$\mathbb{E}[\|\sum_{k=1}^{K}\mathbf{t}_k\|^2] = K\sum_{k=1}^{K}\mathbb{E}[\|\mathbf{t}_k\|^2] - \frac{1}{2}\sum_{i\neq j}\mathbb{E}[\|\mathbf{t}_i - \mathbf{t}_j\|^2]. \tag{A16}$$

Substituting (A16) into (A15) implies that

$$\mathbb{E}[\|\sum_{k=1}^{K}\mathbb{I}_{k\in\mathcal{S}^t}\mathbf{t}_k\|^2] = \frac{KM-M^2}{K(K-1)}\sum_{i=1}^{K}\|\mathbf{t}_i\|^2 + \frac{M(M-1)}{K(K-1)}\|\sum_{i=1}^{K}\mathbf{t}_i\|^2. \tag{A17}$$

By using Assumptions 2 and 4, we have

$$\begin{aligned}\sum_{k=1}^{K}\mathbb{E}[\|\mathbf{t}_k\|^2] = &\sum_{k=1}^{K}\mathbb{E}[\|\sum_{q=0}^{Q-1}[\nabla_\theta F_k(\theta_{k,q}^t,\hat{\mathbf{y}}_k^{t+1}) - \nabla_\theta F_k(\theta^t,\hat{\mathbf{y}}_k^{t+1}) + \nabla_\theta F_k(\theta^t,\hat{\mathbf{y}}_k^{t+1}) \\ &- \nabla_\theta F(\theta^t,\hat{\mathbf{y}}^{t+1}) + \nabla_\theta F(\theta^t,\hat{\mathbf{y}}^{t+1})]\|^2] \\ \le &3QL^2\sum_{k,q}\mathbb{E}[\|\theta^t - \theta_{k,q}^t\|^2] + 3KQ^2\sigma_G^2 + 3KQ^2\mathbb{E}[\|\nabla_\theta F(\theta^t,\hat{\mathbf{y}}^{t+1})\|^2].\end{aligned} \tag{A18}$$

Substituting (A17) and (A18) into (A13), we obtain the final result. □

Lemma A4. *Under Assumptions 2–4, if* $2Q\eta_g^2L^2 \le \frac{1}{Q-1}$, *we have*

$$\begin{aligned}&\sum_{k,q}\mathbb{E}[\|\theta^t - \theta_{k,q}^t\|^2] \\ &\le 4(Q-1)\Big(4KQ^2\eta_g^2\mathbb{E}[[\|\nabla_\theta F(\theta^t,\hat{\mathbf{y}}^{t+1})\|^2] + 4KQ^2\eta_g^2\sigma_G^2 + KQ\eta_g^2\sigma_\theta^2\Big).\end{aligned} \tag{A19}$$

Proof. For any worker $k \in [K]$, we have

$$\begin{aligned}\mathbb{E}[\|\theta^t - \theta^t_{k,q}\|^2] &= \mathbb{E}[\|\theta^t - \theta^t_{k,q-1} + \eta_g g_k(\theta^t_{k,q-1}, \hat{\mathbf{y}}^{t+1}_k)\|^2] \\ &\le \mathbb{E}[\|\theta^t - \theta^t_{k,q-1} + \eta_g F_k(\theta^t_{k,q-1}, \hat{\mathbf{y}}^{t+1}_k)\|^2] + \eta_g^2\sigma_\theta^2 \\ &\le (1 + \frac{1}{Q-1})\mathbb{E}[\|\theta^t - \theta^t_{k,q-1}\|^2] + Q\eta_g^2\mathbb{E}[\|\nabla_\theta F_k(\theta^t_{k,q-1}, \hat{\mathbf{y}}^{t+1}_k)\|^2] + \eta_g^2\sigma_\theta^2, \end{aligned} \tag{A20}$$

where the first inequality is due to Assumption 3 and the second inequality follows from the inequality $2\langle a, b\rangle \le \kappa\|a\|^2 + \frac{1}{\kappa}\|b\|^2$ and setting $\kappa = Q-1$. Furthermore,

$$\begin{aligned}&\mathbb{E}[\|\nabla_\theta F_k(\theta^t_{k,q-1}, \hat{\mathbf{y}}^{t+1}_k)\|^2] \\ &\le 2\mathbb{E}[\|\nabla_\theta F_k(\theta^t_{k,q-1}, \hat{\mathbf{y}}^{t+1}_k) - \nabla_\theta F_k(\theta^t, \hat{\mathbf{y}}^{t+1}_k)\|^2] + 2\mathbb{E}[\|\nabla_\theta F_k(\theta^t, \hat{\mathbf{y}}^{t+1}_k)\|^2] \\ &\le 2L^2\|\theta^t - \theta^t_{k,q-1}\|^2 + 4\mathbb{E}[\|\nabla_\theta F(\theta^t, \hat{\mathbf{y}}^{t+1})\|^2] + 4\mathbb{E}[\|\nabla_\theta F(\theta^t, \hat{\mathbf{y}}^{t+1}) - \nabla_\theta F_k(\theta^t, \hat{\mathbf{y}}^{t+1}_k)\|^2], \end{aligned} \tag{A21}$$

where the last inequality is due to Assumption 2. Substituting (A21) into (A20), with Assumption 4, we have

$$\begin{aligned}\sum_{k,q}\mathbb{E}[\|\theta^t - \theta^t_{k,q}\|^2] \le (1 + \frac{1}{Q-1} + 2Q\eta_g^2L^2)\Big[\sum_{k,q}\mathbb{E}[\|\theta^t - \theta^t_{k,q-1}\|^2] + 4KQ^2\eta_g^2[\|\nabla_\theta F(\theta^t, \hat{\mathbf{y}}^{t+1})\|^2] \\ + 4KQ^2\eta_g^2\sigma_G^2 + KQ\eta_g^2\sigma_\theta^2\Big]. \end{aligned} \tag{A22}$$

Consider $2Q\eta_g^2L^2 \le \frac{1}{Q-1}$; then, we have

$$\begin{aligned}\sum_{k,q}\mathbb{E}[\|\theta^t - \theta^t_{k,q}\|^2] \le (1 + \frac{2}{Q-1})\Big[\sum_{k,q}\mathbb{E}[\|\theta^t - \theta^t_{k,q-1}\|^2] + 4KQ^2\eta_g^2[\|\nabla_\theta F(\theta^t, \hat{\mathbf{y}}^{t+1})\|^2] \\ + 4KQ^2\eta_g^2\sigma_G^2 + KQ\eta_g^2\sigma_\theta^2\Big]. \end{aligned} \tag{A23}$$

Unrolling the recursion, we get

$$\sum_{k,q}\mathbb{E}[\|\theta^t - \theta^t_{k,q}\|^2] \le \sum_{l=0}^{q}(1 + \frac{2}{Q-1})^l\Big(4KQ^2\eta_g^2[\|\nabla_\theta F(\theta^t, \hat{\mathbf{y}}^{t+1})\|^2] + 4KQ^2\eta_g^2\sigma_G^2 + KQ\eta_g^2\sigma_\theta^2\Big). \tag{A24}$$

Since $\sum_{l=0}^{q}(1 + \frac{2}{Q-1})^l \le \frac{Q-1}{2}(1 + \frac{2}{Q-1})^{Q-1} \le 4(Q-1)$ and $1 + x \le \exp(x)$, we have the final result. □

Appendix A.2. The Proof of Theorem 1

Using Lemmas A1–A3, we have

$$\begin{aligned}&\mathbb{E}[F(\theta^{t+1}, \hat{\mathbf{y}}^{t+1})] - \mathbb{E}[F(\theta^t, \hat{\mathbf{y}}^t)] \\ &\le -\frac{\eta Q}{2}\mathbb{E}[\|\nabla_\theta F(\theta^t, \hat{\mathbf{y}}^{t+1})\|^2] + \frac{\eta L^2}{2K}\sum_{k,q}\mathbb{E}[\|\theta^t - \theta^t_{k,q}\|^2] - \frac{\eta}{2K^2Q}\mathbb{E}[\|\sum_{k,q}\nabla_\theta F_k(\theta^t_{k,q}, \hat{\mathbf{y}}^{t+1}_k)\|^2] \\ &\quad + \frac{L\eta^2(K-M)}{2MK(K-1)}\left(3KQ^2\mathbb{E}[\|\nabla_\theta F(\theta^t, \hat{\mathbf{y}}^{t+1})\|^2] + 3KQ^2\sigma_G^2 + 3QL^2\sum_{k,q}\mathbb{E}[\|\theta^t - \theta^t_{k,q}\|^2]\right) \\ &\quad + \frac{\eta^2(M-1)L}{2MK(K-1)}\mathbb{E}[\|\sum_{k,q}\nabla_\theta F_k(\theta^t_{k,q}, \hat{\mathbf{y}}^{t+1}_k)\|^2] + \frac{L\eta^2Q\sigma_\theta^2}{2M} - \frac{\mu\alpha_1}{2K}\sum_{k=1}^{K}\mathbb{E}[\|\hat{\mathbf{y}}^t_k - \hat{\mathbf{y}}^{t+1}_k\|^2]. \end{aligned}$$

When $\eta LK \le \frac{M(K-1)}{K(M-1)}$, we know $\frac{\eta}{2K^2Q} - \frac{\eta^2L(M-1)}{2MK(K-1)} \ge 0$. It leads to

$$\mathbb{E}[F(\theta^{t+1},\hat{\mathbf{y}}^{t+1})]-\mathbb{E}[F(\theta^{t},\hat{\mathbf{y}}^{t})]\leq-\left(\frac{\eta Q}{2}-\frac{L\eta^2(K-M)3Q^2}{2M(K-1)}\right)\mathbb{E}[\|\nabla_\theta F(\theta^t,\hat{\mathbf{y}}^{t+1})\|^2]$$
$$+\left(\frac{\eta L^2}{2K}+\frac{3QL^3\eta^2(K-M)}{2MK(K-1)}\right)\sum_{k,q}\mathbb{E}[\|\theta^t-\theta^t_{k,q}\|^2]$$
$$+\frac{3LQ^2\sigma_G^2\eta^2(K-M)}{2M(K-1)}+\frac{L\eta^2Q\sigma_\theta^2}{2M}-\frac{\mu\alpha_1}{2K}\sum_{k=1}^{K}\mathbb{E}[\|\hat{\mathbf{y}}_k^t-\hat{\mathbf{y}}_k^{t+1}\|^2].$$

Substituting Lemma A4 into the above inequality, we have

$$\mathbb{E}[F(\theta^{t+1},\hat{\mathbf{y}}^{t+1})]-\mathbb{E}[F(\theta^{t},\hat{\mathbf{y}}^{t})]$$
$$\leq-\eta Q\left(\frac{1}{2}-8L^2(Q-1)Q\eta_g^2-\frac{\eta L(K-M)Q}{2M(K-1)}(3Q+48L^2(Q-1)Q^2\eta_g^2)\right)\mathbb{E}[\|\nabla_\theta F(\theta^t,\hat{\mathbf{y}}^{t+1})\|^2]$$
$$+\left(\eta L^2(Q^2(Q-1))\eta_g^2+\frac{24Q^4L^3\eta^2\eta_g^2(K-M)}{M(K-1)}+\frac{3LQ^2\eta^2(K-M)}{2M(K-1)}\right)\sigma_G^2$$
$$+\left(2\eta L^2(Q-1)Q\eta_g^2+\frac{6Q^2(Q-1)L^3\eta^2\eta_g^2(K-M)}{M(K-1)}+\frac{L\eta^2Q}{2M}\right)\sigma_\theta^2$$
$$-\frac{\mu\alpha_1}{2K}\sum_{k=1}^{K}\mathbb{E}[\|\hat{\mathbf{y}}_k^t-\hat{\mathbf{y}}_k^{t+1}\|^2].$$

When $\eta_g^2\leq\frac{1}{64Q(Q-1)L^2}$ and $\eta\leq\frac{M(K-1)}{(3+12Q)QL(K-M)}$, we have

$$8L^2(Q-1)Q\eta_g^2+\frac{\eta L(K-M)Q}{2M(K-1)}(3Q+48L^2(Q-1)Q^2\eta_g^2)\leq\frac{1}{4}.$$

Let $\frac{\eta Q}{4}\leq\frac{\mu\alpha_1}{2K}$; we know

$$\frac{\eta Q}{4}g_t\leq\mathbb{E}[F(\theta^{t},\hat{\mathbf{y}}^{t})]-\mathbb{E}[F(\theta^{t+1},\hat{\mathbf{y}}^{t+1})]+\eta\eta_g^2(L^2(Q^2(Q-1))\sigma_G^2+2L^2(Q-1)Q\sigma_\theta^2)$$
$$+\eta^2\eta_g^2\left(\frac{24Q^4L^3(K-M)}{M(K-1)}\sigma_G^2+\frac{6Q^2(Q-1)L^3(K-M)}{M(K-1)}\sigma_\theta^2\right)$$
$$+\eta^2\left(\frac{3LQ^2(K-M)}{2M(K-1)}\sigma_G^2+\frac{LQ}{2M}\sigma_\theta^2\right).\tag{A25}$$

Summing the above inequality above from 1 to T, we obtain

$$\frac{1}{T}\sum_{t=0}^{T-1}g_t\leq\frac{4(\mathbb{E}[F(\theta^0,\hat{\mathbf{y}}^0)]-\mathbb{E}[F(\theta^T,\hat{\mathbf{y}}^T)])}{\eta QT}+\eta_g^2B_1+4\eta\eta_g^2B_2+4\eta B_3.$$

Since 0 is the lower bound for cross-entropy loss $F(\theta,\hat{\mathbf{y}})$, we obtain the final result.

References

1. McMahan, H.B.; Moore, E.; Ramage, D.; Hampson, S.; y Arcas, B.A. Communication-Efficient Learning of Deep Networks from Decentralized Data. In Proceedings of the 20th International Conference on Artificial Intelligence and Statistics, Fort Lauderdale, FL, USA, 20–22 April 2017; pp. 1273–1282.
2. Yang, Q.; Liu, Y.; Chen, T.; Tong, Y. Federated machine learning: Concept and applications. *ACM Trans. Intell. Syst. Technol.* **2019**, *10*, 1–19. [CrossRef]
3. Zeng, Y.; Wang, Z.; Bai, J.; Shen, X. An accelerated stochastic ADMM for nonconvex and nonsmooth finite-sum optimization. *Automatica* **2024**, *163*, 111554. [CrossRef]

4. Wang, Z.; Zhang, J.; Chang, T.H.; Li, J.; Luo, Z.Q. Distributed stochastic consensus optimization with momentum for nonconvex nonsmooth problems. *IEEE Trans. Signal Process.* **2021**, *69*, 4486–4501. [CrossRef]
5. Stich, S.U. Local SGD converges fast and communicates little. *arXiv* **2018**, arXiv:1805.09767.
6. Yin, Q.; Feng, Z.; Li, X.; Chen, S.; Wu, H.; Han, G. Tackling data-heterogeneity variations in federated learning via adaptive aggregate weights. *Knowl.-Based Syst.* **2024**, *304*, 112484. [CrossRef]
7. Yang, H.; Fang, M.; Liu, J. Achieving linear speedup with partial worker participation in non-iid federated learning. In Proceedings of the International Conference on Learning Representations, Virtual Event, 3–7 May 2021.
8. Li, T.; Sahu, A.K.; Zaheer, M.; Sanjabi, M.; Talwalkar, A.; Smith, V. Federated optimization in heterogeneous networks. In Proceedings of the Conference on Machine Learning and Systems, Austin, TX, USA, 2–4 March 2020.
9. Karimireddy, S.P.; Kale, S.; Mohri, M.; Reddi, S.; Stich, S.; Suresh, A.T. SCAFFOLD: Stochastic controlled averaging for federated learning. In Proceedings of the International Conference on Machine Learning, Virtual Event, 2020; pp. 5132–5143.
10. Wang, J.; Liu, Q.; Liang, H.; Joshi, G.; Poor, H.V. Tackling the objective inconsistency problem in heterogeneous federated optimization. *arXiv* **2020**, arXiv:2007.07481. [CrossRef]
11. Wang, S.; Ji, M. A unified analysis of federated learning with arbitrary client participation. *Adv. Neural Inf. Process. Syst.* **2022**, *35*, 19124–19137.
12. Ribero, M.; Vikalo, H. Reducing communication in federated learning via efficient client sampling. *Pattern Recognit.* **2024**, *148*, 110122. [CrossRef]
13. Cohen, I.; Cozman, F.G.; Sebe, N.; Cirelo, M.C.; Huang, T.S. Semisupervised learning of classifiers: Theory, algorithms, and their application to human-computer interaction. *IEEE Trans. Pattern Anal. Mach. Intell.* **2004**, *26*, 1553–1566. [CrossRef]
14. Zhu, X.J. *Semi-Supervised Learning Literature Survey*; Technical report; Department of Computer Sciences, University of Wisconsin-Madison: Madison, WI, USA, 2005.
15. Chapelle, O.; Scholkopf, B.; Zien, A. Semi-supervised learning. *IEEE Trans. Neural Netw.* **2009**, *20*, 542. [CrossRef]
16. Lee, D.H. Pseudo-label: The simple and efficient semi-supervised learning method for deep neural networks. In Proceedings of the Workshop on Challenges in Representation Learning, ICML, Atlanta, GA, USA, 21 June 2013.
17. Rasmus, A.; Berglund, M.; Honkala, M.; Valpola, H.; Raiko, T. Semi-supervised learning with ladder networks. *Adv. Neural Inf. Process. Syst.* **2015**, *28*, 3546–3554.
18. Laine, S.; Aila, T. Temporal ensembling for semi-supervised learning. *arXiv* **2016**, arXiv:1610.02242.
19. Tarvainen, A.; Valpola, H. Mean teachers are better role models: Weight-averaged consistency targets improve semi-supervised deep learning results. *Adv. Neural Inf. Process. Syst.* **2017**, *30*, 1195–1204.
20. Miyato, T.; Maeda, S.i.; Koyama, M.; Ishii, S. Virtual adversarial training: A regularization method for supervised and semi-supervised learning. *IEEE Trans. Pattern Anal. Mach. Intell.* **2018**, *41*, 1979–1993. [CrossRef] [PubMed]
21. Li, Y.; Wu, B.; Feng, Y.; Fan, Y.; Jiang, Y.; Li, Z.; Xia, S.T. Semi-supervised robust training with generalized perturbed neighborhood. *Pattern Recognit.* **2022**, *124*, 108472. [CrossRef]
22. Berthelot, D.; Carlini, N.; Goodfellow, I.; Papernot, N.; Oliver, A.; Raffel, C. Mixmatch: A holistic approach to semi-supervised learning. *arXiv* **2019**, arXiv:1905.02249.
23. Du, G.; Zhang, J.; Zhang, N.; Wu, H.; Wu, P.; Li, S. Semi-supervised imbalanced multi-label classification with label propagation. *Pattern Recognit.* **2024**, *150*, 110358. [CrossRef]
24. Wang, J.; Ruan, D.; Li, Y.; Wang, Z.; Wu, Y.; Tan, T.; Yang, G.; Jiang, M. Data augmentation strategies for semi-supervised medical image segmentation. *Pattern Recognit.* **2025**, *159*, 111116. [CrossRef]
25. Diao, E.; Ding, J.; Tarokh, V. Semifl: Semi-supervised federated learning for unlabeled clients with alternate training. *Adv. Neural Inf. Process. Syst.* **2022**, *35*, 17871–17884.
26. Albaseer, A.; Ciftler, B.S.; Abdallah, M.; Al-Fuqaha, A. Exploiting Unlabeled Data in Smart Cities using Federated Learning. *arXiv* **2020**, arXiv:2001.04030. [CrossRef]
27. Jeong, W.; Yoon, J.; Yang, E.S.; Hwang, J. Federated Semi-Supervised Learning with Inter-Client Consistency & Disjoint Learning. In Proceedings of the International Conference on Learning Representations, Virtual Event, 3–7 May 2021.
28. Wang, S.; Xu, Y.; Yuan, Y.; Quek, T.Q. Toward Fast Personalized Semi-Supervised Federated Learning in Edge Networks: Algorithm Design and Theoretical Guarantee. *IEEE Trans. Wirel. Commun.* **2023**, *23*, 1170–1183. [CrossRef]
29. Liang, X.; Lin, Y.; Fu, H.; Zhu, L.; Li, X. Rscfed: Random sampling consensus federated semi-supervised learning. In Proceedings of the IEEE/CVF Conference on Computer Vision and Pattern Recognition, New Orleans, LA, USA, 19–24 June 2022; pp. 10154–10163.
30. Zhu, S.; Ma, X.; Sun, G. Two-stage sampling with predicted distribution changes in federated semi-supervised learning. *Knowl.-Based Syst.* **2024**, *295*, 111822. [CrossRef]
31. Cong, Y.; Zeng, Y.; Qiu, J.; Fang, Z.; Zhang, L.; Cheng, D.; Liu, J.; Tian, Z. FedGA: A greedy approach to enhance federated learning with Non-IID data. *Knowl.-Based Syst.* **2024**, *301*, 112201. [CrossRef]

32. Wang, S.; Ji, M. A Lightweight Method for Tackling Unknown Participation Statistics in Federated Averaging. In Proceedings of the International Conference on Learning Representations, Vienna, Austria, 7–11 May 2024.
33. Jhunjhunwala, D.; Sharma, P.; Nagarkatti, A.; Joshi, G. Fedvarp: Tackling the variance due to partial client participation in federated learning. In Proceedings of the Uncertainty in Artificial Intelligence, PMLR, Eindhoven, The Netherlands, 1–5 August 2022; pp. 906–916.
34. Niederreiter, H. *Random Number Generation and Quasi-Monte Carlo Methods*; Society for Industrial and Applied Mathematics: Philadelphia, PA, USA, 1992.
35. Fang, K.T.; Wang, Y. *Number-Theoretic Methods in Statistics*; Chapman and Hall: London, UK, 1994.
36. Zhang, M.; Zhou, Y.; Zhou, Z.; Zhang, A. Model-free subsampling method based on uniform designs. *IEEE Trans. Knowl. Data Eng.* **2024**, *36*, 1210–1220. [CrossRef]
37. Zhou, Z.; Yang, Z.; Zhang, A.; Zhou, Y. Efficient model-free subsampling method for massive data. *Technometrics* **2024**, *66*, 240–252. [CrossRef]
38. Wang, Z.; Wang, X.; Sun, R.; Chang, T.H. Federated semi-supervised learning with class distribution mismatch. *arXiv* **2021**, arXiv:2111.00010. [CrossRef]
39. Fang, K.T.; Li, R.; Sudjianto, A. *Design and Modeling for Computer Experiments*; Chapman and Hall/CRC: Boca Raton, FL, USA, 2006.
40. Fang, K.; Liu, M.Q.; Qin, H.; Zhou, Y.D. *Theory and Application of Uniform Experimental Designs*; Springer: Singapore, 2018.
41. Zhang, A.; Li, H.; Quan, S.; Yang, Z. UniDOE: Uniform Design of Experiments. R Package Version 1.0.2. 2018. Available online: https://cran.r-project.org/src/contrib/Archive/UniDOE/ (accessed on 24 July 2025).
42. Shalev-Shwartz, S.; Singer, Y. *Logarithmic Regret Algorithms for Strongly Convex Repeated Games*; The Hebrew University: Jerusalem, Israel, 2007.
43. Chen, L.; Zhao, D.; Tao, L.; Wang, K.; Qiao, S.; Zeng, X.; Tan, C.W. A credible and fair federated learning framework based on blockchain. *IEEE Trans. Artif. Intell.* **2024**, *6*, 301–316. [CrossRef]

entropy MDPI

Review

A Review: Construction of Statistical Distributions

Kai-Tai Fang [1,2], Yu-Xuan Lin [1,3] and Yu-Hui Deng [1,3,*]

1 Guangdong Provincial Key Laboratory of Interdisciplinary Research and Application for Data Science (IRADS), Beijing Normal-Hong Kong Baptist University, 2000 Jintong Road, Tangjiawan, Zhuhai 519087, China; ktfang@bnbu.edu.cn (K.-T.F.); yuxuanlin@bnbu.edu.cn (Y.-X.L.)
2 The Key Lab of Random Complex Structures and Data Analysis, The Chinese Academy of Sciences, Beijing 100045, China
3 Faculty of Science and Technology, Beijing Normal-Hong Kong Baptist University, 2000 Jintong Road, Tangjiawan, Zhuhai 519087, China
* Correspondence: ivandeng@bnbu.edu.cn; Tel.: +86-0756-362-0618

Abstract

Statistical modeling is fundamentally based on probability distributions, which can be discrete or continuous and univariate or multivariate. This review focuses on the methods used to construct these distributions, covering both traditional and newly developed approaches. We first examine classic distributions such as the normal, exponential, gamma, and beta for univariate data, and the multivariate normal, elliptical, and Dirichlet for multidimensional data. We then address how, in recent decades, the demand for more flexible modeling tools has led to the creation of complex meta-distributions built using copula theory.

Keywords: construction of statistical distribution; distribution family; entropy; function of random variables; mean square error; quasi-Monte Carlo; representative points; statistical distribution

1. Introduction

Statistical distributions form the foundation of probability theory, statistical inference, and predictive modeling. They provide a mathematical framework for describing the randomness, variability, and uncertainty inherent in data. Different types of data—univariate or multivariate, discrete or continuous—require different distributions, including mixture models for complex patterns.

Numerous books have offered comprehensive introductions to useful distributions. The seminal four-volume work by Johnson et al. [1–4] provides an exceptionally detailed encyclopedia of distributions and their interrelations, though its sheer scope can make it challenging for readers to locate specific information efficiently. Other key texts include Fang and Xu's book [5] (in Chinese, which limits its accessibility), Fang et al. [6] focusing treatment on multivariate symmetric distributions, Johnson [7] reviewing statistical simulation for multivariate distributions, and the new work by Fang et al. [8] offering a comprehensive study on representative points of distributions and their applications.

The purpose of this review is to synthesize various methods for constructing statistical distributions. By presenting a unified overview of both traditional and modern techniques, we aim to equip readers with the knowledge to understand existing distributions and develop new ones to meet evolving data modeling needs.

This paper is structured as follows. Section 2 introduces construction methods for univariate distributions, encompassing both traditional and newer models. Section 3 briefly reviews methods for constructing discrete distributions, including both univariate and multivariate frameworks. Section 4.4 then details construction techniques for multivariate statistical distributions, specifically the families of elliptical distributions and meta-distributions created via copula methods. The paper concludes with final remarks in Section 5.

2. Construction of Univariate Statistical Distributions

This section introduces several approaches for constructing univariate continuous distributions:

(1) Distribution families, including location-scale families, the Pearson system, and exponential families;
(2) Functions of random variables via stochastic representations;
(3) Parameter expansion generalizes existing families by adding parameters. For example, normal→ skew normal; exponential → Weibull.
(4) Generalized families via transformation of the cdf. A powerful and prolific approach for generating new families of distributions is through the functional transformation of an existing baseline cdf, $F(x)$. These transformations introduce new parameters, thereby creating more flexible distributions capable of modeling complex data behaviors.
(5) Combination methods, such as mixture distributions, compound distributions, convolutions, and copula-based techniques.

2.1. Distribution Families

A distribution family is defined by a specific structural property. Among many such families, the following three are particularly well established in the literature.

2.1.1. Location-Scale Distribution Family

A distribution $F(x;\mu,\sigma)$ belongs to the location-scale family if its probability density function (pdf) can be expressed as

$$f(x) = \frac{1}{\sigma} f_0\left(\frac{x-\mu}{\sigma}\right), \quad (1)$$

where μ is the location parameter, $\sigma > 0$ is the scale parameter, and f_0 is the standard density of the distribution $Z \sim F(x;0,1)$. This implies that for any $X \sim F(x;\mu,\sigma)$, the standardized variable $Z = \frac{(X-\mu)}{\sigma}$ follows the standard distribution $F(x;0,1)$.

A key property of this family is its invariance under affine transformations, implying that if $X \sim F(x;\mu,\sigma)$, then $a + bX \sim F(x;a+b\mu,|b|\sigma)$. The normal distribution is a classic example of the location-scale distribution. Other prominent examples include the Cauchy and logistic distributions.

- Cauchy distribution: Its pdf is given by

$$f(x;\theta,\lambda) = \frac{1}{\pi\lambda\left[1+\left(\frac{x-\theta}{\lambda}\right)^2\right]},$$

where θ is the location parameter and λ is the scale parameter. Note that the Cauchy distribution does not have a defined mean or variance.
- Logistic distribution: Named for its relationship to the logistic (sigmoid) function, the logistic distribution resembles the normal distribution in shape but possesses heavier

tails. It finds applications in logistic regression, growth models, and economics. Its cumulative distribution function (cdf) is given by

$$F(x;\alpha,\beta)=\frac{1}{1+\exp(-(x-\alpha)/\beta)},\quad x,\,\alpha\in\mathbb{R},\quad \beta>0.$$

There are more other distributions in this category. For further reading, see [9,10].

2.1.2. Pearson Distribution Family

The Pearson family is a system of continuous probability distributions, introduced by Karl Pearson [11], designed to model a wide range of empirical data characterized by properties such as skewness and kurtosis that deviate from the normal distribution. The system is defined by the Pearson differential equation:

$$\frac{df(x)}{dx}=f(x)\frac{x-\lambda}{ax^2+bx+c}, \tag{2}$$

where $f(x)$ is a probability density function and the parameters a,b,c,λ determine the specific distribution type.

Roots of the denominator (ax^2+bx+c) classify distributions into eight or more types listed in Table 1, where type 0 is the normal distribution; type I distribution is the beta distribution; type II distribution curve is a symmetrical U-shaped curve; type III distribution curve is the gamma distribution; type IV distribution curve is skewed heavy-tailed; type V is the shift inverse gamma distribution; type VI is an inverse beta distribution; type VII is the t-distribution. Some references consider more types, like types VIII and IX, which are special cases of the power function distribution, and type X, which is the exponential distribution. More details can be found in Chapter 12 of [1,12].

Table 1. Classification of Pearson distributions.

Type	Condition	Distribution	PDF Example
0	$a=0,b=0$	Normal distribution	$f(x)\propto e^{-(x-\mu)^2/2\sigma^2}$
I	$b^2-4ac>0$	Beta distribution	$f(x)\propto(1+x)^{r_1}(1-x)^{r_2},\lvert x\rvert\leq 1$
II	$b^2-4ac=0,$ $\lambda=-b/2a$	Symmetric beta	$f(x)\propto(1-x^2)^r,\lvert x\rvert\leq 1$
III	$a=0$	Gamma distribution	$f(x)\propto x^{k-1}e^{-x/\theta}.x>0$
IV	$b^2-4ac<0$	Skewed heavy-tailed	Complex form
V	$c=0$	Inverse gamma	$f(x)\propto x^{k-1}e^{-\theta/x},x>0$
VI	$b^2-4ac>0,\lambda\neq$ root	Beta prime, F-distribution	$f(x)\propto x^{r_1}(1+x)^{-(r_1+r_2)}$
VII	$b=0$	Student's t-distribution	$f(x)\propto(1+x^2/\nu)^{-(\nu+1)/2}$

2.1.3. The Exponential Distribution Family

Consider it as a "family" in the biological sense, implying that though its members, such as the normal, exponential, gamma, beta, and Poisson distributions, may appear distinct characteristics, they share a common underlying mathematical structure. This shared "DNA" makes them exceptionally powerful and convenient to use in statistical modeling and machine learning.

Formally, the exponential family comprises distributions whose probability density (or mass) functions can be expressed in the following canonical form:

$$f(x;\boldsymbol{\theta}) = h(x)\exp\left\{\boldsymbol{\theta}^{\top}\mathbf{T}(x) - B(\boldsymbol{\theta})\right\}, \tag{3}$$

where $h(x)$ is a function as base measure that depends only on the data X, not the parameters $\boldsymbol{\theta} = (\theta_1, \ldots, \theta_k)^{\top}$. $\mathbf{T}(x) = (T_1(x), \ldots, T_k(x))^{\top}$ is a sufficient statistic, and $B(\boldsymbol{\theta})$ is a log-partition function and a normalization constant that ensures that the function integrates/sums to 1. $B(\boldsymbol{\theta})$ also generates the moments (mean, variance) of the distribution.

This common structure leads to several powerful properties:

(1) All members have a low-dimensional sufficient statistic $\mathbf{T}(x)$.

(2) In Bayesian statistics, the exponential family always has a natural conjugate prior. This makes Bayesian updating mathematically neat and computationally tractable.

(3) Distributions in the exponential family are the maximum entropy distributions given constraints on the expected values of the sufficient statistics. For example, the normal distribution has the maximum entropy for a given mean and variance.

Further details can be found in references such as [1,9]. Many additional families of univariate distributions have also been cataloged in [1].

2.2. Distributions Produced by a Function of Random Variables

When the distribution of a random variable X or a random vector $\mathbf{X} = (X_1, \ldots, X_k)$ is known, applying a continuous function $Y = g(X)$ or $Y = h(\mathbf{X})$ in order to yield a new distribution is a prevalent distribution construction approach. In this context, the original distribution is termed the initial distribution, while the resulting distribution is called the target distribution. The inverse transformation method [13] is a widely used technique for statistical simulation, based on the following theorem.

Theorem 1. *Let X have a continuous cdf $F(x)$ and a uniform random variable $U \sim U(0,1)$. Then we have*

(a) $F^{-1}(U) \sim F(\cdot)$;

(b) $F(X) \sim U(0,1)$.

Following Theorem 1, we can leverage this connection between any continuous distribution and the uniform distribution to derive the distribution of a transformed random variable $Y = g(X)$. The key insight is to use the probability integral transform from part (b) of the theorem. We know that $F_X(X) \sim U(0,1)$. Therefore, the cdf of the transformation $Y = g(X)$ can be found by relating the event $\{Y \leq y\}$ back to this uniform distribution. Specifically, the cdf of Y is

$$F_Y(y) = P(Y \leq y) = P(g(X) \leq y).$$

The solution to this probability depends on the nature of the function g. For monotonic and differentiable transformations, this approach leads directly to the well-known change of variables formula for the pdf of Y:

$$f_Y(y) = f_X(x)\left|\frac{dx}{dy}\right| = f_X(g^{-1}(y))\left|\frac{d}{dy}g^{-1}(y)\right|,$$

where $x = g^{-1}(y)$ is the inverse function. This formula can be derived by differentiating the cdf $F_Y(y)$, which itself is computed using the distribution of X that Theorem 1 helps us to understand and manipulate through the uniform distribution.

A systematic study and generalization of the inverse transformation method can be found in Li et al. [14]. Numerous distributions have been constructed using this approach. The following are some functions commonly employed in the literature for this purpose.

2.2.1. Transformation of Random Variables

Some transformation examples are presented later.

- Linear transformation $Y = a + bX$, for example, used in the location-scale distributions;
- Power transformation $Y = X^r$, for example, from the normal to the χ^2 distribution by $Y = X^2$;
- Exponential transformation $Y = e^X$, for example, from the normal to the lognormal distribution by $Y = e^X$;
- Inverse transformation $Y = 1/X$, for example, the inverse gamma distribution.
- Transformation $Y = g(X_1, \ldots, X_m)$, for example, the F-distribution and beta distribution are produced by functions of two χ^2 distribution variables.

2.2.2. Order Statistics

These include fundamental objects in statistics, for example, the sample minimum, maximum, and median. They deal with the properties and applications of sorted random samples. Let $X_1, \ldots, X_n$ be a random sample from a population with cdf F and pdf f. The order statistics, denoted by $X_{(1)} \leq X_{(2)} \leq \cdots \leq X_{(n)}$, represent the sorted values of the sample. The cdf of the kth order statistic, $X_{(k)}$, is given by

$$P(X_{(k)} \leq x) = \sum_{j=k}^{n} \binom{n}{j} [F(x)]^j [1 - F(x)]^{n-j}. \tag{4}$$

The density functions for specific order statistics are provided in Table 2. Order statistics have wide-ranging applications, including robust statistics, sample range and interquartile range, quantiles and Q–Q plots, reliability engineering, and non-parametric statistical tests (e.g., the Wilcoxon rank-sum test). A comprehensive introduction to order statistics can be found in [15].

Table 2. Distributions of the order statistics.

Distribution	Density $f(x)$
The general k-th order statistic [1]	$\binom{n}{k-1}[F(x)]^{k-1}[1 - F(x)]^{n-k} f(x)$
Minimum ($X_{(1)}$)	$n[1 - F(x)]^{n-1} f(x)$
Maximum ($X_{(n)}$)	$n[F(x)]^{n-1} f(x)$

[1] Note: The pdf for the median exists in a closed form only when n is odd ($n = 2m + 1$), given by $p_{\text{median}}(x) = \frac{n!}{(m!)^2}[F(x)]^m[1 - F(x)]^m f(x)$. For even n, the median is defined as $\frac{1}{2}(X_{(n/2)} + X_{(n/2+1)})$ and its distribution is derived from the joint distribution of these two order statistics.

2.2.3. Extreme Value Theory (EVT)

EVT is a statistical framework for assessing the probabilities of extreme events. The fundamental result in EVT is the extreme value theorem, stating that the distribution of properly normalized maxima (or minima) converges to one of three types of distributions, regardless of the underlying distribution of the original data. These three types are collectively known as the generalized extreme value (GEV) distribution. The cdf for the GEV is given by

$$F(x) = \exp\left\{ -[1 + \xi(\frac{x - \mu}{\sigma})]^{-1/\xi} \right\}, \text{if } 1 + \xi\frac{x - \mu}{\sigma} > 0, \tag{5}$$

where parameters are μ for location, $\sigma > 0$ for scale, and ξ for shape. The three special cases of the GEV distribution are

- Type I (Gumbel distribution) $Gu(\mu, \sigma)$ light-tailed, with $\xi = 0$. Its pdf is

$$\frac{1}{\sigma}\exp\left\{-\frac{x-\mu}{\sigma} - \exp\left\{-\frac{x-\mu}{\sigma}\right\}\right\}, \sigma > 0.$$

- Type II (Fréchet distribution) heavy-tailed, with $\xi > 0$.
- Type III (Weibull distribution) short-tailed and bounded with $\xi < 0$.

The extreme value distribution has been used in finance, environmental science, engineering, and reliability testing. For a rigorous treatment of the GEV distribution and extreme value theory, see [16].

2.3. Generalized Families Via Transformation of the cdf

Given a baseline cdf $F(x)$, the exponentiated (or power-transformed) family is defined by

$$G(x) = [F(x)]^{\alpha}, \quad \alpha > 0.$$

This construction, detailed in [17], generates a vast range of new distributions. If $X_1, X_2, \ldots, X_n$ is a random sample from $F(x)$, then $G(x)$ is the cdf of the sample maximum, $\max(X_1, \ldots, X_n)$, when $\alpha = n$ is an integer. Notable members include the exponentiated Weibull and exponentiated exponential distributions.

A dual transformation yields the following complementary exponentiated family:

$$G(x) = 1 - [1 - F(x)]^{\beta}, \quad \beta > 0.$$

This is the cdf of the sample minimum, $\min(X_1, \ldots, X_n)$, when $\beta = n$. It is also known as the proportional odds model in survival analysis. Together, the exponentiated and complementary exponentiated families form the foundation of the broader class of maximum–minimum stable distributions.

Further generalizations have been proposed to introduce additional flexibility and skewness. The Alpha Power Family (or T-X family), defined by

$$G(x) = \frac{\alpha^{F(x)} - 1}{\alpha - 1}, \quad \alpha > 0, \alpha \neq 1,$$

effectively introduces skewness to the baseline distribution [18]. A highly flexible generalization is the Kumaraswamy-G family [19], given by

$$G(x) = 1 - [1 - F(x)^{a}]^{b}, \quad a > 0, b > 0.$$

This family, which contains the exponentiated family as a special case ($b = 1$), enjoys the advantage of having a quantile function in a simple closed form.

These methods, along with other systematic frameworks like the T-X family [20], demonstrate that simple transformations of a baseline cdf can serve as an engine for generating numerous new and useful distributions, greatly expanding the toolbox for statistical modeling.

2.4. Combination Methods

There are several approaches to constructing a distribution through combining the existing distributions.

2.4.1. Types of Mixtures

- Finite mixture $f(x) = \sum_{i=1}^{k} w_i f_i(x)$, which has various applications in statistical inference with flexibility in density fitting [21], for example, a mixture of two normals [22] or two Weibull distributions [23].
- Continuous mixture $f(x) = \int f(x;\theta)g(\theta)d\theta$. One example is the scale mixture. A primary method to create such continuous mixtures is through compounding, which we detail in the next section.

The mixing distribution $g(\theta)$ in an infinite mixture is not required to be continuous. When $g(\theta)$ is a discrete distribution, the resulting mixture, often called a countable mixture or discrete mixture, integrates over a countable set of parameters. This approach is technically distinct from the continuous mixture defined above but remains a powerful tool for deriving flexible distributions. Prominent examples of distributions derived from a discrete mixing mechanism include the following:

- The negative binomial distribution, which can be derived as a Poisson-gamma mixture where the Poisson rate parameter is governed by a gamma distribution. While the gamma is continuous, a discrete analogue exists (e.g., a Poisson mixture with a discrete log-gamma distribution would yield a similar over-dispersed count distribution).
- The Student's t-distribution, which is a scale mixture of normal distributions where the precision (inverse variance) parameter follows a gamma distribution.
- The beta-binomial distribution, which arises when the success probability p of a binomial distribution follows a beta distribution.
- The compound Poisson distribution and related models, where the intensity or other parameters are driven by a latent discrete process.

2.4.2. Compounding

It is a fundamental concept in probability theory that a parameter of one distribution is itself a random variable following another distribution (see [1]). This approach generates a more flexible distribution that incorporates uncertainty in the parameter. It is important to note that the marginal distribution resulting from compounding is mathematically equivalent to a continuous mixture distribution, as defined in Section 2.4.1. The compounding framework provides a hierarchical data-generation perspective for the same model. Formally, if $X|\theta \sim F_1(\theta)$ and $\theta \sim F_2(\lambda)$, then the distribution of X is the marginal distribution of a compound distribution. Examples are the beta–binomial, gamma-Poisson (negative binomial), normal–normal, Dirichlet–multinomial, compound Poisson process models. The normal–normal model is as follows:

- First stage (conditional distribution): $X|\mu \sim \mathcal{N}(\mu, \sigma^2)$. The observation X is normally distributed with mean μ and a known variance σ^2;
- Second stage (parameter distribution): $\mu \sim \mathcal{N}(\mu_0, \tau^2)$. The mean μ itself is assumed to be normally distributed with prior mean μ_0 and variance τ^2;
- Compound distribution: The unconditional distribution of $X \sim \mathcal{N}(\mu_0, \sigma^2 + \tau^2)$.

2.4.3. Convolution

The random variable $Z = X + Y$ is termed the convolution of X and Y, and it has a density function given by

$$f_{X+Y}(z) = \int_{-\infty}^{+\infty} f_{X,Y}(x, z-x)dx,$$

where $f_{X,Y}(\cdot,\cdot)$ is the joint density of (X, Y). If X and Y are independent, this simplifies to $f_{X+Y}(z) = (f_X * f_Y)(z) = \int_{-\infty}^{+\infty} f_X(x)f_Y(z-x)dx$.

A distribution of significant practical importance arises when X follows a normal distribution $N(\mu, \sigma^2)$ and Y follows an exponential distribution $\text{Exp}(\lambda)$, with X and Y being independent. This specific convolution forms the cornerstone of the normal–exponential stochastic frontier model [24], widely used in econometrics to measure the efficiency of firms and other decision-making units. In this context, the normal random variable represents the random noise (e.g., measurement error, luck), while the exponential random variable captures one-sided inefficiency.

Then the density function of $Z = X + Y$ is given by

$$f_Z(z; \mu, \sigma, \lambda) = \frac{\lambda}{2} e^{\frac{\lambda}{2}(2\mu + \lambda\sigma^2 - 2z)} \cdot \text{erfc}\left(\frac{\mu + \lambda\sigma^2 - z}{\sqrt{2}\sigma} \right),$$

where $\text{erfc}(z)$ represents the complementary error function defined as

$$\text{erfc}(z) = \frac{2}{\sqrt{\pi}} \int_z^\infty e^{-t^2} dt.$$

2.5. Some Key Univariate Distributions and Related Distributions

The first continuous statistical distribution to be formally studied was the uniform distribution, dating back to Huygens [25]. However, the most historically significant early continuous distribution is the normal distribution, also referred to as the Gaussian distribution. Although the uniform distribution provided the simplest continuous model, it was the normal distribution that first underwent extensive analytical study. The development of the normal distribution emerged later through the work of de Moivre [26] and Gauss [27] during the 18th and 19th centuries. Its fundamental role in error theory and the central limit theorem established it as the cornerstone of continuous probability theory.

2.5.1. Distributions Related to the Normal Distribution

The probability density function of a normal distribution $X \sim N(\mu, \sigma^2)$ is given by

$$f(x; \mu, \sigma) = \frac{1}{\sqrt{2\pi}\sigma} e^{-\frac{1}{2}(\frac{x-\mu}{\sigma})^2}, -\infty < x < \infty, \tag{6}$$

where parameters μ and σ^2 are the mean and variance of X, respectively. When $\mu = 0$ and $\sigma^2 = 1$, the distribution is referred to as the standard normal distribution, denoted by $Z \sim N(0, 1)$. Several distributions derived from the normal distribution are listed in Table 3 and can be constructed as follows:

(1) Lognormal distribution: $X \sim LN(\mu, \sigma^2)$ if $\ln(X) \sim N(\mu, \sigma^2)$;

(2) Skew-normal distribution: proposed by Azzalini [28] with the pdf

$$f(z; \alpha) = 2\phi(z)\Phi(\alpha z), z \in \mathbb{R}, \alpha \in \mathbb{R}, \tag{7}$$

where $\phi(z)$ is the standard normal pdf, $\Phi(\alpha z)$ is is the standard normal cdf evaluated at αz and α is a shape parameter. For more general cases, refer to Table 3. Skew-normal distribution is one of the skew-elliptical distributions, and there are more such distributions including skew-t, skew-Cauchy, skew-logistic, and skew-Laplace distributions; see [29,30]. There is more discussion about this topic in Section 4.6.

(3) Chi-square distribution: If $X_1, \ldots, X_\nu$ are independent and identically distributed (*i.i.d.*) random variables of $N(0, 1)$, then $X = X_1^2 + \ldots + X_\nu^2 \sim \chi^2(\nu)$, the χ^2-distribution with degrees of freedom ν;

(4) Chi distribution: If $X_1, \ldots, X_\nu$ are *i.i.d.* $N(0, 1)$, then $X = \sqrt{X_1^2 + \ldots + X_\nu^2} \sim \chi(\nu)$ the χ-distribution with degrees of freedom ν;

(5) Beta distribution (special case): If $Y \sim \chi^2(2m)$ and $Z \sim \chi^2(2n)$ are independent, then $X = \frac{Y}{Y+Z} \sim Be(m,n)$, referred to Table 3;
(6) Beta prime distribution: If $X \sim Be(\alpha,\beta)$, then $\frac{X}{1-X} \sim BP(\alpha,\beta)$;
(7) Arcsine distribution: It is defined as $Be(\frac{1}{2},\frac{1}{2})$;
(8) F-distribution: If $Y \sim \chi^2(m)$ and $Z \sim \chi^2(n)$ are independent, then $X = \frac{nY}{mZ} \sim F(m,n)$;
(9) t-distribution: If $Y \sim \chi^2(v)$ and $Z \sim N(0,1)$ are independent, then $T = \sqrt{v}\frac{Z}{\sqrt{Y}} \sim t_v$.

Table 3. Some continuous distributions constructed by or closely related to $N(\mu,\sigma^2)$.

Distribution	Notation	Density $f(x)$
Normal	$N(\mu,\sigma^2)$	$\frac{1}{\sqrt{2\pi}\sigma}\exp\left\{-\frac{(x-\mu)^2}{2\sigma^2}\right\}, x,\mu \in \mathbb{R}, \sigma > 0$
Lognormal	$LN(\mu,\sigma^2)$	$\frac{1}{x\sigma\sqrt{2\pi}}\exp\left(-\frac{(\ln x-\mu)^2}{2\sigma^2}\right), x > 0,\ \mu \in \mathbb{R},\ \sigma > 0$
Skew-normal	$SN(\mu,\sigma,\alpha)$	$f(x;\mu,\sigma,\alpha) = \frac{2}{\sigma}\phi\left(\frac{x-\mu}{\sigma}\right)\Phi\left(\alpha\left(\frac{x-\mu}{\sigma}\right)\right), \sigma > 0, x,\mu,\alpha \in \mathbb{R}$
$\chi^2(v)$	$\chi^2(v)$	$[2^{v/2}\Gamma(\frac{v}{2})]^{-1}x^{v/2-1}e^{-x/2}, x > 0, v > 0$
$\chi(v)$	χ_v	$[2^{v/2-1}\Gamma(\frac{v}{2})]^{-1}x^{v-1}e^{-x^2/2}, x > 0, v > 0$
Beta	$Be(a,b)$	$\frac{1}{B(a,b)}x^{a-1}(1-x)^{b-1}, 0 \le x \le 1, a,b > 0$
Beta prime	$BP(\alpha,\beta)$	$\frac{1}{\mathrm{B}(\alpha,\beta)}\frac{x^{\alpha-1}}{(1+x)^{\alpha+\beta}}, x > 0, \alpha,\beta > 0$
Arcsine	arcsine	$\frac{1}{\pi\sqrt{x(1-x)}}, 0 < x < 1$
F	$F(m,n)$	$\frac{1}{\mathrm{B}(\frac{m}{2},\frac{n}{2})}\left(\frac{m}{n}\right)^{\frac{m}{2}}x^{\frac{m}{2}-1}\left(1+\frac{m}{n}x\right)^{-\frac{m+n}{2}}, x > 0, m,n > 0$
Student-t	t_v	$\frac{\Gamma(\frac{v+1}{2})}{\sqrt{v\pi}\Gamma(\frac{v}{2})}\left(1+\frac{x^2}{v}\right)^{-\frac{v+1}{2}}, v > 0, x \in \mathbb{R}$

Note: The title "constructed by" implies a direct derivation from the normal distribution. For distributions like χ^2, χ, F, and t, this direct construction (e.g., as a sum of squares of independent standard normal variables) is most straightforward when their shape/degrees of freedom parameters (v, m, n) are positive integers. The density functions listed here represent the analytic continuations of these distributions to positive real-valued parameters, which are their standard definitions. The beta and arcsine distributions are included due to their relationship with normal random variables via the transformation of ratios or functions thereof.

2.5.2. Distributions Related to the Exponential Distribution

The exponential distribution, defined on the positive real number space, was extensively studied in the early 19th century due to its valuable properties, such as memorylessness and its connection to the Poisson process for modeling rare events (see [1]). Several distributions derived from the exponential distribution are listed in Table 4.

(1) Laplace distribution: Also known as the double exponential distribution, the Laplace distribution extends the exponential distribution symmetrically to the entire real number space, $\mathbb{R}$.
(2) Weibull distribution: The Weibull distribution is formed by introducing location δ and sharp α parameters to the density of the exponential density. It constitutes a flexible family of distributions widely used for modeling time-to-failure, lifespan, and other positive-valued measurements.
(3) Rayleigh distribution: Proposed by Rayleigh [31] for modeling wave amplitudes, the Rayleigh distribution is a special case of the Weibull distribution with $Wei(2,\beta,0)$. It also arises from the normal distribution, $N(0,\sigma^2)$, by $X = \sqrt{Y^2+Z^2} \sim Ray(\sigma)$, where Y and Z are *i.i.d.* $N(0,\sigma^2)$ and $\beta = 2\sigma^2$.

(4) Topp–Leone exponential distribution (TLED): Introduced by [32], the TLED adds a shape parameter α to the exponential distribution, yielding the cumulative distribution function $F(x) = (1 - e^{-2x/\beta})^{\alpha}$. Its density is provided in Table 4. The TLED generalizes certain distributions. For instance, TLED includes the Burr type as $TLED(2, \beta)$ and Frèchet distribution as $TLED(1/2, \beta)$.

Table 4. Some continuous distributions constructed by the exponential distribution.

Distribution	Notation	Density $p(x)$
Exponential	$Exp(\beta)$	$\frac{1}{\beta}e^{-x/\beta},\ x \geq 0, \beta > 0$
Laplace	$Laplace(\mu, \beta)$	$\frac{1}{2\beta}e^{-\frac{\lvert x-\mu\rvert}{\beta}},\ x \in \mathbb{R}, \mu \in \mathbb{R},\ \beta > 0$
Weibull	$Wei(\alpha, \beta, \delta)$	$\frac{\alpha}{\beta}\left(\frac{x-\delta}{\beta}\right)^{\alpha-1} e^{-\left(\frac{x-\delta}{\beta}\right)^{\alpha}},\ x \geq \delta,\ \delta \in \mathbb{R},\ \alpha, \beta > 0$
Rayleigh	$Ray(\beta)$ or $Ray(\sigma)$	$\frac{2x}{\beta}e^{-x^2/\beta},\ x \geq 0,\ \beta = 2\sigma^2$
TLED	$TLED(\alpha, \beta)$	$\frac{2\alpha}{\beta}e^{-2x/\beta}(1 - e^{-2x/\beta})^{\alpha-1},\ x > 0, \alpha, \beta > 0$

It is worth mentioning that the exponential distribution and the Poisson distribution share a fundamental symbiotic relationship within the context of a Poisson process. If the number of events occurring in a fixed time interval follows a Poisson distribution with rate parameter λ, then the waiting time between consecutive events follows an exponential distribution with the same rate parameter $\lambda = \frac{1}{\beta}$. Thus, the former models event counts, and the latter models inter-arrival times.

2.5.3. Distributions Related to the Gamma Distribution

The gamma distribution, $Gamma(\alpha, \beta)$, was formally defined in the 20th century and can be considered as an extension of the exponential distribution. It retains several desirable properties of the exponential distribution, such as additivity: the sum of independently and identically distributed variables $X_i \sim Gamma(\alpha_i, \beta)$ for $i = 1, \ldots, m$ is distributed as $Gamma(\sum_{i=1}^{m} \alpha_i, \beta)$. The gamma distribution is foundational, as the chi-square distribution χ_v^2 is a special case, $Gamma(v/2, 1/2)$, and the beta distribution $Be(a, b)$ can be defined by $\frac{Y}{Y+Z}$, where $Y \sim Gamma(a, 1)$ and $Z \sim Gamma(b, 1)$ are independent. Table 5 lists several important extensions of the gamma distribution.

(1) Location-shift gamma: Adding a location parameter δ forms the three-parameter distribution $Gamma(\alpha, \beta, \delta)$.
(2) Generalized gamma: This distribution exists in several forms. The version shown with shape a, scale d, and power p parameters was introduced by Stacy [33]. It includes several common distributions as special cases: the standard gamma ($p = 1$), the Weibull ($a = 1$), the Rayleigh ($a = p = 2$), and the exponential ($a = p = 1$).
(3) Inverse gamma: Defined as $Y = 1/X$ for $X \sim Gamma(\alpha, \beta)$, this two-parameter distribution is positive-skewed. It is primarily used in Bayesian statistics as the conjugate prior for the variance of a normal distribution.
(4) Beta prime distribution: The ratio X/Y of two independent variables, $X \sim Gamma(\alpha, \theta)$ and $Y \sim Gamma(\beta, \theta)$, follows a beta prime distribution $BP(\alpha, \beta)$.
(5) General beta prime distribution: This is a further extension of the beta prime distribution, incorporating two additional parameters.

Table 5. Some continuous distributions constructed by the gamma distribution.

Distribution	Notation	Density $f(x)$
Gamma	$Gamma(\alpha,\beta)$	$\frac{\beta^\alpha}{\Gamma(\alpha)}x^{\alpha-1}e^{-\beta x},\ x>0,\ \alpha,\beta>0$
Location-shift gamma	$Gamma(\alpha,\beta,\delta)$	$\frac{\beta^\alpha}{\Gamma(\alpha)}(x-\delta)^{\alpha-1}e^{-\beta(x-\delta)},\ x\geq\delta,\ \delta\in\mathbb{R},\ \alpha,\beta>0$
Generalized gamma	$G-gamma(a,d,p)$	$\frac{p}{d^a\Gamma(a/p)}x^{a-1}e^{-(x/d)^p},\ x>0,\ a,d,p>0$
Inverse gamma	$Inv-Gamma(\alpha,\beta)$	$\frac{\beta^\alpha}{\Gamma(\alpha)}x^{-(\alpha+1)}e^{-\beta/x},\ x>0,\ \alpha,\beta>0$
Beta prime	$BP(\alpha,\beta)$	$\frac{1}{\mathrm{B}(\alpha,\beta)}\frac{x^{\alpha-1}}{(1+x)^{\alpha+\beta}},\ x>0,\ \alpha,\beta>0$
General beta prime	$GBP(\alpha,\beta,p,q)$	$\frac{\lvert\alpha\rvert(1+(x/\beta)^\alpha)^{-p-q}(x/\beta)^{p\alpha-1}}{\beta B(p,q)},\ \alpha\in\mathbb{R},\alpha\neq 0,\ p,q,\beta>0,\ x>0.$

2.6. The Generalized Hyperbolic Distribution Family

Schrdinger [34] described the probability distribution of the first passage time in Brownian motion. Thirty years later, Tweedie [35] gave the inverse relationship between the cumulant generating function of the first passage time distribution and that of the normal distribution, and named it the inverse Gaussian (IG) distribution. This new distribution was proposed in the top journal Nature, which shows its importance. The IG distribution, denoted as $IG(\mu,\lambda)$, is defined for $x>0$, $\mu>0$, and $\lambda>0$ by the probability density function:

$$f(x;\mu,\lambda)=\sqrt{\frac{\lambda}{2\pi x^3}}\exp\left\{\frac{-\lambda(x-\mu)^2}{2\mu^2 x}\right\}. \tag{8}$$

The IG distribution models the first passage time of a Brownian motion, making it highly useful for analyzing lifetime data and the frequency of event occurrences in various fields. For a comprehensive reference, see [36]. The IG distribution has many extensions, among which the generalized hyperbolic distribution (GH) is a more general one.

The GH distribution is a continuous probability distribution that represents a highly flexible family of models for describing data with skewness and heavy tails. Its key strength lies in its ability to nest several other important distributions as special or limiting cases, providing a unified framework for statistical modeling. It was introduced by [37] to model the grain size distributions of wind-blown sand. However, its remarkable fit to financial data catapulted it to prominence in financial econometrics and risk management (see [38]).

A random variable X is said to follow a GH distribution $GH(\lambda,\alpha,\beta,\delta,\mu)$ if its pdf is

$$f(x)=C(\lambda,\alpha,\beta,\delta)(\delta^2+(x-\mu)^2)^{(\lambda-0.5)/2}K_{\lambda-0.5}\left(\alpha\sqrt{\delta^2+(x-\mu)^2}\right)\exp(\beta(x-\mu)), \tag{9}$$

where $x\in\mathbb{R}$ and

$$C(\lambda,\alpha,\beta,\delta)=\frac{(\alpha^2-\beta^2)^{\lambda/2}}{\sqrt{2\pi}\alpha^{\lambda-0.5}\delta^\lambda K_\lambda(\delta\sqrt{\alpha^2-\beta^2})},\ \alpha>0,\ |\beta|<\alpha,\ \delta>0,\ \mu,\lambda,\in\mathbb{R}.$$

The parameter λ influences the tail behavior and the subfamily classification; α controls the heaviness of the tails and the steepness; β controls the asymmetry; δ is the scale parameter related to the dispersion; and μ is the location parameter. $K_\lambda(\cdot)$ is the modified Bessel function of the second kind of order λ defined by

$$K_\lambda(x) = \frac{1}{2}\int_0^\infty t^{\lambda-1}\exp\left(-\frac{x}{2}(t+\frac{1}{t})\right)dt.$$

The GH distribution involves many distributions as its special cases: hyperbolic distribution ($\lambda = 1$), normal inverse Gaussian distribution ($\lambda = -0.5$), variance gamma distribution ($\lambda > 0, \delta = 0$), etc. A normal variance-mean mixture distribution, termed the normal inverse Gaussian distribution proposed by [39], is used to construct stochastic processes that appear of interest for statistical modeling purposes, particularly in turbulence and finance. Its pdf is defined as

$$f(x;\alpha,\beta,\delta,\mu) = C(\alpha,\beta,\delta)q\left(\frac{x-\mu}{\delta}\right)^{-1}K_1\left(\alpha\delta q\left(\frac{x-\mu}{\delta}\right)\right)\exp(\beta(x-\mu)), \quad x \in \mathbb{R},$$

where

$$C(\alpha,\beta,\delta) = \frac{\alpha}{\pi}\exp\left(\delta\sqrt{\alpha^2-\beta^2}\right),\ q(t) = \sqrt{1+t^2},$$

and K_1 is the modified Bessel function of the second kind of order 1. The parameters have the following role: $\mu \in \mathbb{R}$ (location) and $\delta > 0$ (scale); $\alpha > 0$ (tail heaviness) controls the steepness of the distribution. A larger α leads to lighter tails and $\alpha > |\beta|$, where β (asymmetry/skewness) controls the skewness. $\beta = 0$ gives a symmetric distribution, $\beta > 0$ implies positive skewness, and $\beta < 0$ implies negative skewness.

The GH distribution is a normal variance-mean mixture of the generalized inverse Gaussian (GIG) distributions. This construction is the source of its flexibility and mathematical tractability. The GIG distribution is a continuous probability distribution that generalizes several important distributions and plays a critical role as a mixing distribution in normal variance-mean mixtures. The GIG distribution denoted by $GIG(\lambda,\chi,\psi))$ is defined by the given pdf

$$f(x;\lambda,\chi,\psi) = \frac{(\psi/\chi)^{\lambda/2}}{2K_\lambda(\sqrt{\psi\chi})}x^{\lambda-1}\exp\left(-\frac{1}{2}\left(\frac{\chi}{x}+\psi x\right)\right), \quad x > 0,\ \chi,\psi \geq 0, \tag{10}$$

where parameter λ determines the shape of the distribution and is deeply connected to the index of the Bessel function. χ is the scale parameter often related to the "left-hand" behavior, with the constraint: $\lambda > 0$ whenever $\chi = 0$. ψ is another scale parameter that is often related to the "right-hand" tail with the constraint: $\lambda < 0$ whenever $\psi = 0$, and $\psi = \chi = 0$ is not allowed. The GIG involves inverse Gaussian distribution ($\lambda = -0.5$), reciprocal inverse Gaussian distribution ($\lambda = 0.5$), and gamma distribution ($\chi = 0, \lambda > 0$).

A random variable Y follows a GH distribution $GH(\lambda,\alpha,\beta,\delta,\mu)$ if it has the following stochastic representation:

$$Y = \mu + \beta X + \sigma\sqrt{X}Z,$$

where $Z \sim N(0,1)$, and $X \sim GIG(\lambda,\chi,\psi)$ is independent of Z. The parameters of the resulting $GH(\lambda,\alpha,\beta,\delta,\mu)$ distribution are identified as follows: $\alpha = \sqrt{\psi\sigma^2+\beta^2}, \delta = \sqrt{\chi}$. By choosing different GIG subfamilies as the mixer, we obtain the different GH subfamilies:

(1) Mixing with the inverse Gaussian ($\lambda = -0.5$) distribution results in the normal inverse Gaussian distribution.

(2) Mixing with the gamma ($\chi = 0, \lambda > 0$) distribution results in the variance gamma distribution.
(3) Mixing with the GIG ($\lambda = 1$) distribution results in the hyperbolic distribution.

2.7. Beta-Generated Distributions

A significant research area is the creation of flexible univariate distribution classes that extend classical models. The beta-generated (BG) distributions by Arnold et al. [40,41] achieve this by merging the beta distribution with a chosen baseline distribution.

Definition 1. *For a baseline cdf $F(x)$ with pdf $f(x)$ on a domain D, the beta-generated (BG) distributions have the following pdf:*

$$g_F(x; a, b) = \frac{1}{B(a,b)} F(x)^{a-1} [1 - F(x)]^{b-1} f(x), \quad x \in D, \quad a > 0, b > 0. \tag{11}$$

We denote this by $X \sim BG(a, b; F)$. The corresponding cdf is derived via the substitution $y = F(t)$:

$$G_F(x; a, b) = \frac{1}{B(a,b)} \int_0^{F(x)} y^{a-1}(1-y)^{b-1} dy = I_{F(x)}(a, b),$$

which is the incomplete beta function ratio.

A key property of the $BG(a, b; F)$ distribution is its stochastic representation:

$$X \stackrel{d}{=} F^{-1}(B), \quad \text{for } B \sim Be(a, b). \tag{12}$$

This representation provides a foundation for applying the generalized inverse transformation method in statistical simulation using representative points. It offers a direct method for simulating from the density (11) and for constructing multivariate extensions. The moments of X are consequently given by

$$E(X^r) = E([F^{-1}(B)]^r), \quad r > 0. \tag{13}$$

The beta-generated family encompasses a wide range of distributions depending on the choice of the baseline F. To demonstrate the flexibility and utility of this class, we select two specific examples. For the generalization of this generating mechanism, see [42].

2.7.1. The Beta-Normal Distribution

If $F(x)$ is the cdf of $N(\mu, \sigma^2)$, the corresponding BG distribution is the beta-normal distribution, denoted as $X \sim BN(a, b; \mu, \sigma)$. As studied by Eugene et al. [43], its cdf is

$$G(x) = \frac{1}{B(a,b)} \int_0^{\Phi(\frac{x-\mu}{\sigma})} t^{a-1}(1-t)^{b-1} dt, \tag{14}$$

where $\Phi(\cdot)$ is the standard normal cdf. For the standard case $BN(a, b; 0, 1)$, the pdf is

$$g(x) = \frac{1}{B(a,b)} \Phi(x)^{a-1} [1 - \Phi(x)]^{b-1} \phi(x), \quad x \in \mathbb{R}. \tag{15}$$

Its moments are given by the formula in (13) (Gupta and Nadarajah [44]).

This four-parameter distribution defines location, scale, and shape, and can be unimodal or bimodal. Its fitting performance has been compared to that of normal mixture models in simulation studies. Note that the beta distribution is a special case of the Dirichlet distribution (cf. Section 4.4.2).

2.7.2. The Beta-Weibull Distribution

The beta-Weibull distribution, denoted by $BW(a, b; c, \gamma)$, has the following pdf:

$$f_{BW}(x) = \frac{1}{B(a,b)} \frac{c}{\gamma} \left(\frac{x}{\gamma}\right)^{c-1} \left[1 - \exp\left\{-\left(\frac{x}{\gamma}\right)^c\right\}\right]^{a-1} \exp\left\{-b\left(\frac{x}{\gamma}\right)^c\right\}, \quad x > 0. \tag{16}$$

A system study on this distribution refer to Famege et al. [45] and Mdziniso [46]. The beta-Weibull distribution includes many useful distributions, including the Weibull distribution ($a = b = 1$), beta-exponential distribution ($c = 1$), Rayleigh distribution ($a = b = 1, c = 2$), two-parameter Burr-type distribution ($b = 1, c = 2$), etc.

The beta-Weibull distribution has many good properties.

(1) The limit of beta-Weibull density (16) is

$$\lim_{x \to \infty} f_{BW}(x) = \begin{cases} \infty, & ac < 1, \\ \frac{c\Gamma(a+b)}{\gamma\Gamma(a)\Gamma(b)}, & ac = 1, \\ 0, & ac > 1. \end{cases}$$

(2) Let $Y \sim Be(a, b)$, then the random variable $X = \gamma[-\log(1 - Y)]^{1/c}$ follows $BW(a, b, c, \gamma)$, where $c, \gamma > 0$. It provides a way to generate a random sample from the BW distribution.

(3) Let Y follow a beta-exponential distribution with parameters (a, b, θ), then random variable $X = \theta(Y/\theta)^{1/c}$ follows a beta-Weibull distribution.

(4) The beta-Weibull distribution is unimodal. The mode is at $x_0 = 1$ whenever $ac < 1$ or $ac = 1$ and $\mathbf{b} \geq (c-1)/2c$. For other cases, x_0 is the solution of the equation

$$bc - (c-1)(x_0/\gamma)^{-c} = c(a-1)[\exp(x_0/\gamma)^c]^{-1}.$$

(5) The rth moments of $BW(a, b, c, \gamma)$ is given by

$$E\left[\left(\frac{X}{\gamma}\right)^r\right] = \frac{1}{B(a,b)} \int_0^\infty t^{r/c}(1 - e^{-t})^{a-1} e^{-bt} dt,$$

by the transformation $t = (x/\gamma)^c$.

3. Construction of Univariate Discrete Distributions and an Approximation

A discrete distribution is characterized by its support points and their probabilities:

$$\begin{array}{c|cccc} X & x_1 & x_2 & \cdots & x_k \\ \hline p_i & p_1 & p_2 & \cdots & p_k \end{array} \tag{17}$$

where the random variable X has support $x_1, \ldots, x_k$ and $P(X = x_i) = p_i, i = 1, \ldots, k$.

3.1. *Classical Univariate Discrete Distributions*

Standard discrete distribution model outcomes from fundamental random processes/trials:

1. Bernoulli(p)/Binomial(n, p): The Bernoulli distribution, Bernoulli(p), models a single trial, and Binomial(n, p) counts successes in n independent trials with sample success probability p.
2. Geometric(p): It models the number of Bernoulli trials needed to obtain the first success, representing the waiting time for a success. It is a special case of the negative binomial (with $r = 1$).

3. Negative Binomial(r, p): As a generalization of the geometric distribution, it models the number of Bernoulli trials needed to achieve r successes. The negative binomial distribution presented here in its classic form (modeling the number of trials) is equivalent to the parameterization modeling the number of failures before the r-th success (with support $y = 0, 1, 2, \ldots$), which is prevalent in many modern software packages and generalized linear models.
4. Poisson(λ): It models the number of events occurring in a fixed interval of time or space, given a constant average rate (λ) and independence between events. It can be derived as a limiting case of the binomial distribution when $n \to \infty$ and $p \to 0$ such that $np \to \lambda$.
5. Hypergeometric(s, n, N, M): It represents the number s of successes in n draws without replacement from a population with N size with M success items, where $\max(0, n - (N - M)) \leq s \leq \min(M, n)$. This differs from the binomial distribution, where trials are independent (i.e., with replacement).

See Johnson and Kotz [47] for an extensive catalog. A guide to selecting common discrete probability distributions is illustrated in Figure 1, with probability mass functions summarized in Table 6.

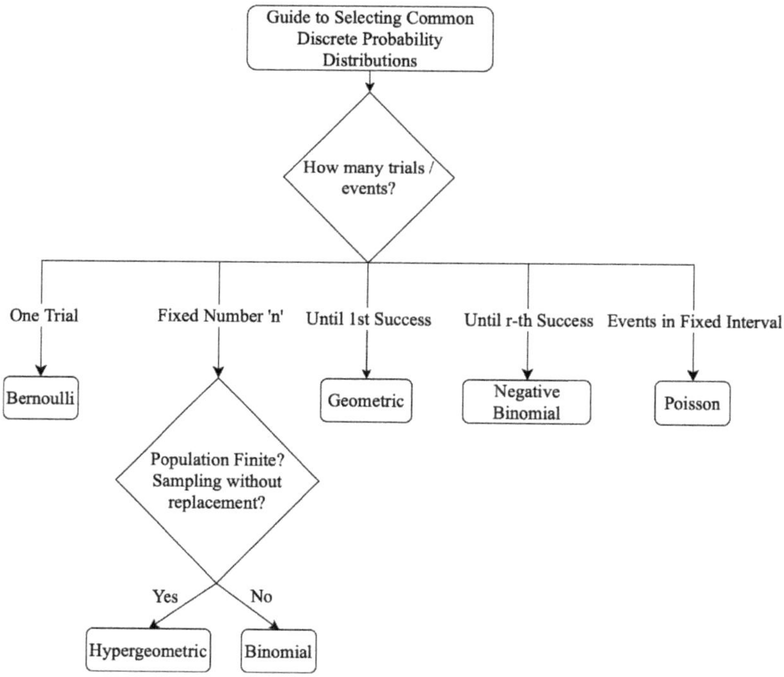

Figure 1. A guide to selecting common discrete probability distributions.

Consider a random variable X following the discrete distribution defined in (17) and a continuous function $g(\cdot)$. The transformed variable $Y = g(X)$ follows a distribution with the following structure:

$$\begin{array}{c|cccc} Y & g(x_1) & g(x_2) & \cdots & g(x_k) \\ \hline p_i & p_1 & p_2 & \cdots & p_k \end{array}. \tag{18}$$

In other words, the law of Y is determined by mapping the support points of X via g while preserving the associated probabilities. This elegant property facilitates the analysis of transformed discrete variables. Li et al. [14] utilized this property to compute nearly representative points for the distribution of $g(X)$.

Table 6. Famous discrete distributions.

Distribution	Support Points	Probability Mass Function $p_i(x)$
Bernoulli(p)	$0,1$	$p_0 = 1-p, p_1 = p$
Binomial(n,p)	$0,1,2,\ldots,n$	$p_i = \binom{n}{i}p^i(1-p)^{n-i}, i = 0,1,2,\ldots,n$
Geometric(p)	$1,2,\ldots$	$p_i = p(1-p)^{i-1}, i = 1,2,\ldots$ (Number of trials until first success)
Negative Binomial(r,p)	$r, r+1,\ldots$	$p_i = \binom{i-1}{r-1}p^r(1-p)^{i-r}, i = r, r+1,\ldots$ (Number of trials until r-th success)
	$0,1,2,\ldots$	$p_i = \binom{i+r-1}{i}p^r(1-p)^i, \quad i = 0,1,2,\ldots$ (Number of failures before r-th success)
Poisson(λ)	$0,1,2\ldots$	$p_i = e^{-\lambda}\frac{\lambda^i}{i!}, i = 0,1,2,\ldots$
Hypergeometric(s,n,N,M)	$\max(0, n-(N-M)),\cdots,\min(M,n)$	$p_i = \binom{M}{i}\binom{N-M}{n-i}/\binom{N}{n}$

Note on alternative derivations and parameterizations: The distributions listed above can often be derived through multiple probabilistic mechanisms, which leads to different (but equivalent) parameterizations and interpretations. These alternative derivations highlight the interconnectedness of discrete probability distributions and provide flexibility in choosing the most appropriate model for a given data-generating process.

3.2. *Distributions Generated by Mixtures*

A powerful method for constructing flexible probability models is through mixture distributions, where the parameter of one distribution is itself governed by another distribution. This approach naturally incorporates heterogeneity and over-dispersion, commonly observed in real-world data.

3.2.1. Poisson Mixtures

When the rate parameter λ of a Poisson distribution is not fixed but follows a continuous distribution $G(\lambda)$ with support on $\mathbb{R}^+$, the resulting marginal distribution is a Poisson mixture. Its probability mass function is given by

$$P(X = k) = \int_0^\infty \frac{e^{-\lambda}\lambda^k}{k!} dG(\lambda), \quad k = 0,1,2,\ldots$$

The most prominent example is the negative binomial distribution, which arises as a Poisson-gamma mixture. Specifically, if

$$X \mid \lambda \sim \text{Poisson}(\lambda) \quad \text{and} \quad \lambda \sim \text{Gamma}(r, \beta = (1-p)/p),$$

then the marginal distribution of X is negative binomial with pmf:

$$P(X = k) = \frac{\Gamma(r+k)}{k!\,\Gamma(r)} p^r(1-p)^k, \quad k = 0,1,2,\ldots$$

This model is widely used for count data where the variance exceeds the mean.

3.2.2. Binomial Mixtures

Similarly, allowing the success probability p of a binomial distribution to vary according to a continuous distribution $F(p)$ on [0,1] leads to a binomial mixture. The marginal pmf is

$$P(X = k) = \int_0^1 \binom{n}{k} p^k(1-p)^{n-k} dF(p), \quad k = 0,1,\ldots,n$$

The beta-binomial distribution is the canonical example, where $p \sim \text{Beta}(\alpha, \beta)$. Its pmf is

$$P(X = k) = \binom{n}{k} \frac{\text{B}(k + \alpha, n - k + \beta)}{\text{B}(\alpha, \beta)}$$

where $\text{B}(\cdot, \cdot)$ is the beta function. This distribution effectively models counts with extra-binomial variation.

Other notable mixtures include the Poisson-inverse Gaussian and the negative binomial-beta distributions [48].

3.3. Distributions Generated by Random Sums

Distributions generated by random sums, also known as compound distributions, provide a framework for modeling the aggregate outcome of a random number of events. Let N be a non-negative integer-valued random variable with pmf $p_N(n)$, and let $\{X_i\}$ be a sequence of *i.i.d.* random variables, independent of N. The random sum is defined as

$$S = X_1 + X_2 + \cdots + X_N, \quad \text{(with the convention that } S = 0 \text{ if } N = 0).$$

The distribution of S is called the compound distribution of N and X_i. Its probability generating function (pgf) is given by $G_S(t) = G_N(G_X(t))$, from which moments and probabilities can be derived.

Prominent examples include the following:

- Compound Poisson distribution: If $N \sim \text{Poisson}(\lambda)$, then S is compound Poisson. This is a highly flexible family used in insurance (to model total claim amounts) and queueing theory. Special cases include the Poisson-exponential and Poisson-gamma (which is equivalent to the negative binomial under a specific parameterization) distributions.
- Geometric sum: If $N \sim \text{Geometric}(p)$, and $X_i \sim \text{Exp}(\theta)$, then $S \sim \text{Exp}(\theta p)$. This result is foundational in renewal theory.

The family of phase-type distributions can also be constructed using random sums of exponential random variables, demonstrating the versatility of this method for generating distributions with specific tail behaviors [49].

3.4. Approximation to Univariate Continuous Distributions by Representative Points

Consider a random variable $X \sim F(x)$, where $F(x)$ is a univariate cumulative distribution function. The empirical distribution function $F_k(x)$ is defined as

$$F_k(x) = \frac{1}{k} \sum_{i=1}^{k} I\{x_i \leq x\}, \tag{19}$$

where I_A is the indicator function of A. The empirical distribution $F_k(x)$ is a discrete distribution with support points $x_1, \ldots, x_k$, each assigned an equal probability mass of $1/k$. It serves as a consistent approximation of $F(x)$, meaning $F_k(x) \to F(x)$ in distribution as $k \to \infty$. This distribution can be represented as

$$\begin{array}{c|cccc} Y_{MC} & x_1 & x_2 & \cdots & x_k \\ \hline p_i & \frac{1}{k} & \frac{1}{k} & \cdots & \frac{1}{k} \end{array}. \tag{20}$$

Alternatively, one can construct other approximations using the so-called representative points (RPs) as support points. For a given distribution $F(x)$ in $\mathbb{R}$, several types of RPs exist, including

- Monte Carlo RPs (MC-RPs): the empirical sample points.
- Quasi-Monte Carlo RPs (QMC-RPs): deterministic points based on low-discrepancy sequences.
- Mean square error RPs (MSE-RPs): points minimizing a mean squared error criterion.

For a univariate continuous distribution $F(x)$, the QMC-RP approximation is given by the following distribution:

$$\begin{array}{c|cccc} Y_{QMC} & F^{-1}(\frac{1}{2k}) & F^{-1}(\frac{3}{2k}) & \cdots & F^{-1}(\frac{2k-1}{2k}) \\ \hline p_i & \frac{1}{k} & \frac{1}{k} & \cdots & \frac{1}{k} \end{array}. \tag{21}$$

MSE-RPs and related approximation distribution is

$$\begin{array}{c|cccc} Y_{MSE} & \xi_1 & \xi_2 & \cdots & \xi_k \\ \hline p_i & p_1 & p_2 & \cdots & p_k \end{array}. \tag{22}$$

where the support points $\{\xi_1, \ldots, \xi_k\}$ are determined by

$$\mathrm{MSE}(\mathcal{Y}) = \int_{-\infty}^{+\infty} \min_i (x - \xi_i^{(k)})^2 p(x) dx = \sum_{j=1}^{k} \int_{I_j} (x - \xi_i^{(k)})^2 p(x) dx, \tag{23}$$

where

$$\begin{aligned} I_1 = (a_1, a_2),\ I_2 = (a_2, a_3),\ \ldots,\ I_k = (a_k, a_{k+1}), \\ a_1 = -\infty,\ a_i = \left(\xi_{i-1}^{(k)} + \xi_i^{(k)}\right)/2,\ i = 2, \cdots, k,\ a_{k+1} = \infty. \end{aligned} \tag{24}$$

Fang and Pan [50] and Fang et al. [8] provided a comprehensive review of the theory, generating algorithms, and applications of representative points in statistical inference.

3.4.1. Difference Between Two Distributions

The Kullback–Leibler (KL) divergence, or relative entropy, of two probability distributions with probability density functions $p(x)$ and $q(x)$ on $\mathcal{X} \subset \mathbb{R}^p$ is defined as the expected logarithmic ratio of densities concerning $p(x)$:

$$D_{KL}(p(\boldsymbol{x})|q(\boldsymbol{x})) = \int_{\mathcal{X}} \log\left(\frac{p(\boldsymbol{x})}{q(\boldsymbol{x})}\right) p(\boldsymbol{x}) d\boldsymbol{x} = E_{p(\boldsymbol{x})}\left[\log\left(\frac{p(\boldsymbol{x})}{q(\boldsymbol{x})}\right)\right]. \tag{25}$$

The KL divergence is non-negative and is equal to 0 if and only if the two distributions are identical.

Now, consider the univariate case. For any discrete distribution, we can find a corresponding density estimator, denoted by $\hat{p}(x)$. Let $F(x)$ be a cdf with pmf $p(x)$, and let $\hat{F}(x)$ with pmf $\hat{p}(x)$ be an approximating distribution. Several criteria in the literature measure the distance between F and $\hat{F}$:

$$\begin{aligned} \text{KL divergence (KL)} : \mathrm{KL}(p \parallel \hat{p}) &= \sum_x \log\left(\frac{p(x)}{\hat{p}(x)}\right) p(x); \\ L^2\text{-norm of pmfs } (L^2 \text{ pdf}) : \|p, \hat{p}\| &= \left(\sum_x [p(x) - \hat{p}(x)]^2\right)^{1/2}; \\ L^2\text{-norm of cdfs } (L^2 \text{ cdf}) : \|F, \hat{F}\| &= \left(\int_{\mathbb{R}} [F(x) - \hat{F}(x)]^2 dx\right)^{1/2}. \end{aligned}$$

Another metric for the distance between $F(x)$ and $\hat{F}(x)$ is the absolute bias index (ABI), which evaluates the overall bias in parameter estimation. For a population distribution $F(x;\boldsymbol{\theta})$ with parameter vector $\boldsymbol{\theta} = (\theta_1, \ldots, \theta_m)$ and its estimate $\hat{\boldsymbol{\theta}} = (\hat{\theta}_1, \ldots, \hat{\theta}_m)$ under $\hat{F}(x)$, the ABI is defined as follows:

$$ABI = \frac{1}{m}\sum_{i=1}^{m}\left|\frac{\theta_i - \hat{\theta}_i}{\theta_i}\right|. \tag{26}$$

3.4.2. Discrete Analogues

Discrete analogs aim to create new discrete distributions that preserve one or more defining characteristics of an original continuous distribution. An approximation $\hat{F}(x)$ is considered successful if it maintains as much information from $F(x)$ as possible, whether measured by the distance between the distributions, the similarity of their moments, or the properties of simulated samples.

As a continuous random variable X can be characterized by its pdf, moments, generating functions, or other features, the construction of a discrete analog Y (with pmf) from X (with density $f(x)$) focuses on matching these properties. The primary methods for this construction, summarized by [51], are classified as follows.

(1) Discrete analogs of the Pearson differential equation. This approach constructs discrete probability distributions by employing difference equations that mirror the structure of the Pearson differential equation, which defines the continuous Pearson family [52,53].

(2) The probability mass function (pmf) of Y retains the form of the pdf of X, and the support of Y is determined from the full range of X. The pmf is defined as

$$P(Y = k) = \frac{f(k)}{\sum_{j=-\infty}^{\infty} f(j)}, \quad k = 0, \pm 1, \pm 2, \ldots.$$

This approach has been used to create discrete analogs of various continuous distributions, including the gamma, general Dirichlet, normal, lognormal, exponential, Laplace, generalized exponential, and gamma distributions [54–56].

(3) The survival function (SF) of Y retains the form of the survival function of X, and the support of Y is determined from the full range of X. The discrete survival function is defined as $S_Y(k) = P(Y \geq k)$, and its corresponding cdf is $F_Y(k) = P(Y \leq k)$, related by $S_Y(k) = 1 - F_Y(k-1)$. This technique has generated numerous discrete distributions, such as the discrete exponential, Weibull, geometric Weibull, normal, Rayleigh, Maxwell, extended exponential, and Lindley distributions [57,58].

(4) The hazard (failure) rate function of Y retains the form of the hazard rate function of X. This method preserves the hazard rate function. For a continuous random variable X with survival function $S_X(x) = P(X \geq x)$ and hazard rate function $\lambda_X(x) = f_X(x)/S_X(x)$, the survival function of the discrete analog Y is given by

$$P(Y \geq k) = \prod_{i=1}^{k-1}(1 - \lambda_X(i)), \quad k = 1, \ldots, m,$$

and its pmf is

$$P(Y = k) = \lambda_X(k)\prod_{i=1}^{k-1}(1 - \lambda_X(i)).$$

This approach has been used to propose new discrete distributions, such as the discrete Lomax, Weibull, and Rayleigh [59].

(5) The moments of Y and X coincide up to a certain order. This method requires that Y and X share the same finite r^{th} moment for $r = 0, 1, \ldots, 2N-1$, and that their cdfs coincide at least at $M+1$ points. The support of the discrete random variable Y is $\{y_1, \ldots, y_{MN}\}$. It has been used to define new discrete uniform, normal, gamma, and beta distributions [60].

There are more other construction methods, for instance, an extensive review on discrete distributions defined for integer data is provided in [61].

4. Multivariate Distributions

The commonly used discrete distributions can be extended to multivariate cases, including multinomial and multivariate negative binomial, hypergeometric, and Poisson distributions.

4.1. Multinomial Distribution

An extension of the binomial distribution is the so-called multinomial distribution. It is the fundamental model for counting events that fall into multiple categories, making it essential in fields like statistics, genetics, machine learning (e.g., topic modeling with naive Bayes), and survey analysis. Considering an experiment consists of n identical, independent trials, each trial results in one of k mutually exclusive and exhaustive categories with probabilities $p_i, i = 1, \ldots, k; p_1 + \cdots + p_k = 1$. Let random vector $\boldsymbol{X} = (X_1, \ldots, X_k)$ follow a multinomial distribution $Multinomial(n; p_1, \ldots, p_k)$. Its probability mass function is

$$P(X_1 = n_1, \ldots, X_k = n_k) = \frac{n!}{n_1! \cdots n_k!}, n_1, \ldots, n_k \in \mathbb{N}_0,\ n_1 + \ldots + n_k = n. \tag{27}$$

The multinomial distribution has many nice properties. One is related to Poisson distribution, that lets $X_1, \ldots, X_k$ be independent and $X_i \sim Poisson(\lambda_i), i = 1, \ldots, k$. Then the conditional distribution of $(X_1, \ldots, X_k | X_1 + \cdots + X_k = n)$ follows $Multinomial(n; p_1, \ldots, p_k)$ where $p_i = \lambda_i / (\lambda_1 + \cdots + \lambda_k), i = 1, \ldots, k$. The multinomial distribution has been used in many statistical applications. One is in the Pearson's chi-square test for goodness-of-fit, using the fact that the test statistic, calculated from observed multinomial counts and expected counts (np_i), follows a chi-square distribution asymptotically (as n grows large).

4.2. Multivariate Hypergeometric Distribution

The multivariate hypergeometric distribution is the generalization of the hypergeometric distribution to more than two categories. It describes the probability of drawing specific numbers of items from each category without replacement. Considering a population with size N, of which $M_1, \cdots, M_k$ are the numbers of items in the k mutually exclusive and exhaustive categories with $\sum_{i=1}^k M_i = N$, suppose that the n random samples are sampling without replacement containing $n_1, \cdots, n_k$ items of each corresponding category. The joint distribution of $\boldsymbol{X} = (X_1, \cdots, X_k)$ has pmf

$$P(X_1 = n_1, \cdots, n_k) = \frac{\prod_{i=1}^k \binom{M_i}{n_i}}{\binom{N}{n}}, \ \sum_{i=1}^k n_i = n,\ 0 \le n_i \le M_i,\ i = 1, \cdots, k. \tag{28}$$

The distribution denoted as $Mult.\ Hypg.(n; M_1, \cdots, M_k)$ is the so-called multivariate hypergeometric distribution. Without requiring the parameters in (28) to be non-negative, multivariate inverse hypergeometric, negative hypergeometric, and negative inverse hypergeometric distributions are then defined; see [62]. One property is that if $\boldsymbol{X}$ and $\boldsymbol{Y}$ are independent and each distributed as $Multinomial(n; p_1, \cdots, p_k)$, then $\boldsymbol{X} | (\boldsymbol{X} + \boldsymbol{Y} = \boldsymbol{N})$ follows $Mult.Hypg.(n, \boldsymbol{N})$.

4.3. Multivariate Poisson Distribution

If the parameters $p_1, \cdots, p_{k-1}$ in the multinomial distribution are allowed to tend to 0, this implies that p_k tends 1 as $n \to \infty$, such that $np_i \to \lambda_i$, $i = 1, 2, \cdots, k-1$. Hence, the probability of obtaining the event $\cap_{i=1}^{k-1}(X_i = n_i)$ tends to

$$P(X_1 = n_1, \cdots, X_{k-1} = n_{k-1}) = \prod_{i=1}^{k-1}\{e^{-\lambda_i}\frac{\lambda_i^{n_i}}{n_i!}\}. \tag{29}$$

This is the joint distribution of $k-1$ mutually independent Poisson random variables with means $\lambda_1, \cdots, \lambda_{k-1}$. The distribution can also be obtained as a limiting form of negative multinomial distributions.

The simplest case, as derived from the multinomial limit, is one of independence, but more flexible distributions allowing for correlation are of greater practical interest. A more general and widely used approach to constructing a multivariate Poisson distribution with a covariance structure is to use a common mixture or latent variable model. A standard construction introduces a set of independent latent Poisson variables and defines the observed variables as their sums.

A classical bivariate Poisson distribution for random variables (X, Y) can be defined as follows:

$$X = Z_1 + Z_0, \quad Y = Z_2 + Z_0,$$

where Z_0, Z_1, Z_2 are independent Poisson random variables with rates $\lambda_0, \lambda_1, \lambda_2 \geq 0$, respectively. The joint probability mass function of (X, Y) is given by

$$P(X = x, Y = y) = \exp(-(\lambda_1 + \lambda_2 + \lambda_0)) \sum_{k=0}^{\min(x,y)} \frac{\lambda_1^{x-k}}{(x-k)!}\frac{\lambda_2^{y-k}}{(y-k)!}\frac{\lambda_0^k}{k!}.$$

The marginal distributions are $X \sim \text{Poisson}(\lambda_1 + \lambda_0)$ and $Y \sim \text{Poisson}(\lambda_2 + \lambda_0)$, and the covariance between X and Y is $\text{Cov}(X, Y) = \lambda_0 \geq 0$. This model can only account for non-negative correlation, which is often sufficient for many applications, such as modeling the number of insurance claims across different policy types or goals scored by two teams in a match.

This construction can be generalized to higher dimensions by introducing more common components, leading to a richer covariance structure [3,63,64]. These correlated multivariate Poisson models are essential tools in modern multivariate count data analysis.

4.4. Continuous Multivariate Distributions

Johnson et al. [4] provided a comprehensive compilation of many multivariate distributions. Johnson [7] offered an in-depth introduction to the generation of multivariate statistical simulations. Palmitesta and Provasi [65] reviewed a range of multivariate distributions and their computer generation methods. Their survey encompassed the Dirichlet distribution, the multivariate Johnson distribution system, multivariate beta and gamma distributions, the multivariate extreme value distribution, the inverse Gaussian multivariate distribution, the Cook–Johnson family of multivariate uniform distributions, and elliptically contoured distributions. They also examined techniques for generating random vectors with specified marginal distributions and correlation matrices. Fang, Kotz, and Ng [6] conducted a comprehensive study on symmetric multivariate distributions. Due to space limitations, this section focuses on selected multivariate distributions from the literature and meta-distributions constructed via copulas, see [66]. For more construction methods for multivariate distribution, see [67].

4.4.1. Stochastic Representation

The traditional definition of the multivariate normal distribution relies on its density function. This approach, however, has several weaknesses:

(i) It assumes that the explicit form of the density function is known.
(ii) It requires the analytical evaluation of high-dimensional integrals to compute probabilities, moments, and marginal distributions.

The stochastic representation operator, denoted by $\stackrel{d}{=}$, is a powerful tool for constructing new distributions. If two random vectors $\mathbf{X}$ and $\mathbf{Y}$ have the same distribution, we write $\mathbf{X} \stackrel{d}{=} \mathbf{Y}$.

Examples

$U \stackrel{d}{=} 1 - U$, where $U \sim U(0,1)$;
$X \stackrel{d}{=} -X$, where $X \sim N(0, \sigma^2)$;
$X \stackrel{d}{=} \mu + \sigma Y$, where $X \sim N(\mu, \sigma^2)$ and $Y \sim N(0,1)$.

Properties

(1) $\mathbf{X} \stackrel{\mathbf{d}}{=} \mathbf{Y} \Rightarrow (f_1(\mathbf{X}), ..., f_m(\mathbf{X})) \stackrel{d}{=} (f_1(\mathbf{Y}), ..., f_m(\mathbf{Y}))$, where f_j are measurable functions. Examples are $\mathbf{X}^\top \mathbf{X} \stackrel{d}{=} \mathbf{Y}^\top \mathbf{Y}$ and $\mathbf{X}/\|\mathbf{X}\| \stackrel{d}{=} \mathbf{Y}/\|\mathbf{Y}\|$.
(2) X, Y, and Z are random variables, $X \stackrel{d}{=} Y$ can imply $X + Z \stackrel{d}{=} Y + Z$, if Z is independent of (X, Y).
(3) If $X + Z \stackrel{d}{=} Y + Z$, and Z is independent of (X, Y), it is not necessary for $X \stackrel{d}{=} Y$.
(4) If Z is independent of (X, Y), then
   a. $X \stackrel{d}{=} Y$ implies $XZ \stackrel{d}{=} YZ$;
   b. $XZ \stackrel{d}{=} YZ$ implies $X \stackrel{d}{=} Y$ under some conditions.
(5) $X \stackrel{d}{=} Y$ if and only if $X^+ \stackrel{d}{=} Y^+$ and $X^- \stackrel{d}{=} Y^-$.

Example 1. *The multivariate normal distribution, denoted by $\mathbf{X} \sim N_p(\boldsymbol{\mu}, \boldsymbol{\Sigma})$, has the following stochastic representation:*

$$\mathbf{X} \stackrel{d}{=} \boldsymbol{\mu} + \mathbf{A}^\top \mathbf{Z}, \tag{30}$$

where $\boldsymbol{\mu} = (\mu_1, \ldots, \mu_p)^\top, \mathbf{A}^\top \mathbf{A} = \boldsymbol{\Sigma}$, and $\mathbf{Z} = (Z_1, \ldots, Z_p)^\top$ with i.i.d. elements $Z_i \sim N(0,1)$. It is easy to find density function, moments, and marginal distributions of $\mathbf{Z}$ and then transfer these to $\mathbf{X}$. For example, from the density function of $\mathbf{Z}$, $\frac{1}{(\sqrt{2\pi})^p} e^{-\frac{1}{2}\mathbf{z}^\top \mathbf{z}}$, it is straightforward to find the density of $\mathbf{X}$ as

$$f(\boldsymbol{x}) = (2\pi)^{-p/2} |\boldsymbol{\Sigma}|^{-1/2} \exp\left\{ -\frac{1}{2} (\boldsymbol{x} - \boldsymbol{\mu})^\top (\boldsymbol{x} - \boldsymbol{\mu}) \right\}. \tag{31}$$

As the mean and covariance of $\mathbf{Z}$ are, respectively, $\mathbf{0}$ and $\boldsymbol{I}_p$, one can immediately find $E(\boldsymbol{X}) = \boldsymbol{\mu}$ and $Cov(\boldsymbol{X}) = \boldsymbol{\Sigma}$, respectively. It is also easy to find that all the marginal and affine transformations of $\boldsymbol{X}$ are normally distributed. For more detailed discussion and applications, see [68].

Many efforts to extend constructing methods from univariate to multivariate, for example, Pearson system, exponential family, and many others, can be found in [4].

4.4.2. Dirichlet Distribution

Let $X_1, ..., X_{m-1}$ and X_m be independent random variables, and $X_i \sim Gamma(\alpha_i)$, $i = 1, ..., m$. Set

$$Y = X_1 + \cdots + X_m, \ Y_j = \frac{X_j}{Y}, j = 1, ..., m.$$

The distribution of $\boldsymbol{Y} = (Y_1, ..., Y_m)^\top$ is called the Dirichlet distribution with parameters $\alpha_1, \ldots, \alpha_m$ and is written as $(Y_1, ..., Y_m) \sim D_m(\alpha_1, ..., \alpha_m)$.

The beta distribution $Be(\alpha, \beta)$ is a special case of Dirichlet distribution. As $Y_1 + \ldots + Y_m = 1$, the random vector $(Y_1, \ldots, Y_m)$ does not have a density on $\mathbb{R}^m$. However, the density of the first $m-1$ components (with respect to Lebesgue measure on the simplex) is given by

$$f(y_1, ..., y_{m-1}) = \frac{1}{B_m(\boldsymbol{\alpha})} \prod_{i=1}^{m} y_i^{\alpha_i - 1}, \ \sum_{i=1}^{m} y_i = 1 \ \ 0 \leq y_i \leq 1, i = 1, \ldots, m,$$

where $\boldsymbol{\alpha} = (\alpha_1, ..., \alpha_m)$ and

$$B_m(\alpha_1, ..., \alpha_m) = \frac{\Gamma(\alpha_1) \cdots \Gamma(\alpha_m)}{\Gamma(\alpha_1 + \cdots + \alpha_m)}.$$

Moreover, Y is independent of $\{Y_j, j = 1, \ldots, m-1\}$.

There is a fundamental relationship between the Dirichlet distribution and the uniform distribution on the unit sphere $S^p = \{\boldsymbol{x} : \boldsymbol{x}^\top \boldsymbol{x} = 1\}$ [68].

Theorem 2. *Suppose that $\boldsymbol{U} \sim U(S^p)$ in $\mathbb{R}^p$. Then $\boldsymbol{U}$ has a stochastic representation*

$$\boldsymbol{U} = \begin{bmatrix} \boldsymbol{U}_1 \\ \vdots \\ \boldsymbol{U}_m \end{bmatrix} \stackrel{d}{=} \begin{bmatrix} D_1 \boldsymbol{U}^{(1)} \\ \vdots \\ D_m \boldsymbol{U}^{(m)} \end{bmatrix}, \tag{32}$$

where $\boldsymbol{U}^{(j)} \in \mathbb{R}^{t_j}$, $t_1 + \cdots + t_m = p$, and

(i) $\boldsymbol{U}^{(j)} \sim U(S^{t_j})$, the uniform distribution on $S^{t_j}, j = 1, \cdots, m$;
(ii) $\boldsymbol{U}^{(1)}, \cdots, \boldsymbol{U}^{(m)}$ and $(D_1, \cdots, D_m)$ are mutually independent;
(iii) $D_j > 0, j = 1, \cdots, m$, and $(D_1^2, \cdots, D_m^2) \sim D_m(t_1/2, \cdots, t_m/2)$.

Based on the Dirichlet distribution, the *multivariate Liouville distribution* is defined on $\mathbb{R}_+^m$ by the stochastic representation $\mathbf{X} \stackrel{d}{=} R\mathbf{Y}$, where $R > 0$ is a random variable independent of $\mathbf{Y}$ and $\mathbf{Y} \sim D_m(\alpha_1, \ldots, \alpha_m)$. For a comprehensive study of the Liouville distribution, see Chapter 6 of [6].

4.4.3. Spherical and Elliptical Distributions

There are a number of equivalent ways to define the spherical distribution. Let $\boldsymbol{X}$ be a $p \times 1$ random vector. The following statements are equivalent [6]:

(i) $\boldsymbol{X} \stackrel{d}{=} \boldsymbol{P}\boldsymbol{X}$ for each $\boldsymbol{P} \in O(p)$, where $O(p)$ is the set of orthogonal matrices of order p;
(ii) The characteristic function (c.f.) of $\boldsymbol{X}$ is of the form $\psi(\boldsymbol{t}^\top \boldsymbol{t})$ for some $\psi \in \Psi_p$ where

$$\Psi_p = \{\psi(\cdot) : \psi(t_1^2 + \ldots + t_p^2) \text{ is a p-dimensional c.f.}\}; \tag{33}$$

(iii) $\boldsymbol{X}$ has a stochastic representation $\boldsymbol{X} \stackrel{d}{=} R\boldsymbol{U}^{(p)}$, where random variable $R \geq 0$ is independent of $\boldsymbol{U}^{(p)}$, $\boldsymbol{U}^{(p)}$ is uniformly distributed on the unit sphere S^p and does not have a density;

(iv) For any $\mathbf{a} \in S^p$ and $\mathbf{b} \in S^p$, we have $\mathbf{a}^\top \boldsymbol{X} \stackrel{d}{=} \mathbf{b}^\top \boldsymbol{X}$.

Theorem 3. *Let $\mathbf{X} \stackrel{d}{=} R\mathbf{U}^{(p)}$ and $P(\mathbf{X} = \mathbf{0}) = 0$. Then*

$$||\mathbf{X}|| \stackrel{d}{=} R, \;\; \mathbf{X}/||\mathbf{X}|| \stackrel{d}{=} \mathbf{U}^{(p)},$$

and they are independent.

Example 2. *The theorem has two immediate applications. First, it provides a method to generate a random sample from the uniform distribution on the sphere, $U(S^p)$: simply sample $\mathbf{X}$ from $N_p(\mathbf{0}, \boldsymbol{I}_p)$ and normalize it to obtain $\frac{\mathbf{X}}{||\mathbf{X}||}$. Second, it allows the mixed moments of $\boldsymbol{U}^{(p)}$ to be easily calculated from the known mixed moments of the standard normal vector $\mathbf{X}$ and the moments of its radius $R = ||\mathbf{X}||$. A detailed discussion can be found in Section 3.1.2 of [6].*

Theorem 4. *Let $\mathbf{X} \sim S_p(\psi)$ denote a spherically symmetric distribution in $\mathbb{R}^p$, characterized by its characteristic function $\psi(\boldsymbol{t}^\top \boldsymbol{t})$ as (33). It is not necessary that $\mathbf{X}$ has a density. The random vector $\mathbf{X} \stackrel{d}{=} R\boldsymbol{U}^{(p)}$ has a density which must be of the form $g(\boldsymbol{x}^\top \boldsymbol{x})$, if and only if the radial variable R has a density, denoted by $f(r)$. The relationship between g and f is given by*

$$f(r) = \frac{2\pi^{p/2}}{\Gamma(p/2)} r^{p-1} g(r^2),$$

where $g(\cdot)$ is called the density generator. We write $\mathbf{X} \sim S_p(g)$.

The necessary condition that $\mathbf{X} \sim S_p(\psi)$ has a density is

$$\int_0^\infty y^{p/2-1} g(y) dy < \infty$$

as

$$\int g(\boldsymbol{x}^\top \boldsymbol{x}) d\boldsymbol{x} = \frac{\pi^{p/2}}{\Gamma(p/2)} \int_0^\infty y^{p/2-1} g(y) dy = 1.$$

Table 7 gives many useful spherical distributions from [6].

Table 7. Some subclasses of p-dimensional spherical distributions.

Type	Density Function $g(\boldsymbol{x}^\top \boldsymbol{x})$ or c.f. $\psi(\boldsymbol{t}^\top \boldsymbol{t})$
Multinormal	$g(\boldsymbol{x}^\top \boldsymbol{x}) = c \exp(-\frac{1}{2}\boldsymbol{x}^\top \boldsymbol{x})$
Kotz-type	$g(\boldsymbol{x}^\top \boldsymbol{x}) = c(\boldsymbol{x}^\top \boldsymbol{x})^{N-1} \exp[-r(\boldsymbol{x}^\top \boldsymbol{x})^s]$, $r, s > 0$, $2N + p > 2$
Pearson type VII	$g(\boldsymbol{x}^\top \boldsymbol{x}) = c(1 + \boldsymbol{x}^\top \boldsymbol{x}/s)^{-N}$, $N > p/2, s > 0$
Multivariate t	$g(\boldsymbol{x}^\top \boldsymbol{x}) = c(1 + \boldsymbol{x}^\top \boldsymbol{x}/v)^{-(p+v)/2}$, $v > 0$
Multivariate Cauchy	$g(\boldsymbol{x}^\top \boldsymbol{x}) = c(1 + \boldsymbol{x}^\top \boldsymbol{x})^{-(p+1)/2}$
Pearson Type II	$g(\boldsymbol{x}^\top \boldsymbol{x}) = c(1 - \boldsymbol{x}^\top \boldsymbol{x})^q$, $q > 0$ for $\boldsymbol{x}^\top \boldsymbol{x} < 1$
Logistics	$g(\boldsymbol{x}^\top \boldsymbol{x}) = c \exp(-\boldsymbol{x}^\top \boldsymbol{x})/[1 + \exp(-\boldsymbol{x}^\top \boldsymbol{x})]^2$
Scale mixture	$g(\boldsymbol{x}^\top \boldsymbol{x}) = c \int_0^\infty t^{-p/2} \exp(-\boldsymbol{x}^\top \boldsymbol{x}/2t) dG(t), G(t)$ a cdf.

Elliptical Distribution

A random vector $\mathbf{X}$ has an elliptical distribution, denoted as $\mathbf{X} \sim EC_p(\boldsymbol{\mu}, \boldsymbol{\Sigma})$, with parameters $\boldsymbol{\mu}$ and $\boldsymbol{\Sigma} = \mathbf{A}^\top \mathbf{A}$, if it can be expressed as

$$\mathbf{X} \stackrel{d}{=} \boldsymbol{\mu} + \mathbf{A}^\top \mathbf{Y} \stackrel{d}{=} \boldsymbol{\mu} + R\mathbf{A}^\top \mathbf{U}^{(p)}, \tag{34}$$

where $\mathbf{Y} \sim S_p(\psi)$ is spherical. This relationship generalizes the way a normal variable $X \sim N(\mu, \sigma^2)$ is constructed from a standard normal $Z \sim N(0,1)$. Consequently, any subclass of spherical distributions in Table 7 defines a corresponding subclass of elliptical distributions.

4.4.4. Approximation to Multivariate Continuous Distributions by Representative Points

For multivariate continuous distributions, the QMC-RPs and MSE-RPs can be defined in a similar way to the univariate case.Suppose that a random vector $\boldsymbol{X} \sim F(\cdot)$ in $\mathbb{R}^n$ has a density function $f(\cdot)$ with a finite mean vector and covariance matrix. A set of points $\Xi = \{\xi_j, j = 1, \cdots, k\}$ is called mean squared error representative points if it minimizes the mean squared error, $\text{MSE}(\Xi) = \int_{\mathbb{R}^n} \min_{j=1,\cdots,k} \|x - \xi_j\|^2 f(x)\, dx$, where $\|\cdot\|$ denotes the L^2-norm. For information regarding the construction of approximation distributions of a continuous multivariate distribution by their QMC-RPs, one can refer to [8,69,70]. For information regarding the construction of approximation distributions of a continuous multivariate distribution by their MSE-RPs, one can refer to [8,70–73]. Due to the complexity of computation in high-dimensional multivariate distribution, the related research works about MSE-RPs of this kind of distribution are limited. Representative points also have many applications for discrete data, especially for discrete massive data. In Chapter 9 of [8], some cases where the sample size is hugely larger than the number of variables have been considered, and some model-based and model-free subsampling methods are included.

4.5. *Basic Statistics Under the Multivariate Population*

Let $\boldsymbol{X}$ follow a multivariate continuous distribution $F(x;\boldsymbol{\theta})$ where $\boldsymbol{\theta}$ represents parameters. A random sample $x_1, \ldots, x_n$ is drawn from this population. The distributions of basic statistics, such as the mean vector, the covariance matrix, and various test statistics, are fundamental to statistical inference and its applications. For example, when the population distribution is multivariate normal, $N_p(\boldsymbol{\mu}, \boldsymbol{\Sigma})$, the standard unbiased estimators for $\boldsymbol{\mu}$ and $\boldsymbol{\Sigma}$ are sample mean and the sample covariance, given, respectively, by

$$\hat{\boldsymbol{\mu}} = \bar{x} = \frac{1}{n}\sum_{i=1}^{n} x_i, \mathbf{S} = \frac{1}{n-1}\sum_{i=1}^{n}(x_i - \bar{x})^\top (x_i - \bar{x}). \tag{35}$$

It is known that $\bar{x} \sim N_p(\boldsymbol{\mu}, \frac{1}{n-1}\boldsymbol{\Sigma})$. Other key related distributions are described below.

Wishart distribution: The Wishart distribution, denoted by $W_p(n, \boldsymbol{\Sigma})$, is the multivariate generalization of the chi-square distribution. It is defined by $W = \sum_{i=1}^{n} \mathbf{Z}_i \mathbf{Z}_i^\top$ and $\mathbf{Z}_i \sim N_p(\mathbf{0}, \boldsymbol{\Sigma})$ are *i.i.d*. The sample covariance matrix $\mathbf{S}$ follows Wishart distribution: $(n-1)\mathbf{S} \sim W_p(n-1, \boldsymbol{\Sigma})$. This distribution was developed by John Wishart [74], who, in his seminal 1928 paper "The Generalised Product Moment Distribution in samples from a normal multivariate population", published in Biometrika, derived the distribution of the matrix of sums of squares and cross-products. A crucial result for normally distributed data is that the sample mean $\bar{x}$ and the sample covariance matrix $\mathbf{S}$ are independent, generalizing the corresponding univariate property.

Distributions of the eigenvalues of $\mathbf{S}$: Unlike the sample covariance matrix itself, the distributions of its individual eigenvalues are complex and do not follow simple, universal forms like the normal or Wishart distributions.

Hotelling's T-squared distribution: It is the multivariate generalization of the Student's t-distribution, used primarily for hypothesis testing on the mean vector. For a random vector $\boldsymbol{X} \sim N_p(\boldsymbol{\mu}, \boldsymbol{\Sigma})$ independent of $\mathbf{S} \sim W_p(n, \boldsymbol{\Sigma})$, the Hotelling's T^2 statistic is denoted as

$$T^2 = n\boldsymbol{X}^\top \mathbf{S}^{-1}\boldsymbol{X}. \tag{36}$$

The resulting T^2 statistic, despite being derived from multivariate data, is a scalar. Therefore, its sampling distribution, denoted by $T^2(p, n, \boldsymbol{\mu})$, is a univariate distribution. When $\boldsymbol{\mu} = \mathbf{0}$, the distribution is central and denoted by $T^2(p, n)$. The T^2 statistic is related to the F-distribution through the following identity: $\frac{n-p+1}{np}T^2(p, n) \sim F(p, n-p+1)$.

Wilks' lambda distribution: This distribution generalizes the beta distribution and is used in multivariate analysis of variance and likelihood ratio tests. Let $A_1 \sim W_p(m, \boldsymbol{\Sigma})$ and $A_2 \sim W_p(n, \boldsymbol{\Sigma})$ be independent. The Wilks' lambda statistic, defined as $\Lambda = \frac{A_2}{A_1+A_2}$, is a scalar. Thus, its sampling distribution, denoted by $\Lambda(p, m, n)$, is a univariate distribution. Wilks' lambda has close relationships with the T^2 distribution and simplifies to an F or beta distribution when $p = 1$.

When the population $\mathbf{X}$ follows an elliptical distribution (a broader class than the normal), deriving the distributions of the aforementioned statistics becomes significantly more challenging. A comprehensive discussion of this topic can be found in [68].

Multivariate L_1-Norm Symmetric Distribution

The elliptical distribution can be regarded as an extension of the multivariate normal distribution. Similarly, the exponential distribution can be generalized to a multivariate setting. Let $X_1, \ldots, X_p$ be *i.i.d.* random variables from the standard exponential distribution, $Exp(1)$ (see Table 4). Consider the random vector $\boldsymbol{X} = (X_1, \ldots, X_p)^\top$ and its L_1-norm defined by $||\mathbf{X}||_1 = |X_1| + \ldots + |X_p|$. Let $\mathbf{U} = \frac{\mathbf{X}}{||\mathbf{X}||_1}$. Fang and Fang [75] defined a class of multivariate distributions via the following stochastic representation:

$$\mathbf{X} \stackrel{d}{=} R\mathbf{U}, \tag{37}$$

where the radial variable R is independent of the directional vector $\mathbf{U}$. This class of distributions was studied systematically in [75,76] and in Chapter 5 of [6].

4.6. Definition by Distribution, Density or Survival Functions

4.6.1. Meta-Skew Symmetric Distributions

A traditional approach to defining a probability distribution is through its distribution function, density function, or survival function. For instance, the multivariate normal distribution in Anderson's book [77] is defined by its density function. A general univariate form of an asymmetric distribution, known as the skew-symmetric family, can be represented as a function that combines a cumulative distribution function and a probability density function; see [78,79].

Definition 2. *A random variable X, whose density function has the form*

$$p(x) = 2f(x)G(w(x)), \tag{38}$$

is called skew symmetric, where $f(x)$ is a density function centrally symmetric about 0, $w(x)$ is an odd real-valued function such that $w(-x) = -w(x)$, and $G(w(\cdot))$ is a cumulative distribution function on $\mathbb{R}$ such that $g = G'$ is an even density function, providing G is differentiable.

4.6.2. Skew-Normal Distribution

The multivariate skew-normal (MSN) distribution, introduced in Table 3, is a fundamental and powerful generalization of both the multivariate normal and the univariate skew-normal distributions. It provides a flexible framework for modeling multivariate data that exhibits asymmetry (skewness).

A p-dimensional random vector $\boldsymbol{Y}$ follows a multivariate skew-normal distribution with location vector $\boldsymbol{\mu}$, positive definite scale matrix $\boldsymbol{\Sigma}$, and skewness vector $\boldsymbol{\alpha}$ if its probability density function is given by

$$f(\boldsymbol{y};\boldsymbol{\mu},\boldsymbol{\Sigma},\boldsymbol{\alpha}) = 2\phi_p(\boldsymbol{y}-\boldsymbol{\mu};\boldsymbol{\Sigma})\Phi(\boldsymbol{\alpha}^\top\boldsymbol{\omega}^{-1}(\boldsymbol{y}-\boldsymbol{\mu})),$$

where $\phi_p(\boldsymbol{z};\boldsymbol{\Sigma})$ is the pdf of p-variate normal distribution with mean $\mathbf{0}$ and covariance matrix $\boldsymbol{\Sigma}$; $\Phi(\cdot)$ is the cdf of $N(0,1)$; $\boldsymbol{\omega}$ is the diagonal matrix formed from the standard deviations of $\boldsymbol{\Sigma}$ (the square roots of the diagonal elements), and the vector $\boldsymbol{\alpha}$ is the shape or skewness parameter vector. It denotes $\boldsymbol{Y} \sim SN_p(\boldsymbol{\mu},\boldsymbol{\Sigma},\boldsymbol{\alpha})$.

The MSN distribution admits an intuitive stochastic representation. Consider a $(p+1)$-dimensional normal random vector $(X_0, \boldsymbol{X}_1^\top)^\top$,

$$\begin{bmatrix} X_0 \\ \boldsymbol{X}_1 \end{bmatrix} \sim N_{1+p}\left[\begin{pmatrix} 0 \\ \mathbf{0} \end{pmatrix}, \begin{pmatrix} 1 & \boldsymbol{\delta}^\top \\ \boldsymbol{\delta} & \boldsymbol{\Sigma} \end{pmatrix}\right]. \quad (39)$$

Here, X_0 is a scalar and $\boldsymbol{X}_1$ is a p-vector. The vector $\boldsymbol{\delta}$ controls the correlation between X_0 and each component of $\boldsymbol{X}_1$. Then

$$Y \stackrel{d}{=} \boldsymbol{\mu} + \boldsymbol{\omega}(\boldsymbol{X}_1 | X_0 > 0) \sim SN_p(\boldsymbol{\mu},\boldsymbol{\Sigma},\boldsymbol{\alpha}),$$

where the skewness parameter $\boldsymbol{\alpha}$ relates to $\boldsymbol{\delta}$ through the following equation:

$$\boldsymbol{\alpha} = \frac{1}{\sqrt{1-\boldsymbol{\delta}^\top\boldsymbol{\Sigma}^{-1}\boldsymbol{\delta}}}\boldsymbol{\Sigma}^{-1}\boldsymbol{\delta}.$$

For comprehensive details on the theory and applications of the multivariate skew-normal distribution, see [80,81].

4.6.3. Skew-Elliptical Distributions

Skew-elliptical distributions form a broad family that generalizes symmetric elliptical distributions by introducing skewness (asymmetry). This extension moves beyond the familiar world of symmetric, bell-shaped curves into the asymmetric realm, providing a principled and mathematically sound framework for modeling a wider range of real-world data patterns. Among these, the skew-t distribution is often a particularly useful starting point for applied work due to its flexibility in handling both skewness and heavy tails.

The general form of the pdf for a skew-elliptical distribution is

$$f(\boldsymbol{z}) = 2f_0(\boldsymbol{z})\Pi(\boldsymbol{z}), \quad (40)$$

where $f_0(\boldsymbol{z})$ is the pdf of a symmetric elliptical distribution (the "parent"), and $\Pi(\boldsymbol{z})$ is a skewing function that maps onto the interval [0, 1] and satisfies $\Pi(\boldsymbol{z}) + \Pi(-\boldsymbol{z}) = 1$. This function controls the direction and amount of skewness. The skew-elliptical family is vast, but several members are particularly important: skew-normal, skew-t, skew-Cauchy, and skew-Laplace distributions. The skew-elliptical distributions are used anywhere that data deviates from symmetry and normality, such as in finance, environmental science, biology, psychometrics, and social sciences. For a comprehensive study, refer to [82].

4.6.4. Definition by Survival Function

The survival function of a random variable $X \sim F(x)$ is defined as $\bar{F}(x) = P(X > x)$. This function is particularly useful in the analysis of biometrical data. Within this domain, the exponential and Weibull distributions play an important role.

A foundational model for dependent failures is the Marshall–Olkin multivariate exponential distribution [83]. Its strength lies in an intuitive shock-based construction and analytical tractability. The model assumes that shocks to the system components arrive according to three independent Poisson processes with rates λ_1, λ_2, and λ_{12}, corresponding to shocks that fatally affect only component 1, only component 2, or both components simultaneously. The arrival times of these shocks, Z_1, Z_2, and Z_{12}, are, therefore, independent exponential random variables with parameters λ_1, λ_2, and λ_{12}, respectively.

We set $X = \min\{Z_1, Z_{12}\}$ and $Y = \min\{Z_2, Z_{12}\}$. The joint survival function of the random vector (X, Y) is defined as $\bar{H}(x, y) = P(X > x, Y > y)$. For any $x, y \geq 0$ the survival function is given by

$$\begin{aligned} \bar{H}(x,y) &= P(Z_1 > x)P(Z_2 > y)P(Z_{12} > \max(x,y)) \\ &= \exp[-\lambda_1 x - \lambda_2 y - \lambda_{12}\max(x,y)]. \end{aligned}$$

Its marginal survival functions are

$$\bar{F}(x) = \exp(-(\lambda_1 + \lambda_{12})x), \text{and } \bar{G}(y) = \exp(-(\lambda_2 + \lambda_{12})y).$$

Hence, X and Y are exponential random variables with parameters $\lambda_1 + \lambda_{12}$ and $\lambda_2 + \lambda_{12}$, respectively. This elegant construction can be extended to higher dimensions.

4.7. *Meta-Distributions via Copula Techniques*

Various statistical distributions play a key role in modeling real-world data. The rapid development of data science has increased the demand for a wider variety of multivariate distributions. A common challenge is to construct a multivariate distribution from given one-dimensional marginal distributions while incorporating a known dependence structure. Such constructions arise not only from statistical theory but also from practical problems, particularly in risk and decision analysis for complex multivariate systems. The copula is a powerful technique designed for this purpose.

Copulas are mathematical functions that fully capture the dependence structure among random variables, offering great flexibility in building multivariate stochastic models. Since their introduction in the 1950s, copulas have gained significant popularity in several applied fields such as finance, insurance, and reliability theory. Nowadays, they are a well-recognized tool for market and credit modeling, risk aggregation, portfolio selection, and more.

The following definition is based on probability theory. For a more general treatment, see [66,84]. As most research works and applications are interested in the copulas with respect to continuous distributions, and it becomes complicated for discrete distributions, this section only covers the continuous case.

Definition 3. *If $C(z_1, \ldots, z_p)$ is the cumulative distribution function on the unit hypercube $[0,1]^p$ with uniform $U(0,1)$ margins, then C is called a copula.*

The following Lemma demonstrates the existence of the copula function.

Lemma 1. *Let $H(x_1, \ldots, x_p)$ be a continuous distribution with p continuous margins F_i on the domain D_i for $i = 1, \ldots, p$. Then there exists a unique copula C such that*

$$C(z_1, \ldots, z_p) = H(F_1^{-1}(z_1), \ldots, F_p^{-1}(z_p)). \tag{41}$$

It is well known that for a given set of p marginal distributions $F_i(x_i)_{i=1}^p$, there exist infinitely many p-dimensional distributions with these margins. If the dependence structure of the joint distribution is known, one may find a unique or a small family of such joint distributions $H(x_1, \ldots, x_p)$. The copula technique is a fundamental tool for this purpose.

Suppose we have p random variables $X_i \sim F_i(x_i)$ for $i = 1, \ldots, p$, and we wish to construct a multivariate distribution H with these margins and a given dependence structure defined by a copula $C(z_1, \ldots, z_p)$. This method is called the copula technique. The resulting distribution is termed a *meta-distribution* and is denoted by $F(C; F_1, \ldots, F_p)$.

Theorem 5. *Sklar's Theorem (Multivariate Case) Let $\mathbf{X}$ be a continuous random vector with joint distribution $H(x_1, \ldots, x_p)$ and continuous marginal distributions F_i on domains D_i for $i = 1, \ldots, p$. Then there exists a unique copula C such that*

$$H(x_1, \ldots, x_p) = C(F_1(x_1), \ldots, F_p(x_p)). \tag{42}$$

Conversely, if C is a copula and $F_1, \ldots, F_p$ are univariate distribution functions, then the function H defined by (42) is a p-dimensional distribution function with margins $F_1, \ldots, F_p$.

If the margins F_i are continuous, then C is unique. The joint density function of $\mathbf{X}$ derived from (42) is given by

$$h(x_1, \ldots, x_p) = c(F_1(x_1), \ldots, F_p(x_p)) \prod_{i=1}^{p} f_i(x_i), \tag{43}$$

where f_i is the probability density function of X_i, and $c(\cdot)$ is the copula density, i.e., the p-th mixed partial derivative of C.

4.7.1. Some Examples of Copula

Many copula examples exist for lower dimensions. This subsection presents selected examples from Nelsen [66] to provide a tutorial for beginners to comprehend the ideas of copula. Examples 3 and 4 have different joint distributions but have the same copula.

Example 3. *Adapted from Nelsen [66]*

Consider the joint distribution

$$H(x, y) = \frac{(x+1)(e^y - 1)}{x + 2e^y - 1}, \; (x, y) \in [-1, 1] \times [0, \infty).$$

Its marginal distributions are $X \sim U(-1, 1)$ with cdf $F(x) = \frac{x+1}{2}$ and $Y \sim Exp(1)$, the standard exponential distribution with cdf $G(y) = 1 - e^{-y}$, and copula

$$C(u, v) = \frac{uv}{u + v - uv}.$$

We now demonstrate how to derive the copula C from H, and, conversely, how to reconstruct H from C, F, G.

Deriving C from H:

Let $u = F(x)$ and $v = G(y)$, which implies $u = \frac{x+1}{2}$ and $v = 1 - e^{-y}$ or $e^y = \frac{1}{1-v}$.

$$\begin{aligned} C(u,v) &= H(F^{-1}(u), G^{-1}(v)) = \frac{(F^{-1}(u)+1)(e^{G^{-1}(v)}-1)}{F^{-1}(u)+2e^{G^{-1}(v)}-1} \\ &= \frac{[(2u-1)+1][e^{-\ln(1-v)}-1]}{2u-1+2e^{-\ln(1-v)}-1} \\ &= \frac{2u(\frac{1}{1-v}-1)}{2u-1+2\frac{1}{1-v}-1} = \frac{2u[1-(1-v)]}{(2u-1)(1-v)+2-(1-v)} \\ &= \frac{uv}{u+v-uv}. \end{aligned}$$

Deriving H from $\{C, F, G\}$:

Note that $e^y = \frac{1}{1-v}$; we have

$$\begin{aligned} H(x,y) &= C(u,v) \\ &= \frac{\frac{x+1}{2}(1-e^{-y})}{\frac{x+1}{2}+1-e^{-y}-\frac{x+1}{2}(1-e^{-y})} \\ &= \frac{(x+1)(1-e^{-y})}{x+1+2(1-e^{-y})-(x+1)(1-e^{-y})} \\ &= \frac{(x+1)(e^y-1)}{(x+1)+2e^y-2} = \frac{(x+1)(e^y-1)}{x+2e^y-1}. \end{aligned}$$

Example 4. *Gumbel's bivariate logistic distribution [85].*

$$H(x,y) = (1+e^{-x}+e^{-y})^{-1}, x, y \geq 0.$$

Its two margins are

$$F(x) = (1+e^{-x})^{-1},\ G(y) = (1+e^{-y})^{-1}.$$

Its copula is

$$C(u,v) = \frac{uv}{u+v-uv},$$

which is identical to the copula in Example 3, despite the marginal distributions being quite different.

For multivariate copulas, higher-dimensional margins are defined as per the following example.

Example 5. *Consider the following three-dimensional distribution H:*

$$H(x,y,z) = \frac{(x+1)(e^z-1)\sin(z)}{x+2e^y-1}, \quad on\ [-1,1]\times[0,\infty]\times[0,\frac{\pi}{2}].$$

Its three one-dimensional marginal distributions are

$$H_1(x) = \frac{x+1}{2}, H_2(y) = 1-e^{-y}, H_3(z) = \sin(z).$$

The three two-dimensional marginal distributions are

$$\begin{aligned} H_{12}(x,y) &= \frac{(x+1)(e^y-1)}{x+2e^y-1}, \\ H_{23}(y,z) &= (1-e^{-y})\sin(z), \\ H_{13}(x,z) &= \frac{1}{2}(x+1)\sin(z). \end{aligned}$$

Example 6. *Fang et al. [86] provided a comprehensive study of the copula defined for $\alpha > 0$ and $\beta \in [0,1]$:*

$$C(u,v;\alpha,\beta) = \frac{uv}{[1-\beta(1-u^{1/\alpha})(1-v^{1/\alpha})]^{\alpha}}. \tag{44}$$

For different values of α and β, we have the following:

1. $\beta = 0$; *U and V are independent.*
2. $\beta = 1$; *it reduces to the bivariate Clayton distribution [87].*
3. $\alpha = 1$; *it reduces to the Ali–Mikhail–Haq copula [88].*

Its multivariate version is given by

$$C(u_1,\ldots,u_n;\alpha,\beta) = \frac{\prod_{i=1}^n u_i}{[1-\beta\prod_{i=1}^n(1-u_i^{1/\alpha})]^{\alpha}}. \tag{45}$$

These examples demonstrate that the copula technique provides a powerful method for constructing numerous new distributions useful for statistical modeling.

4.7.2. Gaussian Copula and Meta-Gaussian Distribution

When $H(\cdot)$ is a multivariate normal distribution, the associated copula is called a Gaussian copula. When $H(\cdot)$ is an elliptical distribution, the corresponding copula is known as an elliptical copula. This family includes the Gaussian copula, the t-copula, and the Kotz-type copula, among others; for a comprehensive overview, see [89].

From the definition of a copula, the Gaussian copula for $N_p(\boldsymbol{\mu}, \boldsymbol{\Sigma})$ is identical to that of $\mathbf{Z} = (Z_1,\ldots,Z_p) \sim N_p(\mathbf{0}, \boldsymbol{R})$, where $\boldsymbol{R}$ is the correlation matrix of $\mathbf{Z}$. Clearly, all marginal distributions of $\mathbf{Z}$ are standard normal $N(0,1)$, yet its components have correlation matrix $\boldsymbol{R} = (r_{ij})$. Denote the cdf of $\mathbf{Z}$ by $G_{\text{normal}}(z_1,\ldots,z_p \mid \boldsymbol{R})$ and define a function C as follows:

$$C_{normal}(u_1,\ldots,u_p) = G_{normal}(\Phi^{-1}(u_1),\ldots,\Phi^{-1}(u_p)),\ (u_1,\ldots,u_p)^\top \in [0,1]^p, \tag{46}$$

where $\Phi(\cdot)$ is the cdf of $N(0,1)$. This function C is the Gaussian copula. Kelly and Krzysztofowicz [90] studied the meta-Gaussian (or meta-normal) distribution. A more detailed analysis can be found in Section 2.6, "Multivariate Gaussian/Normal", of [91].

Definition 4. *The meta-Gaussian or meta-normal distribution with a set of given marginal cdfs $F_1,\ldots,F_p$ is defined by its cdf*

$$F_{X_1,\ldots,X_p}(x_1,\ldots,x_p) = G_{Z_1,\ldots,Z_p}(\Phi^{-1}(F_1(x_1)),\ldots,\Phi^{-1}(F_p(x_p))). \tag{47}$$

We denote this distribution as $\boldsymbol{X} \sim MN_p(\mathbf{0}, \boldsymbol{R}; F_1,\ldots,F_p)$.

The pdf of $MN_p(\mathbf{0}, \boldsymbol{R}; F_1,\ldots,F_p)$ is

$$h(x_1,\ldots,x_p) = c_{normal}(F_1(x_1),\ldots,F_p(x_p))\prod_{i=1}^p f_i(x_i),$$

where c_{normal} is the density of the Gaussian copula and f_i is the pdf corresponding to F_i. In the case where the correlation matrix has all off-diagonal elements equal to ρ, Bouy'e [92] provided illustrative plots for various values of ρ.

Let $\boldsymbol{X} \sim MN_2(\boldsymbol{0}, \boldsymbol{R}; F_1, F_2)$, where the correlation matrix with $\mathrm{Corr}(X_1, X_2) = \rho$. Then the normal copula is given by

$$C_{normal}(u,v) = \frac{1}{2\pi\sqrt{1-\rho^2}} \int_{-\infty}^{\Phi^{-1}(u)} \int_{-\infty}^{\Phi^{-1}(v)} \exp\left\{-\frac{s^2 - 2\rho st + t^2}{2(1-\rho^2)}\right\} dsdt,$$

where $0 \leq u, v \leq 1$.

The correlation coefficient has been used in multivariate analysis for a long time. However, the copula and its related meta-distributions might have different correlation coefficients due to different marginal distributions. Therefore, the so-called "measure of concordance" is considered in the literature. It requests that the copula and its meta-distributions have the same values of the measure of concordance. The Kendall's τ and the Spearman's *rho* are the most popular ones used in the applications. Their definitions can refer to [66]. Spearman's ρ for the binormal copula is given by $\frac{6}{\pi}\arcsin\left(\frac{\rho}{2}\right)$ (see [93]). This result does not extend to other elliptical distributions, which are introduced in the next section.

The meta-normal distribution $\boldsymbol{X} \sim MN_2(\boldsymbol{0}, \boldsymbol{R}; F_1, F_2)$ is given by

$$\begin{aligned} F(x_1, x_2) &= C_{normal}(F_1(x_1), F_2(x_2)) \qquad (48) \\ &= \frac{1}{2\pi\sqrt{1-\rho^2}} \int_{-\infty}^{\Phi^{-1}(F_1(x_1))} \int_{-\infty}^{\Phi^{-1}(F_2(x_2))} \exp\left\{-\frac{s^2 - 2\rho st + t^2}{2(1-\rho^2)}\right\} dsdt. \end{aligned}$$

Mai and Scherer [94], in Example 1.7, discussed the Gaussian copula and meta-Gaussian distributions for the general case $\boldsymbol{X} \sim N_p(\boldsymbol{\mu}, \boldsymbol{\Sigma})$. In this case, the marginal distributions of X_i $(i = 1, \ldots, p)$ are not necessarily identical if the variances $\mathrm{Var}(X_i)$ differ. Now, consider the two-dimensional normal distribution $N_2(\boldsymbol{0}, \boldsymbol{R})$ with correlation matrix $\boldsymbol{R}$ and correlation coefficient ρ. Let $\xi_i = \Phi^{-1}(u_i)$ for $i = 1, 2$. The density of the Gaussian copula, as given in Chapter 7 of [95], is

$$c_{normal}(\xi) = c_{normal}(\xi_1, \xi_2) = |\boldsymbol{R}|^{-1/2} \exp\left(-\frac{1}{2}\xi^\top (\boldsymbol{R}^{-1} - \boldsymbol{I})\xi\right). \qquad (49)$$

This expression can be factorized into two independent components

$$c_{normal}(\xi) = \frac{1}{2\pi\sqrt{1-\rho^2}} \exp\left(-\frac{1}{2}\xi^\top \boldsymbol{R}^{-1}\xi\right) [2\pi \cdot \exp(\frac{1}{2}(\xi_1^2 + \xi_2^2)].$$

The first factor is the density of $N_2(\boldsymbol{0}, \boldsymbol{R})$, while the second factor is the product of the densities of two independent standard normal variables (up to a constant),

$$\sqrt{2\pi}\exp(\tfrac{1}{2}\xi_1^2) \text{ and } \sqrt{2\pi}\exp(\tfrac{1}{2}\xi_2^2).$$

Recently, He et al. [96] derived the covariance matrix of the Gaussian copula and related properties.

4.7.3. Marshall–Olkin Copula

The Marshall–Olkin multivariate exponential distribution was introduced in Section 4.6.4. We now derive its corresponding survival copula, denoted by $\hat{C}_{MO}(u, v)$. We begin by expressing the joint survival function $\bar{H}(x, y)$ in terms of the marginal survival functions $u = \bar{F}(x)$ and $v = \bar{G}(y)$, recalling the relationship $\bar{H}(x, y) = \hat{C}(\bar{F}(x), \bar{G}(y))$, where $\hat{C}$ is the survival copula. Using the identity $\max(x,y) = x + y - \min(x,y)$, we can rewrite the survival function as follows:

$$\begin{aligned}\bar{H}(x,y) &= \hat{C}(\bar{F}(x),\bar{G}(y)) \\ &= \exp[-(\lambda_1+\lambda_{12})x - (\lambda_2+\lambda_{12})y + \lambda_{12}\min(x,y)] \\ &= \bar{F}(x)\bar{G}(y)\min\{\exp(\lambda_{12}x),\exp(\lambda_{12}y)\}.\end{aligned}$$

As $u^{\frac{-\lambda_{12}}{\lambda_1+\lambda_{12}}} = exp(\lambda_{12}x)$ and $v^{\frac{-\lambda_{12}}{\lambda_2+\lambda_{12}}} = exp(\lambda_{12}y)$, let $\alpha = \frac{\lambda_{12}}{\lambda_1+\lambda_{12}}$ and $\beta = \frac{\lambda_{12}}{\lambda_2+\lambda_{12}}$. Obviously, $0 < \alpha, \beta < 1$, and let

$$\begin{aligned} u &= \bar{F}(x) = e^{-(\lambda_1+\lambda_{12})x} = e^{-\lambda_{12}x/\alpha},\ u^{-\alpha} = e^{\lambda_{12}x}, \\ v &= \bar{G}(y) = e^{-(\lambda_2+\lambda_{12})y} = e^{-\lambda_{12}y/\beta},\ v^{-\beta} = e^{\lambda_{12}y}.\end{aligned}$$

The survival copula for the Marshall–Olkin distribution, known as the Marshall–Olkin copula, is given by

$$\begin{aligned}\hat{C}_{MO}(u,v) &= uv\min\left\{u^{\frac{-\lambda_{12}}{\lambda_1+\lambda_{12}}}, v^{\frac{-\lambda_{12}}{\lambda_2+\lambda_{12}}}\right\} = \min\left\{vu^{1-\frac{\lambda_{12}}{\lambda_1+\lambda_{12}}}, uv^{1-\frac{\lambda_{12}}{\lambda_2+\lambda_{12}}}\right\} \\ &= uv\min(u^{-\alpha},v^{-\beta}) = \min(u^{1-\alpha}v, uv^{1-\beta}). \end{aligned} \tag{50}$$

Therefore, the survival copula for the Marshall–Olkin bivariate exponential distribution forms a two-parameter family of copulas given by

$$C_{\alpha,\beta}(u,v) = \begin{cases} u^{1-\alpha}v, & \text{if } u^\alpha \ge v^\beta, \\ uv^{1-\beta}, & \text{if } u^\alpha \le v^\beta. \end{cases} \tag{51}$$

The application of copulas and meta-distributions is a cornerstone of modern quantitative finance, risk management, and many other fields that deal with multivariate dependence. They provide a powerful toolkit for modeling complex relationships beyond simple correlation.

5. Conclusions

The development of statistical distributions, driven by the need to model real data, is a cornerstone of statistical science. With a vast and well-established body of literature, a complete review of construction methods is beyond our scope. This article, instead, focuses on recent advancements in the field, particularly in simulation techniques and computational algorithms. Our aim is to offer readers an expanded perspective on the evolving landscape of statistical distributions.

Author Contributions: Conceptualization, investigation, writing—original draft preparation, resources, supervision, project administration: K.-T.F.; writing—review and editing, visualization: Y.-X.L.; writing—review and editing, funding acquisition: Y.-H.D. All authors have read and agreed to the published version of the manuscript.

Funding: Our work was supported in part by the Guangdong Provincial Key Laboratory of IRADS (grant number 2022B1212010006), in part by National Natural Science Foundation of China (Key Program) (grant number 12231004), and in part by BNBU Research (grant number UICR0600048) at Beijing Normal-Hong Kong Baptist University, Zhuhai, PR China.

Conflicts of Interest: The authors declare no conflicts of interest. The funders had no role in the design of the study; in the collection, analyses, or interpretation of data; in the writing of the manuscript; or in the decision to publish the results.

References

1. Johnson, N.L.; Kotz, S.; Balakrishnan, N. *Continuous Univariate Distributions*, 2nd ed.; John Wiley & Sons: New York, NY, USA, 1994; Volume 1.
2. Johnson, N.L.; Kotz, S.; Balakrishnan, N. *Continuous Univariate Distributions*, 2nd ed.; John Wiley & Sons: New York, NY, USA, 1995; Volume 2.
3. Johnson, N.L.; Kotz, S.; Balakrishnan, N. *Discrete Multivariate Distributions*; John Wiley & Sons: New York, NY, USA, 1997.
4. Kotz, S.; Balakrishnan, N.; Johnson, N.L. *Continuous Multivariate Distributions, Volume 1: Models and Applications*, 2nd ed.; John Wiley & Sons: New York, NY, USA, 2000.
5. Fang, K.T.; Xu, J.L. *Statistical Distribution*; China Higher Education Press: Beijing, China, 2016.
6. Fang, K.T.; Kotz, S.; Ng, K.W. *Symmetric Multivariate and Related Distributions*; Chapman and Hall: London, UK, 1990.
7. Johnson, M.E. *Multivariate Statistical Simulation*; John Wiley & Sons: New York, NY, USA, 1987.
8. Fang, K.T.; Ye, H.; Zhou, Y. *Representative Points of Statistical Distributions and Their Applications in Statistical Inference*; CRC Press: Boca Raton, FL, USA, 2025.
9. Lehmann, E.L.; Casella, G. *Theory of Point Estimation*, 2nd ed.; Springer: New York, NY, USA, 1998.
10. Bickel, P.J.; Doksum, K.A. *Mathematical Statistics: Basic Ideas and Selected Topics*, 2nd ed.; Chapman and Hall/CRC: New York, NY, USA, 2015; Volume 1.
11. Pearson, K.X. Contributions to the mathematical theory of evolution—II. Skew variation in homogeneous material. *Philos. Trans. R. Soc. Lond. A* **1895**, *186*, 343–414.
12. Elderton, W.P.; Johnson, N.L. *Systems of Frequency Curves*; Cambridge University Press: Cambridge, UK, 1969.
13. Hogg, R.V.; McKean, J.W.; Craig, A.T. *Introduction to Mathematical Statistics*, 6th ed.; Prentice Hall: Upper Saddle River, NJ, USA, 2005.
14. Li, Y.; Sun, Z.H.; Fang, K.T. Generalized inverse transformation method via representative points in statistical simulation. *Commun. Stat.-Simul. Comput.* **2024**, *54*, 4519–4545. [CrossRef]
15. David, H.A.; Nagaraja, H.N. *Order Statistics*, 3rd ed.; John Wiley & Sons: Hoboken, NJ, USA, 2004.
16. De Haan, L.; Ferreira, A. *Extreme Value Theory: An Introduction*; Springer: New York, NY, USA, 2006.
17. Al-Hussaini, E.K.; Ahsanullah, M. Exponentiated distributions. *Atlantis Studies in Probability and Statistics*; Atlantis Press: Paris, France, 2015; Volume 21.
18. Mahdavi, A.; Kundu, D. A new method for generating distributions with an application to exponential distribution. *Commun. Stat.-Theory Methods* **2017**, *46*, 6543–6557. [CrossRef]
19. Cordeiro, G.M.; De Castro, M. A new family of generalized distributions. *J. Stat. Comput. Simul.* **2011**, *81*, 883–898. [CrossRef]
20. Alzaatreh, A.; Lee, C.; Famoye, F. A new method for generating families of continuous distributions using the T-X family. *Metron* **2013**, *71*, 6379. [CrossRef]
21. Everitt, B.S.; Hand, D.J. *Finite Mixture Distributions*; Springer: Dordrecht, The Netherlands, 1981.
22. Li, Y.; Fang, K.T.; He, P.; Peng, H. Representative points from a mixture of two normal distributions. *Mathematics* **2022**, *10*, 3952. [CrossRef]
23. Yan, T.; Fang, K.T.; Yin, H. A novel approach for parameter estimation of mixture of two Weibull distributions in failure data modeling. *Stat. Comput.* **2024**, *34*, 221. [CrossRef]
24. Aigner, D.; Lovell, C.K.; Schmidt, P. Formulation and estimation of stochastic frontier production function models. *J. Econom.* **1977**, *6*, 21–37. [CrossRef]
25. Huygens, C. De Ratiociniis in Ludo Aleae. In *Exercitationum Mathematicarum*; Schooten, F.V., Ed.; Elsevier: Leiden, The Netherlands, 1657; pp. 521–534.
26. de Moivre, A. Approximatio ad Summam Terminorum Binomii $(a+b)^n$ in Seriem Expansi. *Misc. Anal.* **1733**, *II*, 1–7.
27. Gauss, C.F. *Theoria Motus Corporum Coelestium in Sectionibus Conicis Solem Ambientum*; Perthes et Besser: Hamburg, Germany, 1809.
28. Azzalini, A. A class of distributions which includes the normal ones. *Scand. J. Stat.* **1985**, *12*, 171–178.
29. Martínez-Flórez, G.; Tovar-Falón, R.; Gómez, H. Bivariate Power-Skew-Elliptical Distribution. *Symmetry* **2020**, *12*, 1327. [CrossRef]
30. Zhou, Y.F.; Lin, Y.X.; Fang, K.T.; Yin, H. The Representative Points of Generalized Alpha Skew-t Distribution and Applications. *Entropy* **2024**, *26*, 889. [CrossRef]
31. Rayleigh, L. On the resultant of a large number of vibrations of the same pitch and of arbitrary phase. *Philos. Mag.* **1880**, *10*, 73–78. [CrossRef]
32. Nadarajah, S.; Kotz, S. Moments of some J-shaped distributions. *J. Appl. Stat.* **2003**, *30*, 311–317. [CrossRef]
33. Stacy, E.W. A generalization of the gamma distribution. *Ann. Math. Stat.* **1962**, *33*, 1187–1192. [CrossRef]
34. Schrdinger, E. Zur theorie der fall-und steigversuche an teilchen mit brownscher bewegung. *Phys. Z.* **1915**, *16*, 289–295.
35. Tweedie, K.C.M. Inverse statistical variates. *Nature* **1945**, *155*, 453. [CrossRef]
36. Seshadri, V. *The Inverse Gaussian Distribution: Statistical Theory and Applications*; Springer: New York, NY, USA, 1999.

37. Barndorff-Nielsen, O.E. Exponentially decreasing distributions for the logarithm of particle size. *Proc. R. Soc. Lond. A Math. Phys. Sci.* **1977**, *353*, 401–419.
38. Eberlein, E.; Keller, U. Hyperbolic distributions in finance. *Bernoulli* **1995**, *1*, 281–299. [CrossRef]
39. Barndorff-Nielsen, O.E. Normal inverse Gaussian distributions and stochastic volatility modelling. *Scand. J. Stat.* **1997**, *24*, 1–13. [CrossRef]
40. Arnold, B.C.; Castillo, E.; Sarabia, J.M. *Conditional Specification of Statistical Models;* Springer Series in Statistics; Springer: New York, NY, USA, 1999.
41. Arnold, B.C.; Castillo, E.; Sarabia, J.M. Conditionally specified distributions: An introduction (with comments and a rejoinder by the authors). *Stat. Sci.* **2001**, *16*, 249–274. [CrossRef]
42. Zografos, K.; Balakrishnan, N. On families of beta-and generalized gamma-generated distributions and associated inference. *Stat. Methodol.* **2009**, *6*, 344–362. [CrossRef]
43. Eugene, N.; Lee, C.; Famege, F. Beta-normal distribution and its applications. *Commun. Stat.-Theory Methods* **2002**, *31*, 497–512. [CrossRef]
44. Gupta, A.K.; Nadarajah, S. On the moments of the beta normal distribution. *Commun. Stat.-Theory Methods* **2005**, *33*, 1–13. [CrossRef]
45. Famege, F.; Lee, C.; Olumolade, O. The beta-Weibull distribution. *J. Stat. Theory Appl.* **2005**, *4*, 121–136.
46. Mdziniso, N.C. The Quotient of the Beta-Weibull Distribution. Master's Thesis, Marshall University, Huntington, WV, USA, 2012.
47. Johnson, N.L.; Kotz, S. *Urn Models and Their Applications;* John Wiley & Sons: New York, USA, NY, 1977.
48. Johnson, N.L.; Kemp, A.W.; Kotz, S. *Univariate Discrete Distributions*, 3rd ed.; John Wiley & Sons: New York, NY, USA, 2005.
49. Ross, S.M. *Introduction to Probability Models*, 11th ed.; Academic Press: Cambridge, MA, USA, 2014.
50. Fang, K.T.; Pan, J. A review of representative points of statistical distributions and their applications. *Mathematics* **2023**, *11*, 2930. [CrossRef]
51. Chakraborty, S. Generating discrete analogues of continuous probability distributions—A survey of methods and constructions. *J. Stat. Distrib. Appl.* **2015**, *2*, 6. [CrossRef]
52. Kemp, A.W. A wide class of discrete distributions and the associated differential equations. *Sankhyā Indian J. Stat. Ser. A* **1968**, *30*, 401–410.
53. Sundt, B.; Jewell, W.S. Further results on recursive evaluation of compound distributions. *ASTIN Bull. J. IAA* **1981**, *12*, 27–39. [CrossRef]
54. Lisman, J.H.C.; Van Zuylen, M.C.A. Note on the generation of most probable frequency distributions. *Stat. Neerl.* **1972**, *26*, 19–23. [CrossRef]
55. Inusah, S.; Kozubowski, T.J. A discrete analogue of the Laplace distribution. *J. Stat. Plan. Inference* **2006**, *136*, 1090–1102. [CrossRef]
56. Kozubowski, T.J.; Inusah, S. A skew Laplace distribution on integers. *Ann. Inst. Stat. Math.* **2006**, *58*, 555–571. [CrossRef]
57. Roy, D. The discrete normal distribution. *Commun. Stat.-Theory Methods* **2003**, *32*, 1871–1883. [CrossRef]
58. Roy, D. Discrete Rayleigh distribution. *IEEE Trans. Reliab.* **2004**, *53*, 255–260. [CrossRef]
59. Krishna, H.; Pundir, P.S. Discrete Burr and discrete Pareto distributions. *Stat. Methodol.* **2009**, *6*, 177–188. [CrossRef]
60. Chakraborty, S.; Chakravarty, D. Discrete gamma distributions: Properties and parameter estimations. *Commun. Stat.-Theory Methods* **2012**, *41*, 3301–3324. [CrossRef]
61. Karlis, D.; Mamode Khan, N. Models for integer data. *Annu. Rev. Stat. Its Appl.* **2023**, *10*, 297–323. [CrossRef]
62. Janardan, K.G.; Patil, G.P. A unified approach for a class of multivariate hypergeometric models. *Sankhyā Indian J. Stat. Ser. A* **1972**, *34*, 363–376.
63. Kocherlakota, S.; Kocherlakota, K. *Bivariate Discrete Distributions;* Marcel Dekker: New York, USA, NY, 1992.
64. Karlis, D. An EM algorithm for multivariate Poisson distribution and related models. *J. Appl. Stat.* **2003**, *30*, 63–77. [CrossRef]
65. Palmitesta, P.; Provasi, C. *Computer Generation of Random Vectors from Continuous Multivariate Distributions;* Dipartimento di Metodi Quantitativi, Università degli Studi di Siena: Siena, Italy, 2001.
66. Nelsen, R.B. *An Introduction to Copulas*, 2nd ed.; Springer: New York, NY, USA, 2006.
67. Balakrishna, N.; Lai, C.D. Construction of bivariate distributions. In *Continuous Bivariate Distributions*, 2nd ed.; Springer: New York, NY, USA, 2009; pp. 179–228.
68. Fang, K.T.; Zhang, Y.T. *Generalized Multivariate Analysis;* Science Press: Beijing, China; Springer: Berlin/Heidelberg, Germany, 1990.
69. Fang, K.T.; Wang, Y. *Number-Theoretic Methods in Statistics;* Chapman & Hall: London, UK, 1994.
70. Pagès, G. *Numerical Probability: An Introduction with Applications to Finance;* Universitext Series; Springer: Berlin/Heidelberg, Germany, 2018.
71. Fang, K.T.; Yuan, K.H.; Benlter, P.M. Applications of number-theoretic methods to quantizers of elliptically contoured distributions, Multivariate Analysis and Its Applications. *IMS Lect. Notes-Monogr. Ser.* **1994**, *24*, 211–225.
72. Tarpey, T.; Flury, B. Self-consistency: A fundamental concept in statistics. *Stat. Sci.* **1996**, *11*, 229–243. [CrossRef]

73. Graf, S.; Luschgy, H. *Foundations of Quantization for Probability Distributions*; Springer: Berlin/Heidelberg, Germany, 2000.
74. Wishart, J. The generalised product moment distribution in samples from a normal multivariate population. *Biometrika* **1928**, *20*, 32–52. [CrossRef]
75. Fang, K.T.; Fang, B.Q. Some families of multivariate symmetric distributions related to exponential distribution. *J. Multivar. Anal.* **1988**, *24*, 109–122. [CrossRef]
76. Fang, K.T.; Fang, B.Q. A characterization of multivariate l_1-norm symmetric distributions. *Stat. Probab. Lett.* **1989**, **7**, 297–299. [CrossRef]
77. Anderson, T.W. *An Introduction to Multivariate Statistical Analysis*; John Wiley & Sons: New York, NY, USA, 1984.
78. Wang, J.; Boyer, J.; Genton, M.G. A skew-symmetric representation of multivariate distributions. *Stat. Sin.* **2004**, *14*, 1259–1270.
79. Arad, F.; Sheikhi, A. Asymmetric distributions based on the t-copula. In Proceedings of the 2022 9th Iranian Joint Congress on Fuzzy and Intelligent Systems (CFIS), Bam, Iran, 2–4 March 2022; pp. 1–3.
80. Azzalini, A.; Valle, A.D. The multivariate skew-normal distribution. *Biometrika* **1996**, *83*, 715–726. [CrossRef]
81. Azzalini, A.; Capitanio, A. Statistical applications of the multivariate skew-normal distribution. *J. R. Stat. Soc. Ser. B Stat. Methodol.* **1999**, *61*, 579–602. [CrossRef]
82. Genton, M.G. (Ed.) *Skew-Elliptical Distributions and Their Applications: A Journey Beyond Normality*; CRC Press: Boca Raton, FL, USA, 2004.
83. Marshall, A.W.; Olkin, I. A multivariate exponential distribution. *J. Am. Stat. Assoc.* **1967**, *62*, 30–44. [CrossRef]
84. Durante, F.; Sempi, C. Chapter 1: Copula theory: An introduction. In *Copula Theory and Its Applications, Proceedings of the Workshop Held in Warsaw, Poland, 25–26 September 2009*; Lecture Notes in Statistics—Proceedings, 198; Springer: Berlin/Heidelberg, Germany, 2010; pp. 3–32.
85. Gumbel, E.J. Multivariate logistic distributions. *Bull. Int. Stat. Inst.* **1961**, *38*, 1–6.
86. Fang, K.T.; Fang, H.B.; von Rosen, D. A family of bivariate distributions with non-elliptical contours. *Commun. Stat. Theory Methods* **2000**, *29*, 1885–1898. [CrossRef]
87. Clayton, U.G. A model for association in bivariate iife tables and its applications in epideniological studies of familial tendency in chronic disease incidence. *Biometrika* **1978**, *65*, 141–151. [CrossRef]
88. Ali, M.M.; Mikhail, N.N.; Haq, M.S. A class of bivariate distributions including the bivariate logistic. *J. Multivar. Anal.* **1978**, *8*, 405–412. [CrossRef]
89. Fang, H.B.; Fang, K.T.; Kotz, S. The meta-elliptical distributions with given marginalis. *J. Multivar. Anal.* **2002**, *82*, 1–15. [CrossRef]
90. Kelly, K.S.; Krzysztofowicz, R. Bivariate meta-gaussian density for use in hydrology. *Stoch. Hydrol. Hydraul.* **1997**, *11*, 17–31. [CrossRef]
91. Joe, H. *Dependence Modeling with Copulas*; CRC Press: London, UK, 2015.
92. Bouyé, E.; Durrleman, V.; Nikeghbali, A.; Riboulet, G.; Roncalli, T. Copulas for Finance—A Reading Guide and Some Applications. Available online: https://ssrn.com/abstract=1032533 (accessed on 1 October 2025).
93. Kruskal, W.H. Ordinal measures of association. *J. Am. Stat. Assoc.* **1958**, *53*, 814–861. [CrossRef]
94. Mai, J.F.; Scherer, M. *Simulating Copulas: Stochastic Models, Sampling Algorithms and Applications*, 2nd ed.; World Scientific: Hackensack, NJ, USA, 2017.
95. Zhang, L.; Singh, V.P. *Copulas and Their Applications in Water Resources Engineering*; Cambridge University Press: Cambridge, UK, 2019.
96. He, P.A.; Fang, K.T.; Ye, H.J. Gaussian copulas and meta Gaussian distributions: A theoretical study. *Stat. Comput.* 2025, *in press*.

entropy

Article

Construction of Space-Filling Asymmetrical Marginally Coupled Designs

Weiping Zhou [1,2,3], Miaomiao Meng [1], Min Li [4,*] and Xue Yang [5,*]

1 School of Mathematics and Computing Science, Guangxi Colleges and Universities Key Laboratory of Data Analysis and Computation, Guilin University of Electronic Technology, Guilin 541004, China; wpzhou@guet.edu.cn (W.Z.); mmyam@mails.guet.edu.cn (M.M.)
2 Center for Applied Mathematics of Guangxi (GUET), Guilin 541004, China
3 Guangxi Academy of Artificial Intelligence, Nanning 530028, China
4 School of Mathematics and Statistics, Qingdao University, Qingdao 266071, China
5 School of Statistics, Tianjin University of Finance and Economics, Tianjin 300222, China
* Correspondence: li_min1212@qdu.edu.cn (M.L.); yangxue_302@163.com (X.Y.)

Abstract

Marginally coupled designs (MCDs) are very suitable for computer experiments with both qualitative and quantitative factors. An MCD consisting of two subdesigns—one for the qualitative factors and the other for the quantitative factors—is said to be symmetrical or asymmetrical when the qualitative factor subdesign is equal-level or mixed-level, respectively. Although symmetrical MCDs have been studied extensively recently, investigations of asymmetrical MCDs are still relatively scarce. In this paper, based on space-filling symmetrical MCDs or space-filling Latin hypercube designs (LHDs), we propose four approaches to constructing a series of space-filling asymmetrical MCDs. The obtained asymmetrical MCDs can inherit the low-dimensional space-filling properties of these symmetrical MCDs or these LHDs. Moreover, the resulting asymmetrical MCDs are flexible in terms of their run sizes. A numerical study is conducted to compare and evaluate the performance of the proposed designs in computer experiments.

Keywords: computer experiment; projection; space-filling property; stratification

MSC: 62K05; 62K99

1. Introduction

Space-filling designs are extremely appropriate for computer experiments that are employed to address complex scientific or engineering problems. Using such designs to plan experiments can spread points in the experimental domain as evenly as possible, which allows every region of the experimental domain to be explored [1,2]. Hence, space-filling designs help to build predictions with high average accuracy when making predictions for unsampled points [3]. Some researchers, such as [4,5], have worked on the construction of space-filling designs using Monte Carlo methods; some scholars have proposed obtaining such designs using entropy criterion optimization (see [3,6–10]); others have constructed such designs based on space-filling properties, such as the maximin distance criterion, discrepancy criterion, and low-dimensional projection [3]. Maximum entropy designs can be approximated as maximin distance designs under the assumption of very weak correlations [3,11,12]. The common goal of Monte Carlo methods, entropy optimization, and space-filling properties is to maximize the information obtained from complex systems using economical run sizes in experiments. Consequently, space-filling designs can be viewed as the interdisciplinary intersection of statistics and information theory. In this paper, we investigate a class of space-filling designs suitable for computer experiments with both qualitative and quantitative factors.

Computer experiments with both qualitative and quantitative factors represent a considerably effective methodology for investigating complex systems and addressing scientific challenges [13–15]. Extensive studies have been conducted on how to efficiently plan such experiments. This goes back to Qian et al. [16] and subsequently Qian [17], who considered systematically planning such experiments using sliced space-filling designs and sliced Latin hypercube designs (SLHDs), respectively. But, these two types of designs can be criticized for their cost–benefit restrictions, namely that the run sizes increase dramatically as the number of qualitative factors grows. For cost-effectiveness, marginally coupled designs (MCDs), with economical run sizes and accommodating a large number of qualitative factors, are proposed by Deng et al. [18]. An MCD consists of two subdesigns, one of which is used to arrange qualitative factors and the other to arrange quantitative factors. In an MCD, the qualitative factor subdesign is commonly an orthogonal array (OA) [19], the quantitative factor subdesign is a Latin hypercube design (LHD) [20], and the latter subdesign is also an SLHD with respect to any qualitative factor in the former subdesign. Since MCDs were proposed, scholars have worked to improve them to have superior properties. Some researchers have worked on optimizing properties of the subdesign for quantitative factors in an MCD, such as improving the low-dimensional space-filling property [21–24] and orthogonality [25]. Others have concentrated on enhancing the stratification property between any l ($l \leq 2$) qualitative factors and all quantitative factors, such as doubly coupled designs (DCDs) [26], group doubly coupled designs (GDCDs) [27], and strongly coupled designs (SCDs) [28]. A design with both qualitative and quantitative factors is classified as symmetrical if the subdesign of qualitative factors is a fixed-level OA. Conversely, such a design is termed asymmetrical when the subdesign of the qualitative factors employs a mixed-level OA. The above MCDs, DCDs, GDCDs, and SCDs are predominantly symmetrical, while asymmetrical designs are relatively rare.

In this paper, we propose four approaches to constructing asymmetrical MCDs based on symmetrical MCDs. When the symmetrical MCDs with low-dimensional space-filling properties in subdesigns of quantitative factors exist, the subdesigns of quantitative factors in the asymmetrical MCDs obtained by Algorithms 1 and 4 can inherit these space-filling properties. The space-filling symmetrical MCDs can be obtained from He et al. [21–23] and Yang et al. [26]. If LHDs with desirable low-dimensional space-filling properties are available, Algorithms 2 and 3 can be employed to create asymmetrical MCDs in which the subdesigns of quantitative factors have the same space-filling properties as those of the LHDs. Orthogonal-array-based LHDs and strong-orthogonal-array-based LHDs have been thoroughly examined in the existing literature [29–35]; therefore, Algorithms 2 and 3 can employ these types of LHDs. Moreover, the obtained asymmetrical MCDs are flexible in terms of their run sizes.

The remainder of the paper is organized as follows. Section 2 gives some definitions and notation. Section 3 proposes several construction methods of asymmetrical MCDs. In Section 4 we conduct a numerical study to verify the performance of the proposed designs. Concluding remarks are provided in Section 5. All proofs and some tables are provided in Appendices A and B, respectively.

2. Definitions and Notation

Throughout this paper, $\mathbf{0}_n$ is an $n \times 1$ vector of zeros, $\mathbf{1}_n$ is an $n \times 1$ vector of ones, and $\mathbf{J}_{u\times q}$ is a $u \times q$ matrix of ones. For two matrices, $A = (a_{ij})_{n\times m}$ and $B = (b_{ij})_{p\times q}$, their Kronecker sum and Kronecker product are defined as $A \oplus B = (a_{ij} + B)_{(np)\times(mq)}$ and $A \otimes B = (a_{ij} \times B)_{(np)\times(mq)}$, respectively. Let $D = (d_{ij})_{n\times m}$ be an $n \times m$ matrix, and for a given integer s, $s \geq 2$, define an $n \times m$ matrix $\psi(D,s)$ as

$$\psi(D,s) = \left(\lfloor d_{ij}/s \rfloor\right)_{n\times m}, \tag{1}$$

where $\lfloor x \rfloor$ represents the largest integer not exceeding x.

Let $GF(s)$ denote the Galois field of order s, with each of the s levels coming from $\{\alpha_0, \alpha_1, \ldots, \alpha_{s-1}\}$, where $\alpha_0 = 0$ and $\alpha_1 = 1$. If s is a prime, $GF(s) = \{\alpha_0, \alpha_1, \ldots, \alpha_{s-1}\}$ simplifies to $GF(s) = \{0, 1, \ldots, s-1\}$. A difference scheme of strength 2 with u rows, v columns, and s levels, denoted by $D(u,v,s)$, is an $u \times v$ matrix with entries taken from $GF(s)$ such that in the vector difference between any two distinct columns, the s levels in $GF(s)$ occur with the same frequency. An $n \times q$ matrix is called an orthogonal array (OA) of strength t, denoted as $OA\left(n, s_1^{q_1} s_2^{q_2} \cdots s_v^{q_v}, t\right)$, $q_1 + q_2 + \cdots + q_v = q$; if (i) the entries of the first q_1 columns are taken from $\{0, 1, 2, \ldots, s_1 - 1\}$, the entries of the next q_2 columns are taken from $\{0, 1, 2, \ldots, s_2 - 1\}$, and so on; (ii) all possible t-tuples occur equally often in any t columns. The $OA\left(n, s_1^{q_1} s_2^{q_2} \cdots s_v^{q_v}, t\right)$ with $s_1 = s_2 = \cdots = s_v = s$ is called a fixed-level or symmetrical OA and denoted by $OA(n, s^q, t)$; otherwise, the array is called a mixed-level or asymmetrical OA. An $n \times p$ matrix is called a Latin hypercube design (LHD) with n runs and p factors, denoted as $LHD(n,p)$, if each column of the matrix contains n levels taken from $\{0, 1, 2, \ldots, n-1\}$ [20]. Let $D = (d_{ij})_{n\times m}$ be a matrix of n runs, m factors, and w levels, and for $2 \leq t \leq m$, the t columns of D are said to achieve t-dimensional stratification on an $s_1 \times \cdots \times s_t$ grid if the t columns can be collapsed into an $OA(n, s_1 s_2 \cdots s_t, t)$, where the w levels are collapsed into s_k levels by $\psi(d_{ij}, w/s_k)$ in Equation (1).

A design $D = (D_1, D_2)$, with D_1 and D_2 representing two subdesigns for qualitative and quantitative factors, respectively, is called a marginally coupled design (MCD) if (i) D_1 and D_2 are an OA and an LHD, respectively, and (ii) the rows in D_2 corresponding to each level of any factor in D_1 form a small LHD. If D_1 and D_2 are an $OA(n, s^q, t)$ and an $LHD(n,p)$, respectively, the MCD is symmetric and denoted by $MCD(n, s^q, p)$; if D_1 and D_2 are an $OA\left(n, s_1^{q_1} s_2^{q_2} \cdots s_v^{q_v}, t\right)$ and an $LHD(n,p)$, respectively, the MCD is asymmetric and denoted by $MCD\left(n, s_1^{q_1} s_2^{q_2} \cdots s_v^{q_v}, p\right)$.

The necessary and sufficient condition for the existence of a symmetrical MCD is presented by Proposition 1 of He et al. [21]. Building upon their work, we can directly derive a necessary and sufficient condition for the existence of an asymmetrical MCD as follows.

Lemma 1. *Suppose $D_1 = (D_{11}, D_{12}, \ldots, D_{1m})$ is an $OA\left(n, s_1^{q_1} s_2^{q_2} \cdots s_m^{q_m}, 2\right)$, where D_{1i} is an $OA\left(n, s_i^{q_i}, 2\right)$ for $i = 1, 2, \ldots, m$, and D_2 is an $LHD(n,p)$; then $D = (D_1, D_2)$ is an $MCD\left(n, s_1^{q_1} s_2^{q_2} \cdots s_m^{q_m}, p\right)$ if and only if $(D_{1i}, \psi(d_2, s_i))$ is an $OA\left(n, s_i^{q_i}(n/s_i), 2\right)$, where d_2 is any column of D_2, and $\psi(d_2, s_i)$ is obtained from Equation (1), $i = 1, 2, \ldots, m$.*

Note that, When $m = 1$, Lemma 1 is transformed into Proposition 1 of He et al. [21].

3. Construction of Asymmetrical MCDs with Low-Dimensional Stratification

This section introduces four construction methods that utilize symmetrical MCDs to construct asymmetrical MCDs. Furthermore, the low-dimensional projection properties of the proposed MCDs are also investigated.

The first method presents a construction for an $MCD(2n, 2^{m-1}4^1, p)$, (D_1, D_2), through an $MCD(n, 2^m, p)$, (A_1, A_2). The key feature of (D_1, D_2) is that the space-filling property of D_2 is determined by that of A_2. Suppose an $MCD(n, 2^m, p)$, denoted as $A = (A_1, A_2)$, is available, where A_1 and A_2 are an $OA(n, 2^m, 2)$ and an $LHD(n, p)$, respectively. For clarity, let the Kronecker sum $\oplus$ in Algorithm 1 be defined over $GF(2)$. Algorithm 1 is as follows.

Algorithm 1 Construction of $MCD(2n, 2^{m-1}4^1, p)$ based on $MCD(n, 2^m, p)$

Step 1. Let $a_{11}^0 = (0,1)^{\mathbf{T}} \otimes \mathbf{1}_n$ and $a_{11}^i = (0,1)^{\mathbf{T}} \oplus a_1^i$ over $GF(2)$, where a_1^i is the ith column of A_1 for $i = 1, 2, \ldots, m$. Obtain a $(2n) \times m$ matrix $D_1 = (a_{11}^1, a_{11}^2, \ldots, a_{11}^{m-1}, 2a_{11}^m + a_{11}^0)$.

Step 2. Construct a $2n \times p$ matrix $\widetilde{D}_2 = \mathbf{1}_2 \otimes A_2$. Obtain a $2n \times p$ matrix D_2 based on $\widetilde{D}_2$ by replacing the 2 entries with level k in each column of $\widetilde{D}_2$ by a random permutation of $\{2k, 2(k+1)-1\}$ for $k = 0, 1, \ldots, n-1$.

Step 3. The resulting design $D = (D_1, D_2)$.

Theorem 1. *For $A = (A_1, A_2)$ in Algorithm 1 and $D = (D_1, D_2)$ generated by Algorithm 1 , the following are true:*

(i) *$D = (D_1, D_2)$ is an $MCD(2n, 2^{m-1}4^1, p)$;*

(ii) *D_2 and A_2 achieve the same low-dimensional stratification.*

Obviously, (i) $A = (A_1, A_2)$ and $D = (D_1, D_2)$ are symmetrical and asymmetrical MCDs, respectively, and (ii) if A_2 achieves stratification in any t dimensions, D_2 also achieves the same t-dimensional stratification as A_2.

Remark 1. *The $MCD(n, 2^m, p)$, $A = (A_1, A_2)$, in Algorithm 1 can be obtained from He et al. [21]. For a given integer λ, $\lambda \geq 1$, an $MCD(8\lambda, 2^{4\lambda}, 4\lambda - 1)$ can be generated by Construction 1 of He et al. [21]; then an $MCD(16\lambda, 2^{4\lambda-1}4^1, 4\lambda - 1)$ (D_1, D_2) exists and D_2 achieves stratification on 2×2 grids. For a given integer u, $u \geq 3$, a space-filling $MCD(2^u, 2^m, 2)$ with $m = 2^{u-2}$ can be obtained through Construction 2 of He et al. [21]; then an $MCD(2^{u+1}, 2^{m-1}4^1, 2)$ (D_1, D_2) exists, and D_2 achieves stratification on $2^{u-1} \times 2$ and $2 \times 2^{u-1}$ grids. For a given integer u, $u \geq 2$, $k = 1, 2$, $m = (3-k)2^{u-2}$, and $p = k(u-1)$, a space-filling $MCD(2^u, 2^m, p)$ can be obtained via Construction 3 of He et al. [21]; then (i) an $MCD(2^{u+1}, 2^{m-1}4^1, p)$ (D_1, D_2) exists, and (ii) D_2 can be partitioned into k disjoint groups of $u-1$ columns; any two distinct columns in D_2 achieve stratification on a 2×2 grid; any two columns from different groups in D_2 achieve stratification on $2^{u-1} \times 2$ and $2 \times 2^{u-1}$ grids. Moreover, $A = (A_1, A_2)$ in Algorithm 1 can also be taken from He et al. [23], and similar results can be obtained.*

Example 1. *Consider $n = 8$, $m = 4$, and $p = 3$, and let $A = (A_1, A_2)$ be an $MCD(8, 2^4, 3)$, which are obtained from Construction 1 of He et al. [21] and listed as follows:*

$$A_1 = \begin{pmatrix} 0 & 1 & 0 & 1 & 0 & 1 & 0 & 1 \\ 0 & 1 & 0 & 1 & 1 & 0 & 1 & 0 \\ 0 & 1 & 1 & 0 & 0 & 1 & 1 & 0 \\ 0 & 1 & 1 & 0 & 1 & 0 & 0 & 1 \end{pmatrix}^{\mathbf{T}} \text{ and } A_2 = \begin{pmatrix} 5 & 4 & 6 & 7 & 0 & 1 & 2 & 3 \\ 7 & 6 & 2 & 3 & 4 & 5 & 1 & 0 \\ 2 & 3 & 4 & 5 & 6 & 7 & 1 & 0 \end{pmatrix}^{\mathbf{T}}.$$

Let a_1^i be the ith column of A_1 for $i = 1, 2, 3, 4$, i.e., $A_1 = (a_1^1, a_1^2, a_1^3, a_1^4)$. Then a_{11}^i for $i = 0, 1, \ldots, 4$ and D_1 are found to be $a_{11}^0 = (0,1)^{\mathbf{T}} \otimes \mathbf{1}_8$, $a_{11}^1 = (0,1)^T \oplus a_1^1$, $a_{11}^2 = (0,1)^T \oplus a_1^2$, $a_{11}^3 = (0,1)^T \oplus a_1^3$, $a_{11}^4 = (0,1)^T \oplus a_1^4$, and $D_1 = (a_{11}^1, a_{11}^2, a_{11}^3, 2a_{11}^4 + a_{11}^0)$, listed as follows:

$$D_1 = \begin{pmatrix} 0 & 1 & 0 & 1 & 0 & 1 & 0 & 1 & 1 & 0 & 1 & 0 & 1 & 0 & 1 & 0 \\ 0 & 1 & 0 & 1 & 1 & 0 & 1 & 0 & 1 & 0 & 1 & 0 & 0 & 1 & 0 & 1 \\ 0 & 1 & 1 & 0 & 0 & 1 & 1 & 0 & 1 & 0 & 0 & 1 & 1 & 0 & 0 & 1 \\ 0 & 2 & 2 & 0 & 2 & 0 & 0 & 2 & 3 & 1 & 1 & 3 & 1 & 3 & 3 & 1 \end{pmatrix}^{\mathbf{T}}.$$

Construct a 16×3 *matrix* $\widetilde{D}_2$ *where* $\widetilde{D}_2 = \mathbf{1}_2 \otimes A_2$*; then we can obtain* D_2 *as follows:*

$$D_2 = \begin{pmatrix} 10 & 8 & 12 & 14 & 0 & 2 & 4 & 6 & 11 & 9 & 13 & 15 & 1 & 3 & 5 & 7 \\ 14 & 12 & 4 & 6 & 8 & 10 & 2 & 0 & 15 & 13 & 5 & 7 & 9 & 11 & 3 & 1 \\ 4 & 6 & 8 & 10 & 12 & 14 & 2 & 0 & 5 & 7 & 9 & 11 & 13 & 15 & 3 & 1 \end{pmatrix}^{\mathrm{T}}.$$

It is easy to check that (D_1, D_2) *is an* $MCD(16, 2^3 4^1, 3)$*. The two-dimensional space-filing properties of* D_2 *can be seen intuitively in Figure 1, i.e., any two distinct columns in* D_2 *achieve stratification on a* 2×2 *grid.*

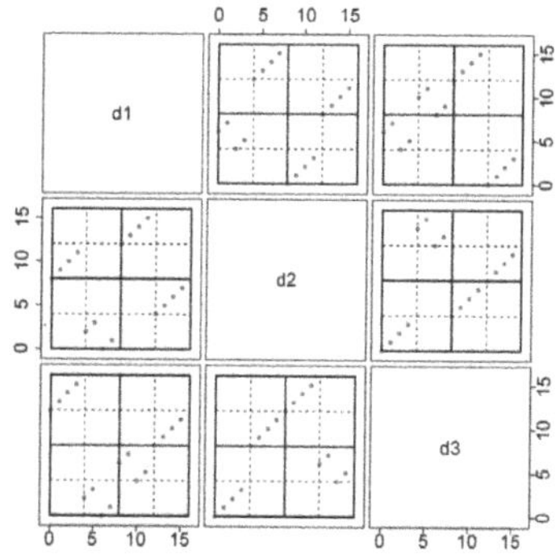

Figure 1. Bivariate projections among the three columns d_1, d_2, d_3 of D_2 in Example 1.

Algorithm 1 provides a way to construct $MCD(2n, 2^{m-1}4^1, p)$s with low-dimensional stratification via $MCD(n, 2^m, p)$s with good properties in low-dimensional projections. In the following, we present an approach to constructing MCDs with $u_1 n$ runs with $u_1 = \lambda s$ and $\lambda \geq 1$. Suppose a difference scheme $D(u_1, v_1, s)$, denoted as Λ_1, and an $MCD(n, s^m, p)$, denoted as $B = (B_1, B_2)$, are available, where B_1 and B_2 are an $OA(n, s^m, 2)$ and an $LHD(n, p)$, respectively. Algorithm 2 offers a method for constructing asymmetrical MCDs, as detailed below.

Algorithm 2 Construction of $MCD\left(nu_1, s^{mv_1^*}n^1, qp\right)$ based on $MCD(n, s^m, p)$

Step 1. Let $\Lambda_1^* = \Lambda_1 \setminus \mathbf{0}_{u_1}$, where $\Lambda_1 \setminus \mathbf{0}_{u_1}$ is the matrix that consists of all columns in Λ_1 except $\mathbf{0}_{u_1}$. Let $v_1^* = v_1 - 1$ if $\mathbf{0}_{u_1}$ is in Λ_1; otherwise, let $v_1^* = v_1$.

Step 2. Construct an $(nu_1) \times (mv_1^* + 1)$ matrix as $D_1 = (\Lambda_1^* \oplus B_1, \mathbf{1}_{u_1} \otimes (0, 1, \ldots, n-1)^{\mathrm{T}})$, where the $\oplus$ operator is based on $GF(s)$.

Step 3. For a given $q \geq 1$, let $D_2 = \mathbf{J}_{u_1 \times q} \otimes B_2 + n\Pi_1 \otimes \mathbf{1}_n$, where Π_1 is an $LHD(u_1, qp)$.

Step 4. The resulting design $D = (D_1, D_2)$.

Theorem 2. *For* Π_1 *from Step 3 of Algorithm 2 and* $D = (D_1, D_2)$ *generated by Algorithm 2, the following are true:*

(i) $D = (D_1, D_2)$ *is an* $MCD\left(nu_1, s^{mv_1^*}n^1, qp\right)$*, if* $\mathbf{0}_{u_1}$ *is in* Λ_1*,* $v_1^* = v_1 - 1$*; otherwise* $v_1^* = v_1$*;*

(ii) D_2 *and* Π_1 *achieve the same low-dimensional stratification.*

The space-filling property of Π_1 plays a critical role in the space-filling property of D_2 in Theorem 2, since $\psi(D_2, n) = \Pi_1 \otimes \mathbf{1}_n$. More precisely, if the LHD Π_1 is based on an OA of strength t, D_2 will have stratification in any t dimensions; if it is based on a strong orthogonal array $SOA(u_1, qp, \theta^3, 3)$ [31], D_2 will achieve stratification on the $\theta \times \theta \times \theta$ grids in any three dimensions; in addition, it can achieve stratification on the $\theta^2 \times \theta$ and the $\theta \times \theta^2$

grids in any two dimensions. The LHD Π_1 can be obtained from orthogonal-array-based LHDs or strong-orthogonal-array-based LHDs [29–35].

Example 2. *Let Λ_1 be a $D(8,8,2)$, $B = (B_1, B_2)$ be an $MCD(4, 2^2, 1)$, and Π_1 be an $LHD(8,3)$ obtained from He et al. [36]:*

$$\Lambda_1 = \begin{pmatrix} 0&0&0&0&0&0&0&0 \\ 0&0&0&1&0&1&1&1 \\ 0&0&1&0&1&0&1&1 \\ 0&0&1&1&1&1&0&0 \\ 0&1&0&0&1&1&0&1 \\ 0&1&0&1&1&0&1&0 \\ 0&1&1&0&0&1&1&0 \\ 0&1&1&1&0&0&0&1 \end{pmatrix}, \quad B = (B_1|B_2) = \left(\begin{array}{cc|c} 0&0&0 \\ 1&1&1 \\ 0&1&2 \\ 1&0&3 \end{array}\right) \text{ and}$$

$$\Pi_1 = \begin{pmatrix} 0&0&0 \\ 2&3&6 \\ 3&6&2 \\ 1&5&4 \\ 6&2&3 \\ 4&1&5 \\ 5&4&1 \\ 7&7&7 \end{pmatrix}.$$

Here, Π_1 qualifies as an $SOA(8,3,8,3)$, according to He et al. [36], meaning that (i) any two distinct columns in Π_1 achieve stratification on 4×2 and 2×4 grids, and (ii) Π_1 can achieve stratification on a $2 \times 2 \times 2$ grid in three dimensions. In Step 1, remove the first column of Λ_1 to obtain the matrix Λ_1^*. Construct a 32×15 matrix D_1 using $D_1 = (\Lambda_1^* \oplus B_1, \mathbf{1}_8 \otimes (0,1,\ldots,7)^T)$, which is listed in Table A1 of Appendix B. For a given $q = 3$, we can also construct D_2 from $D_2 = \mathbf{J}_{8\times 3} \otimes B_2 + 8\Pi_1 \otimes \mathbf{1}_8$, which is provided in Table A1 of Appendix B. It is easy to check that $D = (D_1, D_2)$ is an $MCD(32, 2^{14}8^1, 3)$. The two-dimensional space-filling properties of D_2 can be seen intuitively in Figure 2, i.e., any two distinct columns in D_2 achieve stratification on 4×2 and 2×4 grids. In addition, D_2 achieves stratification on a $2 \times 2 \times 2$ grid in three dimensions.

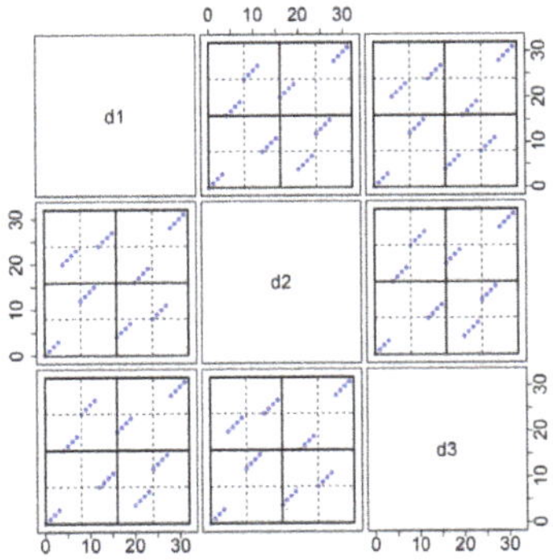

Figure 2. Bivariate projections among the three columns d_1, d_2, d_3 of D_2 in Example 2.

Note that the subdesign of the n level in D_1 just has one column, which is not advisable. To increase the number of columns at level n in D_1, we present Algorithm 3 below, which aims to generate MCDs with $u_2 n$ runs for $u_2 = \lambda s^2$ and $\lambda \geq 1$. Suppose a difference scheme $D(u_2, v_2, n)$, denoted as Λ_2, and an $MCD(n, s^m, p)$, denoted as $C = (C_1, C_2)$, are available, where C_1 and C_2 are an $OA(n, s^m, 2)$ and an $LHD(n, p)$, respectively.

Algorithm 3 Construction of $MCD\left(nu_2, s^m n^{v_2^*}, qp\right)$ based on $MCD(n, s^m, p)$

Step 1. Let $\Lambda_2^* = \Lambda_2 \setminus \mathbf{0}_{u_2}$, where $\Lambda_2 \setminus \mathbf{0}_{u_2}$ is the matrix that consists of all columns in Λ_2 except $\mathbf{0}_{u_2}$. Let $v_2^* = v_2 - 1$ if $\mathbf{0}_{u_2}$ is in Λ_2; otherwise, let $v_2^* = v_2$.

Step 2. Construct an $(nu_2) \times (m + v_2^*)$ matrix as $D_1 = (\mathbf{1}_{u_2} \otimes C_1, \Lambda_2^* \oplus (0, 1, \ldots, n-1)^{\mathrm{T}})$, where the $\oplus$ operator is based on $GF(n)$.

Step 3. For a given $q \geq 1$, let $D_2 = \mathbf{J}_{u_2 \times q} \otimes C_2 + n\Pi_2 \otimes \mathbf{1}_n$, where Π_2 is an $LHD(u_2, qp)$.

Step 4. The resulting design $D = (D_1, D_2)$.

Algorithm 3 presents a method to extend the number of columns at level n in D_1 up to v_2^*. Theorem 3 summarizes the properties of D_1 and D_2 constructed in Algorithm 3.

Theorem 3. *For Π_2 from Step 3 of Algorithm 3 and $D = (D_1, D_2)$ generated by Algorithm 3, the following are true:*

(i) *$D = (D_1, D_2)$ is an $MCD\left(nu_2, s^m n^{v_2^*}, qp\right)$, if $\mathbf{0}_{u_2}$ is in Λ_2; then $v_2^* = v_2 - 1$; otherwise $v_2^* = v_2$;*

(ii) *D_2 and Π_2 achieve the same low-dimensional stratification.*

Theorem 3(ii) illustrates that the space-filling property of D_2 in Algorithm 3 is dependent on that of the LHD Π_2, which means that D_2 may have the desired low-dimensional space-filling property when we choose Π_2 with the low-dimensional space-filling property. The projection properties of D_2 in Algorithm 3 are similar to those of D_2 in Algorithm 2; therefore, Π_2 can also be obtained from orthogonal-array-based LHDs or strong-orthogonal-array-based LHDs.

In Algorithms 2 and 3, the $MCD(n, s^m, p)$s may either be identical or distinct, i.e., $B = (B_1, B_2)$ and $C = (C_1, C_2)$ can be the same or different. If the number of runs in the two difference schemes $D(u_1, v_1, s)$ in Algorithm 2 and $D(u_2, v_2, n)$ in Algorithm 3 is equal, that is, $u_1 = u_2$, then Π_1 in Algorithm 2 and Π_2 in Algorithm 3 can take the same LHD. Next, we construct a new space-filling asymmetrical MCD from Algorithm 3, using the same symmetrical MCD and LHD as in Algorithm 2.

Example 3. *Let Λ_2 be a $D(8, 8, 4)$ as follows:*

$$\Lambda_2 = \begin{pmatrix} 0 & 0 & 0 & 0 & 0 & 0 & 0 & 0 \\ 0 & 3 & 1 & 2 & 0 & 3 & 1 & 2 \\ 0 & 1 & 0 & 1 & 2 & 3 & 2 & 3 \\ 0 & 2 & 1 & 3 & 2 & 0 & 3 & 1 \\ 0 & 0 & 2 & 2 & 1 & 1 & 3 & 3 \\ 0 & 3 & 3 & 0 & 1 & 2 & 2 & 1 \\ 0 & 1 & 2 & 3 & 3 & 2 & 1 & 0 \\ 0 & 2 & 3 & 1 & 3 & 1 & 0 & 2 \end{pmatrix}.$$

Let $C = B$, $C_1 = B_1$, and $C_2 = B_2$, where $B = (B_1, B_2)$ are obtained from Example 2. Here, Λ_2^* is the matrix which deletes the first column of Λ_2. From Steps 1 and 2, we can obtain a 32×9 matrix D_1 using $D_1 = (\mathbf{1}_8 \otimes C_1, \Lambda_2^* \oplus (0, 1, \ldots, 7)^{\mathrm{T}})$, which is presented in Table A2 of Appendix B. Consider the case of $q = 3$ in Step 3. For the $LHD(8, 3)$ Π_2, let $\Pi_2 = \Pi_1$, where Π_1 is obtained from Example 2; then D_2 can be constructed as $D_2 = \mathbf{J}_{8 \times 3} \otimes C_2 + 8\Pi_2 \otimes \mathbf{1}_8$ in Step 3, which is provided in Table A2 of Appendix B. It is easy to check that $D = (D_1, D_2)$ is an $MCD(32, 2^2 4^7, 3)$. The space-filling properties of D_2 are similar to those of D_2 in Example 2 and are therefore omitted here. Note that the addition operations in Step 2 are given as follows (Table 1).

Table 1. Addition table for $GF(4)$ in Example 3.

+	0	1	2	3
0	0	1	2	3
1	1	0	3	2
2	2	3	0	1
3	3	2	1	0

The operation symbol "+" represents addition in the Galois field $GF(4)$.

In Algorithms 2 and 3, the existence of the difference scheme is of great significance. Due to Theorem 6.6, Corollary 6.39 and Theorem 6.63 of Hedayat et al. [19], there exist three types of difference schemes, (i) $D(p^w, p^w, p^v)$; (ii) $D(2s^m, 2s^m, s)$; and (iii) $D(4s^m, 4s^m, s)$, where p is a prime, s is a prime power, and w, v, and m are positive integers, with $w \geq v \geq 1$ and $m \geq 1$. Table 6.67 of Hedayat et al. [19] gives the exact maximal value of v for which a difference scheme $D(\lambda r, v, r)$ exists, for $r = 2, 3, 4, 8, 9$, as listed in Table A3.

The above three algorithms can generate space-filling MCDs with D_1 being an $OA(2n, 2^{m-1}4^1, 2)$, an $OA\left(nu_1, s^{mv_1^*}n^1, 2\right)$ and $OA\left(nu_2, s^m n^{v_2^*}, 2)\right)$, respectively. We introduce another construction for space-filling MCDs with D_1 being an $OA\left(s_1^2, s_1^{m-1}s^{s-1}s_2^1, 2\right)$. Suppose an $OA(s^2, s^{s+1}, 2)$, say E, and an $MCD(s_1^2, s_1^m, p)$ with $s_1 = s^3$, denoted as $M = (M_1, M_2)$, are available, where M_1 and M_2 are an $OA(s_1^2, s_1^m, 2)$ and an $LHD(s_1^2, p)$, respectively (Algorithm 4).

Algorithm 4 Construction of $MCD\left(s_1^2, s_1^{m-1}s^{s-1}s_2^1, p\right)$ based on $MCD(s_1^2, s_1^m, p)$

Step 1. Let $M_1 = (\Omega, \xi)$, where Ω and ξ are the first $(m-1)$ columns and the last column of M_1, respectively. Permute the rows of $M = (M_1, M_2)$ to obtain an MCD, denoted as $\widetilde{M} = (\widetilde{M}_1, \widetilde{M}_2)$ with $\widetilde{M}_1 = (\widetilde{\Omega}, \widetilde{\xi})$, where $\widetilde{\xi} = (0, 1, \ldots, s_1 - 1)^{\mathbf{T}} \otimes \mathbf{1}_{s_1}$.

Step 2. For $s_1 = s^3$, construct two $s_1 \times (s+1)$ matrices F_0 and F_1 based on E, as $F_0 = \mathbf{0}_s \oplus E$ and $F_1 = (0, \ldots, s-1)^{\mathbf{T}} \oplus E$ (**over** $GF(s)$), respectively.

Step 3. Obtain two $s_1^2 \times (s+1)$ matrices Φ_0 and Φ_1 by replacing the levels $0, 1, \ldots, s_1 - 1$ of the $\widetilde{\xi}$ with the 1st, 2nd, …, and s_1th rows of F_0 and F_1, respectively. Let $\Phi_0 = (\phi_0^1, \ldots, \phi_0^{s+1})$ and $\Phi_1 = (\phi_1^1, \ldots, \phi_1^{s+1})$, where ϕ_0^i and ϕ_1^i are the ith columns of Φ_0 and Φ_1, respectively.

Step 4. For $s_1 = s^3$ and $s_2 = s^2$, construct an $OA\left(s_1^2, s_1^{m-1}s^{s-1}s_2^1, 2\right)$ D_1 as

$$D_1 = (\widetilde{\Omega}, \phi_0^1, \ldots, \phi_0^{s-1}, s\phi_0^{s+1} + \phi_1^{s+1}).$$

Step 5. Let $G = \psi(\widetilde{M}_2, s_1)$. Construct three $s_1^2 \times p$ matrices $H = (\phi_1^1, \ldots, \phi_1^1)$, $U = (\phi_0^s, \ldots, \phi_0^s)$ and $V = (\phi_1^2, \ldots, \phi_1^2)$. Let $D_2 = s^3 G + s^2 H + sU + V$.

Step 6. The resulting design $D = (D_1, D_2)$.

Theorem 4. *For $M = (M_1, M_2)$ in Algorithm 4 and $D = (D_1, D_2)$ generated by Algorithm 4, where $s_1 = s^3$ and $s_2 = s^2$, the following are true:*

(i) *$D = (D_1, D_2)$ is an $MCD\left(s_1^2, s_1^{m-1}s^{s-1}s_2^1, p\right)$;*

(ii) *D_2 and M_2 achieve the same low-dimensional stratification.*

Theorem 4(i) shows that the existence of an $MCD\left(s_1^2, s_1^{m-1}s^{s-1}s_2^1, p\right)$ with $s_1 = s^3$ and $s_2 = s^2$ is equivalent to the simultaneous existence of both an $OA(s^2, s^{s+1}, 2)$ and an $MCD(s_1^2, s_1^m, p)$. According to He et al. [21], $m \leq s_1$ in an $MCD(s_1^2, s_1^m, p)$. For a prime h and a positive integer v, if $s = h^v$, there exist an $OA(s^2, s^{s+1}, 2)$ and an $MCD(s_1^2, s_1^{s_1}, p)$.

Theorem 4(ii) tells us that the space-filling property of D_2 in Algorithm 4 is determined by that of M_2 in the initial MCD $M = (M_1, M_2)$. From Theorems 3.1, 3.2 and 3.20 of Hedayat et al. [19], for a prime h and a positive integer v, $s = h^v$, the following three OAs exist: (i) $OA\left(s^3, s^{s^2+s+1}, 2\right)$; (ii) $OA(s^3, s^{s+2}, 3)$ for $h = 2$; (iii) and $OA(s^3, s^{s+1}, 3)$ for an odd prime h. Thus $M = (M_1, M_2)$ can be obtained from Construction 1 of He et al. [21], where M is an $MCD(s_1^2, s_1^{s_1}, s^2+s+1)$ with $s_1 = s^3$, and any two distinct columns of M_2 achieve stratification on an $s \times s$ grid. So any two distinct columns of D_2 in Theorem 4 achieve stratification on an $s \times s$ grid. According to Remark 1 of He et al. [21], for $s_1 = s^3$, M can choose an $MCD(s_1^2, s_1^{s_1}, s+2)$ for s that is a power of 2, and an $MCD(s_1^2, s_1^{s_1}, s+1)$ for an odd prime power s, respectively; furthermore, M_2 achieves stratification in any three dimensions. Hence, the corresponding D_2 in Theorem 4 also possesses a three-dimensional space-filling property.

Based on Algorithm 4, Theorem 4 confirms that asymmetrical MCDs with attractive space-filling properties can be constructed. Next, we give an example to illustrate Algorithm 4 and Theorem 4.

Example 4. *Consider* $s = 2$, $s_1 = 8$, $m = 7$, *and* $p = 2$. *An* $OA(4, 2^3, 2)$ *is given as* $E = (e_1, e_2, e_3)$, *where* $e_1 = (0,0,1,1)^{\mathrm{T}}$, $e_2 = (0,1,0,1)^{\mathrm{T}}$, *and* $e_3 = (0,1,1,0)^{\mathrm{T}}$. *Let* $M = (M_1, M_2)$ *be an* $MCD(64, 8^7, 2)$, *where* M_1 *and* M_2 *are* $OA(64, 8^7, 2)$ *and* $LHD(64, 2)$, *respectively. In Step 1, if we permute the rows of M, we can obtain* $\widetilde{M} = (\widetilde{M}_1, \widetilde{M}_2)$, *which is listed in Table A4 of Appendix B, where* $\widetilde{M}_1 = (\tilde{\Omega}, \tilde{\xi})$ *and* $\tilde{\xi} = (0, 1, \ldots, 7)^T \otimes \mathbf{1}_8$. *Obtain two* 8×3 *matrices* F_0 *and* F_1 *based on E using* $F_0 = \mathbf{0}_2 \oplus E$ *and* $F_1 = (0,1)^T \oplus E$ *over* $GF(2)$. *From Step 3, we can obtain two* 64×3 *matrices,* $\Phi_0 = (\phi_0^1, \phi_0^2, \phi_0^3)$ *and* $\Phi_1 = (\phi_1^1, \phi_1^2, \phi_1^3)$. *For* $s_2 = 4$, *we obtain* $D_1 = (\tilde{\Omega}, \phi_0^1, 2\phi_0^3 + \phi_1^3)$ *in Step 4, and* $G = \psi(\widetilde{M}_2, 8)$ *in Step 5. We also construct three* 64×2 *matrices,* $H = (\phi_1^1, \phi_1^1)$, $U = (\phi_0^s, \phi_0^s)$, *and* $V = (\phi_1^2, \phi_1^2)$. *The resulting designs,* $D_1 = (\tilde{\Omega}, \phi_0^1, 2\phi_0^3 + \phi_1^3)$ *and* $D_2 = 8G + 4H + 2U + V$, *are listed in Table A5 of Appendix B. Next, let* d_1 *and* d_2 *be the first and second columns of* D_2. *It is easy to see that* d_1 *and* d_2 *achieve stratification on an* 8×8 *grid, as shown in Figure 3.*

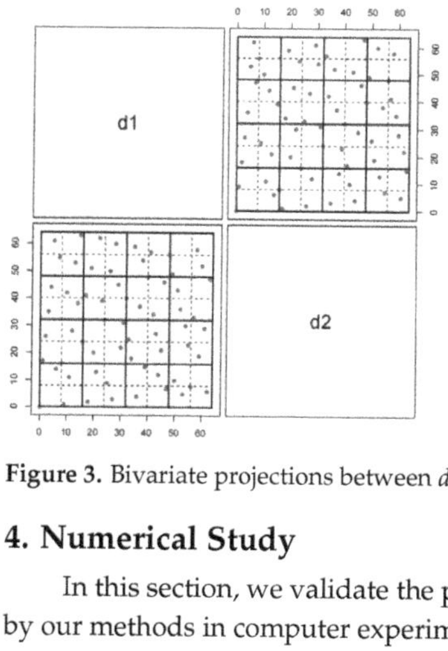

Figure 3. Bivariate projections between d_1 and d_2 of D_2 in Example 4.

4. Numerical Study

In this section, we validate the performance of the asymmetrical MCDs constructed by our methods in computer experiments.

Consider two $MCD(32, 2^2 4^2, 3)$s, taken from Example 3 of this paper and Example 3 of Deng et al. [18], and denote them as MCD1 $= (P_1, P_2)$ and MCD2 $= (Q_1, Q_2)$, respectively. Here, for the $MCD(32, 2^2 4^7, 3)$ $D = (D_1, D_2)$ listed in Table A2 of Example 3 , P_1 consists of the first four columns of D_1, and $P_2 = D_2$. For the $MCD(32, 2^8 4^2, 20)$ $D = (D_1, D_2)$ generated by Construction 3 of Deng et al. [18], as illustrated in their Example 3, Q_1 and Q_2 are taken from the last four columns of D_1 and the first three columns of D_2, respectively.

First, we compare the space-filling properties of the above MCD1 with those of the above MCD2 under the maximum projection criterion [37], the uniformity criterion [38], and the minimum mixed-moment aberration criterion [39]. For MCD1 and MCD2, Table 2 shows the values of the maximum projection criterion ("MaxProQQ"), uniformity criterion ("QQD") and mixed-moment pattern ("MK"). Obviously, MCD1 outperforms MCD2 under the three types of criteria, which implies that MCD1 has better space-filling properties.

Table 2. The values of different designs in the numerical study.

	MaxProQQ	**QQD**	**MK = (MK$_1$, MK$_2$, MK$_3$, MK$_4$)**
MCD1	10.7032	0.0542	(0.3876, 0.2623, 0.2359, 0.2564)
MCD2	12.8260	0.0968	(0.4358, 0.3792, 0.4488, 0.6300)

We next evaluate the performance of MCD1 and MCD2 in building statistical surrogate models. We conduct simulations and generate data for a computer experiment with four qualitative factors, which have two levels, two levels, four levels and four levels, respectively, and three quantitative factors. Its computer model has the following form:

$$y = f_i(x) \times (g_j(x) + h_k(x)) + t_l(x), x = (x_1, x_2, x_3),$$

where i, j, k, and l are the levels for the qualitative factors, $i, j = 1, 2$, $k, l = 1, 2, 3, 4$; $0 \leq x_1, x_2, x_3 \leq 1$ are the values of quantitative factors; and the functions f_i, g_j, h_k, and t_l are as shown below:

$f_1(x) = x_1 + x_2^2 + x_3^3$, $f_2(x) = x_1^2 + x_2 + x_3^3$,

$g_1(x) = cos(x_1) + cos(2x_2) + cos(3x_3)$, $g_2(x) = cos(3x_1) + cos(2x_2) + cos(x_3)$,

$h_1(x) = sin(x_1) + sin(2x_2) + sin(3x_3)$, $h_2(x) = sin(3x_1) + sin(2x_2) + sin(x_3)$, $h_3(x) = sin(2x_1) + sin(x_2) + sin(3x_3)$, $h_4(x) = sin(x_1) + sin(3x_2) + sin(2x_3)$,

$t_1(x) = e^{x_1} + e^{x_2} + e^{x_3}$, $t_2(x) = e^{2x_1} + e^{x_2} + e^{x_3}$, $t_3(x) = e^{x_1} + e^{2x_2} + e^{x_3}$, $t_4(x) = e^{x_1} + e^{x_2} + e^{2x_3}$.

We adopt the easy-to-interpret Gaussian process model first proposed by Xiao et al. [40] to fit the data corresponding to MCD1 and MCD2, and use the root-mean-square prediction error (RMSE) to measure the prediction performance. The RMSE is as follows:

$$\text{RMSE} = \sqrt{\frac{1}{n_t} \sum_{i=1}^{n_t} (y(z_i^*) - \hat{y}(z_i^*))^2},$$

where z_i^* is a test point on the test point set, $i = 1, 2, \ldots, n_t$, and $y(z_i^*)$ and $\hat{y}(z_i^*)$ are the true and predicted responses of the input z_i^*.

According to the RMSE in Figure 4, MCD1 certainly outperforms MCD2 in building statistical surrogate models.

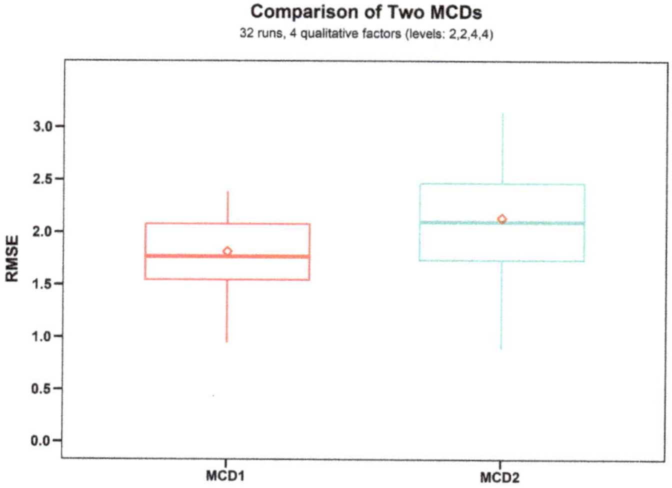

Figure 4. The prediction results of MCD1 and MCD2, where the red square represent the mean of RMSE.

5. Concluding Remarks

Although Construction 3 of Deng et al. [18] constructs asymmetrical MCDs, it does not discuss the space-filling property of the designs for quantitative factors in MCDs. Using simple and easily implementable Algorithms 1–4, the $MCD(2n, 2^{m-1}4^1, p)$, $MCD\left(nu_1, s^{mv_1^*}n^1, qp\right)$, $MCD\left(nu_2, s^m n^{v_2^*}, qp\right)$, and $MCD\left(s_1^2, s_1^{m-1}s^{s-1}s_2^1, p\right)$ with $s_1 = s^3$ and $s_2 = s^2$ are obtained, respectively. Based on symmetrical MCDs with good low-dimensional projection properties in designs for quantitative factors, Algorithms 1 and 4 construct a series of asymmetrical MCDs, which inherit these low-dimensional space-filling properties. Algorithms 2 and 3 make use of the symmetrical MCDs and the space-filling LHDs to generate asymmetrical MCDs with desirable space-filling properties. Compared with Zhou et al. [24], the designs obtained by Algorithms 1–3 are very flexible in terms of their run sizes: (i) if an asymmetrical MCD is constructed by Algorithm 1, the run size of such a design is a multiple of 8; (ii) when constructing the asymmetrical MCDs using Algorithms 2 and 3, their run sizes must be of the form λs^2 for some integer λ.

The number of qualitative factors in an MCD determines its range of applications, so it is important to determine the upper bound of the number of qualitative factors. For the $MCD(2n, 2^{m-1}4^1, p)$ constructed by Algorithm 1, the $MCD\left(nu_1, s^{mv_1^*}n^1, qp\right)$ generated by Algorithm 2, the $MCD\left(nu_2, s^m n^{v_2^*}, qp\right)$ obtained by Algorithm 3, and the $MCD\left(s_1^2, s_1^{m-1}s^{s-1}s_2^1, p\right)$ obtained by Algorithm 4, on the one hand, since $v_i^* = v_i - 1$ or $v_i^* = v_i$ for $i = 1, 2$, the maximum value of v_i^* can be obtained from Table A3. On the other hand, according to Equation (3.2) of [21], it is known that $m \leq n/2$ in $MCD(2n, 2^{m-1}4^1, p)$, $m \leq n/s$ in $MCD\left(nu_1, s^{mv_1^*}n^1, qp\right)$, $m \leq n/s$ in $MCD\left(nu_2, s^m n^{v_2^*}, qp\right)$, and $m \leq s_1$ in $MCD\left(s_1^2, s_1^{m-1}s^{s-1}s_2^1, p\right)$.

Given a small initial MCD $D^{(0)} = \left(D_1^{(0)}, D_2^{(0)}\right)$ with $D_1^{(0)}$ and $D_2^{(0)}$ being an OA and an $LHD(n, p)$, respectively, from Construction 3 of Deng et al. [18], the large MCD $D = (D_1, D_2)$ is found to be $D_1 = D(1) \oplus D_1^{(0)}$ and $D_2 = C \otimes D_2^{(0)} + nH \otimes \mathbf{1}_n$, where $D(1)$ is a difference scheme, $C = (c_{ij})$ is a $u \times f$ matrix with $c_{ij} = 1$, and H is an $LHD(u, pf)$. Obviously, the space-filling property of D_2 depends on H, since $\psi(D_2, n) = H$ from

Equation (1). So we can choose a MCD from this paper as the initial small asymmetrical MCD and select a space-filling H to construct a series of large space-filling asymmetrical MCDs based on Construction 3 of Deng et al. [18].

As we know, orthogonality is extremely important for fitting polynomial models. A natural direction for future work would be to construct good asymmetrical MCDs with orthogonality.

Author Contributions: Conceptualization, W.Z., M.L., and X.Y.; methodology, W.Z. and M.L.; software, W.Z. and M.M.; validation, W.Z. and M.M.; investigation, M.L.; resources, W.Z.; data curation, W.Z.; writing—original draft preparation, W.Z. and M.M.; writing—review and editing, W.Z. and X.Y.; visualization, M.L.; supervision, X.Y.; project administration, X.Y. All authors have read and agreed to the published version of the manuscript.

Funding: This research was funded by the Science and Technology Project of Guangxi (Grant NO. Guike AD23023002), the Special Fund for Scientific and Technological Bases and Talents of Guangxi (Grant NO. Guike AD21075008), the National Natural Science Foundation of China (Grant NO. 12561044), the Innovation Project of GUET Graduate Education (Grant NO. 2025YCXS123), the Shandong Provincial Natural Science Foundation, China (Grant NO. ZR2021QA053), and the General Projects of the National Social Science Fund of China (Grant NO. 23BTJ058).

Institutional Review Board Statement: Not applicable.

Data Availability Statement: The original contributions presented in this study are included in the article. Further inquiries can be directed to the corresponding authors.

Conflicts of Interest: The authors declare no conflicts of interest.

Appendix A. Proofs

To prove Theorem 1, Lemma A1 is given, which is derived from Remark 3 of Li et al. [41].

Lemma A1. *Suppose A^* is an $OA(n, 2^m, 2)$ based on $GF(2)$; then*

$$A = \begin{pmatrix} \mathbf{0}_n & A^* \\ \mathbf{1}_n & A^* + 1 \end{pmatrix}$$

is an $OA(2n, 2^{m+1}, 3)$, where $A^* + 1$ is the matrix obtained by adding 1 (mod 2) to all the entries of A^*.

Proof of Theorem 1. (i) For $i, k = 1, 2, \ldots, m$ and $i \neq k$, $(a_{11}^0, a_{11}^i, a_{11}^k)$ is an $OA(2n, 2^3, 3)$, which follows from Lemma A1. Thus, D_1 is an $OA(2n, 2^{m-1}4^1, 2)$. For $j = 1, 2, \ldots, p$, let a_2^j and d_2^j be the jth columns of A_2 and D_2, respectively. Clearly, a_2^j and d_2^j are an $LHD(n, 1)$ and $LHD(2n, 1)$, respectively. From the construction of a_{11}^i and $\psi(d_2^j, 2) = \mathbf{1}_2 \otimes a_2^j$, we can determine that $(a_{11}^1, a_{11}^2, \ldots, a_{11}^{m-1}, \psi(d_2^j, 2))$ is an $OA(2n, 2^{m-1}n^1, 2)$. Moreover, $(a_{11}^0, a_{11}^i, \psi(d_2^j, 4))$ being an $OA(2n, 2^2(n/2)^1, 3)$ follows, since $a_{11}^i = (0,1)^T \oplus a_1^i$ and $\psi(d_2^j, 4) = \mathbf{1}_2 \otimes \psi(a_2^j, 2)$, and $(a_1^i, \psi(a_2^j, 2))$ is an $OA(n, 2^1(n/2)^1, 2)$. So $(2a_{11}^{m-1} + a_{11}^0, \psi(d_2^j, 4))$ is an $OA(2n, 4^1(n/2)^1, 2)$. Now Part (i) can be proven from Lemma 1.

(ii) According to the construction of D_2, it is easy to see that D_2 and A_2 achieve the same low-dimensional stratification. □

Proof of Theorem 2. (i) D_1 being an $OA\left(nu_1, s^{mv_1^*}n^1, 2\right)$ follows from Theorem 9.15 of Section 9.3 of Hedayat et al. [19]. From Construction 3 of Deng et al. [18], we can find that D_2 is an $LHD(nu_1, qp)$, and $(\Lambda_1^* \oplus B_1, D_2)$ is an $MCD\left(nu_1, s^{mv_1^*}, qp\right)$. Let π_i be the

ith column of $\Pi_1 \otimes \mathbf{1}_n$, $i = 1,2,\ldots,pq$. Since $\psi(D_2,n) = \Pi_1 \otimes \mathbf{1}_n$, and $(\mathbf{1}_{u_1} \otimes (0,1,\cdots n-1)^T, \pi_i)$ for $i = 1,2,\ldots,pq$ is an $OA(nu_1, n^1u_1^1, 2)$, then $(\mathbf{1}_{u_1} \otimes (0,1,\cdots n-1)^T, D_2)$ is an $MCD(nu_1, n^1, qp)$ according to Lemma 1. Then (i) can be obtained straightforwardly.

(ii) From Algorithm 2, it is easy to see that $\psi(D_2,n) = \Pi_1 \otimes \mathbf{1}_n$. Now Part (ii) can be proven. □

Proof of Theorem 3. Let $u_2 = \beta n$ and $n = \eta s$, where β and η are positive integers. $\Lambda_2^* \oplus (0,1,\cdots,n-1)^T$ being an $OA\left(nu_2, n^{v_2^*}, 2\right)$ follows from Lemma 6.27 of Section 9.3 of Hedayat et al. [19]. It is clear that $\mathbf{1}_{u_2} \otimes C_1$ is an $OA(nu_2, s^m, 2)$. For $i = 1,2,\ldots,m$, let c_1^i and $\mathbf{1}_{u_2} \otimes c_1^i$ be the ith columns of C_1 and $\mathbf{1}_{u_2} \otimes C_1$, respectively. Let λ_k be the kth column of $\Lambda_2^* \oplus (0,1,\cdots,n-1)^T$, $k = 1,2,\ldots,v_2^*$. For any $\alpha \in GF(n)$, $(c_1^i, \alpha \oplus (0,1,\cdots n-1)^T)$ then occurs β times in the rows of $(\mathbf{1}_{u_2} \otimes c_1^i, \lambda_k)$, $i = 1,2,\ldots,m$, $k = 1,2,\ldots,v_2^*$, since Λ_2^* is a difference scheme $D(u_2, v_2, n)$. Thus, for $i = 1,2,\ldots,m$, $k = 1,2,\ldots,v_2^*$, $(\mathbf{1}_{u_2} \otimes c_1^i, \lambda_k)$ is an $OA(nu_2, s^1n^1, 2)$. So, D_1 is an $OA\left(nu_2, s^m n^{v_2^*}, 2\right)$. Similarly to the proof of Theorem 2, D_2 is an $LHD(nu_2, qp)$. Let d_i and π_i be the ith columns of D_2 and Π_2, respectively, $i = 1,2,\ldots,pq$. Let c_2^i is the ith column of C_2, where $i = 1,2,\ldots,p$. For $i = 1,2,\ldots,pq$, $\psi(d_i,n) = \pi_i \otimes \mathbf{1}_n$, and there exists k such that $\psi(d_i,s) = \mathbf{1}_{u_2} \otimes \psi(c_2^k,s) + \eta\pi_i \otimes \mathbf{1}_n$, $k = 1,2,\ldots,p$. It is easy to see that for $k = 1,2,\ldots,v_2^*$, $i = 1,2,\ldots,pq$, $(\lambda_k, \psi(d_i,n))$ is an $OA(nu_2, n^1u_2^1, 2)$. For $j = 1,2,\ldots,m$, $k = 1,2,\ldots,p$ and $i = 1,2,\ldots,pq$, $(\mathbf{1}_{u_2} \otimes c_1^j, \mathbf{1}_{u_2} \otimes \psi(c_2^k,s), \pi_i \otimes \mathbf{1}_n)$ is an $OA(nu_2, s^1\eta^1u_2^1, 3)$, since $(c_1^j, \psi(c_2^k,s))$ is an $OA(n, s^1\eta^1, 2)$. Thus $(\mathbf{1}_{u_2} \otimes c_1^j, \psi(d_i,s))$ is an $OA(nu_2, s^1(\eta u_2)^1, 2)$ for $j = 1,2,\ldots,m$ and $i = 1,2,\ldots,pq$. Thus, Theorem 3(i) is true according to Lemma 1, since $u_2 = \beta n$ and $n = \eta s$.

(ii) Similarly to the proof of Theorem 2(ii), it is straightforward to see that (ii) is true. □

To prove Theorem 4, the following two lemmas are given. Following the symbols in Algorithm 4, let $F_0 = (f_0^1, \ldots, f_0^{s+1})$ and $F_1 = (f_1^1, \ldots, f_1^{s+1})$, where f_0^i and f_1^i are the ith columns of F_0 and F_1, respectively.

Lemma A2 is from Wang et al. [42].

Lemma A2. *Suppose f_0^i, f_0^j, f_0^k, f_1^i, f_1^j and f_1^k for $i,j,k = 1,2,\ldots,s+1$, $i \neq j$ are as defined above; then the arrays (f_0^i, f_0^j, f_1^k) and (f_1^i, f_1^j, f_0^k) are $OA(s_1, s^3, 3)$s with $s_1 = s^3$.*

Following the symbols $G = \psi(\widetilde{M}_2, s_1)$, ϕ_0^i and ϕ_1^i, $i = 1,2,\ldots,s+1$ in Algorithm 4, let $G = (g_1, \ldots, g_p)$, where g_i is the ith column of G.

Lemma A3. *For $u = 1,2,\ldots,p$ and $i = 1,2,\ldots,s+1$, suppose g_u, ϕ_0^i, and ϕ_1^i are as defined above; then for $i \neq j$ the arrays $(g_u, \phi_0^i, \phi_0^j, \phi_1^k)$ and $(g_u, \phi_1^i, \phi_1^j, \phi_0^k)$ are $OA(s_1^2, s_1s^3, 4)$s with $s_1 = s^3$.*

Proof of Lemma A3. For $u = 1,2,\ldots,p$, the g_u defined above, and ξ in Step 1 of Algorithm 4, (g_u, ξ) is an $OA(s_1^2, s_1^2, 2)$ according to Proposition 1 of He et al. [21]. Note that after row permutation, $(g_u, \tilde{\xi}) = (\mathbf{1}_{s_1} \otimes (0,1,\ldots,s_1-1)^T, (0,1,\ldots,s_1-1)^T \otimes \mathbf{1}_{s_1})$. It is clear that the arrays $(g_u, \phi_0^i, \phi_0^j, \phi_1^k)$ and $(g_u, \phi_1^i, \phi_1^j, \phi_0^k)$ are $OA(s_1^2, s_1s^3, 4)$s with $s_1 = s^3$, since the arrays (f_0^i, f_0^j, f_1^k) and (f_1^i, f_1^j, f_0^k) are $OA(s_1, s^3, 3)$s with $s_1 = s^3$ according to Lemma A2. □

Proof of Theorem 4. (i) It is clear that D_1 being an $OA\left(s_1^2, s_1^{m-1}s^{s-1}s_2^1, 2\right)$ follows from the expansive replacement method of Section 9.3 of Hedayat et al. [19]. Let g_i and d_i be the ith columns of G and D_2, respectively, where $i = 1,2,\ldots,p$. For $i = 1,2,\ldots,p$, $d_i = s^3g_i + s^2\phi_1^1 + s\phi_0^s + \phi_1^2$. For $i = 1,2,\ldots,p$, d_i being an $LHD(s_1^2, 1)$ follows from Lemma A3. Thus,

D_2 is an $LHD(s_1^2, p)$. From Algorithm 4, it is obvious that $(\widetilde{\Omega}, \psi(d_i, s_1))$ is an $OA(s_1^2, s_1^m, 2)$ for $i = 1, 2, \ldots, p$, based on (M_1, M_2) being an $MCD(s_1^2, s_1^m, p)$ and $G = \psi(\widetilde{M}_2, s_1)$. According to Lemmas A2 and A3, for $i = 1, 2, \ldots, p$, $s_1 = s^3$, $s_2 = s^2$, $(\phi_0^1, \ldots, \phi_0^{s-1}, \psi(d_i, s))$, and $(s\phi_0^{s+1} + \phi_1^{s+1}, \psi(d_i, s_2))$, i is an $OA(s_1^2, s^{s-1}(s^5)^1, 2)$ and an $OA(s_1^2, s_2(s^4)^1, 2)$, respectively. From Lemma 1, $D = (D_1, D_2)$ is an $MCD\left(s_1^2, s_1^{m-1}s^{s-1}s_2^1, p\right)$ with $s_1 = s^3$ and $s_2 = s^2$.

(ii) From Construction 1, it is easy to see that $\psi(\widetilde{M}_2, s_1) = G$ and $\psi(D_2, s_1) = G$. Then (ii) can be obtained straightforwardly. □

Appendix B. Tables

Table A1. $MCD(32, 2^{14}4^1, 3)$ $D = (D_1, D_2)$ in Example 2.

Run	D_1															D_2		
1	0	0	0	0	0	0	0	0	0	0	0	0	0	0	0	0	0	0
2	1	1	1	1	1	1	1	1	1	1	1	1	1	1	1	1	1	1
3	0	1	0	1	0	1	0	1	0	1	0	1	0	1	2	2	2	2
4	1	0	1	0	1	0	1	0	1	0	1	0	1	0	3	3	3	3
5	0	0	0	0	1	1	0	0	1	1	1	1	1	1	0	8	12	24
6	1	1	1	1	0	0	1	1	0	0	0	0	0	0	1	9	13	25
7	0	1	0	1	1	0	0	1	1	0	1	0	1	0	2	10	14	26
8	1	0	1	0	0	1	1	0	0	1	0	1	0	1	3	11	15	27
9	0	0	1	1	0	0	1	1	0	0	1	1	1	1	0	12	24	8
10	1	1	0	0	1	1	0	0	1	1	0	0	0	0	1	13	25	9
11	0	1	1	0	0	1	1	0	0	1	1	0	1	0	2	14	26	10
12	1	0	0	1	1	0	0	1	1	0	0	1	0	1	3	15	27	11
13	0	0	1	1	1	1	1	1	1	1	0	0	0	0	0	4	20	16
14	1	1	0	0	0	0	0	0	0	0	1	1	1	1	1	5	21	17
15	0	1	1	0	1	0	1	0	1	0	0	1	0	1	2	6	22	18
16	1	0	0	1	0	1	0	1	0	1	1	0	1	0	3	7	23	19
17	1	1	0	0	0	0	1	1	1	1	0	0	1	1	0	24	8	12
18	0	0	1	1	1	1	0	0	0	0	1	1	0	0	1	25	9	13
19	1	0	0	1	0	1	1	0	1	0	0	1	1	0	2	26	10	14
20	0	1	1	0	1	0	0	1	0	1	1	0	0	1	3	27	11	15
21	1	1	0	0	1	1	1	1	0	0	1	1	0	0	0	16	4	20
22	0	0	1	1	0	0	0	0	1	1	0	0	1	1	1	17	5	21
23	1	0	0	1	1	0	1	0	0	1	1	0	0	1	2	18	6	22
24	0	1	1	0	0	1	0	1	1	0	0	1	1	0	3	19	7	23
25	1	1	1	1	0	0	0	0	1	1	1	1	0	0	0	20	16	4
26	0	0	0	0	1	1	1	1	0	0	0	0	1	1	1	21	17	5
27	1	0	1	0	0	1	0	1	1	0	1	0	0	1	2	22	18	6
28	0	1	0	1	1	0	1	0	0	1	0	1	1	0	3	23	19	7
29	1	1	1	1	1	1	0	0	0	0	0	0	1	1	0	28	28	28
30	0	0	0	0	0	0	1	1	1	1	1	1	0	0	1	29	29	29
31	1	0	1	0	1	0	0	1	0	1	0	1	1	0	2	30	30	30
32	0	1	0	1	0	1	1	0	1	0	1	0	0	1	3	31	31	31

Table A2. $MCD(32, 2^2 4^7, 3)$ $D = (D_1, D_2)$ in Example 3.

Run	D_1									D_2			Run	D_1									D_2		
1	0	0	0	0	0	0	0	0	0	0	0	0	17	0	0	0	2	2	1	1	3	3	24	8	12
2	1	1	1	1	1	1	1	1	1	1	1	1	18	1	1	1	3	3	0	0	2	2	25	9	13
3	0	1	2	2	2	2	2	2	2	2	2	2	19	0	1	2	0	0	3	3	1	1	26	10	14
4	1	0	3	3	3	3	3	3	3	3	3	3	20	1	0	3	1	1	2	2	0	0	27	11	15
5	0	0	3	1	2	0	3	1	2	8	12	24	21	0	0	3	3	0	1	2	2	1	16	4	20
6	1	1	2	0	3	1	2	0	3	9	13	25	22	1	1	2	2	1	0	3	3	0	17	5	21
7	0	1	1	3	0	2	1	3	0	10	14	26	23	0	1	1	1	2	3	0	0	3	18	6	22
8	1	0	0	2	1	3	0	2	1	11	15	27	24	1	0	0	0	3	2	1	1	2	19	7	23
9	0	0	1	0	1	2	3	2	3	12	24	8	25	0	0	1	2	3	3	2	1	0	20	16	4
10	1	1	0	1	0	3	2	3	2	13	25	9	26	1	1	0	3	2	2	3	0	1	21	17	5
11	0	1	3	2	3	0	1	0	1	14	26	10	27	0	1	3	0	1	1	0	3	2	22	18	6
12	1	0	2	3	2	1	0	1	0	15	27	11	28	1	0	2	1	0	0	1	2	3	23	19	7
13	0	0	2	1	3	2	0	3	1	4	20	16	29	0	0	2	3	1	3	1	0	2	28	28	28
14	1	1	3	0	2	3	1	2	0	5	21	17	30	1	1	3	2	0	2	0	1	3	29	29	29
15	0	1	0	3	1	0	2	1	3	6	22	18	31	0	1	0	1	3	1	3	2	0	30	30	30
16	1	0	1	2	0	1	3	0	2	7	23	19	32	1	0	1	0	2	0	2	3	1	31	31	31

Table A3. The maximum v such that a $D(\lambda r, v, r)$ exists, $r = 2, 3, 4, 8, 9$.

λ	$D(2\lambda, v, 2)$	$D(3\lambda, v, 3)$	$D(4\lambda, v, 4)$	$D(8\lambda, v, 8)$	$D(9\lambda, v, 9)$
	v	v	v	v	v
1	2	3	4	8	9
2	4	6	8	16	18
3	2	9	12	-	27
4	8	12	16	32	36
6	12	18	-	-	54
7	2	-	-	56	-
8	16	24	32	64	72
9	2	27	36	-	81

Table A4. $\widetilde{M} = (\widetilde{M}_1, \widetilde{M}_2)$ in Example 4.

Run	$\widetilde{M}_1$									Run	$\widetilde{M}_1$							$\widetilde{M}_2$	
	$\widetilde{\Omega}$						$\widetilde{\xi}$	$\widetilde{M}_2$			$\widetilde{\Omega}$						$\widetilde{\xi}$		
1	0	0	0	0	0	0	0	0	0	33	0	4	4	4	4	4	4	36	36
2	1	1	2	3	4	5	0	48	56	34	1	2	1	6	0	7	4	28	44
3	2	2	3	4	5	6	0	56	8	35	2	1	6	0	7	3	4	44	20
4	3	3	4	5	6	7	0	8	16	36	3	6	0	7	3	5	4	20	12
5	4	4	5	6	7	1	0	16	24	37	4	0	7	3	5	2	4	12	52
6	5	5	6	7	1	2	0	24	32	38	5	7	3	5	2	1	4	52	4
7	6	6	7	1	2	3	0	32	40	39	6	3	5	2	1	6	4	4	60
8	7	7	1	2	3	4	0	40	48	40	7	5	2	1	6	0	4	60	28
9	0	1	1	1	1	1	1	9	9	41	0	5	5	5	5	5	5	45	45
10	1	0	4	7	2	6	1	41	25	42	1	6	3	2	7	0	5	13	37
11	2	4	7	2	6	5	1	25	1	43	2	3	2	7	0	1	5	37	53
12	3	7	2	6	5	3	1	1	33	44	3	2	7	0	1	4	5	53	29
13	4	2	6	5	3	0	1	33	57	45	4	7	0	1	4	6	5	29	21
14	5	6	5	3	0	4	1	57	17	46	5	0	1	4	6	3	5	21	61
15	6	5	3	0	4	7	1	17	49	47	6	1	4	6	3	2	5	61	5
16	7	3	0	4	7	2	1	49	41	48	7	4	6	3	2	7	5	5	13
17	0	2	2	2	2	2	2	18	18	49	0	6	6	6	6	6	6	54	54
18	1	4	0	5	1	3	2	58	50	50	1	5	7	4	3	1	6	6	22
19	2	0	5	1	3	7	2	50	34	51	2	7	4	3	1	0	6	22	46
20	3	5	1	3	7	6	2	34	2	52	3	4	3	1	0	2	6	46	62
21	4	1	3	7	6	4	2	2	42	53	4	3	1	0	2	5	6	62	38
22	5	3	7	6	4	0	2	42	10	54	5	1	0	2	5	7	6	38	30
23	6	7	6	4	0	5	2	10	26	55	6	0	2	5	7	4	6	30	14
24	7	6	4	0	5	1	2	26	58	56	7	2	5	7	4	3	6	14	6
25	0	3	3	3	3	3	3	27	27	57	0	7	7	7	7	7	7	63	63
26	1	7	5	0	6	2	3	35	11	58	1	3	6	1	5	4	7	23	7
27	2	5	0	6	2	4	3	11	59	59	2	6	1	5	4	2	7	7	31
28	3	0	6	2	4	1	3	59	43	60	3	1	5	4	2	0	7	31	55
29	4	6	2	4	1	7	3	43	3	61	4	5	4	2	0	3	7	55	15
30	5	2	4	1	7	5	3	3	51	62	5	4	2	0	3	6	7	15	47
31	6	4	1	7	5	0	3	51	19	63	6	2	0	3	6	1	7	47	39
32	7	1	7	5	0	6	3	19	35	64	7	0	3	6	1	5	7	39	23

Table A5. $D = (D_1, D_2)$ in Example 4, $h = 2\phi_0^3 + \phi_1^3$.

Run	D_1								D_2		Run	D_1								D_2	
	$\tilde{\Omega}$						ϕ_0^1	h				$\tilde{\Omega}$						ϕ_0^1	h		
1	0	0	0	0	0	0	0	0	0	0	33	0	4	4	4	4	4	0	1	37	37
2	1	1	2	3	4	5	0	0	48	56	34	1	2	1	6	0	7	0	1	29	45
3	2	2	3	4	5	6	0	0	56	8	35	2	1	6	0	7	3	0	1	45	21
4	3	3	4	5	6	7	0	0	8	16	36	3	6	0	7	3	5	0	1	21	13
5	4	4	5	6	7	1	0	0	16	24	37	4	0	7	3	5	2	0	1	13	53
6	5	5	6	7	1	2	0	0	24	32	38	5	7	3	5	2	1	0	1	53	5
7	6	6	7	1	2	3	0	0	32	40	39	6	3	5	2	1	6	0	1	5	61
8	7	7	1	2	3	4	0	0	40	48	40	7	5	2	1	6	0	0	1	61	29
9	0	1	1	1	1	1	0	3	11	11	41	0	5	5	5	5	5	0	2	46	46
10	1	0	4	7	2	6	0	3	43	27	42	1	6	3	2	7	0	0	2	14	38
11	2	4	7	2	6	5	0	3	27	3	43	2	3	2	7	0	1	0	2	38	54
12	3	7	2	6	5	3	0	3	3	35	44	3	2	7	0	1	4	0	2	54	30
13	4	2	6	5	3	0	0	3	35	59	45	4	7	0	1	4	6	0	2	30	22
14	5	6	5	3	0	4	0	3	59	19	46	5	0	1	4	6	3	0	2	22	62
15	6	5	3	0	4	7	0	3	19	51	47	6	1	4	6	3	2	0	2	62	6
16	7	3	0	4	7	2	0	3	51	43	48	7	4	6	3	2	7	0	2	6	14
17	0	2	2	2	2	2	1	3	20	20	49	0	6	6	6	6	6	1	2	49	49
18	1	4	0	5	1	3	1	3	60	52	50	1	5	7	4	3	1	1	2	1	17
19	2	0	5	1	3	7	1	3	52	36	51	2	7	4	3	1	0	1	2	17	41
20	3	5	1	3	7	6	1	3	36	4	52	3	4	3	1	0	2	1	2	41	57
21	4	1	3	7	6	4	1	3	4	44	53	4	3	1	0	2	5	1	2	57	33
22	5	3	7	6	4	0	1	3	44	12	54	5	1	0	2	5	7	1	2	33	25
23	6	7	6	4	0	5	1	3	12	28	55	6	0	2	5	7	4	1	2	25	9
24	7	6	4	0	5	1	1	3	28	60	56	7	2	5	7	4	3	1	2	9	1
25	0	3	3	3	3	3	1	0	31	31	57	0	7	7	7	7	7	1	1	58	58
26	1	7	5	0	6	2	1	0	39	15	58	1	3	6	1	5	4	1	1	18	2
27	2	5	0	6	2	4	1	0	15	63	59	2	6	1	5	4	2	1	1	2	26
28	3	0	6	2	4	1	1	0	63	47	60	3	1	5	4	2	0	1	1	26	50
29	4	6	2	4	1	7	1	0	47	7	61	4	5	4	2	0	3	1	1	50	10
30	5	2	4	1	7	5	1	0	7	55	62	5	4	2	0	3	6	1	1	10	42
31	6	4	1	7	5	0	1	0	55	23	63	6	2	0	3	6	1	1	1	42	34
32	7	1	7	5	0	6	1	0	23	39	64	7	0	3	6	1	5	1	1	34	18

References

1. Santner, T.J.; Williams, B.J.; Notz, W.I. *The Design and Analysis of Computer Experiments*; Springer: New York, NY, USA, 2003. [CrossRef]
2. Fang, K.T.; Liu, M.Q.; Qin, H.; Zhou, Y.D. *Theory and Application of Uniform Experimental Designs*; Springer: Singapore, 2018. [CrossRef]
3. Koehler, J.R.; Owen, A.B. Computer experiments. In *Handbook of Statistics*; Ghosh, S., Rao, C.R., Eds.; Elsevier Science: New York, NY, USA, 1996; Volume 13, pp. 261–308. [CrossRef]
4. Korobov, N.M. The approximate computation of multiple integrals. *Dokl. Akad. Nauk. SSSR* **1959**, *124*, 1207–1210.
5. Niederreiter, H. *Random Number Generation and Quasi-Monte Carlo Methods*; SIAM: Philadelphia, PA, USA, 1992. [CrossRef]
6. Fang, K.T.; Li, R.Z.; Sudjianto, A. *Design and Modeling for Computer Experiments*; Chapman and Hall/CRC: New York, NY, USA, 2006. [CrossRef]
7. Shewry, M.C.; Wynn, H.P. Maximum entropy sampling. *J. Appl. Stat.* **1987**, *14*, 165–170. [CrossRef]
8. Mitchell, T.J.; Scott, D.S. A computer program for the design of group testing experiments. *Commun. Stat. Theory Methods* **1987**, *16*, 2943–2955. [CrossRef]
9. Currin, C.; Mitchell, T.; Morris, M.; Ylvisaker, D. Bayesian prediction of deterministic functions, with applications to the design and analysis of computer experiments. *J. Am. Stat. Assoc.* **1991**, *86*, 953–963. [CrossRef]
10. Lam C.Q. Sequential Adaptive Designs in Computer Experiments for Response Surface Model Fit. Ph.D. Thesis, The Ohio State University, Columbus, OH, USA, 2008. Available online: https://dl.acm.org/doi/book/10.5555/1559257 (accessed on 11 November 2025). [CrossRef]

11. Morris, M.D.; Mitchell, T.J. Exploratory designs for computational experiments. *J. Stat. Plan. Inference* **1995**, *43*, 381–402. [CrossRef]
12. Johnson, M.E.; Moore, L.M.; Ylvisaker, D. Minimax and maximin distance designs. *J. Stat. Plan. Inference* **1990**, *26*, 131–148. [CrossRef]
13. Rawlinson, J.J.; Furman, B.D.; Li, S.; Wright, T.M.; Bartel, D.L. Retrieval, experimental, and computational assessment of the performance of total knee replacements. *J. Orthop. Res. Off. Publ. Orthop. Res. Soc.* **2006**, *24*, 1384–1394. [CrossRef]
14. Huang, H.Z.; Lin, D.K.J.; Liu, M.Q.; Yang, J.F. Computer experiments with both qualitative and quantitative variables. *Technometrics* **2016**, *58*, 495–507. [CrossRef]
15. Cai, X.; Xu, L.; Lin, C.D.; Hong, Y.L.; Deng, X.W. Adaptive-region sequential design with quantitative and qualitative factors in application to HPC configuration. *J. Qual. Technol.* **2024**, *56*, 5–19. [CrossRef]
16. Qian, P.Z.G.; Wu, C.F.J. Sliced space- flling designs. *Biometrika* **2009**, *96*, 945–956. [CrossRef]
17. Qian, P.Z.G. Sliced Latin hypercube designs. *J. Am. Stat. Assoc.* **2012**, *107*, 393–399. [CrossRef]
18. Deng, X.W.; Hung, Y.; Lin, C.D. Design for computer experiments with qualitative and quantitative factors. *Stat. Sin.* **2015**, *25*, 1567–1581. Available online: http://www.jstor.org/stable/24721247 (accessed on 9 December 2025). [CrossRef]
19. Hedayat, A.S.; Sloane, N.J.A.; Stufken, J. *Orthogonal Arrays: Theory and Application*; Springer: New York, NY, USA, 1999. [CrossRef]
20. McKay, M.D.; Beckman, R.J.; Conover, W.J. A comparison of three methods for selecting values of input variables in the analysis of output from acomputer code. *Technometrics* **1979**, *21*, 239–245. [CrossRef]
21. He, Y.Z.; Lin, C.D.; Sun, F.S. On construction of marginally coupled designs. *Stat. Sin.* **2017**, *27*, 665–683. Available online: https://www.jstor.org/stable/26383295 (accessed on 9 December 2025). [CrossRef]
22. He, Y.Z.; Lin, C.D.; Sun, F.S. Construction of marginally coupled designs by subspace theory. *Bernoulli* **2019**, *25*, 2163–2182. [CrossRef]
23. He, Y.Z.; Lin, C.D.; Sun, F.S.; Lv, B.J. Marginally coupled designs for two-level qualitative factors. *J. Stat. Plan. Infer.* **2017**, *287*, 103–108. [CrossRef]
24. Zhou, W.P.; He, W.; Wang, W.; Huang, S.G. Construction of marginally coupled designs with mixed-level qualitative factors. *AIMS Math.* **2024**, *9*, 33731–33755. [CrossRef]
25. Zhou, W.P.; Yang, J.Y.; Liu, M.Q. Construction of orthogonal marginally coupled designs. *Stat. Pap.* **2021**, *62*, 1795–1820. [CrossRef]
26. Yang, F.; Lin, C.D.; Zhou, Y.D.; He, Y.Z. Doubly coupled designs for computer experiments with both qualitative and quantitative factors. *Stat. Sin.* **2023**, *33*, 1923–1942. [CrossRef]
27. Zhou, W.P.; Huang, S.G.; Li, M. Group doubly coupled designs. *Mathematics* **2024**, *12*, 1352. [CrossRef]
28. Liu, M.M.; Liu, M.Q.; Yang, J.Y. Strongly coupled designs for computer experiments with both qualitative and quantitative factors. *Mathematics* **2025**, *13*, 75. [CrossRef]
29. Owen, A.B. Orthogonal arrays for computer experiments, integration, and visualization. *Stat. Sin.* **1992**, *2*, 439–452.
30. Tang, B.X. Orthogonal array-based Latin hypercubes. *Bernoulli* **1993**, *88*, 1392–1397. [CrossRef]
31. He, Y.Z.; Tang, B.X. Strong orthogonal arrays and associated Latin hypercubes for computer experiments. *Biometrika* **2013**, *100*, 254–260. [CrossRef]
32. He, Y.Z.; Cheng, C.S.; Tang, B.X. Strong orthogonal arrays of strength two plus. *Ann. Statist.* **2018**, *46*, 457–468. [CrossRef] [PubMed]
33. Zhou, Y.D.; Tang, B.X. Column-orthogonal strong orthogonal arrays of strength two plus and three minus. *Biometrika* **2019**, *106*, 749–764. [CrossRef]
34. Shi, C.L.; Tang, B.X. Construction results for strong orthogonal arrays of strength three. *Bernoulli* **2020**, *26*, 418–431. [CrossRef]
35. Li, W.L.; Liu, M.Q.; Yang, J.F. Construction of column-orthogonal strong orthogonal arrays. *Stat. Pap.* **2022**, *63*, 515–530. [CrossRef]
36. He, Y.Z.; Tang, B.X. A characterization of strong orthogonal arrays of strength three. *Ann. Statist.* **2014**, *42*, 1347–1360. [CrossRef]
37. Joseph, V.R.; Gul, E.; Ba, S. Designing computer experiments with multiple types of factors: The maxpro approach. *J. Qual. Technol.* **2020**, *52*, 343–354. [CrossRef]
38. Zhang, M.; Yang, F.; Zhou, Y.D. Uniformity criterion for designs with both qualitative and quantitative factors. *Statistics* **2021**, *55*, 90–109. [CrossRef]
39. Xiao, Y.; Zou, N.; Qin, H.; Wang, K. Generalised minimum moment aberration for designs with both qualitative and quantitative factors. *Stat* **2024**, *13*, e684. [CrossRef]
40. Xiao, Q.; Mandal, A.; Lin, C.D.; Deng, X. EZGP: Easy-to-interpret Gaussian process models for computer experiments with both quantitative and qualitative factors. *SIAM/ASA J. Uncertain. Quantif.* **2021**, *9*, 333–353. [CrossRef]

41. Li, P.N.; Wang, C.J.; Jiang, B.C. Group strong orthogonal arrays and their construction methods. *Stat. Pap.* **2025**, *66*, 52. [CrossRef]
42. Wang, C.Y.; Lin, D.K.J.; Liu, M.Q. A new class of orthogonal designs with good low dimensional space-filling properties. *Stat. Sin.* **2025**, *35*, 2057–2073. Available online: https://www3.stat.sinica.edu.tw/statistica/j35n4/J35N406/J35N406.html (accessed on 9 December 2025). [CrossRef]

MDPI AG
Grosspeteranlage 5
4052 Basel
Switzerland
Tel.: +41 61 683 77 34

Entropy Editorial Office
E-mail: entropy@mdpi.com
www.mdpi.com/journal/entropy

www.ingramcontent.com/pod-product-compliance
Lightning Source LLC
Chambersburg PA
CBHW040823250926
51850CB00007BA/1243
* 9 7 8 3 7 2 5 8 7 4 0 6 4 *